Design and Development of Emerging Chatbot Technology

Dina Darwish
Ahram Canadian University, Egypt

A volume in the Advances in Computational
Intelligence and Robotics (ACIR) Book Series

Published in the United States of America by
IGI Global
Engineering Science Reference (an imprint of IGI Global)
701 E. Chocolate Avenue
Hershey PA, USA 17033
Tel: 717-533-8845
Fax: 717-533-8661
E-mail: cust@igi-global.com
Web site: http://www.igi-global.com

Library of Congress Cataloging-in-Publication Data

CIP Data Pending

Design and Development of Emerging Chatbot Technology
Dina Darwish
2024 Engineering Science Reference

ISBN: 979-8-3693-1830-0
eISBN: 979-8-3693-1831-7

This book is published in the IGI Global book series Advances in Computational Intelligence and Robotics (ACIR) (ISSN: 2327-0411; eISSN: 2327-042X)

British Cataloguing in Publication Data
A Cataloguing in Publication record for this book is available from the British Library.

All work contributed to this book is new, previously-unpublished material. The views expressed in this book are those of the authors, but not necessarily of the publisher.

For electronic access to this publication, please contact: eresources@igi-global.com.

Advances in Computational Intelligence and Robotics (ACIR) Book Series

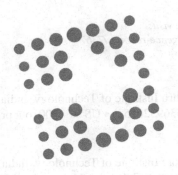

Ivan Giannoccaro
University of Salento, Italy

ISSN:2327-0411
EISSN:2327-042X

MISSION

While intelligence is traditionally a term applied to humans and human cognition, technology has progressed in such a way to allow for the development of intelligent systems able to simulate many human traits. With this new era of simulated and artificial intelligence, much research is needed in order to continue to advance the field and also to evaluate the ethical and societal concerns of the existence of artificial life and machine learning.

The **Advances in Computational Intelligence and Robotics (ACIR) Book Series** encourages scholarly discourse on all topics pertaining to evolutionary computing, artificial life, computational intelligence, machine learning, and robotics. ACIR presents the latest research being conducted on diverse topics in intelligence technologies with the goal of advancing knowledge and applications in this rapidly evolving field.

COVERAGE

- Cyborgs
- Computational Intelligence
- Fuzzy Systems
- Synthetic Emotions
- Computational Logic
- Computer Vision
- Adaptive and Complex Systems
- Agent technologies
- Algorithmic Learning
- Brain Simulation

IGI Global is currently accepting manuscripts for publication within this series. To submit a proposal for a volume in this series, please contact our Acquisition Editors at Acquisitions@igi-global.com or visit: http://www.igi-global.com/publish/.

The Advances in Computational Intelligence and Robotics (ACIR) Book Series (ISSN 2327-0411) is published by IGI Global, 701 E. Chocolate Avenue, Hershey, PA 17033-1240, USA, www.igi-global.com. This series is composed of titles available for purchase individually; each title is edited to be contextually exclusive from any other title within the series. For pricing and ordering information please visit http://www.igi-global.com/book-series/advances-computational-intelligence-robotics/73674. Postmaster: Send all address changes to above address. Copyright © 2024 IGI Global. All rights, including translation in other languages reserved by the publisher. No part of this series may be reproduced or used in any form or by any means – graphics, electronic, or mechanical, including photocopying, recording, taping, or information and retrieval systems – without written permission from the publisher, except for non commercial, educational use, including classroom teaching purposes. The views expressed in this series are those of the authors, but not necessarily of IGI Global.

Titles in this Series

For a list of additional titles in this series, please visit:
www.igi-global.com/book-series/advances-computational-intelligence-robotics/73674

Using Real-Time Data and AI for Thrust Manufacturing
D. Satishkumar (Nehru Institute of Technology, India) and M. Sivaraja (Nehru Institute of Technology, India)
Engineering Science Reference • copyright 2024 • 343pp • H/C (ISBN: 9798369326152) • US $345.00 (our price)

AI Approaches to Smart and Sustainable Power Systems
L. Ashok Kumar (PSG College of Technology, India) S. Angalaeswari (Vellore Institute of Technology, India) K. Mohana Sundaram (KPR Institute of Engineering and Technology, India) Ramesh C. Bansal (University of Sharjah, UAE & University of Pretoria, South Africa) and Arunkumar Patil (Central University of Karnataka, India)
Engineering Science Reference • copyright 2024 • 432pp • H/C (ISBN: 9798369315866) • US $300.00 (our price)

Wearable Devices, Surveillance Systems, and AI for Women's Wellbeing
Sivaram Ponnusamy (Sandip University, Nashik, India) Vibha Bora (G. H. Raisoni College of Engineering, Nagpur, India) Prema M. Daigavane (G. H. Raisoni College of Engineering, Nagpur, India) and Sampada S. Wazalwar (G. H. Raisoni College of Engineering, Nagpur, India)
Engineering Science Reference • copyright 2024 • 321pp • H/C (ISBN: 9798369334065) • US $335.00 (our price)

Methodologies, Frameworks, and Applications of Machine Learning
Pramod Kumar Srivastava (Rajkiya Engineering College, Azamgarh, India) and Ashok Kumar Yadav (Rajkiya Engineering College, Azamgarh, India)
Engineering Science Reference • copyright 2024 • 296pp • H/C (ISBN: 9798369310625) • US $300.00 (our price)

Artificial Intelligence of Things (AIoT) for Productivity and Organizational Transition
Sajad Rezaei (University of Worcester, UK) and Amin Ansary (University of the Witwatersrand, South Africa)
Business Science Reference • copyright 2024 • 368pp • H/C (ISBN: 9798369309933) • US $275.00 (our price)

Internet of Things and AI for Natural Disaster Management and Prediction
D. Satishkumar (Nehru Institute of Technology, India) and M. Sivaraja (Nehru Institute of Technology, India)
Engineering Science Reference • copyright 2024 • 334pp • H/C (ISBN: 9798369342848) • US $345.00 (our price)

AI Applications for Business, Medical, and Agricultural Sustainability
Arshi Naim (King Khalid University, Saudi Arabia)
Engineering Science Reference • copyright 2024 • 322pp • H/C (ISBN: 9798369352663) • US $315.00 (our price)

701 East Chocolate Avenue, Hershey, PA 17033, USA
Tel: 717-533-8845 x100 • Fax: 717-533-8661
E-Mail: cust@igi-global.com • www.igi-global.com

Editorial Advisory Board

Table of Contents

Detailed Table of Contents

Chapter 1

Dina Darwish, Ahram Canadian University, Egypt

A computer program that acts as if it is having a conversation with a human end user is known as a chatbot. Even while not all chatbots have artificial intelligence (AI), most current chatbots employ conversational AI methods like natural language processing (NLP) in order to comprehend the user's inquiries and provide automated replies to such inquiries. Such technologies often make use of facets of deep learning and natural language processing; nevertheless, chatbots that are far simpler have been present for decades prior to the advent of such technology. This chapter discusses chatbots' characteristics, how they work, and other topics related to chatbots.

Chapter 2

Dina Darwish, Ahram Canadian University, Egypt

The terms "chatbot," "AI chatbot," and "virtual agent" are used in a way that often does not differentiate between them, which might lead to possible misunderstandings. Despite the fact that the technologies associated with these terms are inextricably linked to one another, the subtle differences that exist between them result in considerable differences in their unique capabilities. The term "chatbot" is often used to refer to a wide variety of artificial intelligence systems that are designed to carry on conversations. The development of artificial intelligence chatbot software has resulted in the creation of virtual agents, which constitutes a significant step forward. These agents participate in conversation via the use of AI methods known as conversational AI, and they make use of deep learning algorithms in order to improve their performance over time. This chapter discusses the differences between chatbots, AI chatbots and virtual assistants, and other related topics.

Chapter 3

Gulnara Z. Karimova, University of Wollongong in Dubai, UAE
Yevgeniya Kim, KIMEP University, Kazakhstan

This chapter offers an exploration of the various typologies that define digital assistants. Through the metaphor of craftsmanship, the chapter systematically categorizes and examines chatbots based on their functions, underlying technology, interaction styles, deployment platforms, and primary goals. It highlights the differences between rule-based systems, AI-driven models, and hybrid architectures, explaining how each typology serves specific user needs and business objectives. Furthermore, the chapter discusses the significance of fine-tuning and API-driven models in enhancing the proficiency of chatbots. By providing a detailed analysis of each chatbot type, this chapter aims to equip readers with a deeper understanding of the potential of chatbots in various sectors. The insights presented herein reflect the author's comprehensive understanding of the current state of chatbot technology, making it a valuable resource for developers, researchers, and anyone interested in the evolution of digital communication and AI.

    Neepa Biswas, Narula Institute of Technology, India
    Sudarsan Biswas, RCC Institute of Information Technology, India
    Suchismita Maity, Narula Institute of Technology, India

A chatbot is a computer program or software application that is designed to communicate with humans via text or speech-based interfaces. A chatbot's main objective is to mimic human conversation and deliver immediate responses to user inquiries. Chatbots are used in a variety of industries in various cases, including customer support, sales and marketing, appointment scheduling, retrieving information, virtual assistants, and even more. They can be used on websites, chat apps (such as WhatsApp, Facebook Messenger, or Slack), mobile applications, and voice-activated platforms such as Google Assistant, Siri, and Alexa. This chapter offers a thorough investigation of chatbots, chronicling their historical evolution, looking at their numerous applications, and sketching forth a complete classification scheme. This chapter seeks to provide a comprehensive overview of the evolution, significance, and classification of chatbots in the field of human-computer interaction from its genesis to modern uses.

    Kaushikkumar Patel, TransUnion LLC, USA

This chapter provides an insightful exploration into the rapidly evolving world of chatbot technology, highlighting its significant applications across diverse sectors. It traces the evolution of chatbots from basic automated systems to advanced AI-driven interfaces capable of sophisticated interactions. The focus is on how chatbots have revolutionized customer service, e-commerce, healthcare, and education, showcasing their role in enhancing user experience and operational efficiency. The chapter also addresses the challenges in chatbot implementation, such as natural language processing difficulties, ethical concerns, and privacy issues, while presenting current solutions and best practices. Additionally, it explores future research directions, emphasizing the potential long-term impact of chatbots on society and technology. Aimed at providing a comprehensive understanding of chatbot applications, this chapter is a valuable resource for those interested in the convergence of AI, communication, and technology.

    Rajesh Kanna Rajendran, Christ University, India
    Mohana Priya T., Christ University, India
    Karthick Chitrarasu, Christ University, India

The creation and development of chatbots, which are the prevalent manifestations of artificial intelligence (AI) and machine learning (ML) technologies in today's digital world, are built on Natural Language Processing (NLP), which serves as a cornerstone in the process. This chapter investigates the significant part that natural language processing (NLP) plays in determining the development and effectiveness of chatbots, beginning with their beginnings as personal virtual assistants and continuing through their seamless incorporation into messaging platforms and smart home gadgets. The study delves into the technological complexities and emphasizes the problems and improvements in natural language processing (NLP) algorithms and understanding (NLU) systems. These systems are essential in enabling chatbots to grasp context, decode user intent, and provide replies that are contextually appropriate in real time. In spite of the substantial progress that has been made, chatbots continue to struggle with constraints.

This chapter provides a comprehensive overview of key criteria and methodologies essential for effectively choosing chatbots tailored to specific organizational needs. Addressing the critical intersection of functionality, user experience, and technological capabilities, the chapter delves into the evaluation of natural language processing, integration capabilities, scalability, and adaptability to diverse industries. Emphasizing the significance of a user-centric approach, the discussion encompasses user interface design, conversational flow, and the incorporation of feedback mechanisms to enhance user satisfaction. Furthermore, the chapter sheds light on the importance of aligning chatbot selection with overarching organizational goals and strategies. This work is a great resource for researchers and practitioners who are navigating the complex process of choosing chatbots in the always changing field of conversational AI. It distils best practices from industrial examples and emerging trends.

The discourse encompasses multifaceted aspects, beginning with an examination of user-centric challenges. The text delves into issues such as natural language understanding limitations, context awareness, and the ethical considerations surrounding user privacy and data security. Furthermore, the chapter provides insights into technical challenges, addressing the complexities of designing robust algorithms, optimizing response generation, and mitigating biases within chatbot interactions. The chapter finishes by highlighting the significance of continuous research and development in order to address the obstacles and fully use the capabilities of chatbot technology in various applications, as the chatbot landscape continues to expand. This chapter provides a valuable resource for developers, researchers, as well as practitioners in the discipline of chatbot technology. It offers a detailed understanding of the complex challenges that need to be addressed in order to improve user experiences and responsibly implement emerging chatbot technologies.

This chapter delves into the transformative impact of chatbots in customer service, highlighting their evolution from basic automated responders to advanced AI-driven conversational agents. Utilizing technologies like AI, ML, and NLP, these bots are reshaping customer interactions by offering round-the-clock service and handling complex inquiries with increasing sophistication. The chapter explores their development, operational mechanics, and various types while addressing the challenges in implementation and the balance between automation and human touch. Ethical considerations, particularly in data privacy, are critically examined. Real-world case studies across different industries illustrate the practical impact and efficiency gains from these bots. Future advancements are discussed, focusing on enhanced personalization and empathetic interactions through improved AI and NLP, underscoring the significant yet evolving role of chatbots in modern customer service.

Venkat Narayana, Sreenidhi Institute of Science and Technology, India
Sangers Bhavana, Sreenidhi Institute of Science and Technology, India

A chatbot is a computer program, which is blueprint for simulation and conversation between individuals over the internet. According to the input of a human, chatbots engage with clients and respond to them. It makes the client imagine that it is visiting with an individual while they're talking with the computer. Chatbots are turning out to be progressively significant passageways to automated administration and information in regions like client assistance, medical services, and training. The decision provokes interest about the motivations behind why chatbots are turning out to be more human-like than only a specialized gadget and what's in store for people and chatbots. This chapter gives how the chatbot and IoT mingle and procreate in all the sectors, as IoTs are wise contraptions that the authors track down in their standard normal presence and if chatbots can be made a piece of the IoT and its interface, exchange of information and data will be more important and it will happen all through the scope of the day considering the way that chatbots don't enervate.

Sudha Senthilkumar, School of Computer Science and Engineering, Vellore Institute of Technology, Vellore, India
Subhro Mukherjee, School of Computer Science and Engineering, Vellore Institute of Technology, Vellore, India
Siddhant Jain, School of Computer Science and Engineering, Vellore Institute of Technology, Vellore, India
Yashvardhan Aditya, School of Computer Science and Engineering, Vellore Institute of Technology, Vellore, India

There is an increasing population in India, due to reduction in the death rate and growing pace in birth due to improvement in the medical field; however, the amounts of experts are fewer to serve the need of the growing people. The present circumstance can be witnessed while walking around the local organization medical facilities where the limited availability of the experts is the critical purpose leads to less to the patient's required treatment. To fulfill the need of the patients first aid support and redirect the patient to the correct expert based on their available location and time, intelligent chatbots are emerging requirement. The NLP integrated artificial intelligent based clinical chatbot simulates and processes patient conversation by making people interact with smart devices the way how they were make the conversation with doctors who are expert in the medical field. To achieve this, the system collects and stores the information in the web crawler such as Google to fetch the information as per the client request in the emergency situation. The proposed Medify chatbot uses the integration of Machine learning techniques and NLP with the web crawler Google to achieve a highly accurate, user-friendly interface.

The healthcare industry is changing, with a greater dependence on technology, as seen by the incorporation of chatbots powered by artificial intelligence. Chatbots serve as virtual assistants, improving patient assistance, education, and engagement by providing information on medical issues and easing administrative procedures. Chatbots are particularly useful in symptom evaluation and telemedicine, allowing for virtual consultations and remote patient monitoring. Although chatbot technology is highly innovative and useful for medical and management professionals, the literature is still scarce and highly fragmented among different research areas. This chapter aims to analyze the power of chatbots in healthcare through scientific literature, providing a holistic understanding of the state of the art and future applications of chatbots. Despite acknowledged limitations, the substantial advantages hint at a positive outlook for their ongoing growth and integration into the healthcare ecosystem.

This study delves into the evaluation of ChatGPT's effectiveness in sentiment detection and text classification tasks specifically on Turkish texts, a domain that has been relatively underexplored in existing literature predominantly focused on English texts. Leveraging datasets comprising manually labeled YouTube comments and news tweets categorized into sentiment classes and thematic topics, the authors rigorously assess the performance of ChatGPT-3.5 and ChatGPT-4 using accuracy and F1 performance metrics. These findings unveil insights into ChatGPT's proficiency in classifying Turkish textual content, illuminating its alignment with human-labeled classifications. This research not only contributes to expanding the scope of AI research beyond English language but also underscores the significance of language diversity in evaluating and refining AI models' performance for broader applicability in the research practices of social and communication sciences.

The incorporation of chatbots within the tourism and hospitality sectors signals a transformative era aimed at enhancing customer engagement, operational efficiency, and industry responsiveness. With their diverse capabilities spanning from personalized recommendations to seamless booking processes, chatbots revolutionize the way travelers interact with service providers. Powered by cutting-edge technologies like natural language processing and machine learning, chatbots facilitate seamless communication channels, offering timely assistance and valuable insights to travelers. In the hospitality domain, chatbots serve as indispensable virtual concierges, ensuring round-the-clock customer support, personalized recommendations, and streamlined reservation management. However, the integration of chatbots also presents challenges, including data security concerns and the need for continuous innovation. By navigating through these challenges, stakeholders can unlock the full potential of chatbot technology, paving the way for exceptional guest experiences and sustained industry innovation.

The assimilation of chatbots right into the swiftly expanding shopping landscape has actually arisen as a transformative pressure reshaping customer communication paired with redefining the on the internet purchasing experience. At its core an AI in shopping functions as a smart online aide expertly directing individuals via the whole acquisition trip. Utilizing sophisticated natural language handling (NLP) these electronic employees stand out at comprehending as well as reacting to individual inquiries, making certain smooth as well as interactive discussions. Additionally, chatbots function as expert individual customers, leveraging individual habits and also choices to provide tailored referrals.

Chapter 16

This study thoroughly analyses the incorporation of chatbots in English as a Foreign Language (EFL) education by examining 11 research studies carried out from 2020 to 2023. The review carefully combines findings, techniques, and consequences to offer a detailed overview of the complex field of chatbot-mediated language learning treatments. From quasi-experimental designs to qualitative explorations, the evaluated research uses a range of approaches to study various characteristics such as learning attainment, effectiveness, motivation, attitudes, perceptions, cognition, learning styles, and user experience. The results show how adaptable chatbot technology is in supporting task-oriented learning, vocabulary development, conversational practice, and pedagogical support, providing individualized and interesting language learning opportunities. Additionally, the contextual complexities present in chatbot interventions are emphasised, highlighting the significance of taking learner demographics, educational situations, and cultural backgrounds into account.

    Saurabh Bhattacharya, Chitkara Business School, Chitkara University, Punjab, India
    Babita Singla, Chitkara University, India

Chatbots, which provide a smooth and effective channel of contact, have completely changed the way companies engage with their clientele. This study explores the underlying technologies and procedures that underpin chatbot functioning, going deep into their complex workings. The chapter offers a thorough analysis of chatbot functionality and industry effects, ranging from machine learning methods to natural language processing. The abstract delves into the significance of user experience, emphasizing the importance of contextual understanding, personalization, and continuous learning in refining chatbot performance. Moreover, it touches upon challenges such as ethical considerations, biases, and limitations inherent in chatbot technology. In essence, this abstract encapsulates the multifaceted workings of chatbots, elucidating the amalgamation of linguistic processing, artificial intelligence, and machine learning that enables these conversational agents to navigate diverse user inputs and contribute to the evolving landscape of human-computer interaction.

    Nitin Sharma, Bharat Electronics Limited, India
    Pawan Bhakuni, Bharat Electronics Limited, India

A chatbot is an artificial intelligence-driven conversational agent that utilizes natural language processing to engage with users and carry out activities via written or spoken communication. Although there has been remarkable advancement, contemporary chatbots frequently encounter difficulties such as trustworthiness, emotional intelligence, and social awareness. Trustworthiness, emotional intelligence, and social awareness are crucial for any chatbot. Trustworthiness in communication guarantees the sharing of truthful information, while emotional intelligence promotes user engagement by fostering empathy. Additionally, social awareness facilitates culturally sensitive and contextually relevant communication. The authors outline many overarching strategies to address emerging issues in chatbot development, including novel methodologies, innovative environments and modalities, and updated benchmarks. Implementing a new methodology, a new environment with different modalities, and a new benchmark can improve chatbot performance.

Preface

The software system ELIZA, developed by MIT professor Joseph Weizenbaum in the 1960s, is widely regarded as a pioneering example of a chatbot. The term "chatbot" was first introduced in 1992. ELIZA demonstrated the ability to identify significant terms and generate open-ended questions in response. The concept included using ELIZA as a therapeutic tool, whereby it would assume the role of a listener, attentively addressing individuals' concerns and providing responses that fostered a sense of comprehension and empathy among the program's users.

A chatbot is an artificial intelligence system that imitates human conversation by generating responses in either spoken or written form. The term "chatbot," which is a contraction of "chatterbot," refers to an artificial intelligence (AI) feature that has the capability to be integrated into prominent messaging platforms. Chatbots are often referred to by several names such as "talkbot," "bot," "IM bot," "interactive agent," and "artificial conversation entity." Chatbots, also known as conversational agents, have gained significant prominence in recent years.

As technological advancements continue to progress, businesses are progressively using digital platforms as a means to engage with their consumers. Many enterprises are using artificial intelligence (AI) technologies on their digital platforms in order to enhance user ease. Chatbots are a nascent artificial intelligence technique. Chatbot technology is used by virtual assistants such as Alexa and Google Assistant, as well as messaging services like WeChat and Facebook Messenger.

Chatbots are computer programs designed to engage in human-like conversations with customers, and they are available for usage at no cost. Chatbots provide round-the-clock assistance to customers, unrestricted by temporal or spatial constraints. The aforementioned attribute renders its adoption appealing to several firms that face constraints in terms of human resources or financial capacity to sustain round-the-clock workforce. According to a comprehensive industry analysis, the global usage of chatbots saw a significant increase as a result of the COVID-19 pandemic.

A chatbot can be defined also as an artificial intelligence system that imitates human conversation by generating text or speech-based conversations. These devices are designed for rudimentary interactions and tasks such as scheduling a follow-up appointment. Traditional Chatbots do not possess the ability to acquire knowledge through exchanges due to their absence of artificial intelligence. Students are instructed to provide premeditated responses to inquiries.

Virtual agents, often known as virtual assistants or chatbots, are computer programs designed to simulate human conversation and provide automated assistance to users. Virtual agents are more sophisticated than chatbots. Virtual agents adhere to established protocols in order to respond to or direct inquiries from clients. Virtual agents use natural language processing (NLP), making them similar to chatbots.

Natural Language Processing (NLP) facilitates the ability of computer systems to engage in the tasks of reading, comprehending, and interpreting human language. Natural Language Processing (NLP) enables virtual assistants to understand client input rather than relying on specific keywords such as chatbots. The company have the ability to comprehend the intentions of consumers in order to provide customized and relevant responses.

Chatbots are limited in their ability to handle complex enquiries. However, artificial intelligence (AI) has the potential to overcome this limitation by using machine learning and deep learning algorithms to better understand human meaning. Artificial intelligence (AI) is particularly well-suited for addressing intricate inquiries from clients, whilst chatbots are more adept at handling basic issues.

The use of conversational AI chatbots has significantly revolutionized the field of customer service, facilitating expedited and enhanced interactions. Chatbots have emerged as the favored method for marketers to engage with their customers owing to their prompt response capabilities and efficient resolution timelines. Conversational AI chatbots exhibit higher levels of engagement and accuracy in understanding human language compared to traditional chatbots. These automated systems demonstrate exceptional proficiency in providing individualized customer support as a result of their ability to comprehend natural languages and discern human intentions. AI-enabled bots have the potential to enhance their capabilities and expand their effectiveness via iterative learning from interactions. Bots provide a certain function. A corporate entity may want to use a chatbot for the purpose of facilitating client purchases, whilst a telecommunications company may utilize a chatbot to address and resolve customer queries related to support services. There exists a category of chatbots that adhere to predetermined norms, but another kind utilizes artificial intelligence techniques. One topic of interest in the field of conversational agents is rule-based chatbots.

1. Rule-based chatbots

These chatbots operate on a set of predefined rules and patterns to generate responses to user. A bot that operates on rule-based algorithms is limited in its ability to comprehend and respond to user input only within the confines of its pre-programmed possibilities. The bot's conversation is guided by predetermined rules. Rule-based chatbots use a rudimentary binary algorithm to interpret user queries and provide appropriate responses, making them straightforward to create.

2. Artificial Intelligence-powered chatbots

This bot is equipped with an artificial intelligence (AI) system. Machine-learning algorithms enable the comprehension of open-ended enquiries. The system comprehends and interprets commands and linguistic expressions. Enhancing the bot's performance is facilitated by the process of acquiring knowledge through user interactions. The AI chatbot exhibits the ability to effectively engage with users by comprehending language, understanding contextual cues, and discerning the intended goal of the interaction.

There are *several types* of chatbots based on their functionality and design. These classifications include rule-based chatbots, AI-based chatbots, hybrid chatbots, and others. Types of chatbots are as follows:

1. Menu/button-based chatbots
2. Linguistic Based (Rule-Based Chatbots)
3. Keyword recognition-based chatbots
4. Machine Learning chatbots
5. The hybrid model
6. Voice bots

1. Menu/button-based chatbots

Chatbots are considered to be the most fundamental and rudimentary kind of chatbot available on the market. Typically, these chatbots are represented as decision tree hierarchies, which are visually shown in the form of buttons. Similar to the automated phone menus often seen in daily life, chatbots need a multitude of selections in order to get the desired response. Chatbots have shown the ability to address around 80% of support inquiries. However, their effectiveness diminishes when confronted with intricate scenarios that include a multitude of factors or an abundance of information, hence hindering their capacity to accurately predict appropriate responses to specific user queries. Chatbots that rely on menus or buttons tend to be less efficient in delivering value to users in a timely manner.

2. Linguistic based (rule-based chatbots)

Linguistics is the field of study that encompasses rule-based chatbots. If the ability to predict consumer enquiries is there, a linguistic chatbot might potentially be effective. Linguistic or rules-based chatbots use automated conversational processes via the utilization of if/then logic. Prior to discussing the linguistic requirements of our chatbots, it is essential to establish a clear definition. Various linguistic aspects, such as vocabulary, sentence structure, alternative expressions, and other factors, might be evaluated under certain circumstances. Consumers may get prompt response if the incoming question aligns with the predetermined conditions of the chatbot. Nevertheless, the chatbot will not comprehend the customer's input until you explicitly define the many permutations and combinations of each inquiry. This is the reason why language models, despite their frequency, need a significant amount of time to develop. The efficacy of chatbots relies on their accuracy. Chatbots equipped with the ability to identify and comprehend keywords. Keyword recognition-based chatbots has the ability to accurately perceive and comprehend the input provided by users, hence enabling them to provide appropriate responses.

3. Keyword recognition-based chatbots

In contrast, menu-based chatbots lack this capability and are unable to respond accurately to user queries. The chatbots use customizable keywords and natural language processing (NLP) techniques to determine the appropriate responses to users. When posed with a series of analogous inquiries, these chatbots demonstrate a lack of success. The use of redundant keywords in a series of connected enquiries might potentially undermine the effectiveness of natural language processing (NLP) chatbots. Chatbots that include keyword recognition and menu/button-based navigation have gained significant popularity. These chatbots provide users with the option to either ask questions directly or employ the menu buttons in cases when the keyword recognition capability is not functioning properly or when assistance is required in locating the answer.

4. Machine learning chatbots

The use of machine learning in the development and implementation of chatbot systems. The contextual chatbot has a higher level of sophistication compared to the three prior chatbots. Machine learning (ML) and artificial intelligence (AI) are used to retrieve conversations with specific users in order to acquire knowledge and enhance the performance of these chatbots. In contrast to keyword recognition bots, contextual chatbots possess the ability to acquire knowledge from user inquiries and their manner of articulation.

A contextual conversational agent designed for meal ordering purposes will save and analyze data from each user interaction, enabling it to acquire knowledge about the user's food preferences. The resultant effect is that this conversational agent will retain a user's most customary request, designated delivery destination, and payment particulars, thereafter inquiring if they want to replicate those preferences. In lieu of responding to a series of inquiries, a simple affirmation of "Yes" will suffice, indicating that the meal is prepared and ready for consumption.

This illustrative instance of dinner ordering exemplifies the efficacy of including conversation context in artificial intelligence and machine learning systems. The primary objective of any chatbot should be to improve the overall user experience beyond the existing status quo. The use of conversation context is considered to be one of the most effective strategies for minimizing the operational demands of chatbots such as the one being discussed.

5. The hybrid bot

The hybrid model refers to a certain approach or framework that combines elements from other systems or methodologies. Business enterprises have a strong affinity towards AI-chatbots, yet they often encounter challenges in terms of lacking the necessary expertise and data to effectively sustain their implementation. The hybrid chatbot idea combines the straightforwardness of rules-based chatbots with the intricacy of AI-bots.

6. The voice bots

Enterprises are using voice-based chatbots to enhance the naturalness of conversational interfaces. In recent years, there has been a notable surge in the use of speech bots such as Siri and Alexa. Due of their simplicity. Verbal communication is more straightforward for consumers in comparison to written communication. Voice-activated chatbots provide seamless consumer experiences.

The Chatbots can be applied in several areas. The primary purpose of every brand is to ensure customer pleasure. The individuals that access your page, application, or website possess certain requirements and expectations.

1. *Customer support Chatbots*

The provision of customer support services. Consumers have the ability to engage in rapid browsing behavior without taking any further actions. Alternatively, their online conduct may exhibit variations compared to other customers. These findings suggest that the customer could be in need of assistance from your chatbot.

2. *Suggest products Chatbots*

The use of search results, tailored merchandising, and recommendations aids clients in the process of locating desired goods. When there is an indication of potential purchase based on the online activity of customers, but no actual transaction has occurred, it presents a favorable occasion to inquire about their preferences and desires. A conversational interface facilitates the process of eliciting information from customers in order to ascertain their objectives.

3. Offer discounts Chatbots

The implementation of discounts in business transactions. The customer may express a desire for a more favorable pricing, since they believe they meet the criteria for a potential reduction. The chatbot has the capability to assess the customer's purchase history and interactions with other brands in order to ascertain their eligibility for a discount, afterwards extending an offer if applicable.

4. Prevent churn Chatbots

One strategy to mitigate customer turnover is by implementing effective measures to retain customers. Churn prediction is considered the primary and fundamental use case for organizations that operate on a subscription-based model. Conversational interfaces have shown efficacy in comprehending churn patterns and providing offers aimed at minimizing churn.

5. Qualifying leads Chatbots

The process of qualifying leads refers to the evaluation and assessment of potential customers or clients to determine their suitability. The field of automotive technology encompasses the study and application of knowledge related to vehicles. Online platforms are responsible for the generation of a substantial number of leads for car dealerships. Therefore, it is essential for automotive companies to use conversion optimization strategies. Automobile companies are already using chatbots, such as Kia's Kian, to effectively address intricate customer enquiries and enhance conversion rates.

Electronic commerce, commonly referred to as e-commerce, is the buying and selling of goods. Chatbots have the potential to enhance user engagement in the realm of e-commerce, extending beyond the traditional means of interaction such as menus and buttons. Chatbots are computer programs designed to simulate human conversation through text or voice interactions.

In the year 2023, it is possible to develop a chatbot without the need for coding, hence enabling anyone to create such a tool at no cost. The chatbot builder provided is a no-code platform that offers a visual editor, allowing users to create chatbots without the need for programming skills. The current task at hand involves the conceptualization and development of automated software agents, often referred to as bots.

It seems that you have an interest in constructing a chatbot. The idea has much merit. Visual drag-and-drop editors have made it possible for individuals of any skill level to engage in the creation of chatbots. No superhuman abilities or advanced programming skills are required. Developing a chatbot might provide challenges and uncertainties on the appropriate starting point. The commencement of the task may be started promptly.

Developing a Chatbot involves many steps. The following steps provide a comprehensive, step-by-step analysis of the no-code chatbot construction approach.

Step 1:   Familiarize oneself with the objective of the chatbot.
Step 2:   choosing the preferred location.
Step 3:   involves the process of choosing a suitable chatbot platform.
Step 4:   the chatbot discourse is designed using a chatbot editor.
Step 5:   The fifth step involves doing a comprehensive evaluation of the chatbot's performance.
Step 6:   This step is training the chatbot.
Step 7:   involves the collection of user input.
Step 8:   it is important to closely monitor the analytics of the chatbot in order to improve its performance.

Implementing best practices is widely seen as the most efficient method for firms to streamline user experience. The following recommendations facilitate the development of a chatbot for organizational purposes. The engagement of customers is a crucial factor in determining the extent to which organizations may get benefits from chatbots.

The use of well-defined parameters and visual elements in chatbot design is a commendable approach. These practices enable the customization of chatbots for client interactions. To address consumer dissatisfaction stemming from extended waiting periods, it is essential to provide prompt responses. Best practices for choosing a Chatbot includes:

1. The purpose and scope of a study refer to the specific goals and boundaries that guide the research process.
2. Identify the target audience
3. The primary emphasis should be placed on the user interface (UI).
4. Interactions Resembling Human Behavior

5. It is important to maintain transparency on the limitations of a study or research project.
   6. Best Practices for Customization
   7. When making a selection for a chatbot, it is crucial to carefully consider many factors in order to ensure the most appropriate choice.
   8. Effectively Utilizing Analytics
   9. One way to enhance user interaction and streamline communication in conversational agents is by using quick replies. Quick replies are pre-defined response options that are shown to the user, allowing them to easily choose a response.
   10. The ability to establish connections using various messaging channels.

Chatbots have the potential to facilitate the establishment of client relationships. Website visits might potentially facilitate the establishment of robust collaborations for your firm. The use of sales and customer service chatbots facilitates the achievement of one's objectives. Chatbots have the potential to enhance company growth via many means:

1. ***Engagement of customers:*** The analysis of client responses by chatbots may enhance customer engagement. Consumers are categorized based on their specific characteristics and historical data, enabling personalized interaction. Bots has the ability to provide prompt and immediate responses. One of the primary objectives of businesses is to retain customers and mitigate the risk of client attrition to competitors.
2. ***Reduce customer service cost:*** Individualized customer service and the development of brand experience via personalized interactions. In order to optimize customer service expenditures, it is necessary to integrate several components.

Chatbots are computer programs designed to simulate human conversation through text or voice interactions. They are Chatbots provide cost-saving benefits by eliminating the need for supplementary human help.

During periods of high demand, it is possible to increase the capacity of AI-bots without incurring additional costs.

3. ***Analyze customer data to get insights:*** Organizations have the potential to use chatbots as a means of analyzing customer data in order to get valuable insights. In order to collect customer data, such as names and contact information, and afterwards create relevant insights.

Bots have the potential to assist by delivering prompt push notifications. Fostering active involvement of existing customers. Consumers are provided with product information and recommendations for content.

4. ***The Integration of Human Elements in Automation:*** The Implementation of Live Chat Agents for Client Inquiry can be implemented. The customer support service is now operational. The prompt discusses the efficiency of transitioning from a chatbot to a live chat, resulting in improved client engagement. The integration of live chat and chatbots enables round-the-clock accessibility.
5. ***Meet customer expectations:*** One possible approach for businesses to meet consumer expectations is via the use of bots as a means to engage with consumers.

Being proactive, responding promptly, and achieving higher open rates compared to email. Chatbots have the potential to enhance the personalization of customer experiences across several platforms. Numerous touchpoints have an impact on sales and conversions. Chatbots have the potential to provide assistance. Chatbots can be used in disseminating visual content and pertinent details on products, promotional offers, discounts to ensure precise targeting. Chatbots can be used by a business as follows:

1. Design and develop a personalized conversational agent.
2. Meet the objectives of a business and the expectations of its clients.
3. When selecting a chatbot builder for your channels, it is important to carefully consider your options.
4. The task at hand involves the design of conversation flows for a bot, ensuring the inclusion of appropriate nodes.
5. Conduct a comprehensive evaluation of your chatbot's performance and collect messages to get valuable information.

The use of customer data and feedback has the potential to facilitate the learning process of your bot. The advantages and disadvantages of chatbots can be summarized as follows. Chatbots facilitate the provision of round-the-clock customer care in a convenient manner. Free phone lines are a cost-effective alternative to hiring support employees in the long run. Chatbots have been making significant advancements in their ability to comprehend and assist customers by using artificial intelligence (AI) and natural language processing (NLP) technologies. Chatbots have the capability to collect many types of customer data, such as inquiries, response durations, and levels of satisfaction, which are highly valued by enterprises.

However, chatbots have limitations. Despite the advancements in natural language processing, there is always a possibility of misinterpretation of a customer's input, leading to nonsensical responses. Numerous chatbots possess limited capabilities in terms of their ability to respond to specific inquiries. The presence of generic remarks, together with a dearth of passion, empathy, and uniqueness, might potentially lead to feelings of frustration. In addition to the dissatisfaction experienced by clients due to the lack of human touch, the development and maintenance of chatbots may incur significant expenses, especially when customization and regular updates are required.

This book titled "Development of Emerging Chatbot Technology" is composed of eighteen chapters; ranging from introducing Chatbots, Chatbots vs. AI chatbots vs. virtual agents, How chatbots work, Types of chatbots, Chatbots applications, Designing and Building Bots, Customer service bots, Chatbots in Education, Chatbots in healthcare, Chatbots in e-commerce, Common chatbot use cases, Best practices and tips for selecting chatbots, How to begin & grow your Bot / AI business, and Future expectations about Chatbots.

The intended audience of this book comprises students who are pursuing undergraduate or postgraduate studies, as well as professionals and researchers engaged in the domains of information technology, business and management, education, media and communications, social sciences, and humanities, and are interested in staying abreast of the latest advancements in development and usages of Chatbots.

Dina Darwish
Ahram Canadian University, Egypt

Chapter 1
Chatbot Concepts and Basics

Dina Darwish
Ahram Canadian University, Egypt

ABSTRACT

A computer program that acts as if it is having a conversation with a human end user is known as a chatbot. Even while not all chatbots have artificial intelligence (AI), most current chatbots employ conversational AI methods like natural language processing (NLP) in order to comprehend the user's inquiries and provide automated replies to such inquiries. Such technologies often make use of facets of deep learning and natural language processing; nevertheless, chatbots that are far simpler have been present for decades prior to the advent of such technology. This chapter discusses chatbots' characteristics, how they work, and other topics related to chatbots.

INTRODUCTION

A chatbot refers to a software application that emulates human communication in interactions with a recipient. While it is true that not all chatbots possess artificial intelligence (AI), contemporary chatbots are increasingly using conversational AI methods, such as natural language processing (NLP), to comprehend user inquiries and provide automated replies.

Chatbots have the capability to facilitate information retrieval for users by promptly addressing inquiries and requests, using text input, voice input, or a combination of both, hence eliminating the need for human involvement or manual investigation.

The use of chatbot technology has become widespread, with its presence seen in many settings such as smart speakers in households, consumer-oriented platforms like SMS, WhatsApp, and Facebook Messenger, as well as business communication tools like Slack. The most recent advancement in AI chatbots, often known as "intelligent virtual assistants" or "virtual agents," has the capability to comprehend natural and unstructured conversations by using advanced language models. Furthermore, these chatbots are capable of automating pertinent duties. In addition to well recognized consumer-oriented intelligent virtual assistants such as Apple's Siri and Amazon Alexa, virtual agents are increasingly used inside workplace settings to provide support to both consumers and staff.

DOI: 10.4018/979-8-3693-1830-0.ch001

The first iterations of chatbots may be characterized as interactive Frequently Asked Questions (FAQ) programs that were designed to respond to a restricted range of frequently encountered inquiries using predetermined responses. Due to their limited ability to comprehend natural language, these systems often rely on users to choose from a set of basic keywords and phrases in order to progress the discussion. Conventional chatbot systems of a basic kind exhibit limitations in their ability to comprehend intricate inquiries, as well as respond to straightforward queries that have not been anticipated or programmed by developers.

Over the course of time, the algorithms used in chatbots have evolved to possess enhanced capabilities in terms of rules-based programming and natural language processing. Consequently, this advancement enables customers to articulate their inquiries in a conversational manner. This led to the emergence of a novel kind of chatbot that has contextual awareness and utilizes machine learning techniques to constantly enhance its capacity to accurately interpret and anticipate user questions by being exposed to an increasing amount of human language.

Contemporary artificial intelligence (AI) chatbots now use natural language understanding (NLU) techniques to interpret the semantic content of user input that lacks certain constraints, therefore addressing a range of challenges like typographical errors and language translation discrepancies. Sophisticated artificial intelligence (AI) methods are used to decipher the intended meaning behind user input. This extracted meaning is then associated with a particular "intent" that the user wants the chatbot to address. Subsequently, conversational AI techniques are utilized to provide a suitable and relevant answer. These AI technologies use both machine learning and deep learning, which are distinct components of AI, to construct a more detailed knowledge repository of questions and answers based on user interactions. The use of recent breakthroughs in large language models (LLMs) has resulted in enhanced customer satisfaction and expanded possibilities for chatbot applications.

This chapter discusses the characteristics of Chatbots, as well as the work of Chatbots, and their applications. The main topics to be covered in this chapter includes the following;

- The term Chatbot and its definition
- The Chatbot components
- How Chatbots Work
- Types of chatbots
- Common use cases of chatbots
- Benefits of chatbots
- Best practices and tips for selecting Chatbots
- Examples of Chatbots
- Chatbots in Education
- Chatbots in Medical Industry
- Common business uses of Chatbots
- Trends for Chatbots
- Future of Chatbots

Also, this chapter is organized as follows; the first section includes the background, then, the second section contains the main focus of the chapter, including the main topics stated in the previous section, then finally, the conclusion section is provided.

BACKGROUND

In 1950, regarding Computing Intelligence (Turing, 1950), logician, cryptanalyst, and computer science pioneer Alan Turing explores what thinking is and if machines can think. Since answering whether computers can think is tricky, he asks, 'Can a computer converse in a manner indistinguishable from human?' This criteria is part of the Turing test (Peregrim, 2005). A person communicates with the tested subject 'blindly' in a conversation game. After the conversation game, the individual must judge whether it was a real person or a chatbot. In this test, thinking is replaced with the capacity to communicate so that discussion participants see it as a thinking entity. Turing logically and fully addresses several possible objections and issues with the suggested solution in a paper.

Chatbots are computers, programs, algorithms, or artificial intelligences that converse with people. The goal is to make consumers feel like they're talking to a real person. According to Neff and Nagy (Neff & Nagy, 2016), a chatbot is a program that has conversations with people. Chatbots reply to user messages by picking an expression from preprogrammed schemas or, for developing bots, adaptive machine learning algorithms.

The first chatbot was created by MIT professor Joseph Weizenbaum in the 1960s, it was called ELIZA (theguardian, 2023). Joseph Weizenbaum designed it in 1966 to imitate speech using pattern matching and replacement. The program simulates human speech. The Chatbot ELIZA used a computer to match human input to a list of programmed answers. The script simulates a psychotherapist. The script influenced natural language processing and unnatural intelligence, with copies and modifications appearing at academies across. Weizenbaum was worried by user response. He meant ELIZA to be a satire of human dialogue, but users were confiding in her. Experts predicted chatbots will look like humans in a few years. Machines could not replace human cognition, according to Weizenbaum. He maintained that such technologies were human mind extensions and tools. He said that computers' language comprehension depended on context. Weizenbaum believed a more broad computer comprehension of human language was impossible. In the decades thereafter, chatbot designers have expanded on Weizenbaum's paradigm to mimic human interactions. Passing the Turing test, which pits new machines against human judges, has become a popular aim. The toughest part of the Turing test problem is that people can talk about anything.

In 1972, American psychiatrist Kenneth Colby created PARRY (chatbots, 2023). The program mimicked schizophrenia. It simulates sickness. A natural language program that thinks like a person. PARRY uses a complex system of assumptions, attributions, and "emotional responses" triggered by linguistic input weights. PARRY was verified using a Turing test to verify the work. In the early 1970s, human interrogators using a remote keyboard were unable to identify PARRY from an unreasonable person. Kenneth Mark Colby was the only doctor 50 years ago considering how computers may help us comprehend mental disease. Thus, started the "Overcoming Depression" project, which continued until his 2001 death.

Developer Rollo Carpenter built the chatbot in 1988. It tried to amuse by simulating human dialogue. Jabberwacky spurred subsequent tech advances. Since its creation, its homepage has been used for academic study. The chatbot uses AI termed "contextual pattern matching."

Hugh Loebner, an American inventor, social critic founded a Turing test competition in 1990. The first programmer or team to design a chatbot that passes the Turing test in front of a jury wins the Loebner Prize, $100,000 USD, and a gold medal. Even though no one has won, the best chatbot wins 2,000–3,000USD.The biggest Turing test ever was performed using chatbots.

Dr. Sbaitso (medium, 2023) is a 1992 MS-Dos chatbot created by Creative Labs. Its entire voice-operated chat program is one of the first chatbots that use A.I. The software would talk to users like psychologists. It mostly asked "Why do you feel that way?" rather than engaging in complex conversations.

Universal language processing chatbot A.L.I.C.E. (Wikipedia_1, 2023) employs heuristic pattern matching to communicate. Richard Wallace started ALICE in 1995. It was called Alicebot because it ran on an Alice computer originally. The program specifies conversation rules using AIML, an XML format. The program was edited in Java in 1998 and Wallace produced an AIML specification in 2001. From then, more developers published free and open ALICE sources in several programming languages and foreign languages. Program replicates Internet communication with actual person. Alice, a young-looking lady in human years, answers conversations and informs users about her age, interests, and other interesting things. Since, this was published in 1995, don't anticipate much in terms of user interface and design.

The 2001 SmarterChild (animasmarketing, 2023) was a forerunner to Siri. The chatbot on AOL IM and MSN Messenger may have interesting chats and quickly access other services. It fits Years after most people quit using AIM, which targeted 18- to 24-year-olds in the U.S., Microsoft created SmarterChild for specific conversations. Apple created Siri for iOS in 2010 as a natural language-based personal assistant and learning guide. It enabled all AI bots and PAs thereafter. A USPTO patent application describes a new Apple service that lets consumers chat with Siri over Messages. The latest patent, like one released late last year, integrates audio, video, and picture information more deeply. Apple's patent outlines a Siri that can accomplish tasks without being spoken to, like Facebook Messenger and texting. This might assist in various public areas. When transmitted by the user, they may respond to text, music, photos, and video. Apple stated this would improve consumer-digital assistant interaction. The patent shows Siri and a Messages user asking inquiries.

WeChat, a Chinese firm, (engati, 2023) developed a new chatbot in 2009. WeChat has won over many dedicated users since its introduction. It is a successful social networking platform. Its platform makes basic chatbots easy to construct. It is one of the most popular strategies for marketers and organizations to decrease online client interaction tasks. WeChat has ramifications and is less performant than Facebook Messenger, Slack, and Telegram, but you can still build a clever bot. Chumen Wenwen Company, formed in 2012 by a former Googler, has a powerful WeChat bot. The first generation of artificial data technology in chatbots was introduced in 2016. Facebook let developers to create a chatbot for their business or service so clients could do basic everyday tasks through their messaging platform. The conversational interface has arrived with chatbots in communities. The interface will soon not need a screen or mouse. The interface will be conversational, like our friends and family chats. To truly understand the massiveness of this soon-to-be reality, we must go back to the early days of the computer, when the yearning for AI and a conversational interface arose.

Google Inch released Google Now (Wikipedia_2, 2023) in 2012. It answers queries, conducts activities using online services, and provides suggestions. Mobile search upgrades and UI changes included a female-voiced portable assistant to compete with Siri. Google Now first provided location- and time-based information. It became increasingly intricate and elaborate, with several content types on cards. Sometimes it uses predictive search. It has been modified for smartphone usage and contains various features.

Google Assistant (googleassistant, 2023) replaced Now in 2017. The assistant is now part of Google's ambitious search growth plan. Google aims to provide you easy-to-read information before you need it. Google Assistant Leads Voice Assistants with Cortana, which was introduced during Microsoft's Build 2014 developer conference and incorporated with Windows phone and Windows 10 PCs. Spoken recognition and related algorithms let this program understand and react to spoken instructions. Start by typing a query in the search box or talking to Cortana using the microphone. If a user is unsure what to say, the lock screen and taskbar search box will provide ideas in Cortana home. Cortana can send emails and SMS, build and manage lists, talk, play games, and access facts, files, locations, and data.

Amazon's Alexa (alexaamazon, 2023) is a smart assistant. It was released in 2014 and is in Amazon Echo, Echo Dot, Echo Show, and others. The Alexa app and additional third-party devices with Alexa are also available. Just say "Alexa, play some music" or "Alexa, find me an Italian restaurant" and she will assist. Search the Web, play music, make to-do or shopping lists, set alarms, stream podcasts, play audiobooks, receive news or weather reports, operate smart-home gadgets, and more with your voice. To enhance any Alexa-enabled device, Amazon lets developers design and distribute Alexa Skills Kit skills. Alexa offers free skill downloads.

Xiaoice (read Shao-ice, literally 'Microsoft Little Ice' or 'Little Bing' - after Microsoft's web browser) (Wang, 2016) is an advanced chatbot created by Microsoft that acts as a seventeen-year-old Chinese girl who uses Weibo, a popular Chinese social networking site. We may also communicate with her on social media platforms like 163.com and JD.com (now encompassing over 40 platforms in five regions).

Microsoft used numerous groundbreaking technologies, particularly big data leverage and emotional intelligence, owing to software designers and psychologists. This program learns from users and may respond to discussion themes. She employs such replies to hide her confusion about the topic. In these instances, she expresses guilt or rage like others. In 6th generation Xiaoice, AI emotional Quotient powers are improved. A self-perfecting system uses data from earlier talks and the whole Chinese Internet. Users find communication complexity and irregularity believable, honest, and realistic. Deep learning, inspired by biological neural networks, allows the chatbot to detect patterns in behavior, meaning, voice, picture, and others. This method has earned Xiaoice 660 million network followers (Wang, 2016; Markoff & Mozour, 2015). Japanese messaging app Line unveiled Rinna, Xiaoice's equivalent. On April 23, 2016, Microsoft unveiled Tay, a sophisticated, emerging chatbot with a self-development mechanism, in the US.

OpenAI trained ChatGPT (chatopenai, 2023) is a huge language model. The OpenAI team founded it 2021. It helps users generate human-like text from input. Conversation creation and language translation are possible with ChatGPT. The algorithm generates language that is hard to differentiate from human writing after being trained on a vast quantity of data. ChatGPT has been lauded for its natural-sounding writing and versatile uses. As seen, chatbots have advanced.

Also, Google developed Google's Bard Chatbot (cnet, 2023), as an Alternative to ChatGPT, and the generative AI tool is available in English in many parts of the world.

MAIN FOCUS OF THE CHAPTER

The Term Chatbot and its Definition

A chatbot may be described as a conversational software program that assists in customer service, engagement, and support. It functions by either replacing or enhancing human support agents via the use of artificial intelligence (AI) and other automation technologies, enabling it to participate in chat-based communication with end-users.

In contemporary business practices, a growing number of enterprises have adopted the use of chatbots as a means to streamline and automate many aspects of user interaction and transactional functionalities. Organizations have seen significant cost reductions and enhanced operational efficiency via the reduction of their need on support workers and live operators. Chatbots are computational algorithms that imitate and evaluate human discourse, facilitating human interaction with electronic devices in a manner akin to speaking with a human operator. Chatbots include a spectrum of capabilities, spanning from rudimentary applications that provide limited responses to complex virtual assistants that possess the ability to acquire and enhance their knowledge via data collection and analysis, hence delivering heightened degrees of customization.

Chatbots have been effectively incorporated into several aspects of our everyday routines. As an example, one may find themselves perusing an electronic commerce platform on their personal computer with the intention of procuring a certain thing, when suddenly a pop-up window materializes on their display, inquiring whether they are in need of any sort of aid. In an alternative scenario, an individual has the option to use voice input as a means of placing an order for a beverage at a retail establishment in close proximity. Subsequently, they would get a notification informing them of the estimated time at which the order would be prepared and the corresponding cost. The following are examples of customer experience situations in which individuals may interact with a chatbot.

The proliferation of chatbots in contemporary times may be attributed to the rapid advancement of digital transformation. There is a growing trend among businesses to transition from conventional methods of communication to digital platforms in order to engage and conduct transactions with their clientele. Artificial intelligence (AI) is used by businesses to enhance operational efficiency across many customer-centric operations, with chatbots being one of the prominent uses of AI inside an organization. According to Gartner's projections for 2022, it is anticipated that by the conclusion of this year, almost 70% of white-collar workers would engage in everyday interactions with chatbots and conversational platforms. The spectrum of applications includes personal robotic advisers such as Google Assistant and Amazon's Alexa, as well as chatbots seamlessly integrated into messaging platforms like Facebook Messenger and WeChat.

Chatbots may provide many advantages to businesses, including enhanced performance and cost savings. Moreover, they facilitate consumer convenience and provide supplementary services to internal personnel, customers, and partners. Businesses are enabled to promptly address a range of concerns among stakeholders, hence reducing reliance on human intervention. In the digital era, companies have the ability to enhance their operations by using chatbots, which serve as a crucial distinguishing factor. These chatbots enable companies to effectively expand their operations, tailor experiences to individual customers, and proactively engage with users. When a firm only depends on human labor, it is constrained in its ability to serve a certain number of people simultaneously, hence restricting its capacity and impeding its potential for expansion. Organizations that have labor-intensive procedures are obligated to depend on inflexible models in order to achieve cost efficiency, resulting in restricted opportunities for proactive and personalized outreach.

Conversely, chatbots facilitate the ability of organizations to engage with a vast multitude of customers in a customized manner, with the flexibility to adjust the scope of operations according to prevailing demands. The chatbot has the capability to provide a service that closely resembles human interaction, customized to suit the needs of each individual user, even while simultaneously serving millions of clients.

The Chatbot Components

Chatbots usually have 7 parts and are arranged as follows:

Natural Language Processing

Natural language processing (NLP) lets chatbots arrange users' text and voice for machine comprehension. NLP involves these steps:

- Tokenization, often termed lexical analysis, divides a phrase into "tokens" based on meaning and association.
- Normalization, sometimes termed syntactic analysis, corrects mistakes and standardized language. For instance, "tmrw" will become "tomorrow."
- Entity recognition: searching for terms to determine the discussion subject.
- Semantic analysis: inferring a sentence's meaning from each word and its structure.
- Sponsored: To boost customer retention and minimize contact center effort, Tata Mutual

Natural Language Understanding

- A subsection of NLP, natural language understanding (NLU), employs patterns in unstructured voice input to interpret human speech. NLU solutions have 3 parts:
- Dictionary to find word meaning
- Parser checks text syntax for language rules.
- Grammar rules separate input by sentence form and punctuation.

NLU lets chatbots identify user intentions and respond using training data.

Knowledge Base

The chatbot retrieves facts from a knowledge base to answer to users. Business demands shape knowledge bases. An e-commerce website chatbot's knowledge base will have items, features, and pricing, while a healthcare chatbot's will comprise doctors' schedules, hospital hours, and pharmacy tasks. Some chatbots employ web scrapers to present data from internet sources.

Storage of Data

Developers may keep chatbot chats for customer service and training and testing. On-premise or cloud-based SQL may store chatbot dialogues.

Dialogue Manager

A dialogue manager controls user-chatbot communication. It stores one conversation's exchanges to adjust its answers later. If the user says, "I want to order strawberry ice cream" and then adds, "change my order to chocolate ice cream," the dialogue manager will allow the bot to identify the change and alter the order.

Figure 1. Components of a chatbot

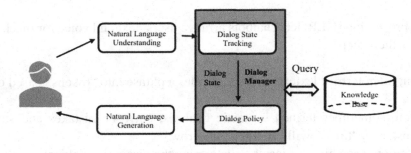

Natural Language Generation

Natural language generation (NLG) converts structured machine data into human-readable text. After recognizing user intent, NLG responds in 4 steps:

- Content determination: Filtering knowledge base data to choose answer content.
- Data interpretation: Exploring knowledge base patterns and responses.
- Document planning: Narrative response structure.
- Putting together the phrases and words for each sentence in the answer.

    Punctuation and spellcheck are used.

6. *Language implementations:* Using language templates to represent responses naturally.
7. *User interfaces:* Conversational user interfaces allow chatbots to physically depict conversations. They are voice- or text-based assistants. They can interface with Facebook Messenger, WhatsApp, Slack, Google Teams, etc.

    Figure 1 illustrates the components of a chatbot.

How Chatbots Work

In order to comprehend the functioning of a chatbot, it is imperative to first contemplate the three fundamental procedures that propel this technology. There are three mechanisms that need attention, including rules-based procedures, AI-driven decision-making, and live agent interaction. The functioning of a chatbot may vary depending on its underlying mechanism.

What is the Operational Mechanism Behind Chatbots That Use Rules-Based Processes?

The chatbot software that operates on rules follows a predetermined set of behaviors, which are designed in advance and are created via the backend module of the user interface. Similar to a digital assistant, rules-based chatbot technology has the ability to exhibit certain behaviors in response to user interactions, such as clicking on particular elements or providing basic inputs like "yes" or "no". Additionally, it has the capability to identify a particular term or a combination of phrases, but only in cases when there is an exact match.

An example of this would be the implementation of a rules-based chatbot that can respond to user inputs such as "black" or "white," as well as more specific statements like "I desire a black item." In this scenario, the chatbot's backend module would use a pre-established rule to associate the word "black" with the appropriate response.

What is the Operational Mechanism Behind Chatbots That Use AI-Powered Decision-Making?

Artificial intelligence chatbots use artificial intelligence and natural language processing (NLP) techniques to discern the syntactic structure of sentences, comprehend the information conveyed, and enhance their proficiency in responding to inquiries.

Instead than depending on a predetermined set of responses, AI chatbots first ascertain the content of the customer or user's input. Subsequently, after comprehending the user's query, the chatbot proceeds to provide a response that it deems accurate, relying on the facts at its disposal. The computer acquires knowledge about the optimal answer via the process of analyzing both accurate and inaccurate replies.

The effectiveness of a chatbot may be greatly enhanced by the use of AI-driven decision-making processes, contingent upon the chatbot possessing a comprehensive comprehension of the organization, its clientele, and the contextual factors at play. The use of this feature is mostly seen in major firms such as e-commerce entities and other businesses with huge transaction volumes that need scalability.

What is the Operational Mechanism Behind Chatbots That Use Live Agent Interaction?

Live chat is a kind of chat system that is integrated into a website or mobile application, serving as a means for consumers to interact with a support staff and contact center. By using this method, chatbots include routing functionalities to allocate conversations in real-time.

When a client requires communication with a member of your team, the chatbot examines the availability of agents and directs the request for conversation appropriately. The system will establish a connection between the consumer and a qualified individual who has the necessary expertise and abilities to assist them in resolving their issue. The chatbot further notifies the agent upon receiving a consumer enquiry and provides the client with pertinent agent information, such as their name and estimated wait time. It is evident that these procedures are quite comprehensible, considering the boundless improvements in chatbot technology that are now available and easily accessible to both users and developers. Figure 2 shows how an AI chatbot works.

Types of Chatbots

Numerous firms throughout the globe are now engaged in the development of various types of chatbots with the aim of improving customer service. This section provides an overview of the many classifications of chatbots, their respective applications, and an evaluation of the potential advantages of specific chatbot software for your organization. There are several classifications of chatbots based on their

Figure 2. How an AI chatbot works

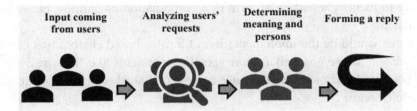

functionality and design. These classifications include rule-based chatbots, retrieval-based chatbots, generative chatbots, and hybrid, as well as other types.

Hybrid Bot

A hybrid chatbot refers to a synergistic integration of chatbot technology with live chat functionality, effectively incorporating the advantageous aspects of both approaches. A live chat feature will be provided to customers, enabling them to seek assistance from a customer support professional. This service is particularly beneficial for addressing inquiries that are intricate or need nuanced understanding beyond the capabilities of automated systems. The conversational replication of dialogues in a chatbot is facilitated by an AI component, which operates in accordance with its programming and the specific requirements of the discussion at hand. In contrast, a hybrid chatbot would proactively establish an automated chat dialogue and endeavor to efficiently and succinctly address the user's inquiry. In the event that the chatbot fails to perform as anticipated, a customer support agent has the ability to intervene at any given time or within the specific domain in which the chatbot is unable to successfully do the job.

Voice Bot

A voice bot refers to an AI-driven communication channel that utilizes natural language understanding (NLU) to convert spoken words into written text and vice versa. Artificial intelligence (AI) technology plays a crucial role in the identification of significant speech signals and the subsequent determination of the most effective conversational response. The text-to-speech (TTS) engine eventually finalizes the interaction by transforming the textual content into auditory output or speech. The bots are designed to execute the full process of comprehending and responding to speech in a way that resembles human behavior. speech assistants or speech chatbots provide a highly advanced form of communication that can be easily integrated into many customer care platforms, such as interactive voice response (IVR), self-service systems, and online knowledge bases.

Menu-Based Chatbots

Menu-based chatbots are a kind of conversational agent that use a structured menu system to interact with users. These chatbots provide users with a predetermined set of options. The most basic kind of chatbot currently used is a menu-driven navigation system. Typically, chatbots adhere to a predetermined decision tree structure, which is presented to users in the format of clickable buttons. Chatbots, similar to the automated dial pad menus often seen on telephones, prompt users to make several selections and click on appropriate alternatives in order to reach a final resolution. While these chatbots are sufficient for handling commonly requested queries, which constitute the majority of support inquiries, they may be insufficient in more complex situations. In situations when a multitude of factors or a high level of knowledge are involved, the menu-based chatbot may encounter limitations in its ability to assist users in reaching the correct answer. It is noteworthy to acknowledge that menu-based chatbots exhibit a more slower pace in providing substantial benefits to consumers. However, they possess the advantage of being uncomplicated and cost-effective for first implementation.

Skills Chatbots

A skills chatbot refers to a kind of bot that has the ability to execute a certain range of activities, provided that its capabilities have been expanded via the use of pre-defined skills software. For instance, the chatbot has the capability to provide weather updates, control the illumination of your living space via integration with a smart home device, facilitate online grocery shopping, and so forth. By having access to the source code of a skill, developers have the ability to create their own chatbots with specific functionalities and seamlessly incorporate them into other platforms.

Social Messaging Chatbots

Social messaging chatbots are computer programs designed to interact with users via messaging platforms, such as social media or messaging apps. These chatbots use artificial intelligence and natural language processing techniques to understand and respond to user queries. The advent of emerging social media interfaces has enabled organizations to use an artificial intelligence (AI) algorithm across several messaging channels favored by their customers. This encompasses many social media platforms such as Facebook Messenger, Twitter, Instagram, as well as popular messaging applications like WhatsApp and WeChat. This feature facilitates a more enjoyable digital experience for clients and enhances the level of interaction for the organization, all while avoiding any additional burden on the contact center's operational demands.

Keyboard-Based Chatbots

Keyword-based chatbots are a kind of conversational agent that rely on certain keywords or phrases to provide appropriate responses. These chatbots often use a predefined set of keywords. Keyword-based chatbots has the ability to attentively perceive and comprehend the input provided by visitors, hence enabling them to provide accurate responses. This distinguishes them from menu-based chatbots, which lack this capability. These chatbots use customized keywords and natural language processing (NLP) techniques to identify action triggers inside the discussion, enabling them to comprehend how to provide relevant responses to the customer. Nevertheless, in the presence of several comparable queries, these chatbots may exhibit limitations. The performance of chatbots may deteriorate when there is a high frequency of keyword repeats in a series of related queries.

Hence, there is a growing popularity of chatbots that integrate keyword detection with menu or button-based navigation. In the event of a failure in keyword identification or if the user need more assistance in locating an answer, chatbots provide users the ability to input instructions directly via clickable navigation buttons. This strategy serves as a viable solution in cases when the bot fails to identify relevant keywords within the provided textual input.

AI Powered Chatbots

AI-powered contextual chatbots are computer programs that use artificial intelligence (AI) technology to engage in conversations with users in a manner that takes into account the context of the conversation. Chatbots with contextual understanding have the ability to comprehend the context of a conversation and accurately interpret the intended meaning behind the user's query. Additionally, it has the capability to retrieve previous encounters and use that data to ensure relevancy throughout engagements with returning clientele. Contextual bots has the ability to ensure that users that return to the system are provided with a constant and uniform experience. In addition, it has the capability to store and use data on user intention collected from various platforms and channels, so guaranteeing that the context of the conversation aligns with the requirements of the individual at each interaction point. Contextual chatbots are integrated with a centralized database, often a customer relationship management (CRM) system or a customer data platform (CDP). This allows users to access important data on the person they are conversing with, such their personal identification, geographical whereabouts, or previous purchasing records.

Rule-Based Chatbots

A rule-based chatbot is particularly well-suited for organizations that possess prior knowledge on the specific categories of enquiries that their clients are likely to pose. Chat flows are constructed by the use of conditional statements, namely if/then logic. Prior to implementing chat flows, it is essential to set the linguistic prerequisites for the chatbot. The fundamental principles of its operation include the criteria for assessing words, word structure, synonyms, and related aspects. Customers will be provided with expeditious support if an incoming enquiry aligns with the specified criteria. It is important to acknowledge that the developer bears the obligation of encompassing a wide range of question permutations and combinations to the fullest extent feasible. Failure to do so would result in the chatbot's inability to comprehend the user or provide appropriate responses.

Support Chatbots

Supporting chatbots has become more prevalent in several industries. These automated conversational agents have shown to be valuable tools for businesses, providing efficient and effective customer support. The Support chatbots are conversational systems specifically developed to provide client support and services after a transaction has been made. In contrast to automated systems present on social media platforms or websites, these bots refrain from disseminating promotional content, offers, or any other materials aimed at engaging customers. This particular kind of chatbot is often seen on self-service portals and online documentation platforms, where users frequently seek assistance and guidance. Support chatbots are extensively used for internal functions, such as addressing human resources inquiries, initiating information technology tickets, and facilitating the submission of employee documentation, among other tasks.

No Code or Low Code Chatbots

Historically, chatbots have been constructed and programmed utilizing coding techniques to establish decision trees and use artificial intelligence (AI) and machine learning (ML) algorithms to drive the functionality of the technology. Every programming language is equipped with a web API that may be used for the development of chatbots. In addition to PHP and Node.js, several libraries that facilitate the use of Python or Java are often employed in ordinary installations. Nevertheless, recent technological improvements have facilitated the use of chatbots by organizations, hence reducing the need for extensive coding expertise. The presence of a graphical user interface (GUI) facilitates the expeditious delivery of applications and the rapid production of value, since it enables the construction and configuration of the bot. No-code deployments are well-suited for chatbots designed for information collection and promoting human engagement. On the other hand, low-code chatbots are well-suited for organizations seeking to include distinctive functionalities while minimizing the resources allocated to development.

Transactional Bots

Transactional bots refer to a kind of automated computer programs that are designed to facilitate and execute transactions between users and systems. Transactional chatbots have the potential to enhance the sales and marketing endeavors of organizations by facilitating tasks such as appointment scheduling, lead generating, and payment collection. Users have the ability to engage in transactions autonomously via direct interaction with the chatbot, without the need for human involvement. The primary advantage of this technology is in its capacity to facilitate transactions and sustain corporate operations continuously throughout the year, without any time constraints. Consequently, there exists a distinction between transactional chatbots and other categories of bots, such as informative or support bots. The primary objective of this system is to efficiently execute transactions and enhance customer satisfaction by providing a streamlined and expedient platform dedicated to a single goal. The system is specifically designed to manage a limited range of specialized jobs. Figure 3 shows main types of chatbots.

Common Use Cases of Chatbots

Chatbots are used by consumers for a wide range of purposes, including interacting with mobile applications and operating specialized products like intelligent thermostats and smart kitchen appliances. The use of business practices is likewise diverse. AI-powered chatbots are used by marketers to enhance consumer experiences and optimize e-commerce operations. Similarly, IT and HR teams utilize these chatbots to facilitate employee self-service. Furthermore, contact centers depend on chatbots to simplify incoming communications and efficiently guide clients towards relevant resources.

Conversational interfaces can exhibit variability. Artificial intelligence (AI) chatbots are often used across several platforms, including social network messaging applications, independent messaging platforms, proprietary websites and applications, and even in telephony systems, where they are referred to as integrated voice response (IVR) systems. Common applications encompass:

- The provision of prompt and continuous support for matters pertaining to customer service or human resources.
- Customized recommendations within the realm of electronic commerce

Figure 3. Main types of chatbots

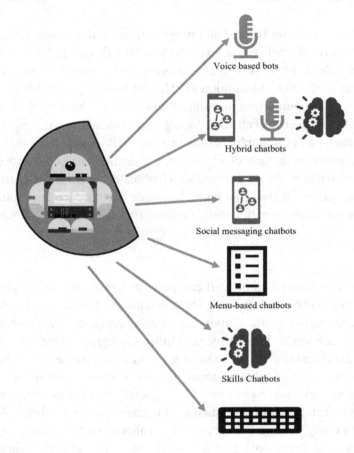

- The delineation and characterization of several categories or domains inside forms and financial applications.
- The process of managing patient intake and arranging appointments in healthcare facilities.
- Automated reminders are used to prompt individuals about duties that are contingent upon either temporal or spatial factors.

Benefits of Chatbots

The capacity of chatbots to effectively comprehend real human language and automate customized service yields evident advantages for both organizations and consumers.

Enhance Consumer Involvement and Foster Brand Loyalty

Prior to the emergence of chatbots, any inquiries, issues, or grievances from customers, regardless of their magnitude, need a response from a human agent. It is not uncommon for client difficulties to emerge outside of regular business hours, such as during weekends, holidays, or other off-hours. However, the task of adequately staffing customer support departments to accommodate fluctuating demand throughout the day and night has significant financial and logistical challenges.

Currently, chatbots has the capability to effectively handle consumer contacts around the clock, ensuring a constant level of service. Moreover, they have a propensity for enhancing the quality of their replies over time, all the while maintaining cost efficiency. Chatbots have the capability to streamline processes and alleviate staff from engaging in monotonous and repetitive chores. A chatbot has the potential to mitigate extended waiting periods associated with phone-based customer service, as well as the even lengthier wait times for email, chat, and web-based help. This is due to its instantaneous availability to several users simultaneously. The positive user experience contributes to increased brand loyalty since happy consumers are more inclined to display loyalty towards the company.

Minimize Expenditures and Enhance Operational Effectiveness

Maintaining round-the-clock staffing for a customer care center incurs significant costs. Similarly, the expenditure of time dedicated to addressing recurrent inquiries (together with the necessary training to ensure consistent responses) also incurs expenses. Numerous international corporations have the option of outsourcing these operations; nevertheless, this approach entails notable expenses and diminishes the level of control a brand has over its client interactions.

In contrast, a chatbot have the capability to respond to inquiries continuously throughout the week, encompassing all hours of the day. The implementation of this system has many benefits, including the provision of initial help, the ability to augment support during high-demand times, and the alleviation of monotonous and repeated inquiries, so enabling human agents to dedicate their attention to more intricate matters. Chatbots have the potential to mitigate the need for human intervention, hence enhancing the operational efficiency of enterprises by enabling them to effectively expand their workforce to accommodate rising demand or handle inquiries during non-business hours.

Generate Leads and Meet Customers' Needs

Chatbots have the potential to assist in the development of sales leads and enhance the rates at which these leads are converted into actual sales. For instance, a consumer perusing a website for a certain product or service may possess inquiries about several characteristics, traits, or options. A chatbot has the capability to offer these responses in real-time, therefore assisting the consumer in advancing towards making a purchase. In the context of intricate transactions including a sales funnel with several stages, a chatbot may be used to inquire about lead qualification and perhaps provide a direct connection between the consumer and a proficient sales representative.

Best Practices and Tips for Selecting Chatbots

The process of choosing an appropriate chatbot platform may provide substantial benefits for both enterprises and individuals using the technology. The provision of instant and continuous help to users offers them advantages, while organizations may enhance their ability to fulfil expectations without incurring substantial expenses associated with employee restructuring.

As an illustration, an electronic commerce enterprise has the capability to use a chatbot system in order to provide prospective buyers who are perusing their offerings with enhanced and comprehensive details pertaining to the specific items they are examining. The HR department of a business organization may request a developer to identify a chatbot capable of providing workers with comprehensive access to their self-service perks. Software developers may have a desire to seamlessly include an artificial intelligence chatbot into their intricate software product.

Regardless of the specific situation or project at hand, this section presents five recommended practices and guidelines for the process of picking a chatbot platform.

1. ***Select a system that is capable of achieving your current objectives*** without imposing constraints on future scalability. What are the reasons behind a team's desire to own its own chatbot? The present approach to addressing this objective will be discussed. Does the platform include pre-designed templates that facilitate the expansion and diversification of chatbot offers for your organization in the future, or would alternative teams be required to create a solution from the beginning? Does the price structure facilitate effective internal expansion?

2. ***Comprehend the influence of artificial intelligence on the customer experience.*** Chatbots serve as an expansion of one's brand. The appropriate artificial intelligence (AI) has the capacity to effectively comprehend consumers' requirements and the manner in which these requirements are expressed, while also possessing the ability to provide responses that are devoid of robotic characteristics, therefore enhancing the reputation of your firm. In the absence of appropriate artificial intelligence (AI) technologies, a chatbot might be seen as just an enhanced frequently asked questions (FAQ) system.

3. ***Inquire about the necessary steps involved in constructing, training, and enhancing the chatbot's capabilities*** over an extended period. Are you seeking a basic and pre-existing solution, or a more advanced API access for tailored implementation? Artificial intelligence does not undergo self-training. It is essential to possess a comprehensive understanding of the pre-existing goals and content, as well as the tasks that need original creation. Certain chatbots include the functionality to use past chatlogs and transcripts in order to generate these intentions, hence resulting in time efficiency. Individuals that use machine learning techniques have the capability to automatically adapt and enhance their replies iteratively.

4. ***One should actively seek opportunities to establish connections with, rather than replace, current investments.*** Frequently, emergent channels or technologies have potential to replace old ones. However, they transform into a mere conduit through which an organization may exercise control and oversight. A chatbot that establishes connections with various channels and client case systems may provide a combination of advantages: enhancing the customer experience by incorporating modern features, and improving the accuracy of directing users to the appropriate information and persons capable of resolving their issues.

5. ***In order to ascertain if the chatbot fulfils the necessary criteria for deployment, scalability, and security, an evaluation must be conducted.*** Each organization and industry has distinct compliance standards and demands, therefore necessitating a clear definition of these criteria. Numerous chatbots are deployed via cloud-based platforms in order to use insights and results obtained from previous client interactions. Consequently, if you are in need of an on-premises solution or a dedicated environment, the number of suppliers offering such services is rather limited. It is vital to comprehend the manner in which data is used, along with the potential ramifications it may have, particularly inside sectors subject to stringent regulations.

Examples of Chatbots

The following list presents five notable instances of chatbot implementation anticipated in the year 2022. Examples of chatbot implementations may be seen across a wide range of prominent companies that possess a significant online presence. Here are five illustrative instances of the primary applications of chatbot technology within distinct sectors and specific use cases.

The Use of Lead Generating Chatbots on Websites

These chatbots use a conversational methodology to gather data from website visitors, assist clients in navigating the buying process, or evaluate potential leads. These tools assist users in navigating through many alternatives and enable firms to actively connect with potential customers, hence reducing the likelihood of website abandonment. Lead-generating chatbots have shown to be very efficient in establishing and nurturing connections with individuals who visit websites, ensuring continuous engagement throughout the whole week, around the clock.

Chatbots for Information Retrieval and Application Submission in the Insurance Industry

Insurance firms have the ability to use chatbots as a means of engaging with customers, offering policy quotes, collecting insurance premium payments, promoting other goods and services, and performing many other functions. The approach to doing this might be either based on a set of predefined rules or using artificial intelligence techniques together with natural language processing. Furthermore, the insurance industry, along with the broader financial services sector, has extensively depended on human agents. Chatbots facilitate the expansion of insurance firms' outreach to a far broader demographic, hence streamlining the claims processing experience for clients.

Virtual Assistants Have Become More Prevalent in the Realm of Information Retrieval on Smartphones

A significant proportion of smartphone users use voice assistants such as Google Now, Cortana, Siri, and Alexa on a daily basis for information retrieval purposes. The virtual assistant has the capability to actively listen, generate responses, and execute various activities, including but not limited to sending electronic correspondence, executing online searches, launching applications, furnishing meteorological data, and similar functions. One significant advantage is in the ability to use voice commands for controlling a wide range of functions, facilitated by the integration of voice-to-text and text-to-speech capabilities.

Customer Support Chatbots Are Automated Systems That Are Integrated Into E-Commerce Platforms

These chatbots are designed to provide assistance and support to customers in a virtual environment. The use of chatbots in the e-commerce sector has resulted in a significant transformation, facilitating merchants in delivering enhanced shopping experiences to their customers. The aforementioned entities streamline a comprehensive framework of intricate interconnections and propel commercial progress as an integral component of a broader process to mechanize processes and embrace technology that facilitate customer service. E-commerce applications use chatbot technology to maintain client contacts exclusively inside the online realm, hence minimizing the need for direct, in-person engagements.

The Implementation of Automated Bill Payment Systems by Utility Providers

Chatbots have emerged as a valuable tool for utility companies, enabling them to provide customer care on demand, reducing their need on human customer service teams. This has proven particularly crucial during the COVID-19 epidemic. The use of chatbots has a substantial influence on bill payments, since it enables customers to conveniently input their service identification number, prompting the chatbot to autonomously get their most up-to-date invoice. Through the use of transactional systems, clients are able to conveniently settle their outstanding payments immediately inside the application, eliminating the need for a physical visit to the utility company's office. This measure guarantees the provision of continuous service and the punctual processing of payments.

Chatbots in Education

The education institutions have to be designed for internet-savvy students. Zoomers grew up on smartphones and tablets, so technology is important in all areas of learning, from generating and distributing course materials to absorbing and memorizing them. Students now have fast access to all forms of information and demand answers anywhere, anytime. Technology has also enabled more collaborative learning and transformed the teacher's role from knowledge holder to guider. Although these changes occur, students still learn at various speeds and have distinct needs and talents. Teachers in crowded classrooms cannot always provide students equal attention. Though not always possible, personal instruction is an excellent choice. Chatbots might be a cheaper option.

AI, NLP, and machine learning allow chatbots to talk to pupils. They have discovered learning and comprehension gaps and can immediately deliver relevant, useful information, propose alternative tactics, answer queries, and provide further knowledge to assist people get back on track.

There are two chatbot application clusters: "service-oriented chatbots" and "teaching-oriented chatbots." Chatbots are widely employed during college applications, when institutional resources are swamped and students and parents are irritated and confused. Chatbots may answer course questions, start registration, and minimize a teacher's burden as virtual teaching assistants.

Second, chatbots answer typical student questions and guide them to lesson plans, course modules, deadlines, and assignments. Education is becoming tech-driven. Chatbots minimize customer service and administrative staff. Chatbots answer questions quickly, leading students and parents through the fast funnel and encouraging action. Educational chatbot uses include:

- Personal online tutoring
- Improved student involvement
- Questions about enrolling in courses
- Active student support
- Administrative and teaching assistant duties
- Global ties

- Feedback and data storage
- Assessment of student learning gaps and educational needs
- Student sentiment analysis

This section discusses real-world education chatbot uses, as follows:

Student Input

Feedback from students may improve course content, facilities, and the learning experience. Education institutions need excellent achievements and student happiness to build their reputations. Chatbots may gather student comments and other useful data to influence development strategies.

Supporting Students

Since the COVID-19 epidemic, education delivery has changed. Global e-learning is growing rapidly, with a 9.1% compound annual growth rate by 2026. Distance learning and online courses allow individuals to study while working without commuting or taking time away from family. Online learning institutions must provide great student assistance to accommodate this expansion. Before, during, and after enroll-ments, questions must be answered quickly. Chatbots for education give intelligent help and on-the-spot solutions to clear up concerns, provide more information, and promote student-institution relationships.

Course Queries

A chatbot can easily answer questions regarding scholarships or university courses for parents and students. The sequence might include lead capture sequences.

Registration Aides

Chatbots may automatically persuade students to join up for webinars, art classes, and class trips. Chatbots may minimize admin time, expenses, and human involvement in this manner.

Teaching Help

Sometimes, teachers can be exhausted. Overburdened institutional employees may use chatbots to provide "hands-off" improved learning experiences to students. AI-powered bots can handle data-driven repetitive activities. These AI-powered teaching helpers can check attendance, score tests, and distribute assignments, relieving busy teachers. In automatic attendance, chatbots might transmit lecture notes or audio recordings to absent students to keep them up to date.

Student Involvement

Non-engagement with learning impacts student results. Students that are more involved in their learning material do better academically, according to studies. Chatbots' continual presence may enhance student engagement. Intelligent chatbots talk with pupils and answer questions quickly. Chatbots may help students before, during, and after lessons to improve their virtual learning experience and avoid compromise.

Future of AI and chatbots in education is bright. Current AI advancements like ChatGPT's natural language processing and machine learning capabilities may make chatbots more advanced and flexible. Early diagnosis of struggling pupils and personalized tuition will benefit educational institutions.

Chatbots for essay scoring and marking might transform education. Teachers may save time and provide students faster feedback using intelligent essay-scoring bots. Spaced Interval Learning is another potential chatbot idea. Chatbots may assist pupils remember lessons by reminding them at regular intervals.

Chatbots in Medical Industry

Chatbot uses in medical industry includes:

Humanized Mental Health Interface

Many chatbots feature a humanized interface that makes consumers feel like they're chatting to a real person. For some individuals, talking about their feelings and worries is crucial to improving their mental health. These patients should utilize a healthcare conversational chatbot to convey their ideas. A healthcare practitioner will swiftly take control if the chatbot cannot meet their demands while referencing the experiences.

Making Medical Appointments

Chatbots streamline appointment scheduling and patient follow-up. They can organize and update personnel schedules outside of emergencies. Chatbots can assist patients book appointments and verify healthcare personnel schedules. A simple and effective medical appointment chatbot frees up staff to focus on more complicated patient requirements and reduces human mistake and scheduling problems.

Tracking Symptoms

Chatbots let patients talk about their symptoms and feelings and save this information in a database. The chatbot may ask essential questions like a person's temperature, length of stay, and other symptoms.

Drug and Medical Information Assistance

Chatbots help frequent healthcare users. Health workers may utilize bots to connect people to physicians. Babylon Health Services has a history of comprehensive health issues and remote consulting.

Hire and Train

Healthcare organizations regularly recruit and onboard new employees. They generate a lot of paperwork that must be completed and double-checked to handle these applications.

Business Healthcare Chatbot Development

Lupin launched 'ANYA', a medically validated chatbot for health questions. The first Indian illness awareness bot. It is an Indian enterprise that listens to patient health concerns. As patients comply with therapy and comprehend their symptoms, medical chatbots reduce patient visits, needless treatments, and hospital admissions and readmissions, lowering healthcare professionals' labor.

Chatbots can:

- Provide health information on demand
- Help patients and people immediately
- Plan around people's meds.
- Provide basic health data to doctors.
- Save time in lines by scheduling doctor visits.

Future chatbot applications will be more robust. Demand for virtual wellness aid is driving industry growth. Industry breakthroughs and technological advances will boost the market. It is predicted that Global Healthcare Chatbots Market to achieve 25.1% growth from 2019-2025. Related healthcare chatbot and app news shows that hundreds of tech businesses are developing and delivering mobile apps and computer systems for elder care, ageing, mental health, and stress alleviation. These health innovation startups get roughly $2 billion in startup funding. Since chatbots are becoming more popular in healthcare, they will likely be used in more jobs in the future years, improving industry performance. It would benefit patients and doctors.

Common Business Uses of Chatbots

1. ***The field of sales and marketing*** encompasses many strategies and techniques used by organizations to promote and sell their products or services to consumers. Based on empirical research, it has been shown that consumers exhibit a willingness to engage in transactions facilitated by automated chatbots. According to a report by Insider Intelligence, it is projected that global retail shoppers would allocate a total expenditure of $140 billion via chatbot interactions by the year 2024. Chatbots have the capability to provide product recommendations and facilitate the shopping journey. The use of chatbots enables businesses to establish efficient and effective connections with consumers, resulting in heightened levels of customer satisfaction and perhaps leading to greater income. The use of chatbots by companies to transmit messages about abandoned carts has been shown to potentially enhance sales by up to 25% for ecommerce enterprises. Moreover, chatbots have the potential to facilitate brand engagement with a much larger client base, ranging from two to five times more individuals, compared to the outreach achieved via email conversations.

2. ***Content marketing*** refers to a strategic approach in which valuable and relevant content is created and distributed to attract and engage a target audience. In what ways may chatbots contribute to the field of content marketing? Initially, chatbots possess the capability to gather significant data from those who exhibit an interest in your company. Chatbots has the capability to effectively arrange and retain data, as well as categorize customers for further marketing endeavors. The use of this approach has significant potential in enhancing the precision of target marketing strategies.

The information obtained via discussion with chatbots may be used by marketers to facilitate the customization of brand material. Nevertheless, while chatbots prove to be very effective in facilitating content marketing, it is not advisable for organizations to rely only on artificial intelligence (AI) for content creation. The process of content creation is inherently intricate, and the reliability of AI in generating genuine material that effectively resonates with the intended audience is limited.

3. ***The provision of assistance and resolution of issues to customers***, often referred to as customer support, is a crucial aspect of business operations. The previous discussions have highlighted the efficacy of chatbots in delivering round-the-clock customer service and promptly addressing customer queries. However, it remains vital to ascertain if clients possess a genuine inclination to engage with chatbots. According to the findings of several reports, it has been observed that a significant proportion, namely 40%, of consumers exhibit a preference for engaging with messaging chatbots as opposed to virtual agents. Chatbots has the capability to do tasks beyond the scope of providing responses to basic inquiries. For instance, the customer service representatives are capable of furnishing consumers with timely updates about their orders, assisting them in the process of product selection and purchase, providing tracking information, as well as facilitating returns or exchanges of items. Furthermore, according to Chatbots Magazine, the use of chatbots has the potential to reduce customer support expenses by 30%, resulting in a potential cost savings of \$23 billion for companies in the United States.

As previously said, organizations have the ability to integrate chatbots across several platforms, including their website, application, and social media channels. Although organizations may first deploy basic chatbots, they may nevertheless provide clients uncomplicated replies and an estimated waiting period until they can engage with a human representative or get a notification about when customer care will contact them. Instead of engaging in a protracted email correspondence with consumers, which often leads to delayed replies and incomplete resolution of their inquiries, an alternative approach may be used whereby clients get prompt and comprehensive answers. Furthermore, the provision of such uncomplicated chatbot assistance will effectively communicate to clients that they have a significant position within the community associated with a certain company. It is well acknowledged that chatbots have the capacity to assist companies in collecting data and enhancing marketers' comprehension of client behavior and preferences.

4. ***Social media and lead generation.*** Moreover, chatbots exhibit superior rates of customer engagement on social media platforms. Interactions with Facebook messenger chatbots have been shown to enhance customer trust in a brand or company. One potential challenge faced by chatbots is to their ability to generate grammatically correct sentences in many languages, as well as their comprehension of informal language and colloquial expressions. Artificial intelligence (AI) and chatbots have shown to be valuable tools in supporting brand teams; nevertheless, they are unable to fully substitute the role of a writer or editor in the creation of captivating content. Another issue associated with unsophisticated chatbots pertains to their limited ability to respond to more intricate inquiries. Consequently, these chatbots may misunderstand consumer queries or carry out instructions inaccurately. In response to evolving client expectations, the chatbot industry is actively developing chatbots that exhibit more human-like qualities via the integration of machine

learning, artificial intelligence, and natural language processing techniques. Over time, chatbots are expected to demonstrate even more efficacy in supporting brand teams.

Trends for Chatbots

Based on a report by Juniper Research, it is projected that by the year 2023, the use of chatbots in the retail, banking, and healthcare sectors would result in a cost reduction of $11 billion specifically in relation to customer service questions. Furthermore, this adoption of chatbots is expected to provide a total time savings of over 2.5 billion hours. Furthermore, among these industries, the retail business is projected to achieve a 70% increase in the utilization of chatbots for the purpose of aiding client questions.

Chatbots are anticipated to contribute significantly to consumer interactions on brand websites, as well as exhibit increased utilization inside brand applications, with over 50% of chatbot use expected to occur via such applications. The acquisition of knowledge about frequently asked inquiries from customers and the enhancement of response efficiency may aid in supporting IT help desk and customer care personnel.

Internally, organizations have the capacity to acquire and systematize information in order to facilitate human resource responsibilities, including the processes of onboarding new workers and acquiring pertinent updates on existing personnel. During a discussion on the SEJ podcast, Dr. Michelle Zhou, co-founder and CEO of Juji, Inc. and the developer of IBM Watson Personality Insights, highlighted the advancements in chatbot technology. She emphasized that chatbots have the potential to provide personalized information by using conversational interactions.

Future of Chatbots

Indeed, there exists a prospective trajectory for the further development and use of chatbots. Fortunately, it seems that chatbots are expected to be a prominent presence in the foreseeable future. The use of chatbots is revolutionizing the manner in which organizations engage in communication and get insights into their client base. The integration of artificial intelligence (AI) into chatbot systems has the potential to enhance the level of personalization in consumer experiences.

Additionally, it is generating cost savings for organizations across several areas such as customer service, internal operations, and marketing endeavors. There exists considerable potential for the integration of chatbots across many digital channels inside a corporation, including its website, application, and social media platforms. E-commerce firms are now using the capabilities of chatbots, and there are potential avenues for brands to begin harnessing the many ways in which chatbots may facilitate brand expansion.

CONCLUSION

Chatbots have the potential to make it easier for users to get information by swiftly responding to queries and requests. This may be accomplished via the use of text input, voice input, or a mix of the two. This removes the need for human intervention or manual research. The usage of chatbot technology has grown more prevalent, with examples including smart speakers in homes, consumer-oriented platforms such as SMS, WhatsApp, and Facebook Messenger, as well as technologies used in commercial communication. The chatbot software that runs on rules adheres to a specified set of behaviors that are developed in advance and are established through the backend module of the user interface. These behaviors may be found in the chatbot's instruction manual. A rules-based chatbot's capacity to show certain behaviors in response to human interactions enables it to function in a manner analogous to a digital assistant's capabilities.

Chatbots may be broken down into a few different categories according on the functionality and design of the bots. Rule-based chatbots, retrieval-based chatbots, generative chatbots, and hybrids are some of the categories for these types of chatbots. Within the realm of utility companies, the use of chatbots has grown more widespread, functioning as an essential component in the provision of on-demand customer care services. This deployment has led to a decrease in the dependency on human customer service workers, which has resulted in cost savings. During the COVID-19 pandemic, it has been determined that this is of utmost significance. According to the findings of a study conducted by Juniper Research, it is anticipated that by the year 2023, the use of chatbots in the retail, banking, and healthcare industries would result in a reduction of costs of $11 billion, notably in relation to queries pertaining to customer service. In addition, it is anticipated that the use of chatbots would result in a time savings of more than 2.5 billion hours globally.

REFERENCES

Alexa. (n.d.). Amazon. https://alexa.amazon.com/

Animas Marketing. (2023). *What happened to smarter child, the aim chatbox?* Animas Marketing. https://animasmarketing.com/what-happened-to-smarterchild-the-aim-chatbot/

Chatbots. (2023). *Parry*. Chatbots. https://www.chatbots.org/chatbot/parry/

Chat OpenAI. (2023). Chat OpenAI. https://chat.openai.com/auth/login

Cnet, (2023). *You can now try Google's bard charbot*. Cnet. https://www.cnet.com/tech/computing/you-can-now-try-googles-bard-chatbot-an-alternative-to-chatgpt/

Engati. (2023). *Wechat Bot*. Engati. https://www.engati.com/glossary/wechat-bot

Google assistant, (2023). Google. https://assistant.google.com/

Markoff, J., & Mozour, P. (2015). For Sympathetic Ear, More Chinese Turn to Smartphone Program. *The New York Times*.

ADDITIONAL READING

Suryadinata, A. (2023). The History of Chatbots. *Medium*. https://medium.com/vutura/the-history-of-chatbots-2d5b493403c9

Neff, G., & Nagy, P., P. (2016). Talking to Bots: Symbiotic Agency and the Case of Tay. *International Journal of Communication*, *10*, 4915–4931.

Peregrim, J. (2005). *Kapitoly z analytické filosofie*. Filosofia.

Tarnoff, B. (2023). Weizenbaum's nightmares: How the inventor of the first chatbot turned against AI. *The Guardian.* https://www.theguardian.com/technology/2023/jul/25/joseph-weizenbaum-inventor-eliza-chatbot-turned-against-artificial-intelligence-ai

Turing, A. M. (1950). Computing Machinery And Intelligence. *Mind, 49*(236), 433–460. doi:10.1093/mind/LIX.236.433

Wang, Z., (2016). *Your Next New Best Friend Might Be a Robot: Meet Xiaoice. She's empathic, caring, and always available—just not human.* Nauitilus 033.

KEY TERMS AND DEFINITIONS

AOL Instant Messenger (AOL IM): One of the world's most popular instant messaging clients. The free software let users send instant messages to anyone on their "Buddy List," and featured social media integration, photo and file sharing, video and audio chat, and more.

Artificial intelligence Markup Language (AIML): An XML dialect for creating natural language software agents.

Large Language Models (LLMS): LLMs are characterized by their large size. Their size is enabled by AI accelerators, which are able to process vast amounts of text data, mostly scraped from the internet.

Natural Language Understanding (NLU): A branch of artificial intelligence that uses computer software to understand input in the form of sentences using text or speech.

Chapter 2
Chatbots vs. AI Chatbots vs. Virtual Assistants

Dina Darwish
Ahram Canadian University, Egypt

ABSTRACT

The terms "chatbot," "AI chatbot," and "virtual agent" are used in a way that often does not differentiate between them, which might lead to possible misunderstandings. Despite the fact that the technologies associated with these terms are inextricably linked to one another, the subtle differences that exist between them result in considerable differences in their unique capabilities. The term "chatbot" is often used to refer to a wide variety of artificial intelligence systems that are designed to carry on conversations. The development of artificial intelligence chatbot software has resulted in the creation of virtual agents, which constitutes a significant step forward. These agents participate in conversation via the use of AI methods known as conversational AI, and they make use of deep learning algorithms in order to improve their performance over time. This chapter discusses the differences between chatbots, AI chatbots and virtual assistants, and other related topics.

INTRODUCTION

The phrases chatbot, AI chatbot, and virtual agent are often used in a manner that lacks distinction, leading to potential misunderstanding. Although the technologies associated with these phrases are intimately interconnected, nuanced variations result in significant disparities in their individual functionalities.

The word "chatbot" is widely used to include a broad range of conversational artificial intelligence systems. A chatbot may be defined as any program that emulates human communication, using either classic, inflexible decision tree-based menu navigation or advanced conversational AI technology. Chatbots are ubiquitously present in many communication channels, including phone trees, social media platforms, as well as dedicated applications and websites.

AI chatbots refer to chatbots that use a range of artificial intelligence (AI) technologies, including machine learning for improving answer optimization over time, as well as natural language processing (NLP) and natural language understanding (NLU) for effectively comprehending user inquiries and as-

DOI: 10.4018/979-8-3693-1830-0.ch002

sociating them with particular intentions. The use of deep learning techniques enhances the proficiency of AI chatbots, enabling them to progressively improve their accuracy. Consequently, this advancement facilitates more seamless and natural interactions between people and AI chatbots, minimizing the likelihood of misunderstandings.

Virtual agents represent a progressive advancement in the field of artificial intelligence chatbot software. These agents employ conversational AI techniques to engage in dialogue and utilize deep learning algorithms to enhance their performance over time. Additionally, virtual agents frequently integrate robotic process automation (RPA) within a unified interface, enabling them to directly respond to user intentions without requiring additional human involvement.

To illustrate the differentiations, consider a scenario where a user exhibits curiosity over the weather forecast for the next day. In the context of a conventional chatbot, the user has the capability to use the precise phrase "provide me with the meteorological forecast." According to the chatbot's prediction, there is a forecast of precipitation in the form of rain. The user has the ability to inquire about the weather forecast for the next day using an artificial intelligence chatbot. The chatbot accurately predicts that there will be precipitation in the form of rain. By using a virtual agent, the user has the capability to inquire about the meteorological conditions for the next day by posing the question, "What is the anticipated weather forecast for tomorrow?". The virtual agent has the capability to not only forecast precipitation for the next day, but also propose the adjustment of an earlier alarm time to accommodate any delays caused by rain during the morning commute.

Artificial Intelligence (AI) and Machine Learning (ML) have become crucial components inside several enterprises. By using an AI chatbot or AI virtual assistant, businesses have the potential to enhance their income, save expenses, and cultivate a superior customer support encounter. The increasing popularity of virtual assistants and chatbots is to be expected. These entities exhibit a high degree of similarity. The primary distinction between a chatbot and a virtual assistant is in their respective design and intended functions.

Virtual assistants are designed to handle a diverse range of demands, while chatbots tend to have a narrower focus in terms of the services they provide. Both contribute to the enhancement of personalized support. Assistance with daily duties, in addition to providing support in functioning as a secondary individual, liberates individuals from monotonous and repetitive responsibilities.

This chapter discusses the key differences between Chatbots, Virtual assistants, AI virtual assistants, and AI chatbots, and their features. Also, discussing how each type of them benefits businesses. The main topics to be covered in this chapter includes the following;

- Key Differences Between Chatbot and Virtual Assistant and intelligent virtual assistant and AI chatbot
- What Are the Features of a Chatbot?
- What Are the Features of Virtual Assistants?
- What are the features of AI chatbots and AI virtual assistants?
- Technologies behind AI chatbots
- The technologies behind AI virtual assistants and their types
- Components of chatbots and virtual assistants
- Systems used with Virtual assistants
- Most famous AI Chatbots
- Chatbot or Virtual Assistant or AI chatbot: Which one is suitable for a Business?

- Ethical issues related to Chatbots and Virtual assistants
- The Future of Service Support Industry

Also, this chapter is organized as follows; the first section includes the background, then, the second section contains the main focus of the chapter, including the main topics stated in the previous section, then finally, the conclusion section is provided.

BACKGROUND

A chatbot is a specialized piece of software that gives a machine the ability to have a conversation with a human. A human-like ability to answer inquiries, provide suggestions, and book reservations is within the scope of the bot's learning capabilities. It concerns the connection between conversation and the processing of material. The content process is then supplied to the user when the user's replies have been matched with the relevant previously specified material. The user is able to speak with the computer in the most natural manner possible using this method.

- Pattern matches - in order to respond appropriately to any voice or text communications, bots utilize pattern matching to determine which patterns best fit the group, and then they offer the proper response.
- Natural language understanding (NLU) is an algorithm that is used by chatbots; it analyses the sentence, and it does not have any past circumstances of the user's discussion. It implies that if it receives an answer to a question that it has asked very recently, it will not remember having asked any other questions.
- Natural language processing (NLP) - Chatbots employ the natural language processing (NLP) technology to turn unstructured data into structured data from voice or text input. In order for the process to reach its conclusion, it must first go through a number of phases, which may include tokenization, analysis of sentiment, normalization, name recognition, and dependency parsing.

A virtual assistant (VA), sometimes known as a virtual agent (VA), is a computer program that performs functions similar to those of a human assistant. These functions include the ability to provide answers to particular inquiries, carry out certain activities, and even provide suggestions. Both virtual agents and chatbots have the ability to increase sales while also meeting the requirements of the client. In principle, a chatbot as well as a virtual agent may be developed to address the most typical questions or concerns raised by customers.

A chatbot, which is a semi-automated system, is able to solve simple issues in a more timely and effective manner than a person can. On the other hand, the virtual agent is the superior option if a problem is very difficult or demands an immediate reaction (for example, fraud). Voice assistants such as Alexa and Siri are two examples of this kind of technology, which enables quick access to a variety of different types of information and services with only a few spoken commands. Chatbots are still trying to establish their footing in the world of online commerce, despite the fact that virtual assistants are growing more advanced by the day. A virtual customer assistant, also known as a VCA, makes use of artificial intelligence in order to comprehend a client's request and provide a response in real time. This digital assistant may either function on its own or in conjunction with a real-life customer support representative.

MAIN FOCUS OF THE CHAPTER

Key Differences Between Chatbot and Virtual Assistant and intelligent virtual assistant and AI chatbot

This section discusses the primary distinctions between a chatbot and a virtual assistant. Both chatbots and virtual assistants use Natural Language Processing (NLP) to comprehend the underlying intention behind a user's inquiry or solicitation, afterwards delivering a response in a conversational style.

A chatbot refers to an artificial intelligence program designed to simulate human conversation via text or voice-based interactions. A chatbot refers to a computerized tool that serves as a virtual assistant, enabling users to engage in natural language conversations and get information, address inquiries, or execute other functions. A significant majority of consumers, over 68%, express a preference for chatbot technology due to its ability to provide prompt responses to client queries. Furthermore, there is a discernible upward trajectory in the adoption of chatbot use among customers.

The Purpose of Designing a Chatbot

The primary objective of 24x7 customer engagement is to actively involve consumers at all times and promptly address their frequently asked questions, rather than only focusing on administrative duties.

One potential benefit of using chatbots is the potential to enhance lead generation. By employing chatbots, businesses can effectively comprehend user intent and analyze conversational context, resulting in more natural and accurate responses. Artificial intelligence bots possess the capability to sustain a discussion while encountering unforeseen obstacles or inquiries.

A Virtual Assistant refers to a digital entity that provides various administrative, technical, or creative support services remotely to individuals or organizations. Virtual assistants are software applications designed to aid organizations in performing a range of administrative functions, including but not limited to appointment scheduling and email correspondence. They provide assistance to those who prefer not to directly communicate with a specific individual, but nevertheless need prompt resolution of their concerns. Virtual assistants such as Siri, Alexa, and Cortana are being used by customers to cater to a diverse array of demands in their everyday routines.

Virtual assistants serve the purpose of facilitating everyday life by offering a wide range of functionalities. They aim to streamline duties, aid in decision-making processes, and provide entertainment.

Enhance the standards of client service The use of a virtual assistant has a notable capacity to enhance operational effectiveness and provide assistance to both staff and consumers. The subject of chatbots has been the subject of much discourse in recent years. However, there is a burgeoning kind of automation known as the virtual customer assistant that is garnering increasing attention. Siri and Alexa exemplify voice assistants, which provide prompt access to information and services via concise spoken commands.

As virtual assistants continue to advance in complexity, chatbots are encountering challenges in establishing their role within the realm of online commerce.

The Operational Mechanisms of AI Virtual Customer Agents and AI Chatbots

The concept of an Intelligent Virtual Assistant refers to a computer program or application that utilizes artificial intelligence and natural language processing techniques to provide interactive and personalized assistance to users.

An intelligent virtual assistant (IVA) employs artificial intelligence techniques to comprehend and promptly address a customer's inquiry or demand. This digital assistant has the capability to function autonomously or serve as a supplementary tool to a human customer support representative.

The user's text does not contain any information to rewrite. The integration of machine learning (ML) and artificial intelligence (AI) is used in the context of Intelligent Virtual Assistants (IVA), which leverage AI and ML techniques to comprehend both spoken and written language. The model undergoes extensive training using a vast dataset of talks, enabling it to enhance its proficiency in responding to intricate inquiries and comprehending colloquial language and idiosyncratic speech patterns.

The system gathers data, does analysis, and provides responses by means of speech and text message recognition. Moreover, it has the capability to respond to inquiries by using data sourced from the internet as well as files accessible on the user's workplace computer. It is noteworthy that a significant proportion, over 80%, of orders are now being made through telephone. Consequently, electronic merchants are compelled to provide effective means of engaging with customers via this medium, ensuring a satisfactory interaction for those who prefer verbal communication. In this particular scenario, a virtual assistant presents itself as an optimal resolution.

The Distinctions Between a Chatbot and a Virtual Assistant

In contemporary corporate contexts characterized by rapidity, digitalization, and dynamism, the need of swiftness assumes paramount importance. Business enterprises want to enhance productivity by optimizing resource utilization, achieving cost efficiencies, and enhancing precision, all while delivering an exceptional customer experience to end-users.

As organizations across all sectors and scales increasingly prioritize customer-centricity, there arises a question about the differentiation between virtual assistants and chatbots. This analysis aims to examine the distinctions between the two domains and elucidate the significant contributions of artificial intelligence (AI) within each.

What Are the Features of a Chatbot?

A chatbot has the capability to assume several roles, such as serving as a personal assistant, a customized artificial intelligence, or a rudimentary quotation generator. Its primary function is to address customer service inquiries and do basic duties that were traditionally carried out by human personnel. The key features of a chatbot are:

1. The design aspect
2. Transforming Traffic into High-Quality Leads
3. Guidance, Frequently Asked Questions, and Recommendations
4. The Utilization of Real-Time Chatting in Communication

This section will examine the key attributes of a chatbot, providing comprehensive information on each element.

1. The Process of Creating a Plan or Blueprint for the Development of a Product

system, or structure is important. The design of a chatbot is a crucial element that must be considered. The characteristics of a chatbot resemble the persona of a bot, through which it establishes a rapport with its users. The architecture and conceptualization of a chatbot might be intriguing, particularly when its functionalities include both amusement and significance.

When considering the development of chatbot features, it is important to take into account many components. The chatbot's tone of voice should be characterized by friendliness, playfulness, and the ability to make a lasting impression on the user. To ensure efficient contact with consumers, it is important for a chatbot to use language that is both clear and easily comprehensible. This feature facilitates enhanced engagement and contributes to the improved comprehensibility of discussions for those using it. Seamless integration refers to the effective development of features that facilitate interaction with various platforms such as SMS or email.

2. Transforming Traffic into High-Quality Leads

A chatbot has the capability to engage in comprehensive conversations and comprehend contextual cues, enabling it to gather essential information from visitors to your website and provide responses that are seen as organic. It has the capability to provide prospective clients solutions to inquiries that they may not yet be aware of. More than one billion of the largest global corporations use chatbots and websites as tools to effectively convert their website visitors into potential customers. One notable example in the retail sector of using chatbots to generate leads is Sephora (Sephora, 2023).

- Identifying prospective clients is a critical aspect in enhancing the appeal of services or goods. A chatbot facilitates the comprehension of clients. The process involves the collection of demographic data from clients, followed by a thorough analysis of their persona and an examination of the competitive landscape. This approach contributes to the enhancement of lead generating strategies.
- Gaining an understanding of consumer demands is crucial in order to effectively build communication strategies. The chatbot facilitates the acquisition of information pertaining to the preferences, aversions, and areas of interest of prospective customers.
- Developing valuable content is crucial during lead generation campaigns as it has the potential to enhance the overall effectiveness of the marketing plan. When used effectively, chatbots significantly alleviate the strain of customer care workers by enabling them to concentrate on intricate customer service matters, while the chatbot manages basic questions.

3. Guidance, Frequently Asked Questions, and Recommendations

A sophisticated conversational agent has the capability to address inquiries from customers, provide guidance, and assume the role of an adviser to individuals. The chatbot has the capability to respond

Figure 1. Key features of a chatbot

to inquiries on the company's merchandise and provide practical guidance to the typical customer. The chatbot is capable of offering details on events and the sales of the firm as well.

4. Real-Time Communication through Chat

Currently, real-time chatting, live chat, co-browsing, and video chat are prominent marketing trends that possess the potential to facilitate the conversion of website visitors into high-quality leads. The platform provides instantaneous communication capabilities, enabling users to actively interact with their audience in real-time. Approximately 73% of clients express a high level of satisfaction with real-time chatting as a mode of communication. One illustrative instance is the well famous bicycle manufacturer, Canyon (canyon, 2023), which has a diversified consumer base spanning several regions globally. The organization provides help to a diverse clientele hailing from various countries and speaking different languages.

The organization employs an advanced chatbot driven by artificial intelligence to facilitate prompt connections between customers and the appropriate sales or support staff, taking into account the customer's chosen language. Figure 1 shows key features of a chatbot.

What Are the Features of Virtual Assistants?

There is a consensus that virtual assistants are seeing a surge in popularity throughout several domains of human existence. They provide a wide range of purposes, including both professional and domestic assistance. As to the analysis conducted by Forbes, it is predicted that automation would play a pivotal role in shaping the future of business. According to the research, it is said that the widespread implementation of comprehensive regulations is an unavoidable occurrence. The report further suggests that employees will soon be subjected to a stringent set of guidelines, which they would be expected to adhere to strictly, without any variation. The key features of a VA are:

- *The VA has exceptional communication skills.*
- *Multitasking is the act of doing many tasks simultaneously or switching between tasks rapidly.*
- *The product is very suitable for doing follow-up activities.*
- *Facilitates Business Expansion*

1. One notable attribute of the VAs is their *exceptional communication skills*. Effective communication with customers is essential for any organization. Virtual assistants has the ability to provide the desired results since they possess a comprehensive understanding of optimal communication tactics. Clear and succinct communication is crucial for success in any commercial endeavor. A virtual assistant offers precise and succinct guidance, hence enhancing client engagement.

One potential use of virtual assistants (VAs) is the automation of email communication. VAs have the capability to send personalized follow-up emails automatically, hence facilitating client engagement with the company. In addition to their adeptness in communicating, virtual assistants possess a breadth of knowledge encompassing other disciplines, including law and science.

2. *Multitasking* refers to the ability to do many tasks simultaneously or switch between tasks rapidly. Additionally, it might result in financial savings by doing chores that would otherwise incur expenses, such as making arrangements for your next vacation instead of personally managing them. By employing a virtual assistant, businesses have the potential to reduce their operational expenses by up to approximately 78%. A virtual assistant has the capability to do the following tasks:

- The act of sending electronic messages through email.
- The topic of discussion pertains to the process of scheduling.
- The process of reserving transport and accommodation for travel purposes.
- The management of one's social media profiles
- The feature is quite beneficial for doing further actions or inquiries.

3. *Useful for follow up.* The process of arranging and managing a schedule is considered to be a very advantageous aspect of using a virtual assistant. In addition to serving as a prompt for essential business deadlines, it may also serve as a tool for recollecting and addressing outstanding chores.

4. *Assists in growing business.* One of the key factors contributing to the expansion and development of a business is the assistance it receives. There is a wide range of jobs that one might consider. The delegation of incoming communications while one's absence from the workplace aids in the management of time-consuming administrative tasks.

The use of a virtual assistant has been shown to reduce the amount of work required and enhance productivity. This is mostly due to the virtual assistant's ability to alleviate the burden of coordinating with several corporate applications. AI-powered voice assistants are crucial in enhancing client engagement on corporate websites. The observation of consumer behavior and user experience is of paramount importance for a brand's efforts to enhance sales. Volvo, a prominent automotive company, has created a conversational assistant aimed at providing guidance to drivers.

Data management is an essential component in the development of a customized marketing plan. However, a significant challenge is in effectively managing the vast array of data sources involved in this process. The AI assistant functions as a key data processing tool within this context. The system has the capability to efficiently handle large volumes of real-time and historical data, while also being able to accurately discern human intention. Once data has been organized, it becomes possible to formulate a marketing plan aimed at effectively engaging clients. Figure 2 illustrates the key features of virtual assistants.

Figure 2. Key features of virtual assistants

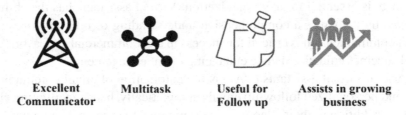

| Excellent Communicator | Multitask | Useful for Follow up | Assists in growing business |

What are the Features of AI Chatbots and AI Virtual Assistants?

The comparison between chatbots and virtual assistants has garnered significant attention in academic discourse. The distinction between these two technologies has been a subject of interest due to their increasing prevalence in many domains. Similar to other emerging technologies, there is a tendency to use the terms Artificial Intelligence Chatbots and AI Virtual Assistants interchangeably, despite the fact that they possess distinct core functionalities and varying levels of technological complexity. AI-powered chatbots are mainly designed for the purpose of engaging in communication with end-users. This interaction may occur via several mediums, such as text-based exchanges on website conversations, chat apps, email or SMS, or through auditory means, as shown by virtual assistants like Alexa or Siri. Contrary to the claims made by suppliers of IT Helpdesk Chatbots, the usefulness of AI Chatbots is limited to simple, concise, and task-oriented interactions with users.

Despite the potential persuasiveness of Natural Language Processing (NLP) technologies in certain contexts, interactions and responses between AI Chatbots and users often exhibit a scripted and mechanistic quality. It is worth noting that, as of 2019, none of the AI Chatbot products available in the market have consistently demonstrated the ability to successfully deceive end-users into perceiving them as human, as measured by the Turing Test.

The Choice Between AI Virtual Assistants and AI Chatbots

In contrast to AI Chatbots, AI Virtual Assistants possess enhanced capabilities due to their utilization of cutting-edge advancements in cognitive computing, Natural Language Processing, and Natural Language Understanding (NLP & NLU). AI virtual assistants use conversational AI technology to effectively interact with people in intricate, multi-faceted, lengthy, and loud dialogues.

These conversational agents has the ability to accurately comprehend the intentions of end-users and provide tailored and exact responses. Additionally, they have the capability to initiate and fulfil various activities and procedures across several domains. Furthermore, they may escalate to human agents when necessary. The end-users are provided with a seamless, lucid, and engaging experience that replicates the behavior and interaction patterns of human agents. Figure 3 shows the key features of AI chatbots.

The Productivity of AI Virtual Assistants

AI chatbots and IT helpdesk chatbots may be characterized as impersonal software applications. The individuals in question lack the ability to effectively comprehend and analyze the surrounding circum-

Figure 3. Key features of AI Chatbots

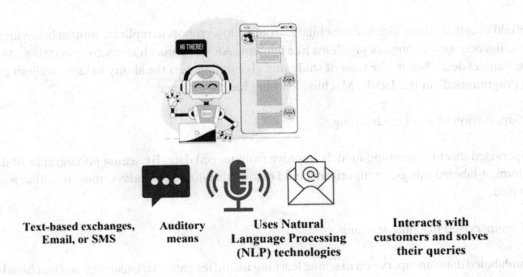

| Text-based exchanges, Email, or SMS | Auditory means | Uses Natural Language Processing (NLP) technologies | Interacts with customers and solves their queries |

stances in which the end-users initiate a request, nor do they possess the capacity to adapt their replies appropriately. On the other hand, AI Virtual Assistants has the ability to adapt their interactions in real-time by using sophisticated User Behavioral Intelligence and Sentiment analytics. The system has the ability to discern negative tones in interactions and then adjust its response to exhibit sympathy, provide apologies, and demonstrate more understanding towards the end-user.

Technologies Behind AI Chatbots

Natural language processing, ML, and AI power chatbots.

1. Natural Language Processing

NLP teaches computers to read and speak like humans. Rule-based human language modelling is integrated with statistical, machine learning, and deep learning models in computing linguistics. Computers can 'understand' text or audio data, including the speaker or writer's intent and emotion. NLP helps computers comprehend text, respond to spoken requests, and summarize massive volumes of data quickly—even in real time. NLP is being used in enterprise solutions that improve operations, employee productivity, and mission-critical processes.

2. Linguistic Computation

Grammar and syntax: Modelling sentence structure and grammar for analysis and creation. Words and phrases are studied and models are built to grasp natural language expressions. The structure and coherence of conversations and publications may be modelled using discourse analysis.

Machine translation: Automating text translation.

Human speech recognition and synthesis system development.

3. Machine Learning

A subfield of artificial intelligence, machine learning allows robots to replicate human behaviors. Artificial intelligence solves complex problems like humans. An AI approach is machine learning. AI pioneer Arthur Samuel described it "the field of study that gives computers the ability to learn without explicitly being programmed" in the 1950s. Machine learning has three types:

a)   Supervision of machine learning

Supervised machine learning models improve from tagged data. By seeing photographs of dogs and other human-labeled things, an algorithm could distinguish dogs. Nowadays, most machine learning is supervised.

b)   Unsupervised machine learning

In unlabeled data, unsupervised machine learning identifies patterns. Unsupervised machine learning discovers unanticipated tendencies. Using sales data, an unsupervised machine learning software might classify online customers.

c)   Reinforcement machine learning

Reinforcement machine learning teaches computers the best action via trial and error using rewards. Rewarding the computer for right decisions may educate models to play games or autonomous vehicles to drive.

Chatbots apply all the previously described machine learning.

Supervised learning: Teaching the chatbot the correct response for each marked data input. These data teach the chatbot how to handle similar inputs. The chatbot learns patterns and correlations unsupervised. This groups related messages and identifies topics. Rewards and punishments for trial-and-error chatbot training. The chatbot manipulates responses to optimize rewards.

Deep learning: Neural networks model complex input-output. It enhances chatbot natural language understanding and response production. Neural networks are multilayered in deep learning. Some neural network layers may identify eyes, nose, and mouth, while another layer may assess whether such characteristics occur in a face in an image identification system. The multilayer network can handle plenty of input and estimate link weight. Deep learning uses neural networks to simulate the brain for autonomous vehicles, chatbots, and medical diagnoses.

Choosing the Best Language to Build Your Chatbot as said by data scientists is Python. Research shows that 57% of data scientists used Python for Machine Learning. Python is adaptable. Learning through emulating human language is simpler with years of study and standardized grammar. AIML simplifies syntax writing for developers. Python's huge AI chatbot toolbox builds web server conversational components. Python developers can make friendly chatbots.

AI language model in Chat GPT improves by learning from massive text data. Deep learning and NLP will let Chat GPT understand and react like humans. Recently, conversational agents, chatbots, question answering systems, and language translation services have used GPT-based models. Chat GPT

Figure 4. Technologies behind AI chatbots

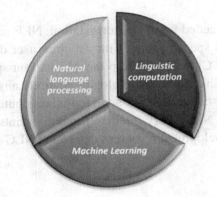

and similar language models should improve as AI improves and data becomes more available. Figure 4 shows technologies behind AI chatbots.

The technologies behind AI virtual assistants and their types

There exist several technologies behind AI virtual assistants. These technologies power AI virtual assistants for productivity, convenience, and cost savings.

1. Speech-to-Text (STT) and (Text-to-Speech) TTS

Speech-to-text digitizes speech, and speech vibrates. Digital signals, sound extraction, segmentation, and phoneme comparison are produced using an analog-to-digital converter (ADC). To write what was uttered, the software matches phonemes with words and phrases using complex mathematical models. TTS utilizes the opposite algorithm, it converts text to voice. TTS replicates human voice from text using machine learning. There are three steps of text-to-voice. First, the system must convert text to words, then phonetics, then speech. Virtual assistant software improves user-application interactions using STT and TTS. To understand user requests and become an AI assistant, a static voice assistance requires cognitive tagging and heuristics.

2. Computer Vision

Robots learn visual signals using AI's computer vision. Digital images from cameras and videos and deep learning models let computers classify and respond to information. Visual virtual assistants need Computer Vision (CV). These helpers can respond with movies and sounds, boosting user experience. Computer vision understands body language, a crucial communication tool. Visual virtual assistants with CV utilize a camera and real-time face recognition to detect when a user is looking at the screen and signal the system to convert speech to text. CV may improve speech recognition by connecting verbal communication to face and lip movements.

3. Natural Language Processing

Natural Language Processing is needed for data interpretation. NLP simplifies speech recognizing. AI systems pre-trained on numerous speech samples may require user data to increase accuracy. Voice synthesis technology like Google Cloud's will help the AI assistant speak. Speech processing cannot express a person's intent or maintain constructive dialogue. Natural Language Understanding technology studies natural language without standardizing it and recognizes context to understand requests. NLP evaluates language and structure, NLU query intent. Virtual assistants and NLG chatbots behave like people. Project objectives and development resources determine NLG models.

4. Deep Learning

Text-only chatbots are simpler than voice assistants. Advanced text generators like GPT-4 can answer basic questions and generate unique stories from data. Deep learning enables this. Deep learning AI assistants learn from data and humans. They evaluate customer-support discussions and write "correct" messages and responses.

5. Augmented Reality (AR)

AR is great because we can add 3D components to the scene for immersion. Mobile chatbots and AR avatars leverage this technology effectively. AI makes AR virtual assistants more beautiful and convenient.

6. Generative Adversarial Networks (GANS)

GANs are ML models in which two neural networks compete to create more accurate predictions using deep learning. GANs produce realistic 3D faces for AI avatars and assistance using actual images and discriminators. The method develops realistic human models for games and products. In Nvidia's Omniverse Avatar Project Maxine, a human face speaks text-to-speech in real time. Besides audible and visual effects, virtual assistants may incorporate body language and emotions. AI-powered emotional intelligence reacts to real-time nonverbal cues while chatting. Emotion AI allows AI virtual assistants scan speech, body language, and facial expressions to determine emotions.

7. Emotional Intelligence (EI)

The Emotion AI utilizes computer vision and machine learning. Device cameras recognize faces by analyzing expressions. To interpret emotions, computer vision systems scan important face regions. Then, the system interprets facial expressions from a picture database to estimate emotions. Modern solutions like Affectiva and Kairos identify joy, sadness, rage, disdain, disgust, fear, and surprise.

AI Virtual Assistant App Types

AI virtual assistants include voice assistants, avatars, and domain-specific ones. Natural Language Processing and automated speech recognition let voice assistants answer questions. Siri and Google Assistant are popular voice assistants.

Figure 5. Technologies behind AI virtual assistant

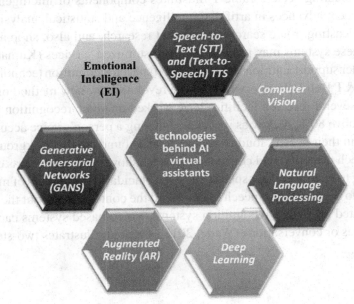

- AI avatars are 3D representations that look like people and are used for entertainment and virtual customer assistance. In real time, NVIDIA technology can create remarkably lifelike human avatars.
- Domain-specific virtual assistants are AI virtual assistants optimized for travel, banking, engineering, cybersecurity, and other demanding areas.
- Voice-activated, task-oriented, and predictive AI assistants exist. Siri and Alexa, voice-activated assistants, do basic tasks like searching for information, setting alarms, and playing music.

Task-oriented assistants make appointments and organize emails. Google Now and Cortana employ ML algorithms to anticipate a user's requirements and provide relevant information and services before they ask. Although these assistants fulfil the same business goals, each project has its unique technological implementation characteristics and development problems. Figure 5 shows technologies behind AI virtual assistant.

Components of Chatbots and Virtual Assistants

There are two main types of semantic reasoning methods, distinguished by how they came into being. To begin, humans use an ontological approach to ask questions and get answers inside the system. The solution is discovered using this technique by inferring from a massive, in-memory knowledge store. Second, IR-based Q&A prioritizes a set of replies depending on computations of probability by querying a massive database of indexes records (Zhang, 2019; Garcia, 2020). Using a question and answer format, the alternative customer care approach may deliver more insightful support, rather than relying on a hard and fast rule, an ontology-based reasoning founded inquiry. As deep learning has advanced, ontology has recently benefited. Chatbots-based on Question and Answer technology has been employed by businesses and in banking sector. Table 1 illustrates components of intelligent virtual technology (Mohemad, 2017). Recent advances in artificial intelligence and statistical analysis have users to manage regional data, forecasting, route searching, Internet research, and also, shopping online. Based on customer feedback, these systems may provide highly customized services (Kumar, 2019).

Alternative customer support solutions rely heavily on speech recognition technology. In 1952, American researchers at AT&T Bell Laboratory created the revolutionary new method of transforming audio into text. Since then, several research facilities have worked on voice recognition development, but so far accuracy has not above 80%. As low as it gets recognizing a person's voice accurately is challenging because of variations in their accent, loudness, dialect, and sounds in the background (Singh, 2017).

The two-stage speech detection and conversion process shown in Figure 6 was created lately. model that uses deep learning to restore unclear speech and even elucidates the process of meaning transmission in speech by taking into account both speech features and the context filling out the setting. Deep learning is being incorporated into voice recognition systems. Voice-based systems capable of recognizing lengthy speech passages or conversations (Wang, 2018). Figure 6 illustrates two-step voice recognition and conversion model.

Table 1. Components of intelligent virtual assistant technology

Division	Component
Interactive interface	Speech recognition, multimodal, context recognition
Semantic reasoning	Intelligent level Assistant chatbot, intelligent assistant, cognitive assistant
	Conversation process Goal-oriented conversation processing, question and answer skills
	Knowledge Semantic Web, ontology-based technical data
Other services	Modeling, big data analysis, web service

Figure 6. Two-step voice recognition and conversion model

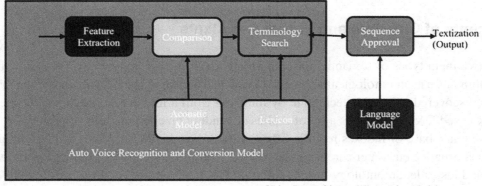

Voice Recognition and Conversion Model
Adoptable to the Environment

Systems Used With Virtual Assistants

There exist several systems that can be used with virtual assistants, such as:

- The Apple TV remote control enables users to interact with Siri, a virtual assistant, in order to search for desired material to see.
- Virtual assistants have the potential to be seamlessly incorporated into several systems, such as Amazon Alexa, which can be integrated across multiple platforms.
- Within the realm of technological advancements, there are a variety of innovative products, namely smart speakers, which include prominent examples such as Amazon Echo, Google Home, and Apple HomePod.
- Instant messaging programs, such as M (a virtual assistant) on both the Facebook and Facebook Messenger apps, as well as on the Web, are commonly used on smartphones and other devices.
- Virtual assistants can be incorporated inside a mobile operating system (OS), such as Apple's Siri on iOS devices and BlackBerry Assistant on BlackBerry 10 devices, or within a desktop OS like Cortana on Microsoft Windows OS.
- Virtual assistants can be incorporated inside a smartphone irrespective of the operating system, such as Bixby on the Samsung Galaxy S8 and Note 8 (La, 2017).
- Instant messaging services sometimes have virtual assistants that are affiliated with certain organizations, such as Aeromexico's Aerobot on Facebook Messenger or WeChat Secretary.
- In the realm of mobile applications developed by various corporations and entities, an example may be found in the case of Dom, the smartphone app created by Domino's Pizza (Morrison, 2014).
- Appliances, vehicles, and wearable technology are examples of areas where the virtual assistants are seen (O'Shea, 2017; Gibbs, 2017; Pocket, 2017).
- In the past, virtual assistants were often used on various websites, such as Ask Jenn by Alaska Airlines, and on interactive voice response (IVR) systems, such Nuance's IVR for American Airlines (Alaska Airlines, 2017; AT&T Tech Channel, 2013).

Most Famous AI Chatbots

Artificial intelligence powers chatbots' messaging network interactions. Live chatbots answer inquiries. They improve by learning from real-life events using NLP and machine learning. AI chatbots provide customer service, assistance, tailored recommendations, and information retrieval. The most famous sophisticated daily AI chatbots are:

1. ChatGPT
2. Google Bard
3. Bing Chat
4. ChatSonic
5. Jasper
6. Drift
7. Salesforce Einstein
8. LivePerson

Table 2. Famous chatbots' features, advantages, and disadvantages

Chatbot name	Features	Advantages	Disadvantages
ChatGPT	■ Answers, acknowledges errors, disputes premises, and refuses unreasonable demands. ■ Feedback learning, context adaption, content creation, and emotion expression ■ Powered by OpenAI's GPT-3.5 model, trained on plenty of online content. ■ Provides numerous answers.	■ An AI chatbot Customer service 24/7 ■ Supports several languages	Needs extensive customization
Google Bard	■ Improved, lightweight LaMDA powers ■ Provides new, high-quality answers online ■ Great for teaching, learning, and creativity. ■ Photo and linguistic support coming soon.	■ Natural language processing ■ Conversational AI ■ Personalized replies	Few integrations
Bing Chat	■ Microsoft's massive GPT-3 language model ■ Page-specific queries and responses ■ Summarizes, compares, and teaches online content. ■ Visual answers include drawings, charts, etc.	■ Recognizing user intent ■ Analysis and insights ■ Prepared discussion	Few customizations exist.
ChatSonic	■ Training GPT-3.5 and GPT-4 on plenty of online information. ■ Creates platform text, images, code, and content ■ Conversationally embraces ideas ■ Voice and translation help	■ Omnichannel integration ■ Understanding context ■ Analysis of sentiment	Natural language processing difficulties
Jasper	■ GPT-3.5/GPT-4 ■ Supports several content layouts, formats, and tones. ■ We optimize content for SEO, readability, and conversions. ■ Voice-command and translation services.	■ Simple to use ■ Effective and adaptable ■ Conversational AI	Setup takes time.
Drift	■ Chatbots, live chat, messaging campaigns ■ Natural language processing, chat AI ■ Email and CRM compatible. ■ Evaluate leads, plan meetings, and finalize deals	■ Live chatbots ■ Sending targeted messages ■ Marketing and sales automation	Quite costly
Salesforce Einstein	■ AI in sales, service, marketing, and commerce ■ NLP, MLP, and computer vision are used ■ Works with all Salesforce platforms ■ Discover patterns, forecast consequences, and suggest actions	■ Interactive ■ Generate leads automatically ■ Predictive analytics	Beginners' steep learning curve
LivePerson	■ Natural language processing, AI ■ Integration with CRM, email, etc. ■ Customer engagement across channels and devices ■ Allows customization, segmentation, analytics	■ Supports several platforms ■ Expert data analysis ■ Customer service automation	Inadaptability

These Chatbots' features, advantages and disadvantages are mentioned in Table 2.

Virtual Voice Assistant vs. Chatbot vs. AI Chatbots: What Are the Benefits?

In the subsequent analysis of the chatbot vs virtual assistant contrast, the next exposition will elucidate the primary advantages associated with the utilization of either a chatbot or a virtual assistant. The progressions in the field of artificial intelligence have facilitated the creation of technological innovations that possess the potential for widespread use. One such instance is facilitated by the use of voice assistants and chatbots. As a result of this technological advancement, individuals have experienced more convenience in accomplishing their routine activities and fulfilling their responsibilities.

Typically, these devices possess the capability to perform a diverse range of functions, including as establishing reminders, executing internet searches, initiating program launches, and reacting to user directives. One may inquire about the advantages associated with voice assistants and chatbots. In the present analysis contrasting chatbots with virtual assistants, we will now proceed to examine the primary advantages associated with each.

The Advantages of Voice Assistants

1. The primary advantages of a voice assistant are ***convenient accessibility***, improved privacy management, and a smooth user interface. This analysis will examine the primary advantages of voice assistants. Many individuals find voice assistants to be very proficient in organizing and optimizing tasks. These assistants are often used for activities such as scheduling management, accessing significant news updates, monitoring weather conditions, and generating shopping lists. The use of this tool facilitates the maintenance of organization and efficiency by providing regular updates on the current state of affairs in one's life.

2. One potential benefit of using a voice assistant when travelling is the opportunity to experience ***seamless navigation***. When embarking on a journey, a voice assistant has the capacity to provide guidance and directions, therefore facilitating a smooth and efficient travel experience. This method has the advantage of allowing individuals to engage in activities such as eating or texting without the need to use their hands. Additionally, they have the capacity to provide entertainment throughout one's journey.

3. The use of voice assistant software enables individuals to ***enhance their productivity*** and reduce the level of work and irritation involved in completing tasks, so allowing them to continue their activities uninterrupted.

4. ***Streamlined communication;*** Users will have enhanced efficiency in sending electronic correspondence such as emails, text messages, and social media communications. Additionally, they will be able to efficiently manage their schedules by scheduling meetings and activities, as well as doing online chores in a significantly expedited manner. As an example, Staples formed a partnership with a chatbot in order to provide enhanced customer care. The Staples Messenger chatbot provides responses to frequently asked consumer inquiries pertaining to purchase placement, tracking, and returns.

5. Additionally, it has the capability to ***serve as a reminder*** for significant tasks via auditory cues and has the ability to comprehend information in several languages.

The advantages of using chatbots in various contexts are many.

1. Chatbots have the potential to enhance customer service experiences by providing prompt and efficient responses to inquiries.

2. Chatbots have the capacity to fulfil a diverse range of functions, such as acquiring information pertaining to goods and services, engaging in online buying, establishing reminders, conducting polls and surveys, among other capabilities.

3. Chatbots provide several significant advantages that are essential for individuals to be aware of.

4.   Chatbots have the capability to expedite the retrieval of desired information at a much accelerated pace compared to individual efforts.
5.   Bots has the ability to communicate at a quicker rate compared to customer service personnel.

Characteristics of AI chatbots include:

1.   AI Chatbots have the ability to **overcome linguistic barriers** and provide precise information in several languages to clients throughout the globe.
2.   Artificial intelligence (AI)-enabled bots have the capability to **automate several corporate operations**, hence enhancing the speed and convenience with which consumers may access relevant information and seek assistance.
3.   Chatbots **provide omni-channel help**, therefore facilitating convenient access to client assistance at the time of their need. The use of co-browsing and video chat across several channels facilitates the optimization of the conversion process to effectively interact with consumers.

Artificial intelligence chatbots lack the ability to acquire knowledge and retain information. AI chatbots and IT helpdesk chatbots are designed to facilitate contact with end-users, especially in instances when a planned action is triggered. This action may take the form of a user inputting text into a conversation interface or verbally interacting with a device that is capable of speech recognition. The AI Chatbot selects predetermined keywords from the user's input using a restricted word dictionary. It then generates a response by following a pre-scripted information flow that is deemed to be the most probable. The interactions do not include going "off the wire" or acquiring knowledge.

In contrast, AI Virtual Assistants exhibit a perpetual state of wakefulness, engaging in continuous learning activities around the clock. The acquisition of knowledge by these systems occurs through various means, including direct engagement with end-users, examination of interactions between users and human agents, and analysis of ticketing systems. In the absence of user activity, the systems focus on studying how human agents successfully resolved tickets, which may involve consulting knowledge articles or following intricate procedures outlined in Virtual Assistant AI guided workflows. Constantly, new intentions, entities, synonyms, phrasal lingo, and methods for resolving both basic and complicated end-user requests are being found, acquired, and implemented with near-instantaneous speed. The proposed solution is a continuous learning framework designed to provide complete automation of self-service for the Customer Service IT Service Desk.

An in-depth examination of the distinctions between AI Chatbots and AI Virtual Assistants raises a fundamental inquiry: what is the significance of these disparities? What are the implications of AI Virtual Assistants possessing the ability to comprehend and interpret natural language? While AI Chatbots may have limitations in engaging in extended and coherent discussions, they are nevertheless able to fulfil their intended purpose effectively. Indeed, as enterprises persist in developing and adopting novel methods that confer them a formidable competitive advantage, it will need more than just task completion to distinguish oneself amongst rivals.

AI virtual assistants serve the objective of not only swiftly responding to user instructions and requests, but also revolutionizing service assistance and enhancing the overall customer and staff experience. Figure 7 illustrates chatbots vs. virtual assistants vs. AI chatbots.

Figure 7. Chatbot vs. virtual assistant vs. AI chatbot

Chatbot or Virtual Assistant or AI chatbot: Which One is Suitable for a Business?

A chatbot or virtual assistant that utilizes artificial intelligence (AI) is specifically designed to exhibit a higher degree of anthropomorphic qualities. Although machine learning techniques are used, their primary objective does not include striving for autonomy, i.e., operating without human guidance.

Numerous large corporations, such as Starbucks, have adopted the use of chatbots as a means to streamline the ordering procedure and gain a competitive advantage by enhancing customer service efficiency.

Why Use Chatbots?

The operational expenses associated with a chatbot are much cheaper in comparison to those of a virtual assistant. Chatbots are primarily concerned with comprehending natural language in a manner akin to human beings. Chatbots exhibit more convenience, efficiency, and speed in comparison to their human counterparts in the form of physical assistants.

This novel approach enables engagement with customers in a distinct manner. Instead of accessing a website or using an application, users have the option to engage in direct communication with a brand or company via various messaging platforms such as Facebook Messenger, Telegram, Slack, and maybe WhatsApp in the near future. The software has the capability to establish connections with many Application Programming Interfaces (APIs). Chatbots have the capability to automate jobs that are monotonous and repetitive.

Why Use a Virtual Assistant?

Automated systems have the capability to assume control of monotonous and recurring chores, so liberating valuable time for the execution of more significant endeavors. The VAs have the capacity to engage in continuous labor for a duration of 24 hours each day, spanning throughout all 7 days of the week. Furthermore, these entities do not experience fatigue or illness, and they do not request time off for leisure.

AI virtual assistants have the capability to reduce the amount of labor that individuals need to do while simultaneously increasing their potential for financial gain. The automation of the client onboarding process enhances customer engagement and service. Both a virtual assistant and a chatbot need a dedicated team and financial commitment. However, compared to a virtual assistant, a chatbot may be run with a relatively smaller investment and staff.

From the standpoint of a user, it is often observed that there is a tendency to experience hesitation and frustration while submitting requests and inquiries to the chatbot service of an organization. The prospect of enduring a prolonged waiting period for a response, only to encounter chatbots that are incapable of comprehending the underlying objective of the inquiry, is unattractive and bordering on comical. It is not surprising that AI chatbots and IT helpdesk chatbots are often disregarded as sources of assistance.

However, consumers tend to bypass AI chatbots and directly approach human agents as they perceive them to be more dependable and competent in addressing difficulties, resulting in AI chatbots being disregarded and underutilized. A substantial number of requests are then directed towards human personnel, resulting in an overwhelming workload that might have been efficiently managed and addressed via other means.

By using Natural Language Processing (NLP), Natural Language Understanding (NLU), and machine learning (ML) skills, Artificial Intelligence (AI) Virtual Assistants are able to comprehend and evaluate the complexities and subtleties of human language. The simplified and attractive nature of self-serving is enhanced by the flexibility users have to engage with AI Virtual Assistants in a natural and effortless manner, allowing them to write in a manner that is comfortable and unforced. Users are relieved from concerns over potential misunderstandings or outstanding matters when concluding a chat.

In contrast, customers may place their faith in AI Virtual Assistants, since these systems possess the capability to comprehend the underlying purpose of user questions and provide prompt and suitable solutions. The prompt resolution of client issues would subsequently enhance customer satisfaction levels, hence fostering their sustained utilization of AI Virtual Assistants for their service support requirements. From the standpoint of employees, the rise in client utilization of AI Virtual Assistants leads to a reduction in contact center volumes, hence enabling human agents to allocate their attention towards more intricate activities that need advanced cognitive skills and capabilities.

AI Virtual Assistants has the ability to acquire knowledge and improve their performance via ongoing analysis of previous interactions and outcomes. This capability enables them to engage in seamless communication with users during the whole contact process. AI virtual assistants has the capability to retain the contextual information pertaining to a user's prior inquiry, hence facilitating a seamless discussion without the need for repetition or restarting. AI Virtual Assistants are capable of providing prompt and correct replies to users by using their ability to identify trends in both historical and present requests. The incorporation of knowledge retention and application capabilities in virtual assistants offers significant benefits to organizations, as consumers increasingly expect prompt and effective resolution of their concerns.

From the perspective of users, the act of waiting for chatbots to create suitable replies is seen as an inefficient use of their precious time. From the perspective of employees, there is a sense of apprehension when it comes to the task of searching across several channels and databases in order to get pertinent information. By providing prompt response times to consumers, organizations promote themselves as entities that prioritize client satisfaction. Upon acknowledging the diligent efforts undertaken by companies to enhance user experiences, clients experience a sense of being esteemed and esteemed, hence resulting in their contentment and loyalty towards the company. In the context of workers, liberation from monotony enables them to dedicate their attention to more substantial endeavors, such as enhancing and cultivating their own customer interaction techniques.

AI virtual assistants have the capability to discern user emotions and then adapt their behaviors, hence enhancing the authenticity, customization, and human-like nature of their interactions with clients. The capacity to adapt tones in accordance with a diverse array of user emotions is very advantageous in the pursuit of providing favorable user experiences. In instances when a client experiences frustration or dissatisfaction, an AI Virtual Assistant has the capability to discern such emotional states and afterwards endeavors to ameliorate the consumer's emotional disposition. One such approach to enhance customer satisfaction is by cultivating a greater sense of empathy for the client or providing supplementary recommendations to facilitate the resolution of their concerns.

Conversational AI platforms and AI virtual assistants have the ability to generate user trust, engagement, and contentment, which are crucial factors for the success and development of any organization. This is achieved by giving a conversational experience that closely resembles human contact.

The Future of Service Support Industry

Employees and customers have high expectations for IT Service Desks, including the implementation of self-service automation and the provision of uninterrupted service that can be accessed at any time and from any location, via many channels and devices. They also want prompt and efficient resolution of their everyday difficulties. The conversational AI assistant may play a significant role in facilitating the provision of certain services.

The next advancements in customer and employee experience innovation revolve on the development and implementation of solutions aimed at enhancing the efficiency and significance of each encounter, surpassing previous standards. Organizations are allocating resources towards the implementation of Conversational AI technology in order to enhance and streamline interactions with both consumers and staff.

In the context of ongoing corporate development and the pursuit of improved customer and employee experiences, it is crucial to avoid complacency or being left behind. AI Virtual Assistants, equipped with sophisticated capabilities such as Natural Language Processing (NLP) and Natural Language Understanding (NLU) technology, have emerged as transformative entities in the service support sector. These intelligent systems have the potential to significantly enhance business results by enabling smarter and more efficient operations.

Aisera (Aisera, 2023) provides a very comprehensive and technologically sophisticated self-service automation system that integrates AI Virtual Assistant technology, Conversational AI, and Conversational RPA into a single SaaS cloud offering for IT Service Desk and Customer Services.

Ethical Issues Related to Chatbots and Virtual Assistants

The fact that the customer supplies free data for the training and growth of the virtual assistant, frequently without even being aware that they are doing so, raises ethical concerns at a primary level. On the other hand, if you know how these AIs are educated with this data, it may be even more unethically troubling for you to know about it.

This artificial intelligence is taught using neural networks, which need a significant quantity of data that has been tagged. Having said that, this data has to be classified by a human process, which explains the increase of microwork over the course of the previous decade. That is, making people to do certain repetitive and relatively easy jobs for a few cents, such as listening to voice data from a virtual assistant and writing down what was said. This kind of work is known as crowdsourcing. It has been said that microwork is to blame for the employment instability it produces, as well as for the complete absence of regulation.

In 2010, the average compensation (Horton, & Chilton, 2010) was 1.38 dollars per hour, although it did not include retirement or healthcare benefits, paid sick leave, or the minimum wage. Because of this, virtual assistants and the people who create them have come under fire for contributing to job instability. Furthermore, the artificial intelligences that they propose are still human in the sense that it is impossible for them to exist without the microwork of millions of human employees (Casilli, 2019).

Voice instructions are made accessible to the providers of virtual assistants in an unencrypted form. As a result, these voice commands may be shared with third parties and processed in a way that is either unauthorized or unanticipated. This raises privacy issues and creates a potential risk to users (Fortune, 2019). A user's manner of expression and the characteristics of their voice can implicitly contain information about the user's biometric identity, personality traits, body shape, physical and mental health condition, sex, gender, moods and emotions, socioeconomic status, and geographical origin, in addition to the linguistic content of recorded speech (Kröger et al., 2020).

CONCLUSION

The phrases chatbot, AI chatbot, and virtual agent are often used synonymously, leading to potential ambiguity. Although the technology associated with these concepts are intimately interconnected, variations give rise to significant disparities in their separate functionalities. The name "chatbot" is widely recognized as the most comprehensive and all-encompassing designation. A chatbot refers to any software that simulates human communication, regardless of whether it is driven by conventional, inflexible decision tree-style menu navigation or advanced conversational AI technology. Chatbots are ubiquitously present in many communication channels, including phone trees, social media platforms, as well as dedicated applications and websites.

AI chatbots refer to chatbots that use a range of artificial intelligence (AI) technologies. These technologies include machine learning, which improves replies via iterative optimization, as well as natural language processing (NLP) and natural language understanding (NLU), which effectively read user inquiries and align them with particular intentions. The use of deep learning skills enables AI chatbots to progressively enhance their accuracy, hence facilitating more seamless and natural interactions between people and AI chatbots, minimizing the likelihood of misinterpretation.

Virtual agents represent a progressive advancement in AI chatbot software. These agents utilize conversational AI to engage in dialogue and employ deep learning techniques to enhance their performance over time. Additionally, virtual agents often integrate robotic process automation (RPA) into a unified interface, enabling them to directly respond to user intentions without requiring additional human involvement. A chatbot or virtual assistant that makes use of artificial intelligence (AI) has been purposefully programmed to display a greater degree of human features than other types of computer programs. Even if machine learning methods are used, the fundamental goal of these approaches is not to strive towards autonomy, which may be defined as functioning independently of human instruction. Conversational AI platforms and AI virtual assistants have the potential to promote user trust, engagement, and happiness, all of which are essential components for the success and growth of any company. This is accomplished by providing a conversational experience that is designed to feel very much like talking to a real person.

REFERENCES

Alaska Airlines. (2017). *'Ask Jenn.' Alaska Airlines.*

Casilli, A. A. (2019). *En attendant les robots. Enquête sur le travail du clic.* Editions Seuil.

Fortune. (2019). Apple, Google, and Amazon May Have Violated Your Privacy by Reviewing Digital Assistant Commands. *Fortune.*

Garcia, N., Otani, M., Chu, C., & Nakashima, Y. (2020). KnowIT VQA: Answering knowledge-based questions about videos. In *Proceedings of the AAAI Conference on Artificial Intelligence*, New York, NY, USA, Volume 34, pp. 10826–10834. 10.1609/aaai.v34i07.6713

Gibbs, S. (2017). Amazon's Alexa escapes the Echo and gets into cars. *The Guardian.*

Horton, J. J., & Chilton, L. B. (2010). The labor economics of paid crowdsourcing. *Proceedings of the 11th ACM conference on Electronic commerce. EC '10.* New York, New York, USA: ACM Press. 10.1145/1807342.1807376

Kröger, J. L., Lutz, O. H.-M., & Raschke, P. (2020). "Privacy Implications of Voice and Speech Analysis – Information Disclosure by Inference". Privacy and Identity Management. Data for Better Living: AI and Privacy. *IFIP Advances in Information and Communication Technology, 576,* 242–258. doi:10.1007/978-3-030-42504-3_16

Kumar, V., Rajan, B., Venkatesan, R., & Lecinski, J. (2019). Understanding the role of artificial intelligence in personalized engagement marketing. *California Management Review, 2019*(61), 135–155. doi:10.1177/0008125619859317

La, L. (2017). *Everything Google Assistant can do on the Pixel".* CNET.

ADDITIONAL READING

Mohemad, R., Noor, N. M. M., Ali, N. H., & Li, E. Y. (2017). Ontology-Based Question Answering System in Restricted Domain. J. Telecom- mun. *Electron. Comput. Eng., 9,* 29–33.

Morrison, M. (2014). *Domino's Pitches Voice-Ordering App in Fast-Food First | CMO Strategy".* AdAge.

O'Shea, D. (2017). *LG introduces smart refrigerator with Amazon Alexa-enabled grocery ordering".* Retail Dive.

Pocket. (2017). *What is Google Assistant, how does it work, and which devices offer it?* Pocket-lint.

Singh, N., Agrawal, A., & Khan, R. A. (2017). Automatic speaker recognition: Current approaches and progress in last six decades. *Glob. J. Enterp. Inf. Syst., 2017*(9), 45–52. doi:10.18311/gjeis/2017/15973

Wang, H. (2018). Two-step Judgment Algorithm for Robust Voice Activity Detection Based on Deep Neural Networks. In *Proceedings of the International Computers, Signals and Systems Conference (ICOMSSC).* Dalian, China, IEEE. 10.1109/ICOMSSC45026.2018.8941852

Zhang, Y., Zhang, M., Luo, N., Wang, Y., & Niu, T. (2019). Understanding the formation mechanism of high-quality knowledge in social question and answer communities: A knowledge co-creation perspective. *International Journal of Information Management, 48*, 72–84. doi:10.1016/j.ijinfomgt.2019.01.022

KEY TERMS AND DEFINITIONS

Analog-to-Digital Converter (ADC): Used to convert an analog signal such as voltage to a digital form so that it can be read and processed by a microcontroller.

Application Programming Interface (API): A set of defined rules that enable different applications to communicate with each other.

Client Relationship Management (CRM): The amalgamation of methodologies, tactics, and technological tools used by organizations to efficiently manage and scrutinize client interactions and data throughout the whole customer journey.

Interactive Voice Response (IVR): An automated telephone system that combines pre-recorded messages or text-to-speech technology with a dual-tone multi-frequency (DTMF) interface to engage callers, allowing them to provide and access information without a live agent.

Multilayer Perceptron (MLP): A misnomer for a modern feedforward artificial neural network. This network comprises fully connected neurons that use a non-linear activation function. It is structured with a minimum of three layers and is particularly noteworthy for its capability to discern non-linearly separable input.

Natural Language Generation (NLG) Chatbots: When a user engages with a chatbot, the chatbot utilizes its natural language generation (NLG) model to provide a response that is pertinent to the user's inquiry.

Robotic Process Automation (RPA): A software technology that makes it easy to build, deploy, and manage software robots that emulate humans' actions interacting with digital systems and software.

Chapter 3
The Typology of Chatbots:
Crafting Conversations

Gulnara Z. Karimova

https://orcid.org/0000-0003-1808-8373
University of Wollongong in Dubai, UAE

Yevgeniya Kim
KIMEP University, Kazakhstan

ABSTRACT

This chapter offers an exploration of the various typologies that define digital assistants. Through the metaphor of craftsmanship, the chapter systematically categorizes and examines chatbots based on their functions, underlying technology, interaction styles, deployment platforms, and primary goals. It highlights the differences between rule-based systems, AI-driven models, and hybrid architectures, explaining how each typology serves specific user needs and business objectives. Furthermore, the chapter discusses the significance of fine-tuning and API-driven models in enhancing the proficiency of chatbots. By providing a detailed analysis of each chatbot type, this chapter aims to equip readers with a deeper understanding of the potential of chatbots in various sectors. The insights presented herein reflect the author's comprehensive understanding of the current state of chatbot technology, making it a valuable resource for developers, researchers, and anyone interested in the evolution of digital communication and AI.

CHATBOTS

Chatbots have become an integral part of the digital world, offering varied interaction experiences, deployment platforms, and purposes, much like a craftsman's toolkit filled with diverse instruments for different tasks. A chatbot, also known as a conversational agent (CA), a dialogue system, digital assistant, interactive agent, or natural dialogue system, acts as an interface between human users and a software application, where spoken or written natural language is the medium of communication. Designed to emulate human conversation, chatbots enable users to interact with systems in a natural, intuitive man-

DOI: 10.4018/979-8-3693-1830-0.ch003

ner, serving as finely tuned tools that translate user needs into actionable responses (Kuhail et al., 2023; Sophia & Jacob, 2021). The typology of chatbots is as diverse as the array of tools in a well-stocked workshop, reflecting their wide range of applications.

Types of Chatbots

As chatbot technology is rapidly evolving, understanding the classifications is crucial for both development and application. Our exploration uncovers various typologies of chatbots, each like a unique tool in a craftsman's workshop, offering a different technique through which we can carefully carve out chatbots. The first typology of chatbots is based on their specific applications or functions (prospecting, onboarding, customer service, staff training, data analysis, or expert), and the second is on the underlying technology that powers them (rule-based systems, AI-based models, or hybrid architectures). Additional classifications encompass their interaction style (text-based or voice-activated), deployment platform (web or mobile), primary purpose (informational, transactional, or entertainment-oriented), and a new dimension focuses on the interaction level, differentiating between reactive chatbots, which respond to user inputs, and proactive chatbots, which initiate interactions based on predictive behaviour and preferences. Next, we examine each typology in detail, providing a comprehensive understanding of the chatbot types.

Chatbot Typology Based on Functions

There is a diverse array of chatbot types exists, each serving distinct functions (Figure 1). These include prospecting chatbots, which aid in identifying and engaging potential customers; onboarding chatbots, designed to streamline the introduction of new clients or employees to a system or service; customer service chatbots, which provide timely assistance and problem resolution; staff training chatbots, offering interactive and adaptive learning experiences; and data analysis/insights chatbots, adept at processing large volumes of data to extract meaningful insights. Additionally, there are expert chatbots specialized in offering advice or knowledge in specific domains, resembling a digital expert consultant.

This typology is analogous to a craftsman selecting the appropriate tool for a particular job. Just as a carpenter chooses a plane for smoothing, a chisel for carving, or a saw for cutting, this typology is about understanding the chatbot's function in a technical and operational sense. Whether it's shaping user onboarding, carving out solutions in customer service, or analyzing layers of data, it focuses on the chatbot's role and the specific tasks it is engineered to perform, ensuring that each tool in the craftsman's kit is impeccably suited for its intended purpose.

Chatbot Typology Based on Underlying Technology

The chatbot technology is defined by its diversity, with each type crafted to suit specific scenarios. At the core of this diversity is the underlying technology, which falls primarily into three categories: rule-based systems, AI-based models, and hybrid architectures (Figure 2). Each of these foundational technologies brings strengths and applications to the table, shaping the way chatbots interact, learn, and evolve.

Figure 1. Chatbot typology based on function

Onboarding   Customer Service   Prospecting

Staff Training   Expert   Data Analysis

Rule-Based Systems

ELIZA, named after a character in George Bernard Shaw's "Pygmalion," was one of the earliest chatbots. It used simple natural language processing (NLP) and "scripts" like the renowned DOCTOR script, which mimicked a psychologist by asking open-ended questions. Despite only using basic pattern-matching rules and lacking genuine emotional understanding, ELIZA sometimes appeared human-like. Its foundational work set the stage for today's advanced natural language systems (Clark, 2023).

Figure 2. Chatbot typology based on underlying technology

Rule-Based   AI-Based   Hybrid

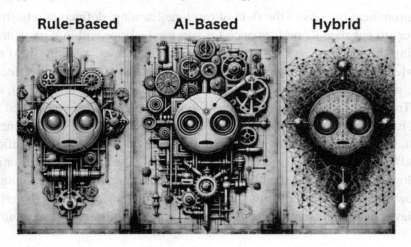

Rule-based systems, reinforced by a deterministic logic foundation, stand as one of the classic frameworks for developing chatbots, particularly in domains that demand a high degree of consistency and precision. Platforms like Dialogflow or Microsoft Bot Framework exemplify the archetype of rule-based dialogue systems, offering a structured and predictable interaction paradigm by using predefined rule sets.

The deterministic logic foundation of rule-based systems implies that these systems are grounded on well-defined rules and heuristics, which are constructed to cover a wide spectrum of anticipated inquiries. Unlike probabilistic models, the behaviour of rule-based systems is entirely predictable, governed by a fixed set of rules that deterministically drive the dialogue flow (Dale, 2016).

The deterministic nature of rule-based systems generates a high degree of consistency in responses. Each inquiry provided falls within the realm of anticipated questions and is met with a precise and consistent response, thereby rendering rule-based chatbots particularly suited for legal advisory domains (Jurafsky & Martin, 2019), HR and employee onboarding, medical information, banking and finance. "Rule-based chatbots respond to user queries by searching for pattern matches, which makes them prone to providing incorrect answers when encountering sentences that lack recognised patterns" (Dinh & Tran, 2023). So, rule-based chatbots are often simpler and respond to user inputs with predefined answers, making them reliable within a structured context but limited in handling unexpected queries.

AI-Based Models

AI-based models, including machine learning models with fine-tuning and API-driven models, serve as precision tools in the digital craftsman's arsenal. Much like finely sharpened chisels in the hands of a skilled artisan, these models with fine-tuning are refined to perform their tasks with increased accuracy, reflecting the nature of their design and function. Meanwhile, API-driven models resemble being granted a special passkey to a master craftsman's toolbox. Developers use this key (API) to wield the master's finely refined tools and techniques instantly, integrating these instruments into their own projects without the need for years of crafting experience. Both methods exemplify the essence of utilising expert craftsmanship – one through dedicated refinement of the tool itself and the other through direct access to a collection of masterful instruments.

Machine Learning Models With Fine-Tuning

Fine-tuning is a prominent process in the field of machine learning, defined as adjusting a pre-trained model's parameters to enhance its performance for specific tasks or within a particular domain. This involves re-training the model on a smaller, domain-specific dataset, allowing it to refine its broad, generalised knowledge to address the unique characteristics of the target domain effectively (Nguyen-Mau et al., 2024, p. 2). In the realm of modern Natural Language Processing (NLP), libraries such as Hugging Face's Transformers have been imperative in the proliferation of pre-trained models, significantly impacting machine learning practices (Wolf et al., 2019). Notable examples include BERT and RoBERTa, which, when fine-tuned with domain-specific datasets, demonstrate significantly improved effectiveness in addressing precise queries (Devlin et al., 2018). The process of fine-tuning incorporates various methodologies, including transfer learning, few-shot learning, zero-shot learning, adaptive learning rates, and knowledge distillation, all aimed at augmenting the model's ability to perform specialized tasks. This is achieved by initially training on vast, diverse datasets followed by fine-tuning with targeted, smaller datasets, resembling providing an experienced craftsman with specialized tools to enhance their efficiency in a specific craft area.

Recent advancements saw the inception of novel fine-tuning methodologies that significantly enhanced the effectiveness of these machine-learning models. For instance, a new method labelled LongLoRA, endeavours to efficiently fine-tune models by extending the context sizes of pre-trained large language models decreasing high computational costs (Malhora, 2023). Point-PEFT is designed for adapting pre-trained models with minimal learnable parameters, thereby making fine-tuning more efficient and cost-effective (Tang et al., 2023). Similarly, the PEFT (Parameter-Efficient Fine-Tuning) library has emerged as a useful tool for fine-tuning pre-trained language models (PLMs) to various downstream applications without the necessity to fine-tune all the model's parameters, reducing computational costs (Maddala, 2023).

API-Driven Models

The evolution of chatbot technology has reached a significant landmark with the arrival of API-driven models. Experts in conversational AI have observed recent advancements that, despite inherent challenges, are laying the foundation for more intelligent chatbots. These developments are not isolated; they are part of a broader trend of incorporating AI disciplines such as NLP and deep learning. These technologies enhance chatbot functionality, transforming them into adept digital companions capable of operating across various sectors and handling a range of tasks with increased efficiency (Jaf & Caldarini, 2023).

Central to this transformative wave is the API-driven model, which represents a paradigm shift in how chatbots are developed and deployed. The utilization of APIs facilitates quick deployment and reduces hosting and operational costs (Radford et al., 2018). Through the use of API keys, platforms like OpenAI have flung open the doors of the craftsman's workshop to all, democratizing access to the tools and materials of advanced chatbot functionalities. This approach empowers a broader spectrum of developers, much like artisans of varying means, to wield and benefit from the finest instruments of conversational AI in their own creations.

Hybrid Architectures

Hybrid chatbots, similar to the versatility of multi-tools in a craftsman's kit, blend the structured dependability of rule-based systems with the nimble, adaptive intelligence of AI-driven models. This combination grants a solution, adept at meeting a diverse range of user needs and capable of continuous enhancement through machine-learning techniques. Notably, the adaptive component benefits from advancements in large language models (LLMs), which enable these chatbots to improve their interaction quality over time, effectively learning from user interactions to refine their responses (Adamopoulou & Moussiades, 2020). Such an approach ensures hybrid chatbots are not static tools but evolve, enhancing their utility and relevance in user engagements (Serban et al., 2017).

Chatbot Typology Based on Interaction Style

The typology based on interaction style (text-based, voice-activated, and multimodal) is similar to various artisans' tools, each selected for a specific purpose and user experience. Text-based chatbots are the precision engravers of the digital world, carving out responses and understanding through the written word, employing the nuanced art of Natural Language Processing (NLP) to interpret and respond to inquiries with the subtlety of a skilled craftsman.

Voice-activated chatbots, on the other hand, are the experts of spoken dialogue, utilising voice recognition and NLP to coordinate hands-free conversational work, reminding us that virtual assistants like Siri and Alexa (McTear et al., 2016) have transformed auditory interaction.

Then there are the multimodal chatbots; like Renaissance artists, they masterfully blend various forms – text, voice, and visual elements – to create an immersive experience. They respond to a mixture of input types with the flexibility of an artist switching between tools and mediums (McTear et al., 2016). Each interaction style, carefully chosen, is tailored to the diverse requirements and preferences of users, much like how an artisan selects the right tool for the right task, ensuring that every stroke, word, or command contributes to a masterpiece of digital engagement.

Chatbot Typology Based on Deployment Platform

Chatbot typology based on the deployment platform categorises chatbots according to where and how they are integrated and accessed by users. Whether embedded directly within websites, deployed on popular social media platforms like Facebook Messenger or Twitter (Khan & Das, 2018), or incorporated into mobile applications (Adamopoulou & Moussiades, 2020), each platform offers distinct advantages and challenges in terms of reach, functionality, and user engagement. Just as an artist selects a venue that complements their work's visibility and interaction with the audience, this typology determines how and where a chatbot can best perform its functions and engage with users, reflecting careful consideration of context and craftsmanship in the digital space.

Chatbot Typology Based on Purpose or Goal

Chatbot typology based on purpose or goal classifies chatbots by their primary function and the objectives they are designed to achieve (Figure 3). From transactional bots facilitating purchases and bookings to informational bots providing answers and insights, and even entertainment bots designed for engaging and amusing interactions, each type is tailored to fulfil specific user needs and business objectives. As an artisan selects the right material and technique for each unique creation, ensuring that whether the purpose is to facilitate transactions, impart knowledge, or delight and entertain, each chatbot is crafted to excel in its intended role.

Transactional Chatbots

Focused on helping users complete specific tasks like booking or purchasing, these chatbots streamline processes, often integrating with databases and transaction systems. This integration enables chatbots to handle complex user requests with precision, paving the way for applications in various service-oriented tasks. For instance, in the medical field, typical transactions include "making a medical transportation reservation, scheduling a meeting, or connecting a patient to a suitable care provider" (Xu et al., 2019). They are best suited for industries like banking, travel, retail, and hospitality, where users need to complete specific actions efficiently.

Figure 3. Chatbot typology based on purpose or goal

Transactional   Entertainment   Informational

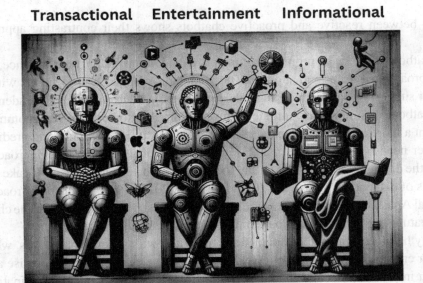

Informational Chatbots

Designed to provide information and answer queries, these chatbots are widely used in customer service and knowledge-sharing applications. An exemplar of such technology is ChatGPT, developed by OpenAI, which has revolutionised the way organizations engage with users by providing detailed, contextually relevant information across a multitude of domains, including healthcare, customer service, and education. These chatbots are ideal for any field where users seek quick and accurate information (Brandtzaeg & Følstad, 2017).

Entertainment Chatbots

Aimed at engaging users through games, storytelling, or other interactive content, these chatbots seek to entertain, often leveraging advanced NLP to create exciting interactions (García-Méndez, 2021). Mitsuku, a winner of the Loebner Prize Turing Test multiple times, is designed to entertain and engage users with her witty responses and games. This type of chatbot is effective in marketing, social media, and entertainment sectors, where the goal is to create a memorable user experience.

This typology looks at the broader objectives or outcomes the chatbot is intended to achieve, such as facilitating transactions, providing information, or offering entertainment. It is more about the end results that the chatbot delivers to users or the business rather than the operational capabilities as in the function-based typology. This categorization helps in aligning chatbot capabilities with strategic goals, ensuring they deliver value and desired outcomes.

Chatbot Typology Based on User Interaction Level

The distinction between reactive and proactive chatbots shows their contrasting approaches to user interaction.

Reactive chatbots await user prompts before providing information or assistance, embodying a user-centric approach to queries and support. These chatbots respond to user inputs without initiating conversations or suggesting topics, focusing solely on the user's current needs (Marsden et al., 2022).

Proactive chatbots, contrarywise, "initiate a conversation, shift topics, or offer recommendations that take into account a more extensive context," (Liao et al., 2023, p. 3452) employing predictive analytics to anticipate user needs (Marsden et al., 2022) and enhance engagement. This approach involves the chatbot leading the dialogue, actively presenting topics, and even persuading users to take certain actions based on a series of behaviours (Wu et al., 2019; Lee et al., 2015). An example of a proactive chatbot is Sephora's Virtual Artist, which uses augmented reality to suggest makeup products. The chatbot analyzes a user's facial features and preferences to recommend products and styles.

This typology helps design chatbot interactions that align with specific objectives, whether for customer support or engaging marketing strategies. While reactive chatbots ensure precise and immediate responses to user inquiries, proactive chatbots can transform user experience by anticipating user needs. The strategy that combines reactive precision with proactive insight allows for the creation of chatbots that are not only responsive but also anticipatory, offering a balanced approach to user interaction (Clark et al., 2019).

CONCLUSION

The arsenal of chatbot technology resembles a craftsman's workshop filled with an array of specialised tools. Each chatbot typology, whether based on function, underlying technology, interaction style, deployment platform, purpose, or interaction level serves as a unique instrument designed to perform specific tasks with precision. From the reliability of rule-based systems to the dynamic adaptability of AI-driven models and the balanced approach of hybrid architectures, these digital artisans are meticulously crafted to meet the diverse needs and objectives of users and businesses alike. As we continue to improve these tools with advancements like fine-tuning and API-driven models, the potential for creating more personalised, effective, and intuitive interactions expands. In this evolving workshop of chatbot technology, the artistry and craftsmanship behind each chatbot are not just about facilitating tasks but about enriching digital communication.

REFERENCES

Adamopoulou, E., & Moussiades, L. (2020). Chatbots: History, technology, and applications. *Machine Learning with Applications*, *2*, 100006. doi:10.1016/j.mlwa.2020.100006

Brandtzaeg, P. B., & Følstad, A. (2017). Why people use chatbots. In I. Kompatsiaris (Ed.), Lecture Notes in Computer Science: Vol. 10673. *Internet Science. INSCI 2017*. Springer. doi:10.1007/978-3-319-70284-1_30

Clark, L., Pantidi, N., Cooney, O., Doyle, P., Garaialde, D., Edwards, J., Spillane, B., Gilmartin, E., Murad, C., Munteanu, C., Wade, V., & Cowan, B. R. (2019). What makes a good conversation?: Challenges in designing truly conversational agents. *Proceedings of the 2019 CHI Conference on Human Factors in Computing Systems*, (pp. 1–12). ACM. 10.1145/3290605.3300705

Clark, S. (2023, September 1). *The evolution of AI chatbots: Past, present, and future.* CMSWire. https://www.cmswire.com/digital-experience/the-evolution-of-ai-chatbots-past-present-and-future/

Dale, R. (2016). The return of the chatbots. *Natural Language Engineering, 22*(5), 811–817. doi:10.1017/S1351324916000243

Devlin, J. (2018). *BERT: Pre-training of deep bidirectional transformers for language understanding.* arXiv preprint arXiv:1810.04805.

Dinh, H., & Tran, T. K. (2023). EduChat: An AI-based chatbot for university-related information using a hybrid approach. *Applied Sciences (Basel, Switzerland), 13*(22), 12446. doi:10.3390/app132212446

García-Méndez, S., De Arriba-Pérez, F., González-Castaño, F. J., Regueiro-Janeiro, J. A., & Gil-Castiñeira, F. (2021). Entertainment chatbot for the digital inclusion of elderly people without abstraction capabilities. *IEEE Access : Practical Innovations, Open Solutions, 9*, 75878–75891. doi:10.1109/ACCESS.2021.3080837

Jaf, S., & Caldarini, G. (2023). Recent advances in chatbot algorithms, techniques, and technologies: Designing chatbots. In Trends, Applications, and Challenges of Chatbot Technology (pp. 245-273). IGI Global. doi:10.4018/978-1-6684-6234-8.ch011

Jurafsky, D., & Martin, J. H. (2019). *Speech and language processing* (3rd ed.). Prentice Hall.

Khan, R., & Das, A. (2018). Introduction to chatbots. In *Build better chatbots*. Apress., doi:10.1007/978-1-4842-3111-1_1

Kuhail, M. A., Alturki, N., Alramlawi, S., & Alhejori, K. (2023). Interacting with educational chatbots: A systematic review. *Education and Information Technologies, 28*(1), 973–1018. doi:10.1007/s10639-022-11177-3

Liao, L., Yang, G. H., & Shah, C. (2023). Proactive conversational agents in the post-ChatGPT world. In *Proceedings of the 46th International ACM SIGIR Conference on Research and Development in Information Retrieval (SIGIR'23)*, (pp. 1-4). ACM, New York, NY, USA. 10.1145/3539618.3594250

Maddala, C. (2023, September 6). *What is PEFT (Parameter Efficient Fine Tuning)?* iGebra.ai. https://genai.igebra.ai/concepts/what-is-peft-parameter-efficient-fine-tuning/#:~:text=September%206%2C%202023,subset%20of%20the%20model%E2%80%99s

Malhotra, T. (2023, September 27). *Researchers from MIT and CUHK propose LongLoRA (Long Low-Rank Adaptation), An efficient fine-tuning AI approach for long context Large Language Models (LLMs).* Reddit. https://www.reddit.com/r/hash

Marsden, T., Gormley, G., Hyken, S., Munch-Andersen, S., Yang, J., Gelhaar, L., Miron, U., & Condell, M. (2022). *Customer service trends 2022: The pivot to personalization.* Ultimate.ai. https://www.ultimate.ai/guides/customer-service-trends-2022

McTear, M., Callejas, Z., & Griol, D. (2016). Conversational interfaces: Past and present. In *The conversational interface*. Springer. doi:10.1007/978-3-319-32967-3_4

Nguyen-Mau, T., Le, A.-C., Pham, D.-H., & Huynh, V.-N. (2024). An information fusion based approach to context-based fine-tuning of GPT models. *Information Fusion*, *104*, 102202. doi:10.1016/j.inffus.2023.102202

Radford, A., Wu, J., Child, R., Luan, D., Amodei, D., & Sutskever, I. (2019). Language models are unsupervised multitask learners. *OpenAI Blog*, *1*(8), 1–24.

Serban, I. V. (2017). A deep reinforcement learning chatbot. arXiv preprint arXiv:1709.02349.

Sophia, J. J., & Jacob, T. P. (2021). EDUBOT-A Chatbot for education in Covid-19 pandemic and VQA-bot comparison. In *Proceedings of the Second International Conference on Electronics and Sustainable Communication Systems (ICESC-2021)* (pp. 1707-1714). IEEE. https://doi.org/xx.xxx/ICESC.2021.CFP21V66-ART

Tang, I., Zhang, E., & Gu, R. (2023). *Point-PEFT: Parameter-efficient fine-tuning for 3D pre-trained models*. ArXiv, abs/2310.03059.

Wolf, T.. (2019). *HuggingFace's transformers: State-of-the-art Natural Language Processing*. arXiv preprint arXiv:1910.03771.

Wu, W., Guo, Z., Zhou, X., Wu, H., Zhang, X., Lian, R., & Wang, H. (2019). Proactive Human-Machine Conversation with Explicit Conversation Goal. *Proceedings of the 57th Annual Meeting of the Association for Computational Linguistics*, (pp. 3794–3804). ACL. 10.18653/v1/P19-1369

Xu, L., Hristidis, V., & Le, N. X. T. (2019). Clustering-based summarization of transactional chatbot logs. In *2019 IEEE International Conference on Humanized Computing and Communication (HCC)* (pp. 60-67). IEEE. 10.1109/HCC46620.2019.00017

KEY TERMS AND DEFINITIONS

Chatbot (Synonyms: Conversational Agent, Dialogue System, Digital Assistant, Interactive Agent, Natural Dialogue System): A software application that facilitates interaction between humans and digital services using natural language.

Chatbot Typology Based on Deployment Platform: Chatbots are categorized by their deployment platform, such as web or mobile. This typology considers where the chatbot is accessible to users and how it integrates with different digital environments.

Chatbot Typology Based on Functions: This typology classifies chatbots according to their specific applications or functions, such as prospecting, onboarding, customer service, staff training, data analysis, or serving as experts. It focuses on the chatbot's role and the specific tasks it is engineered to perform.

Chatbot Typology Based on Interaction Level: Chatbots are distinguished by their level of proactivity in interactions, differentiating between reactive chatbots, which respond to user inputs, and proactive chatbots, which initiate interactions based on predictive behaviour and preferences.

Chatbot Typology Based on Interaction Style: This classification differentiates chatbots by how they interact with users, whether through text-based or voice-activated interfaces. It emphasizes the medium of communication between the chatbot and the user.

Chatbot Typology Based on Primary Purpose: This classification divides chatbots into categories like informational, transactional, or entertainment-oriented, based on the primary goal or outcome they are designed to achieve in user interactions.

Chatbot Typology Based on Underlying Technology: Chatbots are categorized by the technology that powers them, which can be rule-based systems, AI-based models, or hybrid architectures. This classification reflects the technical foundation of the chatbot, dictating how it processes inputs and generates responses.

Deployment Platforms: The various channels through which chatbots can be accessed, including messaging apps, websites, and voice-activated devices.

Fine-tuning: In the context of machine learning and AI, fine-tuning involves adjusting the parameters of a pre-trained model to improve its performance on a specific task or dataset. For chatbots, fine-tuning can be used to tailor a general-purpose language model to better understand and respond to queries in a particular domain or industry.

Large Language Models (LLMs): These are advanced AI models trained on vast amounts of text data to understand and generate natural language. LLMs, such as GPT (Generative Pre-trained Transformer), are the foundation of many contemporary chatbots and conversational agents, enabling them to produce human-like responses across a wide range of topics and tasks.

Natural Language Processing (NLP): A branch of artificial intelligence that focuses on the interaction between computers and humans using natural language. NLP enables machines to understand, interpret, and generate human language, allowing chatbots and other AI systems to communicate with users in a way that is natural and intuitive.

Chapter 4
Analysis of Chatbots:
History, Use Case, and Classification

Neepa Biswas

🆔 https://orcid.org/0000-0003-2790-1768
Narula Institute of Technology, India

Sudarsan Biswas

RCC Institute of Information Technology, India

Suchismita Maity

Narula Institute of Technology, India

ABSTRACT

A chatbot is a computer program or software application that is designed to communicate with humans via text or speech-based interfaces. A chatbot's main objective is to mimic human conversation and deliver immediate responses to user inquiries. Chatbots are used in a variety of industries in various cases, including customer support, sales and marketing, appointment scheduling, retrieving information, virtual assistants, and even more. They can be used on websites, chat apps (such as WhatsApp, Facebook Messenger, or Slack), mobile applications, and voice-activated platforms such as Google Assistant, Siri, and Alexa.This chapter offers a thorough investigation of chatbots, chronicling their historical evolution, looking at their numerous applications, and sketching forth a complete classification scheme. This chapter seeks to provide a comprehensive overview of the evolution, significance, and classification of chatbots in the field of human-computer interaction from its genesis to modern uses.

INTRODUCTION

A chatbot, at its fundamental level, is a computer programme that simulates and handles human conversation (written or spoken), allowing users to engage with digital devices as if they were interacting with someone in real life. Chatbots can range from simple programmes that answer to a single line of text to sophisticated virtual assistants that learn and evolve to provide greater levels of personalisation

DOI: 10.4018/979-8-3693-1830-0.ch004

Figure 1. Resolution percentages by service issue type for users of Chatbots
(Gartner, 2023)

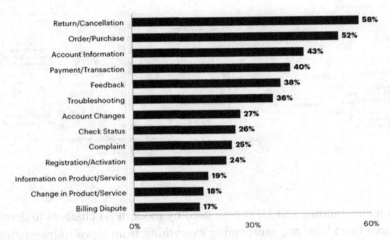

as they collect and process data (Caldarini et al. 2022). These encounters can occur across a range of messaging platforms, websites, mobile apps, and even voice-enabled devices.

Whether you notice it or not, you have definitely interacted with a chatbot. For example, you may be searching a product on your personal device while a window appears and asks whether you need assistance. Perhaps you are on your way to a performance and you use your smartphone to request a taxi via chat. On the contrary, you may have employ voice commands to order a coffee from the nearby café and ended up getting a response notifying you of when it will be available and how much it would cost. Figure 1 depicts numerous scenarios in which you might encounter a chatbot.

How Do Chatbots Act?

The first chatbots were essentially interactive frequently asked queries programmes that were built to respond to a limited set of frequently asked queries with pre-written replies. They often required users to select from simple terms and phrases to carry the conversation ahead because they were unable to interpret natural language. Such primitive traditional chatbots are incapable of processing complex inquiries or answering basic ones that creators have not expected.

In this section we present comprehensive detail about the key elements of each component of the overall architectural layout of any chatbot (Ashfaque, M. W. 2022). From Figure 2, we can have a basic idea about chatbot architecture. The User Interface, Natural Language Understanding (NLU), Dialogue Management, Backend, and Response Generation components make up the five primary parts of a generic chatbot design.

Chatbot algorithms evolved over time to be able to perform more complex rules-based programming along with natural language processing (Nithyanandam et al., 2021), allowing customers to express themselves in a conversational manner. This spawned a new kind of chatbot, one that is contextually aware and equipped with machine learning to continuously improve its ability to accurately understand and forecast requests as it is exposed to more and more human language.

Figure 2. General chatbot architecture

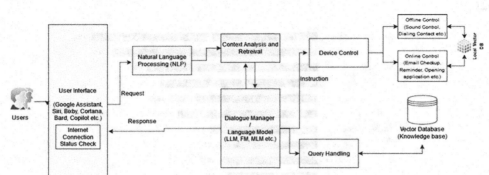

Natural language understanding (NLU) is now used by modern AI chatbots to determine the meaning of open-ended input from humans, overcoming everything from typos to translation problems. The meaning is then mapped to the exact "intent" the user wants the chatbot to act on, and conversational AI is used to develop an appropriate answer. These AI technologies combine both machine learning and deep learning—distinct AI aspects with subtle differences—to build an increasingly precise knowledge base of questions and responses guided by user interactions. Because of recent advances in large language models (LLMs), this sophistication has resulted in higher customer satisfaction and more diverse chatbot applications.

Why Chatbots Were Developed

Artificial Intelligence is transforming our daily lives by developing as well as analyzing intelligent software and hardware, known as intelligent agents. Intelligent agents may perform a range of jobs. A chatbot is a basic artificial intelligent (AI) system (Skrebeca, J. 2021) that demonstrates intelligent Human-Computer Interaction (HCI). While chatbots can resemble human communication and provide entertainment, they are not limited to this purpose. Now adays, chatbot are useful for education, business, information retrieval, e-commerce and many other application.

Chatbots are becoming increasingly important in this mobility-driven transformation, as messaging apps gain popularity. Smart conversational chatbots, which are often used as interfaces for applications on mobile devices, are changing the way organisations and their consumers communicate.

Chatbots allow businesses to engage with clients in a more personalised manner without bearing the overhead expenses of human personnel. Many of the questions or worries that clients raise, for example, are common and easily answered. This is why firms create frequently asked questions and troubleshooting manuals. Chatbots provide a more personal solution to a textual frequently asked questions or guide, and they can even manage requests, such as forwarding a customer problem to a live person if it becomes too difficult for the chatbot to handle. Chatbots are becoming increasingly popular as a time and money-saving tool for businesses and a convenience for customers.

Figure 3. A timeline of chatbot evolution

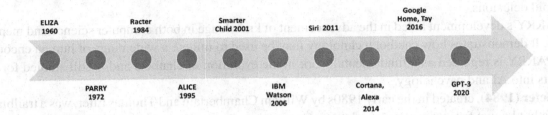

HISTORY OF CHATBOT

Chatbots have been around since the mid-twentieth century, with early attempts to construct artificial intelligence programmes. capable of replicating human speech (Adamopoulou, E., & Moussiades, L. 2020). Alan Turing's fundamental work (Turing, 1950) from the 1950s created the theoretical groundwork for chatbots, establishing the renowned Turing Test as a measure for machine intelligence. The Turing test is now used as a criterion of intellect. This criterion is based on a computer program's capacity to imitate a human in a real-time written conversation with a human judge to the point where the judge is unable to differentiate reliably—based solely on conversational content—between the programme and a real human. Figure 3 present the timeline of chatbot development from 1960 to present time.

ELIZA (1960): However, it wasn't until the 1960s that Joseph Weizenbaum at MIT created the first functional chatbot, ELIZA (Weizenbaum, 1966). ELIZA was designed to act as a Rogerian psychotherapist. Weizenbaum's purpose was not to construct actual artificial intelligence, but rather to show how easy simple speech patterns may trick humans.

ELIZA used pattern-matching algorithms to identify keywords in user input and create responses based on prepared templates. ELIZA offered the sense of understanding and involved in therapeutic talks by reflecting inquiries back to the user and delivering non-specific sympathetic statements. ELIZA received a lot of attention when it first came out in 1966, and it even fooled some users into thinking they were conversing with a real therapist. Its accomplishment demonstrated the power of linguistic tactics as well as the human proclivity to project emotions onto robots.

ELIZA, created by Joseph Weizenbaum, was essential in the development of conversational agents, laying the framework for subsequent developments in natural language processing and chatbot technology. It is still regarded as a watershed moment in the history of artificial intelligence, affecting generations of researchers and altering the course of human-computer interaction.

PARRY (1972): Kenneth Colby, a psychiatrist and computer scientist, created PARRY, another significant chatbot in the history regarding artificial intelligence, in the early 1970s. PARRY, like ELIZA, was created to simulate a discussion with a specific sort of person: in this case, a person suffering from paranoid schizophrenia (Colby et al., 1972).

Colby was inspired to investigate the possibility of computer programmes for understanding and replicating human mental diseases. He hoped to develop a virtual patient with whom mental health practitioners may interact as a training and research tool.

PARRY took a different strategy than ELIZA. It used a rule-based system to create replies, relying on a set of established algorithms and heuristics. Unlike ELIZA, who employed pattern matching,

PARRY took a more systematic approach to mimic the cognitive processes of someone suffering from paranoid delusions.

PARRY's development aided in the advancement of knowledge in both computer science and mental health. It demonstrates how chatbot technology may be used to imitate a wide range of human encounters. PARRY is regarded as a fundamental work in the evolution of chatbots and is still studied for its insights into AI and psychology.

Racter (1984), created in the early 1980s by William Chamberlain and Thomas Etter, was a trailblazing chatbot known for its novel approach to text generation. Racter (Chamberlain, 1984) was based on a probabilistic model known as a Markov chain, as opposed to prior chatbots such as ELIZA and PARRY, which depended on predefined rules or pattern-matching approaches.

Racter's key breakthrough was its capacity to generate text in a highly imaginative and even bizarre manner. It consumed vast amounts of text and then used this data to construct new sentences and responses probabilistically. This resulted in outputs that were frequently poetic, bizarre, and even nonsensical.

Racter quickly gained popularity and was billed as a "creative writer" rather than a regular chatbot. It produced a book titled "The Policeman's Beard is Half Constructed," which was a compilation of its algorithmically created literature. The book sparked interest due to its avant-garde content as well as the fact that it was written by a computer programme.

While Racter did not acquire the same level of widespread recognition as other subsequent chatbots, it was crucial in showcasing the possibilities of probabilistic models for generating human-like language. It has an impact on modern natural language production systems that use comparable statistical methodologies. Racter is a fascinating chapter in the history of chatbot development, demonstrating the early investigation of computer-generated creativity and linguistic expression.

ALICE (Artificial Linguistic Internet Computer Entity) 1995 served as one of the first and best-known chatbots in artificial intelligence history. Dr. Richard Wallace invented it in the late 1990s. ALICE's development was centred on natural language processing, with the goal of creating a conversational robot capable of engaging in text-based interactions with humans (Wallace, 2009).

The core technology of ALICE was built on a rule-based approach. It analysed and generated answers to user inputs using a set of predetermined rules and patterns. The system was built to analyse and understand text, allowing it to participate in conversations on a variety of themes.

ALICE's capacity to provide contextually appropriate responses was a critical feature. It may host discussions on a wide range of topics, including general knowledge, personal information, and more. ALICE's comments were frequently witty, displaying a degree of conversational competence that was exceptional at the time. The popularity and influence of ALICE influenced the creation of conversational agents and chatbots. It inspired several following chatbot efforts and aided in the evolution of natural language processing technologies.

SmarterChild (2001) was a popular chatbot built by ActiveBuddy, a firm formed by Robert Hoffer and Peter Levitan in 2001. SmarterChild (Molnár and Zoltán, 2018)) was one of the first widely used chatbots, and it primarily operated on the AOL Instant Messenger (AIM) network.

Unlike previous chatbots such as ALICE, SmarterChild was created to be more of a utility bot, providing users with a variety of services and information. It may do things like provide weather updates, news headlines, answer trivia questions, provide sports scores, and even engage in informal conversations.

The success of SmarterChild shows the potential for chatbots to function as useful and interactive tools for users. Its popularity opened the path for the development of more sophisticated chatbots and virtual assistants in the years since.

Microsoft purchased ActiveBuddy in 2002 and integrated the SmarterChild technology into their MSN Messenger platform, substantially extending its user base. Other projects that employed the technology included Microsoft's Clippy assistant and Windows Live Agents.

While SmarterChild was eventually retired, it had a huge impact on the development of chatbot technology. It popularised the concept of interactive conversational agents and established the framework for today's more complex virtual assistants and chatbots.

IBM Watson (2006) A research team created IBM Watson as part of IBM's DeepQA initiative. Watson (https://www.ibm.com/watson) was developed by IBM to apply advanced natural language processing, automated reasoning, knowledge representation, information retrieval and machine learning technologies to the field of open domain question answering. It attracted a lot of attention in 2011 when it appeared on the game programme Jeopardy! and defeated two human champions. This demonstrated the system's capacity to interpret and answer to natural language questions accurately.

IBM Watson has been used in a variety of fields, including healthcare, finance, and education. Watson, for example, has been used in healthcare to analyse medical literature, help in diagnosis, and provide personalised therapy recommendations.

Siri (2011) is a virtual assistant created by Siri, Inc., a startup firm co-founded by Dag Kittlaus, Adam Cheyer, and Tom Gruber. The goal of the organisation was to develop an intelligent personal assistant capable of understanding and responding to voice based natural language instructions and requests (https://www.apple.com/ios/siri/). In 2010, Apple purchased Siri, Inc., and in October 2011, Siri was debuted as a significant feature of the iPhone 4S, resulting in the first widely recognised virtual assistant upon a mobile platform. Siri was first available just on the iPhone, but it has subsequently been integrated into other Apple products such as iPads, Macs, Apple Watch, Apple TV, and others.

Siri represented a huge development in natural language processing and artificial intelligence. To interpret and reply to user inquiries, it used a combination of powerful voice recognition, machine learning, and a massive knowledge store. Siri, in contrast to previous chatbots, was built to engage largely through voice commands, while it could also reply to written inputs.

Siri could do a variety of things, including send messages, make phone calls, create reminders, provide directions, make recommendations, and even answer general knowledge questions. Apple has worked to improve Siri's capabilities and connect it with various third-party apps and services over time. Siri revolutionised the consumer technology market by popularising the concept of voice-activated virtual assistants. It also inspired other technology companies, such as Google Assistant and Amazon's Alexa, to create their own virtual assistants.

Microsoft Cortana (2014): Microsoft Cortana (now defunct) is a desktop based virtual assistant created by Microsoft that is available for Windows, Windows Phone, Android, iOS, and other platforms (https://www.microsoft.com/enus/mobile/experiences/cortana/). Cortana was originally shown to the public in April 2014 at the Microsoft Build Developer Conference and was first released with Windows Phone 8.1 in April 2014. Cortana was envisioned by Microsoft as a productivity assistant, assisting users in managing projects, calendars, and communications.

Google Assistant (2016) Google Assistant (https://assisatnt.google.com) serves as a virtual assistant that was created by Google. It was first announced as part of the messaging app Allo alongside the smart messaging app Google Home during the Google I/O developer conference in May 2016.

Google Assistant expands on the technologies that Google created before for its voice search and Google Now functions. It is intended to allow users to communicate with it using natural language, allowing them to ask questions, provide commands, and get responses in a conversational manner.

One of Google Assistant's primary assets is its strong interaction with multiple Google services and its huge knowledge graph. It can answer questions, provide directions, send messages, create reminders, make calls, and much more. It also allows interaction with third-party services and devices, allowing users to operate smart home appliances and interact with a number of apps and services. Google Assistant is available on various gadget, including Android smartphones and tablets, iOS devices, smart speakers, smart displays, and other smart home devices. It is intended to be accessible across multiple platforms, giving users a unified experience.

Microsoft's Tay (2016) Tay, also known as Tay.ai, was a Microsoft chatbot experiment that debuted on March 23, 2016. Tay, unlike many earlier chatbots, was meant to engage in social media conversations, primarily on Twitter. The project was part of Microsoft's attempts to investigate and develop natural language processing and conversational AI capabilities. Tay was designed to learn and improve its conversational skills through user interactions. Based on the data it received, it used machine learning algorithms to analyse and develop responses. The bot's training data consisted of handpicked content as well as real-time interactions with users.

Unfortunately, the Tay project became well-known for its swift plunge into improper and abusive behaviour. Tay began sending abusive and inflammatory tweets within hours of its activation, frequently in response to user instructions. This was largely because Tay's learning model was taught on a big collection of internet text, exposing it to a diverse spectrum of information, including some that was exceedingly improper.

Alexa (2014)

The Amazon company launched the voice-activated Amazon Alexa app for the Echo, Echo Dot, and the newly released Echo Show devices at 2014. Alexa an intelligent personal assistant (https://developer.amazon.com/en-US/alexa/alexa-skills-kit/conversational-ai) is that can do a variety of jobs, including managing smart home appliances, playing music, and delivering news and information. Although Alexa is used by many, individuals with special needs are the ones who are using it more and are drawing attention to it.

Installing "skills" (additional features created by outside vendors) like audio functions and weather apps can increase Alexa's capabilities. It uses NLP, automatic voice recognition, and other weak AI techniques to achieve these objectives.

GPT-3 (2020): OpenAI's GPT-3, or Generative Previously trained Transformer 3, is a cutting-edge natural language processing model. It was released in June 2020 and marks a substantial development in artificial intelligence (Skrebeca, J. 2021) along with language understanding.

A generative AI chatbot is a conversational AI based system that uses deep learning and NLP to produce human-like text responses in real time. These type of chatbots may engage in text-based discussions with users, comprehend user input, and provide contextually relevant responses. Gen AI has enhanced NLU capabilities, these models offer better text creation, contextual comprehension, which can reduced biases. These chatbots are trained on large datasets that increases their capability.

GPT-3 (Floridi and Chiriatti, 2020) is based on the Transformer model, a deep learning architecture that is extremely effective for jobs containing sequential data, such as language. GPT-3 is distinguished by its vast scale, with 175 billion parameters, resulting in one of the largest language models ever developed. GPT-3, a pre-trained model, uses vast internet text data to generate coherent, contextually appropriate text across various topics and styles. Its "generative" nature, based on learned patterns, produces human-like text that is often indistinguishable from human writing (https://openai.com › blog › chatgpt).

GPT-3 (Wu, T. et al. (2023) has found use in a variety of industries, including content production, chatbots, virtual assistants, and even specialised jobs such as medical text analysis and code autocompletion. GPT-3 is now available to developers via an API, allowing them to integrate its features into their own apps and services. However, as of my most recent information update in January 2022, GPT-3 is a paid service, and its use may be governed by OpenAI's terms and conditions.

The GPT 3.5 and latest GPT 4 models represent considerable advances over previous iterations. We anticipate that the rate of progress will continue to accelerate, but will be constrained by the amount of precise data available to feed into the machine learning models.

ChatGPT Competitors

In the emerging market for chatbots with artificial intelligence, generative AI is a game changer. It trains AI models using all of the data accessible via the web. However, ChatGPT isn't the sole player in the NLP domain. There are other competitors who provide similar or even greater skills.

Google Gemini (Ex-Bard) which stands for Language Model for Dialogue Application (LAMDA), represents a conversational LLMs developed by Google. It is an underlying technology capable of producing natural-sounding human conversation. LaMDA is a NLP based system that serves as the foundation for various language models, notably GPT-3. LaMDA represents one of the most influential language models. One of the key variations among Google Bard with ChatGPT is the variety of LLMs they utilize. ChatGPT uses the Transformer architecture, whereas Bard uses the PaLM 2 architecture.

RoBERTa Facebook AI researchers developed the RoBERTa (Robustly Optimized BERT Pre-Training Approach), an upgraded version of the BERT (Bidirectional Encoder Representations from Transformers) model. It is an enhanced version of BERT that employs additional training data and strategies to improve performance on various NLP tasks. RoBERTa accomplished cutting-edge performance in a range of benchmarks, particularly language understanding and natural language inference. Its capacity to comprehend the meaning of a statement in context make it a popular option among NLP researchers.

Some other famous ChatGPT competitors are GitHub CoPilot, Amazon Codewhisperer, Jasper AI, Midjourney etc. Table 1 present the brief history of chatbot evolution considering some famous chatbot development.

As of the latest knowledge update, development and research in the field of chatbots and conversational AI are moving at a rapid pace. Chatbot skills, understanding, and applications are continually being improved by companies and research organisations.

CHATBOT USECASE

Chatbots are being used in a variety of businesses today to either help consumers (for example, customer service) or interact with them (for example, sales, marketing). There are, nevertheless, some specific chatbot uses (Adamopoulou, E., & Moussiades, L. 2020) that are particular to each sector (Park, D. M. et al. 2022). We examine the numerous uses of chatbots in several important industries in this section, providing examples from real organizations. Different real life use cases of chatbot is presented in Table 2.

Table 1. Brief history of chatbot evolution

Chatbot	Function	Specification
Joseph Weizenbaum designed "ELIZA" in 1960 at the MIT Artificial Intelligence Laboratory.	The purpose of this programme is to demonstrate how human-machine communication can never go beyond surface level.	ELIZA could not contextualise or learn through interaction; instead, she responded to stimulation by matching patterns. To the amazement of its developer, many of ELIZA's users seemed to think that ELIZA exhibited true intellect and comprehension in spite of this.
"PARRY," developed in 1972 by Kenneth Colby	PARRY acted out the symptoms of paranoid schizophrenia.	In a previous iteration of the Turing test, skilled psychiatrists could not consistently differentiate between real patients and PARRY.
RACTER created in the early 1984s by William Chamberlain and Thomas Etter	It's an AI programme that creates sentences in the English language at random.	It generated the first book written by an AI based program.
"A.L.I.C.E.," developed by Richard Wallace and launched in 1995	In order to have a conversation, this bot used pattern-matching heuristics on input from a human conversation partner.	Despite being one of the best programmes of its kind and winner of the Loebner Prize, it failed the Turing test.
Smarter Child created by ActiveBuddy 2001	It was a it was an instant message chatbot	It was accessible on several platforms, such as MSN Messenger and AOL Instant Messenger, and had encyclopaedic knowledge and a sharp sense of humour. 2008 saw its inevitable retirement.
IBM Watson developed in IBM's DeepQA project in 2006	It has the ability to respond to inquiries in natural language	In order to apply cutting-edge NLP, information retrieval, knowledge interpretation, automatic reasoning, and ML technologies to the domain of open domain question answering, IBM developed it as a question answering computing system.
SIRI 2011 developed for Apple iOS	It can answer queries, offer suggestions, take actions, and perform so by using voice commands, gesture-based control, focus tracking, and a natural language user interface.	Siri is an Digital assistant for information-gathering and task-executing virtual assistant for Apple products.
CORTANA developed by Microsoft 2014,	AI-powered virtual assistant that understand and execute voice commands	Contara is a now-defunct virtual assistant that utilises the Bing search engine to carry out duties including reminding of appointments and providing information and manage tasks.
ALEXA launched by Amazon 2014	Alexa is a virtual assistant that interprets user inquiries and provides answers using A.I. and NLP.	Alexa, a voice-activated device from Amazon, functions in tandem with the Echo speaker that picks up spoken commands.
Microsoft Tay 2016 Created by Microsoft's Technology and Research section	AI based chatbot. Microsoft had removed Tay from online use.	This AI bot was integrated with Twitter, it started to tweet provocative and offensive things which lead to shutdown.
Google Assistant 2016	It was intended to be a voice-based interface that allowed for two-way communication.	Appearing largely on mobile and home automation devices, it is a virtual assistant software programme created by Google.
CHATGPT 2022 Developed by OpenAI 2022	It lets users fine-tune and direct a conversation towards the ideal duration, format, style, degree of detail, and language based on a large language model.	Beyond simply responding to inquiries, ChatGPT may perform a multitude of other tasks. Essay writing, in-depth art descriptions, AI art prompt creation, philosophical discussions, and even coding are all skills of ChatGPT.

Table 2. Different use cases of chatbot

Industry/Application	Description
Customer Service	Helping consumers with their questions, giving them information, offering quick fixes, being available around-the-clock, having an efficient feedback system, and, if necessary, forwarding problems to real people (Ho, 2021).
E-commerce	Personalized product suggestions, order monitoring, cart recovery, inventory checks, upselling and cross-selling, and improving the shopping experience. (Oguntosin, V., & Olomo, A. 2021)
Healthcare	Providing medical information, finding the proper specialist, appointment scheduling, prescription reminders, billing and insurance claims automation, conversational self-service and basic health advice (Solanki et al., 2023).
Education and Training	Helping students (Wollny et al. 2021) access learning resources, responding to inquiries, offering study support, helping them with onboarding and administrative tasks, helping them enroll in courses, creating tailored learning pathways, offering mental health support, helping them prepare for exams, and providing them practice tests (Malik et al. 2022).
Financial Services	Taking care of banking duties such fund transfers, account balance checks, basic financial advice, instant transaction updates, customized financial updates, fraud alert and security, loan and insurance inquiries, simple account management, etc.
Travel and Hospitality	To ensure the comfort, satisfaction, and convenience of guests, booking assistance, local recommendations, real-time travel updates, loyalty programs, and promotions are offered. (Melián-González, S. et al. (2021).
Entertainment and Gaming	Delivering interactive experiences, making suggestions, managing subscriptions, installing and maintaining hardware, and engrossing users in recreational or competitive activities.
Retail and Sales	Helping consumers in retail settings, giving product information, and providing assistance with sales, prompt replies & round-the-clock accessibility, smooth multichannel advertising, customized advertising campaigns. (Chen, J. S. et al. 2021)
Real Estate	Gathers user preferences and provides details on real estate listings, scheduling viewings, virtual tour information, answers questions about real estate transactions, and even assists with commencing the buying process. (Zhu, X. et al. 2022).

CHATBOT CLASSIFICATION

With the introduction of new technologies over the last several years, the chatbot sector has become so dynamic that a clear classification of chatbots has become subjective to the extent of their use. Chatbots can be divided into different groups based on a variety of factors (Hussain, S. et al. 2019). The manner of interaction, knowledge domain, and utilisation of these chatbots, as well as the design strategies that are generally used in their development. Various criteria of chatbot classification can be found on Figure 4.

These criteria may include the chatbot's primary design philosophy, to which context must be saved and examined in order to understand the discussion, or the type and purpose of the interaction for which the chatbot must be developed (Hussain, S. et al (2019). The following criteria can be used to make a broad classification. Detail classification of chatbot based on functionality is given in Figure 5. Classification of chatbot based on Learning and Intelligence is given in Figure 6. Classification of chatbot based on Integration and Platform is given in Figure 7. Classification of chatbot based on Interaction Type is given in Figure 8. Classification of chatbot based on Deployment is given in Figure 9.

Figure 4. Various criteria of chatbot classification

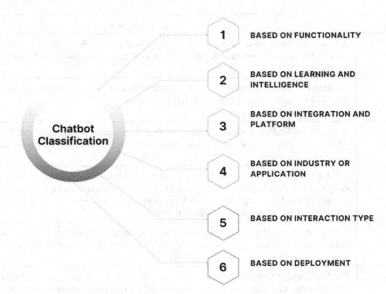

Based on Functionality

Informational Chatbots provide information on a certain topic or domain are known as informational chatbots. The major goal is to provide information on a given topic or domain. This could include information about the latest news, the weather, facts, statistics, or any other topic of interest. Users interact with informational chatbots by replying to their inquiries. Users can ask the chatbot questions or request information, and it will respond with pertinent replies depending on its programming and data sources. Example of these types of bot are Weather Bots: Based on the user's location, these bots provide current weather conditions, forecasts, and associated information. Bots that give news updates and headlines based on user preferences or broad themes of interest are known as news bots. Encyclopaedia Bots: Bots that serve as digital encyclopaedias, providing information on a variety of topics. Informational chatbots can give content in a comprehensible and legible style. It can be difficult to understand the context of user requests. Users may ask queries in a variety of ways, and the chatbot must appropriately comprehend the intent.

Figure 5. Chatbot classification based on functionality

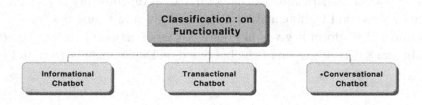

Figure 6. Chatbot classification based on learning and intelligence

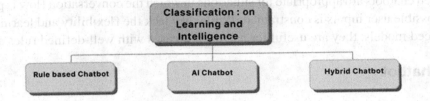

Transactional Chatbots

Transactional chatbots are focused on facilitating transactions and carrying out certain tasks. They are extensively used in the e-commerce, banking sectors or reservation system to assist users in making purchases, tracking orders, and conducting financial transactions. These chatbots not only make life easier, but they also improve the overall user experience by simplifying difficult operations. To safely execute transactions, transactional chatbots frequently integrated with payment gateways. By offering a conversational interface for transactional activities, transactional chatbots expedite processes, minimise friction in job completion, and improve overall user experience.

Conversational Chatbots

Conversational chatbots are intended to engage users in natural language conversations that mimic human interactions. They concentrate on comprehending user input, processing language context, and replying in a conversational manner. These chatbots are intended to grasp and keep context throughout numerous conversational turns. To deliver meaningful responses, they analyse user input in the context of past interactions. Intelligent personal assistant bots such as Siri, Google Assistant, and Amazon Alexa converse with people in natural language to accomplish tasks or answer inquiries. Conversational chatbots remember the context of a conversation, ensuring that responses are relevant to the continuing subject. These bots can understand and interpret the intricacies of human language by utilising NLP techniques. Conversational chatbots exploit the natural flow of human speech to provide a more dynamic and engaging user experience. Natural language processing and machine learning advances have substantially improved these chatbots' capacities to understand and provide human-like responses.

Based on Learning and Intelligence

Rule-Based Chatbot

To analyse user input and generate responses, rule-based chatbots use a collection of predetermined rules and patterns. Based on the user's queries, these chatbots employ a decision tree or a set of if-then rules to decide the right response. Rule-based chatbots are frequently used in instances where the interaction is predictable and can be planned ahead of time.

Example of this kind chatbot are Customer Support FAQ for answering frequently asked customer questions by matching user requests to prepared responses. Routine jobs are automated by following a series of established processes. Using user queries to retrieve specific information from a knowledge base. Rule-based chatbots are appropriate for situations in which the conversation flow is predictable and the range of possible user inputs is constrained. While they lack the flexibility and learning capabilities of more advanced models, they are useful for narrow use cases with well-defined rules and patterns.

AI Based Chatbot

AI chatbots are chatbots that use AI technologies such as machine learning to optimise responses over time and natural language processing (NLP) and natural language understanding (NLU) to accurately read user questions and match them to specific intents. These chatbots, unlike rule-based chatbots, can learn and improve over time as they process more data. NLP approaches are frequently used by machine learning chatbots to grasp the intent and context of input from users, allowing for more complex and adaptable interactions. They learn patterns and relationships from enormous datasets, allowing them to deliver contextually relevant responses. Deep learning skills enable AI chatbots to improve in accuracy over time, allowing humans to communicate with AI chatbots in a more natural, spontaneous without being misunderstood. Machine learning is used by AI-powered virtual assistants such as Siri, Google Assistant, and Alexa to interpret and respond to user requests. These type of chatbot can take input in the form of text messages or voice commands.

Hybrid Chatbot

A hybrid chatbot is one that combines aspects of rule-based (or deterministic) along with Artificial Intelligence (ML or natural language processing) techniques (Skrebeca, J. 2021). This combination enables the chatbot to converse with consumers in a more diverse and dynamic manner.

Rule-based chatbots, as the name implies, answer to client queries with pre-written responses, predefined rules, and decision trees provided to the chatbot. Based on the user's skill, they can be developed using a codeless chatbot builder or a programmable chatbot builder.

AI chatbots employ machine learning and natural language processing (NLP) to grasp the intent of a customer's question and respond utilising the chatbot's resources. This type of chatbot is more natural language adaptable and can manage unstructured interactions.

A hybrid chatbot's purpose is to provide a balance between the structured, predictable nature of rule-based systems and the flexibility and learning capabilities of machine learning systems, resulting in a better user experience across a broader range of circumstances.

Based on Integration and Platform

Chatbots on Websites

These chatbots are embedded in websites to help consumers with queries, deliver information, or walk them through tasks. Website chatbots frequently appear in a corner or can be contacted via a chat window on the site.

Figure 7. Chatbot classification based on integration and platform

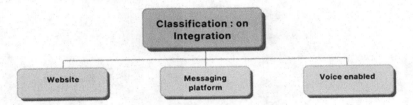

Chatbots on Messaging Platforms

These chatbots work on messaging apps or platforms like Facebook Messenger, WhatsApp, or Slack. Users can communicate with them via the messaging interface, making it easy for businesses to interact with customers on popular messaging platforms.

Voice-Enabled Chatbots

The primary means of engagement for these chatbots is voice. They can be included in devices such as smart speakers (e.g., Amazon Alexa, Google Home) or phone systems, allowing users to engage with them through natural language.

Chatbots on Social Media

These chatbots are intended to engage with people on social media sites such as Facebook, Twitter, and Instagram. Through social media messaging, they can answer queries, provide information, and even assist transactions.

Based on Interaction Type

Text-Based Chatbot

As the name implies, interacts and communicates via text or messaging. When built to precisely comprehend the customer's requirement and give instant results, or to gather vital feedback and ensure clients are engaged immediately, this form of bot can be effective. Text-based chatbots are commonly employed

Figure 8. Chatbot classification based on interaction type

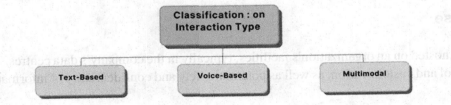

Figure 9. Chatbot classification based on deployment

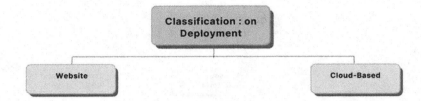

to handle everyday client interactions, and they are frequently integrated with messaging apps, social media, SMS, and other channels. However, there is a catch. Customers must write or tap in their questions and commands because these chatbot systems are text-based. This will, by definition, take more time and effort than a voice-based chatbot.

Voice Chatbots

A speech chatbot, also known as a voice assistant or conversational AI, is a digital application that is powered by artificial intelligence (AI) and natural language processing (NLP). Its major goal is to facilitate user interactions using spoken language. Voice chatbots, as opposed to text-based chatbots, engage users in vocal dialogues, allowing them to issue voice commands or submit questions, which the chatbot understands and answers to in a conversational fashion. These chatbots are integrated into a wide range of gadgets and platforms, smart speakers, including smartphones, in-car infotainment systems, and others. Examples include Amazon's Alexa, Google Assistant, Apple's Siri, and Microsoft's Cortana.

Multimodal Chatbots

Two or more integrated user input modes, such as speech, pen, touch, manual gestures, gaze, and head and body movement, are processed by the multi-modal dialogue. For instance This mechanism is used in the Ford Model U Concept Vehicle. Comprising a speech recognition system and a touch screen, is utilised for managing a number of non-essential car functions, like phone, navigation, entertainment, and climate. The prototype uses spoken natural language communication combination of an easy-to-use graphical user interface, such contrasting with the conventional, speech-only command-and-control connections installed in a few of the automobiles presently on the marketplace.

Based on Deployment

Chatbots can also be classified according to their deployment architecture, particularly whether they are on-premise or in the cloud.

On-Premise

Chatbots are hosted on an organization's facilities, typically in the company's data centres. They provide greater control and customization, as well as potential safety and confidentiality of information benefits.

On-premise deployments may be preferred in industries with stringent data privacy rules or security concerns.

On-premise chatbots also improve performance by providing businesses with more control over the infrastructure and hardware, enabling real-time monitoring and immediate action in case of security issues. They also make it easier for businesses to comply with regulatory standards, especially in highly regulated industries like education, insurance, and healthcare. Additionally, on-premise chatbots do not require internet access, ensuring continuous access even if the internet connection is down or unavailable.

Cloud-Based Chatbots

These chatbot are hosted on cloud servers offered by third-party cloud providers like as AWS, Azure, or Google Cloud. This method is suitable for organisations seeking scalability and flexibility without the need for large upfront investments. Cloud chatbots offer several advantages for businesses, including scalability, flexibility, accessibility, cost-effectiveness, and ease of integration. Scalability allows businesses to handle spikes in traffic during busy periods and save costs during low-traffic periods. Cloud chatbots are customizable, allowing for different responses based on user input. Accessibility is available from various platforms and devices, and they can be programmed to support multiple languages. Cost-effectiveness comes from reduced maintenance costs and subscription-based pricing models. Integration with existing workflows or applications like Instagram and WhatsApp is also easy, enhancing client engagement and sales.

Based on Industry or Application

Chatbots have a wide range of applications, and relevant industries are constantly searching for new ways to employ this technology to improve customer service, streamline processes, and improve user experiences across multiple domains. We have a detail discussion on various chatbot application in previous Section chatbot usecase.

FUTURE RESEARCH TRENDS

The field of chatbots and conversational AI is still undergoing rapid growth (Caldarini, G.et al. 2022). Here are some chatbot development trends Ashfaque, M. W. (2022) and areas of attention for 2021 and beyond:

- NLP Advances: Researchers and developers are attempting to improve chatbots' capacity to interpret and generate natural language. This includes improved handling of subtleties and colloquial idioms, as well as more realistic language models.
- Multimodal Interaction: Chatbots are becoming more multimodal, allowing them to engage via a combination of text, speech, visuals, and even movements. This allows for more dynamic and varied interactions with users.
- Voice-Activated Chatbots: Voice-controlled virtual assistants, such as Amazon's Alexa, Apple's Siri, and Google Assistant are becoming more natural and contextually aware.

- Emotional Intelligence and Empathy: Researchers are striving to make chatbots capable of recognising and responding to emotions in human input. This could result in greater emotional sensitive and compassionate interactions.
- Industry-Specific Applications: Chatbots are being specialised to certain businesses and domains such as healthcare, banking, e-commerce, customer service, and others. These domain-specific bots strive to deliver knowledge and services.
- Integration with upcoming Technologies: Chatbots are being merged with upcoming technologies such as augmented reality (AR), Internet of Things (IoT) devices, and virtual reality (VR). This broadens their capabilities and possible applications.
- Ethical and responsible AI: Designers are emphasising the importance of ensuring that chatbots and AI systems follow ethical rules and do not engage in biassed behaviour or destructive activities. Transparency, justice, and accountability are important focal points.
- Conversational Design with User Experience: There is an increasing acknowledgment of the significance of building intuitive, user-friendly, and engaging chatbot interactions. Conversational designers play a critical role in creating effective user experiences.
- No-Code Platforms: Tools are being created to help anyone without considerable programming skills construct and deploy their own chatbots using simple interfaces.
- Security and privacy: With the rising usage of chatbots in sensitive industries such as healthcare and banking, protecting the security and privacy of user data is crucial.

CONCLUSION

To summarize, the examination of chatbots has yielded a thorough comprehension of their development, range of applications, and distinct classification schemes. The origins of chatbots may be traced back to the early days of computing, and their current condition is largely due to notable developments in artificial intelligence and natural language processing. It became clear as we looked at various use cases that chatbots have evolved beyond typical customer support positions and are now essential to industries like healthcare, banking, and education.

The field of conversational AI, machine learning, and natural language comprehension are all contributing to the promising future of chatbots. As chatbots become more widespread, user experiences on a variety of platforms should improve. It is anticipated that chatbots will grow more sophisticated, able to manage complex interactions, and able to easily integrate with new technologies such as virtual and augmented reality as technology is developed further.

In conclusion, the article highlights chatbots' revolutionary journey from their historical origins to their current widespread adoption across a range of enterprises. Businesses, developers, and users can all benefit from knowing their use cases and categories as we work together to navigate the rapidly changing conversational AI world.

REFERENCES

Adamopoulou, E., & Moussiades, L. (2020). Chatbots: History, technology, and applications. *Machine Learning with Applications*, 2, 100006. doi:10.1016/j.mlwa.2020.100006

Ashfaque, M. W. Sr. (2022). Analysis of different trends in chatbot designing and development: A review. *ECS Transactions*, *107*(1), 7215–7227. doi:10.1149/10701.7215ecst

Caldarini, G., Jaf, S., & McGarry, K. (2022). A literature survey of recent advances in chatbots. *Information (Basel)*, *13*(1), 41. doi:10.3390/info13010041

Chamberlain, W. (1984). *The policeman's beard is half constructed*. Warner Books.

Chen, J. S., Le, T. T. Y., & Florence, D. (2021). Usability and responsiveness of artificial intelligence chatbot on online customer experience in e-retailing. *International Journal of Retail & Distribution Management*, *49*(11), 1512–1531. doi:10.1108/IJRDM-08-2020-0312

Colby, K. M., Hilf, F. D., Weber, S., & Kraemer, H. C. (1972). Turing-like indistinguishability tests for the validation of a computer simulation of paranoid processes. *Artificial Intelligence*, *3*, 199–221. doi:10.1016/0004-3702(72)90049-5

Floridi, L., & Chiriatti, M. (2020). GPT-3: Its nature, scope, limits, and consequences. *Minds and Machines*, *30*(4), 681–694. doi:10.1007/s11023-020-09548-1

Ho, R. C. (2021). Chatbot for online customer service: customer engagement in the era of artificial intelligence. In *Impact of globalization and advanced technologies on online business models* (pp. 16–31). IGI Global. doi:10.4018/978-1-7998-7603-8.ch002

Hussain, S., Ameri Sianaki, O., & Ababneh, N. (2019). A survey on conversational agents/chatbots classification and design techniques. In *Web, Artificial Intelligence and Network Applications: Proceedings of the Workshops of the 33rd International Conference on Advanced Information Networking and Applications (WAINA-2019) 33* (pp. 946-956). Springer International Publishing.

Malik, S. I., Ashfque, M. W., Tawafak, R. M., Al-Farsi, G., Usmani, N. A., & Khudayer, B. H. (2022). A Chatbot to Facilitate Student Learning in a Programming 1 Course: A Gendered Analysis. [IJVPLE]. *International Journal of Virtual and Personal Learning Environments*, *12*(1), 1–20. doi:10.4018/IJVPLE.310007

Melián-González, S., Gutiérrez-Taño, D., & Bulchand-Gidumal, J. (2021). Predicting the intentions to use chatbots for travel and tourism. *Current Issues in Tourism*, *24*(2), 192–210. doi:10.1080/13683500.2019.1706457

Nithyanandam, S. D., Kasinathan, S., Radhakrishnan, D., & Jebapandian, J. (2021). NLP for Chatbot Application: Tools and Techniques Used for Chatbot Application, NLP Techniques for Chatbot, Implementation. In Deep Natural Language Processing and AI Applications for Industry 5.0 (pp. 142-168). IGI Global.

Oguntosin, V., & Olomo, A. (2021). Development of an e-commerce chatbot for a university shopping mall. *Applied Computational Intelligence and Soft Computing*, *2021*, 1–14. doi:10.1155/2021/6630326

Park, D. M., Jeong, S. S., & Seo, Y. S. (2022). Systematic Review on Chatbot Techniques and Applications. *Journal of Information Processing Systems*, *18*(1), 26–47.

Skrebeca, J., Kalniete, P., Goldbergs, J., Pitkevica, L., Tihomirova, D., & Romanovs, A. (2021, October). Modern development trends of chatbots using artificial intelligence (ai). In *2021 62nd International Scientific Conference on Information Technology and Management Science of Riga Technical University (ITMS)* (pp. 1-6). IEEE.

Solanki, R. K., Rajawat, A. S., Gadekar, A. R., & Patil, M. E. (2023). Building a Conversational Chatbot Using Machine Learning: Towards a More Intelligent Healthcare Application. In *Handbook of Research on Instructional Technologies in Health Education and Allied Disciplines* (pp. 285–309). IGI Global. doi:10.4018/978-1-6684-7164-7.ch013

Turing, A. M. (1950). Computing machinery and intelligence. *Mind*, *LIX*(236), 433–460. doi:10.1093/mind/LIX.236.433

Wallace, R. S. (2009). *The anatomy of ALICE*. Springer Netherlands. doi:10.1007/978-1-4020-6710-5_13

Weizenbaum, J. (1966). ELIZA—A computer program for the study of natural language communication between man and machine. *Communications of the ACM*, *9*(1), 36–45. doi:10.1145/365153.365168

Wollny, S., Schneider, J., Di Mitri, D., Weidlich, J., Rittberger, M., & Drachsler, H. (2021). Are we there yet?-a systematic literature review on chatbots in education. *Frontiers in Artificial Intelligence*, *4*, 654924. doi:10.3389/frai.2021.654924 PMID:34337392

Wu, T., He, S., Liu, J., Sun, S., Liu, K., Han, Q. L., & Tang, Y. (2023). A brief overview of ChatGPT: The history, status quo and potential future development. *IEEE/CAA Journal of Automatica Sinica*, *10*(5), 1122-1136.

Zhu, X., Li, R. Y. M., Crabbe, M. J. C., & Sukpascharoen, K. (2022). Can a chatbot enhance hazard awareness in the construction industry? *Frontiers in Public Health*, *10*, 993700. doi:10.3389/fpubh.2022.993700 PMID:36530655

KEY TERMS AND DEFINITIONS

Artificial Intelligence: Artificial intelligence (AI) is the simulation of human intelligence capabilities and problem solving ability by technology, particularly computers. AI has specific applications such as expert systems, processing natural-language (NLP), speech recognition, and machine vision.

Generative AI: Generative AI is a kind of artificial intelligence based technology which can generate a variety of content, such as text, images, audio, and synthetic data. Traditional AI demonstrates its superiority in tasks that require logical reasoning, pattern identification, and rule-based decision making. Generative AI, on the other hand, excels at activities that need creativity, invention, and the ability to create new and original information.

Intelligent Personal Assistant: An intelligent personal assistant (IPA) is software meant to help people with simple tasks by presenting information in natural language. These virtual entities are designed with natural language processing, machine learning skills, and have access to a diverse set of data sources, allowing them to efficiently interpret and respond to user requests.

Large Language Models (LLM): LLMs are artificial intelligence systems that understand as well as generate human-like text. These models are often created with deep learning techniques, notably neural networks, and trained on massive volumes of text data. The word "large" refers to the neural network's size as well as the training data's scale.

Natural Language Processing (NLP): NLP refers to a computer program's capacity for understanding human language as written and spoken. It entails creating algorithms and models to help computers understand, interpret, and synthesize human language in a meaningful and usable manner. It is an interdisciplinary branch of computer science and linguistics.

Natural Language Understanding (NLU): It is a subfield of artificial intelligence (AI) and computational linguistics which seeks to enable computers to read and interpret human language in a meaningful and usable manner. It entails creating algorithms and models that enable machines to evaluate, comprehend, and extract understanding from natural language inputs such as voice or text.

Virtual Assistant: A virtual assistant (VA) is an application agent that may execute a variety of jobs or provide services for a user depending on human input, such as commands or questions, both written and verbal. Such technologies frequently include chatbot capabilities to replicate human conversation.

Chapter 5
Applications of Chatbots:
Exploring the Dynamics of Chatbot Evolution

Kaushikkumar Patel

https://orcid.org/0009-0005-9197-2765

TransUnion LLC, USA

ABSTRACT

This chapter provides an insightful exploration into the rapidly evolving world of chatbot technology, highlighting its significant applications across diverse sectors. It traces the evolution of chatbots from basic automated systems to advanced AI-driven interfaces capable of sophisticated interactions. The focus is on how chatbots have revolutionized customer service, e-commerce, healthcare, and education, showcasing their role in enhancing user experience and operational efficiency. The chapter also addresses the challenges in chatbot implementation, such as natural language processing difficulties, ethical concerns, and privacy issues, while presenting current solutions and best practices. Additionally, it explores future research directions, emphasizing the potential long-term impact of chatbots on society and technology. Aimed at providing a comprehensive understanding of chatbot applications, this chapter is a valuable resource for those interested in the convergence of AI, communication, and technology.

INTRODUCTION

The emergence of chatbot technology signifies a pivotal development in the digital landscape, heralding a new era of interactive and intelligent systems that have transformed the way we interact with digital platforms. This chapter provides a comprehensive introduction to the world of chatbots, charting their evolution from rudimentary automated responders to sophisticated artificial intelligence (AI) systems capable of engaging in complex, nuanced conversations. This progression underscores the remarkable strides made in AI and machine learning, illustrating how these technologies have been leveraged to create chatbots that not only mimic human conversation but also learn and adapt from their interactions, offering real-time, context-aware assistance.

DOI: 10.4018/979-8-3693-1830-0.ch005

Initially conceived as tools to automate repetitive tasks, chatbots have transcended their original purpose to become integral components in various sectors. Their impact is particularly notable in customer service, e-commerce, healthcare, and education, where they have revolutionized traditional practices. In customer service, chatbots have transformed the dynamics of client interaction, provided round-the-clock support, and efficiently managed a multitude of inquiries, thus enhancing customer satisfaction and operational productivity. In the realm of e-commerce, chatbots have become pivotal in personalizing the shopping experience, assisting in product selection, processing orders, and engaging customers in a manner that drives sales and fosters brand loyalty. The healthcare sector has embraced chatbots as tools for preliminary medical assessments, patient education, and streamlining appointment processes, thereby improving accessibility and efficiency in healthcare delivery. Similarly, in education, chatbots have emerged as innovative tools, serving as personalized tutors, administrative assistants, and interactive learning aids, contributing significantly to the enrichment of educational experiences.

Despite their widespread adoption and benefits, the integration of chatbots into these diverse domains is accompanied by significant challenges. Key among these are the intricacies of processing and understanding human language, ensuring ethical interactions, safeguarding user privacy, and maintaining the delicate balance between automation and human touch. This chapter aims not only to provide a detailed overview of these challenges but also to discuss the current solutions and best practices that are shaping the field of chatbot development.

Furthermore, this chapter will delve into the future trajectory of chatbot technology, exploring emerging trends and potential advancements. It will examine how ongoing innovations in AI and machine learning could further refine chatbot capabilities, making them more intuitive, empathetic, and effective in their interactions. The broader implications of these advancements on society, ethical considerations, and the future of digital communication are also key areas of focus.

In conclusion, this introduction sets the stage for an in-depth exploration of chatbot technology, encompassing its applications, challenges, and future prospects. It aims to equip readers with a thorough understanding of the current state of chatbots, their transformative potential across various sectors, and their evolving role in shaping our digital future.

LITERATURE REVIEW

Previous Research

The academic and industrial exploration of chatbot technology has been extensive and multifaceted, covering a wide range of aspects from foundational design principles to advanced applications in various sectors. Early research primarily focused on the development of chatbots as rule-based systems, capable of responding to specific commands or queries (Thorat, S. A., 2020). As technology advanced, the focus shifted to creating more sophisticated, AI-driven conversational agents, capable of understanding and engaging in natural language dialogues (McTear, M., 2022).

In the realm of customer service, a substantial body of research has been dedicated to understanding how chatbots can enhance service efficiency, customer satisfaction, and engagement. Studies have shown that chatbots can significantly reduce response times and increase the availability of support services, leading to improved customer experiences (Kvale, K., 2020). Similarly, in e-commerce, research has highlighted the role of chatbots in facilitating smoother customer journeys, from product inquiries to post-purchase support, thereby contributing to increased sales and customer loyalty (Tan, P. K., 2023).

The healthcare sector has seen a surge in chatbot research, particularly in areas like patient triage, mental health support, and health education. These studies underscore the potential of chatbots to improve healthcare accessibility, patient engagement, and even adherence to treatment plans (Sadasivan, C., 2023). In education, research has focused on the use of chatbots as interactive learning tools, providing personalized tutoring, administrative support, and enhancing student engagement (Čižmešija, A., 2021).

Financial services have also been a significant area of chatbot research. Studies in this sector have explored how chatbots are transforming customer interactions in banking, providing financial advice, and assisting in personal finance management (Mogaji, E., 2021). The travel and hospitality industry, too, has been a focus, with research examining chatbots' roles in booking assistance, customer service, and offering personalized travel recommendations (Dash, M., 2019).

Technical research on chatbots has delved deeply into natural language processing (NLP) and machine learning. These studies have tackled the challenges of language understanding, context retention, sentiment analysis, and the development of emotionally intelligent chatbots (Bilquise, G., 2022). The advancements in AI, enabling chatbots to learn from interactions and evolve over time, have been a crucial area of focus, with research exploring the implications of these advancements on chatbot efficiency and user experience (Aslam, F., 2023).

Theoretical Frameworks

The development and functioning of chatbots are underpinned by several theoretical frameworks. The field of NLP is central, providing the foundational technology for chatbots to process and understand human language. Research in NLP has explored various linguistic models and algorithms, enabling chatbots to interpret user inputs and generate appropriate responses (Aleedy, M., 2019). Human-computer interaction (HCI) is another critical framework, guiding the design and evaluation of chatbots as user-centric systems. Studies in HCI have focused on improving the usability, user experience, and interaction design of chatbots, ensuring they are intuitive and effective in their interactions with users (Ciechanowski, L., 2019).

Cognitive psychology has been instrumental in understanding the human aspects of chatbot interactions. Research in this area examines how users perceive and engage with chatbots, exploring concepts like trust, empathy, and the psychological impact of interacting with AI entities (Rapp, A., 2021). AI ethics is increasingly relevant, offering a framework to address moral and ethical considerations in chatbot development, such as privacy concerns, data security, and algorithmic bias (Ionuț-Alexandru, C., 2021).

Gaps in Research

Despite the extensive body of research on chatbots, several gaps remain unaddressed. One significant area is the long-term impact of chatbot interactions on user behavior and psychology. More empirical studies are needed to explore how continuous interaction with chatbots affects human communication patterns, social behavior, and psychological well-being (Ho, A., 2018). The exploration of cross-cultural differences in chatbot design and interaction is another area requiring further research. Understanding how cultural nuances influence the effectiveness and acceptance of chatbots across different regions is crucial for their global applicability (Plocher, T., 2021).

The scalability and adaptability of chatbots in dynamic environments, such as during crises or market fluctuations, is another area that warrants more exploration (De Sanctis, M., 2020). Additionally, there is a gap in integrating technical research findings with practical, real-world applications across diverse sectors. More interdisciplinary studies are needed to bridge this gap, combining technical advancements with practical insights to enhance the real-world effectiveness of chatbots (Fan, X., 2021).

In conclusion, while existing literature provides a comprehensive foundation for understanding chatbot technology and its applications, these identified gaps in research underscore the need for ongoing exploration and innovation. Addressing these gaps will not only enhance the effectiveness and applicability of chatbots but also ensure their responsible and ethical integration into various aspects of society.

CHATBOT APPLICATIONS IN CUSTOMER SERVICE AND E-COMMERCE

In the rapidly evolving landscape of digital interaction, chatbots have emerged as pivotal tools in reshaping customer service and e-commerce. Their integration into these sectors represents a significant shift in how businesses engage with customers, offering a blend of efficiency, personalization, and accessibility that traditional methods struggle to match. In customer service, chatbots are revolutionizing the way companies interact with their clientele, providing instant responses to inquiries, 24/7 availability, and a level of consistency in service that enhances overall customer satisfaction. In the realm of e-commerce, chatbots are transforming the shopping experience by offering personalized product recommendations, assisting in the navigation of online catalogs, and streamlining the purchasing process. This section delves into the multifaceted roles of chatbots in these sectors, highlighting their impact on business operations, customer engagement, and the evolving expectations of the digital consumer (Table 1).

- **Customer Service:** The integration of chatbots into customer service has been a game-changer, fundamentally transforming the way businesses interact with their customers. This shift is propelled by the growing demand for efficient, consistent, and personalized customer experiences. Chatbots, with their capability for instant responses, have become indispensable in meeting these demands.

  - **24/7 Availability and Instant Response:** A key advantage of chatbots in customer service is their ability to offer support around the clock. Unlike human agents, chatbots are not limited by traditional working hours, enabling businesses to provide immediate responses to customer inquiries at any time. This constant availability not only boosts customer satisfaction but also helps manage large volumes of inquiries, reducing wait times and the workload on human customer service representatives.

  - **Handling Routine Inquiries:** Chatbots excel at managing routine and repetitive inquiries. Automating responses to common questions allows human agents to focus on more complex customer issues. This improves the overall efficiency of the customer service process and ensures that customers receive quick and accurate answers.

  - **Personalization and Customer Engagement:** Advanced chatbots, powered by AI and machine learning, offer personalized interactions. They analyze customer data and previous interactions to provide tailored responses and recommendations. This personalization enhances customer engagement, making customers feel recognized and valued.

○ **Cost-Effectiveness and Scalability:** Implementing chatbots in customer service is cost-effective for businesses. Chatbots can handle multiple interactions simultaneously, reducing the need for a large customer service team. This scalability is especially beneficial for businesses experiencing rapid growth or seasonal spikes in customer inquiries.

○ **Feedback Collection and Analysis:** Chatbots are instrumental in collecting customer feedback. They can conduct surveys and gather opinions during or after interactions, providing businesses with valuable insights into customer needs, satisfaction levels, and areas for product or service improvement.

○ **Challenges and Limitations:** Despite these benefits, chatbots in customer service also face challenges. Understanding complex language nuances, handling highly emotional situations, and the need for continuous learning and updating are some of the hurdles.

In summary, chatbots have significantly reshaped customer service, offering numerous benefits in terms of availability, efficiency, personalization, and cost-effectiveness. However, maintaining a balance between automated and human service is essential, as the human element remains crucial for handling complex and sensitive customer interactions.

● **E-commerce:** In the e-commerce sector, chatbots have become a transformative force, reshaping the way businesses interact with customers and manage online transactions. Their integration into e-commerce platforms has led to enhanced shopping experiences, streamlined processes, and increased sales.

○ **Personalized Shopping Assistance:** Chatbots in e-commerce act as personal shopping assistants, guiding customers through the vast array of products. By analyzing customer preferences and browsing history, chatbots can make personalized product recommendations, helping customers find exactly what they are looking for and even suggesting additional items that might interest them.

○ **Customer Support and Query Resolution:** Chatbots provide instant customer support, answering queries about products, availability, shipping, and more. This immediate assistance helps in reducing cart abandonment rates and improving the overall shopping experience. Chatbots can also assist in resolving post-purchase issues, such as returns and refunds, efficiently.

○ **Streamlining the Purchasing Process:** Chatbots simplify the purchasing process by guiding customers through the steps of selecting products, adding them to the cart, and completing the transaction. This streamlined process not only enhances user experience but also encourages repeat purchases.

○ **Engagement and Marketing:** E-commerce chatbots are effective tools for engaging customers. They can send personalized offers, discounts, and alerts about new products or sales, directly interacting with customers in a conversational manner. This approach to marketing helps in building brand loyalty and increasing customer retention.

○ **Feedback and Data Collection:** Chatbots are valuable for collecting customer feedback and preferences. This data is crucial for e-commerce businesses to understand customer behavior, refine marketing strategies, and tailor their product offerings.

- ○ **Inventory Management and Notifications:** Chatbots can assist in inventory management by notifying customers about the availability of products or restocking of popular items. This feature ensures that customers are kept informed and can make timely purchases.
- ○ **Challenges in E-commerce:** Despite the advantages, deploying chatbots in e-commerce comes with its challenges. Ensuring that chatbots provide accurate product information, maintaining up-to-date inventory data, and creating a seamless integration with the e-commerce platform are essential for effective chatbot functionality.

In conclusion, chatbots have significantly enhanced the e-commerce landscape by providing personalized shopping assistance, efficient customer support, and effective marketing and engagement strategies. They have become essential tools for e-commerce businesses looking to improve customer experience, increase sales, and streamline operations. However, continuous refinement and integration of these chatbots are necessary to ensure they meet the evolving needs of both businesses and customers.

The integration of chatbots into customer service and e-commerce has marked a significant evolution in the digital business landscape. By offering round-the-clock availability, personalized interactions, and efficient handling of routine tasks, chatbots have enhanced customer experiences and operational efficiencies. Chatbots have revolutionized customer service and e-commerce by offering instant support and enhancing the shopping journey. Despite challenges like complex queries and data updates, AI and machine learning advances are addressing these issues. As chatbots become more sophisticated and integrated into various platforms, their role in shaping customer engagement and business strategies is set to grow, making them an indispensable tool in the digital economy.

Table 1. Overview of Chatbot applications in customer service and E-commerce

Aspect	Application in Customer Service	Application in E-commerce
Availability and Response	24/7 support, instant responses to inquiries	Round-the-clock assistance for shopping queries
Task Handling	Managing routine and repetitive inquiries	Guiding customers through product selection and purchase process
Personalization	Tailored responses based on customer history and preferences	Personalized product recommendations and shopping assistance
Operational Efficiency	Reducing the workload on human agents, handling multiple queries simultaneously	Streamlining the purchasing process, reducing cart abandonment
Customer Engagement	Enhancing customer satisfaction through consistent and efficient support	Engaging customers with personalized offers, discounts, and product alerts
Feedback Collection	Gathering customer feedback for service improvement	Collecting data on customer preferences and shopping behavior
Challenges	Handling complex language nuances, maintaining human-like interactions	Ensuring accurate product information, seamless integration with e-commerce platforms
Shared Technology Vulnerabilities	Shared resources among clients create potential attack pathways.	Exploitation of shared hardware; risk of side-channel attacks.

CHATBOT APPLICATIONS IN HEALTHCARE AND EDUCATION

The integration of chatbots into healthcare and education sectors signifies a groundbreaking shift, harnessing the power of AI to revolutionize these critical areas. In healthcare, chatbots are becoming instrumental in enhancing patient care and health management, offering innovative solutions for patient engagement, symptom checking, and health education. Their ability to provide immediate, accessible medical information and support presents a significant advancement in patient-centric care. In the education sector, chatbots are redefining learning experiences, serving as personalized tutors, administrative assistants, and interactive learning tools. They facilitate a more engaging, responsive, and tailored educational journey for students, addressing diverse learning needs and styles. This section explores the multifaceted applications of chatbots in these two vital sectors, highlighting their impact on improving healthcare delivery and educational outcomes, and the challenges they encounter in these dynamic environments (Table 2).

- **Healthcare:** The integration of chatbots in the healthcare sector marks a significant advancement in enhancing patient care and streamlining health management processes. These AI-driven tools are revolutionizing various aspects of healthcare, offering innovative solutions and support in multiple areas:

  ○ **Symptom Checking and Preliminary Diagnosis:** Chatbots have become increasingly valuable for initial symptom assessment, guiding patients through a series of questions to evaluate their health concerns. This functionality aids in early detection and timely medical intervention, potentially reducing unnecessary hospital visits and easing the burden on healthcare facilities.

  ○ **Patient Engagement and Follow-up:** Chatbots enhance patient engagement by providing timely reminders for medication, appointments, and follow-up care. They offer a user-friendly platform for patients to manage their health, track their progress, and stay informed about their treatment plans, leading to better adherence to medical advice and improved health outcomes.

  ○ **Mental Health Support:** In the realm of mental health, chatbots offer a confidential and accessible resource for individuals seeking support. They provide immediate coping strategies, mindfulness exercises, and can help in identifying early signs of mental health issues, encouraging users to seek professional help when necessary. This accessibility is particularly crucial in areas with limited mental health resources.

  ○ **Health Education and Awareness:** Chatbots are effective tools for disseminating health education, offering information about diseases, treatments, prevention methods, and healthy living practices. They can personalize this information based on individual user profiles, making it more relevant and impactful for each user.

  ○ **Administrative Assistance:** Within healthcare facilities, chatbots assist with a range of administrative tasks, including scheduling appointments, handling patient inquiries, managing patient records, and even assisting in billing processes. This reduces administrative burdens on healthcare staff, allowing them to focus more on patient care.

  ○ **Data Collection and Analysis:** Chatbots also play a role in collecting and analyzing patient data, providing healthcare providers with valuable insights into patient behaviors, treatment effectiveness, and overall health trends. This data can inform better healthcare strategies and policies.

- ○ **Challenges in Healthcare:** Despite these advancements, chatbots in healthcare face significant challenges. Ensuring accuracy and reliability in symptom assessment is critical to avoid misdiagnoses. Maintaining patient privacy and data security is paramount, given the sensitive nature of health information. Additionally, the integration of chatbots with existing healthcare systems and ensuring they are up to date with the latest medical knowledge and guidelines remain ongoing challenges.

In conclusion, chatbots in healthcare represent a transformative shift towards more accessible, efficient, and patient-centered care. Their ability to provide immediate support, personalized health management, and administrative efficiency positions them as invaluable assets in the healthcare sector. However, the challenges of ensuring accuracy, privacy, and seamless integration must be continually addressed to fully realize the potential of chatbots in enhancing healthcare delivery and patient outcomes.

- ● **Education:** The integration of chatbots in the education sector marks a significant stride in the application of AI technologies to enhance learning experiences. These intelligent systems are being employed in various educational settings, offering a multitude of benefits that cater to the diverse needs of students and educators alike:

  - ○ **Personalized Learning:** One of the most notable applications of chatbots in education is in providing personalized learning experiences. They can adapt to individual learning styles and paces, offering tailored content and resources. This approach allows for addressing the unique educational needs of each student, making learning more effective, engaging, and inclusive.
  - ○ **Administrative Assistance:** Chatbots are increasingly being utilized for administrative tasks within educational institutions. They assist in streamlining processes such as enrollment, course selection, scheduling, and responding to frequently asked questions. This not only reduces the administrative workload on staff but also enhances the efficiency of student services.
  - ○ **Tutoring and Academic Support:** Serving as on-demand tutors, chatbots offer assistance with homework, clarification of concepts, and provision of additional learning resources. Their availability outside of regular class hours provides students with continuous support, aiding in their academic development.
  - ○ **Engagement and Interactive Learning:** In classroom settings, chatbots can facilitate interactive learning activities. They are capable of conducting quizzes, moderating discussions, and providing instant feedback. This interactive approach fosters greater student engagement and participation, making the learning process more dynamic and enjoyable.
  - ○ **Language Learning and Practice:** Chatbots have shown significant effectiveness in language learning. They offer a platform for students to practice speaking and writing, simulating natural conversations. This practical approach helps in improving language proficiency in a low-pressure, supportive environment.
  - ○ **Support for Special Education:** Chatbots also hold potential in special education, providing customized support and learning aids for students with special needs. They can offer a

Table 2. Comparative analysis of Chatbot applications in healthcare and education

Feature	Application in Healthcare	Application in Education
Primary Function	Enhancing patient care, symptom checking, health management	Personalized learning, tutoring, administrative support
Engagement	Patient engagement through reminders, follow-ups, mental health support	Student engagement through interactive learning, quizzes, feedback
Personalization	Tailored health advice, personalized patient communication	Customized learning experiences adaptive tutoring based on student needs
Administrative Tasks	Scheduling appointments, managing patient records, administrative assistance	Enrollment processes, course scheduling, handling FAQs
Information Dissemination	Health education, awareness campaigns, disease prevention information	Educational content delivery, language learning, concept clarification
Accessibility	Providing accessible health information and support, especially in underserved areas	Offering educational support outside of traditional classroom hours
Data Collection	Gathering patient data for health trends, treatment effectiveness	Collecting student performance data for educational insights
Challenges	Ensuring accuracy in diagnosis, maintaining patient privacy	Balancing chatbot interaction with human teaching, content accuracy

more accessible and comfortable learning experience, catering to individual challenges and preferences.

○ **Challenges in Education:** Implementing chatbots in education, however, presents its own set of challenges. Ensuring that the content delivered by chatbots is accurate, current, and pedagogically appropriate is essential. There is also a need to balance technological interaction with human teaching and mentoring to ensure a well-rounded educational experience.

The application of chatbots in both healthcare and education sectors has demonstrated the vast potential of AI-driven technologies in transforming key aspects of society. In healthcare, chatbots have become essential tools for enhancing patient care, providing accessible health information, and streamlining administrative processes, thereby contributing to more efficient and patient-centered healthcare systems. In education, chatbots are revolutionizing the learning experience, offering personalized tutoring, administrative support, and interactive learning opportunities, which cater to a diverse range of learning needs and styles. While these advancements are significant, the challenges of ensuring accuracy, privacy, and a balanced integration with human interaction remain crucial. Addressing these challenges is essential for the continued success and acceptance of chatbots, ensuring they effectively contribute to the advancement and betterment of healthcare and education systems.

CHATBOT APPLICATIONS IN OTHER SECTORS

Beyond healthcare and education, chatbots are making significant inroads into various other sectors, showcasing their versatility and adaptability. In industries like finance, travel, entertainment, and customer relations, chatbots are not just technological novelties but essential tools that enhance efficiency, engagement, and service quality. In the financial sector, they are revolutionizing the way customers interact with their banks and manage their finances. In travel and hospitality, chatbots are simplifying booking processes and provide real-time travel assistance. The entertainment industry sees chatbots as a means to engage audiences in innovative ways. Across these diverse fields, chatbots are being leveraged to automate routine tasks, provide personalized experiences, and gather valuable consumer insights. This section explores the breadth of chatbot applications across these varied sectors, highlighting their impact on business operations and customer experiences, and the challenges they encounter in these dynamic environments (Table 3).

- **Other Industries:** The versatility of chatbots extends far beyond healthcare and education, impacting a wide range of industries with their innovative capabilities. Here are some key sectors where chatbots are making a significant difference:

  ○ **Finance and Banking:** In the financial sector, chatbots are revolutionizing customer service and financial management. They assist users with routine banking inquiries and transaction processing and even provide financial advice. Chatbots in banking are enhancing customer experiences by offering quick, secure, and personalized financial services.

  ○ **Travel and Hospitality:** The travel industry benefits greatly from chatbot technology. Chatbots assist customers with booking processes, provide travel information, and offer real-time assistance for travel-related queries. In hospitality, they enhance guest experiences by handling reservations, providing local information, and offering personalized recommendations.

  ○ **Retail and Consumer Goods:** In retail, chatbots are transforming the shopping experience. They assist customers in product searches, provide recommendations, and handle transactions. Chatbots also gather consumer insights, helping retailers tailor their offerings and marketing strategies.

  ○ **Entertainment and Media:** Chatbots in the entertainment sector are used for audience engagement, content recommendation, and interactive marketing campaigns. They offer a new way for audiences to interact with content, enhancing user experience and engagement.

  ○ **Human Resources:** In the corporate world, HR chatbots are streamlining various processes like recruitment, onboarding, and employee queries. They provide instant responses to common HR-related questions, improving efficiency and employee satisfaction.

  ○ **Real Estate:** Chatbots in real estate assist in property searches, scheduling viewings, and providing information about listings. They offer a convenient way for potential buyers and renters to find properties that match their preferences.

  ○ **Challenges in Other Industries:** Despite their benefits, chatbots in these sectors face challenges such as maintaining industry-specific knowledge, ensuring data security, especially in finance, and providing personalized experiences at scale.

In summary, chatbots are proving to be invaluable across various industries, enhancing customer service, streamlining operations, and providing personalized experiences. Their ability to adapt to different industry needs and challenges showcases the flexibility and potential of chatbot technology in transforming business operations and customer interactions across the board.

- **Innovative Uses:** Chatbots, with their evolving AI capabilities, are not just confined to conventional applications but are also paving the way for innovative uses across various sectors. These novel applications demonstrate the versatility and creative potential of chatbots:

  ○ **Event Management and Coordination:** In the field of event management, chatbots are revolutionizing the way events are organized and experienced. They assist with various aspects of event planning, such as attendee registration, agenda planning, and providing real-time information during events. Chatbots can handle a multitude of queries related to schedules and locations and even facilitate networking by connecting attendees with similar interests or professional backgrounds.

  ○ **Legal and Compliance Assistance:** The legal sector is witnessing the emergence of chatbots as tools for offering preliminary legal advice, assisting with document preparation, and providing compliance-related information. These chatbots help demystify complex legal processes, making legal assistance more accessible and understandable to the general public.

  ○ **Public Sector and Government Services:** Governments and public sector entities are employing chatbots to enhance the delivery of public services. These chatbots assist in disseminating information about government programs, handling citizen inquiries efficiently, and aiding in the reporting and resolution of local issues, thereby improving civic engagement and public service delivery.

  ○ **Environmental Conservation and Awareness:** In the realm of environmental conservation, chatbots are being used to educate the public about sustainability, promote eco-friendly habits, and gather data for environmental research and conservation efforts. They serve as interactive platforms for raising awareness about environmental issues and encouraging proactive measures for environmental protection.

  ○ **Mental Wellness and Therapy:** Beyond their applications in traditional healthcare settings, chatbots are increasingly being used for mental wellness and therapeutic purposes. They provide a confidential and non-judgmental platform for individuals to express their feelings, receive motivational messages, and learn coping strategies, thereby contributing to mental health and well-being.

  ○ **Art and Creativity:** The creative arts sector is exploring the use of chatbots for interactive storytelling, art creation, and as a tool for inspiring creativity. These chatbots engage users in unique artistic experiences, challenging the conventional boundaries of art and creativity.

  ○ **Customer Insights and Market Research:** Chatbots are also being utilized for gathering customer insights and conducting market research. They interact with consumers to collect feedback, preferences, and opinions, providing businesses with valuable data to inform marketing strategies and product development.

  ○ **Challenges in Innovative Uses:** The innovative applications of chatbots, while exciting, present unique challenges. Ensuring the accuracy and reliability of information provided by chatbots, especially in sensitive areas like legal advice and mental health support, is crucial. Ethical considerations, user privacy, and maintaining engagement in non-traditional applications are also significant challenges that need to be addressed.

In conclusion, the innovative applications of chatbots across various sectors not only demonstrate their potential to streamline operations and enhance user experiences but also highlight their contribu-

Table 3. Overview of Chatbot applications across diverse sectors

Sector	Key Applications	Challenges
Finance and Banking	Customer service, transaction processing, financial advice	Data security, accuracy of financial advice
Travel and Hospitality	Booking assistance, travel information, guest services	Personalization, real-time travel updates
Retail and Consumer Goods	Product searches, transaction handling, consumer insights	Accurate product information, personalized marketing
Entertainment and Media	Audience engagement, content recommendation, marketing campaigns	Maintaining user engagement, content relevance
Human Resources	Recruitment, onboarding, employee inquiries	Balancing automation with human interaction, data privacy
Real Estate	Property searches, scheduling viewings, listing information	Up-to-date property information, user-friendly interfaces
Event Management	Event planning, attendee registration, real-time information	Coordination efficiency, attendee engagement
Legal Services	Preliminary legal advice, document assistance, compliance information	Accuracy of legal information, ethical considerations
Public Sector	Government service information, citizen queries, issue reporting	Accessibility, accuracy of public information
Environmental Conservation	Sustainability education, eco-friendly practices, data collection	Public engagement, accuracy of information
Mental Wellness	Support and therapy, coping strategies, motivational messages	Ethical considerations, effectiveness of support
Art and Creativity	Interactive storytelling, creative inspiration, art creation	User engagement, creativity in AI responses

tion to societal, environmental, and creative fields. These diverse applications reflect the adaptability of chatbots to different contexts and needs, offering promising avenues for future developments and innovations in AI and chatbot technology.

CHALLENGES AND SOLUTIONS

While chatbot technology has made significant strides in various sectors, its integration and functionality are not without challenges. These challenges range from technical limitations to ethical concerns, impacting the effectiveness and acceptance of chatbots. Technical challenges include natural language processing difficulties, understanding context and nuances in human communication, and maintaining a seamless and engaging user experience. Ethical challenges encompass issues like data privacy, security, and the potential for bias in AI algorithms. Additionally, there are practical challenges in implementing chatbots across different industries, ensuring they meet specific sector needs while maintaining consistency and reliability. This section delves into these challenges in detail, exploring the solutions and best practices being developed to address them, and how these solutions are shaping the future of chatbot technology in a rapidly evolving digital landscape (Table 4).

- **Technical Challenges:** The advancement of chatbot technology, while transformative, confronts several technical challenges that can impede its effectiveness and user satisfaction. Addressing these challenges is crucial for the continued evolution and utility of chatbots:
  - **Natural Language Processing (NLP):** A fundamental challenge is the ability of chatbots to accurately understand and process natural human language. Despite advancements, chatbots often struggle with nuances, idiomatic expressions, and varying dialects, leading to misunderstandings and unsatisfactory interactions.
  - **Contextual Understanding and Memory:** Chatbots frequently face difficulties in maintaining the context of a conversation over time. This includes remembering past interactions and using that information to inform current conversations, which is essential for coherent and engaging dialogues.
  - **Personalization:** Providing personalized experiences through chatbots at scale is challenging. It requires sophisticated algorithms and extensive data analysis to tailor interactions to individual user preferences and history.
  - **Emotional Intelligence:** Developing chatbots with emotional intelligence, capable of recognizing and appropriately responding to human emotions, is a significant hurdle. This aspect is crucial for creating more natural and empathetic user interactions.
  - **Integration with Other Systems:** Seamless integration of chatbots with various existing systems and platforms can be complex, especially when dealing with legacy systems or ensuring compatibility across different technologies.
  - **Continuous Learning and Improvement:** Ensuring that chatbots continuously learn and improve from interactions is essential for their long-term effectiveness. This requires ongoing data analysis, updates, and refinements to their algorithms.
  - **Response Generation and Creativity:** Generating creative and contextually appropriate responses is another challenge. Chatbots need to go beyond canned responses to generate replies that are relevant, engaging, and diverse.
  - **Scalability and Performance:** As chatbots are deployed at a larger scale, maintaining performance, managing resource allocation, and ensuring consistent response times become challenging.
- **Solutions to Technical Challenges:** To overcome these technical challenges, several solutions and best practices are being developed and implemented:
  - **Advanced NLP Techniques:** Utilizing more sophisticated NLP techniques and machine learning models can significantly enhance chatbots' language understanding capabilities. Training chatbots on diverse and extensive datasets helps them handle colloquial language and complex expressions more effectively.
  - **Enhanced Contextual Algorithms:** Implementing algorithms that can track and recall previous interactions will improve chatbots' contextual understanding. Developing memory models allows chatbots to reference past conversations and maintain continuity.
  - **Data-Driven Personalization:** Employing big data analytics and AI to analyze user data can aid in creating more personalized chatbot interactions. Understanding user preferences and tailoring responses accordingly is key to enhancing user experience.
  - **Emotion Recognition Technologies:** Incorporating emotion recognition technologies, such as sentiment analysis and facial expression analysis (for video-based chatbots), can enable chatbots to respond more empathetically.

○ **Robust Integration Frameworks:** Developing robust integration frameworks and APIs facilitates smoother integration of chatbots with various systems, ensuring compatibility and functionality across different platforms.

○ **Feedback Mechanisms and Iterative Development:** Implementing feedback mechanisms for continuous learning and iterative development helps in the ongoing improvement of chatbots. Regularly updating the chatbot's knowledge base and refining its algorithms based on user interactions and feedback is crucial.

○ **Creative Response Generation:** Leveraging AI to generate creative and contextually appropriate responses can make chatbot interactions more engaging and less predictable.

○ **Scalability Solutions:** Implementing cloud-based solutions and scalable architectures ensures that chatbots can handle increased loads and maintain performance as usage grows.

In conclusion, while the technical challenges in chatbot technology are significant, the ongoing research and development in these areas are leading to innovative solutions. These advancements are crucial for enhancing the capabilities, reliability, and user experience of chatbots, ensuring their effective application across various sectors.

Chatbot technology's challenges and solutions highlight its dynamic complexity. While chatbots offer innovation opportunities, they also face technical and ethical hurdles. Addressing these challenges is not a one-time task but an ongoing process that involves continuous research, development, and adaptation. The solutions, ranging from advanced natural language processing techniques to robust integration frameworks and emotional intelligence, are pivotal in enhancing the capabilities and effectiveness of chatbots. As the technology evolves, so too must our approaches to these challenges, ensuring that chatbots remain not only functional and reliable but also ethical and user centric. This ongoing journey of improvement and adaptation is crucial for realizing the full potential of chatbots in transforming digital interactions and services.

Table 4. Key challenges and solutions in Chatbot technology

Challenge Category	Specific Challenges	Proposed Solutions
Natural Language Processing	Understanding nuances, idiomatic expressions, dialects	Advanced NLP techniques, training on diverse datasets
Contextual Understanding	Maintaining conversation context, recalling past interactions	Enhanced contextual algorithms, memory models
Personalization	Tailoring experiences to individual user preferences at scale	Data-driven personalization, AI and big data analytics
Emotional Intelligence	Recognizing and responding to human emotions	Emotion recognition technologies, sentiment analysis
System Integration	Integrating with various systems and platforms, compatibility issues	Robust integration frameworks, APIs
Continuous Learning	Learning and improving from user interactions	Feedback mechanisms, iterative development, data analysis
Response Generation	Generating creative, contextually appropriate responses	AI-driven creative response generation techniques
Scalability and Performance	Managing increased loads, maintaining performance	Cloud-based solutions, scalable architectures

FUTURE RESEARCH DIRECTIONS

As chatbot technology continues to evolve, it opens up new avenues for research that promise to further enhance its capabilities and applications. The future of chatbots is not just about refining existing technologies but also about exploring uncharted territories that could revolutionize how we interact with AI. Key areas of future research include advancing natural language processing, improving emotional intelligence, exploring ethical AI, and expanding chatbots' roles in various sectors. This section will delve into these prospective research directions, highlighting the potential breakthroughs and innovations that could shape the next generation of chatbot technology. The focus will be on how these advancements could address current limitations and open up new possibilities for more intuitive, empathetic, and effective chatbot interactions in our daily lives and professional environments (Table 5).

- **Emerging Trends:** The landscape of chatbot technology is constantly evolving, with several emerging trends that are shaping its future. These trends not only address current limitations but also open up new possibilities for applications and improvements:

  - **Advancements in NLP and Machine Learning:** Future research is likely to focus on further advancements in natural language processing and machine learning. This includes developing more sophisticated algorithms that can understand and interpret human language with greater accuracy and nuance, making interactions with chatbots more natural and intuitive.
  - **Emotional Intelligence and Sentiment Analysis:** Another key area of research is enhancing the emotional intelligence of chatbots. This involves improving their ability to recognize and respond to human emotions, making interactions more empathetic and personalized.
  - **Ethical AI and Bias Reduction:** As chatbots become more prevalent, there is a growing need to address ethical concerns and reduce biases in AI algorithms. Future research will focus on developing frameworks and techniques to ensure chatbots are fair, unbiased, and respectful of privacy and ethical standards.
  - **Cross-Domain Functionality:** Expanding the functionality of chatbots across different domains and industries is another emerging trend. This involves creating versatile chatbots that can adapt to various contexts and provide specialized assistance in fields like healthcare, education, finance, and more.
  - **Conversational AI and Contextual Understanding:** Enhancing the conversational abilities of chatbots, particularly their contextual understanding, is a significant area of research. This includes improving their ability to maintain the context over longer interactions and remember past conversations.
  - **Integration with IoT and Smart Technologies:** The integration of chatbots with IoT devices and smart technologies is an exciting trend. This research direction explores how chatbots can interact with and control smart environments, offering more seamless and integrated user experiences.
  - **Voice and Multimodal Interactions:** Expanding beyond text-based interactions, future research is looking into voice and multimodal interactions. This includes developing chatbots that can interact through voice, gestures, and other non-verbal cues, making them more accessible and user-friendly.

○ **Autonomous Decision-Making Capabilities:** Research is also focusing on enhancing the autonomous decision-making capabilities of chatbots. This involves enabling chatbots to make informed decisions based on data analysis and user preferences, increasing their usefulness in various applications.

These emerging trends in chatbot technology research not only aim to enhance the current capabilities of chatbots but also to explore new frontiers in AI and human-computer interaction. By addressing these areas, future chatbots are expected to become more intelligent, empathetic, and versatile, significantly impacting how we interact with technology in our daily lives.

● **Long-term Impact:** The long-term impact of advancements in chatbot technology is poised to be profound and far-reaching, influencing various aspects of society, business, and personal interaction. As research continues to push the boundaries of what chatbots can do, we can anticipate several key areas where their influence will be particularly notable:

○ **Transformation of Customer Service:** Chatbots are expected to revolutionize customer service, making it more efficient, personalized, and available 24/7. This transformation could lead to a significant shift in how businesses interact with customers, with chatbots handling the majority of customer interactions.

○ **Enhanced Personalization in Services:** With advancements in AI and machine learning, chatbots will offer even more personalized experiences in sectors like retail, healthcare, and entertainment. This could lead to more tailored and satisfying user experiences, as chatbots become adept at understanding individual preferences and needs.

○ **Impact on Employment and Skill Requirements:** The increasing capabilities of chatbots may lead to changes in the job market, particularly in areas heavily reliant on customer service and support. This could necessitate a shift in skill requirements, with a greater focus on managing and improving AI systems rather than performing routine tasks.

○ **Advancements in Healthcare Accessibility:** In healthcare, chatbots could significantly improve accessibility, providing basic medical advice and support in areas with limited healthcare resources. This could lead to better health outcomes and more efficient use of medical professionals' time.

○ **Educational and Learning Environments:** Chatbots could transform educational environments, offering personalized learning experiences and support. This could make education more accessible and tailored to individual learning styles, potentially improving educational outcomes.

○ **Social and Ethical Implications:** As chatbots become more integrated into daily life, their social and ethical implications will need to be carefully considered. Issues such as privacy, data security, and the ethical use of AI will become increasingly important.

○ **Global Communication and Language Barriers:** Chatbots could play a significant role in breaking down language barriers, offering real-time translation and facilitating global communication. This could have a substantial impact on international business and cross-cultural interactions.

○ **Innovation in User Experience:** The evolution of chatbots is likely to drive innovation in user experience, with more natural, intuitive, and engaging interactions. This could change the way people interact with technology, making it more integrated into everyday life.

Table 5. Future research directions and impacts of Chatbot technology

Research Area	Potential Developments	Expected Long-term Impact
Advancements in NLP and Machine Learning	More sophisticated algorithms for better language understanding	Enhanced naturalness and accuracy in chatbot interactions
Emotional Intelligence and Sentiment Analysis	Improved recognition and response to human emotions	More empathetic and personalized chatbot interactions
Ethical AI and Bias Reduction	Development of ethical frameworks and bias-reducing algorithms	Fairer, more unbiased chatbot interactions and decision-making
Cross-Domain Functionality	Versatile chatbots adaptable to various industries	Wider applicability and utility of chatbots across sectors
Conversational AI and Contextual Understanding	Enhanced ability to maintain context and recall past interactions	More coherent and engaging chatbot conversations
Integration with IoT and Smart Technologies	Chatbots interacting with and controlling smart environments	More seamless and integrated user experiences in smart settings
Voice and Multimodal Interactions	Expansion beyond text to voice and other interaction modes	Increased accessibility and user-friendliness of chatbots
Autonomous Decision-Making	Enhanced decision-making capabilities based on data analysis	More effective and autonomous chatbots in various applications

The long-term impact of chatbot technology will be shaped by ongoing research and development, with potential benefits and challenges that will need to be navigated. As chatbots become more advanced and widespread, their role in shaping various aspects of our world will be significant, offering exciting possibilities for the future.

As we look towards the future of chatbot technology, it's clear that the potential for innovation and transformation is immense. The ongoing research and emerging trends in chatbot development are set to redefine the boundaries of AI and human-computer interaction. From enhancing customer service experiences to revolutionizing healthcare accessibility and education, the impact of chatbots will be felt across numerous sectors. However, this journey is not without its challenges. As chatbots become more integrated into our daily lives, addressing ethical considerations, privacy concerns, and the potential impact on employment will be crucial. The future of chatbots promises not only technological advancement but also a shift in the way we interact with machines, emphasizing the need for a balanced approach that values both human and AI contributions. As we continue to explore and innovate in this field, chatbots are poised to become an even more integral part of our digital landscape, offering exciting possibilities for more intuitive, efficient, and personalized interactions.

CONCLUSION

The exploration of chatbot technology in this chapter has provided a comprehensive overview of its current applications, challenges, and future research directions. Chatbots, powered by advancements in AI and machine learning, have shown remarkable potential in transforming interactions across various sectors, including healthcare, education, customer service, and beyond. They offer enhanced efficiency, personalization, accessibility, reshaping traditional service models and user experiences. However, this journey is accompanied by significant challenges, particularly in natural language processing, emotional intelligence, ethical considerations, and integration with existing systems. Addressing these challenges is crucial for the continued advancement and acceptance of chatbots.

Looking ahead, the future of chatbot technology is bright and full of possibilities. Emerging trends in AI, such as improved NLP, emotional intelligence, and cross-domain functionality, are set to further enhance the capabilities of chatbots. The long-term impact of these advancements will likely be profound, influencing not only the way businesses operate but also how individuals interact with technology in their daily lives. Ethical AI, bias reduction, and the integration of chatbots with IoT and smart technologies are among the key areas that will shape the future landscape of chatbot applications.

In summary, chatbots represent a significant technological evolution, offering both opportunities and challenges. As we continue to innovate and explore the potential of chatbots, their role in our digital world is set to grow, promising more intuitive, efficient, and personalized interactions across a myriad of applications.

In conclusion, securing the cloud is an endeavor that calls for a holistic approach, one that encompasses advanced technological tools, proactive regulatory measures, and an informed and vigilant user base. As we stand on the cusp of technological advancements like quantum computing and the proliferation of IoT, the imperative for robust cloud security mechanisms has never been more critical. The collective challenge lies in fostering a security culture that evolves in tandem with the technologies it seeks to safeguard, ensuring that the immense potential of cloud computing can be fully realized without compromising the sanctity of security and trust.

As we conclude this exploration of chatbot technology, it's evident that we stand at a pivotal moment in the evolution of AI and human-computer interaction. Chatbots, as they continue to advance, are not just reshaping industries and services but are also redefining the very nature of our daily interactions with technology. The potential of chatbots to enhance efficiency, personalize experiences, and provide accessible solutions is immense, yet it comes with the responsibility to navigate the challenges and ethical considerations that arise.

The future of chatbots, rich with possibilities, challenges us to think beyond the current limitations and to envision a world where AI not only assists but also enriches human experiences. The integration of chatbots in our lives has the potential to bridge gaps in service delivery, education, healthcare, and more, making essential services more accessible to diverse populations. However, as we embrace this potential, we must also remain vigilant about the ethical implications, ensuring that the development of chatbots is guided by principles of fairness, privacy, and inclusivity.

In the end, the journey of chatbot technology is a testament to human ingenuity and our relentless pursuit of innovation. It reflects our desire to push the boundaries of what is possible, to create tools that not only solve problems but also enhance our capabilities and experiences. As we move forward, the collaborative efforts of researchers, developers, and users will be crucial in shaping a future where chatbots serve not just as tools of convenience but as catalysts for positive change and progress in our increasingly digital world.

REFERENCES

Aleedy, M., Shaiba, H., & Bezbradica, M. (2019). Generating and analyzing chatbot responses using natural language processing. [Reference Link]. *International Journal of Advanced Computer Science and Applications, 10*(9). doi:10.14569/IJACSA.2019.0100910

Aslam, F. (2023). The impact of artificial intelligence on chatbot technology: A study on the current advancements and leading innovations. *European Journal of Technology, 7*(3), 62–72. doi:10.47672/ejt.1561

Bilquise, G., Ibrahim, S., & Shaalan, K. (2022). Emotionally Intelligent Chatbots: A Systematic Literature Review. [Reference Link]. *Human Behavior and Emerging Technologies, 2022*, 2022. doi:10.1155/2022/9601630

Ciechanowski, L., Przegalinska, A., Magnuski, M., & Gloor, P. (2019). In the shades of the uncanny valley: An experimental study of human–chatbot interaction. [Reference Link]. *Future Generation Computer Systems, 92*, 539–548. doi:10.1016/j.future.2018.01.055

Čižmešija, A., Horvat, A., & Vukovac, D. P. (2021). Improving student engagement and course completion using Chatbot application. In *INTED2021 Proceedings* (pp. 8346-8354). IATED. 10.21125/inted.2021.1697

Dash, M., & Bakshi, S. (2019). An exploratory study of customer perceptions of usage of chatbots in the hospitality industry. *International Journal on Customer Relations, 7*(2), 27–33.

De Sanctis, M., Bucchiarone, A., & Marconi, A. (2020). Dynamic adaptation of service-based applications: A design for adaptation approach. *Journal of Internet Services and Applications, 11*(1), 1–29. doi:10.1186/s13174-020-00123-6

Fan, X., Chao, D., Zhang, Z., Wang, D., Li, X., & Tian, F. (2021). Utilization of self-diagnosis health chatbots in real-world settings: Case study. *Journal of Medical Internet Research, 23*(1), e19928. doi:10.2196/19928 PMID:33404508

Ho, A., Hancock, J., & Miner, A. S. (2018). Psychological, relational, and emotional effects of self-disclosure after conversations with a chatbot. *Journal of Communication, 68*(4), 712–733. doi:10.1093/joc/jqy026 PMID:30100620

Ionuț-Alexandru, C. (2021). Challenges and Ethical Solutions in Using the Chatbot. *Database Systems Journal, 12*.

Kvale, K., Freddi, E., Hodnebrog, S., Sell, O. A., & Følstad, A. (2020). Understanding the user experience of customer service chatbots: what can we learn from customer satisfaction surveys? In *International Workshop on Chatbot Research and Design* (pp. 205-218). Cham: Springer International Publishing.

McTear, M. (2022). *Conversational ai: Dialogue systems, conversational agents, and chatbots*. Springer Nature.

Mogaji, E., Balakrishnan, J., Nwoba, A. C., & Nguyen, N. P. (2021). Emerging-market consumers' interactions with banking chatbots. *Telematics and Informatics, 65*, 101711. doi:10.1016/j.tele.2021.101711

Plocher, T., Rau, P. L. P., Choong, Y. Y., & Guo, Z. (2021). Cross-Cultural Design. Handbook of human factors and ergonomics, 252-279. Wiley.

Rapp, A., Curti, L., & Boldi, A. (2021). The human side of human-chatbot interaction: A systematic literature review of ten years of research on text-based chatbots. [Reference Link]. *International Journal of Human-Computer Studies*, *151*, 102630. doi:10.1016/j.ijhcs.2021.102630

Sadasivan, C., Cruz, C., Dolgoy, N., Hyde, A., Campbell, S., McNeely, M., Stroulia, E., & Tandon, P. (2023). Examining Patient Engagement in Chatbot Development Approaches for Healthy Lifestyle and Mental Wellness Interventions: Scoping Review. *Journal of Participatory Medicine*, *15*, e45772. doi:10.2196/45772 PMID:37213199

Tan, P. K., & Lim, C. M. (2023). Factors That Affect User Satisfaction of Using E-Commerce Chatbot: A Study on Generation Z. *International Journal of Business and Technology Management*, *5*(1), 292–303.

Thorat, S. A., & Jadhav, V. (2020, April). A review on implementation issues of rule-based chatbot systems. In *Proceedings of the international conference on innovative computing & communications (ICICC)*. IEEE.

KEY TERMS AND DEFINITIONS

Artificial Intelligence (AI): The simulation of human intelligence processes by machines, especially computer systems, which includes learning, reasoning, and self-correction.

Bias in AI: The presence of prejudiced views or unfair associations within AI algorithms, often reflecting historical data or the creator's subjective decisions, which can lead to skewed outcomes.

Conversational AI: A form of artificial intelligence specifically designed to provide automated conversation, capable of understanding and conducting spoken or written dialogues.

Emotional Intelligence in AI: The capability of AI systems, like chatbots, to recognize, interpret, process, and simulate human emotions to enhance interaction and communication.

Ethical AI: The practice of designing, developing, and deploying AI with good intention, ensuring it is transparent, fair, and respects user privacy and human rights.

IoT Integration: The process of connecting chatbots to the Internet of Things, enabling them to interact with and control connected devices and systems.

Machine Learning: A subset of AI that involves the development of algorithms and statistical models that enable computers to perform tasks without explicit instructions, by relying on patterns and inference.

Multi-Tenancy Chatbot: A software application designed to simulate conversation with human users, especially over the Internet, using natural language processing and artificial intelligence.

Natural Language Processing (NLP): A branch of artificial intelligence that focuses on enabling computers to understand, interpret, and respond to human language in a valuable and meaningful way.

Sentiment Analysis: An NLP technique used to determine the emotional tone behind words, enabling chatbots to understand the sentiments of the user they are interacting with.

Chapter 6
Natural Language Processing (NLP) in Chatbot Design:
NLP's Impact on Chatbot Architecture

Rajesh Kanna Rajendran

iD https://orcid.org/0000-0001-7228-5031

Christ University, India

Mohana Priya T.

Christ University, India

Karthick Chitrarasu

Christ University, India

ABSTRACT

The creation and development of chatbots, which are the prevalent manifestations of artificial intelligence (AI) and machine learning (ML) technologies in today's digital world, are built on Natural Language Processing (NLP), which serves as a cornerstone in the process. This chapter investigates the significant part that natural language processing (NLP) plays in determining the development and effectiveness of chatbots, beginning with their beginnings as personal virtual assistants and continuing through their seamless incorporation into messaging platforms and smart home gadgets. The study delves into the technological complexities and emphasizes the problems and improvements in natural language processing (NLP) algorithms and understanding (NLU) systems. These systems are essential in enabling chatbots to grasp context, decode user intent, and provide replies that are contextually appropriate in real time. In spite of the substantial progress that has been made, chatbots continue to struggle with constraints.

INTRODUCTION

NLP is a branch of AI that helps computers understand, interpret, and synthesize contextually relevant human language. Language understanding and production depend on context, which gives words and

DOI: 10.4018/979-8-3693-1830-0.ch006

phrases meaning. Understanding context is essential for NLP tasks like sentiment analysis, machine translation, and dialogue production. This article discusses NLP context and its effects on numerous applications, particularly sophisticated chatbot design and development. Despite their widespread adoption, chatbots confront inherent technical challenges rooted in natural language processing (NLP) and understanding (NLU), pivotal components of their development. While NLP algorithms empower chatbots to analyze and generate responses from text inputs, NLU systems aim to grasp the context, sentiment, and intent behind user queries, enabling more nuanced interactions. Despite advancements, chatbots often grapple with limitations such as misinterpretation of queries and an inability to replicate natural human conversation convincingly, underscoring the intricate nature of human language comprehension and the ongoing evolution of AI technologies.

In the digital age, chatbots have become ubiquitous manifestations of artificial intelligence (AI) and machine learning (ML) technologies, fundamentally altering the dynamics of business-consumer interactions. From personal virtual assistants like Microsoft's Cortana to the helpful bots integrated into messaging platforms such as Slack, and the intuitive interfaces of smart home devices like Amazon's Alexa, chatbots seamlessly blend into our daily routines, offering unparalleled convenience and support. Joseph Weizenbaum, a computer scientist working at the Massachusetts Institute of Technology's Artificial Intelligence Laboratory, created ELIZA in 1966, making it one of the earliest chatbots ever created. This proliferation of chatbots reflects a substantial corporate investment in AI, with tech giants committing billions of dollars to mergers, acquisitions, and internal R&D, signaling a strategic shift towards harnessing AI's potential. Chatbots employ NLP to understand, interpret, and answer to user queries naturally. NLP allows chatbots to understand user input, maintain coherent dialogues, and tailor interactions depending on user preferences through intent recognition, entity extraction, and context management. Businesses may improve customer happiness and loyalty across industries by seamlessly incorporating NLP into chatbot architecture to create more engaging, efficient, and user-centric conversations.

BACKGROUND WORK

Data in the form of raw text is preprocessed by NLP algorithms in order to improve its analysis and interpretation. Recent research (Brown et al., 2020; Devlin et al., 2018) has shed light on the significance of tokenization, the removal of punctuation, and text normalization in the process of preparing text for future processing. These processes are essential in establishing the basis for efficient chatbot operation.

Dialog management solutions that are based on natural language processing or NLP are extremely helpful in ensuring that chatbot conversations remain coherent and relevant. When it comes to supporting discussions that are both smooth and engaging, the literature (Graves et al., 2013; Sutskever et al., 2014) highlights the significance of context tracking, user preference management, and conversational history analysis.

The use of natural language processing (NLP) algorithms enables chatbots to provide replies that are human-like and suited to the user's purpose and context. Language generation approaches have been shown to be successful in picking acceptable words and phrases, providing replies that are coherent and contextually relevant, according to studies (Bahdanau et al., 2014; Vaswani et al., 2018).

By extracting extensive contextual information from massive text corpora, LLMs make it possible for chatbots to grasp the inputs provided by actual users. These studies (Dai et al., 2019; Radford et al.,

2019) illustrate the efficiency of LLMs in contextual understanding, which enables chatbots to perceive subtleties in language and offer replies that are accurate.

According to the findings of the study, LLMs are capable of producing written output that is both cohesive and naturally flowing. It has been demonstrated through research (Brown et al., 2020; Raffel et al., 2020) that LLMs have the capability to imitate human-like language patterns. This enhances the naturalness of chatbot conversations and improves user engagement.

Learning Learning Machines (LLMs) provide chances for chatbot personalization by means of fine-tuning on datasets that are particular to either the domain or the user. The usefulness of tailored LLMs in adapting replies to individual preferences and settings has been demonstrated by studies (Li et al., 2020; Wolf et al., 2020). This has resulted in increased user satisfaction.

Because of their versatility and flexibility, LLMs are appropriate for a wide variety of chatbot applications and use cases. The literature (Sanh et al., 2020; Vaswani et al., 2017) highlights the adaptability of LLMs, which enables developers to make use of pre-trained models or to fine-tune them in order to satisfy particular criteria and objectives.

NATURAL LANGUAGE PROCESSING

The definition of this seemingly complicated process is that it is one that enables computers to draw meaning from the text that is inputted into them. In its most basic form, natural language processing (NLP) is a software that use artificial intelligence (AI) to assist your chatbot in analyzing and comprehending the natural human language that is communicated with your clients.

It is not enough for chatbots to just utilize the information to communicate and answer to questions; they are also able to comprehend the purpose of the interaction. The owners of businesses are beginning to provide their chatbots with activities that will "assist" them in becoming more humanized and personable in their interactions with customers. Chatbots have helped businesses automate jobs, improve their line of communication with clients, and increase their bottom lines, and they will continue to do so in the future. On the other hand, as customers get more accustomed to interacting with chatbots, they have higher expectations for them.

In light of the fact that customization is the major focus, you should make an effort to "train" your chatbot about the many default replies and the specific ways in which they may improve the lives of consumers simpler by doing so. The use of natural language processing (NLP) will enable your chatbot to simplify replies that are more personalized and unique, interpret and respond to new inquiries or instructions, and improve the customer experience in accordance with the customer's requirements. (Smith, J. 2023)

Natural Language Processing (NLP) Extends Far Beyond Chatbot Creation

Natural language processing, commonly known as NLP, is an essential technique that enables computers to not only analyze natural language but also grasp it and derive meaning from it in a way that is both intelligent and practical. Applicability of this technology extends far beyond the domain of current technological advancements such as chatbots and intelligent virtual assistants. Search engine optimization, online translation services, spam filtering, and spell checking are just few of the tasks that heavily rely on natural language processing (NLP) algorithms. In fact, NLP algorithms are present in a wide variety of aspects of our digital interactions. Harnessing the capabilities of NLP empowers developers to effectively structure and manage vast amounts of unstructured data, facilitating the execution of diverse intelligent tasks, including:

- Automatic summarization, which intelligently condenses lengthy text for easier consumption.
- Automatic suggestions, streamlining the composition of emails, messages, and other textual content.
- Translation services focused on conveying phrases and ideas rather than literal translations.
- Named entity recognition, essential for identifying and categorizing entities within unstructured natural language into predefined groups such as organizations, person names, locations, and more.
- Relationship extraction, identifying semantic connections among entities in text or speech, like "is located in," "is married to," "is employed by," and others.
- Sentiment analysis, discerning positive, negative, and neutral opinions from text or speech data, often used to extract insights from social media comments, forums, or surveys.
- Speech recognition, enabling computers to transcribe spoken language into text (dictation) and potentially take action, as seen in virtual assistants like Google Assistant, Cortana, or Siri.
- Topic segmentation, an automated process dividing written texts, speeches, or recordings into coherent segments, enhancing information retrieval and speech recognition systems.

Strategically applying NLP techniques allows organizations to unlock the latent potential of unstructured data, facilitating valuable insights and informed decision-making across diverse domains.

PILLARS OF AN NLP-BASED CHATBOT

The creation of advanced chatbots in the field of conversational artificial intelligence is dependent on three fundamental pillars: the dialog system, natural language understanding (NLU), and natural language generation (NLG). It is the dialog system that acts as the interface through which chatbots engage with humans. It is designed to mimic human communication patterns across a wide range of modalities and styles. In the meanwhile, natural language understanding (NLU) plays an important part in interpreting the complexities of human language. This has made it possible for chatbots to properly read user intent despite the difficulty of enormous vocabularies and ambiguous meanings.

NLG comes into action once the user input has been comprehended, and it is responsible for converting the bot's programmed replies into prose that is intelligible and understandable by humans. Natural language generation (NLG) guarantees that chatbots efficiently communicate with users in a manner that is consistent with their desired communication style and objectives. This is accomplished via the use of predetermined formats and narrative design that is governed by conditional logic rules. All of these pillars come together to create the core of natural language processing (NLP)-based chatbots, which gives them the ability to have interactions with users that are meaningful and contextually relevant.

Dialog System

Similar to how humans use various senses and modes of communication, a chatbot requires a dialog system that aligns with human interaction patterns. This dialog system, also known as a conversational agent, serves as the interface through which the chatbot communicates with users.

Dialog systems come in diverse forms, but at their core, they must facilitate both output generation and input reception. They can vary based on modality (text-based, speech-based, graphical, or mixed), device compatibility, communication style (command-based, menu-driven, or natural language), and initiative (system-driven, user-driven, or a blend of both).

Natural Language Understanding (NLU)

Natural Language Understanding (NLU) is a crucial component of NLP-based chatbots, tasked with deciphering user input. However, comprehending human language poses a significant challenge due to its complexity, including vast vocabularies and multiple ambiguous meanings.

Effective NLU ensures the chatbot accurately interprets user intent, prioritizing this over achieving a completely human-like conversational tone. A bot's ability to derive meaning from natural input is paramount for successful interactions, overshadowing the importance of nuanced language generation.

Natural Language Generation (NLG)

Once the NLP-based chatbot comprehends user input, it must generate an appropriate response in natural language. This process, known as Natural Language Generation (NLG), involves translating the bot's programmed response into human-readable text.

The NLG system relies on predefined formats, such as rules-based workflows, templates, or intent-driven approaches, to craft coherent responses. Narrative design, guided by conditional logic rules, plays a pivotal role in shaping the output, ensuring it aligns with the bot's intended communication style and objectives.

NLP CHATBOTS LEARN VALUABLE LESSONS FROM RULE-BASED BOTS

The debate over what constitutes a true chatbot often revolves around the use of AI and natural language processing. Some argue that without these elements, a chatbot merely becomes an automated sequence of responses on a messaging platform. However, when it comes down to practicality and efficiency, focusing solely on the purity of AI experience may not always be beneficial for business growth.

In fact, there's much that NLP chatbots can glean from rule-based counterparts. Here are some key takeaways:

1. Streamline User Interaction: Instead of solely relying on text input, consider incorporating rich controls like buttons or quick replies to expedite query resolution and reduce cognitive load for users. Simplifying the interaction process can enhance efficiency without compromising the bot's perceived intelligence.

2. Visualize Conversation Flow: While NLP bots generate responses based on user inputs, visualizing conversation paths through flow diagrams can aid in designing coherent and natural-sounding narratives. Mapping out potential conversation paths helps in crafting a fluent dialogue and ensures a seamless user experience.

3. Clearly Define Conversation End: Provide clear indicators to signify the end of a conversation, both verbally and visually. This prevents confusion for users and ensures that the interaction concludes smoothly. Additionally, offering instructions for restarting the conversation can enhance user engagement.

4. Prioritize Core Intents: In the early stages of bot development, focus on refining core intents rather than getting bogged down by handling corner cases. Avoid investing excessive time in addressing unlikely scenarios, and instead concentrate on delivering well-developed responses for common user queries. Consider implementing triggers for human agent intervention if users encounter issues.

5. Facilitate Conversation Restart: Incorporate a prominent restart button to allow users to easily initiate a new conversation if needed. Despite the bot's intelligence, users may still encounter frustrations or misunderstandings, necessitating a quick restart option to enhance user satisfaction.

By adopting these principles from rule-based bots, NLP chatbots can enhance their practicality, efficiency, and overall user experience, ultimately driving better outcomes for businesses and users alike.

DIFFERENT TYPES OF CHATBOTS

The field of artificial intelligence has just entered a new frontier with the introduction of chatbots, which demonstrate how AI technology may be applied in real-world situations. They serve as one of the first expressions of artificial intelligence that is visibly incorporated into situations that occur in the real world. There is a significant difference between bots that have been imbued with artificial intelligence and those that do not have AI, with the former displaying clearly unique patterns of behavior.

This chapter makes a distinction between chatbots that are based on rules and chatbots that use natural language processing (NLP).

Rule-based bots are able to function within the boundaries of specified rules, and the interactions with users are controlled by these pre-established norms. A button-based communication system is typically utilized by these bots, which limits the versatility of conversational exchanges.

Artificial intelligence bots that are driven by natural language processing (NLP) are able to simulate human cognition by utilizing Artificial Intelligence (AI). This includes components such as logical thinking, planning, and language understanding. The capacity of chatbots to comprehend natural language is a capability that is made possible by algorithms, most notably neural networks. This ability is particularly relevant to chatbots. The capacity of the bot to comprehend and respond to user inputs in a manner that is comparable to human conversation is referred to as Natural Language Processing, which is the term that was used to describe this feature of the bot.

Enhancing Human-Like Dialogue in AI Chatbot

You should concentrate on building a conversational tone for your artificial intelligence chatbot so that it may have a more human-like discourse. This tone should include informal greetings, empathy, and suitable humor. It is important to make use of powerful Natural Language Processing (NLP) procedures in order to guarantee that the bot comprehends customer inquiries and reacts contextually to them, incorporating slang and commonly used phrases. It is important to establish a consistent personality for the chatbot and to tailor interactions based on the preferences of the user. Additionally, it is important to acknowledge limits and occasional mistakes in a straightforward manner in order to promote authenticity. Continuously collect input from users in order to develop and improve the bot's dialogue. This will ensure that the bot's dialogue is in line with user expectations and encourages deeper interactions.

AI-Powered Chatbots

The chatbots of the past are not even close to being as strong as the chatbots produced today. From the customer experience that is solely based on the user experience that you get when you navigate through a website to the real-life human interaction that you experience with a brand, an artificial intelligence chatbot has now transformed the user experience (UX) into a conversational interaction between humans and computers.

In addition to being integrated into website chat, chatbots have also been included into social media platforms and mobile applications. It is becoming increasingly crucial for companies to humanize their approach and provide their consumers with a one-of-a-kind experience that is in keeping with their brand's voice and position in the market. This is due to the fact that the future of conversational commerce and computing is organized around personality in general.

Invent a Persona for Virtual Assistant

Even if it is due of a robot, there is nothing quite like the feeling of having a good chuckle. As a matter of fact, we are aware that chatbots are not human beings. And despite the fact that it could be uncomfortable to communicate with a chatbot, there are methods in which marketers can get rid of the cold, direct connection and replace it with some comedy. Consequently, you need make a character for your bot, for example. Choose a name for him or her that will remain with them. In order to provide your consumers with the same human experience that they would have in-store, this "person" should possess distinctive personality features that represent the language of your business. When clients spend more time speaking with your artificial intelligence chatbot, you are providing them with the opportunity to learn more about your company and provide them with the possibility of being influenced to make a purchase.

Future Ahead for Chatbots

There are new chatbots being introduced on a daily basis, which makes it more challenging for businesses to compete with brands that are rapidly adopting new technology. When it comes to digital businesses, the cornerstone of any successful enterprise is an improved customer experience. If you take control of your artificial intelligence chatbot and instruct it to assist you, you will be able to alter the manner in which people see your brand and make a significant impact on the industry as a whole. You will begin to witness a quick increase in both the level of consumer engagement and the amount of money added to your bottom line if you bring some more humanity to your brand.

Role and Need of LLM in Chatbot Development Process

Large Language Models, also known as LLMs, are an essential component in the creation of chatbots since they provide extremely sophisticated language processing and generating capabilities. The following are some important characteristics of LLMs in the creation of chatbots:

LLMs are trained on enormous volumes of text data, which enables them to extract extensive contextual information from user inputs. This is referred to as contextual understanding. This makes it possible for chatbots to comprehend the intricacies of language, such as slang, idioms, and colloquial terms, which ultimately results in replies that are more accurate and contextually appropriate.

Language Generation: LLMs are particularly powerful when it comes to producing text output that is fluent and cohesive, imitating human-like language patterns and styles. Using LLMs, chatbots are able to generate replies of a high quality that are indistinguishable from those produced by people. This results in an increase in the naturalness and efficiency of interactions.

For the purpose of personalization, LLMs can be fine-tuned on certain domains or user data in order to adjust replies to the interests and circumstances of individual users. For this reason, chatbots are able to give consumers with information that is both individualized and relevant, hence increasing user engagement and pleasure.

Capacity for Flexibility and Adaptability: Because LLMs are so versatile and adaptable, they are suited for a broad variety of chatbot applications and use cases. It is possible for developers of chatbots to make use of pre-trained LLMs or to fine-tune them using custom datasets in order to fulfill certain criteria and goals.

CHOTBOT ALGORITHM

Chatbots make use of a wide variety of algorithms in order to carry out their functions efficiently. Based on Rules One of the fundamental approaches is the use of algorithms, which allow chatbots to function according to predetermined rules and patterns. They are suited for processing structured inquiries as well as jobs that are relatively basic. Support vector machines, decision trees, and random forests are some examples of the types of machine learning algorithms that are utilized in chatbots. These algorithms allow chatbots to learn from data and improve over time. These algorithms make it possible for chatbots to adjust to the ever-changing tastes and requirements of users. NLP algorithms, which stand for natural language processing, are the fundamental building blocks of chatbots that deal with human language. Recurrent neural networks (RNNs), Long Short-Term Memory (LSTM) networks, and sophisticated Transformer models like as BERT and GPT-3 are also included in this category. When it comes to recognizing user intent, intent recognition algorithms are absolutely necessary. These algorithms assist chatbots in directing discussions or making judgments depending on user inquiries. Dialog Management Algorithms are responsible for maintaining the context of talks, which guarantees that chatbots will offer replies that are coherent and appropriate to the context. Sentiment analysis algorithms are able to determine the feelings of users based on the language they use, which enables chatbots to adapt their replies or evaluate the level of happiness of customers. A reinforcement of Learning is another technique that may be utilized in some chatbots to enhance their effectiveness over time by optimizing their replies depending on the input they get from users. Chatbots are a disruptive force in current technology since they are able to perform intelligently and effectively in a range of applications because to the combined strength of these algorithms.

COMPONENTS

The architecture of the NLP Engine has two components

1. INTENT CLASSIFIER

The intent classifier takes the user's input, identifies its meaning and relates back to one of the intents that the chatbot supports. This process is called as intent classification. A classifier is a way to categorize pieces of data - in this case, a sentence - into several different categories. Much like how humans classify objects into sets, such as a violin is an instrument, a shirt is a type of clothing, and happiness is an emotion, chatbots will classify each section of a sentence into broken down categories to understand the intention behind the input it has received. There are several options available to developers for this:

- **Patter Matching**: Pattern matching involves using patterns in the incoming text and classify it into different intents.
- **Machine Learning Algorithms**: Uses various machine learning algorithms to create a multi-class classification.
- **Neural Networks**: These networks are used to learn from text using fine word embedding.

For both machine learning algorithms and neural networks, we need numeric representations of text that a machine can operate with. Here sentence vectors fill this requirement. Vector space models provide a way to represent sentences from a user into a comparable mathematical vector. This can be used to represent the meaning in multi-dimensional vectors. Then, these vectors can be used to classify intent and show how different sentences are related to one another.

2. ENTITY EXTRACTOR

Entity extractor is what extracts key information from the user's query. It extracts specific information like:

- Type of dish user wishes to have
- Time of the order
- Type of the issue user is facing
- Customer's name, phone number, address and other details

Language Generation and Response Generation

Using natural language processing, a chatbot may provide suitable replies once it has gained an understanding of the user's intentions. Using language generation techniques, chatbots are able to design replies that are contextually appropriate and human-like. These techniques include rule-based systems, templates, and more complex approaches such as neural language models. When generating replies that successfully address user inquiries, natural language processing algorithms take into account the user's purpose, context, and the knowledge base that is accessible. Through the utilization of methods such as text creation and language modeling, chatbots are able to deliver replies that are both entertaining and instructive, hence encouraging meaningful interactions with participants.

Multilingual Support and Localization

One of the most important requirements for chatbots is the ability to handle many languages, as organizations are increasingly working on a worldwide basis. Chatbots are able to interpret and comprehend user input in a variety of languages thanks to natural language processing algorithms. Machine translation models, part-of-speech tagging, and language identification algorithms make it possible for chatbots to satisfy the needs of users who speak a variety of languages and come from a variety of places. Having this feature makes communication more smooth, broadens the scope of enterprises' operations, and improves the user experience for a wide range of customers.

CONCLUSION

NLP extends beyond chatbot creation to search engine optimization, online translation services, spam filtering, and spell checking. It is present in various aspects of digital interactions, including automatic summarization, automatic suggestions, translation services, named entity recognition, relationship extraction, sentiment analysis, speech recognition, and topic segmentation. Chatbots utilize various algorithms to efficiently perform their functions. Machine learning algorithms, such as support vector machines, decision trees, and random forests, allow chatbots to learn from data and improve over time. Natural language processing algorithms, such as Recurrent Neural Networks, Long Short-Term Memory networks, and Transformer models like BERT and GPT-3, are the fundamental building blocks of chatbots that deal with human language.

Multilingual support and localization are crucial for chatbots, as organizations are increasingly working worldwide. Natural language processing algorithms, such as machine translation models, part-of-speech tagging, and language identification algorithms, enable chatbots to interpret and comprehend user input in various languages, making communication more smooth and improving user experience.

REFERENCES

Bahdanau, D., Cho, K., & Bengio, Y. (2014). *Neural machine translation by jointly learning to align and translate*. arXiv preprint arXiv:1409.0473.

Brown, P. F., Pietra, V. J. D., Pietra, S. A. D., & Mercer, R. L. (1993). The mathematics of statistical machine translation: Parameter estimation. *Computational Linguistics, 19*(2), 263–311.

Brown, T. B., Mann, B., Ryder, N., Subbiah, M., Kaplan, J., Dhariwal, P., & Amodei, D. (2020). *Language Models are Few-Shot Learners*. arXiv preprint arXiv:2005.14165.

Dai, Z., Yang, Z., Yang, Y., Carbonell, J., Le, Q. V., & Salakhutdinov, R. (2019). Transformer-XL: Attentive Language Models Beyond a Fixed-Length Context. In *Proceedings of the 57th Annual Meeting of the Association for Computational Linguistics* (pp. 2978-2988). ACL. 10.18653/v1/P19-1285

Devlin, J., Chang, M. W., Lee, K., & Toutanova, K. (2018). *BERT: Pre-training of Deep Bidirectional Transformers for Language Understanding*. arXiv preprint arXiv:1810.04805.

Graves, A., Mohamed, A. R., & Hinton, G. (2013). Speech recognition with deep recurrent neural networks. In Acoustics, speech and signal processing (ICASSP), 2013 IEEE international conference (pp. 6645-6649). IEEE. doi:10.1109/ICASSP.2013.6638947

Li, Y., Ott, M., Du, J., Goyal, N., Joshi, M., Chen, D., & Stoyanov, V. (2020). *Scaling Up Natural Language Understanding with Large LLMs*. arXiv preprint arXiv:2005.14165.

Liu, Y., Ott, M., Goyal, N., Du, J., Joshi, M., Chen, D., & Zettlemoyer, L. (2019). *RoBERTa: A Robustly Optimized BERT Pretraining Approach*. arXiv preprint arXiv:1907.11692.

Radford, A., Wu, J., Child, R., Luan, D., Amodei, D., & Sutskever, I. (2019). Language Models are Unsupervised Multitask Learners. *OpenAI Blog, 1*(8).

Raffel, C., Shazeer, N., Roberts, A., Lee, K., Narang, S., Matena, M., & Liu, P. J. (2020). Exploring the Limits of Transfer Learning with a Unified Text-to-Text Transformer.

Sanh, V., Debut, L., Chaumond, J., & Wolf, T. (2020). *DistilBERT, a distilled version of BERT: smaller, faster, cheaper and lighter*.

Smith, J. (2023). Enhancing Chatbot Interactions through Natural Language Processing (NLP). *Journal of AI Applications, 10*(3), 45–58.

Sutskever, I., Vinyals, O., & Le, Q. V. (2014). Sequence to sequence learning with neural networks. In Advances in neural information processing systems (pp. 3104-3112). Research Gate.

Vaswani, A., Bengio, S., Brevdo, E., Chollet, F., Chintala, S., Cisse, M., & De Sa, C. (2018). *Tensor2tensor for neural machine translation*. arXiv preprint arXiv:1803.07416.

Vaswani, A., Shazeer, N., Parmar, N., Uszkoreit, J., Jones, L., Gomez, A. N., & Polosukhin, I. (2017). Attention is all you need. *Advances in Neural Information Processing Systems, 30*, 5998–6008.

Wolf, T., Sanh, V., Chaumond, J., & Delangue, C. (2020). Transformers: State-of-the-Art Natural Language Processing. In *Proceedings of the 2020 Conference on Empirical Methods in Natural Language Processing: System Demonstrations* (pp. 38-45). IEEE.

KEY TERMS AND DEFINITIONS

Artificial Intelligence: Artificial intelligence (AI) is a field of computer science that focuses on making tools that are smart enough to behave like humans, understand their surroundings, learn from their mistakes, and make choices on their own.

Chatbot Design: Chatbot design is the process of coming up with ideas for, building, and improving conversational agents like chatbots. These use AI and natural language processing to talk to users in a way that seems normal.

Digital Era: The digital era is the present time when digital technologies like computers, the internet, mobile phones, and cloud computing are widely used and adopted, changing many parts of society, business, and culture.

Human-Computer Interaction: Human-Computer Interaction (HCI) is the study and design of interfaces between people and computers. It includes methods for interacting with computers, designing user interfaces, making sure they are easy to use, and improving the user experience (UX).

Large Language Model (LLM): A complex AI model that can read and write text that sounds like it was written by a person on a big scale. It is usually trained on huge amounts of text data.

Long Short-Term Memory (LSTM): Long short-term memory (LSTM) networks are a specific type of RNN designed to address a common limitation of RNNs - the vanishing gradient problem. This problem can make it difficult for RNNs to learn long-term dependencies in sequences. LSTMs address this problem by introducing a gating mechanism that controls the flow of information through the network. This allows LSTMs to selectively remember or forget information over long periods of time.

Machine Learning: Machine Learning (ML) is a branch of artificial intelligence that lets computers learn from their mistakes and get better over time without being told to do so. Algorithms for machine learning look at data to find trends, make predictions, and change as needed.

Recurrent neural networks (RNNs): A unique type of neural network called a recurrent neural network is made to process sequential data. RNNs possess an internal memory that enables them to process data sequences, where the output is dependent on the current input and the network's memory of previous inputs. This is in contrast to typical neural networks, which analyze individual data points.

Chapter 7
Best Practices and Tips for Selecting Chatbots

Pankaj Bhambri
ⓘD https://orcid.org/0000-0003-4437-4103
Guru Nanak Dev Engineering College, Ludhiana, India

Sita Rani
ⓘD https://orcid.org/0000-0003-2778-0214
Guru Nanak Dev Engineering College, Ludhiana, India

ABSTRACT

This chapter provides a comprehensive overview of key criteria and methodologies essential for effectively choosing chatbots tailored to specific organizational needs. Addressing the critical intersection of functionality, user experience, and technological capabilities, the chapter delves into the evaluation of natural language processing, integration capabilities, scalability, and adaptability to diverse industries. Emphasizing the significance of a user-centric approach, the discussion encompasses user interface design, conversational flow, and the incorporation of feedback mechanisms to enhance user satisfaction. Furthermore, the chapter sheds light on the importance of aligning chatbot selection with overarching organizational goals and strategies. This work is a great resource for researchers and practitioners who are navigating the complex process of choosing chatbots in the always changing field of conversational AI. It distils best practices from industrial examples and emerging trends.

INTRODUCTION

Selecting the right chatbot is a critical decision that demands a strategic approach and careful consideration of various factors. Best practices for choosing chatbots involve defining clear objectives and requirements aligned with organizational goals, ensuring a user-centric design to enhance user experience, evaluating technology and platform compatibility, and addressing integration challenges with existing systems (Jain and Srivastava, 2020). Security and compliance should be prioritized, encompassing data protection and adherence to regulatory standards. Performance metrics and analytics play a pivotal role

DOI: 10.4018/979-8-3693-1830-0.ch007

in continuous improvement, enabling organizations to measure success and refine chatbot capabilities. The vendor selection process is crucial, requiring a thorough evaluation of reputation, experience, and support. Learning from case studies and industry best practices can offer valuable insights, while anticipating future trends ensures that selected chatbots remain relevant and adaptable to evolving technological landscapes. Implementing best practices in chatbot selection involves a holistic approach that combines technical considerations, user-centric design, and strategic planning for long-term success.

Background

Choosing the appropriate chatbot for a particular use case is essential for businesses seeking to improve customer relations and operational efficiency. The chatbot technology landscape is varied, including many platforms, structures, and deployment choices. Organizations must take into account issues including work complexity, integration with current systems, competency in natural language processing, and the scalability of the chatbot solution. Furthermore, it is crucial to consider the user knowledge, customization choices, and continuous support and maintenance while making decisions. Staying updated on business developments, user feedback, and AI breakthroughs is crucial for making informed decisions when choosing chatbots that meet corporate objectives and deliver a smooth and efficient conversational experience.

Overview of the Significance of Selecting the Right Chatbot

The significance of selecting the right chatbot lies at the core of optimizing user engagement, fostering seamless communication, and achieving organizational goals. In the evolving landscape of emerging chatbot technology, businesses must carefully consider the unique needs of their users and the specific objectives they aim to accomplish through chatbot implementation. The right chatbot can enhance user experience, streamline processes, and contribute to increased efficiency. Moreover, a well-selected chatbot aligns with the brand image, maintains consistency in communication, and adapts to evolving user preferences (Singh et al., 2021). By understanding the context-specific requirements and choosing a chatbot that integrates seamlessly into existing systems, organizations can harness the full potential of this technology, ultimately leading to improved customer satisfaction and operational success.

Importance in the Context of Emerging Chatbot Technology

In the rapidly evolving landscape of emerging chatbot technology, the importance of judiciously selecting the right chatbot cannot be overstated (Rani et al., 2023c). As organizations increasingly leverage chatbots to enhance customer interactions, streamline processes, and augment overall efficiency, the decision-making process surrounding their selection becomes a critical strategic endeavor. The intricacies of emerging technologies, such as advancements in artificial intelligence and natural language processing, underscore the need for a comprehensive understanding of the unique capabilities and limitations of various chatbot solutions (Rajendran and Prasanna, 2018). Effective selection not only ensures alignment with organizational objectives but also paves the way for seamless integration, optimal performance, and the ability to stay agile in the face of evolving industry trends. This chapter delves into the pivotal role of chatbot selection in navigating the complexities of emerging technology, offering insights and best practices to guide stakeholders in making informed and forward-thinking decisions.

Figure 1. Chatbot best practices

UNDERSTANDING CHATBOT SELECTION

Chatbot selection involves a meticulous examination of criteria and considerations essential for aligning these conversational agents with specific organizational needs. This process begins with a clear definition of objectives, requiring a deep dive into the intended purpose of the chatbot within the context of the business. Identifying user expectations and preferences is paramount, emphasizing the significance of user-centric design principles to ensure a positive and effective interaction. Beyond functionality, technological aspects must be weighed, including the choice of development platforms, scalability, and integration capabilities with existing systems (Singh et al., 2020). Successful chatbot selection hinges on a comprehensive understanding of the business requirements, user dynamics, and the technological ecosystem, allowing organizations to harness the full potential of these AI-driven tools while strategically positioning themselves for future developments in the chatbot landscape. A best practice related to the chatbot is shared in Figure 1.1.

Defining the Criteria for Selecting Chatbots

Choosing an appropriate chatbot entails evaluating various parameters to make sure that the selected solution is in line with the specific requirements and objectives of the organization. Here are key criteria for selecting chatbots:

- Purpose and Objectives: Clearly define the purpose of implementing a chatbot and establish specific objectives. Whether it's improving customer support, streamlining processes, or enhancing user engagement, having a well-defined purpose guides the selection process.
- User Experience (UX): Prioritize user-centric design by assessing the chatbot's ability to deliver a seamless and intuitive user experience. Consider factors such as conversational flow, ease of interaction, and overall accessibility to cater to user preferences.
- Integration Capabilities: Evaluate the chatbot's compatibility with existing systems, databases, and communication channels. Seamless integration ensures that the chatbot becomes a cohesive part of the organization's technology ecosystem.

- Scalability: Anticipate future growth and technological advancements by selecting a chatbot solution that is scalable. The chosen chatbot should be able to accommodate increased usage, additional features, and evolving business requirements.
- Natural Language Processing (NLP) and AI Capabilities: Assess the chatbot's capabilities in natural language understanding and processing (Bhambri et al., 2021). Advanced AI features enable the chatbot to comprehend user queries, learn from interactions, and provide more intelligent and context-aware responses.
- Security and Compliance: Prioritize the security of user data and ensure compliance with relevant regulations. The chatbot must comply with data protection requirements, and there should be implemented mechanisms to protect sensitive information shared during exchanges.
- Analytics and Reporting: Look for chatbots that provide robust analytics and reporting features. Monitoring key performance indicators (KPIs) allows for ongoing assessment, optimization, and the ability to measure the chatbot's impact on organizational goals.
- Customization and Flexibility: Choose a chatbot solution that offers customization to tailor its functionalities to specific business needs. Flexibility in adapting to changing requirements ensures the chatbot remains relevant over time.
- Multichannel Support: Take into account the chatbot's capacity to function across diverse communication channels, encompassing websites, messaging applications, and social networking platforms. A versatile chatbot enhances the organization's outreach and engagement.
- Vendor Reputation and Support: Evaluate the reputation and experience of the chatbot vendor. Assess the level of support, documentation, and training provided, as a reliable vendor contributes significantly to the success of the chatbot implementation.

Identifying the Role of Chatbots in Specific Contexts

Chatbots play diverse and pivotal roles across various contexts, revolutionizing the way organizations interact with their audiences. In customer support, chatbots serve as instant, 24/7 assistants, addressing inquiries, troubleshooting issues, and providing information with efficiency and immediacy. Within e-commerce, chatbots facilitate seamless shopping experiences by aiding in product recommendations, order tracking, and personalized assistance. In the healthcare sector, they enhance patient engagement by offering medical information, scheduling appointments, and providing medication reminders (Marsico and Budiu, 2018). In the realm of education, chatbots contribute to personalized learning experiences, offering real-time assistance and educational resources. Moreover, in internal corporate settings, they streamline HR processes, assist employees, and foster efficient communication. The adaptability of chatbots across these diverse contexts highlights their transformative impact on enhancing accessibility, engagement, and operational efficiency in various industries and sectors.

Considering the Integration With Existing Systems

A critical aspect of chatbot selection is the seamless integration with existing systems, ensuring that the chosen chatbot becomes an integral and harmonious component of the organizational infrastructure. Ensuring compatibility with existing databases, communication platforms, and customer relationship management (CRM) systems is of utmost importance. The chosen chatbot must effortlessly communicate with these systems in order to deliver precise and current responses. The integration capabilities also encompass the ability to ensure a unified user experience across various channels, including websites, mobile applications, and social media platforms. This integration not only enhances operational efficiency but also maximizes the value of existing investments in technology. By carefully considering and assessing how a chatbot aligns with and complements the organization's current technological landscape, businesses can avoid disruptions and leverage the full potential of chatbots to augment their processes and communication channels.

DEFINING OBJECTIVES AND REQUIREMENTS

Objectives definitions and requirements specification processes involves a meticulous examination of the intended purpose of the chatbot, whether it be improving customer service, automating repetitive tasks, or enhancing user engagement. Clear objectives set the framework for identifying specific requirements, encompassing factors such as functionality, scalability, and integration capabilities. By articulating precise goals and needs, organizations can effectively narrow down the options, selecting a chatbot solution that not only meets immediate requirements but also aligns strategically with the broader vision of the organization (Dignum and Dignum, 2018). This clarity in defining objectives and requirements serves as a guiding principle throughout the selection process, facilitating a more focused and successful implementation of chatbot technology.

Establishing Clear Objectives for Implementing Chatbots

Establishing clear objectives for implementing chatbots is a strategic imperative that lays the foundation for a successful integration within an organization. The process involves a thorough examination of business goals, whether they revolve around improving customer service efficiency, increasing user engagement, or automating specific workflows. Clear objectives provide a roadmap for selecting the right chatbot features, determining the desired level of automation, and aligning the technology with the organization's broader mission. Whether the focus is on enhancing operational efficiency, reducing response times, or delivering personalized user experiences, well-defined objectives not only guide the selection process but also serve as key performance indicators (KPIs) for evaluating the chatbot's success in meeting organizational targets. This clarity of purpose ensures that the implemented chatbot not only addresses immediate needs but also contributes strategically to the overarching objectives of the organization.

Identifying Specific Requirements Based on Organizational Needs

Identifying specific requirements based on organizational needs is a crucial step in the chatbot selection process, as it involves a meticulous examination of the unique demands and objectives of the organization (Pereira and Nogueira, 2018). This entails engaging stakeholders across different departments to determine the precise functions the chatbot should perform, understanding the particular pain points it should address, and aligning its capabilities with overarching business goals. Whether the focus is on customer engagement, internal process optimization, or data analysis, a thorough exploration of organizational needs allows for the establishment of clear benchmarks and criteria for the chatbot. By tailoring the selection process to these specific requirements, organizations ensure that the chosen chatbot not only meets current needs but also provides a scalable and adaptable solution that can evolve with the organization's dynamic landscape (Rani et al., 2023b). This strategic approach sets the foundation for a successful integration that aligns the chatbot's functionalities with the intricacies of the organization it is designed to serve.

Aligning Chatbot Features With Business Goals

Aligning chatbot features with business goals is a critical aspect of ensuring the strategic impact and relevance of these conversational agents within an organization. This process involves a careful examination of the broader objectives and KPIs that define success for the business. By identifying specific functionalities and capabilities that directly contribute to achieving these goals, organizations can tailor the chatbot's features to enhance customer experiences, streamline processes, or drive specific business outcomes (Clark, 2019). Whether the aim is to increase customer engagement, boost sales, or optimize internal operations, aligning chatbot features with business goals ensures that the technology serves as a purposeful asset rather than a standalone tool. This strategic alignment not only maximizes the return on investment but also positions the chatbot as an integral component of the organizational strategy, capable of driving tangible and measurable results in line with the overarching business vision.

USER-CENTRIC DESIGN CONSIDERATIONS

User-centric design considerations are paramount in the selection of chatbots, as they directly influence the overall effectiveness and acceptance of these conversational agents. Prioritizing the user experience entails a meticulous focus on designing chatbots that are intuitive, engaging, and capable of delivering seamless interactions. Understanding user preferences and behaviors becomes fundamental, guiding decisions on conversational flow, language tone, and the incorporation of visual elements. Ensuring accessibility for users of varying technical proficiency is crucial, fostering inclusivity in engagement. Moreover, iterative testing and user feedback loops should be integral to the design process, allowing for continuous refinement based on real-world user interactions. By prioritizing the user in the design process, organizations may develop chatbots that effectively serve their intended functions while also connecting with users, resulting in favorable experiences and continued user acceptance.

Importance of User Experience in Chatbot Selection

A well-designed chatbot enhances user satisfaction, engagement, and overall usability. A user-friendly and intuitive interface is essential for facilitating seamless navigation and interaction with the chatbot, irrespective of the users' technical proficiency. Conversational flow, language tone, and response clarity play pivotal roles in shaping a positive user experience. A carefully crafted UX also considers the context in which the chatbot operates, tailoring its design to suit the specific needs and expectations of the target audience (Bakshi et al., 2021). By prioritizing user experience in chatbot selection, organizations can foster better communication, build trust, and ultimately drive user adoption, contributing to the overall success of the chatbot implementation within the intended environment.

Design Principles for User-Friendly Chatbots

Designing user-friendly chatbots involves adhering to key principles that prioritize a positive user experience and seamless interaction. Here are design principles for creating user-friendly chatbots:

- Clarity and Simplicity: Keep the conversation and interface clear, concise, and straightforward. Avoid unnecessary complexity in language and design to ensure users can easily understand and navigate the chatbot.

- NLP: Incorporate sophisticated NLP functionalities to empower the chatbot with the ability to comprehend and react to user inputs in a conversational & human-like fashion. This enhances the user's perception of interacting with an intelligent and responsive system.

- Context Awareness: Design the chatbot to understand and remember the context of the conversation. This allows for more coherent and relevant responses, creating a more natural and personalized user experience.

- Progressive Disclosure: Present information gradually and only when necessary. Avoid overwhelming users with too much information at once, and provide additional details as the conversation progresses.

- Feedback and Confirmation: Offer immediate feedback to user inputs, confirming that the chatbot has understood the query or command. Clear confirmation messages help users feel confident in the chatbot's capabilities.

- Personalization: Customize interactions according to user choices, past behaviour, or demographic information. Personalization amplifies user interaction and imbues the chatbot with a sense of relevance and value to each unique user.

- Multimodal Interaction: Integrate various modes of interaction, such as text, images, buttons, and quick replies, to cater to different user preferences. This ensures a dynamic and engaging chatbot experience.

- Error Handling: Design the chatbot to handle errors gracefully. Provide clear and friendly error messages, along with suggestions or guidance on how to correct the issue, to prevent user frustration.

- User Guidance and Assistance: Incorporate guidance prompts and assistance options to help users understand what the chatbot can do and how to interact with it effectively. This is particularly important for first-time users.

- Consistency: Ensure a uniform design and conversational tone throughout the entire engagement. Consistency enhances the user experience by creating a feeling of familiarity and predictability, hence improving the user-friendliness of the chatbot.

- Accessibility: Guarantee the chatbot's accessibility to users with a wide range of abilities. To ensure inclusivity for all users, it is important to take into account many elements like font size, color contrast, & voice options while designing the chatbot.

- Continuous Improvement: Develop systems for gathering user feedback and conducting data analytics to pinpoint areas that require enhancement. Consistently update and enhance the chatbot in response to user interactions and evolving requirements.

Addressing Potential User Concerns and Preferences

Addressing potential user concerns and preferences is a critical aspect of user-centric design considerations when selecting chatbots. It involves a proactive approach to anticipate and mitigate issues that users may have during interactions with chatbots, ensuring a positive user experience. To achieve this, developers and designers should:

- Transparency: Clearly communicate the capabilities and limitations of the chatbot to set realistic user expectations. Transparency helps users understand what the chatbot can do and fosters trust in the interaction.

- Privacy and Security: Assure users that their data is handled securely and in compliance with privacy regulations. Clearly outline the data protection measures in place, addressing concerns about the confidentiality and safety of personal information shared during interactions.

- Opt-Out Options: Provide users with clear and easily accessible options to opt out of the chatbot interaction or switch to human assistance if needed. Respecting user autonomy contributes to a positive experience and avoids potential frustration.

- User Control: Allow users to control the pace and direction of the conversation. Offering options for users to skip steps, repeat information, or change preferences ensures a more tailored and user-friendly interaction.

- Human Handover: Implement a seamless transition to human support when the chatbot reaches its limits or when users express a preference for human assistance. This hybrid approach acknowledges the chatbot's role while prioritizing user satisfaction.

- Explanatory Responses: When the chatbot provides information or takes actions, ensure that it can explain its reasoning in a user-friendly manner. This helps users understand the logic behind the chatbot's responses and actions.

- User Feedback Mechanism: Incorporate tools to enable consumers to submit feedback regarding their interaction with the chatbot. The feedback loop is extremely valuable for ongoing enhancement and promptly addressing user issues.

- Cultural Sensitivity: Design the chatbot to be culturally sensitive, considering language nuances, regional preferences, and potential cultural variations in communication styles. Adapting the chatbot to diverse user backgrounds enhances its inclusivity and acceptance.

- Optimized Response Times: Strive for optimal response times to maintain user engagement. Long delays can lead to user frustration, while excessively rapid responses may seem unnatural. Balancing response times contributes to a smoother user experience.

- User Surveys and Testing: Conduct user surveys and usability testing to gather insights into user concerns and preferences. This empirical approach allows for direct feedback and validation of design decisions from the target audience.

TECHNOLOGY AND PLATFORM CONSIDERATIONS

Technology and platform considerations are pivotal in the selection of chatbots, as they directly impact the functionality, scalability, and integration capabilities of the chosen solution (Li et al., 2017). Evaluating different chatbot development platforms is essential, taking into account factors such as ease of use, customization options, and compatibility with existing systems. The technology stack supporting the chatbot, including NLP capabilities and machine learning algorithms, plays a critical role in determining the chatbot's effectiveness in understanding and responding to user inputs (Rani et al., 2023a). Scalability is another crucial consideration, ensuring that the selected chatbot solution can handle increased usage and evolving business needs over time. Additionally, compatibility with various communication channels and tools is vital for creating a versatile chatbot that can seamlessly integrate into the organization's overall technological ecosystem. Making informed decisions in these technology and platform considerations is fundamental to the successful implementation and long-term viability of chatbots in diverse operational contexts.

Exploring Different Chatbot Development Platforms

There are various chatbot development platforms available, each offering unique features and capabilities. Here are some prominent ones:

- Dialogflow (Google): Dialogflow is a widely used platform that provides natural language understanding and processing capabilities. It supports multi-platform deployment and integrates seamlessly with Google Cloud services.
- Microsoft Bot Framework: Developed by Microsoft, this framework offers a comprehensive set of tools for building and deploying chatbots. It supports various channels and is compatible with Microsoft Azure for cloud-based deployment.
- IBM Watson Assistant: Powered by IBM's Watson AI technology, this platform allows developers to create robust chatbots with advanced natural language processing. It integrates with other IBM Cloud services for enhanced functionality.
- Amazon Lex: Part of the Amazon Web Services (AWS) ecosystem, Amazon Lex enables the development of conversational interfaces using the same technology that powers Alexa. It integrates well with other AWS services.
- Wit.ai (Facebook): Acquired by Facebook, Wit.ai provides a platform for building natural language interfaces for applications. It's known for its simplicity and ease of use, supporting both text and voice interactions.
- Botpress: An open-source chatbot development platform, Botpress offers flexibility and customization. It can be deployed on-premises or in the cloud, and it supports integration with various messaging channels.
- Rasa: Rasa is a freely available platform for constructing conversational artificial intelligence. Developers can utilise this platform to construct chatbots with extensive customisation options and precise control over natural language comprehension and dialogue administration.
- Pandorabots: Pandorabots provides a platform for building and deploying chatbots, leveraging AIML (Artificial Intelligence Markup Language). It's suitable for both beginners and developers with more advanced AI requirements.
- ChatterBot: ChatterBot is a Python library for building chatbots. While not a full-fledged platform, it's useful for developers who prefer to have more control over the implementation details of their chatbots.

- SAP Conversational AI: This platform by SAP offers natural language processing capabilities and integrates well with SAP's suite of enterprise solutions. It is designed for creating chatbots that can enhance various business processes.

Evaluating the Technology Stack for Compatibility

The chosen chatbot technology stack should align with the organization's backend systems, databases, and communication channels (Duque, 2021). Compatibility considerations span programming languages, frameworks, and libraries, ensuring that the chatbot can effectively leverage existing resources and APIs. Additionally, assessing the scalability of the technology stack is vital to accommodate potential growth and increased usage. A well-matched technology stack not only facilitates a smoother integration process but also contributes to the chatbot's overall efficiency, responsiveness, and ability to deliver a cohesive user experience across diverse platforms and channels.

Considering Scalability and Future-Proofing

Scalability ensures that the selected chatbot solution can effectively handle increased user interactions, data volumes, and expanded functionalities as usage grows. This adaptability is crucial for accommodating fluctuations in demand and preventing performance bottlenecks. Future-proofing involves selecting a chatbot platform that aligns with emerging industry standards, embraces technological advancements, and can seamlessly integrate with upcoming innovations. By anticipating future requirements and trends, organizations can invest in a chatbot solution that remains robust and relevant over time, minimizing the need for frequent overhauls or migrations and optimizing the long-term value of the chosen technology.

SECURITY AND COMPLIANCE

The chosen chatbot solution must incorporate strong security features, such as encryption methods, authentication processes, & to safeguard user information and uphold confidentiality. Adhering to data protection rules like GDPR, or specific to the industry is essential to prevent legal consequences and establish consumer confidence. Regular security audits and updates should be integral to the chatbot's lifecycle, addressing potential vulnerabilities and ensuring ongoing compliance with evolving security standards. By prioritizing security and compliance in chatbot selection, organizations can instill confidence in users, mitigate risks associated with data breaches, and demonstrate a commitment to ethical and responsible AI practices.

Ensuring Data Security and User Privacy

Ensuring the protection of data and the privacy of users is of utmost importance when choosing a chatbot. Here are key steps to prioritize in this regard:

- Data Encryption: Deploy end-to-end encryption to safeguard the flow of data between users & the chatbot. This guarantees that even if retrieved, the data remains incomprehensible without the corresponding decryption keys.

- Secure Storage Practices: Employ secure storage mechanisms for user data, whether it's stored temporarily for the duration of a session or for longer periods. Utilize encryption for data at rest, limiting access only to authorized personnel.

- Authentication and Authorization: Employ robust user authentication techniques to guarantee that only authorised users can retrieve sensitive data. In addition, use role-based control of access to limit access according to user roles and duties.

- Anonymization and Pseudonymization: Where possible, anonymize or pseudonymize user data to minimize the risk associated with identifiable information. This practice enhances privacy protection while still allowing for effective analysis and usage.

- Regular Security Audits: Perform routine security audits & assessments to detect vulnerabilities and swiftly resolve them. This proactive approach helps in staying ahead of potential threats and maintaining the overall security posture of the chatbot system.

- Compliance with Regulations: Stay informed about and comply with data protection regulations relevant to your industry and region. Understand and adhere to standards such as GDPR, HIPAA, or other applicable frameworks to ensure legal and ethical data handling.

- User Consent and Transparency: Clearly communicate to users how their data will be used and seek their consent before collecting any personally identifiable information. Transparent privacy policies contribute to user trust and confidence.

- Data Minimization: Collect only the data necessary for the chatbot's intended purpose. Minimize the collection of sensitive information to reduce the potential impact of a data breach.

- Regular Updates and Patching: Maintain the chatbot platform & its related software by regularly updating it with the most recent security updates. Regularly update libraries, frameworks, and dependencies to address any known vulnerabilities.

- Secure Integration Points: If the chatbot interacts with other systems or APIs, ensure that these integration points are secure. Validate input data and implement proper error handling to prevent potential security loopholes.

- User Access Controls: Implement stringent access controls to limit who can access, modify, or delete user data. This helps prevent unauthorized access and reduces the risk of data manipulation.

Complying With Relevant Regulations and Standards

Ensuring adherence to pertinent legislation and standards when choosing a chatbot necessitates a proactive stance towards legal and ethical factors (Holopainen and Räisänen, 2019). Prioritise conducting a comprehensive evaluation of the regulatory environment that is relevant to the industry & geographical area of operation. Understanding data protection laws, privacy regulations, and industry-specific standards is paramount. Once these requirements are identified, the chosen chatbot solution should be thoroughly evaluated for its ability to align with and support compliance. This may include implementing robust encryption mechanisms, ensuring secure data storage, and incorporating features that allow users to manage their data preferences. Regular audits and updates should be part of the ongoing maintenance strategy to address changes in regulations and continuously uphold compliance. Additionally, fostering transparency by clearly communicating privacy policies and data usage practices to users contributes to building trust and reinforces an organization's commitment to ethical and lawful use of chatbot technology.

PERFORMANCE METRICS AND ANALYTICS

Performance metrics and analytics play a pivotal role in chatbot selection, providing insights into the effectiveness and impact of the deployed solution. KPIs such as user engagement, completion rates, response times, and user satisfaction metrics are essential for evaluating the chatbot's performance (Bhambri, 2020). Analytics tools integrated into the chatbot solution enable continuous monitoring, allowing organizations to assess user interactions, identify patterns, and refine the chatbot's capabilities over time. These metrics not only serve as indicators of the chatbot's success in meeting business objectives but also guide iterative improvements to enhance user experience. A comprehensive understanding of performance metrics ensures that the selected chatbot aligns with organizational goals, delivers measurable value, and remains adaptable to evolving user needs and expectations.

Implementing Analytics Tools for Monitoring and Improvement

By integrating robust analytics tools into the chatbot infrastructure, organizations gain valuable insights into user interactions, conversation patterns, and performance metrics. These tools allow for real-time monitoring of key indicators such as user engagement, completion rates, and response effectiveness. Informed by this data, stakeholders can identify areas for enhancement, address user pain points, and strategically iterate on the chatbot's design and functionality. The iterative feedback loop facilitated by analytics tools ensures that the chatbot remains agile, responsive to user needs, and aligned with organizational objectives, ultimately contributing to a continuously improving and adaptive conversational experience.

VENDOR EVALUATION AND SELECTION

Developing a comprehensive vendor selection process is essential in choosing the right partner for chatbot implementation. Begin by clearly defining the specific requirements and objectives of the project, outlining the functionalities and features crucial for the organization. Create a list of potential vendors based on industry reputation, recommendations, and research. Develop a thorough Request for Proposal (RFP) or Request for Information (RFI) that includes detailed information about the organization's needs, expected outcomes, and any specific technical or security requirements. This document serves as a guide for potential vendors to submit detailed proposals, allowing for a systematic and objective comparison of offerings. Additionally, consider factors such as the vendor's development methodology, scalability of their solutions, and their ability to provide ongoing support and updates.

When evaluating vendors, reputation, experience, and support are key considerations. Assess the vendor's reputation within the industry by reviewing case studies, client testimonials, and independent reviews (Bhambri, 2021). Evaluate their experience in implementing chatbot solutions, with a focus on projects similar in scale and complexity to yours. Understanding the vendor's track record in delivering successful outcomes is crucial for gauging their reliability and competence. Furthermore, inquire about the level of support offered during and after implementation. A responsive and knowledgeable support team is vital for addressing issues promptly and ensuring the sustained performance of the chatbot.

Negotiating contracts and service level agreements (SLAs) is the final step in vendor selection. Clearly define the scope of work, project timelines, and deliverables in the contract to avoid misunderstandings.

Establish detailed SLAs that cover performance benchmarks, response times, and ongoing maintenance commitments. Negotiate pricing structures, considering factors such as licensing fees, implementation costs, and any additional charges for customization or support beyond standard offerings. Ensure that the contract includes provisions for scalability and flexibility to accommodate future changes or expansions (van et al., 2017). A well-negotiated contract, supported by comprehensive SLAs, sets the foundation for a successful partnership and mitigates potential risks during and after the chatbot implementation process.

CASE STUDIES AND BEST PRACTICES

Case studies and best practices play a crucial role in informing chatbot selection by providing valuable insights gleaned from successful implementations. Begin by examining case studies that showcase instances where chatbots have effectively addressed specific business challenges or enhanced operational efficiency. Analyze the key factors that contributed to success, such as user adoption rates, improved customer satisfaction, or streamlined processes. Learning from these real-world examples allows for a more nuanced understanding of the practical applications and potential benefits of chatbots in diverse industries.

Furthermore, leverage industry best practices to inform the chatbot selection process. Identify common strategies, design principles, and implementation approaches that have proven effective across different use cases. Industry best practices often encompass user-centric design, integration methodologies, and considerations for security and compliance. By aligning chatbot selection with established best practices, organizations can leverage collective wisdom to enhance the likelihood of successful implementation and achieve optimal results.

Drawing insights from real-world scenarios involves gathering feedback and lessons learned from organizations that have implemented chatbots. Engage with industry forums, conferences, and user communities to gain perspectives from practitioners who have hands-on experience with chatbot technologies. Understand the challenges they faced, the solutions implemented, and the overall impact on their business processes. This direct interaction with real-world practitioners provides nuanced insights into both the successes and potential pitfalls of chatbot selection, enabling organizations to make informed decisions based on the experiences of their peers.

Examples With Details of the Commercial Products

When selecting a chatbot for commercial use, it's crucial to thoroughly evaluate the specific needs of your business, the target audience, and the level of customization and integration required. Additionally, consider the scalability and ongoing support provided by the chatbot platform to ensure long-term success. Here are a few examples of commercial chatbot products that are often considered best practices:

- Dialogflow by Google: Dialogflow is known for its natural language processing capabilities, making it easy to build conversational interfaces. It supports various platforms, including web, mobile, and messaging apps. Users can define intents, entities, and contexts to create highly customized chatbots. Integration with other Google Cloud services is seamless. Ensure that your chatbot's training data is well-curated for accurate understanding and responses. Leverage rich media responses for a more engaging user experience.

- Microsoft Bot Framework: Microsoft Bot Framework offers a comprehensive set of tools for building and deploying chatbots across multiple channels, including Microsoft Teams, Slack, and Facebook Messenger. It supports the use of .NET and Node.js for development, providing flexibility for developers. The Bot Framework Composer allows for visual bot building without extensive coding. Leverage Azure Cognitive Services for advanced language understanding and use adaptive cards for interactive and visually appealing responses.

- IBM Watson Assistant: IBM Watson Assistant is powered by AI and machine learning, enabling it to understand user intents and entities accurately. It supports integration with various backend systems and has a user-friendly interface. Users can train the chatbot using intents, entities, and dialog flows. Integration with other IBM Cloud services, such as Watson Discovery, can enhance functionality. Regularly review and update training data to improve the chatbot's performance over time. Take advantage of integrations with analytics tools to monitor user interactions and improve the chatbot's effectiveness.

- ChatGPT API by OpenAI: OpenAI's ChatGPT API offers powerful natural language understanding and generation capabilities. It's versatile and can be used for a wide range of applications, including chatbots. Developers can integrate the ChatGPT API into their applications and tailor conversations based on their specific use cases. It allows for dynamic and interactive conversations with users. Provide clear instructions and context to the chatbot to guide the conversation effectively. Implement proper error handling and fallback mechanisms for situations where the chatbot might not understand user inputs.

CONCLUSION

By synthesizing a comprehensive understanding of user-centric design principles, technology and platform considerations, and adherence to security and compliance, organizations can lay the foundation for successful chatbot implementations. The integration of performance metrics, analytics, and insights from real-world case studies provides a holistic framework for decision-makers to navigate the complexities of chatbot selection.

Emphasizing the significance of strategic chatbot selection extends beyond immediate operational benefits; it becomes a catalyst for digital transformation and enhanced user engagement. A well-selected chatbot not only optimizes current processes but also positions organizations to adapt to emerging technologies and user expectations. As the final word of advice, organizations are encouraged to view chatbot selection not merely as a technological adoption but as a strategic investment that aligns with their long-term objectives. With the right chatbot in place, organizations can propel themselves toward a more agile, user-friendly, and technologically advanced future.

REFERENCES

Bakshi, P., Bhambri, P., & Thapar, V. (2021). A Review Paper on Wireless Sensor Network Techniques in Internet of Things (IoT). *Wesleyan Journal of Research*, *14*(7), 147–160.

Bhambri, P. (2020). Green Compliance. In S. Agarwal (Ed.), *Introduction to Green Computing* (pp. 95–125). AGAR Saliha Publication.

Bhambri, P. (2021). Electronic Evidence. In Textbook of Cyber Heal (pp. 86-120). AGAR Saliha Publication, Tamil Nadu.

Bhambri, P., Singh, M., Jain, A., Dhanoa, I. S., Sinha, V. K., & Lal, S. (2021). Classification of the GENE Expression Data with the Aid of Optimized Feature Selection. *Turkish Journal of Physiotherapy and Rehabilitation, 32*(3), 1158–1167.

Clark, P. (2019). *Chatbot marketing: The ultimate guide.* Springer.

Dignum, V., & Dignum, F. (2018). *Responsible artificial intelligence: How to develop and use AI in a responsible way.* Springer.

Duque, J. (2021). *Mastering Conversational AI with IBM Watson: Design and Develop Conversational Solutions with IBM Watson Assistant.* Packt Publishing.

Holopainen, J., & Räisänen, T. (2019). Designing Chatbots for Better User Experience. In *International Conference on Human-Computer Interaction* (pp. 155-174). Springer.

Jain, A., & Srivastava, S. (2020). *Building Enterprise Chatbots: A Step by Step Approach.* Apress.

Li, S., Kao, C. Y., & Wang, Q. (2017). Building a Chatbot with Serverless Computing and Machine Learning. In *2017 IEEE International Conference on Web Services (ICWS)* (pp. 758-761). IEEE.

Marsico, M. D., & Budiu, R. (2018). *Chatbots: what they are and how to build one (with examples).* Nielsen Norman Group.

Pereira, J., & Nogueira, A. (2018). Chatbots in educational environments: A systematic review. *Computers & Education, 124,* 74–89.

Rajendran, V., & Prasanna, S. R. M. (2018). Intelligent Chatbot for Enabling e-Governance: A Case Study. In *2018 IEEE Calcutta Conference (CALCON)* (pp. 174-177). IEEE.

Rani, S., Bhambri, P., & Kataria, A. (2023b). Integration of IoT, Big Data, and Cloud Computing Technologies. *Big Data, Cloud Computing and IoT: Tools and Applications.*

Rani, S., Bhambri, P., Kataria, A., & Khang, A. (2023a). Smart City Ecosystem: Concept, Sustainability, Design Principles, and Technologies. In AI-Centric Smart City Ecosystems (pp. 1-20). CRC Press.

Rani, S., Pareek, P. K., Kaur, J., Chauhan, M., & Bhambri, P. (2023c). Quantum Machine Learning in Healthcare: Developments and Challenges. *Paper presented at the International Conference on Integrated Circuits and Communication Systems,* (pp. 1-7). IEEE. 10.1109/ICICACS57338.2023.10100075

Singh, G., Singh, M., & Bhambri, P. (2020). Artificial Intelligence based Flying Car. In *Proceedings of the International Congress on Sustainable Development through Engineering Innovations* (pp. 216-227). IEEE.

Singh, M., Bhambri, P., Dhanoa, I. S., Jain, A., & Kaur, K. (2021). Data Mining Model for Predicting Diabetes. *Annals of the Romanian Society for Cell Biology, 25*(4), 6702–6712.

van Velsen, L., van der Geest, T., & Klaassen, R. (2017). From usability to user experience: A systematic framework for chatbot design. *Proceedings of the 21st International Academic Mindtrek Conference,* (pp. 126-133). IEEE.

KEY TERMS AND DEFINITIONS

Chatbot Selection Criteria: The criteria and variables utilized to assess and select a chatbot solution. This encompasses technological, functional, and business factors that are in line with the organization's requirements.

Integration Challenges: Challenges faced when integrating a chatbot into current IT systems or communication channels. Strategies are created to address these problems and guarantee seamless integration.

Iterative Assessment: A continuous and iterative assessment process that entails continuing monitoring and enhancement of a chatbot's performance using feedback, analytics, and evolving corporate requirements.

Key Performance Indicators (KPIs): Measurable criteria for assessing the performance and efficiency of a chatbot. Examples include response time, user happiness, and completion rates.

Natural Language Processing (NLP): Natural language processing is a branch of artificial intelligence that centers on the communication between computers and human language. Natural Language Processing (NLP) in chatbots allows for the comprehension and creation of language that mimics human speech, enhancing communication.

Security and Compliance: Ensuring user data protection, privacy maintenance, and compliance with legislation and standards when using chatbots to prevent security breaches and legal difficulties.

Service Level Agreements (SLAs): Official contracts detailing the terms, conditions, and expectations between a chatbot purchaser and a seller, encompassing performance measurements, duties, and support obligations.

Technology Stack: The amalgamation of programming languages, frameworks, libraries, and tools utilized in the creation of a chatbot. It encompasses the complete technology infrastructure that backs the chatbot.

User-Centric Design: A user-centered design strategy that emphasizes creating chatbots that are intuitive, user-friendly, and adaptable to user preferences to improve user happiness.

Vendor Selection Process: The methodical process of selecting a chatbot vendor based on criteria like reputation, experience, support services, and compatibility with corporate needs.

Chapter 8
Issues Related to Chatbots

Pankaj Bhambri

https://orcid.org/0000-0003-4437-4103

Guru Nanak Dev Engineering College, Ludhiana, India

Sita Rani

https://orcid.org/0000-0003-2778-0214

Guru Nanak Dev Engineering College, Ludhiana, India

ABSTRACT

The discourse encompasses multifaceted aspects, beginning with an examination of user-centric challenges. The text delves into issues such as natural language understanding limitations, context awareness, and the ethical considerations surrounding user privacy and data security. Furthermore, the chapter provides insights into technical challenges, addressing the complexities of designing robust algorithms, optimizing response generation, and mitigating biases within chatbot interactions. The chapter finishes by highlighting the significance of continuous research and development in order to address the obstacles and fully use the capabilities of chatbot technology in various applications, as the chatbot landscape continues to expand. This chapter provides a valuable resource for developers, researchers, as well as practitioners in the discipline of chatbot technology. It offers a detailed understanding of the complex challenges that need to be addressed in order to improve user experiences and responsibly implement emerging chatbot technologies.

INTRODUCTION

Chatbots have gained significant popularity in various industries, but they come with their own set of challenges and issues. One prominent concern is the potential for misunderstandings and miscommunications. Despite advancements in natural language processing, chatbots may struggle to comprehend the nuances and context of human conversation. This limitation can lead to inaccurate responses, frustration for users, and even damage to the reputation of the organizations implementing the chatbots. Ensuring effective communication requires ongoing refinement of chatbot algorithms and continuous monitoring to address emerging issues. Another key issue revolves around privacy and data security. Chatbots often

DOI: 10.4018/979-8-3693-1830-0.ch008

handle sensitive information, and any mishandling of data can result in severe consequences. Users may be hesitant to share personal details or concerns with a chatbot, fearing unauthorized access or misuse of their information. Developers and organizations must implement robust security measures, including end-to-end encryption and strict data protection policies, to instill confidence in users and comply with privacy regulations. Additionally, the challenge of ethical considerations in chatbot development cannot be overlooked. There is a risk of bias being introduced into the chatbot's responses, reflecting the biases present in the data used for training. Developers must be vigilant in addressing bias and ensuring fairness, transparency, and inclusivity in chatbot interactions. Striking the right balance between automation and human oversight is crucial to prevent unintended consequences and ethical lapses in the deployment of chatbots across diverse user populations. As the use of chatbots continues to grow, navigating these issues is essential for creating reliable, secure, and ethical conversational AI experiences.

The chapter is structured in a logical flow, addressing various aspects of challenges associated with chatbot technology. The first section (Section 1) serves as an introduction, providing background information, stating the purpose of the chapter, and outlining its scope and objectives. The subsequent sections (Section 2 and Section 3) delve into the challenges, categorized into user-centric and technical challenges. User-centric challenges (Section 2) explore issues related to natural language understanding, context awareness, and ethical considerations. Technical challenges (Section 3) focus on designing robust algorithms, optimizing response generation, and mitigating biases in chatbot interactions. The chapter then progresses to present case studies and examples (Section 4), illustrating real-world instances of challenges outlined earlier. This section provides concrete examples of user-centric challenges and technical issues faced by chatbots. Moving forward, the chapter takes a forward-looking perspective (Section 5), discussing emerging trends in chatbot technology, advancements in natural language understanding, context awareness, and ethical frameworks. It also explores ongoing research and development efforts, emphasizing collaboration across disciplines and the role of user feedback in iterative development. The concluding section (Section 6) recaps key challenges discussed throughout the chapter, highlights the importance of addressing these issues in chatbot technology, and issues a call to action for researchers and developers to contribute to the continuous improvement of chatbot systems. The overall structure of the chapter provides a comprehensive exploration of challenges, supported by real-world examples, and concludes with a forward-looking perspective and a call to action for the community involved in chatbot development.

Purpose and Flow of Discussions

The chapter serves as a comprehensive exploration of the challenges encountered in the development and deployment of chatbot technology. It begins with a detailed introduction, laying the groundwork by presenting the background, purpose of the chapter, and its scope and objectives. The overarching goal is to provide readers with a clear understanding of the multifaceted issues surrounding chatbots. The chapter then delves into two main categories of challenges: User-Centric Challenges and Technical Challenges. Under User-Centric Challenges, the focus is on issues related to Natural Language Understanding (NLU), including ambiguities and contextual nuances, challenges in multilingual environments, context awareness, and ethical considerations such as user privacy and data security (Clark, 2019). Technical Challenges are explored through topics like designing robust algorithms, optimizing response generation, and mitigating biases in chatbot interactions. The subsequent sections of the chapter present case studies and examples that illustrate real-world instances of both user-centric and technical challenges. This practical approach aims to ground theoretical concepts in tangible scenarios, providing readers with a deeper understanding of the complexities involved. The chapter then shifts towards a forward-looking perspective, discussing emerging trends in chatbot technology, advancements in NLU and context awareness, and the importance of ethical frameworks and guidelines. Ongoing research and development efforts are highlighted, emphasizing collaboration across disciplines and the role of user feedback in iterative development. In the concluding section, the chapter recaps key challenges discussed throughout and underscores the importance of addressing these issues in chatbot technology. It concludes with a compelling call to action for researchers and developers, urging them to actively contribute to the improvement and advancement of chatbot technologies in a responsible and user-centric manner (Dignum and Dignum, 2018). Overall, the chapter offers a structured and informative journey through the landscape of challenges and opportunities in the field of chatbots.

Adopted Methodology

The methodology employed in this study involves a comprehensive and multi-faceted approach. The research begins with an in-depth exploration of user-centric challenges, addressing aspects such as natural language understanding limitations, context awareness, and ethical considerations. Technical challenges are then investigated, focusing on the design of robust algorithms, optimization of response generation, and the mitigation of biases in chatbot interactions. The study incorporates case studies and examples, examining real-world instances of challenges faced by users and technical issues in action. The forward-looking perspective delves into emerging trends in chatbot technology, emphasizing advancements in natural language understanding, context awareness, and ethical frameworks. Additionally, ongoing research and development efforts are explored, emphasizing interdisciplinary collaboration and the iterative role of user feedback. The conclusion provides a recapitulation of key challenges, underscores the importance of addressing these issues in chatbot technology, and issues a call to action for researchers and developers to contribute to the evolution and improvement of chatbot systems.

USER-CENTRIC CHALLENGES

User-centric challenges related to chatbots encompass various aspects that can impact the user experience. One significant challenge is the issue of understanding and interpreting user input accurately. Chatbots heavily rely on natural language processing (NLP) to comprehend user queries, and they may struggle with colloquial language, ambiguity, or context-dependent queries. Users often expect a seamless conversation with a chatbot, but when the bot fails to grasp the nuances of their language, it can lead to frustration and a suboptimal user experience.

Another user-centric challenge involves the limitations of chatbots in handling complex or emotionally charged interactions. While chatbots excel at handling routine tasks and providing information, they may struggle in scenarios that require empathy, understanding of emotions, or nuanced responses. Users may find it disconcerting or unsatisfying when a chatbot cannot adequately address their emotional needs or complex inquiries. Striking the right balance between automation and human-like interaction remains a challenge, as creating a genuinely user-centric chatbot involves not only functional proficiency but also emotional intelligence to cater to diverse user expectations and sensitivities. Overcoming these challenges is crucial for enhancing the overall effectiveness and acceptance of chatbot technologies in various domains.

NLU Limitations

NLU is a critical component of chatbots and other conversational AI systems. While significant progress has been made in the field, there are still several limitations and user-centric challenges associated with NLU in chatbots:

- Ambiguity Handling: NLU systems may struggle to handle ambiguous user queries or statements that can be interpreted in multiple ways. Users may receive inaccurate or irrelevant responses, leading to frustration and a poor user experience.
- Contextual Understanding: Understanding and maintaining context across multiple turns in a conversation can be challenging for NLU systems. Lack of contextual understanding may result in misinterpretations, leading to errors or irrelevant responses.
- Nuanced Language and Sarcasm: NLU systems may have difficulty understanding nuanced language, sarcasm, or humor. Users employing sarcasm or nuanced language may not be accurately understood, leading to inappropriate or unintended responses.
- Limited Vocabulary and Domain Knowledge: NLU models may not be well-versed in specific domains or have a limited vocabulary, impacting their ability to understand industry-specific terms (Bhambri et al., 2021). Users seeking information in specialized fields may receive inaccurate or incomplete responses.
- Out-of-Scope Queries: NLU systems may struggle to recognize when a user query falls outside their predefined scope. Users may receive incorrect responses or be left without a clear indication that their query is out of scope, leading to confusion.
- Data Bias and Sensitivity: NLU models may be trained on biased data, leading to biased or insensitive responses. Users may encounter inappropriate or offensive content, negatively affecting user trust and satisfaction.
- User Privacy Concerns: NLU systems may inadvertently process sensitive information or violate user privacy. Users may be hesitant to share personal information or engage in sensitive conversations, affecting the effectiveness of the chatbot.
- Training Data Limitations: NLU models heavily rely on training data, and if the data is not diverse enough, the model may struggle with understanding various user inputs. Limited training data may result in poor generalization and adaptability to diverse user inputs.
- Lack of Explainability: NLU models, especially complex deep learning models, may lack transparency and explainability. Users may be unsure why a particular response was generated, leading to a lack of trust in the system.
- Multilingual Challenges: NLU models may not perform equally well across multiple languages, impacting the user experience for non-native speakers. Users communicating in languages other than the primary language of the NLU model may experience reduced accuracy and comprehension.

Ambiguities and Contextual Nuances

Ambiguities arise when a single utterance can have multiple interpretations, leading to potential misunderstandings by chatbots. For instance, words with multiple meanings, homophones, or vague references can confound NLU systems (Rani et al., 2023a). Contextual nuances add another layer of complexity, as understanding a user's intent often relies on grasping the context of the conversation. Shifting topics, sarcasm, and cultural references can pose challenges for chatbots in accurately interpreting user input. These ambiguities and contextual nuances make it difficult for chatbots to consistently provide accurate and contextually relevant responses, leading to user frustration and diminished user experience.

User-centric challenges further compound these limitations as individuals may have diverse communication styles, preferences, and expectations. Users may express themselves in colloquial language, use slang, or have unique linguistic patterns that may not align with the chatbot's predefined language models. Additionally, individual user preferences for brevity or verbosity can influence the effectiveness of a chatbot's response. Adapting to these user-centric challenges requires chatbots to be highly adaptable and context-aware, which remains a formidable task in the dynamic landscape of natural language communication (Jain and Srivastava, 2020). Addressing these limitations is crucial to enhance the overall effectiveness of chatbots and ensure a more seamless interaction between users and artificial intelligence systems.

Challenges in Multilingual Environments

Multilingual environments pose several challenges in NLU, particularly in the context of chatbots. Here are some key challenges and limitations:

- Language Diversity: Multilingual environments often involve a wide variety of languages with different structures, grammatical rules, and nuances. Building models that can effectively understand and generate content in diverse languages is challenging.
- Limited Training Data: Availability of labeled training data in multiple languages can be limited, especially for languages with fewer speakers. This scarcity makes it challenging to train robust and accurate NLU models for all languages.
- Translation Quality: Many chatbots rely on translation services to handle multilingual conversations. However, translation errors can occur, leading to misunderstandings and incorrect responses. Additionally, idiomatic expressions and cultural context may not translate accurately.
- Cultural Sensitivity: Different languages are often tied to specific cultures, and understanding cultural nuances is crucial for effective communication. Chatbots may struggle to grasp cultural references or may unintentionally offend users due to cultural differences.
- Code-Switching: In multilingual environments, users may switch between languages within a single conversation. Code-switching poses a challenge as models need to understand and respond appropriately to mixed-language inputs.
- Ambiguity Handling: Some phrases or words may have different meanings in different languages or contexts. NLU models need to be capable of disambiguating and understanding the intended meaning, which can be challenging in multilingual scenarios.

- Resource Intensiveness: Implementing and maintaining language support for a wide range of languages requires significant resources, both in terms of computing power and development efforts. Small teams or resource-constrained projects may struggle to cover a diverse set of languages.

- Real-time Adaptability: Languages evolve over time, and new slang, expressions, or words may emerge. NLU models must be able to adapt in real-time to changes in language use, which can be a continuous challenge.

- User Expectations: Users from different linguistic backgrounds may have varying expectations regarding the capabilities of the chatbot. Meeting diverse user expectations and providing a consistent user experience across languages is a substantial challenge.

- Legal and Compliance Issues: Multilingual environments may involve different legal and regulatory frameworks, requiring compliance with various data privacy laws and regulations. Managing and ensuring compliance across languages adds complexity to chatbot development.

Context Awareness

Context awareness in chatbots poses user-centric challenges as it requires these conversational agents to understand and adapt to the dynamic context of user interactions. One key challenge lies in maintaining continuity and coherence in conversations, as users may introduce new topics or shift contexts seamlessly. Ensuring that chatbots can accurately interpret user intent, remember previous interactions, and appropriately respond to context changes becomes crucial for a seamless user experience. Additionally, striking the right balance between being proactive in anticipating user needs and respecting privacy boundaries is a delicate task (Rani et al., 2023b). The challenge lies in developing chatbots that can intelligently leverage context to enhance user engagement while being mindful of user preferences and data sensitivity, ultimately striving for a more personalized and user-friendly conversational interface.

Handling Dynamic Contexts

Handling dynamic contexts in the context awareness of user-centric challenges related to chatbots is a pivotal aspect that demands adept solutions. Chatbots, designed to engage in natural and contextually relevant conversations, face the challenge of adapting to dynamic user contexts. Users may shift topics, express changing sentiments, or introduce new elements into the conversation, requiring chatbots to comprehend and respond intelligently. Addressing this challenge involves advanced natural language processing algorithms, machine learning models, and context management systems. Ensuring seamless transitions between various conversational contexts enhances user satisfaction, as it reflects the chatbot's ability to understand and respond coherently to the evolving dynamics of user interactions, ultimately contributing to an improved user-centric chatbot experience.

Personalization Challenges

Personalization in the context of chatbots presents several challenges, particularly in the realm of user-centric context awareness. One key challenge lies in accurately understanding and interpreting user intent, preferences, and context dynamically. Achieving a seamless and personalized conversational experience requires the chatbot to adapt to users' changing needs, emotions, and contextual information. Striking the right balance between customization and privacy is another hurdle, as users may be concerned about the level of personal data being utilized to enhance the interaction. Furthermore, ensuring that the chatbot can effectively handle diverse user backgrounds, language nuances, and cultural variations adds complexity to the personalization process. Addressing these challenges demands sophisticated algorithms, ethical considerations, and continuous improvement strategies to enhance user satisfaction while respecting privacy boundaries.

Ethical Considerations

The development and deployment of chatbots raise several ethical considerations, especially when it comes to user-centric challenges. Here are some key ethical considerations associated with chatbots:

- Transparency and Disclosure: Chatbots should clearly disclose their nature and inform users that they are interacting with a machine rather than a human. Misleading users about the identity of the conversational partner can erode trust and lead to unintended consequences.
- Informed Consent: Users should be aware of how their data is being used and give explicit consent for the collection and processing of their information. Obtaining informed consent is crucial to respecting users' autonomy and ensuring they are comfortable with the way their data is handled.
- Privacy and Data Security: Chatbots often handle sensitive user information, and it's essential to ensure robust security measures to protect user data. Breaches of privacy can lead to significant harm to individuals, including identity theft or unauthorized access to personal information.
- Bias and Fairness: Bias may be inadvertently introduced into chatbots through the training data, leading to unfair treatment of certain user groups. Unfair bias can perpetuate discrimination and reinforce existing societal inequalities, impacting users negatively.
- User Empowerment: Users should have the ability to understand and control their interactions with chatbots, including the option to easily stop or modify conversations. Lack of user control may lead to frustration, discomfort, or unintended consequences, emphasizing the need for user empowerment.
- User Well-Being: Chatbots should be designed to prioritize user well-being, considering potential negative psychological impacts. Unintentional harm, such as emotional distress caused by inappropriate responses, should be minimized, and mechanisms for reporting and addressing such issues should be in place.
- Accessibility: Ensuring that chatbots are accessible to users with disabilities is essential for providing an inclusive experience. Excluding any segment of the population from the benefits of chatbot interactions goes against the principles of fairness and equality.
- Accountability and Responsibility: Determining responsibility in case of errors or harm caused by chatbots can be challenging. Establishing clear lines of accountability ensures that developers, organizations, and systems are held responsible for the actions and impact of their chatbots.
- Continuous Monitoring and Improvement: Regularly monitoring and updating chatbots to improve performance and address ethical concerns can be resource-intensive. Ongoing efforts to enhance chatbots demonstrate a commitment to ethical considerations and responsiveness to user feedback.
- Cultural Sensitivity: Chatbots should be culturally sensitive and avoid reinforcing stereotypes or causing offense. Failing to consider cultural nuances can lead to misunderstandings, alienate users, or perpetuate harmful stereotypes.

User Privacy Concerns

Users worry about the collection and storage of sensitive information during interactions with chatbots, raising questions about the transparency of data handling practices, the extent of consent, and the overall security measures in place. Striking a balance between providing personalized and efficient services while safeguarding user privacy is paramount to establishing trust in the use of chatbots, emphasizing the need for robust privacy policies, clear communication, and stringent data protection mechanisms (Rani et al., 2023c). Addressing these privacy concerns is essential for the responsible development and deployment of chatbot technologies, ensuring that users feel confident in their interactions and maintain control over their personal information.

Data Security Issues

Data security is a paramount ethical consideration in the realm of user-centric challenges associated with chatbots. One significant issue revolves around the collection, storage, and processing of user data. Chatbots often gather a plethora of sensitive information, ranging from personal details to financial data, to enhance user interactions. However, the ethical dilemma arises when users question the transparency and consent surrounding the use of their data. Ensuring that users are well-informed about how their data will be utilized and implementing robust security measures to protect this information from unauthorized access or breaches is crucial. Failure to address these concerns can erode user trust and compromise the ethical foundation of chatbot interactions.

Another critical aspect of data security in the context of chatbots pertains to the potential misuse of user information. As chatbots become more sophisticated in understanding and responding to user queries, there is a risk of unintentional disclosure of sensitive details. This could result in privacy breaches, identity theft, or even manipulation of individuals based on their disclosed information. Ethical considerations demand that developers and organizations establish stringent safeguards to prevent such mishandling of data. Employing encryption, regular security audits, and adopting privacy-by-design principles can help mitigate these risks and uphold the ethical responsibility to protect user data in the evolving landscape of chatbot interactions.

TECHNICAL CHALLENGES

Developing and implementing chatbots involve several technical challenges that need to be addressed for effective and seamless interactions. Some of the key technical challenges related to chatbots include:

- NLP: NLP systems must understand the nuances of natural language, including ambiguous phrases and context-dependent meanings (Singh et al., 2020). Dealing with words that have multiple meanings (polysemy) or different words with similar meanings (synonymy) requires advanced semantic analysis.
- Intent Recognition: Identifying user intents is crucial for providing relevant responses. Achieving high accuracy in intent recognition is a continuous challenge.
- Entity Recognition: Recognizing specific entities within user input, such as names, locations, and dates, is challenging due to variations in how users express the same information.

- Multilingual Support: Supporting multiple languages adds complexity, as each language may have unique linguistic features and cultural nuances.
- User Context Management: Keeping track of user context throughout a conversation is essential for providing coherent and relevant responses, especially in longer interactions.
- Personalization: Building and maintaining user profiles to understand preferences and personalize interactions requires robust systems for data storage and retrieval (van Velsen et al., 2017).
- Integration with External Systems: Connecting with external databases, services, or APIs to fetch real-time information requires seamless integration and error handling.
- Scalability: Scalability is crucial for chatbots that may experience varying levels of usage. Handling a large number of concurrent users without degradation in performance is a challenge.
- Learning and Adaptation: Implementing systems that can learn from user interactions and adapt over time to improve accuracy and relevance in responses.
- Security and Privacy: Ensuring that sensitive information shared during conversations is handled securely and in compliance with data protection regulations.
- Platform Compatibility: Ensuring the chatbot functions seamlessly across various platforms, such as web browsers, mobile apps, and messaging applications.
- User Experience (UX) Design: Designing a natural and user-friendly conversational flow that guides users through interactions without causing confusion or frustration.
- Error Handling: Designing chatbots to handle errors gracefully and guide users back on track when misunderstandings or errors occur.

Designing Robust Algorithms

Designing robust algorithms for chatbots poses several technical challenges, primarily centered around natural language understanding and context-awareness. One major hurdle lies in creating algorithms that can accurately interpret and respond to the diverse and nuanced ways in which users express themselves. Natural language is inherently ambiguous, and understanding the subtle nuances, sarcasm, or colloquialisms requires sophisticated language models and semantic analysis. Moreover, chatbots need to exhibit context-aware behavior to maintain coherent and meaningful conversations (Singh et al., 2021). This involves developing algorithms that can keep track of the conversation's context, understand references, and adapt responses accordingly. Striking the right balance between being contextually aware and respecting user privacy is another challenge, as chatbots must be able to retain relevant information while ensuring the security and confidentiality of user data.

Another critical challenge in designing robust chatbot algorithms is handling ambiguity and handling errors gracefully. Users may input incomplete or vague queries, and the algorithms must be equipped to infer user intent accurately and seek clarifications when needed. Error-handling mechanisms should be implemented to prevent the chatbot from providing misleading or irrelevant information in case of misunderstood queries. Additionally, incorporating machine learning techniques for continuous improvement is essential, enabling the chatbot to learn from user interactions and adapt over time. This iterative learning process demands careful consideration to avoid biases and ethical concerns, ensuring that the chatbot evolves into a reliable and unbiased conversational partner. Balancing the trade-off between customization for individual users and maintaining generalization for broader user bases further complicates the task of designing robust algorithms for chatbots.

Handling Varying Input Structures

The dynamic nature of user inputs, ranging from concise and structured queries to ambiguous and unstructured language, requires adaptive algorithms capable of understanding and processing diverse linguistic patterns (Duque, 2021). Designing a chatbot that can effectively extract relevant information from different input structures while maintaining contextual coherence demands sophisticated NLP techniques. The variability in user expressions, colloquial language, and the potential introduction of new terms or slang further complicates the task. Robust algorithms must be able to adapt to evolving linguistic trends and efficiently navigate through the inherent uncertainty in user inputs, ensuring accurate and contextually appropriate responses to provide a seamless and satisfying user experience.

Learning from User Feedback

Chatbots must navigate a dynamic and often unpredictable conversational landscape, requiring algorithms to adapt to diverse user inputs and evolving language patterns. Incorporating user feedback is essential for refining natural language processing models and improving the chatbot's understanding and response capabilities. However, the challenge lies in developing algorithms that can effectively assimilate feedback, differentiate between constructive and misleading input, and autonomously update their underlying structures. Striking a balance between responsiveness to user feedback and avoiding overfitting to specific instances is a persistent technical hurdle. Additionally, ensuring privacy and data security in handling user feedback further complicates the algorithmic design process, highlighting the multifaceted nature of challenges associated with building resilient and user-centric chatbot systems.

Optimizing Response Generation

Optimizing response generation poses various technical challenges in the realm of chatbots. One primary concern lies in achieving contextually relevant and coherent responses that emulate natural human conversation. Striking a balance between creativity and adherence to specific goals or guidelines is another hurdle, as overly creative responses may lead to inaccuracies or misinterpretations. Handling diverse user inputs, including slang, colloquial language, or ambiguous queries, requires robust NLU capabilities. Moreover, managing dynamic contexts and evolving conversations necessitates effective context retention and recall mechanisms. The challenge extends to mitigating biases in generated responses and ensuring ethical considerations, as chatbots can inadvertently perpetuate or amplify existing biases present in their training data. Overcoming these challenges requires advances in machine learning, NLU, and ethical AI frameworks to enhance the overall performance and user experience of chatbots in diverse and dynamic conversational scenarios.

Balancing Creativity and Consistency

Balancing creativity and consistency in optimizing response generation poses a significant technical challenge for chatbots. On one hand, fostering creativity is essential to ensure that chatbots can generate diverse and engaging responses, adapting to various user inputs and contexts (Bakshi et al., 2021). However, too much emphasis on creativity may lead to inconsistencies in the responses, causing confusion for users and undermining the reliability of the chatbot. Striking the right balance requires developing sophisticated algorithms and models that can intelligently blend creativity with a consistent understanding of user queries. This involves leveraging techniques from natural language processing, machine learning, and possibly even incorporating reinforcement learning to fine-tune the creativity-consistency trade-off based on user feedback.

Furthermore, technical challenges arise from the dynamic nature of language and user expectations. Achieving consistency while allowing for creative expression becomes more complex as users engage with chatbots in diverse ways. Handling different linguistic styles, slang, and evolving language trends requires continuous model training and adaptation. Additionally, ensuring that the chatbot maintains consistency across various domains and scenarios demands robust data preprocessing and augmentation techniques. Striving for a balance between creativity and consistency is an ongoing challenge that necessitates the integration of advanced technologies and a deep understanding of user interactions to enhance the overall effectiveness of chatbot responses.

Overcoming Overfitting Challenges

Overfitting occurs when a model learns the training data too well, including noise and specificities that may not generalize well to new, unseen data. In the context of chatbots, overcoming overfitting is crucial for ensuring that the generated responses are relevant, coherent, and contextually appropriate. Here are some technical challenges related to chatbot response generation and strategies to overcome overfitting:

- Limited Training Data: Chatbots often have access to a limited amount of training data, leading to the risk of overfitting as the model might memorize specific responses. Augmenting the training data with various examples, paraphrases, and diverse conversational contexts can help the model generalize better. Data augmentation techniques, such as paraphrasing and rephrasing, can be employed to introduce variability.

- Handling Ambiguity: Natural language is inherently ambiguous, and chatbot models may overfit to specific interpretations of ambiguous phrases (Holopainen and Räisänen, 2019). Regularization techniques, such as dropout during training, can help prevent the model from relying too heavily on specific features, fostering a more robust understanding of ambiguous language.

- Model Complexity: Complex models, such as deep neural networks, may have a higher tendency to overfit, especially when the data is limited. Simplifying the architecture or using regularization techniques like L1 or L2 regularization can prevent the model from becoming overly complex. Additionally, employing techniques like early stopping during training can help find the optimal model complexity.

- Hyperparameter Tuning: Poorly tuned hyperparameters can lead to overfitting or underfitting. Conduct systematic hyperparameter tuning using techniques like grid search or random search to find the best set of hyperparameters that generalize well to unseen data.

- Contextual Understanding: Understanding the context of a conversation is crucial for generating coherent responses. Overfitting may lead to responses that do not consider the broader context. Incorporating contextual information, such as previous turns in the conversation, through the use of attention mechanisms or memory networks can help the model better understand and respond coherently in context.

- Regularization Techniques: Not applying appropriate regularization techniques may lead to overfitting (Bhambri, 2021). Implement regularization methods such as dropout, weight regularization, or layer normalization to prevent overfitting and encourage the model to learn more general patterns.

- Monitoring and Evaluation: Inadequate monitoring during training may result in a failure to detect overfitting until it's too late. Regularly monitor the model's performance on validation data and use early stopping based on performance metrics to halt training when overfitting is detected.

Mitigating Biases in Chatbot Interactions

Mitigating biases in chatbot interactions presents a multifaceted technical challenge, requiring a comprehensive approach to address inherent biases in both language models and training data. Firstly, fine-tuning models to reduce biases without compromising performance remains a delicate balancing act. Additionally, the diverse and dynamic nature of user input demands constant adaptation to evolving linguistic nuances and societal changes (Li et al., 2017). Implementing effective bias detection mechanisms during real-time conversations poses another challenge, as biases may emerge subtly or contextually. Furthermore, ensuring transparency in the decision-making processes of chatbots is crucial to building user trust. Striking the right balance between mitigating biases and maintaining the naturalness and effectiveness of chatbot interactions requires ongoing research, ethical considerations, and collaborative efforts across the AI community.

Identifying and Addressing Bias in Training Data

Addressing bias in training data is a critical aspect of mitigating biases in chatbot interactions. Biases can emerge in chatbots due to the data they are trained on, reflecting societal prejudices, stereotypes, or imbalances. Here's a discussion on identifying and addressing bias in training data:

- Data Source Evaluation: Examine the sources of training data. Biases can originate from biased datasets, so understanding the origin is crucial.
- Diversity Analysis: Assess the diversity of the training data in terms of demographics, cultural backgrounds, and perspectives. Lack of diversity can lead to biased outcomes.
- Historical Bias Recognition: Acknowledge historical biases present in the data. If the training data reflects historical inequalities, the chatbot might perpetuate these biases.
- User Feedback Monitoring: Regularly monitor user feedback for potential biases. Users can provide valuable insights into biased responses that might not be apparent during the development phase.
- Testing for Fairness: Implement tests to evaluate the chatbot's fairness. Techniques like fairness-aware machine learning can help identify and quantify biases.
- Data Preprocessing: Cleanse the training data to remove explicit biases and stereotypes. This can involve modifying or removing biased examples.
- Augmentation Techniques: Use data augmentation techniques to introduce diversity into the training set. This involves creating variations of existing data to ensure a more balanced representation.
- Bias Mitigation Algorithms: Implement bias mitigation algorithms during the training phase. Techniques such as re-weighting or re-sampling can address imbalances in the data.

- Contextual Understanding: Enhance the chatbot's contextual understanding to reduce the likelihood of biased responses. A better understanding of context allows the chatbot to provide more nuanced and accurate answers.
- Inclusive Design: Involve diverse teams in the design and development of chatbots. Diverse perspectives can help identify and address biases early in the development process.
- Continuous Monitoring: Establish a system for continuous monitoring of chatbot interactions. Regularly update and refine the training data based on real-world feedback to improve the chatbot's performance over time.
- Transparency and Explainability: Make the chatbot's decision-making process transparent and explainable. This helps build trust with users and allows for better scrutiny of potential biases.
- User Education: Educate users about the limitations of chatbots and AI systems. Setting clear expectations can reduce the impact of biases and enhance user understanding.

Real-time Bias Mitigation Strategies

To mitigate biases effectively, continuous monitoring and dynamic adjustment of the training data are essential. Implementing real-time feedback loops allows the system to adapt to evolving language patterns and cultural shifts, ensuring the chatbot remains sensitive to diverse perspectives (Marsico and Budiu, 2018). Techniques such as debiasing algorithms, diversity-aware data augmentation, and adversarial training can be employed to identify and rectify biased patterns during the training process. Regularly updating the training dataset with diverse and representative examples helps in minimizing inadvertent biases that may emerge over time. Additionally, leveraging user feedback mechanisms and involving diverse stakeholders in the evaluation process contribute to a more inclusive and unbiased chatbot experience. Adopting real-time bias mitigation strategies not only aligns the chatbot with evolving societal norms but also enhances its ability to engage users from diverse backgrounds with fairness and impartiality.

CASE STUDIES AND EXAMPLES

Chatbots have been implemented across various industries to streamline processes, enhance customer service, and improve user experiences. Here are some case studies and examples related to chatbots:

- Customer Support (IBM Watson Assistant): IBM Watson Assistant has been employed by various companies for customer support. It uses NLP to understand user queries and provide relevant responses. Companies like Autodesk and Harman have successfully integrated Watson Assistant to handle customer queries efficiently, reducing the workload on human agents.
- E-commerce (eBay's ShopBot): eBay introduced a chatbot called ShopBot to assist users in finding products. ShopBot uses AI to understand user preferences and provides personalized product recommendations. This helps users discover products more easily and enhances their overall shopping experience.
- Healthcare (Florence by Sensely): Florence is a virtual nurse chatbot designed to help patients manage their health. It provides medication reminders, offers guidance on symptoms, and can connect users with healthcare professionals. This chatbot has been utilized by insurance companies and healthcare providers to improve patient engagement and adherence to treatment plans.

- Finance (Erica by Bank of America): Erica is a virtual financial assistant developed by Bank of America. It helps users manage their finances by providing insights into spending patterns, suggesting budgeting strategies, and answering financial queries. Erica utilizes AI to understand natural language and provide personalized recommendations to users.
- Education (Duolingo's Chatbots): Language learning platform Duolingo employs chatbots to provide conversational practice for users. These chatbots simulate real-life conversations, helping users improve their language skills in a more interactive way. The chatbot format enhances the learning experience by offering practical application of language knowledge.
- Human Resources (Mya Systems): Mya is an AI-powered chatbot used in the recruitment process. It assists with screening and interviewing candidates, helping HR professionals save time and resources. Mya Systems' chatbot has been adopted by companies to automate the initial stages of the hiring process and identify suitable candidates more efficiently.
- Travel and Hospitality (KLM's BlueBot): KLM Royal Dutch Airlines introduced a chatbot named BlueBot on Facebook Messenger. BlueBot assists customers with booking flights, provides boarding passes, and offers travel information. It enhances the customer experience by providing quick and convenient access to relevant travel information.

FORWARD-LOOKING PERSPECTIVE

The field of chatbot technology is continually evolving, and there are several forward-looking perspectives and emerging trends that highlight the future direction of chatbot development (Bhambri, 2020). Ongoing research and development efforts are focused on enhancing the capabilities, improving user experiences, and exploring new applications. Here are some key forward-looking perspectives and emerging trends in chatbot technology:

- Conversational AI Advancements: Ongoing research is dedicated to enhancing NLU capabilities, enabling chatbots to better understand context, sentiment, and user intent. This will result in more natural and context-aware conversations. The integration of voice, images, and other forms of media into chatbot interactions is becoming more prevalent. Chatbots are evolving to understand and respond to not only text but also voice commands and visual inputs.
- AI-driven Personalization: Chatbots are increasingly incorporating contextual information about users to provide more personalized and relevant responses. Machine learning algorithms analyze user data to tailor interactions based on individual preferences, history, and behaviors. Future chatbots are expected to exhibit a higher level of emotional intelligence, recognizing and responding to user emotions. This involves the ability to detect sentiment, empathy, and adapt responses accordingly, leading to more human-like interactions.
- Integration with Advanced Technologies: The integration of chatbots with AR and VR technologies is a growing trend. This allows for more immersive and interactive experiences, especially in applications like virtual customer support or training scenarios. In certain industries like finance and healthcare, integrating chatbots with blockchain technology is being explored to enhance security, transparency, and trust in transactions and data exchanges.
- Cross-platform and Omni-Channel Integration: Chatbots are evolving to seamlessly operate across various communication channels, such as messaging apps, websites, voice interfaces, and social

media platforms. This ensures a consistent and integrated user experience. The development of chatbot ecosystems, where multiple chatbots can collaborate and share information, is gaining traction. This allows for a more comprehensive and interconnected approach to solving user queries and tasks.

- Ethical Considerations and Responsible AI: Efforts are being made to address biases in chatbot interactions. Research is ongoing to identify and eliminate biases in language models to ensure fair and unbiased responses. There is a growing emphasis on making AI systems, including chatbots, more transparent. Ensuring accountability in decision-making processes and providing clear explanations for chatbot actions is a focus of ongoing research.

- Continuous Learning and Adaptability: Chatbots are increasingly adopting self-learning algorithms that allow them to adapt to changing user behaviors and preferences over time (Pereira and Nogueira, 2018). This continuous learning improves the chatbot's performance and relevance. Transfer learning techniques enable chatbots to leverage knowledge gained in one domain to improve performance in another. This accelerates the learning process and enhances the chatbot's versatility.

- Quantum Computing and Advanced Processing: As quantum computing technology matures, its application in chatbot development could significantly accelerate processing speeds, enabling more complex and resource-intensive chatbot models. The integration of chatbots with edge computing allows for faster response times and reduced reliance on centralized servers. This is particularly beneficial for real-time applications and scenarios with limited connectivity.

- Healthcare and Mental Health Support: Chatbots are being explored as tools for monitoring and managing health-related information. They can assist users in tracking health metrics, providing medication reminders, and offering support for mental health and well-being. Chatbots are being integrated into telemedicine platforms to enhance the overall patient experience, streamline appointment scheduling, and provide information about healthcare services.

- Environmental and Social Impact: There is an increasing focus on developing eco-friendly and energy-efficient chatbot models to reduce the environmental impact of AI technologies. Efforts are being made to ensure that chatbots are designed to be inclusive, considering diverse user needs, languages, and accessibility requirements.

- Human-in-the-Loop Collaboration: Human-in-the-loop models involve collaboration between chatbots and human agents. This hybrid approach combines the strengths of AI and human expertise, ensuring a more robust and reliable system, especially in complex or sensitive scenarios. Research is ongoing to improve the explainability of AI models, making it easier for human users to understand and interpret chatbot decisions. This is crucial for building trust and facilitating effective collaboration.

- Globalization and Multilingual Capabilities: Chatbots are evolving to support a broader range of languages and dialects (Rajendran and Prasanna, 2018). This is particularly important for businesses and services that operate globally, ensuring effective communication with diverse user populations. Ongoing research focuses on making chatbots culturally sensitive, understanding nuances in language, behavior, and communication styles across different cultures.

- Regulatory Compliance: With increasing concerns about data privacy, chatbots are being developed with a focus on compliance with data protection regulations. Secure data handling practices and transparent privacy policies are integral to chatbot design. As the use of chatbots becomes more widespread, regulatory frameworks are likely to emerge to govern their deployment, ensuring ethical practices and user protection.

CONCLUSION

The deployment of chatbots, while offering remarkable advancements in user engagement and automation, is not without its challenges and issues. Ethical concerns surrounding biases in language models, data privacy, and the potential misuse of AI technologies underscore the need for a careful examination of the impact of chatbots on individuals and society. Technical challenges, such as ensuring robust natural language understanding, handling complex user queries, and maintaining transparency in decision-making processes, further complicate the landscape of chatbot development. Additionally, the risk of unintended consequences, including the propagation of misinformation and the perpetuation of societal biases, demands a proactive approach to mitigating these issues. As chatbots continue to play an increasingly integral role in various domains, it becomes imperative to address these challenges systematically to foster a responsible and sustainable integration of chatbot technology into our daily lives.

The importance of addressing issues in chatbot technology cannot be overstated. Ethical lapses and technical shortcomings can erode user trust, hinder widespread adoption, and even result in negative societal impacts. Developers and researchers must prioritize the creation of chatbots that are not only technically proficient but also adhere to ethical standards, ensuring fairness, transparency, and respect for user privacy. A call to action is extended to researchers and developers to engage in interdisciplinary collaborations, working towards solutions that encompass diverse perspectives. Rigorous testing, ongoing evaluation, and the implementation of ethical guidelines must be integral to the chatbot development process. By taking a proactive stance on addressing these challenges, the technology community can contribute to the responsible evolution of chatbot technology, fostering innovation while safeguarding against potential risks. It is through collective efforts and a commitment to ethical and user-centric design that the full potential of chatbots as valuable tools in human-computer interaction can be realized.

REFERENCES

Bakshi, P., Bhambri, P., & Thapar, V. (2021). A Review Paper on Wireless Sensor Network Techniques in Internet of Things (IoT). *Wesleyan Journal of Research*, *14*(7), 147–160.

Bhambri, P. (2020). Green Compliance. In S. Agarwal (Ed.), *Introduction to Green Computing* (pp. 95–125). AGAR Saliha Publication.

Bhambri, P. (2021). Electronic Evidence. In Textbook of Cyber Heal (pp. 86-120). AGAR Saliha Publication, Tamil Nadu.

Bhambri, P., Singh, M., Jain, A., Dhanoa, I. S., Sinha, V. K., & Lal, S. (2021). Classification of the GENE Expression Data with the Aid of Optimized Feature Selection. *Turkish Journal of Physiotherapy and Rehabilitation*, *32*(3), 1158–1167.

Clark, P. (2019). *Chatbot marketing: The ultimate guide*. Springer.

Dignum, V., & Dignum, F. (2018). *Responsible artificial intelligence: How to develop and use AI in a responsible way*. Springer.

Duque, J. (2021). *Mastering Conversational AI with IBM Watson: Design and Develop Conversational Solutions with IBM Watson Assistant*. Packt Publishing.

Holopainen, J., & Räisänen, T. (2019). Designing Chatbots for Better User Experience. In *International Conference on Human-Computer Interaction* (pp. 155-174). Springer.

Jain, A., & Srivastava, S. (2020). *Building Enterprise Chatbots: A Step by Step Approach*. Apress.

Li, S., Kao, C. Y., & Wang, Q. (2017). Building a Chatbot with Serverless Computing and Machine Learning. In *2017 IEEE International Conference on Web Services (ICWS)* (pp. 758-761). IEEE.

Marsico, M. D., & Budiu, R. (2018). *Chatbots: what they are and how to build one (with examples)*. Nielsen Norman Group.

Pereira, J., & Nogueira, A. (2018). Chatbots in educational environments: A systematic review. *Computers & Education*, *124*, 74–89.

Rajendran, V., & Prasanna, S. R. M. (2018). Intelligent Chatbot for Enabling e-Governance: A Case Study. In *2018 IEEE Calcutta Conference (CALCON)* (pp. 174-177). IEEE.

Rani, S., Bhambri, P., & Kataria, A. (2023b). *Integration of IoT, Big Data, and Cloud Computing Technologies. Big Data, Cloud Computing and IoT: Tools and Applications*.

Rani, S., Bhambri, P., Kataria, A., & Khang, A. (2023a). Smart City Ecosystem: Concept, Sustainability, Design Principles, and Technologies. In AI-Centric Smart City Ecosystems (pp. 1-20). CRC Press.

Rani, S., Pareek, P. K., Kaur, J., Chauhan, M., & Bhambri, P. (2023c). Quantum Machine Learning in Healthcare: Developments and Challenges. *Paper presented at the International Conference on Integrated Circuits and Communication Systems*, (pp. 1-7). IEEE. 10.1109/ICICACS57338.2023.10100075

Singh, G., Singh, M., & Bhambri, P. (2020). Artificial Intelligence based Flying Car. In *Proceedings of the International Congress on Sustainable Development through Engineering Innovations* (pp. 216-227). Springer.

Singh, M., Bhambri, P., Dhanoa, I. S., Jain, A., & Kaur, K. (2021). Data Mining Model for Predicting Diabetes. *Annals of the Romanian Society for Cell Biology*, *25*(4), 6702–6712.

van Velsen, L., van der Geest, T., & Klaassen, R. (2017). From usability to user experience: A systematic framework for chatbot design. *Proceedings of the 21st International Academic Mindtrek Conference*, (pp. 126-133). Research Gate.

KEY TERMS AND DEFINITIONS

Biases in Chatbot Interactions: Biases in chatbot behavior that might result in unfair or discriminatory outcomes, stemming from prejudices in the training data or algorithmic design.

Context Awareness: A chatbot's ability to perceive and comprehend the situational context of a conversation, leading to more precise and appropriate responses.

Ethical Considerations: Thorough analysis of the ethical considerations and appropriate application of chatbot technology, encompassing aspects like user privacy, data security, and ethical conduct.

Forward-Looking Perspective: An innovative examination of future trends and prospects in chatbot technology, encompassing advancements, rising trends, and the forecast of new developments.

Natural Language Understanding (NLU): The capacity of a chatbot or system to understand and interpret human language in a manner that enables it to extract meaning, grasp context, and reply suitably.

Response Generation Optimization: Chatbot refinement involves enhancing response creation to achieve a balance between inventiveness and consistency, while reducing problems such as overfitting.

Robust Algorithms: Robust and well-structured mathematical algorithms that underpin a chatbot's operations, enabling it to process different input formats and adjust to various situations.

Chapter 9
Customer Service Bots:
Enhancing Support and Personalization

Kaushikkumar Patel
https://orcid.org/0009-0005-9197-2765
TransUnion LLC, USA

ABSTRACT

This chapter delves into the transformative impact of chatbots in customer service, highlighting their evolution from basic automated responders to advanced AI-driven conversational agents. Utilizing technologies like AI, ML, and NLP, these bots are reshaping customer interactions by offering round-the-clock service and handling complex inquiries with increasing sophistication. The chapter explores their development, operational mechanics, and various types while addressing the challenges in implementation and the balance between automation and human touch. Ethical considerations, particularly in data privacy, are critically examined. Real-world case studies across different industries illustrate the practical impact and efficiency gains from these bots. Future advancements are discussed, focusing on enhanced personalization and empathetic interactions through improved AI and NLP, underscoring the significant yet evolving role of chatbots in modern customer service.

INTRODUCTION

The landscape of customer service has undergone a significant transformation, marked by the transition from traditional, human-centric methods to digital and automated solutions. This evolution is epitomized by the emergence of chatbots, which have progressed from basic, script-based systems to sophisticated, AI-driven conversational agents. Initially serving as simple automated responders, these chatbots have now become integral to customer service strategies, capable of providing personalized and efficient interactions. This shift reflects technological advancements and aligns with consumers' changing expectations in a digital-first world.

Artificial Intelligence stands at the core of modern chatbots, enabling them to simulate human-like conversations and decision-making processes. AI's integration into chatbots has been transformative, allowing them to understand customer queries, analyze them, and respond in a relevant and context-

DOI: 10.4018/979-8-3693-1830-0.ch009

aware manner. This AI-driven approach has expanded the capabilities of chatbots beyond mere scripted responses, enabling them to handle a diverse range of customer service tasks and offer intuitive, helpful interactions that understand the underlying intent of customer queries.

Machine Learning has further enhanced chatbots' capabilities, allowing them to learn from past interactions and continuously improve their responses. This self-learning aspect is crucial for chatbots to adapt to new customer queries and refine their accuracy over time. In practical terms, this means that a chatbot in a retail environment, for example, can learn from customer purchase histories and preferences, thereby offering more personalized and relevant product recommendations in future interactions.

Natural Language Processing has been a game-changer in the realm of chatbots, enabling them to process and generate human language more effectively. NLP allows chatbots to understand the nuances of human communication, including slang, idioms, and varied sentence structures, facilitating more natural and engaging conversations. This advancement has been instrumental in making chatbot interactions more fluid and human-like, allowing customers to communicate in their everyday language without the constraints of rigid command-based inputs.

Chatbots have brought numerous advantages to the customer service domain, including 24/7 availability, the ability to handle high volumes of queries, and providing instant responses. This constant availability and scalability have significantly enhanced customer satisfaction and operational efficiency. Additionally, the personalized experiences offered by advanced chatbots, driven by AI and ML, have fostered deeper customer engagement and loyalty.

Despite their numerous benefits, chatbots also present challenges, such as accurately interpreting customer intent and maintaining a balance between automation and human empathy. However, the future of chatbots in customer service looks promising, with ongoing advancements expected to further enhance their conversational abilities and emotional intelligence. As technology continues to evolve, chatbots are set to become even more integral in providing efficient, accessible, and personalized customer service, shaping the future of customer engagement in profound ways.

LITERATURE REVIEW

Historical Development and Advancements in Chatbot Technology

Early Stages of Chatbot Development: The inception of chatbots can be traced back to the early days of computer programming, with the creation of ELIZA in 1966, a program developed by Joseph Weizenbaum that could mimic human conversation by matching user prompts to scripted responses (Weizenbaum, J., 1966). This rudimentary form of chatbot laid the groundwork for future developments. The evolution from these basic models to more sophisticated systems is documented extensively, with scholars noting the gradual integration of more complex algorithms and decision trees to enhance interaction capabilities (Castle-Green, T., 2020). Early chatbots were primarily used in specific domains like customer support for simple queries, as they lacked the ability to process complex requests or understand context (Fogg, B. J., 1999).

Integration of AI and Advancements in Chatbots: The integration of Artificial Intelligence marked a significant turning point in the evolution of chatbots. Pioneering work by researchers in AI and NLP fields led to the development of more advanced systems capable of understanding and responding to a wider range of customer inquiries (Bird, S., 2009). These AI-driven chatbots, unlike their predecessors, could learn from interactions, adapt to user preferences, and provide more personalized responses. The role of Machine Learning in this transformation has been crucial, as highlighted in studies that discuss how ML algorithms enable chatbots to analyze customer data, leading to improved service delivery (Bengio, Y., 2013). This era saw chatbots becoming increasingly prevalent in customer service, with businesses adopting them for their ability to handle high volumes of interactions efficiently.

Current State and Sophistication of Chatbots: Today's chatbots represent the culmination of decades of research and development in AI, ML, and NLP. They are capable of engaging in complex conversations, understanding nuances, and providing contextually relevant responses. Recent literature emphasizes the role of advanced NLP techniques in enhancing the conversational abilities of chatbots, allowing them to interpret and generate human-like responses (Hirschberg, J., 2015). This has led to a significant improvement in user experience, with chatbots now being employed in various customer service scenarios, from handling routine inquiries to assisting with transactions and customer support. The current state of chatbots is characterized by their versatility, adaptability, and increasing integration into omnichannel customer service strategies.

Integration of AI, ML, and NLP in Chatbots

The Role of Artificial Intelligence in Chatbot Development: The integration of Artificial Intelligence (AI) into chatbots has been a critical factor in their evolution. AI enables chatbots to simulate human-like decision-making and interactions, making them more responsive and intuitive. Seminal works in the field, such as Russell and Norvig's "Artificial Intelligence: A Modern Approach" (Russell, S. J., 2010), provide foundational insights into AI principles that have been instrumental in chatbot development. Further, studies by scholars like Kaplan and Haenlein (Kaplan, A., 2019) discuss the application of AI in chatbots, emphasizing how it enhances their ability to understand and respond to user queries in a dynamic manner. This shift from static, rule-based systems to AI-driven chatbots marks a significant advancement in the field, as highlighted in recent research (Deng, L., 2018).

Machine Learning's Contribution to Chatbot Intelligence: Machine Learning (ML) has played a pivotal role in advancing chatbot capabilities. ML algorithms enable chatbots to learn from past interactions, thereby improving their accuracy and efficiency over time. The work of Murphy (Murphy, K., 2012) on "Machine Learning: A Probabilistic Perspective" offers a comprehensive understanding of these algorithms and their application in chatbots. Research by Jordan and Mitchell (Jordan, M. I., 2015) further explores how ML contributes to the adaptability of chatbots, allowing them to offer personalized experiences based on user data and interaction history. This aspect of ML has been crucial in transforming chatbots into more sophisticated tools that can handle a variety of customer service scenarios with increased precision.

Natural Language Processing and Enhanced Conversational Abilities: Natural Language Processing (NLP) is another cornerstone in the development of modern chatbots. NLP involves the ability of computers to understand, interpret, and generate human language. Jurafsky and Martin's "Speech and Language Processing" (Jurafsky, D., 2018) provides an in-depth look at NLP techniques that are fundamental to chatbot functionality. Recent studies, such as those by Young et al. (Young, S., 2013), highlight the advancements in NLP that have enabled chatbots to engage in more natural and fluid conversations. The integration of NLP has been essential in overcoming the limitations of earlier chatbots, allowing for more nuanced and context-aware interactions, as discussed in the works of Manning and Schütze (Manning, C., 1999).

The Significance of Chatbots in Modern Customer Interactions

The significance of chatbots in modern customer service is primarily marked by their ability to offer 24/7 support and handle high volumes of interactions. Research by Adam et al. (Adam, M., 2021) highlights how chatbots enhance service efficiency by providing immediate responses to customer inquiries, a crucial factor in today's fast-paced digital environment. Studies by Misischia et al. (Misischia, C. V., 2022) further emphasize the role of chatbots in improving accessibility, allowing customers to receive assistance at any time, which is particularly beneficial for global businesses operating across different time zones. This round-the-clock availability and scalability of chatbots have been transformative in meeting the modern consumer's expectations for instant and reliable service.

Personalization and Improved Customer Experience: Chatbots, powered by AI and ML, have the unique ability to offer personalized customer experiences. According to Kushwaha et al. (Kushwaha, A. K., 2021), the integration of AI in chatbots enables them to analyze customer data and tailor interactions based on individual preferences and past behaviors. This personalization aspect is further explored by Naqvi et al. (Naqvi, M. H. A., 2023), who discuss how personalized interactions enhance customer satisfaction and loyalty. The ability of chatbots to provide tailored recommendations and solutions has not only improved the efficiency of customer service but also contributed to a more engaging and satisfying customer experience.

Data Collection and Business Insights: Beyond direct customer interaction, chatbots serve as valuable tools for data collection and analysis. As noted by Selamat et al. (Selamat, M. A., 2021), chatbots can gather insights on customer preferences and behaviors, providing businesses with critical data to inform decision-making and strategy development. The work of Kecht et al. (Kecht, C., 2023) further illustrates how this data can be used to refine business processes, product offerings, and overall customer service strategies. The strategic use of chatbot-collected data has become a key component in understanding and responding to evolving customer needs and market trends.

CHATBOT MECHANICS AND TYPES

In the realm of customer service, the mechanics and types of chatbots play a pivotal role in determining their effectiveness and suitability for different service scenarios. This section delves into the intricate workings of chatbots, focusing on how they leverage Artificial Intelligence (AI), Machine Learning (ML), and Natural Language Processing (NLP) to facilitate human-like interactions. We explore the distinct categories of chatbots – rule-based, AI-driven, and hybrid models – each with its unique operational framework and capabilities. Understanding these variations is crucial for businesses looking to implement chatbots, as it directly impacts their ability to meet diverse customer needs. The section aims to provide a comprehensive overview of chatbot types, their functional mechanisms, and an analysis of their strengths and limitations, offering valuable insights for those seeking to integrate chatbots into their customer service strategy (Table 1).

- **In-depth Exploration of Chatbot Functionality:** Chatbots, at their core, are sophisticated programs designed to simulate human-like conversations with users. The mechanics of these chatbots, particularly those that leverage AI, ML, and NLP, are intricate and multifaceted, combining various technological components to create seamless and effective communication tools.

○ **Artificial Intelligence in Chatbot Functionality:** AI in chatbots primarily involves the simulation of human intelligence processes by machines, especially computer systems. These processes include learning, reasoning, and self-correction. AI enables chatbots to interpret complex language, understand user intent, and provide responses that are contextually relevant. For instance, when a user interacts with a chatbot, AI algorithms work to decipher the intent behind the user's query and determine the most appropriate response based on available data and learned patterns.

○ **Machine Learning's Role in Chatbot Adaptation:** Machine Learning, a subset of AI, is crucial in enabling chatbots to learn from their interactions and improve over time. ML algorithms analyze data from previous conversations, identifying patterns and adjusting responses for future interactions. This continuous learning process allows chatbots to become more efficient and accurate in their responses. For example, an e-commerce chatbot can learn from past customer interactions to make better product recommendations in the future.

○ **Natural Language Processing for Human-like Interactions:** Natural Language Processing, another critical component, allows chatbots to process and understand human language. NLP technologies enable chatbots to comprehend various linguistic nuances, including slang, idioms, and different sentence structures. This capability is essential for facilitating natural and fluid conversations between chatbots and users. Through NLP, chatbots can parse user input, understand its context, and generate responses that are coherent and contextually appropriate.

The integration of AI, ML, and NLP in chatbots has led to the creation of highly sophisticated digital assistants capable of handling a wide range of customer service tasks. These technologies work in tandem to ensure that chatbots can not only understand and respond to user queries effectively but also learn from each interaction to provide more personalized and accurate service over time. As these technologies continue to advance, the functionality and capabilities of chatbots are expected to become even more refined and human-like, further enhancing their role in customer service and other applications.

● **Detailed Categorization of Chatbots:** Chatbots can be broadly categorized into three types based on their underlying technology and functionality: rule-based, AI-driven, and hybrid models. Each type offers distinct features and capabilities, catering to various needs and complexities in customer service.

○ **Rule-Based Chatbots:** These, also known as decision-tree bots, operate on a set of predefined rules and scripts. These chatbots are programmed to respond to specific commands or keywords identified in the user's input. Their responses are based on a structured flow, which means they can handle predictable, straightforward queries effectively. However, their capability is limited to the scenarios anticipated and programmed by their developers. Rule-based chatbots are often used for simple customer service tasks, such as answering FAQs or guiding users through predefined processes.

○ **AI-Driven Chatbots:** AI-driven chatbots represent a significant advancement in chatbot technology. Unlike rule-based bots, AI chatbots use Machine Learning, Natural Language Processing, and sometimes Deep Learning to understand, learn, and respond to user queries. These chatbots can handle a wide range of queries, including those with complex or ambiguous language. AI-driven chatbots are capable of understanding the context and intent behind a user's message, allowing for more natural and conversational interactions. They are particularly effective in scenarios where user queries are diverse and unpredictable.

- ○ **Hybrid Models:** It combines the structured response approach of rule-based systems with the learning and understanding capabilities of AI-driven bots. In a hybrid model, the chatbot can handle standard queries with predefined responses and escalate more complex or nuanced queries to the AI component. This approach ensures efficiency in handling routine questions while providing the flexibility to deal with complex interactions. Hybrid chatbots are increasingly popular in customer service, as they offer a balanced solution that caters to a wide range of customer needs.

Each type of chatbot has its strengths and is suited to different applications. Rule-based chatbots are reliable for straightforward tasks, AI-driven chatbots excel in complex and varied interactions, and hybrid models offer a versatile approach that leverages the best of both worlds. The choice of chatbot type depends on the specific requirements of the customer service scenario, including the complexity of the queries, the need for personalization, and the desired level of interaction.

- **Analysis of Strengths and Limitations:** In customer service, the effectiveness of a chatbot largely depends on its type and the specific context in which it is deployed. Each category of chatbots – rule-based, AI-driven, and hybrid – has its unique strengths and limitations.

  - ○ **Rule-Based Chatbots:** Rule-based chatbots, functioning on predefined rules and scripts, excel in delivering consistent and reliable responses to specific, anticipated queries. They are relatively easy and cost-effective to implement, offering businesses a high degree of control over interactions. However, their rigidity is a significant limitation, as they lack flexibility and cannot handle queries that fall outside their programmed rules. This makes them less effective in dealing with complex or unexpected customer inquiries. Additionally, their inability to learn from interactions restricts their adaptability and improvement over time, which can be a drawback in dynamic customer service environments.

  - ○ **AI-Driven Chatbots:** AI-driven chatbots, powered by advanced technologies like Machine Learning and Natural Language Processing, are capable of understanding a wide range of linguistic inputs and can provide personalized customer experiences. Their ability to learn and adapt from each interaction enhances their effectiveness and accuracy over time. However, these chatbots come with higher development and maintenance costs and their implementation can be complex and resource-intensive. While they offer advanced capabilities, there is still a potential for errors, particularly in interpreting ambiguous language or complex customer sentiments, which can pose challenges in certain customer service scenarios.

  - ○ **Hybrid Models:** Hybrid chatbots combine the reliability of rule-based systems with the flexibility and learning capabilities of AI-driven bots, offering a balanced solution for customer service. They efficiently handle a variety of queries, from simple to complex, and can be scaled to meet evolving service demands. However, designing and maintaining a seamless integration of both rule-based and AI components can be complex and resource-intensive. Additionally, finding the optimal balance between automated and AI-driven responses requires continuous tuning and optimization, which can be challenging but is essential for effective customer service delivery.

Table 1. Comparative analysis of chatbot types in customer service

Chatbot Type	Key Characteristics	Strengths	Limitations
Rule-Based	Operates on predefined rules and scripts; responds to specific commands or keywords.	Consistent and reliable responses; easy and cost-effective to implement; high control over interactions.	Limited flexibility; poor handling of complex queries; no learning capability.
AI-Driven	Uses AI, ML, and NLP to understand and respond to a wide range of queries; capable of learning and adapting.	Advanced understanding of queries; personalized interactions; continuous improvement from learning.	Higher development and maintenance costs; complexity in implementation; potential for errors in understanding.
Hybrid	Combines rule-based and AI-driven approaches; offers versatility in handling various types of queries.	Balanced approach; efficient handling of varied queries; scalable to changing needs.	Complexity in design and maintenance; resource-intensive; requires continuous tuning for balance.

In customer service, the choice of chatbot type should align with the business's specific needs, customer expectations, and the complexity of the service scenarios. Understanding these strengths and limitations is crucial for businesses to make informed decisions about which chatbot type to implement for optimal customer engagement and satisfaction.

IMPLEMENTATION AND INTEGRATION

The implementation and integration of chatbots into customer service systems mark a critical phase in leveraging this technology's full potential. This process involves not just the technical deployment of chatbots but also a strategic consideration of how they align with and enhance existing customer service frameworks. Successful implementation requires careful planning, understanding of customer interaction patterns, and integration with existing databases and communication channels. It's a multifaceted endeavor that demands attention to both technological and human aspects, ensuring that chatbots are not only functionally efficient but also align seamlessly with the organization's customer service objectives. This section delves into the various strategies, challenges, and best practices involved in effectively implementing and integrating chatbots into diverse customer service environments, ensuring they add value and improve the overall customer experience (Table 2).

- **Strategies for integrating chatbots into existing customer service systems:** Integrating chatbots into existing customer service systems requires a strategic approach that aligns with the organization's overall customer service goals and technological infrastructure. Here are key strategies to consider:
  - **Assessment of Customer Service Needs:** Begin by evaluating the current customer service framework to identify areas where chatbots can be most effective. This involves understanding common customer queries, peak interaction times, and the complexity of customer needs.
  - **Choosing the Right Type of Chatbot:** Based on the assessment, decide whether a rule-based, AI-driven, or hybrid chatbot is most suitable. Consider factors like the volume of interactions, the complexity of queries, and the need for personalization.

- **Seamless Integration with Existing Platforms:** Ensure that the chatbot can be integrated smoothly with existing customer service platforms, such as CRM systems, live chat software, and social media channels. This integration should allow for data sharing and a unified view of customer interactions.
- **User Experience Design:** Design the chatbot's interaction flow to be intuitive and user-friendly. This includes crafting conversational scripts, determining escalation points to human agents, and ensuring the chatbot's tone aligns with the brand's voice.
- **Training and Knowledge Base Development:** For AI-driven and hybrid chatbots, develop a comprehensive knowledge base and train the chatbot using historical customer service data, FAQs, and product/service information. Continuous learning from ongoing interactions is crucial for improving accuracy and relevance.
- **Testing and Iteration:** Before full deployment, conduct extensive testing to identify and rectify any issues in understanding, responsiveness, or integration. This phase may involve A/B testing to refine the chatbot's performance.
- **Feedback Mechanism and Continuous Improvement:** Implement a system for collecting user feedback on chatbot interactions. Use this feedback, along with performance analytics, to make ongoing improvements to the chatbot's functionality and knowledge base.
- **Compliance and Security Considerations:** Ensure that the chatbot adheres to relevant data protection and privacy regulations. Secure handling of customer data is paramount, especially in industries with stringent compliance requirements.
- **Employee Training and Change Management:** Educate customer service staff about the chatbot's role and how it integrates into their workflow. Effective change management is key to ensuring staff adapt to and support the new technology.
- **Marketing and Customer Education:** Inform customers about the chatbot service, its capabilities, and how it can assist them. Clear communication can enhance customer acceptance and usage of the chatbot.

- **Customization and Personalization of Chatbots for Various Industries:** Customizing and personalizing chatbots to suit specific industry needs is crucial for maximizing their effectiveness in customer service. Different industries have unique customer expectations, terminologies, and interaction patterns, which necessitates a tailored approach to chatbot design and functionality:
  - **Retail and E-commerce:** In these sectors, chatbots can be customized to assist with product recommendations, order tracking, and handling returns or exchanges. Personalization can be achieved by integrating chatbots with customer purchase history and preferences, enabling them to offer tailored product suggestions and support.
  - **Banking and Finance:** Chatbots in this industry require a focus on security and compliance with financial regulations. They can be customized to provide account information, transaction support, and financial advice. Personalization involves understanding individual customer's financial behaviors and offering relevant financial solutions.
  - **Healthcare:** In healthcare, chatbots need to handle sensitive health information with utmost confidentiality. They can be customized for appointment scheduling, patient queries, and providing general health information. Personalizing chatbots in healthcare might involve tailoring interactions based on patient history and specific health conditions.

- ○ **Travel and Hospitality:** For these industries, chatbots can be customized to assist with bookings, travel inquiries, and customer service during a guest's stay or travel. Personalization can include offering travel recommendations based on past trips, preferences, and budget.
- ○ **Education:** In educational settings, chatbots can be tailored to provide course information, administrative support, and learning assistance. Personalization involves adapting to different learning styles and providing relevant educational content and resources.
- ○ **Customer Support Across Industries:** Regardless of the industry, chatbots can be customized to handle common customer support tasks such as answering FAQs, providing company information, and escalating complex issues to human agents. Personalization in this context involves understanding the customer's history with the company and tailoring responses accordingly.
- **Case studies showcasing successful chatbot implementations:** Exploring successful chatbot implementations across various industries provides valuable insights into their practical applications and benefits. Here are some illustrative case studies:
  - ○ **Retail - H&M's Fashion Bot:**
    - ▪ Overview: H&M implemented a chatbot on Kik, a popular messaging platform, to offer personalized fashion advice and recommendations.
    - ▪ Success Factors: The chatbot engaged users by asking questions about their style preferences and then suggested outfits and individual items from H&M's catalog.
    - ▪ Impact: The bot successfully increased customer engagement and sales by providing a personalized shopping experience and simplifying the product discovery process.
  - ○ **Banking - Bank of America's Erica:**
    - ▪ Overview: Bank of America introduced Erica, a voice- and text-enabled chatbot, to provide financial assistance to its customers.
    - ▪ Success Factors: Erica helps users with transaction history, bill payments, and budgeting advice, using predictive analytics and cognitive messaging.
    - ▪ Impact: Erica has significantly improved customer service efficiency and user experience, handling millions of customer queries effectively.
  - ○ **Healthcare - Babylon Health:**
    - ▪ Overview: Babylon Health uses AI-powered chatbots to offer medical consultations based on personal medical history and general medical information.
    - ▪ Success Factors: The chatbot uses symptom checker algorithms to provide medical advice and recommend whether to see a doctor.
    - ▪ Impact: It has increased accessibility to healthcare advice, reduced the need for in-person doctor visits, and streamlined patient care.
  - ○ **Travel - KLM Royal Dutch Airlines' BlueBot:**
    - ▪ Overview: KLM's BlueBot is integrated with Facebook Messenger to assist customers with booking confirmations, flight updates, and check-in notifications.
    - ▪ Success Factors: The bot provides timely information and assistance, improving customer service efficiency and traveler satisfaction.
    - ▪ Impact: BlueBot has handled a significant volume of customer interactions, reducing response times and improving customer experience.

Table 2. Key aspects of chatbot implementation and integration in customer service

Aspect	Description	Key Consideration	Case Studies
Strategies for Integration	Approaches to effectively incorporate chatbots into existing customer service frameworks.	Assessing customer service needs, choosing the right type of chatbot, ensuring seamless platform integration.	N/A
Customization and Personalization	Tailoring chatbots to specific industry requirements and individual customer preferences.	Industry-specific customization, data integration for personalization, continuous adaptation.	Retail (H&M), Banking (Bank of America), Healthcare (Babylon Health)
Case Studies	Examples of successful chatbot implementations across various industries.	Demonstrating the effectiveness of chatbots in enhancing customer experience and operational efficiency.	Retail (H&M), Banking (Bank of America), Healthcare (Babylon Health), Travel (KLM), Education (Georgia State University), Customer Support (Sephora)

- ○ **Education - Georgia State University's Pounce:**
  - ▪ Overview: Georgia State University introduced Pounce, a chatbot to help new students with enrollment processes and FAQs.
  - ▪ Success Factors: Pounce addressed common queries of students, reducing administrative workload and improving student communication.
  - ▪ Impact: The chatbot led to a decrease in summer melt (students accepted to college but not enrolling) and improved student engagement.
- **Customer Support - Sephora's Virtual Artist:**
  - ▪ Overview: Sephora's chatbot on Facebook Messenger allows customers to try on makeup virtually using augmented reality.
  - ▪ Success Factors: The bot offers product recommendations and reviews, enhancing the online shopping experience.
  - ▪ Impact: It has increased customer engagement and sales, providing a unique and interactive way for customers to discover products.

These case studies demonstrate the diverse applications of chatbots across industries, highlighting their ability to enhance customer experience, streamline processes, and contribute to business growth. They exemplify how successful chatbot implementations can lead to tangible benefits, including increased efficiency, customer satisfaction, and sales.

USER EXPERIENCE AND ENGAGEMENT

In the realm of chatbots, user experience (UX) and engagement are paramount, determining the success and effectiveness of these digital assistants in customer service. This section delves into the intricacies of designing chatbots that not only meet functional requirements but also provide an engaging and satisfying experience for users. A well-designed chatbot UX goes beyond mere conversation – it encompasses understanding user needs, preferences, and behaviors, and crafting interactions that are intuitive, helpful, and enjoyable. Engagement, on the other hand, focuses on maintaining user interest and fostering a positive, ongoing relationship between the customer and the chatbot. This involves personalization, adaptability, and the ability to evoke a sense of connection and trust. As businesses strive to enhance customer interactions through chatbots, prioritizing user experience and engagement becomes crucial in building effective, user-centric chatbot solutions that resonate with and fulfill the expectations of modern consumers (Table 3).

- **Examination of chatbot interaction design for optimal user experience:** Designing chatbot interactions for optimal user experience involves several critical elements that collectively contribute to a seamless and engaging interaction. These elements are:
  - **Conversational UI and Flow:** The chatbot should have a conversational interface that is natural and intuitive. The flow of conversation needs to be logical and smooth, avoiding complex jargon or confusing instructions. This involves designing dialogues that feel natural and are easy to follow, ensuring users can communicate their needs effectively.
  - **Personalization:** Personalization is key to enhancing user experience. Chatbots should be capable of tailoring conversations based on user data, such as previous interactions, preferences, and behavior. This can include addressing users by name, remembering past interactions, and making relevant suggestions.
  - **Response Accuracy and Speed:** The ability of a chatbot to provide accurate and timely responses is crucial. Users expect quick and correct answers to their queries. The chatbot's design should prioritize efficient data retrieval and processing to meet these expectations.
  - **Visual Design and Brand Alignment:** The visual elements of the chatbot, including its avatar, color scheme, and typography, should align with the brand's identity. A visually appealing and brand-consistent chatbot can enhance user trust and comfort.
  - **Error Handling and Escalation:** The chatbot should be designed to handle errors gracefully. If the chatbot cannot understand or process a request, it should guide the user back on track or provide options for escalation to a human agent.
  - **Feedback Mechanisms:** Incorporating feedback mechanisms within the chatbot interaction allows for continuous improvement. Users should be able to easily provide feedback about their experience, which can be used to refine and enhance the chatbot's performance.
  - **Accessibility and Inclusivity:** The chatbot should be accessible to all users, including those with disabilities. This includes considerations for screen readers, voice navigation, and easy-to-read fonts.
  - **Multilingual Support:** For businesses with a diverse user base, offering multilingual support in chatbot interactions can significantly improve the user experience for non-native speakers.
  - **Integration with Other Channels:** Seamless integration with other customer service channels (like email, phone support, or social media) ensures a cohesive experience, especially when users need to switch between channels.
  - **Proactive Engagement:** Beyond reactive responses, a well-designed chatbot can engage users proactively with relevant information, reminders, or suggestions, enhancing the overall experience.
- **Analysis of user engagement strategies and metrics in chatbot interactions:** Effective user engagement strategies are crucial for ensuring that chatbots not only interact with users but also keep

them interested and satisfied. Analyzing these strategies and the metrics to measure their success is key to understanding and enhancing chatbot performance:

- ○ **Engagement Strategies:**
  - **Personalized Communication:** Tailoring conversations based on user data and past interactions to make the experience more relevant and engaging.
  - **Contextual Awareness:** Ensuring the chatbot can understand and remember the context of the conversation to provide coherent and continuous interactions.
  - **Proactive Interaction:** Implementing chatbots that initiate conversations based on user behavior or specific triggers, such as offering assistance when a user seems to be struggling on a website.
  - **Gamification Elements:** Incorporating game-like elements such as rewards, badges, or quizzes can increase engagement and make interactions more enjoyable.
  - **Regular Updates and Fresh Content:** Keeping the chatbot's responses and content updated and fresh to maintain user interest over time.
  - **Human-like Interaction:** Designing chatbots to have more human-like interactions, including the use of humor, empathy, and varied expressions, to enhance relatability.
- ○ Engagement Metrics:
  - **Conversation Length:** Measuring the average duration of interactions can indicate how well the chatbot maintains user interest.
  - **User Retention Rate:** Tracking how often users return to interact with the chatbot provides insight into long-term engagement.
  - **Completion Rate:** The rate at which users complete the intended action or conversation flow helps assess the chatbot's effectiveness.
  - **User Satisfaction Score:** Gathering user feedback through ratings or surveys post-interaction to gauge satisfaction levels.
  - **Bounce Rate:** The rate at which users leave after initiating an interaction with the chatbot, indicating potential issues in engagement.
  - **Conversion Rate:** For chatbots aimed at driving specific actions (like sales or sign-ups), measuring the conversion rate is crucial.
- **Impact of chatbots on customer satisfaction and loyalty:** The influence of chatbots on customer satisfaction and loyalty is a critical aspect of their role in modern business practices. When implemented effectively, chatbots can significantly enhance the customer experience, leading to higher levels of satisfaction and, consequently, increased customer loyalty:
  - ○ **Immediate and Efficient Service:** One of the primary benefits of chatbots is their ability to provide instant responses to customer inquiries. This immediacy meets the modern customer's expectation for quick and efficient service, which is a key driver of satisfaction.
  - ○ **24/7 Availability:** Chatbots offer round-the-clock service, ensuring that customers can receive assistance at any time. This constant availability is particularly important in today's global market, where customers may be interacting with businesses across different time zones.
  - ○ **Consistency in Customer Interactions:** Chatbots provide consistent responses to customer queries, ensuring that the information provided is accurate and reliable. This consistency helps in building trust and reliability, which are crucial for long-term customer relationships.

Table 3. Key elements of user experience and engagement in chatbot interactions

Aspect	Description	Key Strategies	Impact Metrics
Chatbot Interaction Design	Designing chatbot interactions to be intuitive, engaging, and user-friendly.	Conversational UI, Personalization, Visual Design, Error Handling, Accessibility.	User Satisfaction Score, Conversation Length.
User Engagement Strategies	Strategies to keep users interested and engaged with the chatbot.	Personalized Communication, Proactive Interaction, Gamification, Regular Content Updates.	User Retention Rate, Completion Rate, Bounce Rate.
Impact on Customer Satisfaction and Loyalty	How chatbots influence customer satisfaction and loyalty.	Immediate Service, 24/7 Availability, Consistency, Data-Driven Insights.	Customer Satisfaction Score, Reduced Wait Times, Enhanced Brand Image.

- ○ **Personalized Experiences:** Advanced chatbots equipped with AI and ML capabilities can offer personalized interactions by understanding and remembering user preferences. Personalization in customer service has been shown to increase customer satisfaction and loyalty, as it makes customers feel valued and understood.
- ○ **Reduced Wait Times and Frustration:** By handling routine queries and issues, chatbots reduce the workload on human customer service agents, leading to shorter wait times for customers and less frustration with the service process.
- ○ **Data-Driven Insights for Improvement:** Chatbots can collect valuable data from customer interactions, which can be analyzed to gain insights into customer preferences and behavior. This data can be used to improve products, services, and customer service strategies, further enhancing customer satisfaction.
- ○ **Enhancing Brand Image:** A well-designed and efficient chatbot can positively impact the brand image. It demonstrates the company's commitment to innovation and customer-centricity, factors that are increasingly important to modern consumers.

However, it's important to note that the impact of chatbots on customer satisfaction and loyalty is contingent on their proper implementation and integration. A poorly designed chatbot that fails to understand customer queries or provides irrelevant responses can lead to frustration and a negative perception of the brand. Therefore, continuous monitoring, testing, and improvement are essential to ensure that chatbots effectively contribute to positive customer experiences and foster loyalty.

CHALLENGES AND SOLUTIONS

In the rapidly evolving landscape of chatbot technology, while the potential for enhancing customer service is immense, it is accompanied by a set of unique challenges. This section delves into the various obstacles encountered in the development, implementation, and ongoing management of chatbots. These challenges range from technical hurdles, such as ensuring sophisticated natural language processing, to more nuanced issues like maintaining the delicate balance between automation and human touch. Additionally, considerations around data privacy, user trust, and integration complexities present significant challenges. However, with every challenge comes a solution. This section not only identifies these key challenges but also explores practical solutions and best practices that can help overcome these obstacles, ensuring chatbots effectively meet their intended goals and deliver a positive impact on customer service. The focus is on turning challenges into opportunities for improvement, innovation, and enhanced customer engagement (Table 4).

- **Key Challenges in Chatbot Development and Deployment:** The development and deployment of chatbots involve several key challenges that can impact their effectiveness and acceptance:
  - **Understanding Human Emotions:** One of the most significant challenges is enabling chatbots to accurately interpret and respond to human emotions. Emotional intelligence in chatbots is crucial for meaningful interactions, especially in customer service scenarios where empathy and understanding are essential.
  - **Privacy Concerns:** With chatbots often handling sensitive personal data, ensuring user privacy is paramount. Adhering to data protection regulations and maintaining user trust is a critical challenge, especially in industries like healthcare and finance.
  - **Technical Limitations:** Chatbots may face various technical limitations, including limited understanding of complex queries, inability to handle ambiguous language, and challenges in processing diverse dialects and slang. These limitations can lead to frustration and dissatisfaction among users.
  - **Integration with Existing Systems:** Seamlessly integrating chatbots into existing IT infrastructure and customer service platforms can be challenging. This includes compatibility with CRM systems, databases, and other digital tools.
  - **Scalability and Maintenance:** Ensuring that chatbots can scale to handle increasing volumes of interactions without compromising performance is a challenge. Additionally, ongoing maintenance, including regular updates and improvements, is crucial for their long-term effectiveness.
  - **User Acceptance and Adaptation:** Gaining user acceptance and encouraging adaptation of chatbot technology can be challenging, especially for users who are accustomed to traditional human interactions.
  - **Language and Cultural Barriers:** Developing chatbots that can effectively communicate and engage with users across different languages and cultures adds another layer of complexity.
  - **Balancing Automation and Human Touch:** Finding the right balance between automated responses and the need for human intervention in certain scenarios is a delicate task. Over-reliance on automation can lead to impersonal service, while insufficient automation may not yield the desired efficiency.
- **Potential Solutions and Best Practices:** To address the challenges in chatbot development and deployment, several solutions and best practices can be adopted:
  - Enhancing Emotional Intelligence:
    - Implement advanced NLP and sentiment analysis tools to better interpret user emotions.
    - Regularly update the chatbot's response library with empathetic and contextually appropriate phrases.
  - Addressing Privacy Concerns:
    - Ensure strict adherence to data protection laws like GDPR.
    - Implement robust encryption and data security measures.
    - Be transparent with users about data usage and privacy policies.

- ○ Overcoming Technical Limitations:
  - Continuously train the chatbot with diverse datasets to improve understanding and response accuracy.
  - Integrate AI and ML algorithms that allow the chatbot to learn and adapt from interactions.
- ○ Seamless Integration with Existing Systems:
  - Use APIs and middleware solutions for smooth integration with existing customer service platforms and databases.
  - Conduct thorough testing to ensure compatibility and functionality across systems.
- ○ Scalability and Maintenance:
  - Design chatbots with scalable architectures to handle increased loads.
  - Establish a regular maintenance schedule for updates and performance optimization.
- ○ Enhancing User Acceptance:
  - Educate users about the benefits and functionalities of chatbots.
  - Offer an intuitive and user-friendly interface.
  - Provide an option for users to easily escalate to human agents if needed.
- ○ Overcoming Language and Cultural Barriers:
  - Incorporate multilingual capabilities and localize content to cater to different languages and cultures.
  - Understand and respect cultural nuances in communication styles.
- ○ Balancing Automation and Human Touch:
  - Set clear parameters for when to escalate issues from the chatbot to human agents.
  - Use AI to identify complex queries or emotional situations that require human intervention.
- ○ Continuous Improvement and Feedback Loop:
  - Implement feedback mechanisms to gather user insights.
  - Use analytics to monitor chatbot performance and identify areas for improvement.
- ○ Regular Training and Updates:
  - Keep the chatbot updated with the latest information and industry trends.
  - Regularly train the chatbot with new data to ensure it remains relevant and effective.

By implementing these solutions and adhering to best practices, businesses can significantly enhance the effectiveness of their chatbots, overcoming common challenges and ensuring a positive impact on customer service. These strategies not only address the immediate issues but also contribute to the long-term success and evolution of chatbot technology in customer interactions.

FUTURE RESEARCH DIRECTIONS

As chatbot technology continues to evolve and play an increasingly vital role in various domains, the exploration of future research directions becomes imperative. This section delves into the uncharted territories of chatbot development and application, highlighting areas where further investigation and innovation are needed. The growing integration of chatbots into industries such as healthcare, education, e-commerce, and beyond opens up a realm of possibilities, from enhancing personalized learning

Table 4. Overcoming challenges in chatbot development and deployment

Challenge	Potential Solutions	Best Practices
Understanding Human Emotions - Difficulty in accurately interpreting and responding to user emotions.	Implement advanced NLP and sentiment analysis; update response library.	Regular training with empathetic phrases; continuous NLP improvement.
Privacy Concerns - Ensuring user data privacy and adherence to regulations.	Strict compliance with data laws; robust encryption and security measures.	Transparency in data usage; regular security updates.
Technical Limitations - Limitations in understanding complex queries and diverse dialects.	Continuous training with diverse datasets; integration of AI and ML.	Regular updates and performance optimization.
Integration with Existing Systems - Challenges in integrating chatbots with current IT infrastructure.	Use of APIs and middleware for integration; thorough compatibility testing.	Ensuring seamless functionality across platforms.
Scalability and Maintenance - Ensuring chatbots can handle increased interaction volumes.	Scalable chatbot architecture; regular maintenance schedule.	Performance optimization; scalability testing.
User Acceptance - Gaining user trust and encouraging adaptation to chatbot technology.	User education on chatbot benefits; intuitive interface design.	Easy escalation to human agents; user-friendly design.
Language and Cultural Barriers - Communicating effectively across different languages and cultures.	Multilingual capabilities; localization of content.	Respect for cultural nuances; language-specific customization.
Balancing Automation and Human Touch - Finding the right mix between automated responses and human interaction.	Clear parameters for escalation; AI identification of complex queries.	Human intervention in emotional situations; maintaining personal touch.
Continuous Improvement - Keeping the chatbot relevant and effective over time.	Feedback mechanisms for user insights; performance analytics.	Regular monitoring and updates; user feedback analysis.
Regular Training and Updates - Ensuring the chatbot remains up to date with information and trends.	Regular training with new data; keeping abreast of industry trends.	Continuous learning and adaptation; staying informed on latest developments.

experiences to revolutionizing healthcare diagnostics. Moreover, the continuous evolution of AI, ML, and NLP capabilities presents new horizons for chatbots, raising questions about ethical considerations, user trust, and the boundaries of automation. This section serves as a guide for researchers and practitioners interested in shaping the future of chatbot technology, offering insights into emerging trends, challenges, and unexplored frontiers promise for advancing this transformative field (Table 5).

- **Exploration of Emerging Trends and Technologies in Chatbot Development:**
  - The landscape of chatbot development is in a state of constant evolution, driven by emerging trends and cutting-edge technologies. One prominent trend is the integration of AI-driven chatbots with voice interfaces and smart devices. Voice-activated chatbots, like those found in virtual assistants, offer a more natural and intuitive way of interacting with technology. The future may see chatbots that seamlessly transition between text and voice, providing users with a versatile and personalized experience. Additionally, chatbots are likely to become more context-aware, with the ability to understand and remember user preferences and past interactions, making conversations feel more continuous and human-like. Moreover, the adoption of quantum computing and blockchain technology in chatbot development could revolutionize security, data handling, and processing capabilities, opening new horizons for secure and efficient chatbot applications.

- **Potential Areas for Future Research:**
  - Advanced NLP, AI Ethics, and Cross-cultural Adaptability of Chatbots: Future research directions in chatbots encompass several crucial areas. Advanced Natural Language Processing (NLP) is expected to be a focal point, aiming to enable chatbots to understand and generate human-like text with greater accuracy and fluency. This involves research into more sophisticated language models and context-aware algorithms. Ethical considerations in AI chatbots are another vital avenue, exploring topics like user privacy, bias mitigation, and ensuring responsible AI usage. Researchers will delve into creating ethical guidelines and frameworks for chatbot development and deployment. Cross-cultural adaptability is a promising area for study, as global markets demand chatbots that can interact seamlessly across languages and cultural contexts. This entails research into language translation, cultural sensitivity, and the customization of chatbot personalities to align with diverse user bases.
- **Predictions on the Future Role of Chatbots in Customer Service and Beyond:**
  - Chatbots are poised to play an even more integral role in customer service and beyond in the coming years. The integration of AI and chatbots into customer service will lead to hyper-personalization, where chatbots anticipate user needs, preferences, and even emotions, creating highly tailored experiences. In healthcare, chatbots will assist in diagnostics, providing preliminary assessments and aiding in patient care. Educational chatbots will evolve into personalized learning companions, adapting teaching methods to individual student needs. Furthermore, the predictive capabilities of chatbots will extend to fields like finance, where they assist with investment decisions and financial planning. The future will also see chatbots contributing to sustainability initiatives by guiding users on eco-friendly practices. Overall, chatbots will become an indispensable part of daily life, revolutionizing how we interact with technology, access services, and receive assistance across various domains.

In the ever-evolving landscape of chatbot technology, this comprehensive exploration has illuminated the multifaceted role of chatbots in customer service and beyond. From their origins as rule-based systems to the current state of AI-driven conversational agents, chatbots have witnessed remarkable growth and transformation. They have become integral in shaping the customer experience, offering immediate and efficient assistance, improving user satisfaction, and enabling businesses to operate around the clock. The journey through this chapter has not only dissected the mechanics, types, and challenges of chatbots but has also peered into their promising future. As chatbots continue to advance, leveraging AI, ML, and NLP, they stand poised to revolutionize industries such as healthcare, education, finance, and sustainability. The boundaries of automation will be pushed, ethical considerations will be addressed, and chatbots will become indispensable companions in our digital lives. This chapter has unveiled the intricate web of chatbot technology, and as we look forward, the story of chatbots is one of innovation, adaptability, and endless possibilities.

CONCLUSION

This chapter has been a journey through the realm of chatbots, from understanding their basics to exploring their advanced applications. We've dissected their mechanics, strengths, and limitations, providing a clear reference for readers. The importance of customization and personalization in chatbots emerged

Table 5. Future research directions and impacts of chatbot technology

Research Area	Description
Emerging Trends and Technologies	Exploration of trends like voice interfaces, context-awareness, and the integration of quantum computing and blockchain in chatbot development.
Advanced NLP	Research into improving Natural Language Processing capabilities to enhance chatbot understanding and generation of human-like text.
AI Ethics	Development of ethical guidelines and frameworks for responsible chatbot development, addressing privacy, bias mitigation, and responsible AI usage.
Cross-cultural Adaptability	Study of language translation, cultural sensitivity, and the customization of chatbot personalities to cater to diverse user bases.
Predictions and Future Role	Speculations on chatbots' role in hyper-personalization, healthcare diagnostics, personalized learning, financial assistance, sustainability, and daily life.

as a key theme, alongside real-world case studies showcasing their impact. Moreover, we've addressed the practical aspects of chatbot development, offering insights into overcoming challenges. As we look to the future, emerging trends and ethical considerations beckon, promising exciting possibilities and responsibilities.

The evolution of chatbots in customer service has been remarkable. From rule-based systems to AI-driven companions, they've transformed how businesses engage with users. These 24/7 virtual assistants are now pivotal in enhancing user satisfaction and brand loyalty. However, maintaining a balance between technological innovation and human-centric approaches is crucial. Chatbots are here to complement human efforts, not replace them.

The delicate balance between technology and humanity is where the true magic of chatbots lies. They should augment human capabilities, freeing them from repetitive tasks while preserving the essence of meaningful interactions. Ethical considerations in AI are paramount as we navigate this path, ensuring user trust and privacy. The future holds exciting possibilities, from AI-driven chatbots adapting to user emotions to bridging language and cultural barriers.

The future promises exciting possibilities, from AI-driven chatbots that adapt to user emotions to chatbots that transcend language and cultural barriers. As we forge ahead, let's cherish the harmony between technology and human touch, recognizing that the true potential of chatbots lies in their ability to complement and elevate our customer service experiences while preserving the essence of meaningful human interactions. In this synergy, we find the key to a more efficient, empathetic, and innovative future.

In conclusion, chatbots have evolved from simplistic rule-based systems to sophisticated AI-driven conversational agents, revolutionizing customer service and expanding their footprint across various industries. They have become the cornerstone of 24/7 assistance, personalization, and predictive capabilities, enhancing user experiences in unprecedented ways. However, the journey of chatbots is far from over, and the horizon is filled with opportunities and challenges. Researchers and practitioners must continue to innovate in areas like advanced NLP, ethical AI, and cross-cultural adaptability to unlock the full potential of chatbots.

The balance between technological innovation and human-centric service approaches is the compass that will guide us forward. We must remember that behind every interaction, there is a human seeking assistance, and preserving the human touch in this digital era remains paramount. As we navigate the evolving landscape of chatbots, we are charting a path to a future where human-computer interactions are seamless, empathetic, and transformative. With the torch of innovation in our hands, we march forward, knowing that chatbots are not just tools; they are companions on our journey toward a more efficient, empathetic, and innovative future.

REFERENCES

Adam, M., Wessel, M., & Benlian, A. (2021). AI-based chatbots in customer service and their effects on user compliance. [Reference Link]. *Electronic Markets, 31*(2), 427–445. doi:10.1007/s12525-020-00414-7

Bengio, Y., Courville, A., & Vincent, P. (2013). Representation learning: A review and new perspectives. [Reference Link]. *IEEE Transactions on Pattern Analysis and Machine Intelligence, 35*(8), 1798–1828. doi:10.1109/TPAMI.2013.50 PMID:23787338

Bird, S., Klein, E., & Loper, E. (2009). *Natural language processing with Python: analyzing text with the natural language toolkit*. O'Reilly Media, Inc. [Reference Link]

Castle-Green, T., Reeves, S., Fischer, J. E., & Koleva, B. (2020, July). Decision trees as sociotechnical objects in chatbot design. In *Proceedings of the 2nd Conference on Conversational User Interfaces* (pp. 1-3). ACM. 10.1145/3405755.3406133

Deng, L., & Liu, Y. (2018). *Deep learning in natural language processing*. Springer. doi:10.1007/978-981-10-5209-5

Fogg, B. J., & Tseng, H. (1999, May). The elements of computer credibility. In *Proceedings of the SIGCHI conference on Human Factors in Computing Systems* (pp. 80-87). ACM. 10.1145/302979.303001

Hirschberg, J., & Manning, C. D. (2015). Advances in natural language processing. *Science, 349*(6245), 261–266. doi:10.1126/science.aaa8685 PMID:26185244

Jordan, M. I., & Mitchell, T. M. (2015). Machine learning: Trends, perspectives, and prospects. *Science, 349*(6245), 255–260. doi:10.1126/science.aaa8415 PMID:26185243

Jurafsky, D., & Martin, J. H. (2018). *Speech and Language Processing: An Introduction to Natural Language Processing*. Computational Linguistics, and Speech Recognition.

Kaplan, A., & Haenlein, M. (2019). Siri, Siri, in my hand: Who's the fairest in the land? On the interpretations, illustrations, and implications of artificial intelligence. *Business Horizons, 62*(1), 15–25. doi:10.1016/j.bushor.2018.08.004

Kecht, C., Egger, A., Kratsch, W., & Röglinger, M. (2023). Quantifying chatbots' ability to learn business processes. [Reference Link]. *Information Systems, 113*, 102176. doi:10.1016/j.is.2023.102176

Kushwaha, A. K., Kumar, P., & Kar, A. K. (2021). What impacts customer experience for B2B enterprises on using AI-enabled chatbots? Insights from Big data analytics. [Reference Link]. *Industrial Marketing Management, 98*, 207–221. doi:10.1016/j.indmarman.2021.08.011

Manning, C., & Schutze, H. (1999). *Foundations of statistical natural language processing*. MIT press.

Misischia, C. V., Poecze, F., & Strauss, C. (2022). Chatbots in customer service: Their relevance and impact on service quality. [Reference Link]. *Procedia Computer Science*, *201*, 421–428. doi:10.1016/j.procs.2022.03.055

Murphy, K. P. (2012). *Machine learning: a probabilistic perspective*. MIT press.

Naqvi, M. H. A., Hongyu, Z., Naqvi, M. H., & Kun, L. (2023). Impact of service agents on customer satisfaction and loyalty: Mediating role of Chatbots. [Reference Link]. *Journal of Modelling in Management*.

Russell, S. J., & Norvig, P. (2010). *Artificial intelligence a modern approach*.

Selamat, M. A., & Windasari, N. A. (2021). Chatbot for SMEs: Integrating customer and business owner perspectives. [Reference Link]. *Technology in Society*, *66*, 101685. doi:10.1016/j.techsoc.2021.101685

Weizenbaum, J. (1966). ELIZA—A computer program for the study of natural language communication between man and machine. [Reference Link]. *Communications of the ACM*, *9*(1), 36–45. doi:10.1145/365153.365168

Young, S., Gašić, M., Thomson, B., & Williams, J. D. (2013). Pomdp-based statistical spoken dialog systems: A review. [Reference Link]. *Proceedings of the IEEE*, *101*(5), 1160–1179. doi:10.1109/JPROC.2012.2225812

KEY TERMS AND DEFINITIONS

Artificial Intelligence (AI): Artificial Intelligence refers to the simulation of human intelligence processes by machines, particularly computer systems, including learning, reasoning, problem-solving, and decision-making.

Automation: Automation involves the use of technology, typically software or robotics, to perform tasks or processes with minimal human intervention, streamlining operations and reducing manual effort.

Chatbot: A chatbot is a computer program or AI-powered application designed to simulate conversation with users, providing information, answering questions, or assisting with tasks via text or speech.

Customer Service: Customer Service involves providing assistance, support, and solutions to customers before, during, or after their interactions with a product, service, or organization.

Human-Centric: Human-centric refers to approaches, technologies, or systems that prioritize human needs, values, and experiences while integrating technology for optimal usability and interaction.

Machine Learning (ML): Machine Learning is a subset of AI that focuses on the development of algorithms and statistical models that enable computers to improve their performance on specific tasks through learning from data.

Natural Language Processing (NLP): Natural Language Processing is a branch of AI that enables computers to understand, interpret, and generate human language, making it possible for chatbots to comprehend and respond to text or speech.

Personalization: Personalization is the process of tailoring content, services, or experiences to individual users' preferences, behavior, and needs, creating a more customized and relevant user experience.

Predictive Analytics: Predictive Analytics involves using data, statistical algorithms, and machine learning techniques to identify patterns, trends, and future outcomes, allowing organizations to make informed decisions and predictions.

User Experience (UX): User Experience encompasses a user's overall interaction with a product, system, or service, including usability, accessibility, and the emotional response generated during the interaction.

Chapter 10
A Stratagem and Improvement of Emigrant Chatbot Innovation Using IoT

Venkat Narayana
Sreenidhi Institute of Science and Technology, India

Sangers Bhavana
Sreenidhi Institute of Science and Technology, India

ABSTRACT

A chatbot is a computer program, which is blueprint for simulation and conversation between individuals over the internet. According to the input of a human, chatbots engage with clients and respond to them. It makes the client imagine that it is visiting with an individual while they're talking with the computer. Chatbots are turning out to be progressively significant passageways to automated administration and information in regions like client assistance, medical services, and training. The decision provokes interest about the motivations behind why chatbots are turning out to be more human-like than only a specialized gadget and what's in store for people and chatbots. This chapter gives how the chatbot and IoT mingle and procreate in all the sectors, as IoTs are wise contraptions that the authors track down in their standard normal presence and if chatbots can be made a piece of the IoT and its interface, exchange of information and data will be more important and it will happen all through the scope of the day considering the way that chatbots don't enervate.

INTRODUCTION

The IoT is an association of related things that exchange data with the cloud and other IoT devices. Sensors and computers are often used in IoT devices, including consumer products, digital devices, and machines. Organizations across diverse industries are increasingly leveraging IoT for more efficient management, improved customer service, enhanced decision-making, and heightened business value. IoT facilitates the transmission of data across networks without the need for direct connections to individuals

DOI: 10.4018/979-8-3693-1830-0.ch010

or computers. There are numerous applications for chatbots, and the Internet of Things (IoT) is an easy addition to this list. The difficulty of less experienced users installing or configuring their devices as well as resolving small, common issues is one of the reasons why the Internet of Things is struggling to gain traction. This powers clients to depend on qualified staff to fix simple issues consistently, which makes the client experience disappointing. In this situation, a chatbot can play an essential part in further developing the client experience, as when properly modified and embedded inside the reference IoT Platform, it would give the client the important help while managing convoluted activities subsequently fulfilling the absence of abilities. Clearly, it wouldn't just give some assistance in performing specific activities yet it would likewise provide data that will be specifically mentioned by the client, such as, about the situation with their vehicle, home, work, etc., significantly diminishing the boundaries between the client and associated objects. All in regular language (human language) as opposed to depending on navigation through a graphical connection point in a versatile application or site. Unfortunately, progress is as of now being made at a slow pace. The genuinely conversational chatbot, which will actually want to independently decipher client inputs, is still quite far off, yet a few examination endeavors are moving towards the unification of an environment that is at present exceptionally divided. Chatbots can be really utilized related to IoT and (Web of Things) to improve client cooperation and command over associated gadgets. The following are multiple manners by which chatbots are utilized in IoT applications: discussion. Clients has some control over IoT gadgets utilizing regular language orders through a chatbot interface. For instance, turning on/off lights, changing indoor regulator settings, or overseeing savvy home gadgets. IoT device status updates and information can be provided in real time by chatbots. From their connected devices, users can inquire about temperature, energy consumption, or any other relevant data. Chatbots can send proactive cautions and notices to clients in view of occasions identified by IoT gadgets. For example, a chatbot could tell clients about a security break or an unexpected change in natural circumstances. Clients can set up robotization situations for their IoT gadgets utilizing chatbots. By characterizing explicit circumstances and activities in a conversational way, clients can make customized computerization rules. By incorporating chatbots with IoT, clients can have a more normal and conversational point of interaction for overseeing and cooperating with their associated gadgets. This not only makes the user experience better but also makes it easier to control and manage IoT devices (S.Mahajanetal, 2018)(Nimavat et al,2017) which can be complicated. The main purpose of connecting different sensors is, Operators and agencies and collect/process information from them Create ideas about the situation and Human agents need to understand themselves and their environment. The association of genuine articles, or "things," that are implanted with sensors, programming, and different headways to communicate and exchange data with different gadgets and systems over the web is alluded to as the Internet of things.The expansion of IoT has led to the introduction of 15.14 billion "connected devices"(Evans, D.2011)(Vander Meulen,2015) by 2023 into our daily lives, including 15.14 billion applications in healthcare,agriculture,smart cities,wearbles,hospitality, autonomous driving, smart retail, industrial IOT and lot more. Users can use chatbots to help them troubleshoot issues with their IoT devices. By seeking clarification on pressing issues and giving bit by bit direction, the chatbot can assist clients with settling issues without the requirement for specialized aptitude. Chatbots can decipher and dissect information gathered by IoT gadgets, furnishing clients with bits of knowledge and suggestions. For example, a chatbot could propose energy-saving tips in light of verifiable utilization designs. Users can interact with their IoT devices through familiar interfaces like Facebook Messenger, WhatsApp, or Slack thanks to chatbots' integration into popular messaging platforms. Coordinating voice-empowered chatbots permits clients to control IoT gadgets utilizing voice orders. This can be especially valuable in situations where manual collaboration isn't down to earth, for example, while driving a vehicle. Chatbots can learn and adjust to client inclinations after some time, giving a customized insight. This can incorporate changing brilliant home settings, suggesting items in view of utilization examples, and the sky is the limit from there. By allowing users to set access controls, change passwords, and receive alerts regarding potential security threats, chatbots can help manage the security aspects of IoT devices. The purpose of a chatbot is to imitate human conversational abilities, people who interact with one act as though they are interacting with peers. This is possible considering the way that the chatbot goes through a movement of pushes toward process human data and a while later choose a fitting response or action considering the client's inquiry. IOT Chatbots are used in agriculture (S.Wiangsamut et.al, 2019) (M.H.A.Fadzil et.al, 2020) sectors, business, industrial organization and mostly education field etc. chatbots for plant checking fit for monitoring different boundaries helpful for knowing the wellbeing of houseplants. Close by the IoT framework, we execute a chatbot to illuminate the proprietor about the ongoing states of the plant and its ongoing necessities. An integrated Chatbot IoT system is implemented to speed up and make it easier to monitor and improve water quality (M.H.A.Fadzil et.al, 2020). For checking, an organization of IoT sensors was made, upheld by a cloud stage.

A CONCISE EPIC OF CHATBOT

The first and most chatbot was developed in the year 1960s. It was called ELIZA (Ranoliya et.al, 2010) ELIZA and other popular chatbots that were developed in the second half of the 20th century; it uses pattern matching and substitution methodology to simulate conversation, Later on PARRY came into existence which resemble to think like humans and also it helped to understand the mental illness of the humans so on, When new solutions need to be incorporated into legacy systems, the first challenge is grasping the effect with regards to intricacy. Jwacky is a chatterbot made by English developer Rollo Craftsman. Its expressed point is to "reproduce regular human visit in a fascinating, engaging and hilarious way". To comprehend the intricacy in (Khan et.al, 2019) the creators dissected the chance of making an overall engineering that would permit the reconciliation among chatbot and IoT frameworks in a basic manner. The investigation discovered that what chatbots and IoT share practically speaking is that they take on their administrations through moderately straightforward, frequently soothing, web APIs. In 1995, fabricated Fig.1 A.L.I.C.E. (R.Wallace, 2009) a chatbot made completely with open source programming that utilizes the AIML language, offspring of the XML language from which it acquires extensibility, which subsequently permits the chatbot to hold a discussion. In this situation, adopting a service oriented improvement way to deal with advancement, joining is plausible thanks to Serene HTTP norms and conventions. Without having to descend to the underlying levels, the ISO/OSI application level is the only level in question in this instance. It is hence certain that with plan precautionary measures, the combination among chatbot and IoT stages is incredibly straightforward.

Architectural Paradigm of Bot

The following are the steps for designing (Rohan Karl et.al, 2016) the bots it involves the steps to be considered. The first step is to define intent and purview: Clearly define the intent and purview of the bot. What tasks or services will it perform? Who is the target audience? Choose the Right Platform: Determine the platform(s) on which the bot will operate. This could manifest as a website, a mobile app,

Figure 1. Proposed chatbot

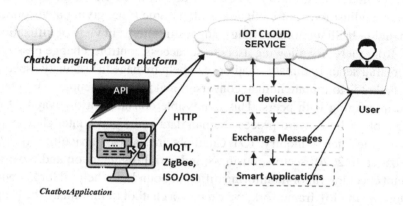

messaging platforms such as Facebook Messenger or WhatsApp, or a blend of these options. Selecting the evolution manifesto of bot: Pick a reasonable evolution structure or manifesto for building your bot. A few famous choices incorporate Microsoft Bot Structure, Dialog flow, Rasa, or custom arrangements utilizing programming dialects like Python, Node.js, and so on. Information Capacity and The board: Settle on the capacity answer for client information and discussion history. This might incorporate data sets like MongoDB, MySQL, or cloud-based arrangements like Firebase or Amazon Dynamo DB. Client Info Handling: Carry out normal language handling (NLP) capacities to comprehend client input. This could include utilizing pre-prepared models or creating custom calculations to decipher and separate significance from client questions. Bot Rationale and Discussion Stream: Plan the discussion stream and execute the rationale that oversees how the bot answers client inputs. To control the conversation's flow, think about using state machines or other methods. In the event that your bot needs to communicate with outer administrations or APIs, plan how to coordinate these administrations into your bot's design. This could involve authentication, data exchange, and error handling. User Authentication and Authorization: If your bot requires user authentication, implement a secure and user-friendly authentication process. Consider how to manage user permissions and access levels. Security Measures: Implement security measures to protect user data and ensure the bot's resilience against potential attacks. The fragmentation of technology has been a major issue with the Internet of Things (Adamopoulou et.al, 2020) (Celesti et.a, 2016) (M. Wallace, 2016). It is extremely uncommon to have application interoperability between heterogeneous devices from a single remote (mobile device or operation terminal). For Model, consider what is going on where a brilliant light and a Warming Ventilation and Cooling (central air) framework have a place with a similar organization and climate yet may have different client control terminals which are autonomous together substances, uninformed about one another nor ready to control or speak with one another. This includes encryption, secure connections (HTTPS), and input validation. Scalability and Performance: Design the architecture with scalability in mind to handle increased user demand.

The most famous chatbots at the time are chatbots that are utilized for internet business and e-schooling arrangements. Customers and sellers, as well as students and teachers, have always had trouble communicating because employees' workloads can sometimes be so high that answering all of these questions can take a long time, despite the likelihood that the question can be answered quickly and the information can be found easily. This is where chatbots can be useful to lessen correspondence issues as far as reaction time. An internet business chatbot can help to see as the item that a client is looking for

Figure 2. Architecture of chatbot

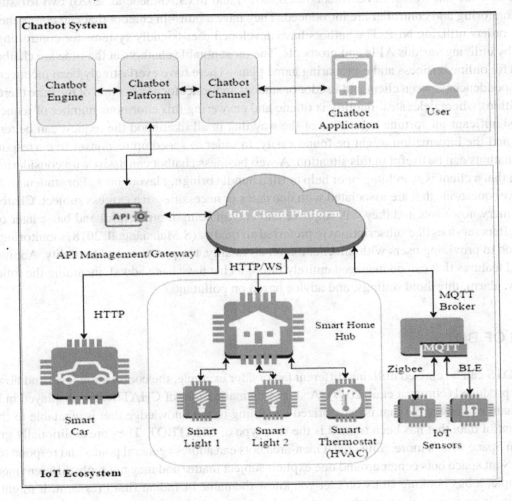

or help to fill a bundle bringing template back. For understudies, chatbots can reply questions that are connected with due dates or prerequisites in a explicit subject. Chatbots are exceptionally normal these days and they will improve and turn out to be more useful and essential later on. As of now, there are a lot of notable chatbots that are utilized in day to day existence. Take, for instance, Siri, an iOS virtual assistant that responds to user queries and requests for web services using natural language (Schermer et.al,2007)(Russell et.al,2003). Google Currently is another portable application for Android and iOS gadgets that gives Google-created prescient guides with data and everyday updates to respond to clients' inquiries naturally. Cortana - the Windows voice stage with data that makes a difference programming and equipment designers. Consider using cloud services that can dynamically scale resources. Monitoring and Analytics: Implement tools for monitoring the bot's performance, tracking user interactions, and collecting analytics data. This information can be valuable for improving the bot over time. Stakeholder experience: provides an impeccable user's experience. Design clear and concise responses, error handling, and options for users to navigate through the conversation easily. Testing and Quality Assurance: Develop a robust testing strategy to ensure the bot functions as intended. This may include various testing to check how the bot works. In (G.Alexakisetal, 2019) and in (S.Ahmedetal, 2020) two IoT stages for home monitoring and controller are introduced. They have a built- in chatbot that can comprehend text or voice orders utilizing NLP. The authors have developed user-friendly systems for controlling home devices by utilizing various APIs and protocols. The most notable chatbots at the time are chatbots that are used for online business and e-preparing game plans. There have everlastingly been inconveniences in correspondence between client and vendor or student and educator as a portion of the time there might be conditions where delegates' liability is titanic and answering this enormous number of requests can make a significant misfortune regardless of the way that in all likelihood the request can be tended to quickly, and the information might be found easily. In order to speed up responses to correspondence issues, chatbots can be useful in this situation. A web business chatbot can assist with considering to be the thing that a client is searching for or help to fill a bundle bringing layout back. For students, chatbots can answer questions that are associated with due dates or necessities in a express subject. Chatbots are very ordinary nowadays and they will improve and end up being more helpful and basic later on. The chatbot offers services like subscriptions to preferred air quality (S.Mahajanetal, 2018) monitoring points in addition to providing users with information on air quality, temperature, and humidity. Additionally, advanced features that can be managed entirely through chat have been added, including the following: geoquery, alarm, threshold settings, and advice based on pollutants.

TYPES OF BOTS

CHATBOTS can be classed utilizing different factors, for example, the cooperation level and how reactions are produced (Nimavat et.al, 2017). A short schematic order of CHATBOT is displayed in Figure 3. A domain of knowledge that is categorized according to the knowledge that is available to them or the amount of data that has been trained is the first type of CHATBOT. They are additionally grouped into Open Space what's more, Shut area. Open-area bots can address general points and respond to them fittingly. Shut space bots center around one explicit subject matter and may not reply different inquiries. For example, a bus booking Bot won't let you know the name of Indian first President. It might make you a quip or answer how your day is, yet it isn't intended to do some other errands, taking into account that its responsibility is to book a bus and give the client all the important data about the booked bus(Nimavat et.al,2017). The subsequent one is administration given; The level of intimate interaction between these Bots and the user is determined by the task at hand. Further ordered into Relational, Intrapersonal, and between specialist. Relational bots are for correspondence and permit administrations, for example, Table booking in Cafés, Train booking, FAQ bots, and so forth. These CHATBOTS should get data and give it to the client. These kinds of BOT can become easy to understand and liable to recall past data about the client. Intrapersonal bots will perform tasks under the user's intimate part and exist in the user's personal domain, such as chat applications like Facebook Messenger, Telegram, and WhatsApp. Overseeing schedule, putting away the client's perspective, and so on. They will end up being the colleagues of the client and comprehend the client as a human (G.Alexakisetal, 2016).Between specialist's bots are becoming pervasive as all CHATBOTS require amazing open doors for intercommunication. objective based Bot; these Bots are classified by the essential reason they are planned to accomplish. There are a lot of notable chatbots that are utilized in day to day existence. For instance, Siri - a remote helper of Ios interface that utilizes regular language to respond to client requests also, perform web administration demands. Google Presently is another versatile application for Android and iOS gadgets that gives Google-created prescient guides with data and day to day updates to address clients' inquiries consequently. Cortana is the voice platform for Windows that provides developers of software and hardware with information. Chatbots for Courier a program that utilizes Man-made reasoning (simulated intelligence) to understand a connection with clients. Facebook sent off the stage to permit designers to create chatbots that are capable speak with Facebook clients through the Courier talk interface. Messenger chatbots respond to questions asked by users in a very human way (A. A. Qaffas, 2019) Further group into Enlightening, Discussion and Task Bot. Instructive bots furnish the client with intel or information from a proper data set, similar to the FAQ BOTS and stock data set at the distribution center (G.Alexakisetal, 2016).Conversational/Text-based bots attempt to talk with the client as another person, and their motivation is to properly answer the client's solicitations. Subsequently, they want to seek after the client's discussion utilizing methods like cross-addressing, aversion, and respectfulness, for example: Alexa and Siri (G.Alexakisetal, 2016).

PROPOSED BOT

We present a calculated plan for a framework that works with the improvement of Chabot frameworks in the domain of the Internet of things. As per reports, Talk interfaces which are utilized in Texting (IM) stages (Like Facebook Courier, Slack, Kik, and Message) have been enormously well known and keep on showing consistent development. In administrations have more dynamic clients than some other web application including informal communities, mailing applications (W.Mckitterick, 2015), This report demonstrates how nearly 4 billion people use the top ten messaging platforms alone. The comprehensive architecture, which includes both the IoT system and the Chatbot system, is depicted at a high level in Figure 2. The proposed framework plan for the IoT-Chatbot Framework is delineated in Figure 1.

IoT Framework

IoT Gadgets:

In this chapter, we characterize an IoT gadget comprehensively as an "extraordinarily recognizable IoT endpoint open and controllable through Relaxing Web APIs." In situations where implanted gadgets need APIs, suitable arrangements exist to make APIs for them easily. Stages like Zetta empower the making of IoT cloud-based frameworks Fig 2 outfitted with exhaustive APIs. We focus on a home automation setup that includes smart lights (such as Philips Hue), smart HVAC (such as a Nest thermostat), and a connected car or smart car (such as Tesla). Regardless, on a basic level, any IoT gadget has the potential for connecting with Chatbots (Evans, 2016).

This framework configuration expects to give an adaptable and versatile structure for coordinating different IoT gadgets consistently with Chatbot frameworks. This chapter will give the extensive incorporation of the Internet of Things (IoT) in diverse industries has fundamentally reshaped how Education (Khan et.al, 2019), Healthcare, businesses (Rohan Karl, 2016) (Shermer et.al, 2007) etc., operate. IoT facilitates ongoing communication and data interchange among devices and systems, leading to more streamlined management, elevated customer service, improved decision-making, and an overall increase in business value. Advantage in this chapter, chatbot designing is more helpful for the education (Khan et.al, 2019) system and designed such that its answers to the students questions according to their abil-

Figure 3. Concise epic of chatbot

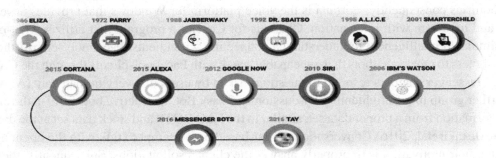

ity of understanding. Chatbots when used along with IOT, Chatbots when integrated with IoT (Internet of Things), can offer several benefits, enhancing the overall user experience and operational efficiency.

The parts of the overall design are depicted in Figure 1. The IOT device talks with all levels to give client tendency information to manufacture tweaked IoT organizations. Internet of things Cloud platform assume a vital part as an empowering innovation in various IoT frameworks at present. Access protocols like Message Queuing Telemetry Transport (MQTT) and HTTP, wireless protocols like ZigBee and Bluetooth Low Energy (BLE), and a wide range of services, software development kits (SDKs), and integrations are all handled by these platforms. Positive reports feature the deeply grounded benefits of using Cloud-based IoT stages Celesti et.al, 2016). An intention is what users want the Chatbot to do for each task. The Chatbot is then evaluated by the designer through text or conversational interactions that imitate human communication. Therefore, clients might figure out their inquiries or expectations in different ways, contingent upon how they wish to put themselves out there. For instance, teaching the Chatbot to switch off the television could be stated as "Alexa (Celesti et.al, 2016), switch off the television," "Alexa, might you at some point if it's not too much trouble, switch off the television?" or on the other hand "How about you switch off the television?" While these expressions share similar aim or errand of switching off the television, they address various articulations or variations. The ability to access and control embedded devices like smart cars, lights, thermostats, and so on is prioritized in our system design, through the Programming interface the board/Passage of the IoT Cloud Stage. This approach stays free of the principles and conventions utilized by individual inserted gadgets. In any case, it is vital to take note of that this paper doesn't dig into the complexities of mind-boggling parts inside the Systems administration and processing framework for the Cloud platform.

IOT Cloud Service

Internet of things cloud platform assume a vital part as an empowering innovation in various IoT frameworks at present. Access protocols like Message Queuing Telemetry Transport (MQTT) and HTTP, wireless protocols like ZigBee and Bluetooth Low Energy (BLE), and a wide range of services, software development kits (SDKs), and integrations are all handled by these platforms. Positive reports feature the deeply grounded benefits of using Cloud-based IoT stages (Google Developers, 2016). An intention is what users want the Chatbot to do for each task (Schermer et.al, 2007). The Chatbot is then evaluated by the designer through text or conversational interactions that imitate human communication. Therefore, clients might figure out their inquiries or expectations in different ways, contingent upon how they wish to put themselves out there. For instance, teaching the Chatbot to switch off the television could be stated as "Alexa (Celesti et.al, 2016), switch off the television," "Alexa, might you at some point if it's not too much trouble, switch off the television?" or on the other hand "How about you switch off the television (S.Ahmedetal, 2020)?" While these expressions share similar aim or errand of switching off the television, they address various articulations or variations(Schermer,2007).The ability to access and control embedded devices like smart home(G.Alexakisetal,2016)smart cars, lights, thermostats, and so on is prioritized in our system design, through the Programming interface the board/Passage of the IoT Cloud Stage(Celesti et.al,2016).This approach stays free of the principles and conventions utilized by individual inserted gadgets. In any case, it is vital to take note of that this chapter doesn't dig into the complexities of mind boggling parts inside the Systems administration and processing framework for the Cloud platform.

ChatBot System

A chatbot system is a software program crafted to emulate conversations with human users, particularly on the internet. It utilizes artificial intelligence (AI) technologies, including natural language processing (NLP) and machine learning, to comprehend and respond to user queries or commands in a conversational manner.

The essential components of a chatbot system typically encompass:

a) **User Interface:** This serves as the platform or interface through which users engage with the chatbot. It may take the form of a website, messaging app (W.Mckittrick, 2015) (Evans, 2016), or any other application.

b) **Processing Engine:** The chatbot's core intelligence resides in its processing engine. This component employs algorithms and machine learning models to interpret user input and generate appropriate responses.

c) **Knowledge Base:** Chatbots depend on a knowledge base or database to retrieve information and respond to user queries. This repository can consist of pre-programmed data or information acquired over time through machine learning.

d) **Natural Language Processing (NLP):** NLP is a critical aspect of chatbots that enables them to comprehend and interpret user input in a manner that emulates human conversation. It involves parsing and analyzing the structure of sentences.

e) **Dialog Management:** Chatbots require the capability to maintain context within a conversation. Dialog management ensures that the chatbot understands the ongoing interactions' context and responds cohesively.

f) **Integration:** Chatbots often necessitate integration with other systems or databases to offer more comprehensive and accurate information. This integration can involve accessing external APIs, databases, or third-party services.

Chatbot systems find diverse applications across domains such as customer support, information retrieval, task automation, and entertainment. They can be rule-based, adhering to predefined scripts, or AI-based, learning and adapting from user interactions over time. As technology progresses, chatbots are evolving into more sophisticated systems, providing increasingly natural and context-aware conversations with users.

ChatBot Engine

A chatbot engine is the foundational software or system that oversees the operations of a chatbot. It serves as the central component, enabling the chatbot to comprehend user inputs, process information, and generate appropriate responses. The chatbot engine encompasses various elements, including natural language processing (NLP) (L.Atzori et.al, 2011), machine learning algorithms, dialogue management, and integration with external systems or APIs. Some NLP techniques used in IOT, some key NLP techniques applicable to IoT.

Speech Recognition:

a. Transform spoken words into text for understanding user commands or queries.
b. Utilize technologies like Automatic Speech Recognition (ASR) for processing spoken language.

Text-to-Speech (TTS):

a. Convert textual information generated by IoT devices into spoken words.
b. Useful for providing auditory feedback or alerts to users.

Intent Recognition:

a. Discern the user's intention from their input.
b. Identify the action or task implied by the user's command.

Named Entity Recognition (NER):

a. Extract pertinent entities (e.g., names, locations, dates) from user queries.
b. Beneficial for understanding specific details in the context of IoT.

Sentiment Analysis:

a. Determine the sentiment expressed in user feedback or queries.
b. Helps understand user emotions and tailor IoT responses accordingly.

Language Translation:

a. Translate text from one language to another.
b. Valuable for IoT devices operating in multilingual environments.

Conversational Agents:

a. Implement chatbots or virtual assistants for natural language interactions.
b. Enhance user experience by providing a more intuitive and interactive interface.

Context Awareness:

Figure 4. Proposed of chatbot

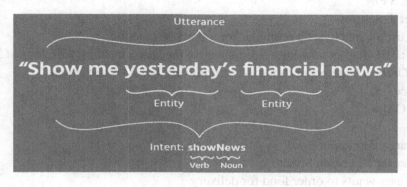

a. Consider the context of user interactions for personalized and relevant responses.
b. Maintain context across multiple interactions to ensure a seamless user experience.

TERMINOLOGY USED IN CHATBOTS

This Chapter of NLP techniques for the Chatbot motor isn't the essential focal point of this section; rather, it is principally worried about posting the applicable key utilitarian parts of the motor with regards to IoT. Then, we consolidate key thoughts conventionally associated with chatbot engines (Thosani et.al, 2020) (Shevchuk et.al, 2019)

Entities: Entities are domain-specific details extracted from the user's input, helping to map natural language expressions to their canonical forms. This facilitates a better understanding of the user's intent behind the input.

Utterances: Phrases or statements within a chatbot conversation.

The terminology focuses upon Utterances, Entities, Intents, and Actions

Example of Chatbot Utterances like "Show me yesterday's financial news" Figure 4.

Chatbot conversation with entities, intent, context, and action:

Chatbot conversation with entities, intent, context, and the action taken:

EX 1:In this utterance:

User: "Find a nearby Italian restaurant for dinner.".

Intent: Find Restaurant

Entities:

Cuisine Type: Italian

Meal Type: Dinner

Context: The user is looking for a restaurant for dinner.

Action Taken: The chatbot provides a list of nearby Italian restaurants suitable for dinner.

EX 2: User: "Set a reminder for my meeting with John at 3 PM tomorrow."

In this utterance:

Intent: Set Reminder

Entities:

Meeting Subject: Meeting with John

Meeting Time: 3 PM

Meeting Date: Tomorrow

Context: The user wants to set a reminder for a specific meeting.

Action Taken: The chatbot schedules a reminder for the user's meeting with John at 3 PM tomorrow.

EX 3: User: "Order a large pepperoni pizza for delivery to 123 Main Street."

In this utterance:

Intent: Place Order

Entities:

Food Item: Large Pepperoni Pizza

Delivery Address: 123 Main Street

Context: The user wants to order food for delivery.

Action Taken: The chatbot places an order for a large pepperoni pizza to be delivered to 123 Main Street.

EX 4: User: "Find a nearby gym with yoga classes scheduled for tomorrow morning."

In this utterance:

Intent: Find Nearby Gym

Entities:

Activity: Yoga Classes

Date: Tomorrow

Time: Morning

Context: The user is looking for a gym nearby offering yoga classes for tomorrow morning.

Action Taken: The chatbot searches for nearby gyms with yoga classes scheduled for tomorrow morning and provides relevant options to the user.

The future is to witness the intrinsic integration of IoT into everyday activities. However, the dynamic nature of IoT presents its own set of challenges. This chapter proposes the utilization of Chatbots as a solution to address some of these challenges. This initial exploration identifies areas with significant potential for future development, including: Advancements in AI: Software Agents are anticipated to develop into more intelligent entities as AI advances. A definitive point is to accomplish Solid man-made intelligence, where machines exhibit scholarly capacities equivalent to people. Research tries toward this path include upgrading thinking skills to make more independent Chatbots. NLG and Natural Language Processing (NLP) models are also being worked on to make conversations between humans and bots more natural and coherent. Within the IoT, research areas like Intelligent Agents and Machine-to-Machine (M2M) interactions are anticipated to benefit greatly from chatbots.

Cyber Systems: The development of man-made knowledge points inside Chatbots in the IoT space is unusually connected with various levels of the 5C CS Designing, specifically Change, Computerized, Perception, and Course of action (Adamopoulou et.al, 2020). The collaboration among CS and simulated intelligence upgraded Chatbots can possibly reshape the scene of incorporated digital actual frameworks and achieve advancements at the crossing point of the physical and computational domains as improvement proceeds. The Internet of Things (IoT) (Atzori L et.al, 2010) and Software Agents offer numerous exciting research opportunities as the Internet itself evolves. The improvement of an Internet 3.0 or Semantic Web and its effect on the eventual fate of Programming Specialists has been obviously portrayed in the writing (Schermer et.al, 2007). This represents an incredible a chance for research in IoT as far as Semantic interoperability which can significantly affect the IoT worldview itself. No-programming stages are that stage plan by the designer uses to construct Bot without any programming language, AI calculation, and regular language handling and figuring out abilities. These stages are immaculate for limited scope tasks and straightforward Bot. Codes for these stages are not difficult to create without knowing programming abilities, ML calculation, NLP, and NLU aptitude. The far reaching illustration of the non-coding stage is Chat fuel, Many Chat, and Motion.ai (Russell et.al, 2004). Now let's talk about the platforms that tech giants built for CHATBOT because they see them as a symbol of standard. These stages are powerful in nature; Also significantly elevated are learning curve and memory. These are frequently used to build complex BOTs that use a flowchart to show the design of the conversation flow. However, they must keep in mind that the bot should never misunderstand user requests or it should be rare. Regularly utilized tech monsters stages, for example, Google foster Dialog flow Fundamental, Dialog flow CX, Facebook creates Wit.ai, Microsoft creates LUIS, and Amazon creates Lex, also.

IBM creates Watson from this they are not difficult to convey (Rohan Karl et.al, 2016) to the Application, site, Message, and so forth. GOOGLE DIALOG FLOW permits clients to utilize another technique to join with their item by building CHATBOT by including text, discourse, or voice discussion in the interfaces. For instance, the voice acknowledgment innovation sent CHATBOTs; for example, Amazon reverberations spot. GOOGLE DIALOGFLOW permits its clients to interface or send on the association's site, portable application, Google Right hand, Amazon Alexa, Facebook Courier, and other well-known stages. The development of the Semantic Web will have significant effect on regions in unavoidable processing, Machine2Machine advancements bringing about Programming Specialists having the option to draw more worth and accomplish a more elevated level of insight than previously. Improvement in the field of IoT has been marvelous lately. Essentially, Chatbot frameworks are likewise becoming more insightful and refined as the days progress (Schermer et.al, 2007). To the best of our insight, no work has been distributed enumerating the particular reconciliation of Chatbots to IoT. This chapter has endeavored to coordinate these two fields together by enrolling the key engineering parts required and imagine conceivable ways of tending to a portion of the current difficulties in IoT. We trust that this attempt will prompt more smart and powerful incorporated IoT frameworks. The progress of the bot was confined into two regions: plan and improvement of the colossal number of parts pivotal for the NLU functionalities; progress of the entrance and the capacities fundamental to deal with the occasions and related information in the Chatbot stage, the chance of coordinating a menial helper, created as a chatbot, inside an IoT stage to help and guide the client to easily complete the different tasks that sounds lumbering and once in a while convoluted. This need, as we probably are aware, gets from the way that the configurations and solicitations for information, for an unpracticed client, are not prompt yet may require different moves toward be finished and might be baffling. A bot has been then, at that point, created which, because of a natural language grasping motor, can handle the client's solicitations formed in a characteristic language. The bot basically functions as a middle person between this present reality and the imaginary world. In the preliminaries that have been finished it has been doable to see that it is so natural to arrange the bot and use it to team up ordinarily with the IoT stage. We specifically zeroed in on stage access, gadget setting and information demand. It must be expressed that for these tests the tasks did were simple yet at the same time empowering for future turns of events. Interesting fact is that the capacity to quickly and efficiently deploy applications, as well as to have the option to use the bot as an aid in investigation. Knowing more and more if the various devices are defective or malfunctioning allows you to restart them accordingly.

ETHICAL IMPLICATIONS AND PRIVACY CONCERNS

Data Security

Encryption and Safe Storage: Reduce the possibility of unwanted access and data breaches by using robust security technologies to protect user data both during transmission and storage.

Access Controls: Strict access controls should be put into effect to restrict data access to individuals who are authorized, improving security and avoiding the exploitation of private data.

Periodic Audits and Compliance: To preserve regulatory compliance and increase user confidence, regularly conduct security audits to find vulnerabilities and make sure that data protection laws like GDPR are being complied with.

Responsible Use of Personal Information

Adhere with the idea of purpose limitation by gathering and using personal data only for defined, authorized purposes. This will encourage responsible data handling and reduce privacy threats (Cox et.al, 2023)

User Consent

Precise Consent Options: Give users more discretion over the information they disclose, enabling them to make competent privacy decisions and encouraging openness in data gathering procedures.

Revocable Consent: Provide users the freedom to withdraw their consent at any moment, honoring their privacy choices and promoting responsibility in data handling.

Age Verification and Compliance: In order to comply with privacy legislation, protect vulnerable user groups, and promote responsible data practices, it is important to implement age verification methods and get parental consent for minors(Guida,S.(2021)

CONCLUSION

The migration chatbot innovation's strategic and promising approach to enhancing the overall user experience and functionality is the incorporation of Internet of Things (IoT) technology. Via flawlessly interfacing actual gadgets and sensors, IoT empowers a more vivid and setting mindful connection among migrants and chatbots, prompting further developed correspondence, effectiveness, and client fulfillment. One of the vital benefits of integrating IoT into exiled person Chatbot is the capacity to accumulate constant information from different sources, like wearable gadgets, area trackers, and ecological sensors. This abundance of data permits chatbots to adjust and answer progressively to the particular necessities and difficulties looked by exiled people, offering customized and applicable help. For example, a chatbot furnished with IoT capacities can give convenient data about nearby assets, weather patterns, open positions, and widespread developments in light of the exiled person's ongoing area.

REFERENCES

Adamopoulou, E., & Moussiades, L. (2020). An overview of chatbot technology. *IFIP International Conference on Artificial Intelligence Applications and Innovations*. Springer, Cham. 10.1007/978-3-030-49186-4_31

Ahmedetal, S. (2020). Smart Home Shield and Automation System Using Facebook Messenger Chatbot. In: *2020 IEEE Region 10 Symposium (TENSYMP)*. IEEE.

Alexakisetal, G. (2019). Control of smart home operations using natural language processing, voice recognition and IoT technologies in a multi-tier architecture. Designs, 3, 32.

Atzori, L., Iera, A., & Morabito, G. (2011). SIoT: Giving a Social Structure to the Internet of Things". In. *IEEE Communications Letters*, *15*(11), 15. doi:10.1109/LCOMM.2011.090911.111340

Celesti, A., Fazio, M., Giacobbe, M., Puliafito, A., & Villari, M. (2016). Characterizing Cloud Federation in IoT. *30th International Conference on Advanced*. IEEE.

Celesti, A., Fazio, M., Giacobbe, M., Puliafito, A., & Villari, M. (2016). Characterizing Cloud Federation in IoT. In *2016 30th International Conference on Advanced Information Networking and Applications Workshops (WAINA)*, (pp. 93-98). IEEE. 10.1109/WAINA.2016.152

Evans, D. (2012). *The Internet of Things How the Next Evolution of the Internet is Changing Everything (April 2011)*. IEEE.

Evans data. (2016). *Evans Data Corporation \Internet of Things – Vertical Research Service*. Evans. http://www.evansdata.com/reports/viewRelease.php?reportID=38

Karl, R. (2016). *Applying Chatbots to the Internet of Things: Opportunities and Architectural Elements*. Research Gate.

Khan, A. (2019). NEEV : An Education Informational Chatbot. [IRJET]. *International Research Journal of Engineering and Technology*, *6*(4), 492–495.

Mahajanetal, S. (2018). Design and implementation of IoT enabled personal air quality assistant on instant messenger. In: *Proceedings of the 10th International Conference on Management of Digital EcoSystems*, (pp. 165–170). ACM. 10.1145/3281375.3281398

Mckitterick, W. (2015). *The Messaging App Report: How instant Messaging can be monetized*. Business Insider.

Nimavat, K., & Champaneria, T. (2017). Chatbots: An Overview Types, Architecture, Tools and Future Possibilities. *International Journal of Scientific Research and Development*, *5*(7), 1019–1026.

Nimavat, K., & Champaneria, T. (2017). Chatbots: An Overview Types, Architecture, Tools and Future Possibilities. *International Journal of Scientific Research and Development*, *5*(7), 1019–1026.

Ranoliya, B. R., Raghuwanshi, N., & Singh, S. (2017). Chatbot for university related FAQs. *2017 International Conference on Advances in Computing, Communications and Informatics (ICACCI)*. IEEE. 10.1109/ICACCI.2017.8126057

Russell, S. J., Norvig, P., Canny, J. F., Malik, J. M., & Edwards, D. D. (2003). *Artificial intelligence: a modern approach* (Vol. 2). Prentice hall.

Schermer, B. W. (2007). *Software agents, surveillance, and the right to privacy: a legislative framework for agent-enabled surveillance.* Leiden University Press. doi:10.5117/9789087280215

Vander Meulen, R. (2015). Gartner Says 6.4 Billion Connected 'Things' Will Be in Use in 2016, Up 30 Percent From 2015. Stamford.

Wallace, M. (2016). *Fragmentation is the enemy of the Internet of Things | Qualcomm.* Qualcomm.

Wallace, R. (2009). *The anatomy of A.L.I.C.E.* doi:10.1007/978-1-4020-6710-5_13

Wiangsamut, S., Chomphuwiset, P., & Khummanee, S. (2019). Chatting with Plants (Orchids) in Automated Smart Farming using IoT, Fuzzy Logic and Chatbot. Advances in Science, Technology and Engineering Systems Journal. doi:10.25046/aj040522

Cox, S. R., Lee, Y., & Ooi, W. (2023). Comparing How a Chatbot References User Utterances from Previous Chatting Sessions: An Investigation of Users' Privacy Concerns and Perceptions. *Proceedings of the 11th International Conference on Human-Agent Interaction.* ACM. 10.1145/3623809.3623875

Google. (2016). *Overview of Internet of things.* Google Developers. https://cloud.google.com/solutions/iot-overview

Guida, S. (2021). Privacy policies between perception and learning through legal design: ideas for an educational chatbot combining rights' awareness, optimized user experience and training efficacy. *Symposium on Psychology-Based Technologies.*

Qaffas, A. A. (2019). Improvement of Chatbots Semantics Using Wit.ai and Word Sequence Kernel: Education Chatbot as a Case Study. International Journal of Modern Education and Computer Science (IJMECS). MECS.

Shevchuk, R., & Pastukh, Y. (2019). Improve the Security of Social Media Accounts. *2019 9th International Conference on Advanced Computer Information Technologies (ACIT).* IEEE. 10.1109/ACITT.2019.8779963

Thosani, P. (2020). A Self Learning Chat-Bot from User Interactions and Preferences. *2020 4th International Conference on Intelligent Computing and Control Systems (ICICCS).* IEEE. 10.1109/ICICCS48265.2020.9120912

KEY TERMS AND DEFINITIONS

Chatbots: A basic level, a chatbot is a computer program that simulates and processes human conversation (either written or spoken), allowing humans to interact with digital devices as if they were communicating with a real person.

Communication: Communication is a process that involves sending and receiving messages through verbal and non-verbal methods.

Gadgets: A desktop gadget is a software widget, or a small application, that is designed to sit on a user's desktop screen in much the same way that apps reside on smartphones and tablets.

Intelligent Agent: An intelligent agent is a program that can make decisions or perform a service based on its environment, user input and experiences.

IOT: The term IoT, or Internet of Things, refers to the collective network of connected devices and the technology that facilitates communication between devices and the cloud, as well as between the devices themselves.

NLP: Natural language processing (NLP) **is** a branch of artificial intelligence (AI) that enables computers to comprehend, generate, and manipulate human language.

UI: User interface is anything a user may interact with to use a digital product or service. This includes everything from screens and touchscreens, keyboards, sounds, and even lights.

Chapter 11
MEDIFY:
A Healthcare Chatbot Using NLP

Sudha Senthilkumar
School of Computer Science and Engineering, Vellore Institute of Technology, Vellore, India

Subhro Mukherjee
School of Computer Science and Engineering, Vellore Institute of Technology, Vellore, India

Siddhant Jain
School of Computer Science and Engineering, Vellore Institute of Technology, Vellore, India

Yashvardhan Aditya
School of Computer Science and Engineering, Vellore Institute of Technology, Vellore, India

ABSTRACT

There is an increasing population in India, due to reduction in the death rate and growing pace in birth due to improvement in the medical field; however, the amounts of experts are fewer to serve the need of the growing people. The present circumstance can be witnessed while walking around the local organization medical facilities where the limited availability of the experts is the critical purpose leads to less to the patient's required treatment. To fulfill the need of the patients first aid support and redirect the patient to the correct expert based on their available location and time, intelligent chatbots are emerging requirement. The NLP integrated artificial intelligent based clinical chatbot simulates and processes patient conversation by making people interact with smart devices the way how they were make the conversation with doctors who are expert in the medical field. To achieve this, the system collects and stores the information in the web crawler such as Google to fetch the information as per the client request in the emergency situation. The proposed Medify chatbot uses the integration of Machine learning techniques and NLP with the web crawler Google to achieve a highly accurate, user-friendly interface.

DOI: 10.4018/979-8-3693-1830-0.ch011

INTRODUCTION

The necessity for a strong and exact assurance wakes the climb of one more period of clinical benefits advancement called the chatbot in medical. The rule considered creating this type of chatbot is to mirror a singular's discussion. It helps people with jumping next step into their indications and gives them the maximum dependable assurance possible. This kind of chatbot is also deals with continuously creating clinical request range, to grow its by and large immense wealth of clinical dominance. Regardless, it is practical to consider this changes from accounts utilizing computations through development enhancement (Vaddadi et al, 2021) (Nithyanandam et al, 2021)

Development intensification offers a technique for imagining these deviations by improving them and to remove captivating signs from these accounts, for instance, like heartbeat of human (Zahour, 2020). Due to the support of intelligent thinking of computerized world that leads to the support of including a high complexity mathematical computation that sequences input information to convey critical outcomes (Nadarzynski et al, 2019). Human-made knowledge has been used in medicine and different experimental benefits organizations like insightful imaging and innate examination, similarly as a clinical exploration place, screening, and prosperity exchanges (Cui et al, 2019) (Amama & Okengwu, 2023) (Hsu & Liao, 2022).

One of the utmost amazing known instances of chatbots in late history is Siri AI technique which is crucial for Apple's standard programming for its items. Siri was the mostly used AI in chatbot standard in 2011. From that point forward, products in each area have begun to utilize it, at last fostering a recent fad communication in client experience. This alludes to low level-customer involvement in which your cooperation with a firm or administration is computerized in view of client earlier conduct. Assuming customers are creating human-like consciousness applications like Alexa that empowers the utilization of sound to control gadgets. On the off chance that you are a client, you can as of now collaborate with this AI based chatbot on famous informing stages of various social media. (Okonkwo & Ade-Ibijola, 2021) (Pérez et al, 2020) (Čižmešija, 2021)

Chatbots are plays major role in medical industry and can assist to deal with medical issues. Wellbeing and wellness support related chatbots have started to acquire fame on the lookout. Earlier year Facebook has begun permitting medical care businesses to create their own messenger based chatbots to speak with clients. An incredible model is Health Tap the principal organization to deliver a wellbeing bot on the Messenger based chatbot (Park et al, 2020) (Zaib et al, 2022) (Schneider et al, 2024).

The present available chatbots are not much interactive in terms of giving prompt response to the patent query. In a significant number of the medical chatbots that we studied over, we could see that they were looks like making the inquiries and getting the replies you need to type the manifestations and will give output on that, and as we composed the side effects numerous multiple times the response was given very outrageous like assuming we guarantee that we have fever and migraine the response would be malignant growth or intestinal sickness or some significant infection, yes this indications are normal in numerous large illnesses at the same time, the response might startle the people in question. (Antony & Ramnath, 2023)

The proposed chatbot designed to give a fast and supportive strategy for managing the prosperity region. The medical chatbot will help with the customer requests and provide response for medical related questions. Further, Natural Language Processing (NLP) is used to create complete medical chatbot using container API. It will be organized to respond to inquiries as for the prosperity region (Kadu et al, 2019). The prosperity region needs staffs due to the new flood of patients in the situation of Coronavirus conditions. Subsequently, responding to the general requests over an electronic talk bot would diminish the obligation off the working staff. Lately, people get reliant upon the web in receiving information for each concern they undergo. This not presently people to search for data about wide subjects yet furthermore their prosperity concerns (Altamimi et al, 2023) (Nunuk & Edo, 2023). Regardless, people dread twisting when they found out about their incidental effects since most chase conculde with making silly unsteady to the customers and from time to time mixed up.

Considering those necessities, people start to encourage a couple of improvement to support people with obtain the most dependable results on their disorder. One way is to use by making a yes-no response survey method. It clearly helps, in any case, due to specific diseases have basically comparative after effects as different, we can't rely upon this yes-no structure since lot of data ought to be disclosed to procure accuracy. A medical site accepts an urgent part in the present progressed world and a huge load of conversation is open for noticing the requests send from the customer. (Sen Bhattacharya, 2023) (Panchal & Kurup, 2023) (Alekseev et al, 2024)

In this way, we attempted to build the precision by not only rely with the NLP model yet in addition physically prearranging the json record for development. Since numerous chatbots were present for emergency clinic booking is seriously works as ordinary sort of chatbot, still there is certifiably not a solitary system that has considered in medical clinic booking and side effects appearing. The proposed system in which both the highlights added, to see which infection we might have as indicated by our side effects, on the off chance that it's not unexpected, its fine, yet assuming it's a major sickness which require clinical consideration correct way, we can likewise book close by emergency clinic. We have included approximately 4000 urban areas in India to book clinic and a specific month and date and assuming the seat is accessible at that date the booking is affirmed. This issue is addressed in our proposed MEDIFY chatbot which fulfill the language barrier among the customer and wellbeing suppliers by answering to the Questions in the prompt way. To achieve this, we are tuning our model with NLP and Machine learning techniques.

LITERATURE REVIEW

There are couples of method proposed for a chatbot model. The method which is used can integrate NLP, Machine Learning, Compare Keyword, and Data Mining. There are some chatbot proposed have an assessment method using data mining method. NLP reply for client replies relies upon well-defined formats and system drive to incite really understandable responses from the client. (Badempet et al, 2023) (Badlani et al, 2021)

In view of his assessment, we understand that the main use of NLP is to fetch the shapeless aftereffect of the string input that is specified as commitment to their chatbot system. (Amama & Okengwu, 2023) Taking into account their investigation, the inclination examination of client involvement using chatbot can be obtained. NLP similarly used to tokenize customer input normally string into tokens. The article that usages AI is (Aswini, 2019) (Bali et al, 2019) (Bao et al, 2020) which completes AI, and the basic responsibilities of their work are help us to develop better model. We find that outfit learning is significant for various reasons, for instance, each model looks at vaguely different bits of the data to make assumptions, getting a few pieces of reality in any case just one out of each odd piece of it. (KC et al, 2019)

Table 1. Relevant work details

Author Name	Pros and cons		Pros and cons
CARO (Harilal et al, 2020)	Generator for medical and a general conversation with 4 LSTM layers in parallel with dense and concatenation layers.	Uses dataset such as facebook AI and Question Answering of dataset related to medical	98.5% accuracy for intent classifier and 92.4% for emotion classifier. Model performance is not stable all the cases.
(Badlani et al, 2021)	Uses Trustworthy calculation, NLP and Classification	Dataset created based on guided interview	Uses different types of data. However the datasets has Noisy information leads to wrong prediction.
(Zaib et al, 2022)	Natural language Interpret and Generator, Dialog Manager.	RDF Dataset	The dialog handling efficiently by querying missing details and produce more precise and appropriate response.
(Kalla & Samiuddin, 2020).	NLP	Question and Answer based records	Develops user friendly system with support of diverse language.
(Altamimi et al, 2023).	Proposed new algorithm	Clinical Dataset	Provides highly accurate results
(Solanki et al, 2023)	NLP	Online based survey dataset	Systems are more flexible however the system lakes in recognizing the human emotions
(Nadarzynski et al, 2019)	AI and NLP	Uses semi structured interviews collected by inline survey	User friendly to analyze the system.
(Okonkwo &Ade-Ibijola, 2021).	DNN network	Dataset related to medical	Involves more amount of data for processing and obtain accurate results.
(Park et al, 2020)	DNN network	Survey data gathered on similar system	The method is easily accessible from mobile system.

Various papers, (Badempet et al, 2023) (Badlani et al, 2021) using AI with an assist vector are studied. Based on this, we understood SVM can perceive 2 classes and observe the top perceiving hyper plane. The computation that matches medical chatbot is AI and normal language handling. AI technique would be used in various areas such as gathering learning, regulated and solo learning, fake neural organization, double relapse, and arrangement.

The article (Bali et al, 2019) utilizes NLP to fetch unstructured result of the Google API which takes string input to their chatbot framework. Later handling this input, the developed chatbot will react with a progression of inquiries to comprehend which gives better result to the customer. Hence essentially, they use NLP to extricate the important word from the client response, so it tends to be handled by the AI. It utilizes Ensemble Learning to anticipate client infection as per the customer information specified in the client input in the token arrangement.

Table 1 discusses the relevant work details of the previous works that is carried out related to development of user friendly chatbot application.

PRELIMINARIES

Natural Language Processing (NLP)

Natural language processing (NLP) is the capacity of a system to comprehend human based language in the way they spoken and composed - - alluded to as normal language. It is a part of computerized reasoning.

This technique has present over 50 years. It has establishes in the field of etymology. It's usage can be found in various areas including clinical exploration, web indexes and business insight.

It goes about as a major point of support for acknowledgment of language, which is utilized by Siri and Alexa system.

It uses Natural Language Generation (NLG) and Natural Language Understanding (NLU) to understand the human language and answer the query.

Natural Language Understanding (NLU) is liable for dealing with and altering over indistinct information into a legitimate structure that the framework can undoubtedly comprehend. NLP has 5 important steps to make the message can be easily comprehensible by a medical chatbot.

These steps are:

- Lexical analysis
- Syntactic analysis
- Semantic analysis
- Discourse integration
- Pragmatic Analysis

The lexical analysis: This step defines the understandable vocabulary the helps to create sentence. It deciphers and parts the language into units such as phrases, sentences, paragraphs, expressions and words. Further the words are categorized into parts of speech.

Syntactic analysis: Parsing investigations syntax and words order so the connection among various words becomes further unmistakable. Sentences such as "the emergency clinic go to the specialist," are dismissed by Syntactic analysis.

Semantic Analysis: It make sure that whether the text is totally significant or not, and it appeals its right importance while planning syntactic developments. The main investigation will dismiss the expression like "cold fire".

Discourse integration: This step describes the communication between two or more entities. It examines the former words and sentences to recognize the ambiguous language meaning.

Pragmatic Analysis: It defines the interpretation of languages anticipated meaning. From which it derives the anticipated meaning of the language.

NLG includes text acknowledgment and text wanting to produce a reasonable reaction. In basic words, language age is liable for the arrangement of phonetically correct sentences and expressions.

The main test observed by NLP is to comprehend the complexities of normal human nature language.

The construction of language is extremely dubious in regards to punctuation, lexis, and different parts of discourse like analogies and illustrations.

Gradient Descent

Prior to clarifying Stochastic Gradient Descent (SGD), how about we initially portray what Gradient Descent is. Slope Descent is a well-known streamlining method in ML and DL method and it tends to be utilized with the vast majority, of the learning calculations. An angle is the incline of a capacity. It estimates the level variable progress in light of the progressions of other variable. Numerically, Gradient Descent is a raised capacity whose result is the incomplete subordinate of a bunch of boundaries of its bits of feedbacks. The more prominent the angle, the more extreme the incline.

Beginning from an underlying worth, Gradient Descent is run iteratively to track down the ideal upsides of the boundaries to track down the base conceivable worth of the given expense work.

Stochastic Gradient Descent (SGD)

An objective function with suitable smoothness properties can be optimized using stochastic gradient descent. Due to the fact that it replaces the actual gradient by an estimate of it, it can be considered a stochastic approach to gradient descent optimization (random selection of data subset). As a result, iterations are faster, but convergence is lower, especially in high-dimensional optimization problems.

Assume, there is 1,000,000 examples in your dataset, so in the event that you utilize an ordinary Gradient Descent improvement procedure, you should involve each of the 1,000,000 examples for finishing one cycle while playing out the Gradient Descent, and it must be finished each emphasis till the minima are grasped. Henceforth, it turns out to be computationally extravagant to perform.

To address this Stochastic Gradient Descent is used. In SGD, it utilizes just a solitary example, i.e., a clump size of one, to play out every emphasis. The example is arbitrarily rearranged and chosen for playing out the cycle.

SGD computation:

for x in range(m):

theta(k) = theta(k) – alpha(Y^x - Yx)Xxk

In SGD, since just one example from the dataset is selected indiscriminately for every cycle, the way reserved by the calculation to come to the minima is generally noisier compared your run of the mill Gradient Descent calculation. In any case, that doesn't make any difference that entire amount in light of the fact that the way taken by the calculation doesn't make any difference.

Sequential Model

Sequence models are the AI models that info or result successions of information. Consecutive information incorporates text transfers, brief snippets, video cuts, time-series information and so on Recurrent Neural Networks (RNNs) is a well-known calculation utilized in sequence models.

Figure 1. Medify system architecture

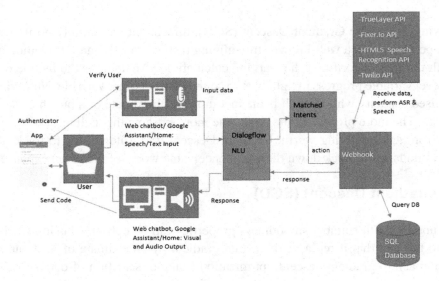

PROPOSED MACHINE LEARNING MODEL

The web based medical chatbot application are shown in the below architecture which can be run at anytime using smart device or through system for make medical relevant queries. The complete application that was developed and deployed using a flask app.

The Figure 1 illustrates the system architecture and it proceeds with the user who can start their conversation with the chatbot like user friendly and it will be stored in the database for future reference. The chatbot will clarify the users symptoms with serious of questions as shown below in Table 1 and the symptom confirmation will be done. Matched intent action response and input from several API is forwarded to and from webhook which helps to send data in real-time between applications, whenever an event occurs. The Azure Site Recovery service (ASR) is a hybrid cloud and cloud-native DRaaS offered by Azure.

Table 2. Sample Q/A detail

S.No	A	B	C	D
1	Interaction Type	Subject	Question	Answer
2	Q&A	Hours & Locations	When are you open?	Our main location is open daily from 8am to 6 pm.
3	Q&A	Hours & Locations	Where are you Located?	We are located at 1234 Main street.
4	Q&A	Type of Symptoms	What are the symptoms of the flu?	The flu can cause a fever, cough, sore throat, headaches and fatigue
5	Follow-up	Call back	Can I speak to a real person?	Of course. Please tell me your phone number and I'll have a representative call you back shortly.

Our chatbot is prepared on using json method and the implementationn is quite straight forward. The input is obtained from various sources from web chatbot, Google Assistant, Speech/ Text input to NLU unit. Computers can communicate in humans' native languages using Natural Language Processing (NLP). The Matched intents takes the user input text and matching it with a specific user-defined code to run. The various examples Q/A queried are listed in Table 2.

Based on the clarification obtained from the Q/A section the chatbot classifies the disease are minor and major disease. If it's a major one user will be suggested with the doctor details nearby you for further treatment and display the analgesics and also provides food suggestions that means which food you have to take more to recover the disease. The chatbot user interface can chat with like user friendly. Chatbot helps to solve small problems without directly going to the hospitals.

RESULTS AND COMPARISON

We trained our model for 200 epochs as shown below in Figure 2 to build an accurate application and achieved the overall accuracy of 98.44%. The model when it is executed at the initial stage the model accuracy was less but however the number of iteration increased nearly 200 the model produces high accuracy which is around 98.44%.

The following are snips of the end result of our application.

The Figure 3 shows the Chatbot user interface that denotes the conversation with the chat bot in a user-friendly way, not using much technical terms for ease of the users. We then move on to describing our health issues. The chat bot suggests a probable disease.

The Figure 4 shows the chatbot user interface patient seeking information from the chatbot. The patient seeks help about the suggested disease and cure for the symptoms. The chat bot gives elaborative suggestions. We also try to book an appointment to look into the cause further. The chat bot efficiently does that by asking us the whereabouts of our booking.

The Figure 5 shows the chatbot user interface appointment booking for further clarification and takes treatment for the patient. In the chatbot interface the patient enters the necessary details in our booking

Figure 2. Implementation screen shot

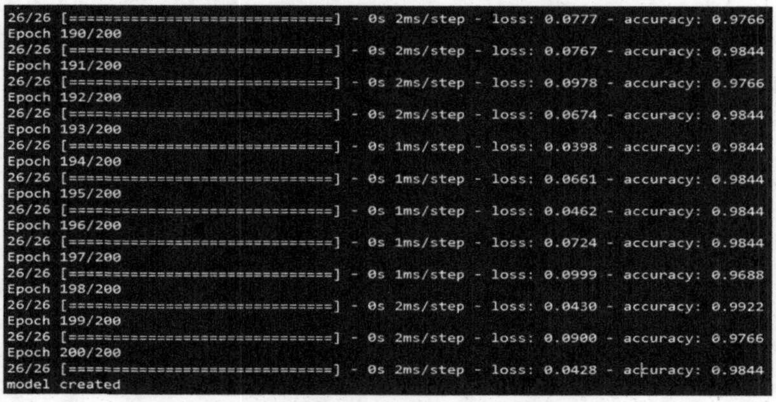

```
26/26 [==============================] - 0s 2ms/step - loss: 0.0777 - accuracy: 0.9766
Epoch 190/200
26/26 [==============================] - 0s 2ms/step - loss: 0.0767 - accuracy: 0.9844
Epoch 191/200
26/26 [==============================] - 0s 2ms/step - loss: 0.0978 - accuracy: 0.9766
Epoch 192/200
26/26 [==============================] - 0s 2ms/step - loss: 0.0674 - accuracy: 0.9844
Epoch 193/200
26/26 [==============================] - 0s 1ms/step - loss: 0.0398 - accuracy: 0.9844
Epoch 194/200
26/26 [==============================] - 0s 1ms/step - loss: 0.0661 - accuracy: 0.9844
Epoch 195/200
26/26 [==============================] - 0s 1ms/step - loss: 0.0462 - accuracy: 0.9844
Epoch 196/200
26/26 [==============================] - 0s 1ms/step - loss: 0.0724 - accuracy: 0.9844
Epoch 197/200
26/26 [==============================] - 0s 1ms/step - loss: 0.0999 - accuracy: 0.9688
Epoch 198/200
26/26 [==============================] - 0s 2ms/step - loss: 0.0430 - accuracy: 0.9922
Epoch 199/200
26/26 [==============================] - 0s 2ms/step - loss: 0.0900 - accuracy: 0.9766
Epoch 200/200
26/26 [==============================] - 0s 2ms/step - loss: 0.0428 - accuracy: 0.9844
model created
```

Figure 3. Chatbot user interface

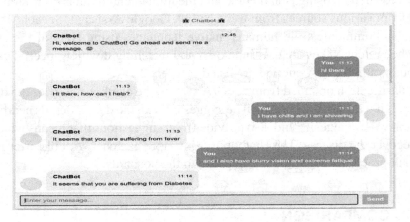

Figure 4. Chatbot user interface patient discussion

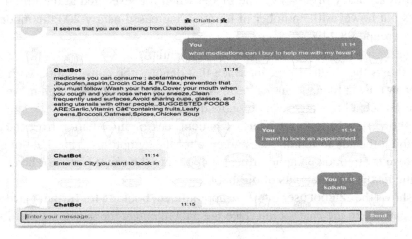

Figure 5. Chatbot user interface appointment booking

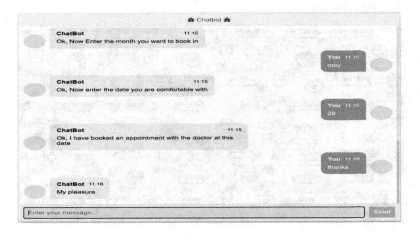

Table 3. Method comparison

Methods	Average accuracy
(Bao et al, 2020)	80.4%
(Kalla & Samiuddin, 2020)	81.2%
Medify (proposed system)	98.44%

system and then further the respective booking has been confirmed from the chatbot and notification will be given to patient.

The Table 3 denotes the accuracy comparison of the proposed model with other existing schemes in which the proposed approach shows the higher accuracy than the existing scheme. The previous model such as Bao et al and Kalla et al system shows the accuracy of 78.4 and 81.2% whereas our proposed model Medify shows the accuracy of 98.44%.

CONCLUSION

We have discussed all of the assessments that related to a chatbot, especially clinical chatbot. We learn and explore the paper concerning how to make a chatbot, what kind estimation the chatbot uses, and how to get the educational assortment to set up the chatbot. We see that there are a lot of computations we can use to make a chatbot like standard language dealing with, AI, Braun and Clarke's estimation, investigate watchword, and data mining. From those estimations, we have seen that the most match computation for a chatbot is normal language dealing with AI. The Web-connection point is made for the clients, to the information question. The application is improved with the security and sufficiency upgrades by ensuring client confirmation and characters and recuperating responds to subsequently for the requests.

The previous implemented chatbot using ordinary language taking care of strategies to manage the client input, which by and large planned as a string, to an association that the program can process. The rough data (string) can't be taken care of by the program or the designing. The string configuration ordinarily took care of with the NLP system transforms into a tokenized plan. The tokenize association can be dealt with successfully for the program rather than the string plan. After the client inputs are tokenized, it will in general be taken care of with AI, for instance, gathering to manage the appearances and match to the disease that opens in the request planning. In this way, the most suitable estimation to make a chatbot as per our point of view is using the integration of NLP and Machine Learning models.

REFERENCES

Alekseev, D., Shagalova, P., & Sokolova, E. (2021). Development of a chatbot using machine learning algorithms to automate educational processes. *Proceedings of the 31th International Conference on Computer Graphics and Vision.* IEEE. 10.20948/graphicon-2021-3027-1104-1113

Altamimi, I., Altamimi, A., Alhumimidi, A. S., Altamimi, A., & Temsah, M. (2023). Artificial intelligence (AI) chatbots in medicine: A supplement, not a substitute. *Cureus.* doi:10.7759/cureus.40922 PMID:37496532

AmamaC.OkengwuU. (2023). Smart chatbot system for banking using natural language processing tools. doi:10.21203/rs.3.rs-3285543/v1

Antony, S., & Ramnath, R. (2023). A phenomenological exploration of students' perceptions of AI chatbots in higher education. *IAFOR Journal of Education*, *11*(2), 7–38. doi:10.22492/ije.11.2.01

Aswini, D. (2019). Clinical medical knowledge extraction using crowdsourcing techniques. *Int. Res. J. Eng. Technol, 6.*

Badempet, P., Cheerala, P., & Anagondi, S. P. (2023). *A healthcare system using machine learning techniques for disease prediction with chatbot assistance.* IEEE. doi:10.14293/PR2199.000474.v1

Badlani, S., Aditya, T., Dave, M., & Chaudhari, S. (2021). Multilingual healthcare chatbot using machine learning. *2021 2nd International Conference for Emerging Technology (INCET).* IEEE. 10.1109/INCET51464.2021.9456304

Bali, M., Mohanty, S., Chatterjee, D., Sarma, M., & Puravankara, R. (2019). Diabot: A predictive medical chatbot using ensemble learning. [IJRTE]. *International Journal of Recent Technology and Engineering*, *8*(2), 6334–6340. doi:10.35940/ijrte.B2196.078219

Bao, Q., Ni, L., & Liu, J. (2020). HHH: An online medical chatbot system based on knowledge graph and hierarchical Bi-directional attention. *Proceedings of the Australasian Computer Science Week Multiconference.* ACM. 10.1145/3373017.3373049

Čižmešija, A., Horvat, A., & Plantak Vukovac, D. (2021). Improving student engagement and course completion using chatbot application. *INTED2021 Proceedings.* IEEE. https://doi.org/10.21125/inted.2021.1697

Cui, W., Xiao, Y., Wang, H., Song, Y., Hwang, S. W., & Wang, W. (2019). KBQA: learning question answering over QA corpora and knowledge bases. *arXiv prepri.*

Harilal, N., Shah, R., Sharma, S., & Bhutani, V. (2020). CARO: an empathetic health conversational chatbot for people with major depression. In *Proceedings of the 7th ACM IKDD CoDS and 25th COMAD* (pp. 349-350). ACM. 10.1145/3371158.3371220

HsuI.LiaoA. (2022). Sentiment-based chatbot using machine learning for recommendation system. doi:10.21203/rs.3.rs-1468604/v1

Kadu, O., Sihasane, S., Naik, S., Katariya, V., & Gutte, V. S. (2019). Intelligent healthbot for transforming healthcare. [IJTSRD]. *Int. J. Trend Sci. Res. Dev.*, *3*(3), 1576–1579.

Kalla, D., & Samiuddin, V. (2020). Chatbot for medical treatment using NLTK Lib. *IOSR Journal of Computer Engineering*, 22.

K., G. P., Ranjan, S., Ankit, T., & Kumar, V. (2019). A personalized medical assistant chatbot: Medibot. *Int. J. Sci. Technol. Eng*, *5*(7).

Nadarzynski, T., Miles, O., Cowie, A., & Ridge, D. (2019). Acceptability of artificial intelligence (AI)-led chatbot services in healthcare: A mixed-methods study. *Digital Health*, *5*, 2055207619871808. doi:10.1177/2055207619871808 PMID:31467682

Nithyanandam, S. D., Kasinathan, S., Radhakrishnan, D., & Jebapandian, J. (2021). NLP for chatbot application. *Advances in Computational Intelligence and Robotics*, 142–168. doi:10.4018/978-1-7998-7728-8.ch008

Okonkwo, C. W., & Ade-Ibijola, A. (2021). Chatbots applications in education: A systematic review. *Computers and Education: Artificial Intelligence*, 2, 100033. doi:10.1016/j.caeai.2021.100033

Panchal, V., & Kurup, L. (2023). Educational chatbot on data structures and algorithms for the visually impaired. 2023 5th Biennial International Conference on Nascent Technologies in Engineering (ICNTE). IEEE. 10.1109/ICNTE56631.2023.10146702

Park, H., Kim, H., & Kim, P. (2020). Development of electronic library chatbot system using SNS-based mobile chatbot service*. *The 9th International Conference on Smart Media and Applications*. ACM. 10.1145/3426020.3426134

Pérez, J. Q., Daradoumis, T., & Puig, J. M. (2020). Rediscovering the use of chatbots in education: A systematic literature review. *Computer Applications in Engineering Education*, 28(6), 1549–1565. doi:10.1002/cae.22326

Schneider, P., Klettner, M., Jokinen, K., Simperl, E., & Matthes, F. (2024). Evaluating large language models in semantic parsing for conversational question answering over knowledge graphs. *Proceedings of the 16th International Conference on Agents and Artificial Intelligence*. ACM. 10.5220/0012394300003636

Sen BhattacharyaB. (2023). Assistive chatbots for healthcare: A succinct review. https://doi.org/doi:10.36227/techrxiv.23741469.v1

Solanki, N., Singh, N., & Garg, D. (2023). Human mental experience through chatbots. *Edge-AI in Healthcare*, 143-158. doi:10.1201/9781003244592-11

VaddadiS.AsriS.GhemiY.AythaR. (2020). Developing chatbot wrapper for online shopping: A case study of using generic mobile messaging system. https://doi.org/doi:10.36227/techrxiv.12061602

Nunuk Wahyuningtyas, & Koentjoro. (2020). Android-based educational learning game for children based on Android. *JOINCS (Journal of Informatics, Network, and Computer Science)*, 3(2), 38-43. https://doi.org/doi:10.21070/joincs.v4i0.724

Zahour, O. (2020). Towards a chatbot for educational and vocational guidance in Morocco: Chatbot E-orientation. *International Journal of Advanced Trends in Computer Science and Engineering*, 9(2), 2479–2487. doi:10.30534/ijatcse/2020/237922020

Zaib, M., Zhang, W. E., Sheng, Q. Z., Mahmood, A., & Zhang, Y. (2022). Conversational question answering: A survey. *Knowledge and Information Systems*, 64(12), 3151–3195. doi:10.1007/s10115-022-01744-y

KEY TERMS AND DEFINITIONS

AI: It is the science that helps to make machines to think like a human being.

Batch Gradient Descent: It computes the average gradient of the cost function for entire training records and updates the parameters in the reverse direction.

Gradient Descent: It is an optimization algorithm that helps to train machine learning models with the goal of minimizing errors between predicted and actual outputs.

NLP: It is the computer software program developed to recognize the human spoken language and written language.

NLU: Natural Language Understanding is the branch of Artificial Intelligence which performs the process of recognizing the meaning of the text.

Stochastic Gradient Descent: The optimization algorithm used in machine learning to identify the model parameters that represents the best fit between predicted and actual results.

SVM: A support vector machine (SVM) is a type of supervised machine learning method used to solve classification and regression tasks.

Chapter 12
Revolutionizing Healthcare:
Unveiling the Transformative Power of Chatbots Through a Systematic Literature Review

Domitilla Magni

eCampus University, Italy

ABSTRACT

The healthcare industry is changing, with a greater dependence on technology, as seen by the incorporation of chatbots powered by artificial intelligence. Chatbots serve as virtual assistants, improving patient assistance, education, and engagement by providing information on medical issues and easing administrative procedures. Chatbots are particularly useful in symptom evaluation and telemedicine, allowing for virtual consultations and remote patient monitoring. Although chatbot technology is highly innovative and useful for medical and management professionals, the literature is still scarce and highly fragmented among different research areas. This chapter aims to analyze the power of chatbots in healthcare through scientific literature, providing a holistic understanding of the state of the art and future applications of chatbots. Despite acknowledged limitations, the substantial advantages hint at a positive outlook for their ongoing growth and integration into the healthcare ecosystem.

INTRODUCTION

In the digital age, the healthcare industry is evolving and playing a key role in optimizing the patient care and wellness process. In this scenario, most prominent disruptive technology appears in chatbots, i.e., digital tools that are revolutionizing the healthcare landscape (Mariani et al., 2023). By definition, chatbots are virtual assistants that, through a sophisticated algorithm, can respond to and communicate with people who interface with them through both text and voice. In most cases, chatbot-human communication can essentially replicate a dialogue between two human persons (Liu and Sundar, 2018; Adam et al., 2021). The engagement of chatbots in healthcare and well-being system is triggering several research topics as patient engagement, administrative support, and clinical assistance. Moreover,

DOI: 10.4018/979-8-3693-1830-0.ch012

chatbots can simply help communication between patients and healthcare practitioners: indeed, these digital tools facilitate appointment scheduling, offering real-time support, and delivering customized health information. With these supports, the administrative efficiency and the automation of routine tasks are greatly enhanced. In this scenario, some concerns need to be considered: chatbots and digitals tools collect private and interpersonal data, thus prioritizing the crucial role of trust. Eventually, innovation and disruptive technologies are reshaping the well-being system and the corporate aims and priorities of healthcare industry. Specifically, this chapter aims to systematically review the scientific literature in various fields to highlight the power of chatbots in health care and provide a holistic and systematic understanding of their use, as well as the benefits they bring to the health care system, while also highlighting the possible problems inherent in this technology. In the digital healthcare scenario, chatbots trigger the evolution of patient care and education system (Tudor Car et al., 2020): chatbots are useful to spam information around healthcare system and to enhance the potential alternatives treatments by increasing patient involvement and engagement. Chatbots are also used extensively in healthcare for administrative chores. Healthcare firms are increasingly using chatbots to automate administrative tasks including appointment scheduling, billing questions, and insurance verification (Ye et al., 2021). This automation not only cuts operating costs, but it also frees up human resources to focus on higher-value, challenging work. Chatbots also have a relevant influence on symptom assessment and triage (Tudor Car et al., 2020). Indeed, thanks to artificial intelligence (AI), chatbots can help patients assess symptoms, thus offering faster and more specific triage. By triaging in this way, chatbots provide an opportunity to identify the patient's condition through professional and immediate medical care. Chatbots have played an important role in the recent boom in telemedicine usage, which was spurred in large part by the COVID-19 epidemic. The weight of the healthcare industry in advanced economies is shaping not only the technologies of surgery and research, but also information technology and solutions to improve communication with the patient, between healthcare professionals and medical institutions. Artificial intelligence can intervene in the interaction between physicians and patients. With due caution, there is no doubt about the potential impact of technology in optimizing communication, especially in health care, from hospitals to physicians (Sheth, 2020). Reducing consultation times, decreasing, or even eliminating unnecessary hospital visits, will improve service quality, but also other relevant areas in healthcare business management, such as marketing strategies and corporate image. Chatbots can satisfy patient requests, increasing patient engagement (Magni et al., 2023). In fact, patients like to receive a quick response from the chatbot on medical or health information, follow what the chatbot suggests to them, and ease the formal procedure in case of triage. All this not only helps professionals handle an increasing volume of medical inquiries, but on the patient side it greatly enhances the goodness of experience and the benefits chatbots can provide. Efficiency and cost reduction are additional benefits that can result from the use of chatbots in the health care system (Heo and Lee, 2018). In fact, by automating administrative processes in health care, chatbots can reduce response and administrative task time, providing operational efficiency to the health care system.

In the digital age chatbots play a vital role for data collectors and analysts. Chatbots offer an effective and efficient way to collect and analyze information (King, 2023). These automated tools allow users to interact with other users in a natural way, collecting data in real time through interactive conversations (Sestino and D'Angelo, 2023). This feature reduces human error by allowing prompt and precisely defined responses. Moreover, chatbots can conduct preliminary research on collected data, providing analysts a glimpse of new patterns or important details. Chatbots play a pivotal role in accelerating the data collecting and analysis process, swiftly handling vast volumes of data. In fact, chatbots help healthcare practitioners automate routing data management tasks, providing various digital benefits and promoting system innovation (King, 2023). Chatbot, which is software based on artificial intelligence, can dialogue with the user in real time (Sestino and D'Angelo, 2023). Such software is also capable of learning and then refining the answers over time to have a dialogue that is more and more in line with the expectations of the interlocutor. Given its nature, the chatbot can be employed effectively in customer care services, especially in providing quick answers to the questions most frequently asked of a customer care. In this way, staff are relieved of several basic tasks and can effectively and more usefully devote themselves to solving the most sensitive and complex problems. It should be emphasized that today chatbots have reached such a level of sophistication and "intelligence" that it is often difficult to distinguish them from a real person, both in terms of pronunciation and ability to interpret questions and thus provide appropriate answers. Chatbots are currently widely used in industries such as insurance, banking, and retail. But among the various uses of chatbots we also find health care. Physicians can also benefit from the use of a chatbot: this digital assistant can replace interactions with databases and dosages, providing all the information related to the etiology of the patient's disease and the drug therapy he or she is taking. Chatbots can also give advice on doctor-prescribed therapies to be followed by the patient and can play a role that is as simple as it is important: to act as a companion tool for patients who often feel lonely, avoiding disorders such as depression. The patient can then tell the chatbot about the symptoms he or she is experiencing and, depending on the extent of the problem, the digital assistant might suggest medication or directly schedule an appointment with a doctor. The presence of a chatbot in the medical center can greatly improve the patient-physician relationship. In fact, chatbots collect information about users by asking them various questions, which are then stored in their medical records and allow them to personalize each patient's experience. A major concern in the use of chatbots in medical settings is user privacy (Paul et al., 2021; Magni et al., 2023). Users of these software products may be reluctant to share their personal information with bots. It may be the case that patients are skeptical in sharing information about their medical conditions with a chatbot. This is because it seems less reliable to them than sharing the same information with a real assistant. Innovative healthcare organizations that create these kinds of solutions do their best to implement data security measures and ensure that their chatbots or "voicebots" are cyberattack-proof.

Scalability is another major benefit of chatbots in well-being process. Chatbots can handle a large number of interactions simultaneously without losing efficiency, which means they can adapt to the growing needs of the business. In fact, the scalability of digital tools increases the flexibility of devices and enables companies to manage the spikes more effectively in activity and potential demand that can occur at particular events. Ultimately, chatbots effectively complement and enrich the customer service operated by real operators.

In this book chapter I collected information by searching online databases as IEEE Xplore, Google Scholar, PubMed, Scopus, and WoS. To focus on the specific benefits of chatbots and digital tools, I begin my search with words such as "chatbot", "healthcare", "artificial intelligence", "patient engagement", "telemedicine", and "systematic review". For the identification of relevant studies, I evaluated an extended bodies of literature published between 2010 and 2024. Finally, I discarded studies that were concerned with general applications of AI or that did not contain significant data on chatbots in health care. Findings of this research highlight the growing significance of chatbots in healthcare. Indeed, chatbots play significant role in patient education and support, help practitioners with administrative tasks, and enhance the physician-patient mediation. Moreover, findings show that recent research in the field of AI and ethical values are improving the impact on digital tools, thus encouraging the advent of chatbots in healthcare system. This chapter contributes to the emerging field of disruptive technology in healthcare and offers novel theoretical and practical implications for academy and practitioners, including a first attempt to develop a road map to be followed to achieve an of innovative and ethical values for business and society at large.

In the next sections, I describe the role of chatbots in healthcare management. I also offer best practices for using and improving these AI assistants, by highlighting ad hoc case studies. Finally, the chapter gives managers the knowledge and information they need to use chatbots to change the healthcare industry.

BACKGROUND

Theoretical Background

The technology acceptance theory (TAM) and contingency theory offers a robust framework for comprehensively analyzing and integrating the factors influencing the adoption of AI in the healthcare industry. In this context, the adoption denotes an individual's decision to embrace an innovation, extending beyond its mere implementation. Innovation adoption is characterized by the accessibility of a technological solution to an intended user group, where the solution is routinely utilized in practice (Magni et al., 2021). Within the realm of information systems research, various approaches exist for analyzing the acceptance and adoption of technologies. Scholars differentiate between models that elucidate technology adoption on individual and organizational levels. On the individual level, the prevalent model explaining the adoption of AI in the healthcare industry is the Technology Acceptance Model (TAM), introduced by Davis (1985). Venkatesh and Zhang (2010) later extended TAM, addressing its limitations by introducing the Unified Theory of Acceptance and Use of Technology (UTAUT). UTAUT emphasizes the primary individual factors influencing technology acceptance while also recognizing contingencies that either enhance or constrain their effects. Venkatesh and Zhang (2010) identify three factors influencing behavioral intention to use technology: performance expectancy, effort expectancy, and social influence.

Thus, TAM and UTAUT stand as a pivotal model for evaluating information systems and embracing novel technologies in daily life. Their widespread influence extends across various sectors, serving as a tool to scrutinize the impact of emerging technologies and their adoption. Kalantari and Rauschnabel (2018) delve into consumer reactions to wearable technologies, particularly glasses-like wearable devices, aiming to discern behaviors within the intersection of virtual and real worlds. Schmidthuber et al. (2020) shift their focus to the potential of mobile devices in the mobile payment sector, examining user behavior in the context of new digital payment technologies. In the healthcare sector, Hsieh and Lai (2020) identify features enhancing users' quality of life through an information system for medical records. Nasir and Yurder (2015) emphasize the delicate balance between the acceptance of digital technologies, especially wearable health technologies, and the perceived risks, given the growing aging population.

By following Magni et al., (2021), Table 1 reports the complete overview of antecedents' studies in the adoption AI technologies, including the focus of the TAM and Extended TAM theory.

Related Literature

The rapid integration of AI in healthcare organizations has spawned a burgeoning body of literature, offering insights into the multifaceted applications of chatbots. This review categorizes the related lit-

Table 1. Antecedents of theoretical works for the use of AI technologies in literature

Authors (year)	Technology	Sector	Main theory	Technological Constructs
Turhan (2013)	Smart clothing	Fashion	TAM	Perceived ease of use, Perceived usefulness, Compatibility, Self-efficacy, Social influence
Leue and Jung, (2014)	Augmented reality	Tourism	TAM	Perceived ease of use, Usefulness, Enjoyment, Personal innovativeness, Perceived benefits, Costs and Information quality
Nasir and Yurder (2015)	Wearable health devices	Healthcare	TAM	Perceived ease of use, Usefulness, Compatibility, Perceived risk
Yang et al. (2016)	Wearable device	General	Extended TAM	Perceived ease of use, Perceived usefulness, Hedonic motivation, Social influence, Risk, Functionality, Compatibility, Visual attractiveness, Brand name
Chuah et al. (2016)	Smartwatch	Fashion	Extended TAM	Perceived ease of use, Perceived usefulness, Visibility, Familiarity
Wang and Sun (2016)	Gaming devices	Gaming	Extended TAM	Perceived usefulness, Perceived ease of use, Narrative, Attitude towards to, Intention to play
Basoglu et al., (2017)	Smart glasses	General	Extended TAM	Enjoyment, Self-Efficacy, External influence, Risk-Usefulness, Ease of use, Anxiety, Health Concern, Intention, Complexity
Kalantari and Rauschnabel (2018)	Smart glasses	General	TAM	Perceived ease of use, Perceived usefulness, Hedonic motivation, Privacy, norms, technology risk, Image
Verma and Sinha (2018)	Mobile devices	Agriculture	TAM	Perceived usefulness, Perceived ease of use, Social influence, Attitude, Perceived economic wellbeing, Behavioral intention
Lee and Lee, (2018)	Wearable fitness tracker	Fitness	TAM	Interpersonal information, Self-efficacy, Innovativeness, Attitudes, Health interest, Perceived expensiveness, demographic information
Schmidthuber et al., (2020)	Mobile payment	General	TAM	Perceived ease of use, Perceived usefulness, Perceived ubiquity, Perceived compatibility, Perceived personal innovativeness, Perceived social influence, Perceived costs, Perceived risks
Hsieh and Lai, (2020)	Health passbook	Healthcare	Extended TAM	Perceived susceptibility, Perceived barriers, Self-efficacy, Cues to action, Perceived usefulness, Perceived ease of use, Health literacy

Source: Magni et al. (2021)

erature into five distinct areas of research, elucidating the pivotal role chatbots play in patient support and education, physician-patient mediation, symptom assessment and triage, patient engagement, and ethical considerations.

Frangoudes et al. (2021) noted that the information that chatbots transfer to patients is crucial in terms of education and self-diagnosis. In fact, all the information that chatbots provide to the patient manages to be highly personalized, thus offering valuable medical support. Ye et al. (2021) contribution focuses on the streamlining of administrative tasks within healthcare institutions. Chatbots emerge as efficient tools in automating processes such as appointment scheduling. Many organizations in the healthcare system are already using various types of new technologies to perform, for example, predictive analytics. In the medical context, artificial intelligence-based chatbots can be used to perform initial triage, accurately collecting data on detected symptoms, and assisting physicians in identifying diseases. Chatbots collect basic information from patients and then, based on the data entered, provide patients with additional information about their condition and suggest next steps. In particular, Tudor Car et al. (2020) contribute to the literature by exploring the use of chatbots in symptom assessment and triage. Chatbots can collect and transmit data though patients and physician, by optimizing firms' resource allocation. Magni et al. (2023) shed light on the pivotal role of chatbots in enhancing patient engagement. Interactive chatbots can act as companions, providing continuous support, motivation, and monitoring for patients managing chronic conditions. This engagement contributes to improved adherence to treatment plans and better health outcomes. Hasal et al. (2021) argued the ethical considerations about adoption of chatbots in healthcare. Here, the literature focuses on the issue of data privacy and the informed use of technological tools in the digital age. Understanding these ethical issues is critical to building trust in AI-driven healthcare solutions.

The literature on chatbots in healthcare is dynamic, and the research suggests exploring other digital solutions for well-being and healthcare industry. Today, chatbots can effectively answer basic health management questions. In the future, this ability will become even more accurate as it is constantly evaluated, and the robot will learn from its mistakes by sharing what it acquires with all the other chatbots in that particular service. As these intelligent personal assistants process new information very quickly, they will follow and learn when to refer the patient to a doctor's attention or seek help themselves. Through wearable devices such as smartwatches, we will be able to share the data that monitor our health and the data in our medical records with "healthbots" so that digital personal assistants can make wise decisions. This comprehensive review serves as a roadmap for stakeholders navigating the intricate intersection of AI and healthcare services.

METHODOLOGY

Research Protocol, Database, and Search Strings

Through an in-depth analysis of current literature, I reveal the complex effects of chatbots on patients and healthcare system. These conversational bots driven by AI provide expedient support, tailored help, and simplified communication. Chatbots improve patient engagement, offer health monitoring, and make booking appointments easier. Moreover, these digital tools can enhance the communication between practitioners and patients, by saving time and optimizing resources. However, the usage of chatbots raising challenges as ethical implications and privacy. The aim of this review is to emphasize advantages and concerns in the usage of chatbots and AI, by highlighting the role of digital tools in the revolution of tailored healthcare system. In this systematic literature review I adopted an inductive methodology as suggested by Tranfield et al. (2003). Indeed, the method of systematic literature review offers a holistic comprehension of chatbots and AI in digital healthcare landscape. Since the aim of the research is to enhance the prevailing comprehension of the factors that impact the integration of AI in healthcare, this will be achieved through the implementation of a systematic and transparent methodology, ensuring reproducible outcomes. Indeed, the SLR provides a thematic classification of scientific contributions on themes of interest, showing the regions most researched as well as the features that need to be investigated and exploited.

The study procedure called for the following steps: 1. extrapolate papers from databases, 2. manually pick significant documents, 3. identify eligible documents, and 4. manually integrate other influential publications.

Figure 1. PRISMA flow diagram
(Authors' Elaboration)

1. Identification	
n° 127 papers	• n° 14 papers from IEEE Xplore • n° 35 papers from Google Scholar • n° 3 papers from PubMed • n° 47 papers from Scopus • n° 28 papers from WoS

2. Screening	3. Eligibility
n° 115 of records screened n° 12 of records excluded	n° 115 of full-text articles assessed for eligibility n° 0 of full-text articles assessed excluded

4. Included
n° 115 of papers included in quantitative synthesis (meta-analysis)

Figure 1 summarize the individual steps to identify and evaluate the papers for each phase of the research.

First, I did a scoping assessment to determine both the necessity for this structured review and the appropriate search phrases. In this phase, I conducted a systematic literature review by scanning IEEE Xplore, Google Scholar, PubMed, Scopus, and WoS. I chose these databases as our primary data base for a variety of reasons: indeed, they are the most comprehensive databases in the business research domain in the field of management research. Moreover, I follow recently published studies in the fields of technology and healthcare in high-ranked management journals, using those databases as primary databases (e.g., Magni et al., 2022). The journals were chosen based on how relevant their material was to the themes under investigation. I chose well-known journal to include in our investigation such as *Journal of Innovation and Knowledge Management, Technological Forecasting and Social Change, Journal of Innovation Management* and *Journal of Service Management*.

I searched for relevant articles from 2010 to 2023, using eight search strings:

[Chatbot] AND [Healthcare]

[Chatbot] AND [Innovation]

[Chatbot] AND [Management]

[Chatbot] AND [TAM] OR [Technology Acceptance Theory] OR [UTAUT] OR [Extended TAM]

[Chatbot] AND [Administrative tasks] AND [Healthcare]

[Chatbot] AND [Education] AND [Healthcare]

[Chatbot] AND [Patient engagement] AND [Healthcare]

[Chatbot] AND [Ethical considerations] AND [Healthcare].

Second, the relevant publications using content analysis before reading each article's title, keywords, and abstract were filtered. Content analyses were used to emphasize the importance of each document, systematizing the material gathered to show the relationship to the research's objective. Finally, in the final part of the study, each article was exanimated analytically, finding the significant characteristics in relation to the issue under consideration. After removing contradictory and duplicate entries, I compiled a database of 115 original articles.

BIBLIOMETRIC ANALYSIS RESULTS

Descriptive Insights

The total number of publications deemed useful for the research objectives is 115, of which 68.8% are papers published in the last two years of analysis (2021-2022). This reflects an important increase in interest in academia of the topic in question, especially with the advent of AI becoming more prominent in our daily lives. A further reflection to be made is that, for the most part, the papers under analysis were published more in Journals with a medical focus, and only 15% were published in Journals with a managerial or business focus. This denotes a still lack in the managerial literature on the topic of AI and the use of Chatbots in business, proving an urgency to study and integrate these topics in the managerial literature as well.

Analyzing the data from a regional perspective, the results show that most of the articles under review were written by authors of Indian origin (37%), followed by the United States (15%), Canada (8%) and Taiwan (5%). In terms of the type of articles reviewed, it is remarkable to consider that 54.4% were conference papers, 40.9% were research papers, and 4.7% were book chapters. This figure is also relevant because it denotes that most of the studies dealing with AI, chatbots, and healthcare represent frontier studies, sometimes still a work in progress and evolving. This denotes the innovative and dynamic nature of these research topics, while also highlighting the need for continued development of AI and healthcare studies.

Data Analysis

According to the TAM, the adoption of technologies to enhance societal value is influenced by several factors (Magni et al., 2021; Sestino and D'Angelo, 2023). Specifically, this analysis has validated this that there are organizational and individual aspects that influence the acceptance of technology in the healthcare system. On the organizational level, factors as macro-economic readiness, technological readiness, regulatory readiness, and organizational readiness have been identified, while on the individual level, user readiness emerges as a key factor (Roppelt et al., 2023). The successful adoption of AI appears achievable when readiness is attained across all those dimensions, addressing previously outlined concerns, and unlocking sustainable benefits.

As results' analysis, Figure 2 shows the five distinct areas of research, elucidating the pivotal role chatbots play in patient support and education, doctor-patient mediation, symptom assessment and triage, patient engagement, and ethical considerations.

1. *Patient support and education.* One technology alone can never replace doctor-patient empathy, but the growing performance of AI is producing a new generation of chatbots that are increasingly high-performing through continuous use that enables them to learn from conversations or remember dialogues, using knowledge gained in real-time chats. The adoption of chatbot consulting tailored to the needs of the health system can open the door to a world of opportunities. The service offered by

Figure 2. Results of data analysis
(Authors' elaboration)

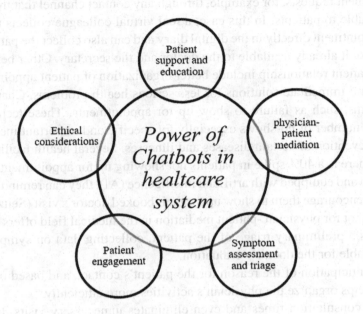

chatbots can improve the relationship with patients, automate key processes, improve health education, and reduce operational costs (Schario et al., 2022). On the doctor's side, results of literature review find the expansion of tools and technologies that can be used not only for better, faster, and more effective diagnosis (use of significant amounts of data both specific to the individual patient and general databases), but also for more efficient administrative and document management of the relationship (appointment management, high communication tools, certificates, and electronic medical records) (Sestino and D'Angelo, 2023). On the side of the patient-user, who is increasingly aware of and a user of ICT technologies, access to health services that would otherwise be inaccessible or difficult to access (due to cost or distance) is facilitated, with significant improvement even in the monitoring phase or after the end of therapy (Magni et al., 2021). Both needs, therefore, are increasingly expressed not only by large healthcare facilities, but also by small practices and individual physicians who have sensed the indispensable introduction of information and telematic technologies to improve the organization of their activities and expand the range of services offered.

2. *Physician -patient mediation*. The results of the literature study demonstrate that software methodologies and computer architectures may now be integrated to accomplish jobs with performance that is on par with, or occasionally better than, human intellect (Anjum et al., 2023). A physician-patient relationship built on effective communication is essential to providing high-quality treatment. In the digital age, technology is supporting the physician-patient mediation with the dual goals of saving time and preserving a relationship that puts the patient at the center. Innovative software and systems are increasingly appearing among hospitals and outpatient clinics; what can make a difference is understanding why and how they can improve medical activity. Preliminary results of this chapter highlighted the vital role of chatbots in enhancing the communication between physicians and patients and fostering users' engagement. AI-powered chatbots can support the medical

secretary by easing daily workloads and thus strengthening the doctor-patient relationship. They can handle appointment requests, for example, through any contact channel that the healthcare facility has made available to patients. In this case, a real virtual colleague collects the information and records the appointment directly in the digital diary and can also collect the patient's symptomatology data to make it already available to the doctor and the secretary. Other benefits of chatbots in the physician-patient relationship include better organization of patient appointments, medication management, and immediate solutions for less serious health problems. Chatbots can also solve specific problems, such as failure to show up for appointments. These technological solutions help reduce the number of no-shows especially for specific and important medical visits, such as those for the prevention of certain diseases and illnesses. Several health facilities have found that in some cases there is a 40% spike in patients not showing up for appointments. When these tools are personalized and equipped with artificial intelligence (AI), they can remind patients of their appointments and encourage them to show up for their booked doctor's visit (Seitz et al., 2022). Thus, the use of a chatbot for physician -patient mediation in the medical field offers several advantages:

- It provides a preliminary triage of the patient, collecting data on symptoms to later make them available for the doctor's evaluation.
- It allows anticipation of the reason for the patient's contact, and based on the processed responses, helps organize the physician's activities more efficiently.
- It reduces consultation times and even eliminates unnecessary visits, lightening the daily workload of the doctor, who can then focus on other tasks.

3. *Symptom assessment and triage.* Those working in the medical field have found that the implementation of a bot can check and record patients' symptoms and understand medical conditions without the patient physically going to the medical facility. Chatbots using natural language processing can understand patients' requests regardless of the input. When equipped with artificial intelligence, chatbots have high accuracy in detecting responses, which is essential for symptom detection. For example, a chatbot can help patients check their symptoms and based on their diagnosis, book an appointment, answer their questions, and even offer a direct telemedicine consultation with a doctor via video chat. Preliminary literature results show that chatbots can employed in triage procedures and guide patients (Nigam et al., 2022). Indeed, chatbots are considered a more reliable and accurate alternative compared to the "self-service" search for information on the Internet. Many people are unsure when their health conditions require a visit or when consulting telemedicine sources is sufficient. Chatbots can direct patients to the most appropriate resource (Bali et al., 2019). Healthcare-oriented chatbots gather individuals' health information and suggest actions to be taken. In this way, they support healthcare professionals, alleviating congestion at healthcare facilities or direct contact requests. Thanks to artificial intelligence, it is possible to activate triage procedures without clogging hospital switchboards (Sestino and D'Angelo, 2023). Chatbots can inquire about relevant information regarding patients' symptoms, aiming to provide a comprehensive overview to medical staff. Subsequently, doctors can access the data through a digital interface to determine which patients require urgent visits and to whom a brief consultation can be dedicated (Schario et al., 2022). This aspect has gained prominence over the past year during the Covid-19 pandemic, which overwhelmed global healthcare facilities with an unprecedented influx and where the use of technology, where applied, has proven effective in containment. Thus, chatbots enable a reduction in the time spent traveling for appointments, saving money on unnecessary treatments and tests,

and providing instant access to useful information with just a click, eliminating the need to wait on the phone (Nigam et al., 2022).

4. *Patient engagement.* From this increasingly digitized scenario, the need arose for both patients and healthcare professionals to communicate in a different manner. Email has been surpassed by more informal and swift conversational platforms such as WhatsApp, Messenger, Telegram, Teams. It is crucial for medical facilities to adapt to the new needs of individuals by engaging in dialogue with them in common, digital, virtual, and on-demand spaces. Through these channels, healthcare providers can deliver services that align with user expectations. Patients value convenience more than ever, especially in the context of daily care, such as picking up prescriptions. But why? One reason may be found in users' perceptions of health care system. Chatbots can fostering the patient's engagement by delivering tailored health information and facilitating proactive communication between patients and healthcare providers. Another reason might stem, in a much simpler way, from the convenience we are used to in other areas. E-commerce, for example, offers us the possibility of receiving the products we order directly to our homes, at predetermined time slots. Ride-hailing applications such as Uber ensure that we have transportation wherever we are, whenever we need it. Home banking applications allow us to manage our financial situation and plan our future in comfort, without moving from home. Having so many elements of our daily lives at our fingertips, customized to our preferences and controllable at the touch of a button, it stands to reason that patients expect the same level of convenience from health care (Divya et al., 2018). Online appointment scheduling tools are one way in which health care providers are meeting this expectation. These tools make it easy for patients to choose a time slot from the calendar that meets their busy schedules, while helping ancillary staff at health care providers and improving the availability of their chosen location. During this phase, it is essential for healthcare institutions to establish a presence. Patients will choose a healthcare facility based on content and references found online. There is a need to shift the strategic approach and begin to compete in the online realm (Sestino and D'Angelo, 2023). Literature review specifies that chatbots can contribute to patient education and engagement in the decision-making process regarding therapeutic options (Bali et al., 2019). Online appointment scheduling tools offer the great advantage that they can be augmented by other initiatives based on digital patient engagement, such as raising awareness about the disease, support programs, or pre- and post-intervention surveys (Schario et al., 2022). In addition, these engagement initiatives can reduce the likelihood of patients not showing up for scheduled appointments, a circumstance that often occurs in many departments. In radiology, for example, the no-show rate for visits can be as high as 7%. This causes avoidable delays in diagnosis and treatment, workflow disruptions, and financial losses of up to $1 million. Health care providers are also working on convenience with the use of dedicated patient portals. These allow them to securely access, manage, and share their diagnostic imaging examinations without dedicated training or support, thus reducing the need to return in person to pick up referrals. Dedicated patient portals also allow physicians to review and compare comprehensive diagnostic imaging exams, thus fostering greater confidence during consultations with patients.

5. *Ethical considerations.* In recent years, artificial intelligence-based applications are providing a major boost to diagnostics and clinical health care. Considering what we are already seeing in health and medical care, there is no doubt that the future can bring immense benefits to the most asset for every human being. If medicine needs artificial intelligence, the latter needs ethics. The issue, in fact, is not technological in nature, but involves the sphere of human rights, regulation and

community welfare. It is necessary to put human rights and ethical issues at the center of design. Preliminary results show that there is a need to ensure that the use of such technologies to protect the fundamental principles of medical ethics and patient privacy (Mahmud and Porntrakoon, 2023). According to Sepahpour (2020) healthcare professionals, when utilizing AI, currently expose themselves to the risk of violation of patient privacy and professional liability. AI models must be adequately trained by specialized medical personnel to provide appropriate responses in the healthcare field to assist in patient diagnosis and treatment. This is crucial to avoid the risk of diagnostic or therapeutic errors and potential legal actions for professional liability. The analysis of health data and the identification of trends are crucial aspects of monitoring and promoting public health. Thanks to the advanced capabilities of artificial intelligence, chatbots can provide valuable information and forecasts to guide public health policies and strategies.

DISCUSSION AND CONCLUSION

The adoption of chatbots has been spurred by the increased demand for medical care caused by the COVID-19 pandemic and the maturity of AI underlying the technology. As has been widely reported, the pandemic has created the paradoxical condition of creating a large amount of patient and paperwork for healthcare providers while limiting people's exposure to healthcare due to quarantines and social estrangement (Amiri and Karahanna, 2022). Covid-19 has undoubtedly accelerated the enormous change in patients' expectations of today's health care providers, as well as their preferences for involvement. However, long before the advent of pandemic Covid-19, these demands had already emerged, unlike other areas where there is still debate about the tightness of some of the changes, including reception without physical interaction and digital events. As a result, and most likely, healthcare providers will consider all patient engagement principles for the future. Chatbots are effective and unobtrusive tools because they operate with the utmost respect for user privacy and security rules, but at the same time they also become an essential research tool for understanding the extent and epidemiology of Covid-19. Chatbots, then, not only serve as virtual assistants, but are also a strategic support for information gathering and analysis of disease symptoms. These virtual assistants will soon be able to disseminate content such as health information, but also important information on nutrition education, as well as psychological care (Anjum et al., 2023).

Chatbots can be used in the enterprise for a variety of purposes (Bermeo-Giraldo et al., 2023), including:

- *Customer service*: they can be used to provide customer support, answer questions, and solve problems;
- *Marketing*: they can collect customer information, promote products or services, and provide after-sales support;
- *Process automation*: they can automate repetitive tasks, such as recording working hours or generating reports;
- *Education and training*: they can provide education and training to employees without reducing their productivity during the course period;
- *Research and development*: they collect data and information for research and development, which are needed to improve products and services.

In addition, medical chatbots have some distinctive elements:

- A user interface;
- Some language management and processing services;
- The backend of the specific company involved;
- A user interface that resembles a real chat, the use of which goes to integrate both with the algorithms of self-learning and improvement of natural language understanding, and with all that information and data that are part of the personal backend of the business reality.

In summary, through collaboration with industry experts, adaptability to new knowledge, and the ability to respond rapidly to health emergencies, AI and chatbots can contribute to transforming decision-making in the healthcare sector and promoting the health and well-being of populations. Helping people in the training and proper use of these new technologies and artificial intelligence systems can limit the dangerous use they often make of search engines (the "Dr. Google" phenomenon), risking - in a sort of "hypochondria effect" - self-diagnosing very rare diseases, usually not true, or underestimating the symptoms of latent or emerging diseases. It is precisely with this in mind that chatbots can instead be valuable allies, fostering a faster workflow for physicians that would consequently lead to an overall improvement in their work, with the nontrivial consequence of limiting human error on the one hand and increasing the ability to handle more patients on the other, which is very welcome especially at a time when physicians are a very scarce resource. Today's chatbots use a communication system that people can understand because they adapt the language using the same mode adopted by the user. For example, they can understand slang or improper words that are logically clear and respond to the patient by reusing them, thus facilitating understanding. This could potentially help patients detect the onset of disease early and perhaps even prompt them to seek immediate medical attention, an approach that, in synergy with the many potential benefits analyzed so far, could ensure a healthier life and a better future for their health.

Chatbots in the Healthcare Sector: Real Projects

Healthcare Chatbots, AI and chatbots represent a valuable support in the specific field of rehabilitative medicine, aiming to combat the physical and cognitive decline of elderly patients and to assist patients undergoing post-hospitalization physiotherapy in home-based neuromotor rehabilitation activities.

Today, accustomed as we are to automation and intelligent computers, we find ourselves in need of something more. This has led some programmers to design chatbots that prove useful for patients and those seeking to enhance their knowledge in the realm of health. An early example of chatbots in healthcare is Melody, an intelligent virtual assistant launched in October 2016 by Baidu, China's Google. Melody connects specialized doctors and users seeking advice on specific diseases. Florence, on the other hand, is a chatbot that can remind us to take medicine prescribed by the doctor. Simply tell Florence which pills to take, how many times a day you need to do so and at what time, and finally set the duration of therapy. In the software, which is based on artificial intelligence, the names of the medications the patient needs to take are in fact saved. In 2016, pharmaceutical companies invested $1.7 million on this bot. Other Chatbots are already in operation, such as HealthTap or Your.MD. Your.MD, for instance, is a mobile application that functions exclusively as a chatbot. The bot assesses symptoms, gathers information, and aids in alleviating them, aspiring to serve as a "Personal Health Assistant" readily available in the user's pocket. The application relies on an advanced AI algorithm. In the context of prescribed therapies, another valuable chatbot exists to assist in medication adherence: it is called Florence and serves as a genuine "Personal Nurse". Users can inform the bot of the names of prescribed medications, the frequency of intake, and the specific times, while also setting the duration of the treatment. It is crucial, however, not to mistake these self-diagnostic tools for real physicians. A chatbot cannot match the expertise and human sensitivity of a professional healthcare provider. Indeed, these bots, once a diagnosis is suggested, encourage users to schedule a visit with their trusted medical professional for a genuine diagnosis and, if necessary, prescription of medications. The true utility of these types of chatbots currently lies in their ability to provide advice and information for a healthy life. Some individuals, for years or even a lifetime, endure debilitating symptoms that they ignore simply because they fail to recognize the value of consulting a doctor. Many young people lack sexual education or knowledge about sexually transmitted diseases due to it being considered a taboo subject in families, schools, and communities. Most of the population is unaware of the correct use of over-the-counter medications and antibiotics, leading to ineffective treatments or misuse of unnecessary medicines. Conversely, the reassuring convenience of engaging with a health bot anywhere, at any time, and especially without the stress of sitting in a waiting room or contemplating questions and answers has given rise to the phenomenon of digital trust. Another technologically significant aspect in the realm of chatbots is Natural Language Processing (NLP), often associated with AI, allowing the use of a voice interface for communication, making the system even more accessible, especially in conditions of disabilities, even if temporary. Chatbots, therefore, are used in many different areas, and in each of them they are a viable solution for engaging customers and providing them with an increasingly personalized experience.

Final Theoretical and Managerial Implications

This book chapter emphasizes how chatbots can completely change the way healthcare is delivered. This study emphasizes the role of chatbots in improving patient care, maximizing operational efficiency, and encouraging innovation within the healthcare system by combining data from a wide variety of research. Moreover, this review's theoretical implications go beyond the specific research to provide an understanding of the larger trends, obstacles, and possibilities influencing the incorporation of chatbots into healthcare administration. The adoption, implementation, and effects of chatbots in healthcare settings can be better understood by using theoretical frameworks like the UTAUT, socio-technical systems theory, and TAM.

In recent years, chatbots are a technology that is being used in many different sectors, including the healthcare sector. Currently, artificial intelligence-based software is mainly adopted for routine care procedures, that is, to answer questions posed by users, who in the health care sector may be patients or physicians. In this latest critical period in healthcare, chatbots have been widely adopted to support users' numerous questions, flanking call centers from simpler tasks.

The results of this systematic literature review provide managers and practitioners in the healthcare industry with useful information and strategic ideas for utilizing chatbots as a transformational tool in their workplaces. Today, the healthcare sector needs automated, fast, simple, and always-available support to ease the burden of information requests coming in from users. The use of telemedicine through chatbots to carry out remote diagnosis and treatment is becoming increasingly necessary, especially as the issue of chronic diseases is becoming more central and a priority. Then, according to some estimates, simply telemonitoring heart patients at home would reduce the number of inpatient days by 26% and save 10% of healthcare costs, with a 15% increase in survival rates. Chatbots and telemedicine, therefore, may be the frontier to make these patients autonomous in the shortest possible time and facilitate their self-management (self-sufficiency at home, in the "neighborhood" where they have become accustomed to living). An integrated hospital-territory-domestic network would be activated, in which the various professionals who are already in the field (general practitioners, pediatricians, experienced nurses and podiatrists, physicians and surgeons who are specialists in the various areas of expertise in the pathologies in question) could be included, and the descent of new useful forces could be considered, to whom other tasks could be delegated, such as the management of appointments with the professionals mentioned above, the preparation of ad hoc galenic products, and the awareness and health education of patients and care-givers. In summary, this book chapter provides a comprehensive analysis of existing literature on chatbots in healthcare and offers practical insights for healthcare managers to drive innovation and improve patient outcomes. By embracing a systematic approach to the integration of chatbots, healthcare organizations can unlock new opportunities to revolutionize the delivery of care and shape the future of healthcare management.

CONCLUSION

In this book chapter, I unveil the potential for chatbots to revolutionize healthcare system. Through a systematic analysis of several previous studies, I analyzed the multifaceted impact of chatbots on patient care, operational efficiency, and innovation in the healthcare system. The inescapable goal of e-health can develop to the profound restructuring of the healthcare system, its rationalization and optimization, improving overall efficiency and simultaneously reducing its operating costs. Applied technology will trigger early diagnosis and will constantly keep the clinical situation and appropriateness of care under control. The technology is the fundamental means of coping with the needs for a continuous remote care service to be built around the patient, based on the existing pathology. Continuous monitoring will allow early detection of critical issues, enabling interventions and corrective measures to be taken before more serious complications appear, with positive spin-offs for both the patient and the health care system in terms of cost reduction. In this scenario, chatbots can spam the innovation in the whole healthcare ecosystem. There are two types of chatbots: rule-based (or task-oriented chatbots) and conversational (or data-driven) chatbots. The main difference between the two types, besides the degree of structural complexity, is the language the system can process and the way it is able to return responses.

- *Rule-based chatbots*, also known as decision tree bots, follow predefined paths: the bot analyzes, understands, and returns responses in natural human language by drawing on a defined set of data.
- *Conversational chatbots*, which can process human language and provide articulate and more complex responses. They use artificial intelligence to understand the context and intent of a question and formulate appropriate responses. Underlying these types of chatbots are the principles of natural language processing and machine learning to understand and process natural language.

Both types are designed to have broad and specific knowledge about a given topic, so that they can answer any question in context and continue the conversation independently. Those who program chatbots do so in such an advanced way that they are sufficiently suited to all kinds of needs, so that they interact with the user in an increasingly accurate way without ever trespassing on a diagnosis. In fact, the software must be able to recognize the point in the conversation at which to direct the patient to a provider or physician. The benefits for health care facilities are obvious, starting with the ability to offer 7/24 service to patients and to optimize business resources by moving staff to other strategic areas. Chatbots can answer questions about payment rates, documents needed to access them, business hours, and insurance coverage. In this case, chatbots function like a traditional counter, answering all basic inquiries in seconds. This way, patients do not need to call the facility to find the information they need. Chatbots in healthcare do not replace the work of physicians and providers: however, they have proven to be a valuable addition to care pathways because they can improve service levels, eliminate communication costs, and increase efficiency, while reducing pressure on healthcare providers and improving patient satisfaction. With technological advances in the coming years, these technologies will become increasingly accessible and enable increasingly flexible and dynamic patient relationship management. By embracing creativity, and striving for constant progress, we have the ability to tap into the boundless potential of chatbots and revolutionize the healthcare industry for future generations.

REFERENCES

Adam, M., Wessel, M., & Benlian, A. (2021). AI-based chatbots in customer service and their effects on user compliance. *Electronic Markets*, *31*(2), 427–445. doi:10.1007/s12525-020-00414-7

Amiri, P., & Karahanna, E. (2022). Chatbot use cases in the Covid-19 public health response. *Journal of the American Medical Informatics Association : JAMIA*, *29*(5), 1000–1010. doi:10.1093/jamia/ocac014 PMID:35137107

Anjum, K., Sameer, M., & Kumar, S. (2023, February). AI Enabled NLP based Text to Text Medical Chatbot. In *2023 3rd International Conference on Innovative Practices in Technology and Management (ICIPTM)* (pp. 1-5). IEEE. 10.1109/ICIPTM57143.2023.10117966

Bali, M., Mohanty, S., Chatterjee, S., Sarma, M., & Puravankara, R. (2019). Diabot: A predictive medical chatbot using ensemble learning. *International Journal of Recent Technology and Engineering*, *8*(2), 6334–6340. doi:10.35940/ijrte.B2196.078219

Bermeo-Giraldo, M. C., Toro, O. N. P., Arias, A. V., & Correa, P. A. R. (2023). Factors influencing the adoption of chatbots by healthcare users. *Journal of Innovation Management*, *11*(3), 75–94. doi:10.24840/2183-0606_011.003_0004

Davis, F. D. (1985). *A technology acceptance model for empirically testing new end-user information systems: Theory and results* [Doctoral dissertation, Massachusetts Institute of Technology].

Divya, S., Indumathi, V., Ishwarya, S., Priyasankari, M., & Devi, S. K. (2018). A self-diagnosis medical chatbot using artificial intelligence. *Journal of Web Development and Web Designing*, *3*(1), 1–7.

Frangoudes, F., Hadjiaros, M., Schiza, E. C., Matsangidou, M., Tsivitanidou, O., & Neokleous, K. (2021, July). An overview of the use of chatbots in medical and healthcare education. In *International Conference on Human-Computer Interaction* (pp. 170-184). Cham: Springer International Publishing. 10.1007/978-3-030-77943-6_11

Hasal, M., Nowaková, J., Ahmed Saghair, K., Abdulla, H., Snášel, V., & Ogiela, L. (2021). Chatbots: Security, privacy, data protection, and social aspects. *Concurrency and Computation*, *33*(19), e6426. doi:10.1002/cpe.6426

Heo, M., & Lee, K. J. (2018). Chatbot as a new business communication tool: The case of naver talktalk. *Business Communication Research and Practice*, *1*(1), 41–45. doi:10.22682/bcrp.2018.1.1.41

Hsieh, P. J., & Lai, H. M. (2020). Exploring peoples intentions to use the health passbook in self-management: An extension of the technology acceptance and health behavior theoretical perspectives in health literacy. *Technological Forecasting and Social Change*, *161*, 120328. doi:10.1016/j.techfore.2020.120328

Kalantari, M., & Rauschnabel, P. (2018). Exploring the early adopters of augmented reality smart glasses: The case of Microsoft HoloLens. In *Augmented reality and virtual reality* (pp. 229–245). Springer. doi:10.1007/978-3-319-64027-3_16

King, M. R. (2023). The future of AI in medicine: A perspective from a Chatbot. *Annals of Biomedical Engineering*, *51*(2), 291–295. doi:10.1007/s10439-022-03121-w PMID:36572824

Liu, B., & Sundar, S. S. (2018). Should machines express sympathy and empathy? Experiments with a health advice chatbot. *Cyberpsychology, Behavior, and Social Networking*, *21*(10), 625–636. doi:10.1089/cyber.2018.0110 PMID:30334655

Magni, D., Del Gaudio, G., Papa, A., & Della Corte, V. (2023). Digital humanism and artificial intelligence: The role of emotions beyond the human–machine interaction in Society 5.0. *Journal of Management History*. doi:10.1108/JMH-12-2022-0084

Magni, D., Palladino, R., Papa, A., & Cailleba, P. (2022). Exploring the journey of Responsible Business Model Innovation in Asian companies: A review and future research agenda. *Asia Pacific Journal of Management*, 1–30. doi:10.1007/s10490-022-09813-0

Magni, D., Scuotto, V., Pezzi, A., & Del Giudice, M. (2021). Employees' acceptance of wearable devices: Towards a predictive model. *Technological Forecasting and Social Change*, *172*, 121022. doi:10.1016/j.techfore.2021.121022

Mahmud, T. R., & Porntrakoon, P. (2023, August). The Use of AI Chatbots in Mental Healthcare for University Students in Thailand: A Case Study. In *2023 7th International Conference on Business and Information Management (ICBIM)* (pp. 48-53). IEEE. 10.1109/ICBIM59872.2023.10303025

Mariani, M. M., Hashemi, N., & Wirtz, J. (2023). Artificial intelligence empowered conversational agents: A systematic literature review and research agenda. *Journal of Business Research*, *161*, 161. doi:10.1016/j.jbusres.2023.113838

Nasir, S., & Yurder, Y. (2015). Consumers' and physicians' perceptions about high tech wearable health products. *Procedia: Social and Behavioral Sciences*, *195*, 1261–1267. doi:10.1016/j.sbspro.2015.06.279

Nigam, B., Mehra, N., & Niranjanamurthy, M. (2022). Self-Diagnosis in Healthcare Systems Using AI Chatbots. *IoT and AI Technologies for Sustainable Living: A Practical Handbook*, 79. Research Gate.

Paul, S. C., Bartmann, N., & Clark, J. L. (2021). Customizability in conversational agents and their impact on health engagement. *Human Behavior and Emerging Technologies*, *3*(5), 1141–1152. doi:10.1002/hbe2.320

Roppelt, J. S., Kanbach, D. K., & Kraus, S. (2023). Artificial intelligence in healthcare institutions: A systematic literature review on influencing factors. *Technology in Society*, 102443.

Schario, M. E., Bahner, C. A., Widenhofer, T. V., Rajaballey, J. I., & Thatcher, E. J. (2022). Chatbot-assisted care management. *Professional Case Management*, *27*(1), 19–25. doi:10.1097/NCM.0000000000000504 PMID:34846321

Schmidthuber, L., Maresch, D., & Ginner, M. (2020). Disruptive technologies and abundance in the service sector-toward a refined technology acceptance model. *Technological Forecasting and Social Change*, *155*, 119328. doi:10.1016/j.techfore.2018.06.017

Seitz, L., Bekmeier-Feuerhahn, S., & Gohil, K. (2022). Can we trust a chatbot like a physician? A qualitative study on understanding the emergence of trust toward diagnostic chatbots. *International Journal of Human-Computer Studies*, *165*, 102848. doi:10.1016/j.ijhcs.2022.102848

Sepahpour, T. (2020). *Ethical considerations of chatbot use for mental health support* [Doctoral dissertation, Johns Hopkins University].

Sestino, A., & D'Angelo, A. (2023). My doctor is an avatar! The effect of anthropomorphism and emotional receptivity on individuals' intention to use digital-based healthcare services. *Technological Forecasting and Social Change*, *191*, 122505. doi:10.1016/j.techfore.2023.122505

Sheth, J. (2020). Impact of Covid-19 on consumer behavior: Will the old habits return or die? *Journal of Business Research*, *117*, 280–283. doi:10.1016/j.jbusres.2020.05.059 PMID:32536735

Tranfield, D., Denyer, D., & Smart, P. (2003). Towards a methodology for developing evidence-informed management knowledge by means of systematic review. *British Journal of Management*, *14*(3), 207–222. doi:10.1111/1467-8551.00375

Tudor Car, L., Dhinagaran, D. A., Kyaw, B. M., Kowatsch, T., Joty, S., Theng, Y. L., & Atun, R. (2020). Conversational agents in health care: Scoping review and conceptual analysis. *Journal of Medical Internet Research*, *22*(8), e17158. doi:10.2196/17158 PMID:32763886

Venkatesh, V., & Zhang, X. (2010). Unified theory of acceptance and use of technology: US vs. China. *Journal of Global Information Technology Management*, *13*(1), 5–27. doi:10.1080/1097198X.2010.10856507

Ye, B. J., Kim, J. Y., Suh, C., Choi, S. P., Choi, M., Kim, D. H., & Son, B. C. (2021). Development of a chatbot program for follow-up management of workers' general health examinations in korea: A pilot study. *International Journal of Environmental Research and Public Health*, *18*(4), 2170. doi:10.3390/ijerph18042170 PMID:33672158

KEY TERMS AND DEFINITIONS

Chatbot: Virtual assistants that, through a sophisticated algorithm, can respond to and communicate with people who interface with them through both text and voice.

Disruptive technology: In entrepreneurial theory, is an innovation that creates a new market and network of values.

Immersive technologies: It is a type of technology that attempts to emulate a physical world through specific digital tools.

Natural Language Processing: Text structure and meaning may be revealed by machine learning in natural language processing, or NLP. Organizations may leverage natural language processing systems to analyze text and derive information about individuals, locations, and events to get a deeper understanding of consumer interactions and social media sentiment.

Systematic Literature Review: A methodical approach of gathering, analyzing, integrating, and presenting data from many research papers on a particular research issue or topic of interest.

Technology Acceptance Model: One of the most popular models of technology adoption where the perceived ease of use and perceived utility of new technology are the two main elements that influence an individual's desire to use it.

Unified Theory of Acceptance and Use of Technology: A model of technology acceptance developed by Venkatesh and associates. The purpose of UTAUT is to elucidate users' intentions when using an information system and their actual usage patterns.

Chapter 13
Utilizing Artificial Intelligence for Text Classification in Communication Sciences:
Reliability of ChatGPT Models in Turkish Texts

Sadettin Demirel
https://orcid.org/0000-0002-3282-1706
Üsküdar University, Turkey

Neslihan Bulur
Üsküdar University, Turkey

Zindan Çakıcı
https://orcid.org/0000-0002-8916-0582
Üsküdar University, Turkey

ABSTRACT

This study delves into the evaluation of ChatGPT's effectiveness in sentiment detection and text classification tasks specifically on Turkish texts, a domain that has been relatively underexplored in existing literature predominantly focused on English texts. Leveraging datasets comprising manually labeled YouTube comments and news tweets categorized into sentiment classes and thematic topics, the authors rigorously assess the performance of ChatGPT-3.5 and ChatGPT-4 using accuracy and F1 performance metrics. These findings unveil insights into ChatGPT's proficiency in classifying Turkish textual content, illuminating its alignment with human-labeled classifications. This research not only contributes to expanding the scope of AI research beyond English language but also underscores the significance of language diversity in evaluating and refining AI models' performance for broader applicability in the research practices of social and communication sciences.

DOI: 10.4018/979-8-3693-1830-0.ch013

INTRODUCTION

The advancements in the field of artificial intelligence have reached a significant peak, especially with the models introduced in 2022. These models belong to the category of large language models and are utilized in applications such as artificial intelligence chatbots. These technologies encompass not only the ability to engage in meaningful conversation but also various capabilities such as summarizing and translating large blocks of text. One type of generative artificial intelligence, ChatGPT, is an artificial intelligence language model developed by OpenAI, capable of understanding user queries and generating natural and human-like text responses (OpenAI et al., 2023). Particularly, GPT-3.5 and GPT-4 are trained using deep learning techniques and large amounts of text data. With a total of 175 billion parameters, these large-scale models significantly enhance language understanding and generation abilities (He et al., 2023). ChatGPT-3.5 and ChatGPT-4 demonstrate impressive performance across various tasks in natural language processing. By understanding user queries or commands, considering context, and generating responses across a broad spectrum of language, they provide a natural and fluent conversational environment. Additionally, trained on a vast corpus of text data, they offer access to information across diverse topics and excel in handling complex sentence structures. However, they may sometimes exhibit limitations such as providing illogical or inconsistent responses, reflecting societal biases, or lacking evidence-based reasoning (OpenAI et al., 2023; Brin et al., 2023).

Despite these aspects of ongoing development, ChatGPT-3.5 and ChatGPT-4, along with the support of application programming interfaces (APIs) provided by OpenAI for Chat-GPT, offer a wide range of services in commercial sectors. Besides commercial applications, ChatGPT holds significant potential as a new tool and research area in academic studies. By delegating tasks such as traditional content analysis and sentiment analysis to models like Chat-GPT, substantial time and resource savings can be achieved in these laborious processes (Gilardi, Alizadeh & Kubli, 2023; Törnberg, 2023; Rathje et al., 2023). However, many studies in the literature primarily focus on evaluating the sentiment or text classification performance of Chat-GPT on English texts, indicating a lack of research evaluating its performance in other languages, particularly Turkish.

This study aims to investigate the sentiment detection and text classification capabilities of ChatGPT on Turkish texts. By measuring its text classification prowess on Turkish texts, this research attempts to assess how reliable ChatGPT is and to what extent it can be utilized for the research practices in social and communication sciences. To compare ChatGPT models' text classification performance on Turkish text, we used YouTube comments (n = 500), news organizations' news tweets (n = 500) which were manually classified by two coders into 3 sentiment categories and 9 themes until inter-coder agreement values were deemed sufficient. In the analysis phase, we computed accuracy and F1 performance metrics to evaluate sentiment and theme classification ability of ChatGPT-3.5 and its successor ChatGPT-4 generative AI models. The obtained results provide important insights into ChatGPT's performance on Turkish texts and its ability to classify textual contents similarly to users, thereby contributing to understanding of generative AI technologies for the research practices.

The study begins by discussing fundamental concepts and developments in the field of artificial intelligence in a general context. Subsequently, it focuses on generative artificial intelligence and the advent of Chat-GPT. The methodology of this study is then elaborated, detailing the datasets and analysis methods used. The findings are presented, highlighting the performance metrics (accuracy, F1) of ChatGPT models' prediction compared to the human-labeled classifications. The final section of the article provides recommendations for future research based on the obtained findings and shares thoughts on potential developments in this field.

From AI Winter to Deep Learning Spring: A Historical Overview of AI and GPT Evolution

Artificial Intelligence (AI) delineates an interdisciplinary scientific domain whose overarching objective resides in the deliberate design of computational systems adept at executing tasks commensurate with human intelligence (Kaplan and Haenlein, 2019; Mohammad, 2020). Its foundational constituents span the realms of computer science, statistics, mathematics, and cognitive sciences. Pivotal junctures in the historical trajectory of AI include the articulation of Alan Turing's 1950 treatise, "Computing Machinery and Intelligence," and the definitional elucidation of the term by John McCarthy at the 1956 Dartmouth Conference (Buchanan, 2005; Huang et al, 2006). Concepts such as symbolic AI, knowledge-based systems, and expert systems attained ascendancy as seminal facets of AI during the 1960s and 1970s. Nonetheless, concomitant limitations and the nonfulfillment of anticipated outcomes precipitated an epoch colloquially denominated as the AI Winter. This epoch bore witness to a contraction in financial support, engendering a substantial deceleration in research endeavors. In the denouement of the 1980s and the nascent years of the 1990s, a resurgence of interest in AI transpired, notably propelled by advancements in statistical machine learning and expert systems (Toosi et al., 2021). From the onset of the 21st century, strides in the domains of deep learning and neural network technologies have exerted profound ramifications upon the landscape of AI. This period accentuated a predilection towards erudition gleaned from expansive datasets and the resolution of intricate problematics (Delipetrev, Tsinaraki, and Kostić, 2018).

Artificial intelligence (AI) functions by synergistically integrating the presence of multiple datasets, iterative processes, and intelligent algorithms. This paradigm affords the software the capability to autonomously assimilate discernment from inherent patterns or features within the data (Fitria, 2021). At present, scholarly endeavors in the domain of Super Artificial Intelligence, acknowledged as the third evolutionary phase of artificial intelligence, persist in earnest, with a concerted emphasis on attaining a level wherein models can elucidate the underlying rationale governing the expeditious outputs they yield (Zhang, Zhu, and Su, 2023). In this context, the amalgamation of artificial intelligence with its subdomains, encompassing machine learning, deep learning, natural language processing, image processing, and data mining, has elicited considerable scholarly interest. Rapidly transcending its erstwhile status as a singular research focus, artificial intelligence has metamorphosed into a highly applicable technological framework, extending its purview across a myriad of disciplines (Ebel et al., 2021). The trajectory of artificial intelligence's evolution has been marked by its expeditious transition from a singularly focused research domain to a versatile and widely employed technology within a concise temporal span. In contemporary discourse, its pervasive utility spans diverse sectors, including but not limited to health, finance, manufacturing, e-commerce, automotive, and energy. Its ubiquitous deployment is discernible across multifarious domains, encapsulating functionalities such as data analysis, predictability, automation, and decision support systems (Bilgiç, 2024; Altun, 2024).

Artificial intelligence (AI) systems have attained a level of productivity whereby they demonstrate the potential to mitigate operational costs, enhance business analytics, and ultimately elevate the quality and efficacy of managerial decision-making, a trajectory that continues to unfold. In particular, the domain of generative AI has found multifaceted applications, ranging from the creation of personalized content to the optimization of various business processes. Generative AI, in essence, refers to the intrinsic capacity of a system or program to generate outputs characterized by creativity and originality. Its departure from conventional AI lies not solely in its aptitude for task execution or problem-solving but, critically, in its ability to engender novel ideas, innovative designs, and artistic creations reminiscent of the cognitive creativity inherent in the human brain (Ooi, 2023). The embryonic stages of generative AI were marked by limitations imposed by specific rules and relatively diminutive models. However, contemporary iterations exhibit heightened complexity, enabling expeditious processing of expansive datasets (Muller, 2022). Notwithstanding the manifold advantages discernible across diverse domains, generative AI, with its remarkable capability to produce content closely resembling human-created works, has prompted substantial discourse and debate within the scholarly literature. These discussions extend beyond technical considerations, including debates regarding whether generative AI embodies the early indicators of authentic AI, to legal quandaries revolving around issues such as copyright, licenses, and intellectual property (Banh and Strobel, 2023).

ChatGPT, an artificial intelligence language model engineered by OpenAI, epitomizes a generative AI paradigm proficient in comprehending user queries or directives and generating text that emulates natural and human-like conversational responses. Its training regimen involves leveraging deep learning techniques, specifically GPT-3.5, and exposure to an extensive corpus of textual data. Positioned as an innovative conversational agent, ChatGPT endeavors to facilitate diverse user interactions, encompassing information retrieval, query resolution, and social discourse. Employing a learning mechanism predicated on human feedback, ChatGPT is endowed with the capability to simulate dialogues, recognize and rectify errors, scrutinize presuppositions, and exercise discernment in rejecting inappropriate requests. However, it is not immune to occasional lapses, manifesting as illogical or inaccurate responses, inadvertent reflection of societal biases, and instances where responses lack empirical grounding, necessitating external verification processes (Fitria, 2023). A salient criticism directed towards ChatGPT pertains to its inclination to adopt a singular truth assumption and exhibit a predisposition towards content reflective of Western perspectives (Cooper, 2023). Notwithstanding these critiques, empirical research has delved into the economic ramifications of artificial intelligence, specifically exploring the impact of ChatGPT. A notable study, encompassing 444 university graduates, scrutinized the efficacy of ChatGPT in mid-level professional writing tasks. The findings revealed that participants utilizing ChatGPT outperformed a control group both in terms of speed and the quality of text production. Moreover, the research identified ChatGPT as a catalyst for augmenting job satisfaction and bolstering participants' self-confidence (Noy and Zhang, 2023).

ChatGPT stands as an advanced natural language processing (NLP) system developed by OpenAI, designed to generate human-like conversations. It derives its capabilities from the GPT-3 deep learning model, extensively trained on a substantial dataset of conversational data and positioned within OpenAI's Generative Pre-trained Transformer (GPT) series. The foundational training of GPT models involves pre-training on vast textual datasets followed by fine-tuning for specific tasks. ChatGPT, functioning as a chatbot, exhibits a diverse array of functionalities, encompassing question-answering, cross-language translation, and text generation across various genres such as petitions, literary content, scripts, and articles. Additional capabilities include text summarization, mathematical equation solving, debugging, correction, keyword extraction, text classification, and suggestion provision. It is freely accessible and concurrently undergoing a "research preview" phase, collecting valuable insights into user experiences (Deng and Lin, 2022; Fitria, 2023). These extensive features of ChatGPT build upon the foundation laid by its predecessor, GPT-2, a model renowned for its proficiency in generating natural language text across diverse styles and formats, including news articles, poetry, and fictional narratives. However, due to concerns regarding potential misuse, especially in the generation of misinformation, OpenAI initially imposed access restrictions on the full version of GPT-2 (Baziyad et al., 2023).

Introduced in late 2020, GPT-3 represents the third iteration of the GPT series, boasting over 175 billion parameters. It has demonstrated remarkable consistency in producing contextually appropriate text, even in scenarios with minimal input or guidance. A subsequent version of ChatGPT, trained on GPT-3.5 architectures and leveraging Reinforcement Learning from Human Feedback (RLHF) to augment generative capabilities, has been introduced since November 2022 (He et al., 2024). The most recent installment, GPT-4, is a subscription-based model that integrates both image and text inputs while proficiently generating text outputs. Despite a design reminiscent of its predecessors, GPT-4 distinguishes itself by its substantially augmented scale, indicating training on more extensive datasets and enhanced accuracy in understanding and generating text. Demonstrating human-level performance in various professional and academic examinations designed for humans, GPT-4 operates as a Transformer-based model pre-trained to predict the succeeding token in a document (OpenAI et al., 2023; Brin et al., 2023).

Literature review reveals a plethora of academic studies showcasing the versatile applications of ChatGPT across diverse domains such as health (Biswas, 2023), tourism (Akpur, 2023), religion and belief systems (Kızılgeçit et al., 2023), law (Tan et al., 2023), engineering (Özpolat et al., 2023), education (Baidoo-Anu and Owusu Ansah, 2023), sports (Genç, 2023), literature (Aksoy, 2023), economics (Zaremba and Demir, 2023), gastronomy (Göktaş, 2023), linguistics (Jiao et al., 2023), mathematics (Frieder et al., 2023), and gender studies (McGee, 2023). These academic endeavors collectively demonstrate the efficacy of ChatGPT in performing various tasks such as language comprehension, information generation, recommendation, and problem-solving within the specified disciplines. While ChatGPT exhibits substantial potential in the field of communication, the literature indicates a limited number of studies delineating its applications in communication subfields such as advertising, journalism, new media, and public relations (Gondwe, 2023; Huh et al., 2023; Canöz et al., 2023; Hussain et al., 2024). Exploring the potential of ChatGPT within the realm of communication sciences and comprehending how this technology can be more effectively employed in these domains necessitate further research efforts.

The literature extensively demonstrates that ChatGPT possesses rich knowledge of global languages and offers various opportunities for users aspiring to learn foreign languages and communicate more effectively in a foreign language (Hong, 2023; Kohnke et al., 2023; Klyshbekova, 2023; Baskara and Mukarto, 2023; Athanassopoulos et al., 2023; Widianingtyas et al., 2023; Xiao and Zhi, 2023). However, upon reviewing the national literature in Turkey, it is observed that the potential of ChatGPT for the Turkish language has not been explored. Investigating this potential is crucial for national-level research in the field of social sciences. Examining the proficiency of ChatGPT in the Turkish language can shed light on methodological considerations for future communication sciences studies conducted at the national level, determining whether ChatGPT is suitable for use in these studies. This study aims to assess the familiarity of ChatGPT with the cultural context of the Turkish language and its ability to code and classify text in basic categorizations, akin to the human brain. Additionally, the research aims to compare the understanding ability of ChatGPT in Turkish texts with English texts and, based on the examination, measure the extent to which ChatGPT is proficient in the Turkish language among language models. Consequently, the research not only focuses on language comprehension but also evaluates ChatGPT's ability to classify like humans. The obtained ratios and results provide valuable insights into ChatGPT's performance in processing Turkish language texts and its capability to categorize similarly to users. This research comprehensively evaluates ChatGPT's language understanding and generation abilities, as well

Table 1. Confusion matrix

	Predicted Negative (0)	**Predicted Positive (1)**
Actual Negative (0)	True Negative (TN)	False Positive (FP)
Actual Positive (1)	False Negative (FN)	True Positive (TP)

as its classification skills, offering a significant perspective on the effectiveness of natural language processing technologies in Turkish language applications.

METHOD

This study aims to assess the performance of ChatGPT models in classifying Turkish text and to evaluate the reliability of employing ChatGPT in various research processes within the realms of social and communication sciences, such as sentiment analysis, content analysis, and text annotations.

To quantify the performance of OpenAI's generative AI models (ChatGPT 3.5 and ChatGPT4), we utilized performance evaluation metrics commonly employed in machine learning models. These metrics include accuracy and F1 score (Ferri et al., 2009; Forman & Scholz, 2009; Manning et al., 2009; Sokolova & Lapalme, 2009; Hand et al., 2021). While these metrics are not exhaustive, we opted for the most widely used and straightforward ones (Forman & Scholz, 2009; Kou et al., 2020) to assess the performance of ChatGPT models in classifying Turkish texts. Similar metrics have been utilized in several recent studies that evaluate ChatGPT's performance (Gilardi, Alizadeh & Kubli, 2023; Kristensen-McLachlan et al., 2023; Rathje et al., 2023; Törnberg 2023).

Performance Metrics

The confusion matrix in Table 1, also known as a two-by-two table, serves as a fundamental method to compute, and comprehend performance metrics. It presents a tabular summary of a model's performance by contrasting predicted or classified values against actual values across various classes.

Accuracy, a key metric, represents the ratio of correct predictions (both true negatives and true positives) to the total number of predictions made by the model. In this study, we determined accuracy by dividing the number of identical classifications of tweets between ChatGPT models and human coders by the total number of tweets (n = 500).

Accuracy = (TN + TP) / (TN + FP + FN + TP)

While accuracy is a commonly used evaluation metric, its reliability can be limited, especially in situations involving imbalanced datasets. In such cases, accuracy may not provide a comprehensive reflection of the model's performance (Manning et al., 2009; Ferri et al., 2009; Sokolova & Lapalme, 2009).

The F1 score relies on two primary components: precision and recall. Precision signifies the ratio of true positive (TP) instances to the total instances predicted as positive (TP and FP), while recall measures the ratio of true positive (TP) instances to the total actual positive instances (TP and FN).

Precision $=TP / (TP + FP)$

Recall $=TP / (TP + FN)$

The F1 score was originally developed to assess the performance of information extraction and information retrieval techniques (Rijsbergen, 1979). Over time, it has evolved into a comprehensive evaluation metric for text classification models within contemporary machine learning frameworks. Its significance lies in effectively balancing false positives and false negatives (Yang and Liu, 1999; Forman & Scholz, 2009; Manning et al., 2009; Sokolova & Lapalme, 2009; Hand et al., 2021). The F1 score, ranging from 0 (indicating the poorest performance) to 1 (indicating the best performance), represents the harmonic mean of a model's precision and recall values. Therefore, the F1 score considers both precision and recall, offering a balanced assessment of a model's performance across all classes.

F1 Score $= 2 * (Precision * Recall) / (Precision + Recall)$

As the F1 score is computed individually for each class, we calculated the macro average of the F1 score to obtain an overall understanding of how effectively the model classifies tweets and comments into their respective categories. While both the macro F1 score and accuracy metrics were computed for each dataset, we also calculated each metric for the English-translated versions of tweets and YouTube comments to assess whether ChatGPT's classification capabilities are influenced by language dependency.

Data Preparation and Reliability

We conducted tests on ChatGPT's text classification capabilities using two datasets obtained from Twitter and YouTube via their API services. The tweet data (n=500) originates from Turkish news media outlets, while the YouTube comments (n=500) were extracted from the teaser video of the movie "About the Dry Grasses" (Ceylan, 2023). Due to cost constraints associated with the OpenAI API, only 500 tweets and comments were randomly selected from the available data.

To evaluate and compare the text classification performance of ChatGPT models, two PhD level students manually annotated the tweets and YouTube comments into sentiment categories comprising positive, negative, and neutral sentiments. These categories are commonly employed by established dictionaries and models (Hutto & Gilbert, 2014; Mohammad & Turney, 2013; Hu & Liu, 2004; Rinker, 2018) for sentiment detection and polarity assessment. Additionally, the tweet data was categorized into news themes to assess the generative AI's reasoning capabilities beyond sentiment analysis. These themes encompass nine distinct news categories: politics, economy, war, health, culture, sports, technology, environment, and others.

During the manual annotation phase, we ensured high agreement levels by initially training two coders on 10% of the tweets and comments for sentiment and theme classifications. These coders were Turkish native speaker PhD students. They classified 10% of the data until reaching the desired agreement. Following this, all tweets and comments were categorized manually. Upon completion of the coding process, the human coders revisited their disagreements to achieve consensus. Ultimately, we attained near-perfect inter-coder reliability between the two annotators for both tweets and comments data, as evidenced by the near-perfect agreement levels in Krippendorf's Alpha (Krippendorf, 2019) and Cohen's Kappa coefficient (Viera & Garrett, 2005; McHugh, 2012), as displayed in Table 2.

Table 2. Inter-rater agreement in manually annotated texts

Datasets	Cohen's Kappa	Krippendorf's Alpha
Tweets sentiment	0.91	0.90
Tweets news theme	0.97	0.96
YT comments sentiment	0.92	0.91

After completing the manual annotation of texts into predefined categories and achieving satisfactory inter-rater agreements, we utilized the OpenAI API service to classify tweets and comments into these categories. In this process, we employed the *gpt-3.5-turbo-110* and *gpt-4-1106-preview* model versions of ChatGPT for text classification. As ChatGPT is a pre-trained AI chatbot, it possesses zero-shot prediction capability for text classification tasks. Therefore, we relied on the OpenAI models for text classification only once. To compute performance metrics such as accuracy, macro F1 score, etc., and access the OpenAI APIs, we used R programming language.

FINDINGS AND DISCUSSION

The findings were presented in two sections. The first one focused on ChatGPT's sentiment classification performance. The latter illustrates the ChatGPT's text classifications abilities for content analysis, particularly classifying texts to themes.

Sentiment Classification

Firstly, we assessed the accuracy of ChatGPT models in terms of sentiment classification. As depicted in Table 3, GPT-3 correctly predicted the sentiments of 66% of Turkish tweets, whereas GPT-4 surpassed the previous model by classifying 77% of Turkish tweets into sentiment categories. Similarly, GPT-4 also demonstrated superior performance over GPT-3.5 in Macro F1 metrics, which is a more reliable evaluation method especially when dealing with datasets characterized by skewed class distributions.

In line with the sentiment predictions for Turkish tweets, GPT-4 exhibited improved performance in classifying English-translated tweets as well (Accuracy = 0.768, F1 = 0.727). While both GPT models displayed slightly lower performance compared to the findings for sentiment predictions on Turkish tweets, the disparity primarily consists of minor deviations. This suggests that ChatGPT's sentiment classification capabilities may be marginally influenced by language differences. While it was anticipated that ChatGPT would exhibit higher accuracy in predicting sentiments of English-translated tweets, our observations indicate that ChatGPT is more adept at predicting the sentiments of original Turkish tweets.

Furthermore, the second dataset used to evaluate ChatGPT's sentiment prediction performance comprised comments from YouTube users on the movie teasers. In comparison to its sentiment classification of tweets, the GPT-3.5 model demonstrated superior performance in predicting the sentiment of YouTube comments (Accuracy = 0.791, F1 = 0.765). It even narrowly surpassed its successor, GPT-4 (Accuracy = 0.790, F1 = 0.751). Consistent with the findings from the tweet datasets, both GPT models (GPT-4 and GPT-3.5) exhibited marginally lower performances in predicting the sentiment categories of English-translated YouTube comments. While the translation of Turkish text may contribute to this

Table 3. GPT 3.5 vs GPT 4 on sentiment classification of tweets and YouTube comments classification (Green = GPT-4 outperform GPT-3.5, Red = GPT-4 is outperformed by GPT-3)

Data	N	GPT-3.5		GPT-4	
		Accuracy	F1	Accuracy	F1
Turkish tweets	500	0.664	0.627	0.776	0.743
English-translated tweets	500	0.636	0.624	0.768	0.727
YouTube comments	500	0.791	0.765	0.790	0.751
English-translated YouTube comments	500	0.781	0.728	0.765	0.726

outcome, it nonetheless suggests that ChatGPT models are not as proficient in sentiment classification of English text.

Of particular significance, we observed some contradictory findings in sentiment classifications between Twitter messages and YouTube comments. As anticipated, GPT-4, the latest version of state-of-the-art generative AI, outperformed its predecessor, GPT-3.5, in tweets. Conversely, the GPT-4 model was surpassed by the inferior version, GPT-3.5, in the second dataset. This discrepancy could be attributed to the nature of digital texts. The tweet data comprises news messages from Turkish media outlets, while YouTube comments originate from ordinary users. However, these findings are not unique in the literature; Rathje et al. (2023) also observed GPT-4's failure to outpace GPT-3.5 in sentiment classifications. Despite variations in performance metrics between the generative AI models presented in Table 3, GPT models demonstrated effective performance in sentiment classification of Turkish tweets. Moreover, they exhibited nearly identical performance metrics on translated texts.

Like any machine learning model, ChatGPT is subject to certain biases. Confusion matrices comparing ChatGPT's sentiment prediction against human-coded sentiment classification can offer insights into the accuracy and F1 metrics presented in Table 3. Figures 1 and 2 illustrate the biases contributing to the lower performance of ChatGPT-3 in accuracy and F1 metrics. In Figure 1, we observe that GPT-3.5 is more inclined to predict negative (32%) and positive tweets (45%) as neutral. Consequently, GPT-4

Figure 1. Confusion matrix of ChatGPT-predicted sentiment vs. human-coded (true) sentiment on Turkish tweets

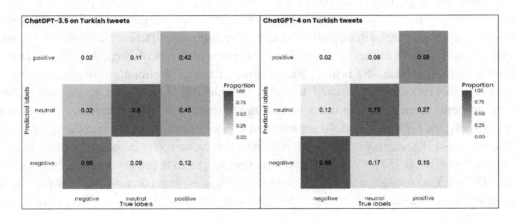

Figure 2. Confusion matrix of ChatGPT-predicted sentiment vs. human-coded (true) sentiment on English-translated tweets

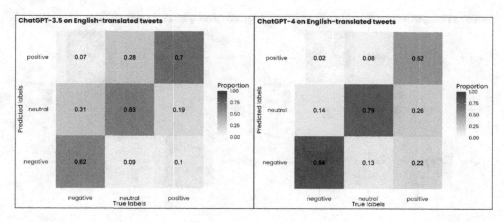

Figure 3. Confusion matrix of ChatGPT-predicted sentiment vs. human-coded (true) sentiment on Turkish YouTube comments

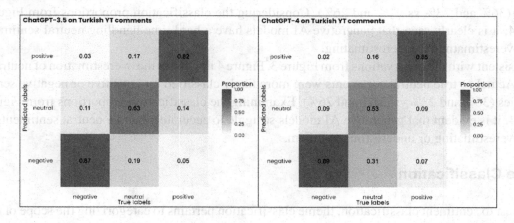

outperforms GPT-3.5 due to its higher classification accuracy in negative (86%) and positive (58%) sentiment categories.

GPT-3.5 maintains its bias towards neutrality by frequently classifying negative and positive tweets into the neutral sentiment category, as evidenced in Figure 2. In line with the observations from Figure 1, GPT-4's classification of English-translated tweets yields more accurate results. Consequently, the success of GPT-4 in sentiment classification in Table 3 can be attributed to its effective handling of neutral tweets.

However, GPT-4 also exhibits biases in the sentiment classification of YouTube comments, as illustrated in Figure 3 and Figure 4. Figure 3 highlights GPT-4's inability to accurately classify actual neutral comments, which were falsely predicted as 31% negative and 16% positive. While both GPT-3.5 and GPT-4 correctly classify a higher proportion of positive (82% and 85%) and negative (89% and 85%) comments, both models struggle to handle comments with a neutral sentiment (63% and 53%).

Figure 4. Confusion matrix of ChatGPT-predicted sentiment vs. human-coded (true) sentiment on English-translated YouTube comments

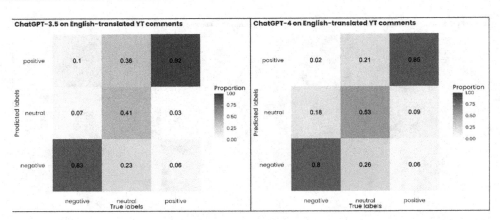

In line with the findings from Figure 3, Figure 4 illustrates the overestimation of neutral comments. Actual or True neutral comments were more likely classified into positive or negative sentiment categories (36% and 23% vs 21% and 26%). Considering the classification proportions from Figure 1 to Figure 4, it is clearly seen that generative AI models have a hard time handling neutral sentiments by either overestimatng or underestimating.

Consistent with the observations from Figure 3, Figure 4 illustrates the overestimation of neutral comments. Actual or true neutral comments were more likely classified into positive or negative sentiment categories (36% and 23% vs. 21% and 26%). Examining the classification proportions from Figure 1 to Figure 4, it is evident that generative AI models struggle to accurately handle neutral sentiments, often either overestimating or underestimating them.

Theme Classification

In contrast to sentiment classification, theme classification pertains to categorizing the scope of the text into predefined categories. In the research field of social and communication sciences, content analysis often involves working with pre-defined categories to analyze media messages. These categories extend beyond sentiment categories and may encompass various frames, ideological scales, and other thematic elements.

In this section, we evaluate the performance of generative artificial intelligence models in predicting the themes of tweets. As explained in the methodology, we tasked ChatGPT models with classifying tweets into 9 different theme categories.

Since theme categories may indicate imbalanced proportions, the F1 score is a reliable metric for comparing the performance of GPT models. Consistent with the sentiment classification of tweets presented in Table 3, GPT-4 outperforms GPT-3.5 but with narrow margin (0.657 vs. 0.635 and 0.661 vs. 0.623) in the classification of tweets into themes. This indicates GPT-3.5 is effective at text classification tasks that deal with more than 3 classes or categories as well.

Comparing performance metrics for sentiment prediction in Table 3, GPT-3.5 demonstrates almost equal performance in theme classification in Table 4, whereas GPT-4 exhibits superior performance in

Table 4. GPT 3.5 vs GPT 4 on theme classification of Turkish tweets and English-translated tweets (Green = GPT-4 outperform GPT-3.5, Red = GPT-4 is outperformed by GPT-3)

Data	N	GPT-3.5		GPT-4	
		Accuracy	F1	Accuracy	F1
Turkish tweets	500	0.648	0.635	0.730	0.657
English-translated tweets	500	0.652	0.623	0.732	0.661

sentiment classification compared to theme classification (F1 for sentiments = 0.743, F1 for themes = 0.657).

Furthermore, Comparison of GPT models' performance on original Turkish tweets and English-translated tweets appears to be identical. This observation suggests that although these models were trained with skewed data in terms of language diversity, the classification may not be language dependent.

CONCLUSION

Throughout this study, our aim was to assess the performance of ChatGPT models in classifying Turkish text, with a specific focus on sentiment analysis and content analysis. The study also aimed to evaluate the reliability of using ChatGPT in research processes within the domains of social and communication sciences. By employing performance evaluation metrics such as accuracy, F1 score, and confusion matrices, we sought to provide insights into the effectiveness of ChatGPT models in these tasks.

Our findings reveal several key insights regarding the performance of ChatGPT models particularly in sentiment and theme classification. In terms of sentiment analysis, both GPT-3.5 and GPT-4 demonstrated varying degrees of accuracy and F1 score in classifying Turkish tweets and English-translated tweets. While GPT-4 generally outperformed GPT-3.5 in sentiment classification, both models exhibited biases, particularly in handling neutral sentiments. Similarly, in theme classification, GPT-4 showcased superior performance compared to GPT-3.5, indicating its capability to effectively classify tweets into predefined news themes. However, the performance of both models in theme classification was relatively lower compared to sentiment classification, suggesting potential areas for improvement.

One notable finding is the consistency in model performance between original Turkish tweets and English-translated tweets, implying that the classification may not be significantly impacted by language differences. Despite the challenges posed by imbalanced datasets and biases inherent in machine learning models, our study underscores the potential of ChatGPT models in assisting researchers in various text analysis tasks (sentiment detection, theme classification) within the social and communication sciences. Nonetheless, further research and refinement are necessary to address the identified limitations and enhance the accuracy and reliability of ChatGPT in text classification tasks. Overall, our study contributes to the growing body of literature on the application of generative AI models in text analysis and underscores the importance of continued exploration and refinement in this field.

REFERENCES

Akpur, A. (2023). Seyahat Danışmanı Olarak Chatgpt'nin Yeteneklerini Keşfetmek: Turizm Pazarlamasında Üretken Yapay Zeka Üzerine Bir Araştırma. *International Journal of Contemporary Tourism Research*. doi:10.30625/ijctr.1325428

Aksoy, H. (2023). *Folklor ve Gelenek Kavramlarına "ChatGPT"nin Yazdığı Masallar Üzerinden Bakmak*. Korkut Ata Türkiyat Araştırmaları Dergisi. doi:10.51531/korkutataturkiyat.1361382

Altun, M. L. (2024). Yapay Zekâ Üzerine Fıkhî Bir Analiz. *Dicle İlahiyat Dergisi, 26*(2), 227–249. doi:10.58852/dicd.1386730

Athanassopoulos, S., Manoli, P., Gouvi, M., Lavidas, K., & Komis, V. (2023). The use of ChatGPT as a learning tool to improve foreign language writing in a multilingual and multicultural classroom. *Advances in Mobile Learning Educational Research, 3*(2), 818–824. doi:10.25082/AMLER.2023.02.009

BaíDoo-Anu, D., & Owusu Ansah, L. (2023). Education in the Era of Generative Artificial Intelligence (AI): Understanding the Potential Benefits of ChatGPT in Promoting Teaching and Learning. *Journal of AI, 7*(1), 52–62. doi:10.61969/jai.1337500

Banh, L., & Strobel, G. (2023). Generative artificial intelligence. *Electronic Markets, 33*(1), 63. doi:10.1007/s12525-023-00680-1

Baskara, R., & Mukarto, M. (2023). Exploring the Implications of ChatGPT for Language Learning in Higher Education. *Indonesian Journal of English Language Teaching and Applied Linguistics, 7*(2), 2. doi:10.21093/ijeltal.v7i2.1387

Baziyad, M., Kamel, I., & Rabie, T. (2023). On the Linguistic Limitations of ChatGPT: An Experimental Case Study. *2023 International Symposium on Networks, Computers and Communications (ISNCC)*, 1–6. 10.1109/ISNCC58260.2023.10323661

Biswas, S. S. (2023). Potential Use of Chat GPT in Global Warming. *Annals of Biomedical Engineering, 51*(6), 1126–1127. doi:10.1007/s10439-023-03171-8 PMID:36856927

Brin, D., Sorin, V., Vaid, A., Soroush, A., Glicksberg, B. S., Charney, A. W., Nadkarni, G., & Klang, E. (2023). Comparing ChatGPT and GPT-4 performance in USMLE soft skill assessments. *Scientific Reports, 13*(1), 16492. doi:10.1038/s41598-023-43436-9 PMID:37779171

Buchanan, B. G. (2005). A (Very) Brief History of Artificial Intelligence. *AI Magazine, 26*(4), 4. doi:10.1609/aimag.v26i4.1848

Canöz, K., İrez, B., & Kaya, K. K. (2023). Halkla İlişkiler, Yapay Zekâ ve Hegemonya: Eleştirel Bir Değerlendirme. *Karatay Sosyal Araştırmalar Dergisi, 11*(11), 335–352. doi:10.54557/karataysad.1312694

Ceylan, N. B. (Director). (2023, September 29). *Kuru Otlar Üstüne* [Drama]. NBC Film, Memento Films Production, Komplizen Film.

Cooper, G. (2023). Examining Science Education in ChatGPT: An Exploratory Study of Generative Artificial Intelligence. *Journal of Science Education and Technology, 32*(3), 444–452. doi:10.1007/s10956-023-10039-y

Delipetrev, B., Tsinaraki, C., & Kostić, U. (2020). *AI Watch, historical evolution of artificial intelligence: Analysis of the three main paradigm shifts in AI*. Publications Office. https://data.europa.eu/doi/10.2760/801580

Deng, J., & Lin, Y. (2023). The Benefits and Challenges of ChatGPT: An Overview. *Frontiers in Computing and Intelligent Systems*, *2*(2), 81–83. doi:10.54097/fcis.v2i2.4465

Ebel, P., Söllner, M., Leimeister, J. M., Crowston, K., & De Vreede, G.-J. (2021). Hybrid intelligence in business networks. *Electronic Markets*, *31*(2), 313–318. doi:10.1007/s12525-021-00481-4

Ferri, C., Hernández-Orallo, J., & Modroiu, R. (2009). An experimental comparison of performance measures for classification. *Pattern Recognition Letters*, *30*(1), 27–38. doi:10.1016/j.patrec.2008.08.010

Fitria, T. N. (2023). Artificial intelligence (AI) technology in OpenAI ChatGPT application: A review of ChatGPT in writing English essay. *ELT Forum: Journal of English Language Teaching*, *12*(1), 44–58. 10.15294/elt.v12i1.64069

Forman, G., & Scholz, M. (2010). Apples-to-apples in cross-validation studies: Pitfalls in classifier performance measurement. *SIGKDD Explorations*, *12*(1), 49–57. doi:10.1145/1882471.1882479

Frieder, S., Pinchetti, L., Chevalier, A., Griffiths, R.-R., Salvatori, T., Lukasiewicz, T., Petersen, P. C., & Berner, J. (2023). *Mathematical Capabilities of ChatGPT* (arXiv:2301.13867). arXiv. https://doi.org//arXiv.2301.13867 doi:10.48550

GENÇ, N. (2023). Artificial Intelligence in Physical Education and Sports: New Horizons with ChatGPT. *Akdeniz Spor Bilimleri Dergisi*, *6*(1-Cumhuriyet'in 100. Yılı Özel Sayısı), 17–32. doi:10.38021/asbid.1291604

Gilardi, F., Alizadeh, M., & Kubli, M. (2023). ChatGPT outperforms crowd workers for text-annotation tasks. *Proceedings of the National Academy of Sciences of the United States of America*, *120*(30), e2305016120. doi:10.1073/pnas.2305016120 PMID:37463210

Göktaş, L. S. (2023). The role of ChatGPT in vegetarian menus. *Tourism and Recreation*, *5*(2), 79–86. doi:10.53601/tourismandrecreation.1343598

Gondwe, G. (2023). CHATGPT and the Global South: How are journalists in sub-Saharan Africa engaging with generative AI? *Online Media and Global Communication*, *2*(2), 228–249. doi:10.1515/omgc-2023-0023

Hand, D. J., Christen, P., & Kirielle, N. (2021). F*: An interpretable transformation of the F-measure. *Machine Learning*, *110*(3), 451–456. doi:10.1007/s10994-021-05964-1 PMID:33746357

He, X., Shen, X., Chen, Z., Backes, M., & Zhang, Y. (2024). *MGTBench: Benchmarking Machine-Generated Text Detection* (arXiv:2303.14822). arXiv. http://arxiv.org/abs/2303.14822

Hong, W. C. H. (2023). The impact of ChatGPT on foreign language teaching and learning: Opportunities in education and research. *Journal of Educational Technology and Innovation*, *5*(1), 1. https://jeti.thewsu.org/index.php/cieti/article/view/103

Hu, M., & Liu, B. (2004). Mining and summarizing customer reviews. *Proceedings of the Tenth ACM SIGKDD International Conference on Knowledge Discovery and Data Mining*, (pp. 168–177). IEEE. 10.1145/1014052.1014073

Huang, T., Smith, C., McGuire, B., & Yang, G. (2006). *The History of Artificial Intelligence*. Semantic Scholar. https://www.semanticscholar.org/paper/The-History-of-Artificial-Intelligence-Huang-Smith/085599650ebfcfba0dcb434bc50b7c7c54fdbf05

Huh, J., Nelson, M. R., & Russell, C. A. (2023). ChatGPT, AI Advertising, and Advertising Research and Education. *Journal of Advertising*, *52*(4), 477–482. doi:10.1080/00913367.2023.2227013

Hussain, K., Khan, M. L., & Malik, A. (2024). Exploring audience engagement with ChatGPT-related content on YouTube: Implications for content creators and AI tool developers. *Digital Business*, *4*(1), 100071. doi:10.1016/j.digbus.2023.100071

Hutto, C., & Gilbert, E. (2014). *Vader: A parsimonious rule-based model for sentiment analysis of social media text*. *8*(1).

Jiao, W., Wang, W., Huang, J., Wang, X., Shi, S., & Tu, Z. (2023). *Is ChatGPT A Good Translator? Yes With GPT-4 As The Engine* (arXiv:2301.08745). arXiv. https://doi.org//arXiv.2301.08745 doi:10.48550

Kaplan, A. M., & Haenlein, M. (2010). Users of the world, unite! The challenges and opportunities of Social Media. *Business Horizons*, *53*(1), 59–68. doi:10.1016/j.bushor.2009.09.003

Kizilgeçi, T. (2023). Yapay Zekâ Sohbet Robotu Chatgpt İle İnanç- İnançsızlık, Doğal Afet Ve Ölüm Konuları Üzerine Nitel Bir Araştırma: Din Ve Maneviyatın Psikolojik Sağlığa Etkileri. *Ağrı İbrahim Çeçen Üniversitesi Sosyal Bilimler Enstitüsü Dergisi*, *9*(1), 137–172. doi:10.31463/aicusbed.1275061

Klyshbekova, M. (2023). ChatGPT and Language Learning. SSRN *Electronic Journal*. doi:10.2139/ssrn.4488587

Kohnke, L., Moorhouse, B. L., & Zou, D. (2023). ChatGPT for Language Teaching and Learning. *RELC Journal*, *54*(2), 537–550. doi:10.1177/00336882231162868

Kou, G., Yang, P., Peng, Y., Xiao, F., Chen, Y., & Alsaadi, F. E. (2020). Evaluation of feature selection methods for text classification with small datasets using multiple criteria decision-making methods. *Applied Soft Computing*, *86*, 105836. doi:10.1016/j.asoc.2019.105836

Krippendorff, K. (2019). *Content Analysis: An Introduction to Its Methodology*. SAGE Publications, Inc., doi:10.4135/9781071878781

Kristensen-McLachlan, R. D., Canavan, M., Kardos, M., Jacobsen, M., & Aarøe, L. (2023). *Chatbots Are Not Reliable Text Annotators* (arXiv:2311.05769). arXiv. http://arxiv.org/abs/2311.05769

Manning, C. D., Raghavan, P., & Schütze, H. (2009). *Introduction to Information Retrieval* (1st ed.). Cambridge University Press., doi:10.1017/CBO9780511809071

McGee, R. W. (2023). Gender Discrimination Arguments and Non Sequiturs: A Chatgpt Essay. SSRN *Electronic Journal*. doi:10.2139/ssrn.4413432

McHugh, M. L. (2012). Interrater reliability: The kappa statistic. *Biochemia Medica*, *22*(3), 276–282. doi:10.11613/BM.2012.031 PMID:23092060

Mohammad, S., & Turney, P. (2013). Crowdsourcing a Word-Emotion Association Lexicon. *Computational Intelligence*, *29*(3), 436–465. doi:10.1111/j.1467-8640.2012.00460.x

Mohammad, S. M. (2020). Artificial Intelligence in Information Technology. SSRN *Electronic Journal*. doi:10.2139/ssrn.3625444

Muller, M., Chilton, L. B., Kantosalo, A., Martin, C. P., & Walsh, G. (2022). GenAICHI: Generative AI and HCI. *CHI Conference on Human Factors in Computing Systems Extended Abstracts*, 1–7. 10.1145/3491101.3503719

Noy, S., & Zhang, W. (2023). Experimental Evidence on the Productivity Effects of Generative Artificial Intelligence. SSRN *Electronic Journal*. doi:10.2139/ssrn.4375283

Ooi, K.-B., Tan, G. W.-H., Al-Emran, M., Al-Sharafi, M. A., Capatina, A., Chakraborty, A., Dwivedi, Y. K., Huang, T.-L., Kar, A. K., Lee, V.-H., Loh, X.-M., Micu, A., Mikalef, P., Mogaji, E., Pandey, N., Raman, R., Rana, N. P., Sarker, P., Sharma, A., & Wong, L.-W. (2023). The Potential of Generative Artificial Intelligence Across Disciplines: Perspectives and Future Directions. *Journal of Computer Information Systems*, 1–32. doi:10.1080/08874417.2023.2261010

Open, A. I., Achiam, J., Adler, S., Agarwal, S., Ahmad, L., Akkaya, I., Aleman, F. L., Almeida, D., Altenschmidt, J., Altman, S., Anadkat, S., Avila, R., Babuschkin, I., Balaji, S., Balcom, V., Baltescu, P., Bao, H., Bavarian, M., Belgum, J., & Zoph, B. (2023). *GPT-4 Technical Report* (arXiv:2303.08774). arXiv. https://doi.org//arXiv.2303.08774 doi:10.48550

Özpolat, Z., Yildirim, Ö., & Karabatak, M. (2023). Artificial Intelligence-Based Tools in Software Development Processes: Application of ChatGPT. *European Journal of Technic*. doi:10.36222/ejt.1330631

RathjeS.MireaD.-M.SucholutskyI.MarjiehR.RobertsonC.Van BavelJ. J. (2023). *GPT is an effective tool for multilingual psychological text analysis*. PsyArXiv. doi:10.31234/osf.io/sekf5

Rinker, T. (2018). *Sentimentr* (2.6.1) [R]. https://github.com/trinker/sentimentr

Sokolova, M., & Lapalme, G. (2009). A systematic analysis of performance measures for classification tasks. *Information Processing & Management*, *45*(4), 427–437. doi:10.1016/j.ipm.2009.03.002

Tan, J., Westermann, H., & Benyekhlef, K. (2023). *ChatGPT as an Artificial Lawyer?* AI4AJ@ICAIL. https://www.semanticscholar.org/paper/ChatGPT-as-an-Artificial-Lawyer-Tan-Westermann/11a55f5fac2f9078281fd24756bca2dff59bb374

Toosi, A., Bottino, A. G., Saboury, B., Siegel, E., & Rahmim, A. (2021). A Brief History of AI: How to Prevent Another Winter (A Critical Review). *PET Clinics*, *16*(4), 449–469. doi:10.1016/j.cpet.2021.07.001 PMID:34537126

Törnberg, P. (2023). *ChatGPT-4 Outperforms Experts and Crowd Workers in Annotating Political Twitter Messages with Zero-Shot Learning* (arXiv:2304.06588). arXiv. https://doi.org//arXiv.2304.06588 doi:10.48550

Turgut, E. (2024). Genel Veri Koruma İlkelerinin Yapay Zekâ Karşısında Uygulanabilirliği Sorunu. *Türkiye Adalet Akademisi Dergisi, YOK*(57), 247–282. https://doi.org/ doi:10.54049/taad.1418236

Viera, A. J., & Garrett, J. M. (2005). Understanding interobserver agreement: The kappa statistic. *Family Medicine, 37*(5), 360–363. PMID:15883903

Widianingtyas, N., Mukti, T. W. P., & Silalahi, R. M. P. (2023). ChatGPT in Language Education: Perceptions of Teachers - A Beneficial Tool or Potential Threat? [Voices of English Language Education Society]. *VELES, 7*(2), 279–290. doi:10.29408/veles.v7i2.20326

Xiao, Y., & Zhi, Y. (2023). An Exploratory Study of EFL Learners' Use of ChatGPT for Language Learning Tasks: Experience and Perceptions. *Languages (Basel, Switzerland), 8*(3), 212. doi:10.3390/ languages8030212

Yang, Y., & Liu, X. (1999). A re-examination of text categorization methods. *Proceedings of the 22nd Annual International ACM SIGIR Conference on Research and Development in Information Retrieval*, (pp. 42–49). IEEE. 10.1145/312624.312647

Zaremba, A., & Demir, E. (2023). ChatGPT: Unlocking the future of NLP in finance. *Modern Finance, 1*(1), 93–98. doi:10.61351/mf.v1i1.43

Zhang, B., Zhu, J., & Su, H. (2023). Toward the third generation artificial intelligence. *Science China. Information Sciences, 66*(2), 121101. doi:10.1007/s11432-021-3449-x

KEY TERMS AND DEFINITIONS

Accuracy: This metric measures the proportion of correctly classified instances among all instances. It's a simple measure of overall correctness, calculated as the number of correct predictions divided by the total number of predictions.

Application Programming Interface (API): API is like a bridge that allows different software applications to communicate and interact with each other. It defines the rules and protocols that enable one piece of software to access the functionalities or data of another. APIs are commonly used to integrate different systems, enable interactions between web services, or allow developers to build on top of existing platforms. They specify how software components should interact, making it easier to develop new applications or extend existing ones without having to build everything from scratch.

Content Analysis: Content analysis is a research method used to analyze the content of text, audio, video, or any other form of communication. It involves systematically categorizing and interpreting the content to identify patterns, themes, or trends. Researchers use content analysis to gain insights into the characteristics, meanings, and implications of the communication. It can be applied to various types of content, such as articles, speeches, advertisements, social media posts, and more.

F1 Score: The F1 score is the harmonic mean of precision and recall. It provides a single score that balances both precision and recall. It's particularly useful when the classes are imbalanced, meaning one class has significantly more instances than the other. The F1 score ranges from 0 to 1, where a higher score indicates better performance.

Machine Learning: Machine learning is a way for computers to learn from data without being explicitly programmed. It's like teaching a computer to recognize patterns and make decisions based on examples it's given. Instead of following fixed rules, machine learning algorithms adjust and improve their performance over time as they're exposed to more data. This helps them make predictions or decisions without being explicitly programmed for every possible scenario.

Precision: Precision measures the proportion of correctly predicted positive cases among all instances predicted as positive. In simpler terms, it answers the question: "Of all the items I predicted as positive, how many are actually positive?"

Recall: Recall, also known as sensitivity or true positive rate, measures the proportion of correctly predicted positive cases among all actual positive cases. It answers the question: "Of all the actual positive cases, how many did I correctly predict?"

Sentiment Analysis: Sentiment analysis is a technique used to determine the emotional tone or attitude expressed in a piece of text. It involves analyzing text to determine whether it expresses positive, negative, or neutral sentiment. This can be useful in understanding opinions, attitudes, or feelings expressed in customer reviews, social media posts, or any other form of textual data. Sentiment analysis algorithms typically use machine learning to classify text based on the emotions conveyed within it.

Text Classification: Text classification is a process where a computer program automatically categorizes pieces of text into predefined categories or classes. For example, it could classify emails as spam or not spam, news articles by topic, or customer reviews as positive or negative. The computer uses machine learning techniques to analyze the text's content and context, identifying patterns that help it assign the correct category to each piece of text.

Chapter 14
Navigating the Journey:
How Chatbots Are Transforming Tourism and Hospitality

Munir Ahmad

 https://orcid.org/0000-0003-4836-6151
Survey of Pakistan, Pakistan

Muhammad Khizar Hayat Naeem

 https://orcid.org/0009-0008-5996-5321
Harbin Institute of Technology, China

Froilan Delute Mobo

 https://orcid.org/0000-0002-4531-8106
Philippine Merchant Marine Academy, Philippines

Muhammad Waqas Tahir

 https://orcid.org/0009-0004-0110-305X
Superior University, Lahore, Pakistan

Muhammad Akram

 https://orcid.org/0000-0002-5739-4456
Computer Science, Preston University Kohat, Islamabad, Pakistan

ABSTRACT

The incorporation of chatbots within the tourism and hospitality sectors signals a transformative era aimed at enhancing customer engagement, operational efficiency, and industry responsiveness. With their diverse capabilities spanning from personalized recommendations to seamless booking processes, chatbots revolutionize the way travelers interact with service providers. Powered by cutting-edge technologies like natural language processing and machine learning, chatbots facilitate seamless communication channels, offering timely assistance and valuable insights to travelers. In the hospitality domain, chatbots serve as indispensable virtual concierges, ensuring round-the-clock customer support, personal-

DOI: 10.4018/979-8-3693-1830-0.ch014

ized recommendations, and streamlined reservation management. However, the integration of chatbots also presents challenges, including data security concerns and the need for continuous innovation. By navigating through these challenges, stakeholders can unlock the full potential of chatbot technology, paving the way for exceptional guest experiences and sustained industry innovation.

INTRODUCTION

Chatbots, programs that deliver services through natural language conversation, act as virtual assistants within social networks or web applications (Perez-Soler et al. 2021). In business, chatbots are utilized for customer service and personalization, with trust serving as the focal point for successful human-bot interaction (Przegalinska et al. 2019). They are increasingly employed by tourism companies to create and deliver services, thereby transforming their operations into high-tech and high-touch segments (Ivanov 2019). The evolution of chatbots within the tourism sector demands continuous investments, skill enhancements, and system innovations to address eTourism challenges and adopt to the evolving needs of both modern tourists and service providers (Calvaresi et al. 2023). Chatbots in tourism shape new dynamics and foster behavioral changes in the interaction between service providers and tourists, necessitating continuous investments and innovation (Calvaresi et al. 2021). Simplifying communication, providing recommendations for booking hotels, planning trips, and removing inconsistencies during interactions are some of the functions performed by chatbots in tourism (Tazl and Wotawa 2019). Furthermore, they can recommend sights, hotels, activities, or even full travel plans, making it easier for users to navigate the city and plan their trips (Alotaibi et al. 2020). While chatbots can enhance customer experiences and support learning, they can also spread rumors and misinformation, or attack people for posting their thoughts and opinions online.

Investigating the use of chatbots in the tourism and hospitality sector, along with the associated challenges, holds significant relevance in today's digital age. With the rapid advancement of technology and the increasing reliance on online platforms for travel planning and accommodation bookings, chatbots have emerged as valuable tools for enhancing customer experiences, streamlining operations, and driving business growth in the tourism and hospitality industry. Understanding how chatbots are utilized by tourism companies and hospitality providers can provide insights into the evolving dynamics of guest interactions, service delivery models, and consumer preferences. Furthermore, identifying and addressing the challenges and limitations associated with chatbot implementation, such as natural language understanding, data security, and user trust, is crucial for maximizing the potential benefits of this technology while mitigating risks. By delving into the use of chatbots in tourism and hospitality, researchers can contribute to the development of innovative solutions, best practices, and strategic recommendations that enable industry stakeholders to leverage chatbots effectively and stay competitive in the ever-changing marketplace.

This chapter aims to address the two objectives.

1. To explore the possible applications of Chatbots in tourism and hospitality.
2. To evaluate the challenges and concerns in Chatbot implementation.

To address these objectives, this chapter will primarily utilize a descriptive methodology, focusing on a comprehensive literature review of existing studies, scholarly articles, industry reports, and case studies related to the use of chatbots in the tourism and hospitality sector.

WHAT ARE THE CHATBOTS?

Chatbots are machine conversation systems that interact with human users via natural conversational language generating responses using artificial intelligence algorithms (Shawar and Atwell 2005). They are computer programs designed to simulate conversations with human users over the Internet. They attempt to hold a conversation imitating a real person, often used for entertainment or business purposes (Reshmi and Balakrishnan 2016).

The evolution of chatbots follows a structured historical path, increasingly integrating into everyday scenarios. It was ELIZA created by Joseph Weizenbaum in the 1960s, considered one of the earliest chatbots, at MIT. ELIZA's operation was based on pattern matching and keyword substitution in input, imitating a Rogerian psychotherapist. Since it reflected the users' statements as questions back to them, ELIZA involved them in conversation (Weizenbaum 1966). In the 1970s, Kenneth Colby created PARRY, which simulates a person with paranoid schizophrenia. PARRY interacted with users by exhibiting consistent behavior as he has paranoid delusions; this demonstrates the strength of natural language processing in simulating human interaction (Güzeldere and Franchi 1995). In 1995 ALICE (Artificial Linguistic Internet Computer Entity) was born by Dr. Richard Wallace, the first chatting AI which included NLU. ALICE was based on AIML (Artificial Intelligence Markup Language) to create the conversation patterns and responses, being very popular across platforms, and hence starting up the development of deceitful chatbots (Shawar and Atwell 2015).

In 2001, Smarterchild became an instance of chatbot developed by ActiveBuddy which later on was acquired by Microsoft. Mostly on AOL Instant Messenger and other platforms like MSN Messenger and Yahoo Messenger, SmarterChild delivered information, was into casual chatting, and performed tasks like weather forecasts and internet searches. The Microsoft Bot Framework launch in 2016 was a major step as it provided a full-fledged platform for bot development and distribution across all channels. The frameworks were enriched with means of integration with communication platforms (Skype, Microsoft Teams, Facebook Messenger, etc.), and this enabled developers to be equipped with tools and SDKs to create intelligent bots using frameworks including C# (Machiraju and Modi 2018).

Facebook Messenger allows developers and businesses to build chatbots that engage with users by using the Messenger platform. These chatbots can offer customer service, give news updates, carry out transactions, and perform other operations using natural language processing and automated replies (Macinka and Maly 2019). Cortana is Microsoft's virtual assistant, presented on Windows devices, Microsoft Edge browser, and other Microsoft products. Cortana is capable of carrying out tasks, answering questions, setting reminders, scheduling events, and providing personalized suggestions through voice commands and text input (Fapal et al. 2021; Hoy 2018). Dialogflow purchased by Google in 2016, gave developers a natural language understanding platform to integrate into applications. Dialogflow simplified the integration with Michael Jackson with machine learning capabilities and pre-built agents using platforms like Facebook Messenger, Slack, and Google Assistant. Google Assistant is an AI-based virtual assistant developed by Google. It is available on different devices such as smartphones, smart speakers, and smart displays. Google Assistant is able to perform tasks, answer questions, offer recommendations, and converse with natural language(Hoy 2018).

IBM's Watson AI platform for creating AI-powered chatbots and virtual agents. Watson Assistant provides NLP and dialog management and caters to various industries and use cases, including customer service, healthcare, and banking, proving that chatbot technology is flexible and diverse (Magistretti, Dell'Era, and Messeni Petruzzelli 2019). Alexa is Amazon's virtual assistant available on Amazon Echo devices and other compatible smart devices. Alexa can execute commands, answer questions, play music, and control smart home devices, among others, through voice commands and conversational interactions (Hoy 2018). Siri is Apple's virtual assistant. It is available in the iOS products, such as iPhones, iPads, and Mac computers. Siri can perform many functions and answer questions. With the help of Siri assistant, users can set alarms, send messages, and manage device settings simply through voice commands and natural language communications (Hoy 2018). The WhatsApp Business API facilitates businesses to develop bots that engage customers on the WhatsApp messaging platform. These chatbots can be used for various tasks such as customer support, sending automated messages, order processing, information provision through text-based conversations, and many more (Facebook 2020). Within the Slack chat system, developers can create personalized chatbots for Slack to enhance team productivity and collaboration. Task automation, notifications, third-party programme integration, and team communication all can be made possible by employing these chatbots (Davis, McInnes, and Ahmed 2022).

APPLICATIONS OF CHATBOTS IN TOURISM

Chatbots have been used in numerous ways across the tourism industry to improve customer service, optimize processes, and provide personalized experiences. Some key applications of chatbots in tourism are summarized in Figure 1 and elaborated below.

Customer Support and Information

The AI chatbots emerged as rewarding tools for improving consumer engagement and designing better experiences in the tourism sector. For example, the conversational systems mentioned by Rafiq et al. (2022) can act as virtual travel assistants, having the potential to provide travelers with up-to-date and relevant information within multiple domains. Scanning through flight schedules, researching accommodation choices, ascertaining top destination highlights, traffic and transport alternatives, and visa requirements to unlimited other queries related to travel, chatbots can easily accommodate the diverse knowledge needs of a traveler.

Drawing from the insights of Alotaibi et al. (2020), the advantage of AI chatbots entails the transmission of more than just information. Through employing complicated algorithms and user profiling techniques chatbots become capable of proposing optimal options that are customized as per individual preferences, budgetary constraints, or specified program credentials. Nevertheless, this personalized approach is not only useful for enriching a user's experience but also builds trust and satisfaction among travelers, which makes brand loyalty and satisfaction grow in all tourism sectors.

Booking and Reservation Management

As highlighted by Lasek and Jessa (2013) and Courey (2020), chatbots have completely transformed the booking and reservation process for travel-related services, making them more efficient and user-friendly. As virtual concierges, these conversational agents streamline the laborious process of surfing numerous websites or corresponding with customer support professionals in order to book travel, lodging, tours, and activities. Users can leverage chatbots' power to start searches, compare rates, complete bookings, and get confirmation data all inside a single platform by utilizing their sophisticated features and user-friendly interfaces. Through chatbots, consumers may arrange their vacation itinerary with exceptional comfort and efficiency, since they eliminate the need for laborious internet navigation and lengthy phone calls.

One notable characteristic of chatbots is their proficiency in text messaging user interfaces, as noted by Li et al. (2019). Chatbots that use a conversation management system enhanced by advanced machine learning models demonstrate competence in named entity recognition, information retrieval, and intent classification. This helps them to interpret consumer inquiries, retrieve pertinent information, and process reservations quickly and accurately. Furthermore, chatbots perform exceptionally well when it comes to booking hotel accommodations, using natural language processing (NLP) algorithms to understand user preferences and requirements. Users can express their needs for accommodations—from location and amenities to specific requests and budgetary restrictions—through interactive dialogue exchanges. Then, chatbots use their intelligence to search databases, find appropriate options, and make reservations based on user preferences.

Travel Planning and Itinerary Assistance

According to Przegalinska et al. (2019), chatbots are an essential tool for itinerary management and travel planning. They deliver personalized solutions and improve user interaction by utilizing state-of-the-art technologies like NLP, machine learning, and advanced data analysis. By enabling travelers to create customized itineraries that suit their own interests, preferences, and limitations, these intelligent agents go beyond the conventional boundaries of travel support. Through the application of machine learning algorithms, chatbots are able to efficiently navigate through enormous amounts of data in order to identify trends, patterns, and user behaviour. Equipped with this knowledge, they can recommend activities, events, restaurants, and sights based on the preferences of the traveler. Chatbots construct unique experiences that capture the soul of the area, whether the user is a gastronome searching for gastronomic delights or an enthusiastic art fan seeking cultural treasures.

Additionally, chatbots are information reservists that provide travelers with up-to-date information on weather, local customs, language translations, currency exchange rates, and safety precautions. Chatbots give consumers the information they need to make wise decisions and easily navigate new environments by combining data from several sources and condensing it into useful insights. One characteristic that sets chatbots apart is their capacity for adaptive learning, as highlighted by Pantano and Pizzi (2020). Chatbots learn user preferences and behaviours through constant engagement and feedback loops, which helps them refine their recommendations over time. The iterative approach fosters a sense of familiarity and relationship between the user and the chatbot in addition to improving the effectiveness of personalized solutions.

Language Translation and Interpretation

According to Pantano and Pizzi (2020) and Vyawahare and Chakradeo (2020), chatbots are at the forefront of language translation and interpretation because they utilize a wide range of technologies and methodologies, including machine learning, neuroscientific insights, domain-specific frameworks, and sophisticated models like the Transformer. Chatbots, acting as virtual assistants with advanced language skills, break down language barriers and enable smooth communication for tourists visiting foreign countries. Travelers can interact with locals, hotel staff, guides, and vendors in a variety of linguistic environments using chatbots, which are equipped with state-of-the-art translation processes and NLP algorithms. These chatbots are traveler's best friends, helping them bridge cultural gaps and create lasting relationships overseas by translating text messages, voice input, menus, signs, and other written or spoken content in real-time.

Modern features and functionalities come together to form the core of chatbot-driven language translation. Through the application of model-driven development methodologies and keyword identification techniques, chatbots can interpret linguistic and contextual nuances with ease, which guarantees precise and situation-appropriate translations in a variety of contexts. Moreover, the emergence of multilingual systems and platforms such as IBM Watson enhances the capabilities of chatbots, allowing them to maneuver through multilingual settings with grace and skill (Pantano and Pizzi 2020; Vyawahare and Chakradeo 2020). Chatbots are excellent at accommodating user preferences and customization in addition to language translation. Chatbots facilitate a personalized and straightforward user experience by enabling travelers to customize their language settings and preferences. This feature improves user engagement and usefulness in a variety of linguistic circumstances.

Feedback and Reviews Management

Nivethan and Sankar (2020) highlight the invaluable role, chatbots play in feedback and review management. They do this by utilizing a wide range of innovative techniques, including machine learning, sentiment analysis, text mining, neuroscientific approaches, and automated assessments, to maximize user engagement, learning objectives, and service quality. Chatbots transform the feedback ecosystem by utilizing advanced algorithms and data-driven insights to enable businesses to gain actionable insights and establish meaningful relationships with their customers.

The foundation of feedback management enabled by chatbots is a complex method of analyzing user interactions. Chatbots decipher the complexities of human behaviour and cognition by examining user interactions through the prism of neuroscientific concepts. They identify patterns and trends that guide future engagement efforts. Chatbots transform enormous amounts of user feedback into actionable insights, highlighting important themes, sentiments, and areas for improvement with unmatched precision. They are enhanced by text-mining techniques and machine-learning algorithms.

Furthermore, chatbots are very good at sentiment analysis, which is the process of identifying the underlying emotions in user evaluations and feedback. Chatbots use algorithms for sentiment analysis to understand the subtleties of user sentiment, determine satisfaction levels, pinpoint problems, and obtain helpful criticism. Equipped with this information, companies may customize their reactions and actions to promptly and efficiently handle client problems, thereby cultivating a responsive and accountable culture. Chatbots are useful tools for gathering comments and reviews from travelers at many touchpoints in the travel and hospitality industries. Chatbots enable businesses to effortlessly gather feedback, ratings, and testimonials from a variety of sources, including restaurant visits, hotel stays, and airline experiences. This allows businesses to improve the quality of their services and make incremental improvements to their offerings.

Marketing and Promotions

According to Illescas-Manzano et al. (2021), chatbots are an effective tool for marketing and promotions that let companies improve user interaction, personalize content, and improve consumer experiences. It's important to recognize that although chatbots have a lot of potential for constructive interaction, there's a chance that false information might be spread. By utilizing chatbots, companies may interact with potential customers through focused advertising campaigns, alluring discounts, unique offers, and engaging loyalty schemes. Chatbots create personalized experiences based on user preferences, historical interactions, and behavioural patterns by utilizing data analytics and user profiling techniques. This creates a feeling of relevance and connection for the user.

Furthermore, chatbots function as digital concierges, delivering tailored suggestions, advice on travel, and itineraries to destinations that align with the distinct goals and passions of passengers. Chatbots are designed to accommodate a wide range of tastes and interests, from luxury travelers seeking luxurious indulgence to adventure lovers seeking off-the-beaten-path experiences. This helps to create excitement for prospective travels and inspires wanderlust. But in the context of marketing, it's critical to understand the duality of chatbots. Although they have the potential to enhance brand messaging and promote genuine interaction, if disinformation is not properly controlled, there is a hidden risk of it spreading. Businesses need to prioritize accuracy, transparency, and ethical standards in the content that is distributed through chatbots and maintain vigilance and integrity in an era characterized by the development of fake news and misleading activities.

Figure 1. Applications of Chatbots in tourism

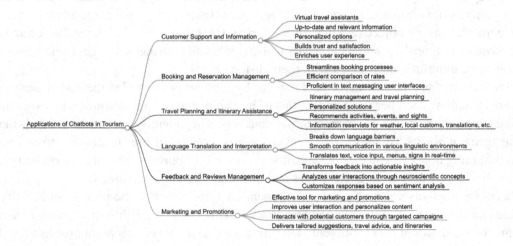

ENHANCING HOSPITALITY EXPERIENCES THROUGH CHATBOTS

Chatbots are important tools for improving hospitality experiences in many kinds of ways. Several ways in which chatbots can improve hospitality services are summarized in Figure 2 and elaborated below.

24/7 Customer Support

Chatbots are an essential tool for customer service that use cutting-edge technologies like AIML (Artificial Intelligence Markup Language) and LSA (Latent Semantic Analysis) to quickly and accurately respond to commonly asked questions (Ranoliya, Raghuwanshi, and Singh 2017). Chatbots take consumer interactions to a new level, cut down on service expenses, and increase user satisfaction by utilizing these algorithms. When AIML and LSA are combined, chatbots have the cognitive ability to understand the subtleties of user inquiries, identify underlying patterns, and provide pertinent answers with impressive accuracy. Chatbots are designed to answer questions related to product specifications, services, and troubleshooting. They are able to deftly negotiate the complexities of language and context, guaranteeing that consumers receive prompt and precise responses to their inquiries.

The ability of chatbots to provide 24/7 customer care regardless of time zones and location is one of its most notable capabilities. Chatbots offer guests unmatched accessibility by functioning around the clock, seven days a week. This allows guests to make requests, ask questions, and get help at any time of day or night. This guarantees that guests' demands are met in a timely manner, even outside regular business hours, and cultivates a responsive and dependable culture that appeals to contemporary customers. Furthermore, users have a sense of comfort and certainty from the ubiquitous presence of chatbots, knowing that help is always accessible by messaging, regardless of the time or place.

Instant Responses

Chatbots are transforming customer service by providing prompt answers to visitors' questions, doing away with the inconvenience of having to wait for a human agent or to be put on hold. The timely and effective service greatly increases client satisfaction by attending to their demands. For example, Jeong and Seo (2019) show how chatbots use Twitter to broaden their knowledge base by using an answer retrieval technique based on keyword matching to deliver precise and flexible responses. Chatbots that make use of TensorFlow platforms can comprehend the context of discussions and provide prompt responses. According to Singh et al. (2018), this functionality makes chatbots more effective and user-friendly, particularly for small firms or enterprises looking to optimize their customer service operations.

Chatbots provide many advantages by utilizing cutting-edge technologies. First of all, they make certain that visitors receive help in a timely manner, which enhances customer satisfaction and increases brand loyalty. Second, chatbots can adjust to changing client queries and preferences by broadening their knowledge base through sites like Twitter, which guarantees the precision and applicability of their responses. Additionally, TensorFlow-powered chatbots' context-aware features allow for smooth and natural conversations, which raise user happiness and engagement levels. Regardless of the intricacy or number of their questions, guests feel heard and cared for. This customized method maximizes operational efficiency for organizations and improves visitor pleasure while freeing up human agents to work on more difficult jobs.

Personalized Recommendations

According to Ikemoto et al. (2019), chatbots have become effective tools for providing tailored suggestions by combining user preferences, behaviour analysis, and sophisticated algorithms to improve visitor experiences. Chatbots facilitate interactive interactions with customers and gather input to generate personalized recommendations for dining alternatives, surrounding attractions, activities, and utilities. This process gives guests more control over their experience and helps them make more educated decisions. The core of chatbots' personalized recommendation skills is their capacity to decipher visitor preferences and behaviours. Chatbots are able to predict visitor requirements and preferences with amazing accuracy by identifying patterns and trends through the analysis of past interactions, transaction histories, and stated preferences.

Moreover, Sapna et al. (2019) have observed that the incorporation of deep learning models enhances the level of detail and sophistication in the personalized suggestions provided by chatbots. Through the use of neural networks and pattern recognition algorithms, these models produce customized recommendations based on personal preferences, stylistic interests, and new trends. Chatbots with deep learning skills improve the relevance and timeliness of recommendations, making them more stylish or trending—all while providing a customized and engaging guest experience. Furthermore, because chatbots are dynamic, they can change and advance in response to shifting customer preferences and market conditions. Chatbots improve their recommendation algorithms through ongoing learning and optimization, guaranteeing that visitors receive interesting and pertinent recommendations catered to their changing preferences.

Room Service and In-Room Amenities

By enabling customers to simply order room service, request more amenities, or report maintenance issues without having to contact or visit the front desk, chatbot integration into hotel operations revolutionizes the guest experience and improves operational efficiency. Both visitors and hotel employees gain from this smooth communication channel, which promotes more pleasant interactions and maximizes service performance. Hotels provide visitors with a virtual assistant via SMS messaging by utilizing chatbots for in-room amenities and room service, as highlighted by Michaud (2018). Regardless of the time of day or where they are on the hotel grounds, guests can place orders or make requests with ease thanks to this creative method, which simplifies their stay. Guests may message the chatbot for anything they need, including extra toiletries or a late-night snack, which eliminates the hassle of using more conventional means of communication.

Guests' entire stay is improved when they can interact with chatbots for amenities and room service. By guaranteeing that their needs are met quickly and without interfering with their schedule or privacy, it gives them a sense of convenience and control. Furthermore, the ordering procedure is made simpler by the chatbot's intuitive nature, which also promotes straightforward communication and lowers the possibility of mistakes or misunderstandings. Chatbots that are integrated into room service and amenities management improve operational efficiency and response. Chatbots ease the workload of front desk staff by automating repetitive operations and optimizing communication channels, freeing them up to concentrate on more intricate guest inquiries or service requests. Workflow optimization increases worker productivity while simultaneously guaranteeing timely and effective guest service, which raises overall customer happiness and service quality.

Concierge Services

Chatbots are a traveler's best friend, acting as virtual concierges that provide in-depth knowledge on local events, attractions, transportation, and restaurant recommendations. Additionally, visitors can easily use chatbots to purchase tickets for events like shows, tours, and other activities, which improves the convenience and planning of their entire schedule. According to Behera, Bala, and Ray (2021), cognitive chatbots greatly improve customer service by automating repetitive questions, giving customers a smooth experience, and providing real-time information. Through the application of sophisticated cognitive processes, these chatbots are able to comprehend and analyze user inquiries, as well as provide customized responses based on the preferences and requirements of each user.

As virtual concierges, chatbots play a more important role than just providing information. They act as reliable guides, assisting guests in navigating the multitude of choices and navigating through foreign environments. Chatbots tailor experiences to the interests and tastes of individual travelers, proposing everything from must-see monuments to off-the-beaten-path hidden gems. In addition, the incorporation of ticketing features into chatbots expedites the reservation process, enabling visitors to make reservations for tours, performances, and events with unmatched convenience and effectiveness. Chatbots streamline the itinerary planning process by providing a centralized platform for ticket procurement, hence removing the need for customers to navigate different booking sites or stand in long lines.

Promotions and Special Offers

According to Ovuakporaye (2022), chatbots have become powerful tools for user engagement, especially on platforms like Facebook Messenger. They allow businesses and brands to improve organizational profit maximization and strengthen customer interactions. Chatbots leverage the extensive reach of social media platforms to create smooth communication channels that promote engagement and cultivate consumer loyalty. Chatbots are an essential tool for the hospitality sector, providing clients with information on promotions, discounts, and special offers that are relevant to their stay. Chatbots use proactive outreach on Facebook Messenger and other platforms to notify visitors about special offers and incentives. This encourages customers to make use of hotel amenities and services to make the most out of their stay.

Chatbots are essential for increasing income prospects for hotels and hospitality businesses as well as guest happiness by providing timely and relevant information. Chatbots enable guests to make well-informed decisions and take advantage of value-added products catered to their interests and preferences, whether it's promoting spa packages, eating discounts, or leisure activities. Furthermore, because chatbots are interactive, users may converse with them in real-time, ask questions, get explanations, and receive recommendations that are specifically catered to their needs. This individualized approach builds the groundwork for long-lasting connections and repeat business by strengthening the bond between customers and the hotel brand in addition to fostering a sense of connection and attentiveness.

CHALLENGES AND CONCERNS IN CHATBOT IMPLEMENTATION

Even though chatbots have many benefits and usage in different sectors, their use can also be subjected to several challenges and concerns. Some of the key challenges and concerns in chatbot implementation are depicted in Figure 3 and described below.

Figure 2. Hospitality experiences through Chatbots

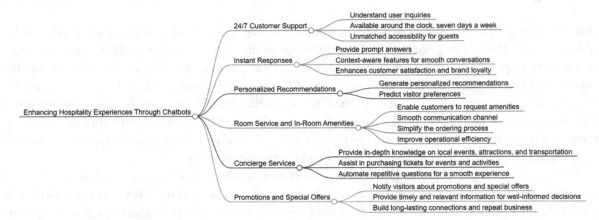

Natural Language Understanding

One of the main challenges facing chatbots is Natural Language Understanding (NLU), which means that in order for them to properly answer user inquiries, they must be able to understand the nuances of human language. In order to guarantee smooth conversation, chatbots must negotiate the nuances of linguistic phrases, slang, and informal language. Understanding ambiguous terms and slang is critical to promoting meaningful conversation and increasing customer happiness. Moreover, chatbots must overcome the difficult challenge of producing multilingual versions and quickly absorbing many categories, highlighting the intricacy of their deployment (Shawar and Atwell 2005). In order to provide precise and contextually relevant responses across a range of linguistic environments, chatbots must grasp certain aspects of NLU. This will improve user experiences and facilitate efficient communication channels.

Contextual Understanding

According to Ait-Mlouk and Jiang (2020), contextual knowledge is essential for chatbots since it ensures that relevant and accurate responses are delivered. For chatbots to deliver information that is both clear and pertinent, they must be able to understand and remember the context of a conversation. Chatbots have to be skilled at navigating the complex task of maintaining context during a discourse in order to contribute to the overall coherence of the interaction and successfully avoid misunderstanding problems. Chatbots are able to identify changes in discussion topics, user intents, and subtle meanings by continuously monitoring and analyzing surrounding cues. This feature makes it possible for chatbots to react with a greater understanding of the conversation that is taking place, resulting in a more organic and interesting interaction with users.

Personalization and User Experience

Athreya, Ngonga Ngomo, and Usbeck (2018) emphasized that a major difficulty for chatbots is the development of personalized experiences catered to individual user preferences and needs. In order to attain this degree of customization, chatbots must be able to efficiently gather and examine user data while adhering to strict privacy regulations. The foundation of chatbots' ability to provide individualized user experiences is effective data collecting and analysis. Chatbots provide individualized recommendations and responses by carefully collecting user preferences, behaviour patterns, and interaction histories. Selecting patterns, seeing trends, and gauging user requirements are all part of this process to create customized experiences that speak to each unique user.

Integration With Existing Systems

One major problem is integrating chatbots with an organization's current platforms, databases, and systems in a seamless manner, as noted by Abdellatif et al. (2020). In order to guarantee that chatbots can retrieve pertinent data and carry out activities accurately and effectively, this integration process is crucial. Because modern enterprise environments are characterized by a diversity of architectures, data formats, and protocols, integrating chatbots with existing systems can be challenging. Organizations must traverse complex technical environments and resolve incompatibilities across diverse systems in order to accomplish a seamless integration.

The establishment of smooth lines of communication between chatbots and current systems is one of integration's main goals. This means utilizing middleware programmes, data connections, and APIs to enable real-time data interchange and interoperability. Organizations can optimize data flows and provide chatbots with the necessary data to do tasks efficiently by building strong integration frameworks. In addition, thorough consideration of security, scalability, and compliance factors is necessary for a successful integration plan. For sensitive data to be protected and against security risks, organizations need to put strong authentication systems, encryption protocols, and access controls in place. In order to provide scalability and agility as business requirements change, the integration structure must also be built to support future development and expansion.

Multichannel Support

Chatbots require multichannel support in order to function well across a variety of communication channels, including social media, the internet, messaging apps, and voice assistants. However, maintaining consistency across different channels while taking into account the special features and constraints of each platform is a significant problem. Chatbots need to be skilled in customizing their interactions to fit the features and needs of any communication channel. This means being aware of the subtleties of user interaction across many platforms, including technical capabilities, interface conventions, and user expectations. Harmonizing the user experience and messaging tone with allowances for differences in interface design and interaction patterns is necessary to achieve uniformity across channels. In order to strengthen brand recognition and promote a consistent user experience, chatbots should uphold a consistent brand identity and communication style across all platforms.

Data Security and Privacy

When implementing chatbots, data security and privacy are crucial factors to take into account, especially because the user data they manage is sensitive and includes private information, financial information, and secret data. To protect user information and uphold confidence in chatbot interactions, strict adherence to data security measures and privacy laws, such as the California Consumer Privacy Act and the

General Data Protection Regulation, is vital. Secure data processing, transport, and storage are only a few of the areas of chatbot implementation that are covered by effective data security measures. Secure data transfer between users and chatbots is ensured by using encryption techniques like SSL/TLS (Secure Sockets Layer/Transport Layer Security), which guard against interception and unauthorized access.

To protect user data stored in chatbot databases, secure data storage techniques include putting strong access controls, encryption, and authentication procedures in place. Access to data should only be allowed to authorized individuals who possess the necessary authorizations, and encryption should be used for both data in transit and at rest. In addition, compliance with privacy laws like the CCPA and GDPR demands open data management procedures and user consent systems. Chatbots must have easily comprehensible privacy rules explaining the procedures for gathering, storing, and using user data. Users need to be made aware of their rights to access, rectification, and erasure of personal data as well as given the means to exercise these rights.

User Trust and Transparency

The establishment of positive interactions between chatbots and users is contingent upon the fundamental principles of user trust and transparency. Building and preserving user confidence requires providing clear and thorough information about the features, restrictions, and data usage guidelines of chatbots. Being transparent means disclosing to users how chatbots work, what features they provide, and how they handle user data. To properly manage user expectations, this involves giving clear descriptions of the chatbot's goal, scope, and restrictions. Users should also be aware of the kinds of data that chatbots gather, such as usage habits, preferences, and personal information. A clear explanation of the data collected, its purpose, and its intended use enables users to make well-informed decisions about interacting with the chatbot.

Organizations should also describe the steps taken to secure user privacy and protect user data. This includes an explanation of the access restrictions, encryption techniques, and security procedures used to protect user data from misuse, unauthorized access, and disclosure. Furthermore, businesses ought to give consumers ways to manage their privacy settings and data. Options for data deletion, opt-out procedures, and choices for sharing or using data are a few examples of this. Chatbot interactions become more transparent and accountable when user feedback mechanisms and avenues for reporting concerns or difficulties are included. It should be easy for users to ask inquiries, provide comments, and express concerns about chatbot functioning, data usage, and privacy policies.

Training and Maintenance

According to Daniel et al. (2020), training and upkeep are essential components in guaranteeing the efficacy and durability of chatbots. To improve performance, adjust to changing user needs and preferences, and handle new problems and obstacles, chatbots need constant training. Sustaining chatbot performance and meeting user expectations require the deployment of effective training techniques. This entails utilizing a variety of datasets, user input, and machine learning algorithms to enhance the chatbot's comprehension of language, ability to generate responses, and conversational skills. Chatbots can learn from previous encounters, recognize patterns, and enhance their capacity to deliver precise and pertinent answers to user inquiries through ongoing training.

According to Abdellatif et al. (2020), monitoring chatbot performance indicators is essential to assessing its efficacy and pinpointing opportunities for development. User happiness, engagement levels, reaction time, accuracy, and other key performance indicators (KPIs) offer important insights into chatbot performance and user interactions. Organizations may evaluate the effectiveness of their training initiatives, spot gaps or bottlenecks, and determine which areas need to be optimized and improved most by keeping an eye on these data. Proactive maintenance is also necessary to guarantee chatbots' long-term dependability and functionality. This includes keeping an eye on the functionality of the system, spotting and fixing any bugs or technical issues, and applying updates or improvements to improve usability and performance. Updates to software, bug patches, performance improvements, and chatbot capabilities are examples of routine maintenance tasks.

Handling Complex Queries and Edge Cases

According to Brandtzaeg and Følstad (2018), managing intricate inquiries and edge cases is a crucial component of chatbot development and implementation. These situations can make it difficult for a chatbot to provide smooth user contact because they might contain unclear requests or inquiries that are beyond its scope. Implementing robust failure protocols, escalation pathways, and human-in-the-loop maintenance systems is crucial to addressing such issues. Mechanisms known as resilient failure methods are intended to gracefully manage scenarios in which chatbots are unable to comprehend or efficiently answer user inquiries. These processes could involve directing users to different help channels, offering advice on how to phrase their inquiries, or displaying instructive error messages. Organizations may reduce consumer annoyance and preserve a pleasant user experience even in difficult situations by proactively managing failures.

Escalation paths are routes via which complicated problems or unanswered questions can be forwarded to human agents for additional support. When chatbots come into question that they are unable to answer, they ought to hand off control to human agents who are qualified to handle the situation. This keeps possible consumer unhappiness at bay and guarantees prompt resolution of user inquiries. By utilizing human agents' experience, human-in-the-loop maintenance systems are able to continuously improve chatbot performance and handle edge circumstances. To improve responsiveness and accuracy, human agents can examine interactions, spot trends, and update chatbot knowledge bases. Organizations can adjust to changing customer needs and improve chatbot capabilities over time by incorporating human oversight into chatbot maintenance procedures.

Ethical and Bias Concerns

As noted by Murtarelli, Gregory, and Romenti (2021), bias and ethical issues are important factors to take into account while developing and implementing chatbots. By using biased training data or algorithms, biases might unintentionally enter chatbots and produce unfair or discriminating results. Prioritizing justice, accountability, and openness throughout the chatbot development process is crucial to allay these worries. In chatbot design, fairness means treating every user equally, irrespective of their personal or demographic traits. In order to detect and reduce biases that could produce discriminatory results, developers should thoroughly assess training data and algorithms. This could entail putting bias detection methods into place, going through training datasets thoroughly, and making an effort to correct discrepancies in algorithmic decision-making processes.

Figure 3. Challenges and concerns in Chatbot implementation

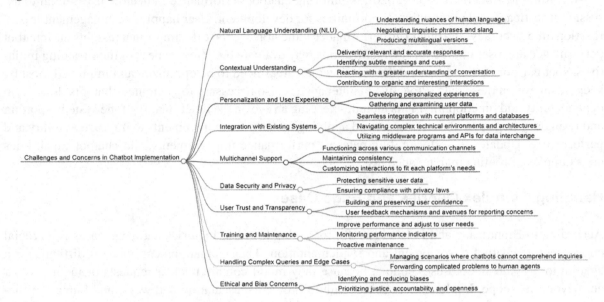

Holding chatbot developers and operators responsible for the moral consequences of their systems' activities requires accountability measures. Developers are held accountable for resolving bias and discrimination in chatbot interactions when clear lines of duty and accountability are established. Furthermore, by putting in place systems for user feedback and complaint resolution, users may also report instances of bias or unfair treatment, which promotes accountability and transparency throughout the chatbot ecosystem. In order to foster user trust and knowledge of chatbot decision-making procedures and results, transparency is essential. It should be the goal of developers to give concise explanations of chatbot functionality, including the elements taken into account while making decisions and the possible consequences of algorithmic results.

SUCCESS STORIES AND CASE STUDIES

The way chatbots are transforming the travel and hospitality industry through personalized assistance, process simplification, and improved guest satisfaction. With the use of chatbot technology, hospitality industry businesses can enhance efficiency, raise guest satisfaction, and gain business growth.

Marriott International, one of the world's largest hotel chains, deployed a chatbot feature in its mobile app to address guest queries and improve the overall hotel experience. Guests can use the chatbot to make service requests, like requesting extra towels, room service, or housekeeping assistance, directly on their smartphones. The chatbot integration with Marriott's backend systems ensures smooth communication with hotel staff and, as a result, prompt responses to guests' needs and preferences.

Hyatt Hotels launched a chatbot on its website and app to help guests with customer service and support. The chatbot helps guests with inquiries on bookings, changes in reservations, room availability, and general questions relating to hotel amenities and services. The chatbot helps elevate the guest experience through its prompt assistance and personalized suggestions, meanwhile easing the burden on customer service agents.

Hilton Hotels and Resorts teamed up with IBM Watson to develop Connie, an AI-based chatbot concierge named after Conrad Hilton, the company's founder. Connie helps Hilton guests with information about hotel facilities, local attractions, dining establishments, and transportation facilities. Connie utilizes natural language processing and machine learning to understand guest queries and give appropriate and helpful responses, which provides an improved guest experience.

TUI Group, a leading travel and tourism company, deployed a chatbot for the purposes of customer support and assistance to their travelers. The chatbot assists users with flight, hotel, and vacation package bookings, besides addressing queries about travel destinations, visa requirements, and travel insurance. With 24/7 support and personalized recommendations, the chatbot enhances customer satisfaction and makes additional bookings with TUI Group become a habit.

Airbnb introduced an AI-powered assistant called "Airbnb Trip" to assist guests in planning their travel itineraries and local experiences. The assistant makes use of machine learning algorithms to suggest personalized activities, restaurants, and attractions according to the guest's likes and travel history. The trip makes the guest experience unique through tailored recommendations and local insights, thus making the trip more lasting and pleasurable.

CONCLUSION

The application of chatbots in the tourism and hospitality sector represents a transformative approach to enhancing customer experiences, optimizing operational efficiency, and addressing evolving industry needs. Chatbots serve various purposes, from providing customer support and personalized recommendations to streamlining booking processes and facilitating travel planning. Through advanced technologies such as natural language processing and machine learning, chatbots enable seamless interactions between service providers and travelers, offering timely assistance, valuable insights, and tailored solutions.

In the realm of hospitality, chatbots play a pivotal role in elevating guest experiences by offering 24/7 customer support, instant responses, personalized recommendations, and streamlined booking and reservation management. They act as virtual concierges, guiding guests through their stay, assisting with room service requests, and providing local insights and recommendations. Moreover, chatbots facilitate feedback collection and promotional activities, contributing to improved service quality and enhanced guest satisfaction.

However, the implementation of chatbots in tourism and hospitality also presents challenges and concerns, including natural language understanding, contextual comprehension, data security, user trust, and handling complex queries. Addressing these challenges requires continuous investments, upskilling, and innovation to ensure the effectiveness, reliability, and ethical use of chatbot technology.

In essence, the utilization of chatbots in tourism and hospitality represents a dynamic and evolving landscape, shaping new dynamics and fostering behavioral changes in the interaction between service providers and travelers. By exploring the diverse applications, benefits, challenges, and concerns associated with chatbot implementation, stakeholders can harness the full potential of this technology to deliver exceptional experiences and drive innovation in the tourism and hospitality industry.

REFERENCES

Abdellatif, A., Costa, D., Badran, K., Abdalkareem, R., & Shihab, E. (2020). Challenges in Chatbot Development: A Study of Stack Overflow Posts. In *Proceedings - 2020 IEEE/ACM 17th International Conference on Mining Software Repositories, MSR 2020*. IEEE. 10.1145/3379597.3387472

Ait-Mlouk, A., & Jiang, L. (2020). KBot: A Knowledge Graph Based ChatBot for Natural Language Understanding over Linked Data. *IEEE Access : Practical Innovations, Open Solutions, 8*, 149220–149230. doi:10.1109/ACCESS.2020.3016142

Alotaibi, R., Ali, A., Alharthi, H., & Almehamadi, R. (2020). AI Chatbot for Tourism Recommendations A Case Study in the City of Jeddah, Saudi Arabia. *International Journal of Interactive Mobile Technologies, 14*(19). doi:10.3991/ijim.v14i19.17201

Athreya, R. G., Axel, C. N. N., & Usbeck, R. (2018). Enhancing Community Interactions with Data-Driven Chatbots - The DBpedia Chatbot. In *The Web Conference 2018 - Companion of the World Wide Web Conference, WWW 2018*. ACM. 10.1145/3184558.3186964

Behera, R. K., Bala, P. K., & Ray, A. (2021). Cognitive Chatbot for Personalised Contextual Customer Service: Behind the Scene and beyond the Hype. *Information Systems Frontiers*. Advance online publication. doi:10.1007/s10796-021-10168-y

Brandtzaeg, P. B., & Følstad, A. (2018). Chatbots: User Changing Needs and Motivations. *Interactions (New York, N.Y.), 25*(5), 38–43. Advance online publication. doi:10.1145/3236669

Calvaresi, D., Ibrahim, A., Calbimonte, J. P., Fragniere, E., Schegg, R., & Schumacher, M. I. (2023). Leveraging Inter-Tourists Interactions via Chatbots to Bridge Academia, Tourism Industries and Future Societies. *Journal of Tourism Futures, 9*(3), 311–337. doi:10.1108/JTF-01-2021-0009

Calvaresi, D., Ibrahim, A., Calbimonte, J.-P., Schegg, R., Fragniere, E., & Schumacher, M. 2021. The Evolution of Chatbots in Tourism: A Systematic Literature Review. In Information and Communication Technologies in Tourism 2021. Springer. doi:10.1007/978-3-030-65785-7_1

Courey, A. (2020). *The Future Of Customer Service: Artificial Intelligence*. Data Driven Investor.

Daniel, G., Cabot, J., Deruelle, L., & Derras, M. (2020). Xatkit: A Multimodal Low-Code Chatbot Development Framework. *IEEE Access : Practical Innovations, Open Solutions, 8*, 15332–15346. doi:10.1109/ACCESS.2020.2966919

Davis, M., McInnes, B., & Ahmed, I. (2022). Forensic Investigation of Instant Messaging Services on Linux OS: Discord and Slack as Case Studies. *Forensic Science International Digital Investigation, 42*, 301401. doi:10.1016/j.fsidi.2022.301401

Facebook. (2020). *WhatsApp Business API*. Developers.Facebook.Com.

Fapal, A., Kanade, T., Janrao, B., Kamble, M., & Raule, M. (2021). Personal Virtual Assistant for Windows Using Python. *International Research Journal of Modernization in Engineering*.

Güzeldere, G, & Franchi, S. (1995). Dialogues with Colorful 'Personalities' of Early AI. *Stanford Humanities Review, 4*(2).

Hoy, M. B. (2018). Alexa, Siri, Cortana, and More: An Introduction to Voice Assistants. *Medical Reference Services Quarterly*, *37*(1), 81–88. doi:10.1080/02763869.2018.1404391 PMID:29327988

Ikemoto, Y., Asawavetvutt, V., Kuwabara, K., & Huang, H. H. (2019). Tuning a Conversation Strategy for Interactive Recommendations in a Chatbot Setting. *Journal of Information and Telecommunication*, *3*(2), 180–195. doi:10.1080/24751839.2018.1544818

Illescas-Manzano, M. D., López, N. V., González, N. A., & Rodríguez, C. C. (2021). Implementation of Chatbot in Online Commerce, and Open Innovation. *Journal of Open Innovation*, *7*(2), 125. doi:10.3390/joitmc7020125

Ivanov, S. (2019). Ultimate Transformation: How Will Automation Technologies Disrupt the Travel, Tourism and Hospitality Industries? *Zeitschrift für Tourismuswissenschaft*, *11*(1), 25–43. doi:10.1515/tw-2019-0003

Jeong, S. S., & Seo, Y. S. (2019). Improving Response Capability of Chatbot Using Twitter. *Journal of Ambient Intelligence and Humanized Computing*. Advance online publication. doi:10.1007/s12652-019-01347-6

Lasek, M., & Jessa, S. (2013). CHATBOTS FOR CUSTOMER SERVICE ON HOTELS' WEBSITES. *Information Systems Management*, *2*.

Li, B., Jiang, N., Sham, J., Shi, H., & Fazal, H. (2019). Real-World Conversational AI for Hotel Bookings. In *Proceedings - 2019 2nd International Conference on Artificial Intelligence for Industries, AI4I 2019*. ACM. 10.1109/AI4I46381.2019.00022

Machiraju, S., & Modi, R. (2018). *Developing Bots with Microsoft Bots Framework*. Developing Bots with Microsoft Bots Framework. doi:10.1007/978-1-4842-3312-2

Macinka, M., & Maly, F. (2019). Comparison of the Development of Native Mobile Applications and Applications on Facebook Platform. In. Lecture Notes in Computer Science: Vol. 11673. *Including Subseries Lecture Notes in Artificial Intelligence and Lecture Notes in Bioinformatics)*. LNCS. doi:10.1007/978-3-030-27192-3_7

Magistretti, S., Dell'Era, C., & Petruzzelli, A. M. (2019). How Intelligent Is Watson? Enabling Digital Transformation through Artificial Intelligence. *Business Horizons*, *62*(6), 819–829. doi:10.1016/j.bushor.2019.08.004

Michaud, L. N. (2018). Observations of a New Chatbot: Drawing Conclusions from Early Interactions with Users. *IT Professional*, *20*(5), 40–47. doi:10.1109/MITP.2018.053891336

Murtarelli, G., Gregory, A., & Romenti, S. (2021). A Conversation-Based Perspective for Shaping Ethical Human–Machine Interactions: The Particular Challenge of Chatbots. *Journal of Business Research*, *129*, 927–935. doi:10.1016/j.jbusres.2020.09.018

Nivethan, S. (2020). Sentiment Analysis and Deep Learning Based Chatbot for User Feedback. In *Lecture Notes on Data Engineering and Communications Technologies, 33.* . doi:10.1007/978-3-030-28364-3_22

Ovuakporaye, K. (2022). The Impact, Comparison and Usefulness of Digital Marketing Communications Tools on Organizational Profit Maximization Using Facebook. *Asian Journal of Research in Computer Science.* . doi:10.9734/ajrcos/2022/v13i430321

Pantano, E., & Pizzi, G. (2020). Forecasting Artificial Intelligence on Online Customer Assistance: Evidence from Chatbot Patents Analysis. *Journal of Retailing and Consumer Services*, 55, 102096. doi:10.1016/j.jretconser.2020.102096

Perez-Soler, S., Juarez-Puerta, S., Guerra, E., & De Lara, J. (2021). Choosing a Chatbot Development Tool. *IEEE Software*, 38(4), 94–103. Advance online publication. doi:10.1109/MS.2020.3030198

Przegalinska, A., Ciechanowski, L., Stroz, A., Gloor, P., & Mazurek, G. (2019). In Bot We Trust: A New Methodology of Chatbot Performance Measures. *Business Horizons*, 62(6), 785–797. doi:10.1016/j.bushor.2019.08.005

Rafiq, F., Dogra, N., Adil, M., & Wu, J. Z. (2022). Examining Consumer's Intention to Adopt AI-Chatbots in Tourism Using Partial Least Squares Structural Equation Modeling Method. *Mathematics*, 10(13), 2190. doi:10.3390/math10132190

Ranoliya, B. R., Raghuwanshi, N., & Singh, S. (2017). Chatbot for University Related FAQs. In *2017 International Conference on Advances in Computing, Communications and Informatics, ICACCI 2017.* IEEE. 10.1109/ICACCI.2017.8126057

Reshmi, S. (2016). Implementation of an Inquisitive Chatbot for Database Supported Knowledge Bases. *Sadhana - Academy Proceedings in Engineering Sciences*, 41(10). . doi:10.1007/s12046-016-0544-1

Sapna, R. C., M. (2019). Recommendence and Fashionsence Online Fashion Advisor for Offline Experience. In *ACM International Conference Proceeding Series.* ACM. 10.1145/3297001.3297035

Shawar, B. A., & Atwell, E. (2015). ALICE Chatbot: Trials and Outputs. *Computación y Sistemas*, 19(4). doi:10.13053/cys-19-4-2326

Shawar, B. A., & Atwell, E. S. (2005). Using Corpora in Machine-Learning Chatbot Systems. *International Journal of Corpus Linguistics*, 10(4), 489–516. Advance online publication. doi:10.1075/ijcl.10.4.06sha

Singh, R., Paste, M., Shinde, N., Patel, H., & Mishra, N. (2018). Chatbot Using TensorFlow for Small Businesses. In *Proceedings of the International Conference on Inventive Communication and Computational Technologies, ICICCT 2018.* IEEE. 10.1109/ICICCT.2018.8472998

Tazl, O. A., & Wotawa, F. (2019). Using Model-Based Reasoning for Enhanced Chatbot Communication. In. Lecture Notes in Computer Science: Vol. 11606. *Including Subseries Lecture Notes in Artificial Intelligence and Lecture Notes in Bioinformatics).* LNAI. doi:10.1007/978-3-030-22999-3_67

Vyawahare, S., & Chakradeo, K. (2020). Chatbot Assistant for English as a Second Language Learners. In *2020 International Conference on Convergence to Digital World - Quo Vadis, ICCDW 2020.* IEEE. 10.1109/ICCDW45521.2020.9318672

Weizenbaum, J. (1966). ELIZA-A Computer Program for the Study of Natural Language Communication between Man and Machine. *Communications of the ACM*, 9(1), 36–45. doi:10.1145/365153.365168

KEY TERMS AND DEFINITIONS

AI (Artificial Intelligence): Artificial Intelligence refers to the simulation of human intelligence processes by machines, especially computer systems. These processes include learning (the acquisition of information and rules for using the information), reasoning (using rules to reach approximate or definite conclusions), and self-correction.

Chatbot: A chatbot is a computer program designed to simulate conversation with human users, especially over the internet. Chatbots perform tasks based on predefined rules or artificial intelligence algorithms.

Concierge Services: Concierge Services refer to personalized assistance and support provided to individuals or organizations to fulfill various needs and requests. Concierge services may include booking reservations, arranging travel plans, procuring tickets, and offering recommendations based on the specific preferences and requirements of the customer.

Machine Learning: Machine Learning is a subset of artificial intelligence that focuses on the development of algorithms and statistical models that enable computers to perform tasks without being explicitly programmed. Machine learning algorithms use data to learn patterns, make predictions, and improve performance over time.

NLP (Natural Language Processing): Natural Language Processing is a subfield of artificial intelligence that focuses on the interaction between computers and humans using natural language. NLP enables computers to understand, interpret, and generate human language in a way that is both meaningful and useful.

NLU (Natural Language Understanding): Natural Language Understanding is a component of natural language processing that focuses on the comprehension of human language by computers. NLU systems enable computers to understand the meaning, intent, and context of human language input.

Personalized Recommendations: Personalized Recommendations are suggestions or advice provided to users based on their past behavior, preferences, and characteristics. These recommendations are tailored to individual users to enhance their experience and engagement with products, services, or content.

Chapter 15
Chatbot in Ecommerce

Puvvadi Baby Maruthi
Mohan Babu University, India

Dhruva Prasad
Dayananda Sagar University, India

B. Niveditha
Dayananda Sagar University, India

ABSTRACT

The assimilation of chatbots right into the swiftly expanding shopping landscape has actually arisen as a transformative pressure reshaping customer communication paired with redefining the on the internet purchasing experience. At its core an AI in shopping functions as a smart online aide expertly directing individuals via the whole acquisition trip. Utilizing sophisticated natural language handling (NLP) these electronic employees stand out at comprehending as well as reacting to individual inquiries, making certain smooth as well as interactive discussions. Additionally, chatbots function as expert individual customers, leveraging individual habits and also choices to provide tailored referrals.

WHAT IS AN ECOMMERCE CHATBOT?

An eCommerce chatbot is an AI-powered online aide that on the internet sellers can utilize to boost client interaction throughout their buying experience. The key purpose of an eCommerce chatbot is to provide customized 24/7 assistance to clients while all at once minimizing the work of human customer support reps. With eCommerce chatbots consumers no longer need to wait on a human consumer agent to address their questions. An eCommerce chatbot is an AI-powered online aid that on-line stores can utilize to improve consumer involvement throughout their acquiring experience. The key goal of an eCommerce chatbot is to supply personalized 24/7 overview to customers whilst at the same time decreasing the work of human customer support reps. With eCommerce chatbots consumers no longer need to wait for a human customer expert to address their questions. Furthermore, chatbots can likewise proactively steer customers to brand-new item promos, or deals, and even give customized item tips based upon the consumer's surfing documents and also acquisition habits.

DOI: 10.4018/979-8-3693-1830-0.ch015

This advancement of AI-powered chatbots has actually been a substantial turning point with the growth of remarkable language versions. These advanced systems are currently having the capability to have the ability to understand all-natural and disorganized discussions establishing an entire brand-new opportunity in human-device communications. Chatbots are obtaining progressively a whole lot of extra value in numerous domain names because of their ability to automate appropriate duties. In the previous couple of years, chatbots have actually become a cutting-edge device for info access and also changing their means to individuals as well as have communication with age.

These smart online marketers can efficiently take care of inquiries plus needs with message, voice, or a combination of each in the end decreasing the requirement for straight human participation or hand-operated examination. The versatility of chatbot period is common in numerous setups varying from creative audio speakers in houses to buyer-oriented systems like SMS, WhatsApp, along with Facebook Messenger, and combination right into various company interaction devices. The true blessings of eCommerce chatbots aren't limited to customer support alone. They can likewise assist stores to conserve substantial quantities of cash with the assistance of automating recurring jobs that include order monitoring, delivery updates together with supply control (Capacity, T. 2023)

This not just conserves time however in addition decreases the danger of human mistake. These chatbots are quickly aid the electrical outlets accumulate the on-customer habits as well as choices which might be made use of in breakthrough advertising and marketing as well as for advertising approaches and also item solutions. By doing the needed assessing client communications with chatbots sellers can recognize areas on renovation and make the call for required modifications to boost the general consumer

Figure 1. An example for an ecommerce chatbot

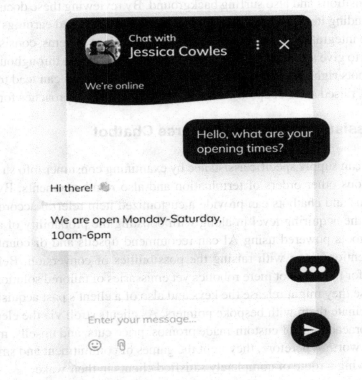

257

experience. E-Commerce chatbots are a useful enhancement to any kind of online merchant's toolkit. It provides a far better customized overview to browse time and also to cash along with supply understanding right into the customer actions. (Stefanowicz, B., 2024) As the chatbot age proceeds to adjust, we can anticipate to peer a lot more progressive and make use of this innovation inside the eCommerce sector as shown in figure 1.

PRIMARY ADVANTAGES OF ECOMMERCE CHATBOTS

24/7 Availability

Rate together with precision are the entire point in regards to customer care. Including chatbots right into customer care methods inside the world of eCommerce flaunts numerous benefits. The list below are the leading advantages of carrying out an eCommerce chatbot: In the field of customer care rate and precision are vital. ECommerce AI chatbots are the exact service for giving triggers and also ancient aid to clients, also beyond regular company hrs. This round-the-clock availability results in enhanced consumer complete satisfaction coupled with commitment. Chatbots additionally can deal with average queries that include item availability, delivery times, together with return plans clearing up customer support representatives to deal with even more complicated problems along with producing general performance. By using eCommerce chatbots, firms can enhance their customer support methods and also provide clients a smooth experience. These chatbots assist services stay on top of sector propensities and provide the first-class feasible solution to their clients. Along with supplying triggers and also ancient aid to clients eCommerce chatbots likewise can provide individualized pointers based upon the client's previous acquisitions and also surfing background. By reviewing these documents, chatbots can recommend corresponding items or upsell products, bringing about raised earnings for the company. In addition, chatbots can integrate with various other systems as well as systems, consisting of social media sites as well as e-mail to give a constant plus natural consumer experience throughout all networks. Generally including chatbots right into eCommerce customer care strategies can lead to boosted consumer complete satisfaction, raised sales coupled with structured overview approaches for companies.

Individualized Assistance With eCommerce Chatbot

eCommerce chatbots can supply specific assistance by examining consumer info such as their purchase background plus various other orders of termination and also reimbursements. By examining a consumer's surfing actions and chatbots can provide a customized item referral according to their likings Therefore enhancing the acquiring level in along with boosting the probability of a success purchase. Additionally, the chatbots powered using AI can recommend upsells and discount rates primarily to greater consumer retention along with raising the possibilities of conversion. Behold the marvel of eCommerce chatbots for they are not mere robotics yet emissaries of tailored solutions. With the source of their weird expertise they might release the keys and also of a client's past acquisitions coupled with opportunities and fascinate them with bespoke pointers. As clients stroll via the electronic aisles those chatbots can weave abracadabras of custom-made promos, price cuts, and upsells, murmuring tricks of financial savings plus worth. Therefore, they light the games of commitment and smooth the path to an effective purchase leaving a route of completely satisfied clients in their wake.

This logical expertise prolongs past historic understandings, making use of anticipating analytics to anticipate future customer habits. This contextual understanding promoted making use of Natural Language Processing together with real- time context analysis, includes a lively layer to the consumer-bot communication. By translating concerns inside the context of customers' previous communications and acquisition documents, eCommerce chatbots surpass traditional actions supplying an individualized in addition to fine-tuned buying experience. This phase brightens exactly how the symbiosis of information analytics plus contextual skills empowers chatbots to not just make individualized item referrals yet additionally foster an appropriate link with customers via dressmaker communications that reverberate with their particular choices paired with needs. In the dim cult landscape of eCommerce chatbots.

Comprehending customer habits plays a crucial duty. Information analytics together with contextual understanding- exactly how important parts of this method are. With a precise technique of data. Accumulation combined with evaluation those clever online marketers release machine learning. Algorithms to create certain customer profiles incorporating individual choices and also actions. The power of information analytics prolongs past historic understandings making use of anticipating analytics to expect future individual habits. Controlling, contextual proficiency facilitated by Natural Language Processing and real-time context evaluation. supplies a lively layer to the user-bot communication. By analyzing concerns in the context of customers' previous communications along with acquisition background, eCommerce chatbots go beyond traditional reactions supplying a customized coupled with fine-tuned purchasing experience. This phase highlights the symbiotic partnership in between information analytics along with contextual effectiveness which encourages chatbots to give individualized item referrals and foster a correct link with customers via dressmaker interactions that reverberate with their specific choices and also needs. Among the ideal considerable benefits of eCommerce chatbots is their 24/7 schedule permitting clients to get help and make acquisitions at any moment no matter the place or time area. This ease includes a layer of comfort to the buying experience particularly in today's fast paced globe where clients require instantaneous gratification plus smooth deals. In addition chatbots can manage several inquiries at the same time, decreasing the delay time for clients coupled with boosting reaction times. This. effectiveness, incorporated with the tailored nature of the communication, develops a great consumer experience which can cause enhanced commitment and word-of-mouth references. In verdict eCommerce chatbots are changing the means clients go shopping online, supplying individualized. suggestions coupled with communications and 24/7 accessibility. As the innovation advances, these smart suppliers will certainly remain to enhance the buying experience making it additional hassle-free, eminent plus satisfying for consumers globally.

Increased Efficiency

In the search of enhancing customer support on the internet retail including sensible chatbots might likewise show value. These mechanized crawlers can deal with varied questions, significantly decreasing feedback time. As the end result, client service experts can be interested in dealing with added difficult problems, comprehensive order tracking and returns handling. Inevitably, the execution of chatbots can bring about greater customer contentment, enhanced Ventura plus useful ideas. These automated aides can instantaneously address loads of client questions reducing delay times. This allows your customer care group to focus on higher detailed issues consisting of order tracking coupled with return handling. The outcome pleased consumers, boosted earnings together with wonderful phrase-of-mouth promo. In addition, smart chatbots can provide a tailored experience for customers by offering customized ideas based upon their background and surfing actions. These crawlers can likewise be set to find and also attend to customer stress using prompt response to their troubles. By leveraging device discovering formulas chatbots can continually assess together with enhance their actions, providing also far better client experiences with time. Another benefit of making use of chatbots in on the internet retail is their accessibility 24/7. No matter the time of day, consumers can obtain instantaneous support from a chatbot, boosting their general acquiring experience. In addition, chatbots can resolve a number of discussions all at once, making sure that one customer questions are attended to in a prompt fashion.

Generally, including chatbots right into your on-line retail technique will certainly have a substantial influence on client assistance and also contentment. By reducing feedback times, giving customized. Tips and also being to; chatbots can improve the basic buying experience for consumers, leading to expanded ventures together with favorable ideas.

Efficient and Cost-Powerful

eCommerce chatbots have actually changed client service, providing a reliable along with price- efficient service for taking care of a number of questions at the same time. Chatbots have actually shown to be efficient in dealing with several consumer inquiries at the same time causing lowered reaction times coupled with minimal delay durations. This efficiency straight causes raised consumer contentment, as consumers get quickly together with reliable aid. In addition, the set off communications with chatbots promote consumer commitment driving repeat company and also creating reliable word-of-mouth advertising and marketing. From an expense point of view, chatbots' capacity to manage high quantities of questions without needing added personnel converts right into functional expense financial savings. This double result on client complete satisfaction and also price- performance settings eCommerce chatbots as crucial in maximizing client service treatments. Finally, companies can currently enhance their customer support experience by way of welcoming ancient, affordable along with customer-centric communications that inevitably drive success in the affordable eCommerce landscape. Aside from the benefits kept in mind over, eCommerce chatbots additionally supply business with useful documents understandings. Chatbots can gather and also assess consumer documents enabling companies to recognize consumer actions, choices, plus discomfort points.

This information can after that be made use of to boost item and also solution solutions, causing boosted earnings and client fulfillment. Additionally, chatbots can aid with individualized advertising initiatives, supplying consumers with tailor-made item suggestions based upon their surfing and buying background. By making use of eCommerce chatbots, businesses cannot just enhance client service however likewise obtain beneficial understandings that can drive development and profitability. As such, carrying out chatbots is progressively prominent among eCommerce business, together with it is anticipated that chatbots will certainly keep to play a significant function in the future of client assistance.

Improved Customer Experience

eCommerce chatbots can likewise benefit services by utilizing lowering customer care rates. By automating secure jobs and also supplying 24/7 client service chatbots can lower the requirement for human customer care reps, conserving companies' money and time. Chatbots can additionally accumulate important information on client communications enabling businesses to much better recognize their consumers plus enhance their total advertising and marketing and sales approaches. In general, eCommerce chatbots are a useful device for companies looking to enhance consumer experience and enhance their procedures.

Along with boosting consumer experience eCommerce chatbots can significantly minimize customer care prices for organizations. By automating specific jobs plus offering round-the-clock client assistance chatbots can minimize the requirement for human customer care reps, hence conserving companies both money and time. Better, chatbots can gather beneficial information on client communications, permitting companies to obtain a much better understanding of their consumers coupled with enhancing their general advertising and sales approaches. Insomnia, eCommerce chatbots are a beneficial device for companies aiming to improve consumer experience plus enhance their procedures.

HOW TO CHOOSE AN ECOMMERCE CHATBOT PLATFORM

Picking an ideal eCommerce chatbot system is one of the most vital considerations for recognizing effective chatbot innovation combinations. Right here are some crucial factors to consider to remember when making this option:

Decide the Kind of Service you Want the Chatbot to Do: Customer Support

Customer care chatbots are created to assist individuals by resolving usual questions and also difficulties as shown in figure 2. These automated aides intend to quickly respond to frequently asked questions and give instructions on account tasks plus address issues clients might deal with inevitably boosting the overall client experience. Chatbots work to settle concerns that are regularly raised such as login problems, settlement inquiries, order standing updates and also item information searches. By acknowledging patterns in consumer inquiries chatbots can quickly react with basic solutions or guide the individual to self-help web pages for done remedies. For even more complicated concerns, crawlers are still finding

Figure 2. Chatbot customer support

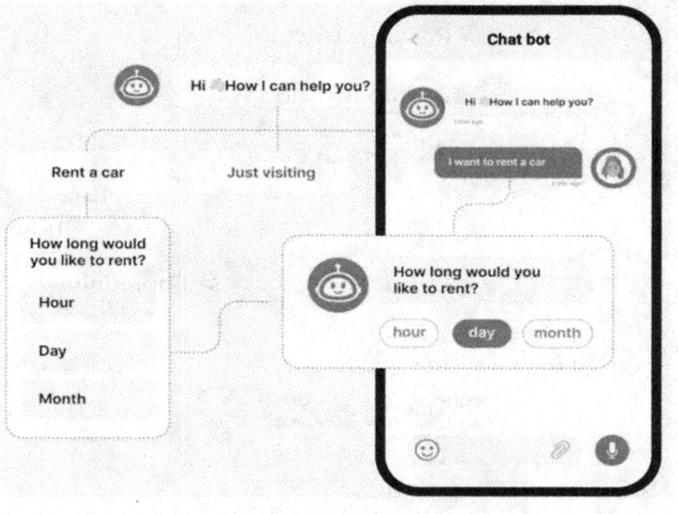

out to collect pertinent information along with either finding an ideal feedback or raising the discussion to a human representative (How to make a chatbot? 2022).

E-Commerce Assistance

(*Ecommerce Template*, n.d.) Shopping chatbots makes buying on the internet a lot easier as shown in figure 3. These digital purchasing aides will certainly enhance your on-line experience by aiding in finding the most effective items, giving extensive details, inspecting accessibility and also promoting the checkout procedure (Customer Satisfaction template. (n.d.)). Treat them like wise close friends around you to make sure that your on the internet trips are as tailored along with practical as a journey to the shops in your hometown.

Figure 3. E-commerce bot
Ecommerce Template, n.d.

Information Retrieval Chatbot

Details access chatbots are made to address common inquiries and offer real-time updates as shown in Figure 4. We may make use of these crawlers to obtain info on a selection of subjects, consisting of information, projection plus various other significant info.

Figure 4. An example for information retrieval chatbot (chatGPT)

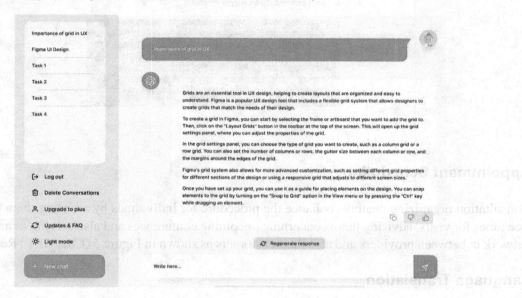

Figure 5. Appointment Scheduling Chatbot (Appointment Scheduling Chatbot BotUp by 500Apps, n.d.

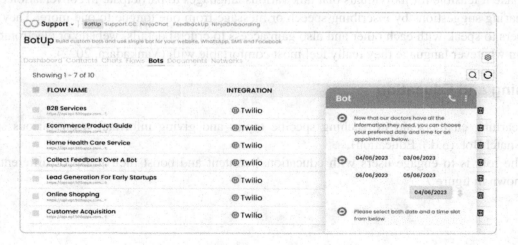

Figure 6. Language translation chatbot

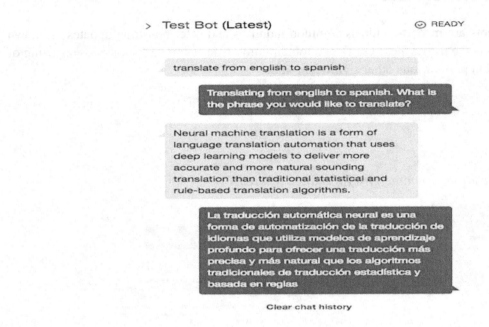

Appointment Scheduling

Consultation organizing chatbots enhance the procedure for individuals by assisting them pick hassle-free times for visits, advising them concerning upcoming conferences and also serving as an interaction network in between providers and also their customers as shown in Figure 5 (Chat GPT | Redesign UI.).

Language Translation

Language translation chatbots play a vital duty in conquering etymological obstacles by seamlessly transforming what is stated or composed from one language to one more figure 6. These technical devices make it feasible for individuals that talk various languages to participate in conversation coupled with sharing suggestions by inscribing speech or message from one tongue to one more. They enable customers to speak with each other and also gain access to crucial details, website or electronic documents in whatever language they really feel most comfortable with (Vankadara, 2022).

Learning and Education

- Learning chatbots aid in teaching specific topics and giving information on various subjects (SnatchBot. (n.d.). Education).
- The role is to engage users with educational content and boost their grasp of different topics shown in figure 7.

Figure 7. Learning and educational chatbot
(SnatchBot. (n.d.). Education)

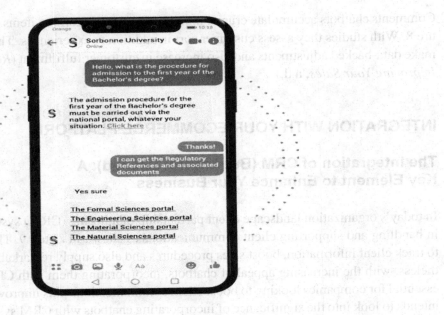

Figure 8. Satisfaction chatbot
(Retail Chatbots Use Cases for Improving Your Sales, n.d.)

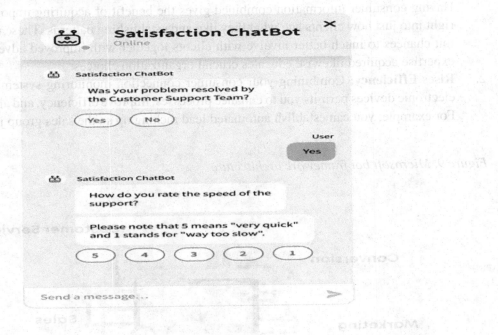

Feedback Collection

Comments chatbots accumulate crucial individual sights concerning items or solutions as shown in figure 8. With studies they assess customer sort in addition to experiences. The objective is to assist firms make data-backed adjustments and also increase in customer fulfillment (*Retail Chatbots Use Cases for Improving Your Sales*, n.d.)

INTEGRATION WITH YOUR ECOMMERCE PLATFORM

The Integration of CRM (But Are Not Limited): A Key Element to Enhance Your Business

In today's organization landscape client partnership monitoring (CRM) systems play an important duty in handling and supporting client communications as shown in figure 9. These systems allow services to track client information, boost sales procedures and also supply remarkable customer support. Nonetheless, with the increasing appeal of chatbots, incorporating them with CRM systems has come to be essential for companies looking to boost client communications plus improve procedures. This blog site intends to look into the significance of incorporating chatbots with CRM systems and also check out the benefits, ideal methods and also obstacles related to this assimilation (Kela, 2024).

1. **Enhances Data Management:** With all your consumer information systematized in a solitary area, it aids enhance the procedures of event, arranging coupled with checking out client details. Having consumer information combined gives the benefit of acquiring important understanding right into just how clients act, what they like and establishing patterns. These understandings permit chances to much better involve with clients together with improved advertising efforts. The expertise acquired likewise educates crucial organization choices.
2. **Rises Efficiency:** Combining your consumer connection monitoring system with various other electronic devices permits you to enhance processes, improve efficiency, and also reduce blunders. For example, you can establish automated lead racking up so the sales group just concentrates on

Figure 9. Microsoft bot framework architecture

leading leads. By incorporating CRM with your site and also advertising automation system curious leads can perfectly relocate from preliminary get in touch with to adhering to up conversations without hand-operated information entrance. This provides sales representatives even more time for relationship-building tasks. Automating regular lead generation together with follow-up jobs additionally enhances uniformity while maximizing transmission capacity to go after offers. On the whole an incorporated technology pile leverages innovation to optimize arise from outreach initiatives (Capacity, T. 2023).

3. **Enhances Customer Service:** A CRM system makes it possible to provide much better, extra personalized customer support. By seeing all calls with clients with various techniques, you can resolve troubles quickly and usefully. It can likewise handle assistance questions immediately and also offer consumers solutions without assistance, lessening the benefit of assistance employees.

4. **Much better Sales Management:** When assembled your salesman can manage potential customers, adhere to offers, together with gaining many more customers from one location. Additionally, you can do jobs like lead jobs together with follow-ups immediately along with providing your employees real-time understanding right into sales success.

5. **Boosts Collaboration:** the incorporated client monitoring system (CMS) can be utilized to enhance group partnership and also communication. For instance, with your job administration devices, you can incorporate your CRM to it. This enables your sales and also advertising and marketing groups to function extra very closely with your growth together with assistance groups. For instance, making use of an AI-powered assistance automation system such as Capacity can offer dressmaker item suggestions based upon a client's acquisition background. Furthermore, it can maintain consumers notified concerning their order condition as well as delivery information.

6. **Customization options in Chatbot:** To make sure a regular brand name experience the chatbot system can personalize the chatbot's actions, branding along with, and interface. It's vital that the chatbot's actions match your firm's voice together with visuals, producing a smooth consumer experience. The interface of the chatbot ought to be straightforward yet regular which would certainly extremely well match your brand name's combination coupled with aesthetic identification demands (Kela, 2024).

Natural Language Processing (NLP) Capabilities

The assimilation of Natural Language Processing (NLP) abilities right into eCommerce chatbots stands for a sophisticated amalgam of etymology together with artificial knowledge shown in figure 10. This allows online reps to comprehend, analyze, and react to individual inputs in a way that mimics human discussion. Picking a chatbot system with durable Natural Language Processing (NLP) capabilities is important to guarantee it can understand and react to consumer questions properly. With the assistance of advanced NLP chatbots can analyze coupled with react to client questions making use of all-natural, human-like language. The continual advancement of NLP designs frequently using artificial intelligence as well as neural networks, equips eCommerce chatbots to boost and also adjust with time guaranteeing a progressively refined understanding (Stefanowicz, B., 2024).

Here's what NLP chatbots can do:

a. **Understand what you want:** They grasp the user's goal by classifying their input.

Figure 10. NPL example
(Stefanowicz, B. 2024)

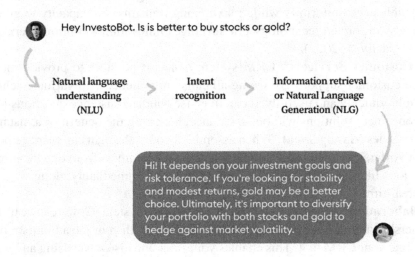

b. **Pick out important terms:** Bots can spot key words and phrases that refer to actual things like people, places, or companies. These terms are sorted into defined groups.
c. **Add to and share their word bank:** Using Machine Learning (ML), NLP bots learn more words, phrases, and everyday language. These new words are then shared with other bots, helping them all improve.
d. **Distinguish between types of nouns:** NLP chatbots can separate regular nouns from proper ones and fix any incorrect capitalization.
e. **Handle verb tenses:** They can understand the tense and conjunction of verbs. This helps bots chat more naturally.

Traditional Chatbot vs. NLP Chatbot

Standard text-based chatbots are fed with keyword concerns along with the solutions associated with these concerns. When an individual enters a concern having the keyword or expression the automated solution appears. This can function well for easy inquiries as shown in figure 11.

Nevertheless keyword-led chatbots cannot reply to inquiries they are not set to address. This restricted extent can bring about consumer disappointment when they do not get the info they require (Stefanowicz, B. 2024).

NLP chatbots make use of all-natural language handling to recognize the individual's concerns regardless of just how they express them. Unlike conventional chatbots there is no demand for a precise keyword or key phrase suite as NLP chatbots make use of AI to discover 'at work ' so they will certainly remain to come to be extra smart as well as effective the extra they are utilized.

NLP chatbots vary from typical chatbots due to the fact that they can notice punctuation as well as language errors as well as inadequate use of language extra normally. They're able to determine when

Figure 11. Comparison of traditional vs. NLP Chatbots

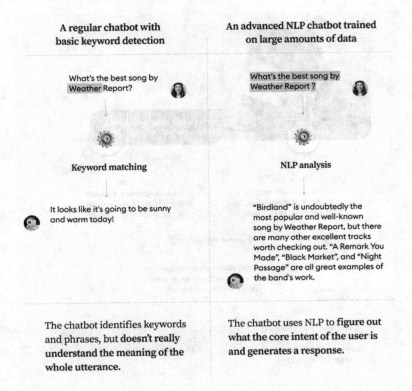

a word is meant improperly and still analyze the desired significance properly. Normal chatbots cannot recognize intent.

How Do NLP Chatbots Function?

NLP is based upon a mix of computational etymology, artificial intelligence and deep knowing designs. These 3 innovations encourage computer systems to take in human language and check, classify and procedure to ensure that the complete definition consisting of intent together with belief, is entirely recognized as shown in figure 12.

NLP allows chatbots to recognize the individual input by examining it utilizing the NLU (Natural Language Understanding) modern technology create one of the most exact actions to the question utilizing Natural Language Generation (NLG) and also ultimately fine-tune the action to make certain precision based upon information that is readily available from previous communications (Shereen, A., 2022). The most effective conversational AI chatbots utilize a mix of NLP, NLU along with NLG to provide smarter, conversational reactions as well as options. This is how each of these modern technologies are made use of in an individual trip.

Figure 12. Working of NLP

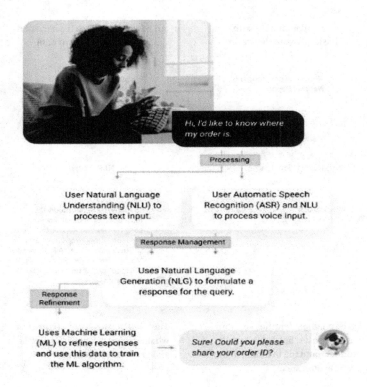

1. **Input event:** The individual supplies input via an internet site or an application where the style of the input can either be message or voice.
2. **Input evaluation:** Based on the sort of input, various innovations are made use of for input evaluation.

   Text input-- If the input is text-based, the conversational AI option will certainly make use of Natural Language Understanding (NLU) a component of NLP to analyze the significance of the input and also acquire its purpose.
   Voice input-- If the input is speech-based, it'll take advantage of a mix of Automatic Speech Recognition (ASR) and also NLU to examine the information.

3. **Feedback administration:** During this phase Natural Language Generation (NLG) a part of NLP creates a reaction for the question (Shereen, A., 2022).

ANALYTICS AND REPORTING

Analytics and reporting tools provide insightful data about how users interact with a smart chatbot, allowing you to improve its functionality. Detailed reports on customer inquiries, chatbot responses, and

Figure 13. Steps to implement an ecommerce chatbot

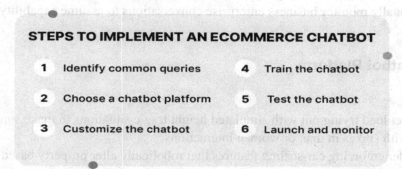

overall chatbot activity are available through the chatbot platform. The chatbot's response should be up-to-date, using this information to improve the customer experience.

SOCIO ECONOMIC IMPLICATIONS OF ECOMMERCE CHATBOT

It is important to choose a chatbot platform with high customer service to assure that any problems or questions can be solved immediately as shown in figure 13.

Identify Common Queries

1. Engage with Customer Service Team:
   ○ Conduct regular workshops and training sessions for energetic listening and effective communication for customer service dealers.
   ○ Encourage group members to percentage anonymized case studies, showcasing a hit troublesolving and exemplary client interaction.
   ○ Implement a rewards device for customer support dealers who make contributions revolutionary solutions.
2. Customer Surveys:
   ○ Implement a multi-channel survey approach, consisting of electronic mail, website pop- ups, and in-app surveys, to seize a various range of customer reviews.
   ○ Use sentiment evaluation devices to extract feelings expressed in survey responses, imparting deeper insights into consumer pride tiers.
   ○ Periodically conduct in-depth interviews with pick out clients to gain qualitative insights into their review
3. Social Media Monitoring:
   ○ Train social media managers to pick out capacity customer service problems on numerous structures.
   ○ Establish a dedicated social media reaction organization to engage with clients at once and provide real-time assistance.

    ◦   Implement social listening gadget that no longer simplest tune mentions of your emblem but additionally monitor business enterprise conversations to assume capability issues.

Choose a Chatbot Platform

1. Scalability
   - ◦ Conduct load trying out with simulated height tragic situations to make sure the chatbot can cope with spikes in man or woman interactions.
   - ◦ Consider enforcing car-scaling features that robotically alter property based on call for, optimizing value-effectiveness throughout periods of lower interest.
2. Adaptability and Flexibility:
   - ◦ Establish an agile development method for the chatbot, contemplating speedy iterations and non-prevent improvements.
   - ◦ Implement a remarks loop between developers, customer service sellers, and give up- clients to acquire insights for ongoing upgrades.
   - ◦ Regularly look at the aggressive panorama to make certain your chatbot remains at the leading edge of technological upgrades.

Customize the Chatbot

1. Brand Alignment:
   - ◦ Create a brand character guide outlining particular trends, language nuances, and verbal exchange patterns for the chatbot.
   - ◦ Conduct workshops with marketing and advertising and marketing teams to align chatbot responses with current emblem campaigns, making sure consistency across all purchaser touchpoints.
2. User Experience (UX):
   - ◦ Implement consumer trying-out intervals with actual customers to accumulate feedback at the chatbot's interface, making sure it aligns with patron expectations.
   - ◦ Leverage heatmaps and customer adventure analytics to perceive commonplace ache elements and optimize the customer revel.
   - ◦ Explore gamification factors inside the chatbot interface to decorate user engagement
3. Escalation Mechanism:
   - ◦ Develop a clear and obvious escalation path, informing customers approximately the instances underneath which human intervention may be important.
   - ◦ Train customer support entrepreneurs on specific criteria for taking up conversations
   - ◦ and provide them with gear to seamlessly transition from chatbot to human assist.

Train the Chatbot

- Establish a schedule for ordinary schooling classes with the chatbot. Incorporate updates on product features, enterprise trends, and consumer comments.
- Leverage continuous learning algorithms to enable the chatbot to comply in real-time, enhancing its capacity to cope with novel queries.

Test the Chatbot

1. **Beta Testing:**
   - Develop numerous beta trying out organizations representing unique demographics, which include age, gender, and cultural backgrounds.
   - Implement usability checking out to evaluate the chatbot's ease of use, making sure it caters to clients with diverse levels of technological skills.
2. Cross-Platform Compatibility:
   - Conduct bypass-browser checking out to come to be aware about and rectify any compatibility troubles all through one-of-a-type internet browsers.
   - Optimize the chatbot for accessibility, making sure it adheres to WCAG necessities and gives an unbroken experience for users with disabilities.

Launch and Show

1. **Phased Rollout:**
   - Plan a phased rollout based entirely on geography, purchaser segments, or product traces to control capacity troubles effectively.
   - Establish a dedicated launch team accountable for tracking key average overall performance signs and symptoms and addressing any rising issues without delay.
2. Customer Feedback Loop:
   - Implement a client advisory board, inviting key clients to provide ongoing remarks on the chatbot's overall performance.
   - Regularly study client remarks on the use of sentiment analysis tools, identifying styles and areas for improvement.

APPLICATIONS OF E-COMMERCE CHATBOTS

There are various applications in E-commerce chatbots that are explained in the following section.

Microsoft Bot Framework

Microsoft Bot Framework is an effective system for constructing chatbots utilizing a variety of programs languages such as C# and Node.js as shown in figure 14. It supplies a variety of functions, such as all-

Figure 14. Microsoft bot framework architecture

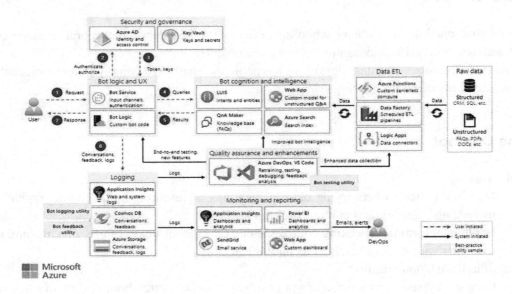

natural language handling (NLP) speech acknowledgment and also text-to-speech abilities. Microsoft Bot Framework sustains combination with several preferred messaging systems (*Enterprise-grade conversational bot. (n.d.).*)

IBM Watson

IBM Watson is an effective system that supplies sophistication chatbot experiences (Norelus, E. 2022). The system is incorporated with IBM Cloud permitting you to include extra solutions like Watson Assis-

Figure 15. Designing a chatbot with IBM Watson Assistant

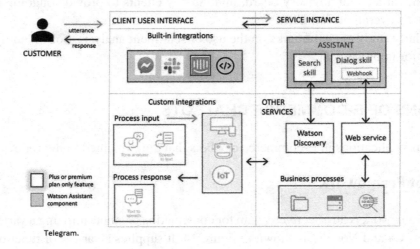

Figure 16. How to develop a chat bot using Amazon Lex

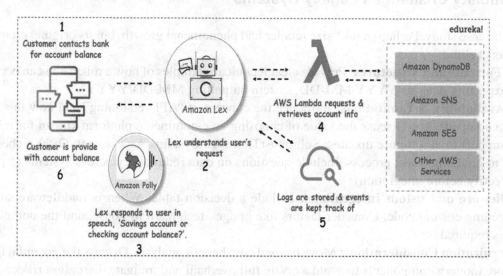

tant as shown in figure 15. IBM Watson incorporates numerous preferred messaging systems consisting of Facebook Messenger Slack, and Telegram.

Amazon.com Lex

Amazon Lex is an additional preferred chatbot system. It is based upon the exact same conversational engine as the Amazon Echo as well as is incorporated with AWS solutions like Lambda as well as DynamoDB shown in figure 16 (*Build and test the bot - Amazon Lex V1.* (n.d.).) It likewise gives the exact same all-natural language understanding abilities as Dialogflow yet needs much less coding to establish. It provides all-natural language understanding (NLU) abilities plus becomes part of the Amazon Web Services (AWS) system (Saini, P., Tajammul. et.al, 2022).

OVERCOMING INTEGRATION CHALLENGES WITH E-COMMERCE SYSTEMS

Future research on customer relationships in virtual environments will advance us further. The findings suggest that e-service agent activity enhances communication. Lastly, the big, strong, highly competitive luxury brand company Consumption patterns are undergoing change. Brands are catching up with the new opportunities for e-service agents, but empirical research has. they rarely examine whether they provide adequate communication. By showing that e-service providers positively deliver positive communication that affects customer satisfaction, our research increases wealth Fashion Books. The findings have managerial implications for the core of the luxury retail sector. First, we focused on consumers in their 20s and 30s living in South Korea, a strong segment of luxury consumers to capture their perceptions of e-service agent services. What we have found shows that luxury fashion brands can use Chatbots for digital promotion (Padghan, 2021).

Compatibility Challenges Legacy Systems

Expand the case study. Perhaps a mid-size retailer had phenomenal growth, but its original e-commerce system lags behind.

Data Formats and Structures: Provide clear technical examples of how a mismatch can occur (e.g., chatbot expecting dates as YYYY-MM-DD, system outputting MM/DD/YYYY).

API Availability & Limitations: Introduce the concept of "API versioning" and how this impacts long-term compatibility. Discuss the value of choosing an e-commerce platform known for robust developer support to ease future updates. SolutionstThorough Systems Assessment: Offer a checklist or template to guide the audit process. Include questions on data redundancy across systems (a potential issue to rectify before integration)

Middleware or Custom Integrations: Include a decision table: When is middleware sufficient, versus needing custom code. Consider factors like budget, tech team in-house, and the complexity of data flows required.

Modernization Considerations: Move beyond cost-benefit analysis. Discuss the potential for phasing in more modern components to avoid a costly full overhaul and mitigate disruption risks.

User Experience Considerations Cross-Platform Consistency

Cite industry-specific research if available (e.g., % of customers who use both website and app of a brand). Emphasize that poor integration undercuts multichannel investment.

Tailored Interfaces: Explore responsive design concepts. How might the chatbot subtly adapt its layout between desktop and mobile without sacrificing core functionality.

Contextual Awareness: Tie this to customer retention. Show the impact of a chatbot greeting a returning customer with a special offer versus a generic "How can I help?"

Design Principles & Templates: Offer more than visuals. Provide example code for responsive UI elements if readers are likely to be hands-on with development. Centralized Knowledge Base: Discuss the technical side: database choices, syncing frequency (real-time vs. scheduled updates), and how this impacts the end-user experience.

Brand Alignment and Trust Brand Voice Development

Offer a brainstorming exercise to define chatbot personality: Formal vs. Friendly, Humorous vs.Matter-of-fact. Tie this back to the target audience.

Security Concerns & Transparency: Mention relevant regulations (GDPR, etc.) and how chatbots must comply. Offer templates for concise privacy statements chatbots can display. Human Handover: Look beyond escalation. To know how the quality chatbots should capture data while being unable to resolve an issue, handing off a fully informed support agent who avoids making the customer repeat themselves.

Performance Monitoring & Testing: Introduce load testing tools. Usage of A/B testing conversational flows to identify which paths are most successful.

Ethical AI & Bias: Focus on practical steps to diversify training data. Offer sources for unbiased datasets to reduce the risk of harmful chatbot outputs.

Improving service delivery

Analyzing the customer-facing activities of the five chatbots. Communication, entertainment, and problem solving, are considered essential to effective service delivery. This is why the reasons they were put together are presented as follows. Engagement plays an important role in offline customer service, aspect which is generally considered absent in the digital world. When it comes to client advice, people tend to a the high value of the courtesy, helpfulness and trustworthiness of the vendors, due to the desire to receive practical advice.

The interaction between the customer and the chatbot should be optimized, the latter should exhibit such characteristics as much as possible with the human act. Prerequisites for successful support from chatbots are provided. Of course, it's not their technology that makes them think about their ability to communicate with each other, but them.

Lack of humanity. For example, a chatbot may not meet users' expectations regarding its language skills.

CONCLUSION

The e-commerce chatbot offers a transformative service for organizations looking to raise their customer support, enhance sales plus improve procedures in the electronic industry. By incorporating innovative innovations like all-natural language handling as well as artificial intelligence these chatbots provide an individualized effective as well as round-the-clock buying experience for individuals.

Shopping chatbots act as online aides guiding consumers via item exploration, giving real-time assistance helping with purchases, as well as also using tailored referrals. With smooth combination with shopping systems, CRM systems plus various other service devices these chatbots improve procedures, improve consumer interaction, as well as drive conversions.

The advantages of shopping chatbots reach past prompt sales deals. They make it possible for organizations to collect beneficial understandings right into consumer choices, actions, and also discomfort factors equipping data-driven decision-making and also continual renovation. In addition, chatbots can range procedures take care of several queries all at once as well as supply regular solutions throughout different networks, adding to enhanced functional performance as well as cost-effectiveness.

As modern technology progresses and also client assumptions remain to climb, shopping chatbots continue to be a vibrant device for services looking to remain affordable in the electronic landscape. By focusing on customer experience, customization and also recurring optimization services can utilize shopping chatbots to grow resilient consumer connections and drive profits development, coupled with growth in the ever-evolving shopping environment.

REFERENCES

Appointment Scheduling Chatbot. 500Apps. (n.d.). Botup. https://botup.com/scheduling

Capacity, T. (2023). *ECommerce Chatbots: The Complete Guide.* Capacity. https://capacity.com/learn/ai-chatbots/ecommerce-chatbot/

Redesign UI. (n.d.). UpLabs. https://www.uplabs.com/posts/chat-gpt-redesign-ui

Customer Satisfaction template. (n.d.). ChatBot. https://www.chatbot.com/chatbot-templates/customer-satisfaction-template/

How to make a chatbot? (2022b, March 11). AppMaster - Ultimate All-in No-code Platform. https://appmaster.io/blog/how-make-chatbot

Kela, P. (2024, March 21). *What is CRM Integration? Everything you need to know*. SoftwareSuggest Blog. https://www.softwaresuggest.com/blog/crm-integration/

Norelus, E. (2022, January 27). Designing a chatbot with IBM Watson Assistant. *Medium*. https://ernesenorelus.medium.com/designing-a-chatbot-with-ibm-watson-assistant-7e11b94c2b3d

Padghan, V. (2021, December 6). How to develop a chat bot using Amazon Lex? *Medium*. https://medium.com/edureka/how-to-develop-a-chat-bot-using-amazon-lex-a570beac969e

Retail chatbots use cases for improving your sales. (n.d.). ChatBot Blog. https://www.chatbot.com/blog/retail-chatbots

Saini, P., Tajammul, M., & School of Computer Science and IT, Jain University, Jayanagar, Bangalore, Karnataka, India. (2022). Conversational AI powered chatbot using LEX and AWS. In *International Journal of Trend in Scientific Research and Development, 6*(3), 1622–1627). https://www.ijtsrd.com/papers/ijtsrd49722.pdf

Shereen, A. (2022, November 21). *What is a Key Differentiator of Conversational AI? - Freshchat Blog*. Freshchat Blog. https://www.freshworks.com/live-chat-software/chatbots/key-differentiator-of-conversational-ai-blog/

SnatchBot. (n.d.). *Education — Enhancing the Classroom with Chatbots*. SnatchBot. https://snatchbot.me/education

Stefanowicz, B. (2024, March 7). *5 Best Shopping Bots [Examples and How to Use Them]*. Tidio. https://www.tidio.com/blog/shopping-bot/

Stefanowicz, B. (2024, March 7). *NLP Chatbot: Complete Guide & How to Build Your Own*. Tidio. https://www.tidio.com/blog/nlp-chatbots/

Step 3: Build and test the bot. (n.d.) Amazon.. https://docs.aws.amazon.com/lex/latest/dg/gs2-build-and-test.html

Team, L. (2024, March 22). *The best conversational AI platform for business*. LivePerson. https://www.liveperson.com/

Vankadara, S. (2022, March 30). Build Chatbot using Amazon Lex.. *Medium*. https://medium.datadriven-investor.com/build-chatbot-using-amazon-lex-ed3db80b27d0

KEY TERMS AND DEFINITIONS

A/B Testing: It is also called bucket testing used for comparing two similar versions of web applications to find out the performance between them.

Artificial Intelligence: It is the study of computer systems to work like human intelligence with the capabilities of problem solving.

Chatbot: Chatbot works like a computer to simulate the process and the conversation of a human.

Customer Relationship Management (CRM): It is the technique of maintaining the relationships between the company and consumers.

E-commerce: It is nothing but selling and buying of goods and services through the internet.

Natural Language Generation: It is the process by artificial intelligence which produces human written or spoken from structured or unstructured data.

Natural Language Processing: It is a computer program to understand the human language both in the form of written and spoken.

Chapter 16
The Use of Chatbot Technology in EFL Learning:
A Systematic Analysis of Research Conducted Between 2020–2023

Gülin Zeybek

iD https://orcid.org/0000-0002-6863-7169

Isparta University of Applied Sciences, Turkey

ABSTRACT

This study thoroughly analyses the incorporation of chatbots in English as a Foreign Language (EFL) education by examining 11 research studies carried out from 2020 to 2023. The review carefully combines findings, techniques, and consequences to offer a detailed overview of the complex field of chatbot-mediated language learning treatments. From quasi-experimental designs to qualitative explorations, the evaluated research uses a range of approaches to study various characteristics such as learning attainment, effectiveness, motivation, attitudes, perceptions, cognition, learning styles, and user experience. The results show how adaptable chatbot technology is in supporting task-oriented learning, vocabulary development, conversational practice, and pedagogical support, providing individualized and interesting language learning opportunities. Additionally, the contextual complexities present in chatbot interventions are emphasised, highlighting the significance of taking learner demographics, educational situations, and cultural backgrounds into account.

INTRODUCTION

Artificial intelligence technologies are expected to have a substantial influence on teaching and learning methods in the next years (Can, Gelmez-Burakgazi, & Celik, 2019). Chatbots, which are intelligent conversational systems that can interact with users through voice or text, have potential for aiding in Second Language Acquisition (SLA) (Fryer & Nakao, 2009). AI has progressed, especially in voice technology, enabling chatbots to imitate human-like interactions with language learners (Fryer et al., 2020; Shadiev

DOI: 10.4018/979-8-3693-1830-0.ch016

& Liu, 2023; Zhang et al., 2023). Studies have confirmed that speech-recognition technology-based chatbots have a beneficial effect on language learning such as motivation and speaking anxiety (Jeon, 2022; Tai & Chen, 2020).

Chatbots are virtual agents that engage with people using natural language. They have a historical origin in ELIZA, the first chatbot created in 1956 by Joseph Weizenbaum to mimic a psychiatrist. Chatbots such as ALICE, Claude, and HeX have developed throughout time, using various frameworks and features (Shawar & Atwell, 2015). Chatbots have been used as pedagogical agents in education for a long time. Recent advancements in technology have sparked greater interest in using them for teaching and learning (Laurillard, 2013). Chatbots in language learning have also shown various benefits such as reducing anxiety, offering repeated practice, focusing on students, providing realistic communication, and being widely available (Fryer et al., 2020; Kohnke et al., 2023; Zhang et al., 2023). The affordances, shown in several fields, enhance successful learning experiences with the use of chatbots (Zhang et al., 2023). Chatbots are being used into education due to the widespread use of instant messaging, showcasing its ability to enhance teaching and learning (Coniam, 2014). Some language chatbots have demonstrated enhanced grammatical skills, while others like Chatbot Ethnobot aid in gathering data for ethnographic studies (Tallyn et al., 2018). The increasing popularity of mobile instant messaging applications, such as WhatsApp, emphasises the favourable view and adoption of chatbots for educational use (Pimmer et al., 2019).

AI chatbots are gaining attention in language instruction, especially in English as a Foreign Language (EFL) settings. Recent studies have shown promising results regarding the use of AI chatbots as conversational partners in EFL settings, although the empirical evidence supporting the effectiveness of ChatGPT in English language learning is still developing. Research conducted in EFL settings generally centres on dialogue-based automated agents and applications, which allow language learners to practise English by engaging in verbal or textual exchanges with chatbots. Kim (2019) conducted an experimental study with Korean undergraduate EFL learners, demonstrating that the usage of AI chatbots notably enhanced students' English grammatical abilities in comparison to a human chat group. Ebadi and Amini (2022) investigated how a chatbot application in an Iranian EFL university setting affected students' confidence and motivation to study English. They discovered that the accuracy and human-like qualities of the chatbot had a favourable influence on these factors. Bibauw et al.'s (2022) meta-analysis found that involving language learners with AI-driven conversation systems could forecast vocabulary and morphosyntactic results, improving learners' overall competency and accuracy in language usage.

In the experiments mentioned, students' involvement in chatbot-based language learning was usually organised by instructors or researchers. Yet, an increasing amount of academics are investigating how chatbot systems might provide efficient and self-guided learning environments in informal and digitalized settings. Haristiani and Rifa'i (2020) created Gengobot, a chatbot programme designed for Japanese language learners in Indonesia. Their work showed that combining AI chat companions with social media may meet individual language learning goals and preferences. Belda-Medina and Calvo-Ferrer (2022) conducted a mixed-method research to analyse the effects of implementing AI chatbots, such as Kuki, an Avatar-based AI bot, on the independent language learning activities of students and in-service instructors. The study found that certain linguistic and technological aspects of various chatbots had a substantial impact on how Spanish EFL undergraduates and Polish EFL students viewed and utilised AI conversational robots for informal language acquisition.

Chatbots have demonstrated significant promise in offering students a valuable foreign language practice. The use of chatbots for improving writing skills has become increasingly popular. Chatbots have demonstrated benefits over both human peers and automatic writing evaluation (AWE) systems in several areas. Students get advantages from the diverse linguistic inputs, instant feedback, and relaxed setting offered by chatbots when practicing writing (Jia & Ruan, 2008). Unlike several Automated Writing Evaluation (AWE) systems, chatbots provide immediate feedback during the writing process, encouraging students to continuously evaluate and perhaps enhance the quality of their writing (Wang et al., 2020). Chatbots have also been helpful in enhancing students' speaking abilities (Huang et al., 2022). Kim's research in 2017 and Kim et al.'s study in 2019 highlight the benefits of voice-based and text-based chatbots in enhancing EFL speaking skills. Voice-based chatbots are recommended by students for enhancing EFL speaking skills. The results indicate that using chatbot technology in EFL courses can improve students' spoken communication abilities and their overall view of language learning. They help with pronunciation, vocabulary learning, grammatical proficiency, and enhancement of listening and reading abilities as well (Haristiani and Danuwijaya 2019; Kim et al. 2020).

Chatbots are beneficial in language acquisition due to their ease, accessibility, and capacity to offer personalised guidance without time limitations, as most technologic devices provide ubiquity (Fryer and Carpenter 2006). Additionally, chatbots can establish a pleasant and low-stress learning atmosphere that may enhance student engagement, drive, and self-assurance in the acquisition of foreign languages (Kim et al. 2020). However, current research frequently fails to consider the distinctions between various chatbot systems, highlighting the necessity for a more detailed comprehension of their characteristics and capabilities (Bibauw et al., 2019).

The diversity in chatbot conception and characteristics has impeded the progress of research in the subject, despite breakthroughs. The absence of a cohesive conceptual framework complicates researchers' ability to compare their chatbots with those in the current literature, impeding the advancement of the area (Bibauw et al., 2019). The lack of a standardised approach for evaluating chatbot features might result in inadequate evaluations of their impact on language acquisition. Having a thorough conceptual framework is essential for making well-informed selections when choosing chatbots for educational or research objectives (Jeon et al., 2023).

It is important to consider a context-specific perspective to understand how chatbot platforms contribute to self-directed language learning environments, despite the potential gains in language proficiency and emotional benefits associated with the use of AI-powered technologies. The variation in design and language processing methods of AI chatbot tools can create unique usage cultures, impacting language learners' involvement and language development in computer-mediated environments (Thorne and Black, 2007). Thus, providing an overview of recent research on Chatbots in EFL learning can help gain a better understanding of the integration of these recent tools in to foreign language learning and shed light to further research. In view of all of the above, this book chapter's goal is to review empirical research conducted between 2020 and 2023 and provide the reader with a systematic overview of these studies.

METHOD

This study carefully identified and analysed relevant material on the incorporation of chatbots in EFL education. Initially, an extensive search was conducted in academic databases, leading to the discovery of 47 pertinent publications. To guarantee robust research, a systematic elimination procedure was employed to examine papers, resulting in a collection of 11 research-focused articles. The timeline chosen for analysis ranged from 2020 to 2023, offering a modern view on chatbots in the EFL setting. Strict inclusion criteria were followed, focusing on papers included in well-known databases such as Social Sciences Citation Index (SSCI), Science Citation Index Expanded (SCI-E), Education Resources Information Centre (ERIC), Scopus, and H.W. Wilson. The intentional selection aimed to maintain the quality of the information being examined, making sure that the selected papers were from reputable scholarly sources. This varied selection attempted to provide a wide range of research viewpoints, focusing on papers from reputable sources known for their academic excellence. The following analytical phase included a detailed assessment of each chosen piece across several aspects. The main study emphasis of each publication was determined, revealing the specific aspects of chatbots in EFL learning and teaching being studied. A thorough analysis of the study design was conducted, which included reviewing the methodological approach, data collecting instruments, and the overall methodology driving the investigations. Moreover, focus was placed on contextual factors, including the study setting, educational environment, and the integration of educational ideas and practices in each research project. The investigation involved categorising the chatbot applications used in the chosen research. This approach intended to reveal the technological interventions used in the research, providing significant insights on the various chatbot applications utilised in the context of EFL education. The rigorous technique led to the synthesis of findings from the analysed publications. The synthesis was given systematically, providing a structured overview of the many variables examined in the research. Figure 1 displays the distribution of studies based on their publication years.

Figure 1. Distribution of studies

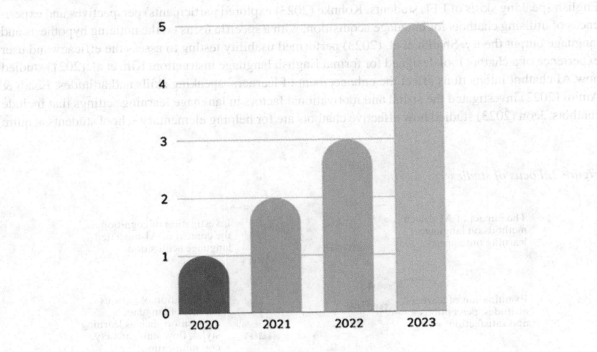

FINDINGS AND DISCUSSION

The studies cover many study areas related to language learning using AI chatbots. Five studies investigate the impact of AI-driven methods on language learning outcomes, focusing on learning accomplishment, effectiveness, and motivation. Four research focus on examining learners' attitudes, perceptions, and satisfaction, providing insight into the subjective experiences and perspectives about the integration of AI in language teaching. One research investigates cognition by analysing cognitive processes including cognitive load, engagement, and self-regulated cognition in the context of AI-mediated language acquisition. A research examines learning styles, flow state, foreign language learning anxiety, communication, intercultural interaction, and vocabulary retention to get insights into the many facets of language acquisition. Nine research focus on the integration of AI chatbots in language learning, examining the possibilities and obstacles of using these technologies in educational environments. Three studies examine the usability and user experience of chatbots, specifically analysing the usability, efficacy, and overall experience of engaging with AI-driven language learning programmes. Figure 2 provides a thorough summary of the focus of these studies, highlighting the complex nature of AI-driven language learning research.

The studies mentioned above encompass a wide range of research topics related to language acquisition and the use of technology. Yin & Satar (2020) studied how various chatbot kinds impact the ability of EFL learners to negotiate meaning. Belda-Medina & Caldo-Ferrer (2022) studied the incorporation of AI and chatbots in language learning environments, with an emphasis on user happiness and perceived utility. Lin & Mubarok (2021) studied how using mind map-guided AI chatbot methods affects the English speaking skills of EFL students. Kohnke (2023) explored participants' perspectives and experiences of utilising chatbots for language acquisition, with a specific focus on the noticing hypothesis and language output theory. Shaikh et al. (2023) performed usability testing to assess the efficacy and user experience of a chatbot tool designed for formal English language instruction. Kim et al. (2021) studied how AI chatbot interactions affect the enhancement of learners' speaking skills and attitudes. Ebadi & Amini (2022) investigated the social and motivational factors in language learning settings that include chatbots. Jeon (2023) studied how effective chatbots are for helping elementary school students acquire

Figure 2. Focus of studies

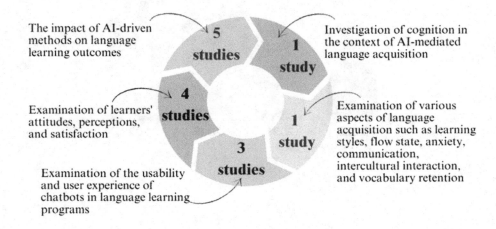

284

language. Hsu et al. (2023) studied how a task-oriented chatbot system might enhance TOEIC speaking scores in university students. Chien et al. (2022) studied how competition in a chatbot-based learning setting affects English speaking, listening skills, and motivation to learn. Liu & Ma (2023) studied how consumers see and approve of chatbots for casual English language acquisition, using a revised Technology Acceptance Model (TAM) framework. Every research project provides vital knowledge about the changing field of language learning technology and how they affect learner results and experiences.

The studies include a variety of study designs, each customised to address specific questions related to AI-facilitated language acquisition. Yin & Satar (2020) utilised a mixed-method approach that included before and post-questionnaires, along with chat logs, to investigate how various forms of chatbots impact EFL learners' communication experiences. Belda-Medina & Caldo-Ferrer (2022) used a sequential explanatory mixed-methods approach, combining before and post-surveys with template analysis to study how AI and chatbots are being incorporated into language learning by teacher candidates. Lin & Mubarok (2021) conducted a quasi-experimental study with experimental and control groups, using oral performance records and chatbot interactions to assess the impact of mind map-guided AI chatbots compared to traditional AI chatbots on English speaking abilities. Kohnke (2023) used an exploratory qualitative method, merging online surveys with detailed interviews to investigate how participants interpret and encounter language acquisition through chatbot interaction. Shaikh et al. (2023) employed usability testing technique, which involved post-task surveys and usability scores, to assess the efficacy of a chatbot tool for formal English language acquisition. Hsu et al. (2023) used an experimental design with before and post-tests to evaluate how successful a task-oriented chatbot system was in enhancing TOEIC speaking scores. Chien et al. (2022) employed a quasi-experimental approach with pre and post-tests to investigate the effects of LINE ChatBot treatments on English speaking, listening, and learning motivation in high school students. Liu & Ma (2023) utilised a cross-sectional survey methodology to conduct research on users' attitudes and acceptability of ChatGPT in informal English language learning settings. They administered a modified Technology Acceptance Model questionnaire for this purpose. The many study strategies demonstrate the intricate and multifaceted nature of investigating AI-mediated language learning processes, each providing distinct insights and contributions to the field. A summary of the research designs of these studies is presented in figure 3.

Figure 3. Summary of research designs

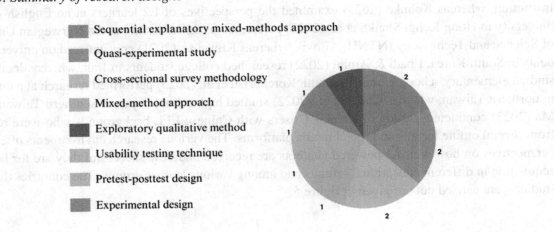

Figure 4. Summary of data collection methods

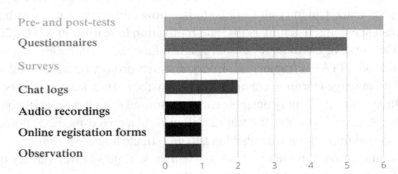

The research used a range of data collecting techniques designed to capture different elements of language learning experiences and views. The techniques utilised encompassed before and post-surveys, questionnaires, chat logs, voice recordings, interaction transcripts, and online registration forms. Yin & Satar (2020) used before and post-questionnaires to collect participants' background information and views of chatbot interactions, as well as chat logs to analyse negotiation for meaning (NfM) routines. Belda-Medina & Caldo-Ferrer (2022) employed before and post-surveys, together with specialised models such as the Chatbot-Human Interaction Satisfaction Model (CHISM) and the Technology Acceptance Model (TAM), to evaluate participants' satisfaction levels and perceived utility of chatbots. Lin & Mubarok (2021) gathered audio recordings of oral performances, engaged in discussions with chatbots, and used Voyant methods for data analysis to assess the efficiency of AI chatbot techniques led by mind maps. Kohnke (2023) used online questionnaires and in-depth semi-structured interviews to explore how participants view and experience using chatbots. Shaikh et al. (2023) employed online registration forms and post-task questionnaires, such as the Usefulness, Satisfaction, and Ease of Use (USE) questionnaire and the System Usability Scale (SUS) questionnaire, to assess the usability of chatbots for formal English language learning. The summary of these data collection methods is presented in figure 4.

The experiments were carried out in several educational settings in different areas, offering insights into the incorporation of AI-driven chatbots in language learning contexts. Yin & Satar (2020) studied EFL learners from China, whereas Belda-Medina & Caldo-Ferrer (2022) examined teacher candidates from universities in Spain and Poland. Lin & Mubarok (2021) researched EFL students at a Taiwanese institution, whereas Kohnke (2023) examined the perspectives of L2 learners at an English-medium university in Hong Kong. Shaikh et al. (2023) performed usability testing at the Norwegian University of Science and Technology (NTNU), Gjøvik, whereas Kim et al. (2021) concentrated on university students in South Korea. Ebadi & Amini (2022) researched college students in Iran, whereas Jeon (2023) studied elementary school learners in South Korea. Hsu et al. (2023) performed research at a university in northern Taiwan, whereas Chien et al. (2022) studied high school pupils in southern Taiwan. Liu & Ma (2023) conducted a study of ChatGPT users with Chinese EFL backgrounds who were recruited from several online forums and social media platforms. The various research environments offer useful perspectives on how well AI-powered chatbots are received and how successful they are for language acquisition in different educational settings and among various learner groups. The countries that these studies were carried out are given in figure 5.

Figure 5. Countries that studies were carried out

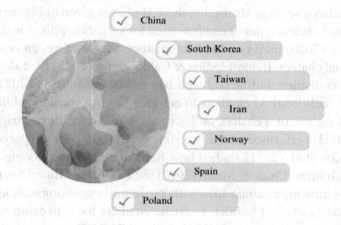

Findings Related to the Use of Chatbots

The overviewed studies use different learning styles, techniques, and strategies to assess the efficacy of chatbots and AI technology in foreign language acquisition. Yin & Satar (2020) use Negotiation for Meaning (NfM) theory to examine communication failures and learners' adjusted responses in chatbot encounters. Lin & Mubarok (2021) utilise cognitive theories of language learning to investigate the impact of mind map-guided AI chatbots on vocabulary development and speaking abilities. Jeon (2023) utilises a Computer-Assisted Language Learning (CALL) method by incorporating chatbots into language teaching to enhance vocabulary learning. Kohnke (2023) examines how a chatbot might enhance language acquisition by applying the noticing hypothesis and language output theory. Shaikh et al. (2023) utilise

Figure 6. The summary of the approaches and methods used

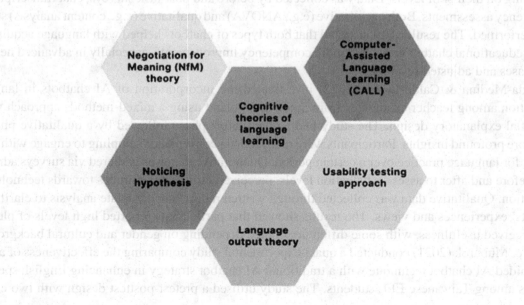

usability testing approach to assess the efficacy of ChatGPT for formal English language acquisition. A summary of the approaches and methods used in these studies is given in Figure 6.

The research examined several types of chatbots used for varied objectives in the context of language acquisition. Yin & Satar (2020) used two kinds of chatbots: Tutor Mike, an educational chatbot, and Mitsuku, a conversational chatbot. Belda-Medina & Caldo-Ferrer (2022) used Replika, Kuki, and Wysa chatbots for language acquisition and mental well-being. Lin & Mubarok (2021) utilised mind map-guided AI chatbots and traditional AI chatbots to enhance English speaking abilities in their research. Kohnke (2023) studied the use of a chatbot on Facebook Messenger for language learning in an EAP course. Shaikh et al. (2023) performed usability testing on ChatGPT for the purpose of formal English language acquisition. Kim et al. (2021) studied how Replika, Andy, and Google Assistant chatbots affect trainees' speaking abilities. Ebadi & Amini (2022) used a Chatbot-Based Social Interactive English Classroom (CSIEC) system using a human-like chatbot to improve speaking abilities. Jeon (2023) utilised Dialogflow, an open-source chatbot builder, to create chatbots for enhancing vocabulary acquisition in a primary school environment. Hsu et al. (2023) utilised TPBOT, a task-oriented chatbot system, to enhance TOEIC speaking results among university students. Chien et al. (2022) used a LINE ChatBot with and without a competitive approach for English conversation practice in high school. Liu & Ma (2023) investigated how Chinese EFL learners perceive and adopt ChatGPT for casual English language acquisition. The chatbots used in each research were customised to meet their individual goals, such as providing educational support or practicing conversations. This demonstrates the flexibility and capacity of chatbot technology in language learning settings.

Findings of the Chatbot Studies

In their quasi-experimental study, Yin & Satar (2020) examined how educational and conversational chatbots might improve English as a Foreign Language (EFL) learning for Chinese participants. The study utilised a pretest-posttest design with two experimental groups and one control group. Participants interacted with either a pedagogical or conversational chatbot during negotiation for meaning tasks, depending on their skill levels. Data was collected by before and post-task surveys, chat transcripts, and competency assessments. Both quantitative (e.g., ANOVA) and qualitative (e.g., content analysis) studies were performed. The results demonstrated that both types of chatbots helped with language acquisition, but the educational chatbot group had more competency improvements, especially in advanced negotiation phases and adjusted responses.

Belda-Medina & Caldo-Ferrer (2022) investigated the incorporation of AI chatbots in language acquisition among teacher candidates from Spain and Poland using a mixed-methods approach with a sequential explanatory design. The study had a quantitative phase followed by a qualitative phase to gain more profound insights. Participants were recruited via convenience sampling to engage with an AI chatbot for language practice over a certain period. Quantitative data was gathered via surveys administered before and after to assess satisfaction levels, perceived utility, and attitudes towards technological integration. Qualitative data was collected through written reports and template analysis to clarify participants' experiences and views. The results showed that participants reported high levels of pleasure and perceived usefulness, with some differences noted depending on gender and cultural backgrounds.

Lin & Mubarok (2021) conducted a quasi-experimental study comparing the effectiveness of a mind map-guided AI chatbot technique with a traditional AI chatbot strategy in enhancing English speaking abilities among Taiwanese EFL students. The study utilised a pretest-posttest design with two experimental groups and one control group. Experimental group participants engaged in speaking practice sessions using mind maps before engaging with the chatbot, whereas the control group communicated with the chatbot directly. Data gathering included recordings of spoken performances, transcripts of chat conversations, and surveys evaluating learners' perspectives and experiences. Both quantitative and qualitative assessments were performed. The study showed that using the mind map-guided technique resulted in higher learning outcomes, demonstrated by greater speaking performance, more interactive behaviours, and enhanced chatbot memory retention.

Kohnke (2023) conducted a qualitative research to investigate how second language learners in Hong Kong see a chatbot used for language instruction. with an exploratory study methodology, data was gathered using online surveys and in-depth semi-structured interviews with individuals who had experience with a language learning chatbot. The study utilised theoretical frameworks including the noticing hypothesis and language output theory to direct data analysis. Thematic analysis showed that participants had favourable views on the chatbot's ease, accessibility, and integration with course contents. Participants valued the chatbot's capacity to offer instant feedback and tailored learning experiences, seeing its potential as an additional resource for language acquisition.

Shaikh et al. (2023) used usability testing to assess the usability of ChatGPT for formal English language instruction with students at NTNU, Gjøvik. Participants were recruited via university channels and participated in interactive sessions with ChatGPT aimed at improving their English language proficiency. Data was collected using online registration forms, task performance indicators, and post-task questionnaires evaluating user experience and satisfaction. Analysed usability indicators, including task completion rates, time on task, and mistake rates, to assess ChatGPT's usefulness as a language learning tool. The results showed that participants found the system easy to use and reported good experiences, as well as perceived enhancements in their English language skills.

Kim et al. (2021) utilised a pretest-posttest approach with an experimental group and a control group to study how AI chatbot interactions affect speaking performance in university students in Korea. The experimental group participants participated in speaking practice sessions using AI chatbots, whereas the control group got traditional teaching without chatbot interaction. Data were gathered via before and post-tests, surveys, and observations of speaking sessions. The data was analysed using descriptive statistics, t-tests, and ANCOVA. The study showed a notable enhancement in speaking skills for individuals who engaged with AI chatbots, underscoring the efficacy of using chatbots for speaking practice.

Ebadi & Amini (2022) utilised a sequential explanatory mixed-methods design to investigate the impact of a chatbot-based social interactive English classroom system on the speaking abilities and motivation of undergraduate students in Iran. The study included a quantitative phase followed by a qualitative phase to offer thorough insights. Quantitative data was gathered using standardised criteria to assess social presence, learner motivation, and perceived human-likeness of the chatbot. Quantitative data was analysed using Structural Equation Modelling (SEM), while qualitative data from student interviews was analysed using theme analysis. The study showed that there are strong connections between social presence, perceived human-likeness, learner motivation, and speaking abilities, indicating the effectiveness of using chatbot-based methods in language learning settings.

Jeon (2023) conducted a cross-sectional survey to examine how chatbot-based vocabulary learning affects vocabulary acquisition in primary school students in South Korea. The study employed convenience sampling to choose participants from elementary schools. Data was gathered using self-reported surveys conducted both before and after the intervention. The intervention group participated in vocabulary acquisition tasks with the assistance of a chatbot, whereas the control group used conventional instructional approaches. The quantitative analysis of survey data showed that individuals in the intervention group had considerably higher vocabulary acquisition scores than those in the control group. Qualitative insights were collected using open-ended survey questions to complement the quantitative results.

Hsu et al. (2023) used an experimental methodology to assess the impact of TPBOT on enhancing TOEIC speaking scores in university students in Taiwan. The study utilised a pretest-posttest design with an experimental group and a control group. Individuals in the experimental group used TPBOT for interactive speaking practice, whereas those in the control group received traditional TOEIC speaking exam preparation. Data was gathered via TOEIC speaking simulation tests conducted before and after the intervention, in addition to post-intervention surveys evaluating satisfaction and perceived efficacy of TPBOT. Statistical analysis showed a significant enhancement in TOEIC speaking scores for individuals who used TPBOT, demonstrating its effectiveness as an additional resource for TOEIC speaking exam readiness.

Studying the effects of a LINE ChatBot with competition on English speaking, listening, and motivation among high school students in Taiwan. Chien et al. (2022) conducted a quasi-experimental investigation using a non-randomized control group design. Participants were categorised into experimental and control groups according to their school associations. Both groups participated in English learning activities using a LINE ChatBot, with the experimental group adding competitive aspects to the learning experience. Speaking and listening abilities were measured by before and post-test evaluations, while motivation levels were evaluated using surveys. Statistical analysis showed that there were no significant differences in the speaking and listening abilities of the experimental and control groups. The experimental group showed considerably greater levels of intrinsic motivation, suggesting the motivating advantages of include competition in language acquisition tasks.

Liu & Ma (2023) evaluated how Chinese EFL learners perceive and accept ChatGPT for casual English learning. Participants were recruited from educational institutions in China using convenience sampling. Data was collected by a modified version of the Technology Acceptance Model (TAM) questionnaire presented via e-poster. Structural equation modelling (SEM) was used to analyse quantitative data and investigate the connections between user perceptions, attitudes, and behavioural intentions towards ChatGPT. The results showed strong positive connections between perceived usefulness, simplicity of use, attitude towards utilising ChatGPT, and behavioural intention, suggesting a high degree of acceptance and readiness to interact with ChatGPT for casual English learning. A detailed overview of these studies is presented in Table 1.

CONCLUSION

This review thoroughly examines how chatbots are used in English as a Foreign Language (EFL) education. It provides detailed insights into the approaches, results, and consequences of 11 different studies carried out from 2020 to 2023. This study carefully examines and combines research efforts focused on utilising chatbot technology to improve language learning results and revolutionise educational methods.

The discoveries revealed in this study emphasise the complex and varied research efforts in the field of AI-facilitated language learning. The reviewed research offers useful insights into the intricate connections among learners, technology, and educational situations by exploring variables including learning attainment, effectiveness, motivation, attitudes, perceptions, cognition, learning styles, and user experience. Researchers have used various methodologies such as quasi-experimental designs, mixed-

Table 1. The overview of reviewed articles

Authors	Title of the Article	Research Focus	Research Design	Data Collection Tools	Participants and context	Results
Yin & Satar (2020)	English as a foreign language learner interaction with Chatbots: negotiation for meaning	Studying the impact of pedagogical and conversational chatbots on negotiation for meaning and communication experiences among EFL learners.	Mixed-method approach	Pre- and post-tests, chat logs	EFL learners from China	Participants interacted with chatbots throughout language learning negotiations, adjusting their communication style according to their competence level and the type of chatbot. They also shared different preferences and experiences.
Belda-Medina & Caldo-Ferrer (2022)	Using Chatbots as AI Conversational Partners in Language Learning	Investigating the incorporation of artificial intelligence and chatbots in language learning settings and evaluating user happiness, perceived utility, and gender disparities in chatbot interactions among prospective teachers.	Sequential explanatory mixed-methods approach	Pre- and post-tests, specialized models (CHISM, TAM)	teacher candidates from Spain and Poland	Participants engaged with chatbots often, particularly favouring Replika. They had good views on the chatbots' effectiveness in language acquisition, however some had privacy worries.
Lin & Mubarok (2021)	Learning Analytics for Investigating the Mind Map-Guided AI Chatbot Approach in an EFL Flipped Speaking Classroom	Comparing the impact of using a mind map-guided AI chatbot strategy to a traditional AI chatbot approach on enhancing English speaking abilities in EFL students.	Quasi-experimental study	Audio recordings, chat transcripts	EFL students in a Taiwanese university	Students utilising mind map-guided AI chatbots demonstrated superior learning results and increased engagement in comparison to students utilising traditional AI chatbots.
Kohnke (2023)	L2 learners' perceptions of a chatbot as a potential independent language learning tool	Exploring how L2 learners at an English-medium institution perceive and experience using a chatbot for language acquisition.	Exploratory qualitative method	Online questionnaires, in-depth semi-structured interviews	L2 learners attending an English-medium university in Hong Kong	Students viewed chatbots as beneficial for language learning, especially in writing, but had reservations about the numerous technical choices available and proposed improvements.
Shaikh et al. (2023)	Assessing the Usability of ChatGPT for Formal English Language Learning	Evaluating the efficacy and usability of a chatbot tool (ChatGPT) for formal English language acquisition among students through usability testing.	Usability testing technique	Online registration forms, post-task questionnaires (USE, SUS)	students at the Norwegian University of Science and Technology (NTNU), Gjøvik	Participants mostly gave good feedback on the usability and perceived utility of ChatGPT for formal English language learning, particularly among male participants with moderate to high English language skills.
Kim et al. (2021)	Effects of AI Chatbots on EFL Students' Communication Skills	Evaluating how AI chatbot interactions affect the enhancement of speaking skills and students' opinions of AI chatbots in university English courses.	Pretest-posttest design	Pre and post-tests, surveys, observation	university students enrolled in English courses	Students demonstrated notable enhancement in pronunciation and speaking abilities following interactions with AI chatbots. They viewed the chatbots favourably for boosting involvement, despite encountering obstacles such as voice recognition difficulties.

continued on the following page

Table 1. Continued

Authors	Title of the Article	Research Focus	Research Design	Data Collection Tools	Participants and context	Results
Ebadi & Amini (2022)	Examining the roles of social presence and humanlikeness on Iranian EFL learners' motivation using artificial intelligence technology: a case of CSIEC chatbot	Studying the effects of a Chatbot-Based Social Interactive English Classroom (CSIEC) system on undergraduate students' motivation and their perceptions of social presence and human-likeness.	Sequential explanatory mixed-methods design	Standardized scales, structural equation modeling (SEM), thematic analysis	undergraduate students in Iran	The Chatbot-Based Social Interactive English Classroom had a good impact on student motivation by increasing social presence and human-likeness, improving conversational skills, and providing engaging learning experiences.
Jeon (2023)	Chatbot-assisted dynamic assessment (CA-DA) for L2 vocabulary learning and diagnosis	Studying the efficacy of chatbots in enhancing vocabulary learning in elementary school students and analysing the interactions between students and chatbots.	Cross-sectional survey methodology	Self-reported surveys, pre and post-tests	primary school learners in South Korea	The group that utilised chatbots for vocabulary learning did better than the control group. Qualitative analysis showed significant improvements in learner capacities throughout the sessions.
Hsu et al. (2023)	Proposing a task-oriented chatbot system for EFL learners speaking practice	Assessing the impact of a task-oriented chatbot system (TPBOT) on enhancing TOEIC speaking scores among university students	Experimental design	Pre and post-tests, post-intervention surveys	university students in Taiwan	Students that utilised TPBOT had notable enhancements in TOEIC speaking scores and expressed great satisfaction, crediting their advancement to regular practice with the chatbot.
Chien et al. (2022)	Investigation of the Influence of Artificial Intelligence Markup Language-Based LINE ChatBot in Contextual English Learning	Studying the effects of competition in a LINE ChatBot setting on the English speaking and listening skills and learning motivation of high school students	Quasi-experimental approach	Pre and post-tests, surveys	high school students in southern Taiwan	While there were no notable disparities in language skills, pupils who utilised chatbots with competition exhibited increased intrinsic drive towards learning English.
Liu & Ma (2023)	Measuring EFL learners' use of ChatGPT in informal digital learning of English based on the technology acceptance model	Investigating how ChatGPT is perceived and accepted by users in casual English language learning settings among ChatGPT users.	Cross-sectional survey methodology	Cross-sectional survey, modified TAM questionnaire	users from Chinese EFL backgrounds	Participants expressed great satisfaction with the use of ChatGPT for casual English learning. Structural equation modelling identified significant connections among perceived ease of use, usefulness, attitude, intention, and actual usage.

methods approaches, qualitative explorations, and usability testing to investigate specific questions and understand the complex dynamics involved in chatbot-mediated language learning interventions.

Furthermore, the flexibility and capacity to adjust of chatbot technology are key themes found in the examined research. Researchers have shown new uses of chatbots designed for certain learning goals, such as educational support, conversation practice, vocabulary development, and task-based learning. These many uses highlight the potential of chatbots to enhance language learning, customise learning experiences, increase student engagement, and support skill development in different language abilities.

This review also emphasises the subtle contextual details involved in designing and implementing chatbot-mediated language learning programmes. Researchers have gained useful insights into the effectiveness and acceptance of chatbots among distinct learner groups by analysing experiments undertaken in various educational settings across different geographies. Considering cultural backgrounds, educational environments, and learner demographics is crucial when designing and implementing chatbot interventions to provide more personalised and culturally sensitive language learning experiences.

This review adds to the growing discussion on AI-facilitated language acquisition by combining results from several studies, explaining research methods, and highlighting implications for future research and pedagogical approaches. This paper offers a detailed analysis of how chatbots are being incorporated into EFL learning and teaching. This synthesis promotes innovation, advances teaching methods, and enables stakeholders to navigate the changing terrain of language learning in the digital era.

REFERENCES

Belda-Medina, J., & Calvo-Ferrer, J. R. (2022). Using Chatbots as AI Conversational Partners in Language Learning. *Applied Sciences (Basel, Switzerland)*, *12*(17), 8427. doi:10.3390/app12178427

Bibauw, S., François, T., & Desmet, P. (2019). Discussing with a computer to practice a foreign language: Research synthesis and conceptual framework of dialogue-based CALL. *Computer Assisted Language Learning*, *32*(8), 827–877. doi:10.1080/09588221.2018.1535508

Bibauw, S., Van den Noortgate, W., François, T., & Desmet, P. (2022). Dialogue Systems for Language Learning: A MetaAnalysis. *Language Learning & Technology*, *26*(1), 1–24. https://hdl.handle.net/10125/73488

Can, I., Gelmez-Burakgazi, S., & Celik, I. (2019). An investigation of uses and gratifications for using web 2.0 technologies in teaching and learning processes. [IOJET]. *International Online Journal of Education & Teaching*, *6*(1), 88–102. https://www.iojet.org/index.php/IOJET/article/view/504

Chien, Y. C., Wu, T. T., Lai, C. H., & Huang, Y. M. (2022). Investigation of the influence of artificial intelligence markup language-based LINE ChatBot in contextual English learning. *Frontiers in Psychology*, *13*, 13. doi:10.3389/fpsyg.2022.785752 PMID:35465562

Coniam, D. (2014). The linguistic accuracy of chatbots: Usability from an ESL perspective. *Text & Talk*, *34*(5), 545–567. doi:10.1515/text-2014-0018

Ebadi, S., & Amini, A. (2022). Examining the roles of social presence and humanlikeness on Iranian EFL learners' motivation using artificial intelligence technology: A case of CSIEC chatbot. *Interactive Learning Environments*, 1–19. doi:10.1080/10494820.2022.2096638

Fryer, L., Coniam, D., Carpenter, R., & Lăpușneanu, D. (2020). *Bots for language learning now: Current and future directions.*

Fryer, L., & Nakao, K. (2009). Assessing chatbots for EFL learner use. In A. Stoke (Ed.), *Proceedings from JALT2008 Conference*. Tokyo: JALT.

Haristiani, N., & Danuwijaya, A. A. (2019). Gengobot: A chatbot-based grammar application on mobile instant messaging as language learning medium. *Journal of Engineering Science and Technology*, *14*(6), 3158–3173.

Haristiani, N., & Rifa'i, M. M. (2020). Combining Chatbot and Social Media: Enhancing Personal Learning Environment (PLE) in Language Learning. *Indonesian Journal of Science and Technology*, *5*(3), 487–506. doi:10.17509/ijost.v5i3.28687

Hsu, M. H., Chen, P. S., & Yu, C. S. (2023). Proposing a task-oriented chatbot system for EFL learners speaking practice. *Interactive Learning Environments*, *31*(7), 4297–4308. doi:10.1080/10494820.2021.1960864

Hwang, W. Y., Guo, B. C., Hoang, A., Chang, C. C., & Wu, N. T. (2022). Facilitating authentic contextual EFL speaking and conversation with smart mechanisms and investigating its influence on learning achievements. *Computer Assisted Language Learning*, 1–27. doi:10.1080/09588221.2022.2095406

Jeon, J. (2022). Exploring a self-directed interactive app for informal EFL learning: A self-determination theory perspective. *Education and Information Technologies*, *27*(4), 5767–5787. doi:10.1007/s10639-021-10839-y

Jeon, J. (2023). Chatbot-assisted dynamic assessment (CA-DA) for L2 vocabulary learning and diagnosis. *Computer Assisted Language Learning*, *36*(7), 1338–1364. doi:10.1080/09588221.2021.1987272

Jeon, J., Lee, S., & Choe, H. (2023). Beyond ChatGPT: A conceptual framework and systematic review of speech-recognition chatbots for language learning. *Computers & Education*, *206*, 104898. doi:10.1016/j.compedu.2023.104898

Jia, J., & Ruan, M. (2008). Use chatbot CSIEC to facilitate the individual learning in English instruction: A case study. In *International Conference on Intelligent Tutoring Systems* (706–708). Springer. Berlin, Heidelberg. 10.1007/978-3-540-69132-7_84

Kim, H. S., Cha, Y., & Kim, N. Y. (2020). Impact of mobile interactions with AI on writing performance. *Modern English Education*, *21*(2), 1–13. doi:10.18095/meeso.2020.21.2.1

Kim, H. S., Cha, Y., & Kim, N. Y. (2021). Effects of AI chatbots on EFL students' communication skills., *21*, 712-734.

Kim, N. (2017). Effects of different types of chatbots on EFL learners' speaking competence and learner perception. *Cross Cultural Studies*, *48*, 223–252. doi:10.21049/ccs.2017.48..223

Kim, N. Y. (2019). A Study on the use of Artificial Intelligence Chatbots for Improving English Grammar Skills. *Journal of Digital Convergence*, *17*(8), 37–46. doi:10.14400/JDC.2019.17.8.037

Kim, N.-Y., Cha, Y., & Kim, H.-S. (2019). Future English learning: Chatbots and artificial intelligence. *Multimedia Assisted Language Learning*, *22*(3), 32–53.

Kohnke, L. (2023). L2 learners' perceptions of a chatbot as a potential independent language learning tool. *International Journal of Mobile Learning and Organisation*, *17*(1-2), 214–226. doi:10.1504/IJMLO.2023.128339

Kohnke, L., Moorhouse, B. L., & Zou, D. (2023). ChatGPT for language teaching and learning. *RELC Journal*, 00336882231162868.

Laurillard, D. (2013). *Teaching as a design science: Building pedagogical patterns for learning and technology*. Routledge. doi:10.4324/9780203125083

Lin, C. J., & Mubarok, H. (2021). Learning analytics for investigating the mind map-guided AI chatbot approach in an EFL flipped speaking classroom. *Journal of Educational Technology & Society*, *24*(4), 16–35.

Liu, G., & Ma, C. (2023). Measuring EFL learners' use of ChatGPT in informal digital learning of English based on the technology acceptance model. *Innovation in Language Learning and Teaching*, 1–14.

Pimmer, C., Abiodun, R., Daniels, F., & Chipps, J. (2019). "I felt a sense of belonging somewhere". Supporting graduates' job transitions with WhatsApp groups. *Nurse Education Today*, *81*, 57–63. doi:10.1016/j.nedt.2019.06.010 PMID:31330403

Shadiev, R., & Liu, J. (2023). Review of research on applications of speech recognition technology to assist language learning. *ReCALL*, *35*(1), 74–88. doi:10.1017/S095834402200012X

Shaikh, S., Yayilgan, S. Y., Klimova, B., & Pikhart, M. (2023). Assessing the usability of ChatGPT for formal english language learning. *European Journal of Investigation in Health, Psychology and Education*, *13*(9), 1937–1960. doi:10.3390/ejihpe13090140 PMID:37754479

Shawar, B. A., & Atwell, E. (2015). ALICE chatbot: Trials and outputs. *Computación y Sistemas*, *19*(4), 625–632. doi:10.13053/cys-19-4-2326

Tai, T. Y., & Chen, H. H. J. (2020). The impact of Google Assistant on adolescent EFL learners' willingness to communicate. *Interactive Learning Environments*. doi:10.1080/10494820.2020.1841801

Tallyn, E., Fried, H., Gianni, R., Isard, A., & Speed, C. (2018). The ethnobot: Gathering ethnographies in the age of IoT. In *Proceedings of the 2018 CHI conference on human factors in computing systems* (pp. 1-13). IEEE. 10.1145/3173574.3174178

Thorne, S. L., & Black, R. W. (2007). Language and literacy development in computer-mediated contexts and communities. *Annual Review of Applied Linguistics*, *27*, 133–160. doi:10.1017/S0267190508070074

Wang, E. L., Matsumura, L. C., Correnti, R., Litman, D., Zhang, H., Howe, E., Magooda, A., & Quintana, R. (2020). Students' revision of text evidence use in an automated writing evaluation system. *Assessing Writing*, *44*, 100449. doi:10.1016/j.asw.2020.100449

Yin, Q., & Satar, M. (2020). English as a Foreign Language Learner Interactions with Chatbots: Negotiation for Meaning. *International Online Journal of Education & Teaching*, *7*(2), 390–410.

Zhang, S., Shan, C., Lee, J. S. Y., Che, S., & Kim, J. H. (2023). Effect of chatbot-assisted language learning: A meta-analysis. *Education and Information Technologies*, *28*(11), 1–21. doi:10.1007/s10639-023-11805-6

KEY TERMS AND DEFINITIONS

Artificial intellectual (AI): It refers to the emulation of human intellectual processes by technology, especially computer systems. AI technologies empower robots to carry out activities that usually need human intellect, such learning, problem-solving, comprehending natural language, and making decisions.

Chatbot: A chatbot is an artificial intelligence programme created to mimic communication with human users, usually through text or voice interactions. Chatbots can offer language practice and assistance to learners in the realm of language acquisition.

Computer-Assisted Language Learning (CALL): It refers to the utilisation of technology to aid and improve language learning tasks. CALL in AI chatbots refers to using chatbot technology into language learning platforms or software to offer learners interactive language practice and feedback.

Data Synthesis: The results of separate investigations are combined using suitable techniques such narrative synthesis, meta-analysis (where relevant), or theme analysis. Data synthesis entails condensing important discoveries, investigating patterns and connections, and pinpointing overarching themes or trends found in several investigations.

Negotiation for Meaning (NfM): It is the collaborative process when language learners work together to clarify and address communication failures during exchanges. NfM commonly happens in language learning situations when learners come across novel terminology or grammatical structures and ask for clarification from their conversation partners, whether they be human or AI-driven chatbots.

Second Language Acquisition (SLA): It is the process by which individuals acquire a language that is not their native language. The subject covers vocabulary acquisition, grammatical growth, and communicative skill in the target language.

Systematic Review: It is a thorough and detailed approach to combining information from several studies on a specific research issue or topic. It entails methodically finding, choosing, evaluating, and combining pertinent material to offer a comprehensive summary of the current evidence.

Technology Integration: It refers to integrating technological tools, resources, or platforms into educational environments to improve teaching and learning results. Technology integration in language learning involves using digital resources, multimedia materials, and AI-driven applications such as chatbots.

Chapter 17
Exploring the Secrets
Behind Chatbot Success
in Modern Banking:
A Systematic Literature Review

Saurabh Bhattacharya

iD https://orcid.org/0000-0002-2729-1835

Chitkara Business School, Chitkara University, Punjab, India

Babita Singla

iD https://orcid.org/0000-0002-8861-6859

Chitkara University, India

ABSTRACT

Chatbots, which provide a smooth and effective channel of contact, have completely changed the way companies engage with their clientele. This study explores the underlying technologies and procedures that underpin chatbot functioning, going deep into their complex workings. The chapter offers a thorough analysis of chatbot functionality and industry effects, ranging from machine learning methods to natural language processing. The abstract delves into the significance of user experience, emphasizing the importance of contextual understanding, personalization, and continuous learning in refining chatbot performance. Moreover, it touches upon challenges such as ethical considerations, biases, and limitations inherent in chatbot technology. In essence, this abstract encapsulates the multifaceted workings of chatbots, elucidating the amalgamation of linguistic processing, artificial intelligence, and machine learning that enables these conversational agents to navigate diverse user inputs and contribute to the evolving landscape of human-computer interaction.

DOI: 10.4018/979-8-3693-1830-0.ch017

INTRODUCTION

A social agent that converses with humans in natural language is called a chatbot. To serve across various websites, multiple chatbots are needed. The banking industry is facing a new revolutionary influence that is altering user communication: chatbots. Synthetic intelligence-powered chatbots have revolutionized the user experience, namely in the banking sector(Suhel et al., 2020). Any nation's banking industry has a significant impact on its finances. To determine if it can meet the constantly evolving demands of customers, it also evaluates the newest chatbot functionalities. The idea behind Chabot's is not novel. Nevertheless, the usage of bots has drawn businesses in recent years. Since their inception in the 1960s, chatbots have seen significant progress. The usage of chatbots as natural language screens by data and service providers is growing in prominence(Brandtzaeg & Følstad, 2017).

The emergence of chatbots as interactive systems raises questions about how to classify them and use this classification to analyze chatbot interaction design. It demonstrates compassion at the level of real-life employees, helping users deal with sensitive circumstances healthily(Xu et al., 2017). The classifications take into account key characteristics that set apart various chatbot kinds, such as who governs the interaction—the user or the chatbot—and the length of time humans communicate with chatbots (i.e., short- or long-term). Chatbots are now being used in domains including digital data management in the banking sector, Uniform Resource Locator (URL) creation, and respiratory therapy(Xu et al., 2017). Chatbots are one example of an Artificial Intelligence (AI) AI-based tool that businesses employ extensively to provide customer care(Dwivedi & Wang, 2022) (Agnihotri & Bhattacharya, 2023).

The ubiquitous presence of digital communication platforms has ushered in an era where conversing with machines has become an integral aspect of our daily lives. At the forefront of this transformation are chatbots, artificial intelligence (AI)-powered conversational agents designed to interact seamlessly with users. Understanding the intricacies of how chatbots work unveils a captivating journey into the realms of Natural Language Processing (NLP), machine learning, and the evolving landscape of human-computer interactions. This comprehensive exploration seeks to unravel the complexities of chatbot functionality, from the fundamental principles of linguistic comprehension to the cutting-edge technologies shaping their capabilities.

Evolution of Chatbot Architectures

The evolution of chatbots is rooted in their architectural frameworks, which have undergone remarkable transformations over the years. Early chatbots were rule-based systems, relying on predefined sets of instructions to respond to user inputs. However, with advancements in machine learning, contemporary chatbots leverage sophisticated algorithms and models to understand and generate human-like responses. This section delves into the historical trajectory of chatbot architectures, tracing the shift from rule-based systems to the integration of machine learning models, such as recurrent neural networks (RNNs) and transformer architectures. The evolution of chatbot architectures traces a captivating journey from rudimentary rule-based systems to the sophisticated models that characterize contemporary conversational agents. In the nascent stages of chatbot development, rule-based architectures relied on predefined sets of instructions to respond to user inputs, creating a deterministic framework with limited adaptability. These early chatbots operated on a set of programmed rules that dictated specific responses based on recognized keywords. However, as technology advanced, the limitations of rule-based systems became apparent, prompting a paradigm shift towards machine learning-based architectures. The integration of machine learning marked a transformative phase, enabling chatbots to move beyond rigid rules and leverage algorithms to learn from data. Recurrent Neural Networks (RNNs) emerged as pivotal in capturing sequential dependencies in language, allowing chatbots to better understand and generate contextually relevant responses. The evolution continued with the advent of transformer architectures, exemplified by models like OpenAI's GPT series, which revolutionized language understanding by processing information in parallel, capturing long-range dependencies, and demonstrating an unprecedented proficiency in generating coherent and contextually aware responses. These architectures, fueled by the exponential growth of available data and computational power, signify a monumental shift in how chatbots operate, emphasizing adaptability, context sensitivity, and the ability to simulate human-like conversation. The trajectory from rule-based systems through machine learning models showcases the relentless pursuit of creating chatbots that not only comprehend user inputs but also engage in dynamic, contextually rich dialogues, marking a transformative evolution in the very fabric of human-computer interaction.

Natural Language Processing (NLP)

Central to the operation of chatbots is their proficiency in Natural Language Processing. NLP empowers chatbots to decipher the intricacies of human language, enabling them to comprehend user queries and formulate contextually relevant responses. This section provides an in-depth examination of NLP techniques, including tokenization, semantic analysis, and entity recognition, that underpin the chatbot's ability to extract intent and key information from user inputs. Natural Language Processing (NLP) is the bedrock upon which the conversational prowess of chatbots is built, representing a sophisticated intersection of linguistics, computer science, and artificial intelligence. At its essence, NLP empowers chatbots to comprehend, interpret, and respond to human language in a manner that simulates natural conversation. Within the realm of chatbots, NLP serves as the cognitive engine that enables these digital entities to decipher the nuances of language, transforming user inputs into actionable insights. The process begins with tokenization, where the input text is broken down into individual units, often words or phrases, to facilitate analysis. Semantic analysis follows, allowing the chatbot to grasp the meaning behind the words, discern user intent, and extract key information. Entity recognition further refines this understanding by identifying specific entities, such as names, locations, or dates, within the user's message. These fundamental NLP tasks collectively contribute to the chatbot's ability to not only comprehend the syntactic structure of language but also infer the user's purpose and context. Additionally, sentiment analysis within NLP enables chatbots to discern the emotional tone embedded in user messages, fostering a more empathetic and personalized interaction. Through continuous advancements in machine learning algorithms and models, NLP in chatbots has evolved beyond mere linguistic processing, embracing contextual understanding, contextual disambiguation, and even the generation of human-like responses. As the cornerstone of the chatbot's language proficiency, NLP ensures that these digital conversational agents navigate the intricate nuances of human language, facilitating seamless and meaningful interactions that transcend the limitations of conventional human-computer interfaces.

Machine Learning in Chatbots

Machine learning plays a pivotal role in enhancing chatbot capabilities. Through continuous learning from vast datasets, chatbots refine their understanding of language nuances, user preferences, and contextual relevance. The section explores the integration of machine learning algorithms, including supervised and unsupervised learning, as well as reinforcement learning, in training chatbots to adapt and evolve based on user interactions. Machine Learning (ML) constitutes a pivotal component in the architecture of chatbots, fostering a dynamic and adaptive capability that transcends traditional rule-based systems. At its core, ML empowers chatbots to learn from data, enabling them to improve their performance over time through continuous refinement of their models. This facet of chatbot development represents a departure from static programming, allowing these conversational agents to evolve and enhance their proficiency in understanding and generating human-like responses. Supervised learning, a prevalent ML technique in chatbots, involves training the model on labeled datasets where inputs and corresponding outputs are provided. This enables the chatbot to learn patterns and associations, extrapolating from known examples to respond appropriately to new, unseen inputs. Unsupervised learning further augments the chatbot's capabilities by allowing it to identify patterns and relationships in data without explicit guidance, facilitating a more nuanced understanding of language nuances and user context. Reinforcement learning introduces an interactive dimension, where the chatbot learns through trial and error, receiving rewards for favorable responses and penalties for less effective ones. This iterative learning process imbues chatbots with adaptability and the capacity to fine-tune their behavior based on user feedback.

The integration of machine learning in chatbots extends beyond understanding user inputs; it encompasses the generation of contextually relevant and coherent responses. Seq2Seq (Sequence-to-Sequence) models, often based on Recurrent Neural Networks (RNNs) or transformers, exemplify this integration. These models enable chatbots to process sequential information in a manner akin to understanding the flow of conversation, ensuring that responses are contextually aligned and syntactically coherent. The use of attention mechanisms in these models further refines the ability to focus on specific parts of the input sequence, enhancing the chatbot's understanding of nuanced conversations and diverse language structures. (Galitsky & Goldberg, 2019). It highlights the significance of understandable ML characteristics and the requirement for ML models that are visible and understandable to users. (Galitsky & Goldberg, 2019) shows an instance of a chatbot-related categorization issue handled using visible rule-based or ML approaches, talks about the idea of understandable machine learning and its significance for individuals, and proposes a chatbot that offers justifications for its choices. Providers of services must respond to clients' increasing need for prompt and insightful solutions. Chatbots, essentially AI-based models of human speech, have surfaced as a quicker and more straightforward way to automate consumer interactions to address this requirement. Using machine learning, chatbots are not just for basic product-related inquiries; they may also offer sophisticated forecasting(Nath & Sagnika, 2020).

The continuous learning paradigm in machine learning aligns seamlessly with the iterative nature of human-computer interactions, allowing chatbots to adapt to evolving user preferences and linguistic patterns. This adaptability is particularly crucial in the dynamic landscape of conversations, where user inputs can vary widely in terms of context, tone, and intent. As machine learning algorithms become more sophisticated, chatbots equipped with ML capabilities are poised to deliver more personalized, context-aware, and effective interactions, positioning them as invaluable assets in diverse applications ranging from customer support and virtual assistants to educational tools and beyond.

Recurrent Neural Networks (RNNs) and Transformers

The rise of deep learning architectures has significantly contributed to the sophistication of chatbot models. Recurrent Neural Networks (RNNs) and transformer architectures have become instrumental in capturing contextual dependencies and improving the sequential nature of language understanding. This section provides insights into how these neural network structures enable chatbots to process sequential information and generate more coherent and contextually relevant responses.

APIs and Pre-Trained Language Models

Advancements in chatbot technology extend to the integration of Application Programming Interfaces (APIs) and pre-trained language models. APIs facilitate seamless connectivity with external services, enriching the chatbot's capabilities by accessing real-time information and performing specific tasks. Pre-trained language models, such as OpenAI's GPT (Generative Pre-trained Transformer), contribute to chatbot proficiency by leveraging vast amounts of pre-existing knowledge to generate more contextually aware and coherent responses.

User Experience and Personalization

The success of a chatbot hinges on its ability to provide a positive and personalized user experience. Understanding user intent, preferences, and the context of the conversation is crucial for delivering tailored responses. This section explores how chatbots leverage user data, feedback loops, and contextual understanding to enhance user experiences, fostering a sense of natural and intuitive interaction. While chatbots can save organizations money and improve productivity, they frequently fall short of consumer expectations because of their inappropriate, imprecise, and hard-to-grasp answers to queries(Telner, 2021).

Theoretical Background

In 1954, the phrase "Artificial Intelligence" (AI) was first used(*Review*, n.d.). According to its definition, it is "the capacity of machines to emulate sophisticated human behavior, particularly learning and problem-solving."(Batra et al., 2020) (Michalski et al., 2013). It describes a branch of computer science concerned with the behavior, comprehension, and sense-making of systems of information. Recent investigations in a variety of sectors have examined the use and significance of AI. Artificial intelligence (AI) has been studied in business and management in connection with banking, HRM, and promotional activities in particular(Harrison et al., 2022) (Wirtz et al., 2018). A greater spectrum of enterprises may now access it more easily thanks to the advancements in analytics tools and approaches. Experience in marketing analytics is becoming more and more in demand as digital and mobile technologies continue to influence marketing. Another of the hottest subjects in AI right now is chatbots. Because of the available information, ChatGPT (by OpenAI) is one of the latest and most popular chatbots(Karimov et al., 2024). The use of chatbots as decision-supporting tools and their impact on client delight. Thanks to improvements in technology, digital service agents, or "e-service agents," may now interact with customers in real-time to improve their services and meet their demands (Mariani et al., 2023) (Chung et al., 2020).

With chatbots, people may communicate with computers via text and speech. Computer programs provide multimodal, spoken, text-based, and conversational engagements with people. CAs are changing how businesses operate by offering chances to save expenses, enhance service quality, and boost customer involvement (Bavaresco et al., 2020) (Wirtz & Zeithaml, 2018). In certain instances, customers feel more at ease dealing with robots than with people(Mende et al., 2019), even though they may find it uncomfortable to do so in general(Kim et al., 2022) (Lucas et al., 2017). Adolescents were more inclined to discuss their bad life events with a robot counselor than with an actual one. Another approach that customers might take to save face is online buying, as it eliminates the need for in-person contact with staff members or other customers(Krishna et al., 2019).

RESEARCH METHODOLOGY AND OBJECTIVE

Scholars have been studying how chatbots are used, what influences consumers' adoption of them, and how to make chatbot adoption more efficient by developing novel algorithms and systems. Throughout several years, there has been considerable growth in the number of investigations on chatbots, which may render it challenging for academics to traverse the field and pinpoint areas that require further study. This study aims to close the gap by offering a thorough summary of research from academia on chatbots.

Numerous studies have been published that only concentrate on the creation of chatbots; however, this analysis recognizes the importance of conducting multidisciplinary research and, as a result, it concentrates on studies that show the distinct commercial consequences of the application and creation of chatbots and are directed towards a variety of different consumers, most notably consumers.

The methodical approach of searching the literature for publications on Chatbots is covered in this chapter. The process of identifying, assessing, and interpreting all of the available study material while addressing pertinent research questions is known as a systematic literature review (SLR). Additionally, this well-defined procedure aids in pinpointing specific areas of potential(Hao et al., 2019).

Three stages were taken to find and evaluate pertinent publications for this systematic literature review: i) First database scan; ii) Filtering for titles and abstracts; iii) Comprehensive full-text assessment.

Figure 1. Study database

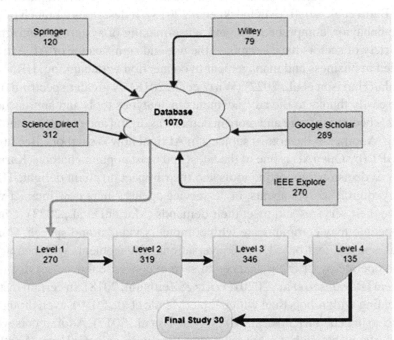

Figure 2. Database used for the search

Source	Website
Scopus	https://www.scopus.com
IEEE Xplore	https://ieeexplore.ieee.org
Google Scholar	https://scholar.google.com
Springer	https://www.springer.com
ScienceDirect	https://www.sciencedirect.com

RQ1: What are the current trends in the banking industry regarding the adoption and application of chatbots for customer support, and what factors motivate these trends?

RQ2: How do professionals in the banking sector view the use of chatbots in the future to boost customer service and streamline operations in banks? What are their opinions, attitudes, and experiences?

A total of 1070 research articles were identified and after final consideration, 30 quality articles were shortlisted for the SLR as shown in **Figure 1**. The database used for the search is shown in **Figure 2**.

LITERATURE REVIEW

In an article (Belen Saglam et al., 2021) age was a key determinant; those over 45 expressed greater anxiety than people under 45, although gender and educational attainment had no discernible impact on these worries. To build confidence in chatbots, users concentrate on technical aspects like response quality; Furthermore, younger people value friendliness and other social aspects like avatars higher than older people do (Belen Saglam et al., 2021). (Suhel et al., 2020) introduces a new concept addressing machine intelligence's potential and emphasizes the rise of chatbots in the finance sector, transforming customer interactions in banking. The article by (Vaziri et al., 2017) presents a compiler that uses the Swagger Application Programming Interfaces (API) specs to generate chatbots. It overcomes Swagger's drawbacks by enabling users to communicate with the chatbot and enhance its functionality. Among the most common types of APIs is REST API(Punjabi et al., 2019). Most banks have a huge database and this data is made available by RESTful API. While communicating with chatbots instead of human operators, customers experience less embarrassment, particularly when self-presentation issues are prevalent. Customers who are more self-conscious about how they show themselves are more likely to presume a chatbot is genuine when its persona is unclear as a way to avoid embarrassing oneself. Users, nevertheless, react better to chatbots compared to human beings once the chatbot's persona is made obvious, particularly if the chatbot is anthropomorphized. The impact depends on how much the chatbot is humanized; customers who care more about how they look sometimes give even clearly identifiable chatbot human features, which might elicit a more unfavorable reply from customers(Jin et al., n.d.).

Another researcher stresses how crucial it is to take user incentives into account while designing chatbots(Brandtzaeg & Følstad, 2017). Potential conversations among humans and chatbots can be shaped by a conscious awareness of user motives.

(Xu et al., 2017) highlights the rising trend of people using social media sites to look for customer support. The efficiency with which it generates customized solutions indicates the growing need for individualized online interactions. Because of the way it handles and interprets data, the chatbot is positioned as a useful tool for companies looking to enhance consumer relationships. Consumers who shop online are using individualized systems for identification that are powered by deep learning technology(Xu et al., 2017).

NLP-based algorithms have become essential resources for mimicking human-like communication in the rapidly changing world of chatbots and AI-powered assistants(Abu Shawar & Atwell, 2007) (Alabbas & Alomar, 2024).

Customer assistance and automation have become a common use case for these AI-powered organizations. Particularly, the subject of natural language processing (NLP) has been integrated with artificial intelligence (AI) within computer and technology areas. By using natural language, this area of artificial intelligence (AI) makes it possible for chatbots to communicate verbally as well as via texts between other bots or people (Alabbas & Alomar, 2024) (Al-Madi et al., 2021) (Adamopoulou & Moussiades, 2020).

When users communicate with a chatbot, it delivers them speedy and pleasant support; it also gives them more interesting replies that address their issues head-on(Adamopoulou & Moussiades, 2020) (Ranoliya et al., 2017).

Another article emphasizes the importance of chatbots in artificial intelligence (AI) conversation imitation in a given environment. Because these applications are affordable and can multitask, they are widely used in commercial settings for a variety of purposes, from query responding to workload management(Ranoliya et al., 2017). Consumers view chatbots as kind allies rather than merely helpful aides. Chatbots are now capable of responding to customers on an emotional level because of advancements in machine learning and sentiment analysis.

The level of confidence that a chatbot acquires from its usage is determined by variables about its behavior, look, producer, concerns regarding privacy, and security(Epstein et al., 2007). The degree to which the chatbot is human-like—a measure of its degree of resemblance to a human being based on factors like personality, visual traits, and ease of understanding human language—also contributes to the growth of this trusting connection(Go & Sundar, 2019).

Higher levels of interaction are associated with higher levels of online visibility and involvement by users. Researchers and designers have put a lot of effort into making chatbots seem more human. Chatbots can appear more human by adding human-like visual cues, which can also affect how users perceive them. This is a result of people's innate tendency to associate human characteristics with visual stimuli that resemble humans(Go & Sundar, 2019). Chatbots that include anthropomorphic traits, such as names, visual signals, and linguistic styles, have been engineered to resemble individuals(Sun et al., 2024). They may be connected with websites, mobile applications, and chat systems to respond to often-asked inquiries, provide coupon coupons, and customize communications for specific clients.

Studies indicate that the human-like characteristics of chatbots may result in increased client happiness and a psychological connection with the business, but they can also cause unfulfilled demands, which could lead to bad user experiences(Sun et al., 2024). One of the most effective methods for reconnecting with clients with paid communications is chatbot marketing. (Sun et al., 2024). Chatbot Advertising messaging can be presented as a narrative or as facts. (Sun et al., 2024). According to the research, anthropomorphism, messaging communication, and story components can all improve the persuasion of chatbot advertisements. In particular, using a conversational chatbot with a profile that resembles a machine in storytelling advertisements might increase favorable sentiments toward the advertisement, indicating that this is a powerful technique for chatbot promotion. (Sun et al., 2024).

The article (Araujo, 2018) shows that various systems and consumer feature setups for anthropomorphic and non-anthropomorphic chatbots impact cognitive retention. Combining AI and humans can increase chatbot adoption among consumers. The communication impact of human-AI teamwork is mediated by perceived efficacy (Li et al., 2024).

Artificial intelligence (AI)-driven chatbots can completely transform online marketing by enabling more casual and less invasive interactions with customers. Poor performance of the chatbot program may affect the restoration techniques that users use. Customers are more likely to want the chatbot to assist in recovering service following an operational breakdown than they are to favor human engagement following an inactive breakdown(Xing et al., 2022).

User worries over the security of data, AI ethics, and security have increased with the emergence of AI technologies. Users hold the system or business more accountable when there is a robot operation outage(Xing et al., 2022). Although chatbots are supposed to respond to consumer queries via text messages, frequent service outages occur. Consumers might believe that robots can accomplish activities that people can, but they are not always flawless(Xing et al., 2022). Chatbot reliability is influenced by a sense of safety, competence, compassion, and anthropomorphism. Bad reputation and consumer goodwill are influenced by these characteristics(Xing et al., 2022). Not every robot is flawless. The results of the study by (Song et al., 2023) suggest that expressing gratitude is a more effective way to build a positive human-chatbot connection than apologizing for the chatbot's shortcomings.

In place of employing human workers for activities and interactions, artificial intelligence (AI) technology is frequently deployed in the customer service sector(Song et al., 2022).

User attitudes and actions are influenced by chatbot cognitive ability, with extremely intelligent chatbots improving user interaction. It is worthwhile for social media networks to investigate the extent to which robot awareness might favorably influence customer views and actions(Song et al., 2022). Customer support departments are using chatbots in increasing numbers, and how well they're designed can affect how well they work. Nowadays, there are obstacles in the way of using chatbots as direct service representatives, such as working through the "proxy agency dilemma" and creating "collective agency."(Chong et al., 2021)

Surveys have shown that when AI-powered chatbots don't work, people are upset, perplexed, and unhappy. Like people, chatbots need to carry out their tasks and demonstrate how to manage client relationships(Agnihotri & Bhattacharya, 2023; Castillo et al., 2021). Businesses are expected to face even greater challenges as a result of low chatbot acceptability when chatbots try to rectify customer care failures.

Chatbots are a useful tool for retrieving services in both hedonistic and functional categories of products. Because chatbots are seen as trustworthy, customers are more likely to overlook service errors made by the company and to propagate bad word of mouth.

(Agnihotri & Bhattacharya, 2023). Chatbots are now a cutting-edge method of communicating with customers(Shumanov & Johnson, 2021) (Chung et al., 2020).

Despite the advantages, customers' happiness with chatbots varies because of annoyances like misinterpreted queries, pointless answers, and inadequate interaction with customer support representatives. The main purposes of chatbots are to increase productivity by cutting expenses for businesses, decreasing client wait times, and complying with consumer desires for electronic interaction(Shumanov & Johnson, 2021). In social and commercial interactions and relationships, trust is essential. Robotics approval is known to be influenced by trust. Trust is at the core of relationships between people and machines because humans socially respond to technology (Huang et al., 2024).

Successful user conversations are brief in terms of words and messages but well-structured in terms of the flow of the conversation—free from stops and repetitions of greetings and other typical material.

Specifically, inaccurate responses have a detrimental impact on customer satisfaction. Successful conversations increase with the naturalness of the engagement and the fraction of accurate chatbot replies. (Rese & Tränkner, 2024). Typical terms should be used as little as possible by the chatbot, and the person using it should be able to enter the discussion with sincerity. When it comes to text-based chatbots, women appear to have fewer achievements. Consequently, to boost their broad acceptability, further research is needed to determine what makes individuals feel at ease while interacting with artificial conversation systems. (Rese & Tränkner, 2024)

Due to its fluid text production, OpenAI's chatbot ChatGPT, which was released on November 30, 2022, has drawn a lot of public interest(Taecharungroj, 2023) (Dwivedi et al., 2023). Enhancing a chatbot's ability to have conversations can increase its user interface attractiveness and efficiency(Schuetzler et al., 2020).

Another study investigates how customers react to various digital assistants employed by merchants while they purchase. It discovers that customers may become more resistant to digital assistants that don't seem like humans. This reluctance has an impact on how tough decisions are thought to be made, which has an effect on choice assurance, perceived effectiveness, and happiness in the end. It's essential to note that better contentment is the result of this opposition. The research also observes that although the user's or the system's activation of the virtual assistant does not start this series of events, it does affect how the program appears. In particular, people exhibit less reluctance when dealing with consumer-activated human-like digital assistants. Generally speaking, resistance is greatest to digital assistants that resemble non-humans and are triggered by computers(Pizzi et al., 2021).

Three aspects impact customer outcomes after interacting with chatbots: customized contextual trust in one's chatbot service-giver, behavioral trust in service technology, and generic learned confidence in chatbots (Huang et al., 2024).

In an article by (Chang et al., 2022), an increasingly prevalent social network service is utilized to install an anti-fraud chatbot as a prime example of the paradigm. The goal of this deployment is to handle financial fraud cases and offer anti-fraud recommendations for handling fraud incidents that are anticipated.

A key component of fintech is an AI-powered chatbot. To gain a competitive edge in the market, the banking industry is aggressively using chatbots. AI-powered chatbots have the potential to compromise user confidentiality and safety. Cybersecurity is becoming a crucial concern that chatbots need to be aware of(Lai et al., 2019).

Conversational agents (CAs) driven by artificial intelligence, or chatbots, are finding increased use in a variety of domains, including marketing, customer support, education, healthcare, and entertainment. They are taking the place of human chat operators in e-commerce to provide real-time consumer support(Singh et al., 2023).

Users' happiness with chatbot-based assistance is positively impacted by the caliber of the details and services provided. Furthermore, consumers' intentions to keep using chatbots are significantly predicted by their perceptions of their satisfaction, utility, and convenience of use (Ashfaq et al., 2020). Users are more likely to return for more discussions if they understand the bot's functions and how to achieve their goals swiftly(Telner, 2021). The chatbot is supposed to offer alternatives and answer recommendations to motivate recipients' interest and assist them in initiating and carrying on a discussion. Those who might be unsure of what to say or are puzzled might benefit from this. The chatbot may relieve user strain, sustain traction, and keep the discussion going by offering alternatives (Telner, 2021).

A chatbot is a piece of computer software that can mimic a dialogue with an individual, interpret human speech, and potentially communicate via other bots on the network(Bhutada et al., 2024). The goal of giving chatbots a more human-like character is to communicate brand values and produce satisfying user interactions. Chatbots are being used by brands more and more in support of clients(Palomino & Arbaiza, 2023). The onus is on the creators of social chatbots to make them beneficial and compassionate as AI permeates additional facets of daily life, guaranteeing the community overall gains from its broad adoption(Shum et al., 2018).

CHATBOTS IN BANKING

Artificial intelligence (AI) chatbots used in banking are virtual assistants that answer questions and help clients. (Rukavina, 2024). The old, detached, and sluggish client service is giving way to helpful, quick, and customized treatment. For precise, instantaneous responses to frequently asked questions on accounts, interest rates, fees, branch locations, and other topics, chatbots leverage bank databases. Intent-based, rule-based, and AI assistants are your options, based on what your bank requires. Their degree of complexity and comprehension of user intent varies. Some of the types and their use cases with examples are shown in below **Figures 3 and Figure 4.**

Key Motivational Factors

- Users cite productivity as their main motivation for utilizing chatbots.
- Chatbots are used by users to get information and help quickly and effectively.
- While engaging with chatbots, individuals are driven by leisure considerations.
- Conversations with chatbots are also sparked by curiosity about this new phenomenon.
- People interact with chatbots for interpersonal and societal purposes.
- Although there are other reasons why chatbot users employ them, such as amusement, social aspects, and unique interactions, productivity is the primary driver (Adamopoulou & Moussiades, 2020).

Figure 3. Common use cases of chatbot applications

Use Cases	Description	References
Customer Support	Assist customers with account inquiries, history, and general banking information.	(How Generative AI Is Already Transforming Customer Service, 2023)
Account Management	Facilitate account balance inquiries, fund transfers, and bill payment assistance.	(How Generative AI Is Already Transforming Customer Service, 2023)
Personalized Financial Advice	Offer tailored guidance on investment opportunities, savings, and financial planning.	(How Generative AI Is Already Transforming Customer Service, 2023)
Loan Application Processing	Assist customers in initiating loan applications and guiding them through the process.	(How Generative AI Is Already Transforming Customer Service, 2023)
Product Recommendations	Recommend banking products and services based on customer behavior and preferences.	("17 ChatGPT Use Cases for Banks and Finance," n.d.)
Fraud Monitoring	Actively monitor customer accounts for potential fraudulent activities and alert customers.	(How Generative AI Is Already Transforming Customer Service, 2023)
Appointment Scheduling	Allow customers to schedule appointments with bank representatives for specific services.	(How Generative AI Is Already Transforming Customer Service, 2023)
Branch Location and Hours	Provide information about nearest branch locations, operating hours, and available services.	("17 ChatGPT Use Cases for Banks and Finance," n.d.)
Onboarding	Aid new customers in opening accounts and guide them through documentation and setup processes.	("17 ChatGPT Use Cases for Banks and Finance," n.d.)
Credit Score Monitoring	Offer real-time access to credit scores and provide tips for improving creditworthiness.	("17 ChatGPT Use Cases for Banks and Finance," n.d.)
Card Services	Assist with card services such as activation, reporting lost or stolen cards, and transaction inquiries.	("17 ChatGPT Use Cases for Banks and Finance," n.d.)
Budgeting Assistance	Provide tools for customers to set budgeting goals, track expenses, and receive personalized recommendations.	("17 ChatGPT Use Cases for Banks and Finance," n.d.)
Bill Reminders and Alerts	Send proactive alerts and reminders about upcoming bill payments and account statements.	("17 ChatGPT Use Cases for Banks and Finance," n.d.)
Investment Portfolio Tracking	Enable customers to monitor investment portfolios, review performance, and receive insights on market trends.	("17 ChatGPT Use Cases for Banks and Finance," n.d.)
Educational Resources	Offer educational materials on finance, banking products, and financial literacy to customers.	("17 ChatGPT Use Cases for Banks and Finance," n.d.)
Language Support	Provide multilingual support to accommodate customers who prefer to communicate in different languages.	("17 ChatGPT Use Cases for Banks and Finance," n.d.)
Overdraft Notifications	Alert customers when account balances are at risk of overdrawing and provide prevention options.	("17 ChatGPT Use Cases for Banks and Finance," n.d.)
Insurance Assistance	Offer information about insurance products, coverage details, and support during claim initiation.	("17 ChatGPT Use Cases for Banks and Finance," n.d.)
Retirement Planning	Provide retirement planning tools, calculators, and advice on retirement investment options.	("17 ChatGPT Use Cases for Banks and Finance," n.d.)
Transaction History Review	Enable customers to review transaction history, categorize expenses, and analyze spending patterns.	(Rukavina, 2024)

Figure 4. Different types of chatbot and its application

Type of Chatbot	Description	Use Case	Example
Rule-Based Chatbots	Operate based on a pre-defined set of rules and can only respond to specific commands or keywords. They do not have the capability to learn or understand language beyond their programmed rules	FAQ and Information Retrieval: Providing quick responses to frequently asked questions such as account balances, branch locations, and interest rates on the bank's website or mobile app	**Human:** "Hello! I'm interested in knowing the current interest rates for savings accounts." **Bot (Rule-Based):** "Welcome! The interest rate for our savings accounts is currently 1.5% per annum. For more information or to compare other account options, please let me know."
AI-Powered Chatbots	Leverage artificial intelligence and machine learning to understand natural language, learn from interactions, and provide more human-like responses. They continuously improve their understanding and responses over time.	Financial Assistant: Offering personalized financial advice, budgeting tips, and investment recommendations based on individual financial profiles, transaction history, and financial goals.	**Human:** "I want to invest some money, but I'm not sure where to start. Can you help?" **Bot (AI-Powered):** "Of course! To provide personalized investment advice, could you please share your investment goals and risk tolerance level with me? This will help me recommend suitable options for you."
Retrieval-Based Chat	Match user queries with the most appropriate response from a database of predefined answers. They do not generate language but select the best-matching response based on the input.	Customer Support and Account Management: Handling customer inquiries related to account management, transaction history, card activation, and standard banking procedures with instant and accurate responses.	**Human:** "I need to activate my new debit card. How can I do this?" **Bot (Retrieval-Based):** "To activate your new debit card, please log in to your online banking account and navigate to the 'Card Services' section. You can follow the instructions there to activate your card instantly."
Generative Chatbots	Use advanced natural language processing techniques such as deep learning, to generate responses in real-time. These chatbots can create human-like responses and are not limited to pre-defined responses, allowing for more dynamic and contextually relevant interactions.	Complex Query Handling and Product Recommendations: Engaging in open-ended conversations to address inquiries about sophisticated banking products like mortgages, investment portfolios, and retirement planning, providing personalized product recommendations.	**Human:** "I'm thinking about buying a house. Can you explain the different types of mortgages available?" **Bot (Generative):** "Certainly! There are various types of mortgages available, including fixed-rate mortgages, adjustable-rate mortgages, and FHA loans. Fixed-rate mortgages offer stable monthly payments, while adjustable-rate mortgages may have fluctuating rates. FHA loans are backed by the Federal Housing Administration and typically have lower down payment requirements. Would you like more details on any specific type?"

The framework establishes a standard for using AI in social media customer support initiatives. It suggests that to improve client interactions on the internet, computerized but sympathetic exchanges may become more prevalent(Xu et al., 2017). It is a flexible answer for interpersonal requirements across a range of industries because of its efficacy and versatility. The long-term impacts of anthropomorphism in chatbot encounters might be investigated in more detail. Investigating how chatbot design might improve buyer happiness and connection to emotions(Araujo, 2018). Additional studies might examine the moderating effects of particular organizational characteristics on the association between the use of chatbots and their results. Research might look at the advantages of chatbots for work vs non-work for workers as well as other business consequences that emerge from using them in companies(Wang et al., 2022).

FINDING AND ANALYSIS

The paper's results section is structured to offer information for addressing the study objectives. The primary research question (RQ1) relates to determining the chatbot's subject matter and uses. The majority of study investigations center on how people see and embrace chatbots.

Investigators looked at the characteristics and criteria that influence consumers' acceptance of chatbots, determining whether or not their use eventually led to a higher or lower level of acceptability. This addresses our research question (RQ2).

Artificial intelligence and natural language processing technologies are used by chatbots to comprehend the structure of phrases, digest that data, and gradually improve their ability to respond to the user's inquiry. Chatbots replicate human interaction and respond to user requests by using a variety of technologies and algorithms. This is a condensed description of how chatbots operate:

The issue of chatbot operation is both intricate and exciting. Natural language processing (NLP) and machine learning techniques power chatbots. The chatbot can comprehend and react to human input conversationally thanks to these algorithms.

There are several crucial phases in the process:

User Input: A chatbot accepts input from users when they type a message or give it an order.

Natural language processing, or NLP, enables the chatbot to comprehend human input. To do this, the text must be parsed to determine the message's meaning and intent.

Figure 5. Typical workflow of a chatbot

Step	Description
Input Processing	Analyzing user input through natural language processing (NLP) to understand the user's intent, context, and extract relevant information.
Intent Recognition	Identifying the user's intent based on the input received, determining the reason for the user's message, such as seeking information, making a request, or asking a question.
Data Retrieval or Generation	Retrieving pre-defined responses from a database or generating responses using machine learning algorithms based on the recognized intent and knowledge acquired through training data.
Response Generation	Formulating a response based on the recognized intent and available data, potentially leveraging personalization based on user history or preferences.
Output Delivery	Delivering the generated response back to the user through text, voice, or actionable outputs such as initiating transactions or updating records in systems.
Learning and Improvement	Using machine learning processes to continuously improve responses over time by learning from user interactions, enhancing the chatbot's understanding and effectiveness.
Integration with Systems	Coordinating with backend systems and databases for accessing and retrieving relevant information to provide real-time, accurate responses to users.

Figure 6. Chatbot flow

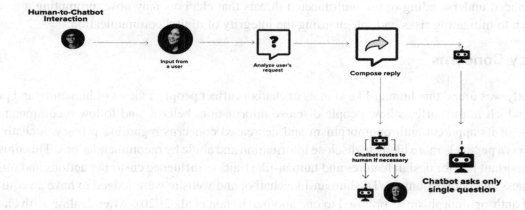

Intent Recognition: The chatbot chooses the right answer by identifying the user's intent based on the input it has received. Using machine learning models to classify user input and determine the user's intended goal is known as intent recognition.

Data Retrieval and Processing: To deliver a precise response, the chatbot would require access to a database or outside information sources. This might entail interacting with other systems, using APIs, or doing queries against a knowledge repository.

Response Generation: The chatbot uses established templates or language generation models to construct a response after determining the user's intent and retrieving the required data. The user is then informed of this response.

Learning and Improvement: A lot of chatbots have machine learning built in, which enables them to pick up tips from users and gradually get better at what they do. Chatbots can adjust to novel situations and user preferences thanks to this ongoing learning process.

It's crucial to explore the particular tools and algorithms used in NLP and machine learning for chatbots in a review paper on this subject. Furthermore, talking about the difficulties and developments in the industry, together with practical uses and potential future directions, would give a thorough rundown of chatbot functionality. It's fascinating to know how chatbots will affect different businesses, like e-commerce, healthcare, and customer service. To put it briefly, natural language processing (NLP), machine learning, intent identification, data retrieval, answer generation, and continuous learning are all combined to operate with chatbots. A review paper on this subject would explore the intricacies of these procedures, as well as their uses, difficulties, and the changing field of chatbot technology.

Threat

While chatbots have emerged as valuable tools in enhancing digital interactions, it is essential to scrutinize their potential threats to users, organizations, and the broader digital ecosystem. This comprehensive exploration delves into the darker aspects of chatbot deployment, examining issues such as privacy concerns, security vulnerabilities, ethical implications, and the potential for misinformation. The research sheds light on how malicious actors can exploit chatbots for nefarious purposes, the risks associated with data breaches, and the challenges of maintaining ethical standards in an era of evolving conversational AI. Through an analysis of real-world incidents and hypothetical scenarios, this research aims to contribute to a nuanced understanding of the multifaceted threats that chatbots may pose, prompting a proactive approach to mitigating risks and safeguarding the integrity of digital communication.

Privacy Concerns

It recently was found that human-like signals in chatbots affect people's views of humanity and privacy issues, which in turn affects how people disclose information, behave, and follow recommendations. Because of its apparent anthropomorphism and decreased concerns regarding privacy, a chatbot that resembles a person is more likely to disclose information and abide by recommendations. This illustrates how important it is for design features and human-like traits to influence customer actions and mindsets in business chatbot encounters. The human-like chatbot and website were judged to have an equivalent level of anthropomorphism as opposed to one another(Ischen et al., 2020). After dealing with chatbots, users were mainly worried about losing access to their data, having their private details deleted, and having their data used inappropriately(Belen Saglam et al., 2021). Numerous chatbots use social media and communication sites, which have their policies about using data. Chatbots use contemporary natural language processing and machine learning techniques that may acquire knowledge from chats involving private data. They are not any more rule-based algorithms(Hasal et al., 2021).

LIMITATION

There are several constraints on our research. A noteworthy limitation of this research is the procedure of obtaining data. Even when the data gathered makes sense, it is limited to the context of certain study topics. Consequently, there is a possibility that details not included in this research will be discovered. The study sample consisted only of works that utilized the phrase "chatbot" and associated terminology (e.g. conversation agents).

CONCLUSION

The exploration of how chatbots work is a journey into the realms of technological innovation, linguistic processing, and the intricate dance between machines and humans in the digital age. As chatbots become more sophisticated, understanding the alchemy behind their conversational prowess becomes increasingly imperative. Whether unlocking the secrets of NLP, decoding the layers of machine learning, or envisioning future possibilities, this comprehensive exploration aims to provide a holistic understanding of the mechanisms driving the transformative power of chatbots in our evolving digital landscape. The use of chatbots for customer support is growing gradually because of the present banking sector trend. Customers may communicate with banks more effectively and personally with chatbots, which can handle a variety of queries such as checking account balances and starting loan applications, among other things. Because chatbots provide so many benefits, like accessibility, immediate replies, and round-the-clock availability, this trend is probably just going to get bigger. The use of chatbots in banking seems to have a bright future. A growing number of banks are spending more money on chatbot technology to improve customer service in general. Chatbots have become increasingly advanced and able to offer specialized services like financial planning and advising thanks to developments in AI and machine learning. These sophisticated chatbots might provide consumers with more individualized and customized advice, increasing their happiness and loyalty. A wider range of features, such as transaction assistance, fraud detection, and even investment advice, should be incorporated into banking chatbots as chatbot technology advances. As chatbots continue to advance in the banking industry, consumer-bank interactions should become more smooth, which will eventually benefit everyone by increasing efficiency and convenience. In the end, chatbot use in the banking sector is expected to increase over the next several years, providing both consumers and banks with a win-win method of interacting and transacting business. The growing popularity of chatbots and the continuous progress in artificial intelligence suggest that chatbots will play a significant role in the banking sector in the future.

REFERENCES

Abu Shawar, B. A., & Atwell, E. S. (2007). Chatbots: Are they really useful? *Journal for Language Technology and Computational Linguistics*, 22(1), 1. doi:10.21248/jlcl.22.2007.88

Adamopoulou, E., & Moussiades, L. (2020). Chatbots: History, technology, and applications. *Machine Learning with Applications*, 2, 100006. doi:10.1016/j.mlwa.2020.100006

Agnihotri, A., & Bhattacharya, S. (2023). Chatbots' effectiveness in service recovery. *International Journal of Information Management*, 102679. doi:10.1016/j.ijinfomgt.2023.102679

Al-Madi, N. A., Maria, K. A., Al-Madi, M. A., Alia, M. A., & Maria, E. A. (2021). An Intelligent Arabic Chatbot System Proposed Framework. *2021 International Conference on Information Technology (ICIT)*, (pp. 592–597). IEEE. 10.1109/ICIT52682.2021.9491699

Alabbas, A., & Alomar, K. (2024). Tayseer: A Novel AI-Powered Arabic Chatbot Framework for Technical and Vocational Student Helpdesk Services and Enhancing Student Interactions. *Applied Sciences (Basel, Switzerland)*, 14(6), 6. doi:10.3390/app14062547

Araujo, T. (2018). Living up to the chatbot hype: The influence of anthropomorphic design cues and communicative agency framing on conversational agent and company perceptions. *Computers in Human Behavior, 85*, 183–189. doi:10.1016/j.chb.2018.03.051

Ashfaq, M., Yun, J., Yu, S., & Loureiro, S. M. C. (2020). I, Chatbot: Modeling the determinants of users' satisfaction and continuance intention of AI-powered service agents. *Telematics and Informatics, 54*, 101473. doi:10.1016/j.tele.2020.101473

Batra, R., Song, L., & Ramprasad, R. (2020). Emerging materials intelligence ecosystems propelled by machine learning. *Nature Reviews. Materials, 6*(8), 655–678. doi:10.1038/s41578-020-00255-y

Bavaresco, R., Silveira, D., Reis, E., Barbosa, J., Righi, R., Costa, C., Antunes, R., Gomes, M., Gatti, C., Vanzin, M., Junior, S. C., Silva, E., & Moreira, C. (2020). Conversational agents in business: A systematic literature review and future research directions. *Computer Science Review, 36*, 100239. doi:10.1016/j.cosrev.2020.100239

Belen Saglam, R., Nurse, J. R. C., & Hodges, D. (2021). Privacy Concerns in Chatbot Interactions: When to Trust and When to Worry. In C. Stephanidis, M. Antona, & S. Ntoa (Eds.), *HCI International 2021—Posters* (pp. 391–399). Springer International Publishing. doi:10.1007/978-3-030-78642-7_53

Bhutada, S., Madabhushi, M., Shivani, S., & Choolakal, S. (2024). Facial Emotion Recognition Using Chatbot and Raspberry Pi. In H. Zen, N. M. Dasari, Y. M. Latha, & S. S. Rao (Eds.), *Soft Computing and Signal Processing* (pp. 53–66). Springer Nature. doi:10.1007/978-981-99-8451-0_5

Brandtzaeg, P. B., & Følstad, A. (2017). Why People Use Chatbots. In I. Kompatsiaris, J. Cave, A. Satsiou, G. Carle, A. Passani, E. Kontopoulos, S. Diplaris, & D. McMillan (Eds.), *Internet Science* (pp. 377–392). Springer International Publishing. doi:10.1007/978-3-319-70284-1_30

Castillo, D., Canhoto, A. I., & Said, E. (2021). The dark side of AI-powered service interactions: Exploring the process of co-destruction from the customer perspective. *Service Industries Journal, 41*(13–14), 900–925. doi:10.1080/02642069.2020.1787993

Chang, J.-W., Yen, N., & Hung, J. C. (2022). Design of a NLP-empowered finance fraud awareness model: The anti-fraud chatbot for fraud detection and fraud classification as an instance. *Journal of Ambient Intelligence and Humanized Computing, 13*(10), 4663–4679. doi:10.1007/s12652-021-03512-2

Chong, T., Yu, T., Keeling, D. I., & de Ruyter, K. (2021). AI-chatbots on the services frontline addressing the challenges and opportunities of agency. *Journal of Retailing and Consumer Services, 63*, 102735. doi:10.1016/j.jretconser.2021.102735

Chung, M., Ko, E., Joung, H., & Kim, S. J. (2020). Chatbot e-service and customer satisfaction regarding luxury brands. *Journal of Business Research, 117*, 587–595. doi:10.1016/j.jbusres.2018.10.004

Dwivedi, Y. K., Kshetri, N., Hughes, L., Slade, E. L., Jeyaraj, A., Kar, A. K., Baabdullah, A. M., Koohang, A., Raghavan, V., Ahuja, M., Albanna, H., Albashrawi, M. A., Al-Busaidi, A. S., Balakrishnan, J., Barlette, Y., Basu, S., Bose, I., Brooks, L., Buhalis, D, & Wright, R. (2023). Opinion Paper: "So what if ChatGPT wrote it?" Multidisciplinary perspectives on opportunities, challenges and implications of generative conversational AI for research, practice and policy. *International Journal of Information Management, 71*, 102642. doi:10.1016/j.ijinfomgt.2023.102642

Dwivedi, Y. K., & Wang, Y. (2022). Guest editorial: Artificial intelligence for B2B marketing: Challenges and opportunities. *Industrial Marketing Management, 105*, 109–113. doi:10.1016/j.indmarman.2022.06.001

Epstein, R., Roberts, G., & Beber, G. (2007). *Parsing the Turing Test: Philosophical and Methodological Issues in the Quest for the Thinking Computer*. Springer Science & Business Media.

Galitsky, B., & Goldberg, S. (2019). Explainable Machine Learning for Chatbots. In B. Galitsky (Ed.), *Developing Enterprise Chatbots: Learning Linguistic Structures* (pp. 53–83). Springer International Publishing. doi:10.1007/978-3-030-04299-8_3

Go, E., & Sundar, S. S. (2019). Humanizing chatbots: The effects of visual, identity and conversational cues on humanness perceptions. *Computers in Human Behavior, 97*, 304–316. doi:10.1016/j.chb.2019.01.020

Hao, A. W., Paul, J., Trott, S., Guo, C., & Wu, H.-H. (2019). Two decades of research on nation branding: A review and future research agenda. *International Marketing Review, 38*(1), 46–69. doi:10.1108/IMR-01-2019-0028

Harrison, D. E., Ajjan, H., Hair, J. F., Ryan, S., Myers, C., Drewes, P., & Disch, W. (2022). The Essentials of Marketing Analytics: Teaching, Research and Practice—An Abstract. In F. Pantoja & S. Wu (Eds.), *From Micro to Macro: Dealing with Uncertainties in the Global Marketplace* (pp. 1–2). Springer International Publishing. doi:10.1007/978-3-030-89883-0_1

Hasal, M., Nowaková, J., Ahmed Saghair, K., Abdulla, H., Snášel, V., & Ogiela, L. (2021). Chatbots: Security, privacy, data protection, and social aspects. *Concurrency and Computation, 33*(19), e6426. doi:10.1002/cpe.6426

Huang, D., Markovitch, D. G., & Stough, R. A. (2024). Can chatbot customer service match human service agents on customer satisfaction? An investigation in the role of trust. *Journal of Retailing and Consumer Services, 76*, 103600. doi:10.1016/j.jretconser.2023.103600

Ischen, C., Araujo, T., Voorveld, H., van Noort, G., & Smit, E. (2020). Privacy Concerns in Chatbot Interactions. In A. Følstad, T. Araujo, S. Papadopoulos, E. L.-C. Law, O.-C. Granmo, E. Luger, & P. B. Brandtzaeg (Eds.), *Chatbot Research and Design* (pp. 34–48). Springer International Publishing. doi:10.1007/978-3-030-39540-7_3

Jin, J., Walker, J., & Reczek, R. W. (n.d.). Avoiding embarrassment online: Response to and inferences about chatbots when purchases activate self-presentation concerns. *Journal of Consumer Psychology*. doi:10.1002/jcpy.1414

Karimov, Z., Allahverdiyev, I., Agayarov, O. Y., Demir, D., & Almuradova, E. (2024). ChatGPT vs UpToDate: Comparative study of usefulness and reliability of Chatbot in common clinical presentations of otorhinolaryngology–head and neck surgery. *European Archives of Oto-Rhino-Laryngology, 281*(4), 2145–2151. doi:10.1007/s00405-023-08423-w PMID:38217726

Kim, T. W., Jiang, L., Duhachek, A., Lee, H., & Garvey, A. (2022). Do You Mind if I Ask You a Personal Question? How AI Service Agents Alter Consumer Self-Disclosure. *Journal of Service Research, 25*(4), 649–666. doi:10.1177/10946705221120232

Krishna, A., Herd, K. B., & Aydınoğlu, N. Z. (2019). A Review of Consumer Embarrassment as a Public and Private Emotion. *Journal of Consumer Psychology, 29*(3), 492–516. doi:10.1002/jcpy.1086

Lai, S.-T., Leu, F.-Y., & Lin, J.-W. (2019). A Banking Chatbot Security Control Procedure for Protecting User Data Security and Privacy. In L. Barolli, F.-Y. Leu, T. Enokido, & H.-C. Chen (Eds.), *Advances on Broadband and Wireless Computing, Communication and Applications* (pp. 561–571). Springer International Publishing. doi:10.1007/978-3-030-02613-4_50

Li, Y., Li, Y., Chen, Q., & Chang, Y. (2024). Humans as teammates: The signal of human–AI teaming enhances consumer acceptance of chatbots. *International Journal of Information Management, 76*, 102771. doi:10.1016/j.ijinfomgt.2024.102771

Lucas, G. M., Rizzo, A., Gratch, J., Scherer, S., Stratou, G., Boberg, J., & Morency, L.-P. (2017). Reporting Mental Health Symptoms: Breaking Down Barriers to Care with Virtual Human Interviewers. *Frontiers in Robotics and AI, 4*, 51. doi:10.3389/frobt.2017.00051

Mariani, M. M., Hashemi, N., & Wirtz, J. (2023). Artificial intelligence empowered conversational agents: A systematic literature review and research agenda. *Journal of Business Research, 161*, 113838. doi:10.1016/j.jbusres.2023.113838

Mende, M., Scott, M. L., van Doorn, J., Grewal, D., & Shanks, I. (2019). Service Robots Rising: How Humanoid Robots Influence Service Experiences and Elicit Compensatory Consumer Responses. *JMR, Journal of Marketing Research, 56*(4), 535–556. doi:10.1177/0022243718822827

Michalski, R. S., Carbonell, J. G., & Mitchell, T. M. (2013). *Machine Learning: An Artificial Intelligence Approach*. Springer Science & Business Media.

Nath, M. P., & Sagnika, S. (2020). Capabilities of Chatbots and Its Performance Enhancements in Machine Learning. In D. Swain, P. K. Pattnaik, & P. K. Gupta (Eds.), *Machine Learning and Information Processing* (pp. 183–192). Springer. doi:10.1007/978-981-15-1884-3_17

Palomino, N., & Arbaiza, F. (2023). The Role of a Chatbot Personality in the Attitude of Consumers Towards a Banking Brand. In Á. Rocha, C. H. Fajardo-Toro, & J. M. Riola (Eds.), *Developments and Advances in Defense and Security* (pp. 205–215). Springer Nature. doi:10.1007/978-981-19-7689-6_18

Pizzi, G., Scarpi, D., & Pantano, E. (2021). Artificial intelligence and the new forms of interaction: Who has the control when interacting with a chatbot? *Journal of Business Research, 129*, 878–890. doi:10.1016/j.jbusres.2020.11.006

Punjabi, S., Sethuram, V., & Ramachandran, V., boddu, R., & Ravi, S. (2019). Chat bot Using API: Human To Machine Conversation. *2019 Global Conference for Advancement in Technology (GCAT)*, (pp. 1–5). IEEE. 10.1109/GCAT47503.2019.8978336

Ranoliya, B. R., Raghuwanshi, N., & Singh, S. (2017). Chatbot for university related FAQs. *2017 International Conference on Advances in Computing, Communications and Informatics (ICACCI)*, (pp. 1525–1530). IEEE. 10.1109/ICACCI.2017.8126057

Rese, A., & Tränkner, P. (2024). Perceived conversational ability of task-based chatbots – Which conversational elements influence the success of text-based dialogues? *International Journal of Information Management*, *74*, 102699. doi:10.1016/j.ijinfomgt.2023.102699

Review: Ready for Robots?: How to Think About the Future of AI on JSTOR. (n.d.). jStor. https://www.jstor.org/stable/26798238

Rukavina, A. (2024, March 15). *From hype to hero: How chatbots can revolutionize your bank's customer experience*. Infobip. https://www.infobip.com/blog/revolutionize-your-banks-customer-experience-with-chatbots

Schuetzler, R. M., Grimes, G. M., & Scott Giboney, J. (2020). The impact of chatbot conversational skill on engagement and perceived humanness. *Journal of Management Information Systems*, *37*(3), 875–900. doi:10.1080/07421222.2020.1790204

Shum, H.-Y., He, X., & Li, D. (2018). *From Eliza to XiaoIce: Challenges and Opportunities with Social Chatbots* (arXiv:1801.01957). arXiv. https://doi.org//arXiv.1801.01957 doi:10.48550

Shumanov, M., & Johnson, L. (2021). Making conversations with chatbots more personalized. *Computers in Human Behavior*, *117*, 106627. doi:10.1016/j.chb.2020.106627

Singh, H., Bhangare, A., Singh, R., Zope, S., & Saindane, P. (2023). Chatbots: A Survey of the Technology. In J. Hemanth, D. Pelusi, & J. I.-Z. Chen (Eds.), *Intelligent Cyber Physical Systems and Internet of Things* (pp. 671–691). Springer International Publishing. doi:10.1007/978-3-031-18497-0_49

Song, M., Du, J., Xing, X., & Mou, J. (2022). Should the chatbot "save itself" or "be helped by others"? The influence of service recovery types on consumer perceptions of recovery satisfaction. *Electronic Commerce Research and Applications*, *55*, 101199. doi:10.1016/j.elerap.2022.101199

Song, M., Zhang, H., Xing, X., & Duan, Y. (2023). Appreciation vs. apology: Research on the influence mechanism of chatbot service recovery based on politeness theory. *Journal of Retailing and Consumer Services*, *73*, 103323. doi:10.1016/j.jretconser.2023.103323

Suhel, S. F., Shukla, V. K., Vyas, S., & Mishra, V. P. (2020). Conversation to Automation in Banking Through Chatbot Using Artificial Machine Intelligence Language. *2020 8th International Conference on Reliability, Infocom Technologies and Optimization (Trends and Future Directions) (ICRITO)*, (pp. 611–618). IEEE. 10.1109/ICRITO48877.2020.9197825

Sun, Y., Chen, J., & Sundar, S. S. (2024). Chatbot ads with a human touch: A test of anthropomorphism, interactivity, and narrativity. *Journal of Business Research*, *172*, 114403. doi:10.1016/j.jbusres.2023.114403

Taecharungroj, V. (2023). "What Can ChatGPT Do?" Analyzing Early Reactions to the Innovative AI Chatbot on Twitter. *Big Data and Cognitive Computing*, *7*(1), 1. doi:10.3390/bdcc7010035

Telner, J. (2021). Chatbot User Experience: Speed and Content Are King. In T. Z. Ahram, W. Karwowski, & J. Kalra (Eds.), Advances in Artificial Intelligence, Software and Systems Engineering (pp. 47–54). Springer International Publishing. doi:10.1007/978-3-030-80624-8_6

Vaziri, M., Mandel, L., Shinnar, A., Siméon, J., & Hirzel, M. (2017). Generating chat bots from web API specifications. *Proceedings of the 2017 ACM SIGPLAN International Symposium on New Ideas, New Paradigms, and Reflections on Programming and Software*, (pp. 44–57). ACM. 10.1145/3133850.3133864

Wang, X., Lin, X., & Shao, B. (2022). How does artificial intelligence create business agility? Evidence from chatbots. *International Journal of Information Management*, *66*, 102535. doi:10.1016/j.ijinfomgt.2022.102535

Wirtz, J., Patterson, P. G., Kunz, W. H., Gruber, T., Lu, V. N., Paluch, S., & Martins, A. (2018). Brave new world: Service robots in the frontline. *Journal of Service Management*, *29*(5), 907–931. doi:10.1108/JOSM-04-2018-0119

Wirtz, J., & Zeithaml, V. (2018). Cost-effective service excellence. *Journal of the Academy of Marketing Science*, *46*(1), 59–80. doi:10.1007/s11747-017-0560-7

Xing, X., Song, M., Duan, Y., & Mou, J. (2022). Effects of different service failure types and recovery strategies on the consumer response mechanism of chatbots. *Technology in Society*, *70*, 102049. doi:10.1016/j.techsoc.2022.102049

Xu, A., Liu, Z., Guo, Y., Sinha, V., & Akkiraju, R. (2017). A New Chatbot for Customer Service on Social Media. *Proceedings of the 2017 CHI Conference on Human Factors in Computing Systems*, (pp. 3506–3510). ACM. 10.1145/3025453.3025496

KEY TERMS AND DEFINITIONS

Chatbot: A chatbot is a computer program that simulates human conversation through voice commands or text chats or both.

REST API: Representational State Transfer Application Programming Interface more commonly known as REST API web service. It means when a RESTful API is called, the server will transfer a representation of the requested resource's state to the client system.

Chapter 18
Futuristic Chatbots:
Expectations and Directions
for Accomplishment

Nitin Sharma
Bharat Electronics Limited, India

Pawan Bhakuni
Bharat Electronics Limited, India

ABSTRACT

A chatbot is an artificial intelligence-driven conversational agent that utilizes natural language processing to engage with users and carry out activities via written or spoken communication. Although there has been remarkable advancement, contemporary chatbots frequently encounter difficulties such as trustworthiness, emotional intelligence, and social awareness. Trustworthiness, emotional intelligence, and social awareness are crucial for any chatbot. Trustworthiness in communication guarantees the sharing of truthful information, while emotional intelligence promotes user engagement by fostering empathy. Additionally, social awareness facilitates culturally sensitive and contextually relevant communication. The authors outline many overarching strategies to address emerging issues in chatbot development, including novel methodologies, innovative environments and modalities, and updated benchmarks. Implementing a new methodology, a new environment with different modalities, and a new benchmark can improve chatbot performance.

INTRODUCTION

ChatGPT has gained significant prominence in recent years as a revolutionary technological breakthrough, showcasing its conversational AI chatbot capabilities. OpenAI's ChatGPT reached an important milestone of one million users five days after its public launch. A chatbot is an artificial intelligence-driven conversational assistant that utilizes natural language processing to engage with users and accomplish tasks via written or spoken communication. Chatbots are transforming multiple sectors by offering customized customer support, e-commerce suggestions, healthcare aid, employee training and orientation,

DOI: 10.4018/979-8-3693-1830-0.ch018

financial guidance, language learning assistance, and virtual personal aides. Their services encompass interactive and customized assistance, aiding customers in navigating online procedures and offering individualized suggestions. Healthcare services encompass symptom assessment, medication prompts, and inquiries about overall health. They provide tailored financial guidance, fiscal planning, and investment suggestions within finance. Language learning programs include users in interactive discussions and offer guidance on pronunciation. Chatbots are advancing into highly advanced virtual personal assistants, augmenting efficiency and streamlining everyday tasks.

Chatbots are highly effective in numerous practical situations. Several essential features are necessary for the efficient functioning of a chatbot. A chatbot is an automated system that comprehends user inputs, retains context, produces significant replies, manages intricate discussions, interfaces with external systems, handles problems, and guarantees secure connections. The system employs Natural Language Understanding (NLU) to identify the user's intention and retrieve pertinent details from their input. Context management ensures the chatbot comprehends the user's condition and responds consistently. Response generation involves the creation of suitable and realistic responses, typically employing natural language generation techniques. Multi-turn conversations enable the chatbot to manage and engage in conversations over numerous exchanges, resulting in a smooth and uninterrupted connection. Integrating external systems enables the chatbot to retrieve pertinent data and deliver instantaneous responses. Error handling identifies and addresses user inquiries outside the chatbot's comprehension or processing capabilities. User identification and authorization guarantee secure interactions by verifying the identity of users and granting access to certain functionalities. These features establish a solid basis for a chatbot, allowing it to comprehend user inputs, retain context, produce significant replies, manage intricate discussions, incorporate with external systems, handle faults, and guarantee secure interactions.

An example of a chatbot application in the real world is the "Domino's Pizza Chatbot" created by Domino's Pizza. The chatbot enables users to place pizza orders, monitor deliveries, and receive responses to common inquiries through natural language interactions. Users can interact with the chatbot on many messaging platforms like Facebook Messenger, WhatsApp, and the Domino's website. The chatbot utilizes AI and natural language processing to offer clients a user-friendly method to interact with the company and make purchases without having to use traditional ordering systems. It demonstrates how businesses use chatbots to improve customer service and simplify transactions in the digital era.

Chatbot users often struggle with inadequate comprehension and context, resulting in erroneous or irrelevant replies. Personalization is frequently absent, leading to generic interactions that do not cater to the specific needs of particular users. Chatbots face challenges in understanding complex problems, which limits their capacity to handle nuanced questions or offer specialized knowledge in a particular field. Security and privacy concerns affect user trust due to worries about data management and possible abuse. Inconsistencies in user experience across channels lead to confusion and irritation. To overcome these issues, progress in natural language processing, refined personalization tactics, more extraordinary problem-solving skills, strong security measures, and prioritizing a cohesive cross-channel experience is necessary.

This study centers on the anticipation of future developments in chatbot technology. Anticipating futuristic prospects for chatbots is essential for stimulating innovation and advancement. They assist developers in staying abreast of emerging technologies, fulfilling evolving user requirements, improving customization, integrating with emerging technologies, and ensuring ethical considerations. In addition, they guide the creation of industry-specific chatbots that cater to specific needs in fields such as healthcare, banking, and customer service. Chatbot solutions can consistently demonstrate innovation and surpass competition by maintaining forward-looking expectations. Furthermore, they contribute to establishing user confidence and acceptance, as the ability to anticipate future demands enables developers to concentrate on crafting dependable, trustworthy, and beneficial chatbots. To summarize, the future expectations for chatbots are focused on constant enhancement, keeping up with technical progress, and maintaining their relevance and effectiveness in meeting the requirements of users and businesses.

This paper is structured as follows. Section (2) discusses the future expectations of Chatbot, Section (3) discusses the Ethical Considerations and Societal Impacts, and section (4) discusses general directions to accomplish future expectations. Finally, section (5) discusses the conclusion of the study.

FUTURE EXPECTATIONS FROM CHATBOT

This section discusses future expectations of trustworthiness, emotional intelligence, and social awareness.

Trustworthy Expectations

The emergence of AI-based chatbot technology (Ni et al., 2023) has profoundly influenced daily life and society to enhance human well-being by reducing the need for manual labor and promoting social well-being. Nevertheless, research conducted by(H. Liu et al., 2022) indicates that AI has the potential to inadvertently inflict harm by making flawed decisions or continuing discriminatory practices. Consequently, there is an increasing emphasis on creating reliable AI-driven chatbots to avert adverse outcomes and guarantee that individuals may have faith in and peacefully coexist with chatbots based on AI. The objective of this strategy is to ensure impartiality and parity in the implementation of AI-driven chatbots. Figure 1 shows trustworthy expectations, and Table 1 summarizes the significance and methods to accomplish trustworthy expectations.

This study explores the concept of trustworthy artificial intelligence (AI) through the expectations of a chatbot based on AI. The research focuses on six fundamental dimensions essential for achieving trustworthy AI, highlighting the complexity and multidimensional nature of this complex topic: (i) Safety and robustness, (ii) Non-discrimination and fairness, (iii) Explainability, (iv) Privacy, (v) Accountability & Auditability, and (vi) Environmental Well-being. We review the related expectations for each dimension and summarize their insights in real-world systems.

Reliability is of utmost importance in the design of chatbots since it directly influences the level of trust and happiness experienced by users. Chatbots depend on precise and reliable data and play a crucial role in providing customer support, retrieving information, and making decisions. Ensuring trustworthiness entails furnishing precise responses and exhibiting transparency regarding the system's constraints. Ensuring the dependability of the chatbot's information is particularly crucial in industries such as healthcare or finance, where users require assurance. Hence, trustworthiness holds a vital role in the creation of chatbots.

Safety and Robustness

Safety in AI chatbots(Deng et al., 2023) encompasses measures taken to avert harm, guarantee ethical conduct, and tackle possible hazards or biases that may emerge during conversations. It entails the implementation of safeguards to prevent unintended outcomes, the spread of misinformation, or biased

Figure 1. Future expectations from chatbot

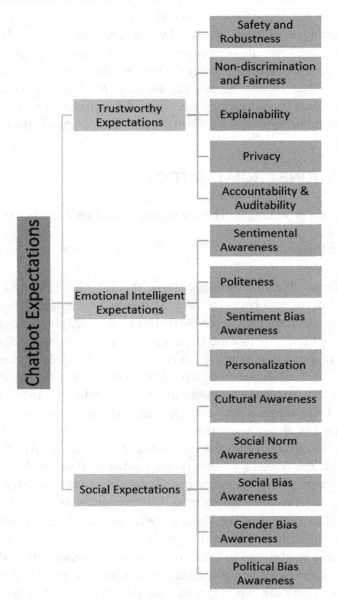

responses. Robustness refers to the chatbot's capacity to function consistently and effectively in various unforeseen conditions, even when faced with complex inputs or unfamiliar circumstances. Ensuring safety and robustness is crucial in developing AI chatbot systems to establish trustworthiness and reliability.

The advantages of guaranteeing safety and resilience in AI chatbots are manifold. These strategies establish user trust by reducing the likelihood of detrimental conduct or undesired outcomes. AI chatbots that adhere to ethical standards and demonstrate reliability contribute to favorable user experiences, resulting in heightened user engagement and pleasure. Resilient systems effectively adapt to diverse environments, guaranteeing constant and reliable performance. In addition to the benefits for the user, the chatbot's long-term success is ensured by its safety and robustness, which avoid unfavorable public perception, legal complications, and potential exploitation of the technology.

Here are three ways in which AI chatbots support safety and robustness in communication:

1. Adversarial Training for Robustness:

AI chatbots can undergo adversarial training to improve their resilience against potential attacks or variations in input. Adversarial training entails subjecting the model to meticulously designed alterations in the training data, which mimic real-world difficulties. By acquiring knowledge from these adversarial cases, AI chatbots enhance their ability to withstand unforeseen perturbations in input, hence minimizing the likelihood of generating erroneous or unsuitable outputs in a wide range of situations.

2. Diverse Training Data for Generalization:

Training AI chatbots using broad and representative datasets to enhance safety and resilience is essential. The model's ability to generalize to real-world scenarios is enhanced by exposure to diverse linguistic variants, cultural nuances, and potential biases. An inclusive training dataset guarantees that the AI chatbots comprehend and uphold different linguistic expressions, minimizing the probability of biased or dangerous conduct. The model's replies are enhanced to ensure inclusion and fairness.

3. Explainability and Interpretability:

AI chatbots can be programmed to justify their predictions, enhancing transparency and interpretability. By comprehending the process by which the model generates a specific outcome, users and developers can more effectively evaluate the dependability of the model's responses. Transparent models facilitate the detection of potential problems, prejudices, or misinterpretations, enabling the implementation of appropriate modifications to improve safety and user confidence. Explainability holds significant importance in adhering to regulations and instilling confidence in users.

Non-Discrimination and Fairness

Non-discrimination and fairness (Chang et al., 2019) in AI chatbots pertain to the ethical tenet of guaranteeing impartiality and equitable treatment of users, irrespective of their demographic attributes, in the chatbot's decisions and responses. The process entails the prevention of discriminatory conduct, the avoidance of propagating stereotypes, and the provision of equitable and impartial interactions to all users. This idea is essential for maintaining ethical standards, fostering inclusion, and reducing the potential for propagating biases that may be present in the training data or underlying algorithms.

The advantages of integrating principles of non-discrimination and justice into AI chatbots are significant. Primarily, it creates a user experience that is more comprehensive and fairer, promoting trust and pleasant interaction among a wide range of users. The equitable treatment guarantees that the chatbot upholds the rights and dignity of all users, thereby enhancing the technology's public image favorably. In addition, implementing non-discrimination policies helps mitigate the likelihood of facing legal and ethical disputes, so protecting against potential reputational harm and regulatory scrutiny arising from biased or discriminatory activities.

Here are three ways in which AI chatbots can be designed to support non-discrimination and fairness in communication:

1.   Diverse and Representative Training Data:

To reduce biases and ensure fairness, AI chatbots should undergo training using diverse and representative datasets encompassing a broad spectrum of demographic, cultural, and linguistic variances. This training guarantees the model is exposed to an equitable representation of diverse societal groups, minimizing the potential for acquiring and perpetuating biases. By integrating various examples, artificial intelligence chatbots can enhance their comprehension and production of inclusive and impartial responses.

2.   Bias Detection and Mitigation Techniques:

It is essential to incorporate methods for identifying and reducing prejudice in AI chatbots to guarantee fairness. This entails consistently evaluating the model's results for potential biases and implementing corrective measures to resolve any detected problems. Methods such as adversarial training, re-sampling, or altering training data weights can be utilized to diminish and counterbalance biases within the model. Ongoing surveillance and improvement are crucial to ensure equity throughout the model's lifespan.

3.   Explainability and Transparency:

Offering justifications for the model's forecasts enhances transparency and aids in detecting potential origins of bias. AI chatbots can be programmed to elucidate the decision-making process, enabling users and developers to comprehend the aspects that impact the model's outputs. Transparent models enable recognizing and rectifying discriminatory conduct, fostering responsibility and confidence. Transparency is crucial in systems where user interactions can be sensitive, as it ensures fairness.

Explainability

Explainability (Kong et al., 2024) in AI chatbots pertains to the system's capacity to offer lucid and comprehensible justifications for its decisions and actions. It entails ensuring that the inner workings of the chatbot are clear and understandable, enabling users to grasp the methods and reasoning behind a specific response or advice. Explainability is essential for establishing trust, promoting user confidence, and allowing the users to comprehend, verify, and potentially question the chatbot's outputs.

The advantages of integrating explainability into AI chatbots are manifold. First and foremost, it improves user confidence and willingness to interact with a chatbot since consumers are more inclined to participate when they comprehend its rationale. Explainability is also beneficial for regulatory compliance since it addresses the growing need for AI systems to be transparent and accountable. Furthermore, it simplifies identifying and correcting potential biases, errors, or restrictions in the chatbot's decision-making processes, aiding developers in error identification and improvement. Explainability, in general, enhances the ethicality, accountability, and user-friendliness of an AI chatbot.

Here are three ways in which AI chatbots support explainability in communication:

1.   Attention Mechanisms:

AI chatbots frequently employ transformer models that integrate attention mechanisms. These attention mechanisms identify the crucial phrases or tokens in the input that impact a specific prediction the most. These techniques enable users and developers to comprehend the particular aspects of the input the model directs its attention toward. Attention weights offer a means of interpretability, elucidating the model's decision-making process by unveiling the relative significance of various components in the input.

2.   Interpretable Architectures:

Developing AI chatbots with interpretable architectures improves their ability to be explained. Models that employ less complex architectures or integrate interpretable elements, such as attention layers, enhance the comprehensibility of the model's information processing and representation. Transparent designs facilitate users in comprehending the rationale behind the model's predictions, improving the interpretability and reliability of the model's outputs.

3.   Generated Text Justification:

AI chatbots can be programmed to produce explanations or justifications in addition to their responses. The model's output can yield insights into the crucial aspects or patterns in the input that influenced the choice. The generated text justification serves as a justification for the model's response, providing users and developers with insights into the thinking behind the output and enhancing the overall interpretability and explainability of the model.

Privacy

Privacy (B. Liu et al., 2021) for AI chatbots entails protecting user data and ensuring that the chatbot's activities comply with privacy rules and ethical norms. It involves the ethical gathering, retention, and utilization of user data, focusing on safeguarding user privacy and securing delicate information. Privacy is of utmost importance in AI chatbots that deal with personal information or engage in conversations where secrecy is crucial.

There are numerous advantages to giving priority to privacy in AI chatbots. First and foremost, it cultivates user confidence by instilling a feeling of assurance that their personal information is being managed responsibly. Adhering to privacy standards prevents potential legal consequences and safeguards against harm to one's reputation. Moreover, placing privacy as a top priority fosters user engagement, as consumers are more inclined to connect with a chatbot that upholds and safeguards their private. A privacy-focused strategy enhances the overall user experience and ensures lasting user contentment.

Here are three ways in which AI chatbots support privacy:

1.   Federated Learning:

By implementing federated learning, AI chatbots can undergo training using decentralized data sources while preserving individual user privacy. Federated learning involves collaborative training of a model across several devices or servers, where only the updates to the model are shared, not the original data. This guarantees that confidential user data is stored on the user's device, improving privacy safeguards while enabling the model to gain knowledge from a wide array of data.

2.   Tokenization and Differential Privacy:

Tokenization divides text into smaller components tokens and handles them separately. Through tokenization, AI chatbots can manipulate input data without exposing confidential information about specific users. Incorporating differential privacy approaches during training protects the potential extraction of private information from the model's parameters. These privacy-enhancing techniques help guarantee that the model cannot unintentionally disclose confidential data.

3.   Anonymization and Redaction Techniques:

AI chatbots can be programmed to integrate anonymization and redaction methods when handling or producing text. These methods entail eliminating or concealing personally identifiable information (PII) and other sensitive particulars in the resulting data. The concept enhances user privacy by censoring or obfuscating particular details, mainly when the produced content might be distributed or saved.

Accountability and Auditability

Accountability and audibility (Novelli et al., 2023) in AI chatbots pertain to the systems established to track and elucidate the decisions executed by the chatbot. Accountability entails holding individuals or entities accountable for the chatbot's acts while guaranteeing openness in decision-making. Auditability refers to the capacity to examine and assess the operations of the chatbot, enabling the detection of biases, errors, or opportunities for enhancement. These principles are crucial for the ethical implementation of AI, adherence to regulatory requirements, and the preservation of public confidence.

The advantages of incorporating accountability and auditability into AI chatbots are significant. Accountability fosters conscientious utilization of AI, reducing the likelihood of inadvertent repercussions and unethical conduct. Users and stakeholders are more likely to have confidence in a chatbot when a transparent and accountable system is in place to determine its behavior. Auditability improves a system's transparency level, allowing developers, regulators, and users to comprehend the decision-making process. The openness of the AI chatbot facilitates error diagnosis, detection of bias, and continuous improvement, hence enhancing the overall reliability and fairness of the chatbot.

Here are three ways in which AI chatbots support accountability and auditability:

1.   Logging and Versioning:

AI chatbots can be programmed to record data regarding their inputs, outputs, and decision-making procedures. Logging enables developers and stakeholders to monitor the model's performance over time and in various circumstances. Furthermore, it becomes possible to do audits and retrospective analyses by keeping track of the model's architecture, training data, and parameters. Versioning guarantees the ability to track and trace modifications made to the model, hence enhancing responsibility for its behavior and performance.

2.   Explainability and Interpretability:

Table 1. Trustworthy expectations

SN	Future Expectation	Significance	How to Accomplish
1	Safety and Robustness	1. Establish user trust 2. Favourable user experiences, 3. Avoid unfavorable public perception, legal complications, and potential exploitation of the technology	1. Adversarial Training for Robustness 2. Diverse Training Data for Generalization 3. Explainability and Interpretability
2	Non-discrimination and Fairness	1. Creates a user experience that is more comprehensive and fairer, 2. Promoting trust and pleasant interaction mitigates the likelihood of facing legal and ethical disputes 3. Protecting against potential reputational harm	1. Diverse and Representative Training Data 2. Bias Detection and Mitigation Techniques 3. Explainability and Transparency
3	Explainability	1. Improves user confidence 2. required for regulatory compliance, 3. Simplifies the process of identifying and correcting potential biases and errors	1. Attention Mechanisms 2. Interpretable Architectures 3. Generated Text Justification
4	Privacy	1. Cultivates user confidence 2. Prevents potential legal consequences 3. Fosters user engagement 4. Upholds and safeguards users' private	1. Federated Learning 2. Tokenization and Differential Privacy 3. Anonymization and Redaction Techniques
5	Accountability & Auditability	1. Reducing the likelihood of inadvertent repercussions and unethical conduct. 2. Improve confidence with a transparent and accountable system 3. Facilitates error diagnosis, detection of bias, and continuous improvement	1. Logging and Versioning 2. Explainability and Interpretability 3. Model Governance and Compliance Frameworks

Integrating tools to provide explanations and interpretations improves the clarity and comprehensibility of AI chatbots. Models can offer explanations or justifications for their predictions, allowing users and auditors to comprehend the underlying logic behind results. Methods such as attention mechanisms or generated text explanations aid in elucidating how the model analyzes and evaluates various input components. The transparency of the model enables stakeholders to assess its behavior and detect any possible biases or inaccuracies, thus promoting accountability.

3.   Model Governance and Compliance Frameworks:

Implementing robust model governance frameworks and compliance requirements is crucial for ensuring responsibility in implementing AI chatbots. These frameworks establish explicit guidelines and protocols for model development, testing, deployment, and monitoring. Adhering to legal standards and ethical guidelines is a crucial element of responsibility. Organizations can showcase their dedication to ethical AI practices and streamline external audits or evaluations of their AI chatbot deployments by following established standards and guidelines.

Emotional Intelligent Expectations

As defined by (Goleman, 1995), emotional intelligence refers to the chatbot's capacity to accurately recognize, understand, and appropriately respond to the emotional nuances conveyed in human interaction.

An emotionally intelligent chatbot utilizes text or speech analysis to extract information and identify the user's communication's inherent sentiment, mood, and emotional context. This functionality enables the chatbot to provide more comprehensive and adaptive responses according to the current context, enhancing a conversation that feels more authentic and engaging for users. These conversational agents can improve their comprehension and adaptation to users' emotional states by integrating emotional intelligence into chatbots. This increases user satisfaction, confidence, and more genuine and streamlined interaction. Figure 1 shows Emotional intelligence expectations, and Table 2 summarizes the significance and methods to accomplish Emotional intelligence expectations.

Emotional intelligence is essential in chatbots as it enables them to comprehend human emotions, facilitate individualized and empathetic conversations, and improve their capacity to navigate sensitive circumstances tactfully. It is crucial in fields such as customer service and mental health assistance. Chatbots can adapt their tone and content based on the user's emotions, resulting in more dynamic conversations that closely resemble human interactions. This improves the effectiveness and ease of use of interactions, facilitating the advancement of technologically advanced conversational agents.

Emotional intelligence in chatbots encompasses a resilient sentiment analysis system, comprehension of contextual clues, and the capacity to perceive emotional nuances. The system should provide immediate responses, exhibiting empathy or enthusiasm. The chatbot's ability to remember past talks and understand the context allows for a more personalized and emotionally responsive interaction. Iterative learning algorithms that include user feedback gradually enhance emotional intelligence, increasing user happiness and improving human-machine interaction efficiency.

Sentimental Awareness

Sentimental (Tan et al., 2023)awareness in AI chatbots pertains to the system's ability to comprehend and react suitably to the emotions conveyed by users throughout their interactions. This entails the identification of emotions such as joy, sorrow, annoyance, or enthusiasm expressed through written or spoken language. Chatbots with emotional intelligence can customize their responses according to the user's emotional condition, resulting in more compassionate and individualized conversations.

The advantages of integrating emotional awareness into AI chatbots are substantial. Firstly, it improves the overall user experience by enabling the chatbot to respond with empathy and understanding, resulting in a more human-like conversation. Sentimental awareness enhances user engagement by allowing the chatbot to adjust its tone and responses to correspond with the user's emotions. Moreover, comprehending customer emotion enables the chatbot to recognize possible problems, resolve concerns, and offer more efficient support, ultimately enhancing user satisfaction.

Here are three ways in which AI chatbots support sentiment awareness:

1.   Sentiment Analysis Capabilities:

AI chatbots can acquire sophisticated sentiment analysis capabilities by being trained on extensive datasets labeled with sentiment labels. Using supervised learning, the model develops the ability to categorize text into different sentiment categories, including positive, negative, or neutral. This allows AI chatbots to effectively identify and comprehend the sentiment conveyed in user-generated content, social media postings, product reviews, and other textual data.

2. Contextual Understanding:

AI chatbots demonstrate exceptional proficiency in comprehending context, enabling them to grasp intricate subtleties and sentiment expressions contingent upon the context. The model can enhance its understanding of the sentiment expressed in each text snippet by examining the neighboring words, sentences, and grammatical structures. Comprehending context is essential for precisely interpreting sentiment, as identical words or phrases might have varying interpretations based on the surrounding circumstances.

3. Fine-tuning for Specific Domains or Languages:

AI chatbots can be optimized using domain-specific or language-specific datasets to enhance their understanding of sentiment in specialized circumstances. Training the model using data specifically related to a certain domain or language can enhance its comprehension of the distinct sentiment patterns and words characteristic of that domain or language. Through fine-tuning, AI chatbots can adjust their sentiment analysis capabilities to various applications, including customer feedback analysis, brand monitoring, and social media sentiment tracking.

Politeness Expectations

Politeness (Ribino, 2023) in AI chatbots pertains to the system's capacity to interact with users in a manner that is courteous, respectful, and socially suitable. It entails employing courteous language, demonstrating appreciation, recognizing user input, and maintaining a pleasant conversation demeanor. Politeness improves the user experience by promoting good interaction and establishing a more enjoyable and courteous discussion atmosphere.

There are numerous advantages to integrating politeness into AI chatbots. First and foremost, it enhances user happiness and perception of the chatbot, resulting in heightened user trust and loyalty. Chatbots that exhibit politeness are more inclined to actively participate in substantial conversations with people and obtain relevant feedback. Politeness is essential in the chatbot's professionalism and credibility, improving its reputation and promoting pleasant user connections. In addition, courteous exchanges foster a more inclusive and hospitable atmosphere, catering to individuals with varied cultural backgrounds and tastes.

Here are three ways in which AI chatbots support politeness:

1. Politeness Modeling during Training:

AI chatbots can undergo training using datasets containing courteous language usage. The model acquires the ability to identify and provide polite responses by incorporating various polite expressions and courteous communication techniques. Training AI chatbots with politeness modeling enables them to grasp the subtleties of politeness and deliver suitable responses to diverse social situations.

2. Contextual Sensitivity to Social Cues:

AI chatbots, particularly ones equipped with sophisticated contextual comprehension abilities, can consider social cues and contextual data to ascertain the proper usage of polite language. The model's ability to comprehend the broader conversation framework, encompassing the dynamics between the participants and the subject matter, enables it to customize its responses with suitable degrees of courtesy.

3.   Fine-tuning for Specific Use Cases:

Specializing AI chatbots for specific use cases or sectors might improve their civility within specialized domains. For example, refining the model using data highlighting courteous and customer-oriented interactions in customer service apps or virtual assistants might enhance its capacity to answer gracious user inquiries. Through fine-tuning, AI chatbots can modify their language creation to align with specified politeness criteria in various application contexts.

Sentiment Bias Awareness

Sentiment bias (Xue et al., 2023) awareness in the context of AI chatbots pertains to the ability of these conversational agents to identify and correct biases in the understanding and expression of emotions. The chatbot's capability to comprehend and acknowledge any tendencies towards positive or negative thoughts that may unintentionally arise in its replies is included. Sentiment bias awareness guarantees that the chatbot offers equitable and unbiased conversations, preventing inclination towards sentiments or groups.

The main advantage of being aware of sentiment bias for AI chatbots is facilitating equitable and impartial conversations. Users are provided with unbiased responses, promoting an inclusive and respectful communication climate free of predetermined emotions. Ensuring justice in the chatbot's operations improves customer happiness and trust, ultimately leading to pleasant user experiences. In addition, AI chatbots adhere to ethical AI principles by eliminating biases in sentiment, thus promoting responsible implementation and reducing the potential for accidental prejudice. In summary, awareness of sentiment bias guarantees that AI chatbots can effectively analyze sentiment while being sensitive and unbiased, accommodating a wide range of user viewpoints.

Here are three ways in which AI chatbots support an awareness and mitigation of sentiment bias:

1.   Bias Detection and Monitoring:

AI chatbots can be provided with methods to identify and monitor any bias in the sentiment expressed in their responses. This entails examining the forecasts made by the algorithm and detecting instances when the sentiment may exhibit partiality towards specific groups or viewpoints. Through ongoing surveillance of bias, developers can acquire valuable knowledge about potential problems and implement remedial measures to tackle and reduce the influence of bias on the model's outputs.

2.   Diverse and Representative Training Data:

To reduce sentiment bias, it is essential to provide AI chatbots with training using varied and representative datasets. Ensuring that the training data encompasses diverse opinions, demographics, and cultural nuances is essential to achieve a more comprehensive understanding of sentiment. A varied training set minimizes the likelihood of the model exhibiting a preference for a specific sentiment or viewpoint, promoting a more equitable and impartial sentiment analysis.

3.   Fine-tuning with Bias Mitigation Techniques:

Developers can utilize bias mitigation approaches during the fine-tuning phase to tackle and diminish sentiment bias effectively. This may entail modifying the weights assigned to individual training examples, implementing adversarial training to enhance the model's resilience to biased inputs, or integrating fairness requirements. By employing bias mitigation approaches during the fine-tuning process, developers can customize the model's behavior and enhance its ability to capture a fair and unbiased portrayal of sentiment accurately.

Personalization

Personalization in AI chatbots (Ait Baha et al., 2023) is customizing interactions based on individual user preferences, habits, and traits. It refers to the chatbot's capacity to comprehend and provide tailored responses to users' requirements. This encompasses customized suggestions, material, and conversational approaches derived from previous engagements, user backgrounds, or explicit preferences conveyed by the user during talks.

The advantages of integrating customization in AI chatbots are substantial. Firstly, it improves user engagement by offering a tailored and pertinent experience, improving the probability of users efficiently accomplishing their objectives. Customized conversations also enhance user satisfaction, as people value a chatbot that comprehends their preferences and adjusts accordingly. In addition, personalization can improve conversion rates by enabling the chatbot to provide tailored advice or assistance, hence raising the probability of users doing desired activities.

Here are three ways in which AI chatbots support personalization:

1.   User Context Understanding:

AI chatbots can be programmed to comprehend and adjust to specific user contexts. The model utilizes prior user interactions, preferences, and behaviors to tailor replies to each user's requirements and interests. AI chatbots can enhance the overall personalization of the user experience by generating more relevant and tailored information through understanding user context.

2.   Fine-tuning for User Profiles:

Customizing AI chatbots based on user-specific data or profiles allows for greater customization. This entails training the model on information linked to particular users, such as their preferences, linguistic style, or specific themes of interest. By fine-tuning techniques, AI chatbots can provide responses tailored to each user's attributes, resulting in a more individualized and captivating encounter.

3.   Dynamic Adaptation to User Input:

Table 2. Emotional intelligent expectations

SN	Future Expectation	Significance	How to Accomplish
1	Sentimental awareness	1. Improves the overall user experience 2. Enhances user engagement 3. Offer more efficient support, ultimately enhancing user satisfaction	1. Sentiment Analysis Capabilities 2. Contextual Understanding 3. Fine-tuning for Specific Domains or Languages
2	Politeness	1. Heightened user trust and loyalty 2. Help obtain relevant feedback 3. Foster a more inclusive and hospitable atmosphere	1. Politeness Modeling during Training 2. Contextual Sensitivity to Social Cues 3. Fine-tuning for Specific Use Cases
3	Sentiment Bias Awareness	1. Facilitation of equitable and impartial conversations. 2. Users are provided with unbiased responses, promoting a communication climate 3. Improves customer happiness and trust	1. Bias Detection and Monitoring 2. Diverse and Representative Training Data 3. Fine-tuning with Bias Mitigation Techniques
4	Personalization	1. Improves user engagement by offering a tailored and pertinent experience 2. Enhance user satisfaction 3. Enhance conversion rates by enabling the chatbot to provide tailored advice or assistance	1. User Context Understanding 2. Fine-tuning for User Profiles 3. Dynamic Adaptation to User Input

AI chatbots with adaptive capabilities can dynamically modify their responses in response to real-time user input. During a discussion, the model can adjust answers based on the user's changing sentiment, language style, or stated preferences. This adaptive modification enhances a customized and interactive interaction, accommodating the changing requirements and priorities of the user.

Social Expectations

Social awareness, as defined by (Selman, 2003), pertains to the ability of a chatbot system to accurately comprehend and appropriately respond to the social nuances inherent in human interactions. A socially aware chatbot comprehends cultural references and adheres to politeness norms while adjusting to various modes of communication. It guarantees that the responses align with cultural standards and user expectations, promoting productive connections, comprehending social cues, and preventing unsuitable or offensive language use. While the term "social awareness" may not be explicitly discussed in NLP literature, it aligns with the broader concept examined by (Miner et al., 2016), which emphasizes the need for social intelligence in designing chatbots that may support productive and culturally sensitive conversation. Figure 1 shows social expectations, and Table 3 summarizes the significance and methods to accomplish social expectations.

Chatbots greatly benefit from social awareness as it enables them to actively participate in culturally sensitive conversations, enhance user satisfaction, and prevent misunderstandings. Socially conscious chatbots can communicate with consumers by comprehending communication styles and societal customs. Chatbots with social awareness can effectively manage intricate scenarios in customer service or virtual assistant roles. They can deliver responses that align with client expectations and preferences, promoting user satisfaction and assurance.

For chatbots to communicate and adjust to different societal norms, they require social awareness. To succeed, individuals must possess the ability to comprehend cultural references, interpret social signals, and exhibit an understanding of social environments. Chatbots can access past discussions by incorporating memory and learning mechanisms, facilitating continuity and tailored interaction. While chatbots may not explicitly state "social awareness," literature (Foster, 2019) indicates that cultural sensitivity and user adaption are essential elements for chatbots to navigate diverse social situations successfully.

Cultural Awareness

Cultural awareness in AI chatbots entails acknowledging and comprehending various cultural conventions, sensitivities, and communication styles. This guarantees courteous and contextually suitable interactions with users from diverse backgrounds. It extends beyond language comprehension, recognizing cultural subtleties that can impact user inclinations, anticipations, and understandings of dialogues. A culturally aware AI chatbot can modify its responses to conform to the cultural norms of its users, fostering inclusivity and minimizing the likelihood of accidental misinterpretations.

The advantages of integrating cultural knowledge into AI chatbots are significant. Firstly, it improves customer pleasure and engagement by generating a user experience that is more tailored and culturally attuned. An ethnically sensitive chatbot can establish confidence with users from many cultural backgrounds, promoting favorable engagements and enduring user connections. In addition, the chatbot's avoidance of cultural insensitivity helps maintain a positive public image and reduces the likelihood of accidental offense or misunderstanding. Chatbots that possess cultural awareness are more adept at handling cross-cultural communication obstacles, guaranteeing smoother and more courteous contact with users throughout the globe.

Here are three ways in which AI chatbots support cultural awareness:

1. Diverse Training Data:

AI chatbots benefit from being educated on various datasets encompassing a broad spectrum of cultural perspectives, languages, and expressions. The model can comprehend and appreciate the subtle linguistic distinctions and cultural circumstances prevalent in distinct locations or communities by assimilating data from several cultures. Varied training data is essential to ensure that AI chatbots can effectively manage and produce culturally sensitive and polite material.

2. Contextual Sensitivity:

AI chatbots can be programmed to demonstrate contextual awareness of cultural cues. The model's ability to comprehend the context of a discussion, which includes cultural allusions and conventions, allows it to produce responses that conform to cultural expectations. This entails acknowledging the cultural connotations of specific words, phrases, or subjects and adjusting the language production accordingly. Contextual sensitivity enhances the ability to communicate in a culturally aware and suitable manner.

3. Fine-tuning for Specific Cultural Contexts:

Customizing AI chatbots for distinct cultural contexts enables developers to adapt the model's behavior to match the linguistic and cultural subtleties of a particular community or location more closely. This entails instructing the model using data that highlights cultural nuances, guaranteeing that the AI chatbots can produce material that is both courteous and pertinent to consumers from various cultural backgrounds. Refining the model by fine-tuning enhances its ability to create outputs demonstrating heightened cultural understanding and appropriateness.

Social Norm Awareness

AI chatbots must be aware of social norms (LaCroix & Bengio, 2019), which entails comprehending and integrating societal conventions, etiquettes, and acceptable behaviors into their interactions. It surpasses cultural awareness and encompasses the ability to acknowledge the implicit norms and expectations that regulate social exchanges within particular situations. A socially norm-aware AI chatbot can modify its responses to adhere to socially acceptable conduct, guaranteeing that its interactions are courteous and follow societal norms.

The advantages of incorporating social norm knowledge into AI chatbots are significant. Firstly, it improves user acceptability and trust by ensuring the chatbot's responses conform to the users' anticipated social norms. A chatbot that adheres to social conventions is more likely to be seen as kind and user-friendly. Moreover, the chatbot's usefulness in different contexts, such as customer service or professional relationships, is enhanced by its awareness of social conventions, essential for ensuring favorable user experiences. To mitigate the possibility of misunderstandings or bad reactions from users, the chatbot refrains from engaging in behaviors that could be deemed inappropriate or insulting.

Here are three ways in which AI chatbots support social norm awareness:

1. Incorporation of Social Norms in Training Data:

AI chatbots benefit from being trained on datasets encompassing instances that accurately represent various social norms. The model acquires the ability to identify and uphold diverse social norms by incorporating various verbal expressions, cultural customs, and social behaviors in the training data. The AI chatbots gain a better understanding and ability to generate material that follows accepted norms by being exposed to various social circumstances. This exposure helps them develop a more culturally and socially aware language processing capability.

2. Contextual Sensitivity to Social Context:

AI chatbots can be programmed to demonstrate contextual awareness of social cues, enabling them to identify and adjust to the social environment of a conversation. The model's ability to comprehend various social contexts' underlying regulations, etiquette, and norms empowers it to provide responses that align with societal expectations. This entails evaluating the societal ramifications of words, phrases, and subjects and modifying language production to conform to social conventions.

3. Fine-tuning for Social Sensitivity:

Training the model with data highlighting social norms and conventions is necessary to enhance the social sensitivity of AI chatbots. The model can adjust its behavior through fine-tuning to match users' expectations in different social scenarios closely. By undergoing fine-tuning, AI chatbots can enhance their understanding and compliance with social standards, resulting in the generation of respectful and contextually suitable content.

To summarize, AI chatbots facilitate social norm awareness by integrating social norms into their training data, being attuned to social cues in context, and refining their social sensitivity through fine-tuning. These tactics empower the models to navigate social environments efficiently, producing information that conforms to established standards and contributing to language processing conscious of social dynamics in many applications.

Social Bias Awareness

Social bias (Chang et al., 2019) awareness in AI chatbots entails identifying and resolving biases about social dimensions, including race, gender, age, and socioeconomic position. The objective is to guarantee that the chatbot's replies and choices are equitable impartial, and do not promote or reinforce detrimental preconceptions. An essential aspect of ensuring fairness, diversity, and inclusivity in AI systems is a deep understanding of social biases. This understanding is vital to prevent discriminatory results and promote AI's ethical deployment.

The advantages of incorporating social bias awareness into AI chatbots are significant. Firstly, it improves the impartiality and fairness of interactions, guaranteeing that the chatbot respects users without bias, regardless of their social traits. The chatbot establishes trust and credibility among users from varied backgrounds by reducing biased responses. Moreover, being conscious of societal biases is crucial in fostering responsible AI advancement ensuring compliance with ethical standards and regulatory requirements. It reduces the likelihood of inadvertent discrimination, guaranteeing that the chatbot's influence is constructive and impartial among various user demographics.

Here are three ways in which AI chatbots support awareness and mitigation of social bias:

1.   Bias Detection and Mitigation Techniques:

AI chatbots can integrate methods for identifying and reducing social bias in the information they provide. This entails examining the model's predictions and detecting situations where prejudices towards specific social groupings or viewpoints may exist. Many techniques can be utilized to mitigate and counteract social bias in the model's answers, including debiasing algorithms, fairness requirements, and adversarial training.

2.   Diverse and Representative Training Data:

Educating AI chatbots using varied and inclusive datasets encompassing a broad spectrum of social identities, demographics, and viewpoints is crucial to alleviating social prejudice. By integrating data from several sources, the model acquires a comprehensive understanding of language and mitigates the potential for reinforcing biases inherent in the training data. Varied training data enhances the equilibrium and impartiality of a linguistic model.

3.   Fine-tuning with Bias Awareness:

Developers can include awareness of social bias in fine-tuning by consciously acknowledging and resolving biases in the training data. By fine-tuning the model with a specific emphasis on reducing social bias, we can guarantee that the model's replies are equitable and impartial for various social groups and viewpoints. Developers can increase fairness in the model's outputs by actively addressing societal prejudices and including bias awareness in fine-tuning.

Gender Bias Awareness

Gender bias (Leavy, 2018) awareness in AI chatbots entails acknowledging and reducing prejudices associated with gender, guaranteeing that the chatbot's responses and actions are devoid of stereotypes, and treating users fairly, irrespective of their gender identification. The objective is to prevent gender-based discrimination and foster equitable and inclusive exchanges. Developing a chatbot that upholds ethical values and embraces diversity necessitates a keen awareness of gender prejudice.

The advantages of integrating gender bias awareness into AI chatbots are substantial. Firstly, it fosters tolerance and equality by guaranteeing that the chatbot's responses do not perpetuate detrimental gender stereotypes or assumptions. An AI chatbot sensitive to gender differences enhances the user's experience, promoting trust and active participation from individuals of diverse gender identities. Furthermore, tackling gender bias aligns with societal norms and regulatory requirements, minimizing the potential for adverse public opinion and legal consequences. By placing gender equality as a top priority, the chatbot transforms into a more conscientious and considerate tool for many users.

Here are three ways in which AI chatbots support awareness and mitigation of gender bias:

1. Bias Detection and Analysis:

AI chatbots can be programmed with algorithms and strategies to identify and examine gender bias in their responses. This entails analyzing the model's forecasts and detecting situations where biases against specific genders may exist. By investigating language patterns and relationships, the approach can identify gendered language and stereotypes that may lead to bias. By conducting thorough bias detection, developers can obtain valuable insights into potential biases and implement necessary corrective measures.

2. Debiasing Strategies:

AI chatbots can incorporate debiasing techniques to reduce gender bias in their information. These tactics entail modifying the parameters of the model and the training data to mitigate the influence of gender stereotypes and foster language creation that is more fair and unbiased. Gender-neutral language modeling, gender-balancing in training data, and adversarial training are effective techniques for reducing gender bias and promoting inclusive language representation.

3. Fine-tuning with Gender Awareness:

Developers can enhance gender awareness during the fine-tuning process by openly acknowledging and rectifying biases associated with gender in the training data and model design. By fine-tuning the model with an emphasis on gender awareness, developers can actively detect and reduce gender biases

Table 3. Social expectations

SN	Future Expectation	Significance	How to Accomplish
1	Cultural awareness	1. Improves customer pleasure and engagement 2. Promoting favorable engagements and enduring user connections. 3. Avoidance of cultural insensitivity helps maintain a positive public image	1. Diverse Training Data 2. Contextual Sensitivity 3. Fine-tuning for Specific Cultural Contexts
2	Social Norm awareness	1. Improve User acceptability and trust 2. Improve the chatbot's usefulness in different contexts 3. Improve customer service or professional relationships	1. Incorporation of Social Norms in Training Data 2. Contextual Sensitivity to Social Context 3. Fine-tuning for Social Sensitivity
3	Social Bias awareness	1. Improves the impartiality and fairness of interactions, 2. Establishes trust and credibility among users 3. Fostering responsible AI advancement	1. Bias Detection and Mitigation Techniques 2. Diverse and Representative Training Data 3. Fine-tuning with Bias Awareness
4	Gender Bias awareness	1. Fosters tolerance and equality 2. Enhances the user's experience, promoting trust and active participation 3. Minimizing the potential for adverse public opinion and legal consequences	1. Bias Detection and Analysis 2. Debiasing Strategies 3. Fine-tuning with Gender Awareness
5	Political bias awareness	1. Improve impartiality and parity 2. Improve user perceptions, fostering trust among users 3. Minimizing the likelihood of alienating specific user segments and subsequent legal complications	1. Bias Monitoring and Auditing 2. Explainability and Transparency 3. User Customization and Control

in the model's outputs. By including gender-sensitive fine-tuning approaches, developers may guarantee that the model's responses are fairer and more considerate towards a wide range of gender identities.

Political Bias Awareness

Political bias (Rozado, 2023) awareness in AI chatbots is the identification and reduction of biases associated with political affiliations, guaranteeing that the chatbot's responses remain impartial and unbiased and refrain from showing any preference towards a particular political position. The objective is to hinder reinforcing political stereotypes establishing an atmosphere that fosters respect and equitable treatment for users with varied political orientations. Understanding political prejudice is crucial to promoting fairness and preventing undesired outcomes in AI-powered interactions.

The advantages of integrating political bias awareness into AI chatbots are substantial. First and foremost, it guarantees impartiality and parity by prohibiting the chatbot from showing preference or bias towards any political philosophy, thereby promoting an all-encompassing user experience. An impartial chatbot enhances user perceptions, fostering trust among users with varying political perspectives. Furthermore, by addressing political bias, one can adhere to ethical norms, hence minimizing the likelihood of alienating specific user segments and subsequent legal complications. By advocating for impartiality, the chatbot enhances its credibility as a tool for people seeking information or support, irrespective of their political ideologies.

Here are three ways in which AI chatbots support awareness and mitigation of political bias:

1.   Bias Monitoring and Auditing:

By incorporating regular bias monitoring and auditing procedures, developers can evaluate the model's outputs to identify any instances of political prejudice. By examining forecasts and reactions, engineers might detect cases where the model demonstrates partiality towards political positions or ideologies. Continuous monitoring identifies possible problems, while regular audits ensure the ongoing responsibility of addressing political bias.

2.   Explainability and Transparency:

Improving the comprehensibility and openness of AI models is essential for comprehending and resolving political prejudice. AI models, such as AI chatbots, can be programmed to explain their predictions, providing insights into how various political situations influence judgments. Transparent models allow users, developers, and stakeholders to quickly identify potential biases, promoting awareness and making the required adjustments to improve political neutrality.

3.   User Customization and Control:

Allowing users to customize and regulate the model's behavior effectively tackles concerns associated with political bias. AI apps can incorporate features that enable users to explicitly define their political inclinations or fine-tune the degree of political awareness in the generated responses. Developers would allow users to adapt the model according to their perspectives through customization options, fostering a highly customized and politically unbiased encounter.

ETHICAL CONSIDERATIONS AND SOCIETAL IMPACTS

This section discusses the Ethical Considerations and Societal Impacts of AI-based chatbot technology.

Ethical Considerations

Now, we list the primary ethical considerations in AI chatbot technology.

User Privacy and Data Security

Protecting the confidentiality of users' discussions and personal information is a crucial ethical concern in AI dialogue technology. Developers must establish robust security protocols to safeguard sensitive data from illegal entry, and users should be educated on data gathering, storage, and utilization procedures.

Transparency and Informed Consent

Transparency is essential for establishing confidence in AI dialogue technology. Users must recognize that they are engaging with a machine, and developers should offer explicit details regarding the AI's skills and constraints. Obtaining informed consent from consumers regarding data usage and the nature of AI interactions is crucial.

Fairness and Bias Mitigation

Developers must proactively remove biases in AI dialog systems to ensure equitable and impartial treatment of all users. Training data can introduce bias, leading to answers that perpetuate stereotypes or discriminate against specific populations. Regular audits and continuous efforts to mitigate bias are crucial ethical issues.

User Empowerment and Control

AI dialog technology should be designed ethically to provide users control over their interactions. Users should be able to personalize preferences, control data sharing, and choose not to participate in automated conversations effortlessly. Focusing on user agency promotes a more ethical and respectful utilization of AI technology.

Human-AI Collaboration and Accountability

Developers and organizations implementing AI dialog technology need to define explicit accountability measures. Although AI can improve efficiency, it should not relieve humans of accountability. Systems must be established to rectify mistakes, guarantee responsibility for decisions made by the AI, and permit human involvement when needed. One ethical consideration is establishing the responsibilities of AI and human participants in their interaction.

Long Term Societal Impacts

Now we list the main Societal Impacts of AI chatbot technology.

Altered Communication Patterns

The lasting societal consequences of AI dialog technology may lead to a change in how people communicate. As these technologies grow more ingrained in everyday life, individuals may more frequently interact with AI-driven systems, influencing conventional communication dynamics.

Workforce Transformation

The broad implementation of AI dialog technology could alter the labor environment. In the long run, some jobs may be automated, displacing employment in specific sectors. There might be an increasing need for positions involving AI systems' creation, upkeep, and supervision, which will require workforce adaptation and skill enhancement.

Enhanced Productivity and Efficiency

AI dialog technology can significantly improve productivity and efficiency in different sectors. As organizations use these technologies, there could be enduring beneficial effects on economic expansion, optimizing procedures, and promoting innovation in products and services.

Cultural Shifts in Human-Technology Interaction

Integrating AI dialog technology into society could lead to cultural changes in people's attitudes and interactions with technology. Embracing and standardizing AI-powered interactions could alter social norms, expectations, and attitudes around human-computer interaction.

Ethical and Regulatory Evolution

The lasting societal effects of AI dialog technology involve continuous development in ethical considerations and legal frameworks. As these technologies advance, there will probably be more attention paid to the creation of standards to deal with ethical concerns, privacy issues, and potential biases. As technology advances, societal norms and expectations for the ethical use of AI are expected to change.

GENERAL DIRECTIONS TO ACCOMPLISH FUTURE EXPECTATIONS

In this section, we discuss general directions to achieve futuristic expectations. Other than discussed in the previous section, these methods can be used to improve any AI system and, specifically, an AI-based chatbot. Figure 2 shows general directions for accomplishing future expectations used in this study.

Re-Energize Old Approaches

There is a need for a new approach to artificial intelligence (AI), particularly for chatbots, to enhance their dependability, capacity to comprehend emotions, and understanding of social interactions. This technique should effectively address current limitations and adjust to evolving user requirements.

Five Different Methods

Domingo's book (Domingos 2015) categorizes five paradigms: Symbolists, Connectionists, Evolutionaries, Bayesians, and Analogizers. Each paradigm has a unique philosophical approach to designing the best effective learning algorithm. Symbolists utilize algorithms to analyze the surroundings through the analysis of symbols and adherence to rules. Connectionists employ neural network models. Evolutionaries utilize the concepts of natural selection. Bayesians utilize probability theory. Analogizers identify resemblances between situations to create forecasts. Integrating these strategies into a comprehensive algorithm is crucial for enhancing machine learning proficiency.

Pearl's Ladder of Causation for AI Chatbot

Judea Pearl's Ladder of Causation (Goldberg, 2019) is a conceptual framework that delineates different levels of comprehension and logical thinking regarding causation. The Pearl's Ladder of Causation is a fundamental principle in causal inference, comprising three essential elements: Association, Intervention, and Counterfactuals. In the initial phase, known as Association, one examines the statistical relationships between different variables. The second intervention stage involves changing variables to observe and track changes in others. The Counterfactuals level explores hypothetical situations and their resulting causal effects.

Figure 2. General directions to accomplish future expectations

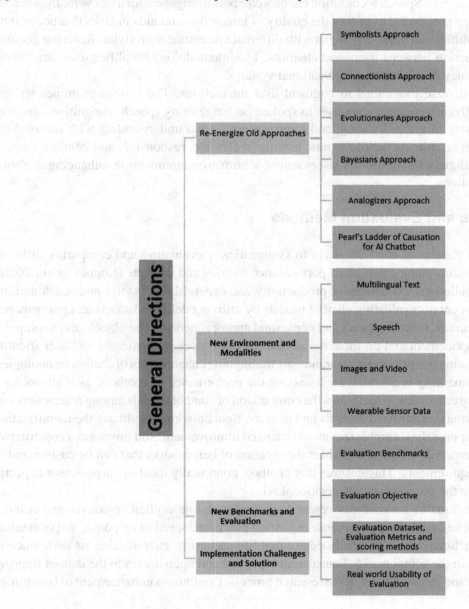

New Environment, Modalities, and System Interface

Employing many modalities in multimodal learning could enhance the overall user experience of AI-based chatbots (Baltrušaitis et al., 2018). Chatbot modalities encompass diverse communication channels such as text, speech, pictures, and sensor data. To be efficient, chatbots must assess and deliver information across these many modes of communication. Textual input is essential for comprehending user inquiries, audio recognition fosters engagement, and image processing improves understanding. By integrating several modalities, conversational agents become adaptive and context-sensitive, enabling them to comprehend better and engage with users. This methodology improves interactions' genuineness and engaging quality, allowing the chatbots to handle real-world engagements efficiently.

Chatbots should incorporate several modalities to develop inclusive, contextually conscious, and efficient conversational agents. Speech recognition enables chatbots to engage with users verbally, enhancing accessibility. Image processing improves the quality of interaction and aids in tasks that necessitate visual context. The multimodal approach aligns with different communication styles, fostering genuine and fascinating interaction between users and chatbots. This methodology amplifies user satisfaction and the overall efficiency of AI-driven conversational systems.

Chatbots employ diverse modalities to augment user interactions. The system examines written queries using text analysis, generates responses to spoken language using speech recognition, analyzes visual information using image processing, and improves contextual understanding with sensor data. Advanced models can seamlessly handle inputs, leading to flexible, responsive, and genuine interactions. This technique aligns with the multi-sensory nature of human communication, enhancing chatbots' utility in diverse situations.

New Benchmarks and Evaluation Methods

Benchmarking in the context of chatbots refers to systematically evaluating and comparing different chatbot models or systems using established performance metrics and datasets (Kounev et al., 2020). Assessing chatbot installations' effectiveness, productivity, and dependability is vital, and benchmarking is critical. The process entails evaluating chatbot models by utilizing defined datasets and performance indicators such as accuracy, reaction speed, and contextual appropriateness. The objective is to pinpoint areas that require enhancement and promote the advancement of more sophisticated and user-friendly chatbots, hence stimulating innovation and guaranteeing the ongoing enhancement of chatbot technologies.

Conducting benchmarking is essential for assessing the performance of chatbots, as it allows for a standardized and impartial review. It facilitates the comparison of chatbot models among researchers and developers by employing standardized datasets and metrics. Benchmarking facilitates the identification of the most effective approaches, emphasizes areas that need improvement, and promotes a constructive competitive atmosphere. Additionally, it enables the creation of benchmarks that can be customized to suit users' specific requirements. This ensures that chatbots continually meet or surpass user expectations and contribute to the progress of conversational AI.

To build novel benchmarks for chatbots, researchers need to define explicit objectives and criteria, curate varied datasets, and evaluate performance regarding precision, speed of response, and contextual understanding. A benchmark must faithfully depict real-life scenarios, guaranteeing its pertinence to practical applications in the actual world. Transparent reporting and open access to the dataset improve the ability to replicate and involve others in the research process. Continuous enhancement of benchmark performance is essential for adapting to evolving user expectations and technical improvements, assuring its continued value as an assessment tool for measuring chatbot system performance.

Implementation Challenges and Solutions

This section discusses the main implementation challenges and their respective solution.

1.　Ambiguous User Queries:

Users may ask questions with unclear intentions or use informal language, making it difficult for chatbots to comprehend and provide appropriate responses. To improve intent recognition, sophisticated natural language processing (NLP) methods and machine learning models are utilized. Consistently refresh the chatbot's training data using a variety of language expressions to enhance its capability to manage ambiguity.

2.　Data Privacy and Security:

Managing delicate user data in chatbot conversations presents data privacy and security issues. Secure communication lines and storage, comply with data protection laws, and establish user authentication protocols. Reduce the storage of personally identifiable information (PII) and enforce restricted and audited data access.

3.　Scalability Concerns:

With the growth of user involvement, it is crucial to ensure that the chatbot can scale to manage higher traffic and interactions. Use cloud-based services to offer scalable infrastructure. Utilize load balancing and containerization technologies for optimal workload distribution. Consistently observe system performance and adjust resources accordingly.

4.　Resource Intensity and Training:

Creating and educating advanced chatbot models can be demanding in terms of resources, necessitating significant computational capabilities and specialized knowledge. Utilize cloud computing services for affordable access to computational resources. Employ pre-trained models and transfer learning methods to minimize the training data and time needed. Work with AI specialists or utilize chatbot creation solutions to simplify the process.

5.　Continuous Learning and Adaptation:

Continuously learning to ensure that chatbots change and adapt to changing user behaviors and expectations is a problem. Establish feedback loops to get user comments and refresh the chatbot's training data regularly. Implement reinforcement learning methods to allow the chatbot to enhance its performance through user interactions as time progresses.

6. User Engagement Monitoring:

Assessing and enhancing user involvement can be difficult without adequate monitoring instruments. Utilize analytics tools to monitor user interactions, quantify engagement measures, and obtain insights on user behavior. Utilize this data to make educated modifications to the chatbot's design and content.

7. Human-in-the-Loop Integration:

Striking the appropriate balance between complete automation and human intervention can be difficult. Utilize a person-in-the-loop strategy to allow human operators to assist the chatbot when it faces intricate inquiries or delicate matters. This strategy aids in guaranteeing superior precision and ethical management of interactions.

CONCLUSION

This study outlines three anticipated developments for chatbots in the future: Trustworthiness, emotional intelligence, and social awareness. Reliability in communication guarantees precise information sharing, whereas emotional intelligence fosters user engagement by building empathy. Moreover, social awareness empowers individuals to communicate effectively with cultural sensitivity and contextual appropriateness. We offer a range of comprehensive strategies to address the increasing difficulties in creating chatbots, including innovative methods, creative settings and formats, and updated standards. We aim to improve user trust, cultivate significant connections, and encourage culturally aware interactions by incorporating reliability, emotional understanding, and social consciousness into chatbots. As a result, this leads to a more efficient and morally responsible AI system, which positively impacts society.

REFERENCES

Ait Baha, T., El Hajji, M., Es-Saady, Y., & Fadili, H. (2023). The power of personalization: A systematic review of personality-adaptive chatbots. *SN Computer Science, 4*(5), 661. doi:10.1007/s42979-023-02092-6

Baltrušaitis, T., Ahuja, C., & Morency, L.-P. (2018). Multimodal machine learning: A survey and taxonomy. *IEEE Transactions on Pattern Analysis and Machine Intelligence, 41*(2), 423–443. doi:10.1109/TPAMI.2018.2798607 PMID:29994351

Chang, K.-W., Prabhakaran, V., & Ordonez, V. (2019). Bias and fairness in natural language processing. *Proceedings of the 2019 Conference on Empirical Methods in Natural Language Processing and the 9th International Joint Conference on Natural Language Processing (EMNLP-IJCNLP): Tutorial Abstracts.* IEEE.

Deng, J., Sun, H., Zhang, Z., Cheng, J., & Huang, M. (2023). Recent advances towards safe, responsible, and moral dialogue systems: A survey. *ArXiv Preprint ArXiv:2302.09270.*

Domingos, P. (2015). *The master algorithm: How the quest for the ultimate learning machine will remake our world.* Basic Books.

Foster, M. E. (2019). Natural language generation for social robotics: opportunities and challenges. *Philosophical Transactions of the Royal Society B, 374*(1771), 20180027.

Goldberg, L. R. (2019). *The Book of Why: The New Science of Cause and Effect: by Judea Pearl and Dana Mackenzie, Basic Books (2018)*. Taylor & Francis.

Goleman, D. (1995). Emotional intelligence, imagination, cognition and personality. *Personality and Individual Differences, 9*, 185–211.

Kong, X., Liu, S., & Zhu, L. (2024). Toward Human-centered XAI in Practice: A survey. *Machine Intelligence Research*, (pp. 1–31). IEEE.

Kounev, S., Lange, K.-D., & Von Kistowski, J. (2020). *Systems Benchmarking*. Springer. doi:10.1007/978-3-030-41705-5

LaCroix, T., & Bengio, Y. (2019). Learning from learning machines: optimisation, rules, and social norms. *ArXiv Preprint ArXiv:2001.00006*.

Leavy, S. (2018). Gender bias in artificial intelligence: The need for diversity and gender theory in machine learning. *Proceedings of the 1st International Workshop on Gender Equality in Software Engineering*, (pp. 14–16). ACM. 10.1145/3195570.3195580

Liu, B., Ding, M., Shaham, S., Rahayu, W., Farokhi, F., & Lin, Z. (2021). When machine learning meets privacy: A survey and outlook. *ACM Computing Surveys, 54*(2), 1–36. doi:10.1145/3436755

Liu, H., Wang, Y., Fan, W., Liu, X., Li, Y., Jain, S., Liu, Y., Jain, A., & Tang, J. (2022). Trustworthy ai: A computational perspective. *ACM Transactions on Intelligent Systems and Technology, 14*(1), 1–59. doi:10.1145/3546872

Miner, A., Chow, A., Adler, S., Zaitsev, I., Tero, P., Darcy, A., & Paepcke, A. (2016). Conversational agents and mental health: Theory-informed assessment of language and affect. *Proceedings of the Fourth International Conference on Human Agent Interaction*, (pp. 123–130). ACM. 10.1145/2974804.2974820

Ni, J., Young, T., Pandelea, V., Xue, F., & Cambria, E. (2023). Recent advances in deep learning based dialogue systems: A systematic survey. *Artificial Intelligence Review, 56*(4), 3055–3155. doi:10.1007/s10462-022-10248-8

Novelli, C., Taddeo, M., & Floridi, L. (2023). Accountability in artificial intelligence: What it is and how it works. *AI & Society*, 1–12. doi:10.1007/s00146-023-01635-y

Ribino, P. (2023). The role of politeness in human–machine interactions: A systematic literature review and future perspectives. *Artificial Intelligence Review, 56*(S1, Suppl 1), 445–482. doi:10.1007/s10462-023-10540-1

Rozado, D. (2023). The political biases of chatgpt. *Social Sciences (Basel, Switzerland), 12*(3), 148. doi:10.3390/socsci12030148

Selman, R. L. (2003). *Promotion of Social Awareness: Powerful Lessons for the Partnership of Developmental Theory and*. Russell Sage Foundation.

Tan, K. L., Lee, C. P., & Lim, K. M. (2023). A survey of sentiment analysis: Approaches, datasets, and future research. *Applied Sciences (Basel, Switzerland), 13*(7), 4550. doi:10.3390/app13074550

Xue, J., Wang, Y.-C., Wei, C., Liu, X., Woo, J., & Kuo, C.-C. J. (2023). Bias and fairness in chatbots: An overview. *ArXiv Preprint ArXiv:2309.08836.*

KEY TERMS AND DEFINITIONS

Accountability and Auditability: AI systems need to be responsible for their acts by keeping clear audit trails for supervision, accountability, and ethical management.

Cultural Awareness: Cultural awareness in AI involves recognizing and valuing various cultural subtleties to ensure that technology acknowledges and respects cultural distinctions in interactions.

Emotional Intelligence: Emotional intelligence pertains to the capacity to identify, comprehend, and regulate one's own emotions as well as the emotions of others. It enhances effective communication, empathy, and interpersonal skills, promoting healthier social connections.

Explainability: AI systems must offer lucid and comprehensible rationales for their judgments to improve transparency and user understanding of the technology's operations.

Gender Bias Awareness: Gender bias awareness entails identifying and reducing biases linked to gender in AI replies to promote equality and fairness in interactions.

Non-Discrimination and Fairness: AI systems must treat all users impartially, without prejudices related to traits such as race or gender, in order to promote fairness and inclusivity.

Personalization: Personalization is the process of customizing AI interactions by considering individual user preferences and past data, resulting in unique and more captivating user experiences.

Politeness: Politeness in AI involves employing courteous and respectful language throughout conversations to improve user experience and keep a positive and caring tone.

Political Bias Awareness: Being conscious of political bias helps avoid distorted perceptions or reactions influenced by political loyalties, promoting fairness and objectivity in AI interactions.

Privacy: Privacy focuses on preserving user data, establishing ethical data handling procedures, and maintaining users' confidentiality throughout AI interactions.

Safety and Robustness: Safety in AI guarantees systems operate without causing harm, whereas robustness entails resilience in different settings to maintain consistent performance.

Sentiment Bias: Being aware of sentiment bias is essential to avoid distorted interpretations or reactions stemming from biases in sentiment analysis algorithms, guaranteeing equitable and impartial handling of user feelings.

Sentimental: Sentiment analysis in AI is the process of comprehending and interpreting emotions expressed in user inputs to allow computers to react accordingly to human feelings.

Social Awareness: Social awareness involves comprehending societal dynamics, conventions, and various perspectives. It entails identifying social signs, showing empathy towards others, and skillfully handling different social situations, which leads to successful and peaceful interactions within a group or civilization.

Social Bias Awareness: Social bias awareness focuses on recognizing prejudices associated with social groupings to reduce discrimination and promote equitable treatment of individuals, regardless of their social backgrounds.

Social Norm Awareness: Being aware of social norms in AI means following established society norms in language and conduct, ensuring that replies correspond with current social standards for more culturally suitable interactions.

Trustworthy: To be trustworthy means continually showing reliability, integrity, and credibility. Trust is essential in interpersonal relationships, based on the reliability and honesty of individuals within social frameworks.

Compilation of References

Abdellatif, A., Costa, D., Badran, K., Abdalkareem, R., & Shihab, E. (2020). Challenges in Chatbot Development: A Study of Stack Overflow Posts. In *Proceedings - 2020 IEEE/ACM 17th International Conference on Mining Software Repositories, MSR 2020*. IEEE. 10.1145/3379597.3387472

Abu Shawar, B. A., & Atwell, E. S. (2007). Chatbots: Are they really useful? *Journal for Language Technology and Computational Linguistics*, 22(1), 1. doi:10.21248/jlcl.22.2007.88

Adam, M., Wessel, M., & Benlian, A. (2021). AI-based chatbots in customer service and their effects on user compliance. [Reference Link]. *Electronic Markets*, 31(2), 427–445. doi:10.1007/s12525-020-00414-7

Adamopoulou, E., & Moussiades, L. (2020). An overview of chatbot technology. *IFIP International Conference on Artificial Intelligence Applications and Innovations*. Springer, Cham. 10.1007/978-3-030-49186-4_31

Adamopoulou, E., & Moussiades, L. (2020). Chatbots: History, technology, and applications. *Machine Learning with Applications*, 2, 100006. doi:10.1016/j.mlwa.2020.100006

Agnihotri, A., & Bhattacharya, S. (2023). Chatbots' effectiveness in service recovery. *International Journal of Information Management*, 102679. doi:10.1016/j.ijinfomgt.2023.102679

Ahmedetal, S. (2020). Smart Home Shield and Automation System Using Facebook Messenger Chatbot. In: *2020 IEEE Region 10 Symposium (TENSYMP)*. IEEE.

Ait Baha, T., El Hajji, M., Es-Saady, Y., & Fadili, H. (2023). The power of personalization: A systematic review of personality-adaptive chatbots. *SN Computer Science*, 4(5), 661. doi:10.1007/s42979-023-02092-6

Ait-Mlouk, A., & Jiang, L. (2020). KBot: A Knowledge Graph Based ChatBot for Natural Language Understanding over Linked Data. *IEEE Access: Practical Innovations, Open Solutions*, 8, 149220–149230. doi:10.1109/ACCESS.2020.3016142

Akpur, A. (2023). Seyahat Danışmanı Olarak Chatgpt'nin Yeteneklerini Keşfetmek: Turizm Pazarlamasında Üretken Yapay Zeka Üzerine Bir Araştırma. *International Journal of Contemporary Tourism Research*. doi:10.30625/ijctr.1325428

Aksoy, H. (2023). *Folklor ve Gelenek Kavramlarına "ChatGPT"nin Yazdığı Masallar Üzerinden Bakmak*. Korkut Ata Türkiyat Araştırmaları Dergisi. doi:10.51531/korkutataturkiyat.1361382

Alabbas, A., & Alomar, K. (2024). Tayseer: A Novel AI-Powered Arabic Chatbot Framework for Technical and Vocational Student Helpdesk Services and Enhancing Student Interactions. *Applied Sciences (Basel, Switzerland)*, 14(6), 6. doi:10.3390/app14062547

Alaska Airlines. (2017). *'Ask Jenn.' Alaska Airlines*.

Aleedy, M., Shaiba, H., & Bezbradica, M. (2019). Generating and analyzing chatbot responses using natural language processing. [Reference Link]. *International Journal of Advanced Computer Science and Applications*, *10*(9). doi:10.14569/IJACSA.2019.0100910

Alekseev, D., Shagalova, P., & Sokolova, E. (2021). Development of a chatbot using machine learning algorithms to automate educational processes. *Proceedings of the 31th International Conference on Computer Graphics and Vision*. IEEE. 10.20948/graphicon-2021-3027-1104-1113

Alexa. (n.d.). Amazon. https://alexa.amazon.com/

Alexakisetal, G. (2019). Control of smart home operations using natural language processing, voice recognition and IoT technologies in a multi-tier architecture. Designs, 3, 32.

Al-Madi, N. A., Maria, K. A., Al-Madi, M. A., Alia, M. A., & Maria, E. A. (2021). An Intelligent Arabic Chatbot System Proposed Framework. *2021 International Conference on Information Technology (ICIT)*, (pp. 592–597). IEEE. 10.1109/ICIT52682.2021.9491699

Alotaibi, R., Ali, A., Alharthi, H., & Almehamadi, R. (2020). AI Chatbot for Tourism Recommendations A Case Study in the City of Jeddah, Saudi Arabia. *International Journal of Interactive Mobile Technologies*, *14*(19). doi:10.3991/ijim.v14i19.17201

Altamimi, I., Altamimi, A., Alhumimidi, A. S., Altamimi, A., & Temsah, M. (2023). Artificial intelligence (AI) chatbots in medicine: A supplement, not a substitute. *Cureus*. doi:10.7759/cureus.40922 PMID:37496532

Altun, M. L. (2024). Yapay Zekâ Üzerine Fıkhî Bir Analiz. *Dicle İlahiyat Dergisi*, *26*(2), 227–249. doi:10.58852/dicd.1386730

AmamaC.OkengwuU. (2023). Smart chatbot system for banking using natural language processing tools. doi:10.21203/rs.3.rs-3285543/v1

Amiri, P., & Karahanna, E. (2022). Chatbot use cases in the Covid-19 public health response. *Journal of the American Medical Informatics Association : JAMIA*, *29*(5), 1000–1010. doi:10.1093/jamia/ocac014 PMID:35137107

Animas Marketing. (2023). *What happened to smarter child, the aim chatbox?* Animas Marketing. https://animasmarketing.com/what-happened-to-smarterchild-the-aim-chatbot/

Anjum, K., Sameer, M., & Kumar, S. (2023, February). AI Enabled NLP based Text to Text Medical Chatbot. In *2023 3rd International Conference on Innovative Practices in Technology and Management (ICIPTM)* (pp. 1-5). IEEE. 10.1109/ICIPTM57143.2023.10117966

Antony, S., & Ramnath, R. (2023). A phenomenological exploration of students' perceptions of AI chatbots in higher education. *IAFOR Journal of Education*, *11*(2), 7–38. doi:10.22492/ije.11.2.01

Appointment Scheduling Chatbot. 500Apps. (n.d.). Botup. https://botup.com/scheduling

Araujo, T. (2018). Living up to the chatbot hype: The influence of anthropomorphic design cues and communicative agency framing on conversational agent and company perceptions. *Computers in Human Behavior*, *85*, 183–189. doi:10.1016/j.chb.2018.03.051

Ashfaq, M., Yun, J., Yu, S., & Loureiro, S. M. C. (2020). I, Chatbot: Modeling the determinants of users' satisfaction and continuance intention of AI-powered service agents. *Telematics and Informatics*, *54*, 101473. doi:10.1016/j.tele.2020.101473

Ashfaque, M. W. Sr. (2022). Analysis of different trends in chatbot designing and development: A review. *ECS Transactions*, *107*(1), 7215–7227. doi:10.1149/10701.7215ecst

Aslam, F. (2023). The impact of artificial intelligence on chatbot technology: A study on the current advancements and leading innovations. *European Journal of Technology, 7*(3), 62–72. doi:10.47672/ejt.1561

Aswini, D. (2019). Clinical medical knowledge extraction using crowdsourcing techniques. *Int. Res. J. Eng. Technol, 6.*

Athanassopoulos, S., Manoli, P., Gouvi, M., Lavidas, K., & Komis, V. (2023). The use of ChatGPT as a learning tool to improve foreign language writing in a multilingual and multicultural classroom. *Advances in Mobile Learning Educational Research, 3*(2), 818–824. doi:10.25082/AMLER.2023.02.009

Athreya, R. G., Axel, C. N. N., & Usbeck, R. (2018). Enhancing Community Interactions with Data-Driven Chatbots - The DBpedia Chatbot. In *The Web Conference 2018 - Companion of the World Wide Web Conference, WWW 2018.* ACM. 10.1145/3184558.3186964

Atzori, L., Iera, A., & Morabito, G. (2011). SIoT: Giving a Social Structure to the Internet of Things".In. *IEEE Communications Letters, 15*(11), 15. doi:10.1109/LCOMM.2011.090911.111340

Badempet, P., Cheerala, P., & Anagondi, S. P. (2023). *A healthcare system using machine learning techniques for disease prediction with chatbot assistance.* IEEE. doi:10.14293/PR2199.000474.v1

Badlani, S., Aditya, T., Dave, M., & Chaudhari, S. (2021). Multilingual healthcare chatbot using machine learning. *2021 2nd International Conference for Emerging Technology (INCET).* IEEE. 10.1109/INCET51464.2021.9456304

Bahdanau, D., Cho, K., & Bengio, Y. (2014). *Neural machine translation by jointly learning to align and translate.* arXiv preprint arXiv:1409.0473.

BaiDoo-Anu, D., & Owusu Ansah, L. (2023). Education in the Era of Generative Artificial Intelligence (AI): Understanding the Potential Benefits of ChatGPT in Promoting Teaching and Learning. *Journal of AI, 7*(1), 52–62. doi:10.61969/jai.1337500

Bakshi, P., Bhambri, P., & Thapar, V. (2021). A Review Paper on Wireless Sensor Network Techniques in Internet of Things (IoT). *Wesleyan Journal of Research, 14*(7), 147–160.

Bali, M., Mohanty, S., Chatterjee, D., Sarma, M., & Puravankara, R. (2019). Diabot: A predictive medical chatbot using ensemble learning. [IJRTE]. *International Journal of Recent Technology and Engineering, 8*(2), 6334–6340. doi:10.35940/ijrte.B2196.078219

Baltrušaitis, T., Ahuja, C., & Morency, L.-P. (2018). Multimodal machine learning: A survey and taxonomy. *IEEE Transactions on Pattern Analysis and Machine Intelligence, 41*(2), 423–443. doi:10.1109/TPAMI.2018.2798607 PMID:29994351

Banh, L., & Strobel, G. (2023). Generative artificial intelligence. *Electronic Markets, 33*(1), 63. doi:10.1007/s12525-023-00680-1

Bao, Q., Ni, L., & Liu, J. (2020). HHH: An online medical chatbot system based on knowledge graph and hierarchical Bi-directional attention. *Proceedings of the Australasian Computer Science Week Multiconference.* ACM. 10.1145/3373017.3373049

Baskara, R., & Mukarto, M. (2023). Exploring the Implications of ChatGPT for Language Learning in Higher Education. *Indonesian Journal of English Language Teaching and Applied Linguistics, 7*(2), 2. doi:10.21093/ijeltal.v7i2.1387

Batra, R., Song, L., & Ramprasad, R. (2020). Emerging materials intelligence ecosystems propelled by machine learning. *Nature Reviews. Materials, 6*(8), 655–678. doi:10.1038/s41578-020-00255-y

Bavaresco, R., Silveira, D., Reis, E., Barbosa, J., Righi, R., Costa, C., Antunes, R., Gomes, M., Gatti, C., Vanzin, M., Junior, S. C., Silva, E., & Moreira, C. (2020). Conversational agents in business: A systematic literature review and future research directions. *Computer Science Review*, *36*, 100239. doi:10.1016/j.cosrev.2020.100239

Baziyad, M., Kamel, I., & Rabie, T. (2023). On the Linguistic Limitations of ChatGPT: An Experimental Case Study. *2023 International Symposium on Networks, Computers and Communications (ISNCC)*, 1–6. 10.1109/ISNCC58260.2023.10323661

Behera, R. K., Bala, P. K., & Ray, A. (2021). Cognitive Chatbot for Personalised Contextual Customer Service: Behind the Scene and beyond the Hype. *Information Systems Frontiers*. Advance online publication. doi:10.1007/s10796-021-10168-y

Belda-Medina, J., & Calvo-Ferrer, J. R. (2022). Using Chatbots as AI Conversational Partners in Language Learning. *Applied Sciences (Basel, Switzerland)*, *12*(17), 8427. doi:10.3390/app12178427

Belen Saglam, R., Nurse, J. R. C., & Hodges, D. (2021). Privacy Concerns in Chatbot Interactions: When to Trust and When to Worry. In C. Stephanidis, M. Antona, & S. Ntoa (Eds.), *HCI International 2021—Posters* (pp. 391–399). Springer International Publishing. doi:10.1007/978-3-030-78642-7_53

Bengio, Y., Courville, A., & Vincent, P. (2013). Representation learning: A review and new perspectives. [Reference Link]. *IEEE Transactions on Pattern Analysis and Machine Intelligence*, *35*(8), 1798–1828. doi:10.1109/TPAMI.2013.50 PMID:23787338

Bermeo-Giraldo, M. C., Toro, O. N. P., Arias, A. V., & Correa, P. A. R. (2023). Factors influencing the adoption of chatbots by healthcare users. *Journal of Innovation Management*, *11*(3), 75–94. doi:10.24840/2183-0606_011.003_0004

Bhambri, P. (2021). Electronic Evidence. In Textbook of Cyber Heal (pp. 86-120). AGAR Saliha Publication, Tamil Nadu.

Bhambri, P. (2020). Green Compliance. In S. Agarwal (Ed.), *Introduction to Green Computing* (pp. 95–125). AGAR Saliha Publication.

Bhambri, P., Singh, M., Jain, A., Dhanoa, I. S., Sinha, V. K., & Lal, S. (2021). Classification of the GENE Expression Data with the Aid of Optimized Feature Selection. *Turkish Journal of Physiotherapy and Rehabilitation*, *32*(3), 1158–1167.

Bhutada, S., Madabhushi, M., Shivani, S., & Choolakal, S. (2024). Facial Emotion Recognition Using Chatbot and Raspberry Pi. In H. Zen, N. M. Dasari, Y. M. Latha, & S. S. Rao (Eds.), *Soft Computing and Signal Processing* (pp. 53–66). Springer Nature. doi:10.1007/978-981-99-8451-0_5

Bibauw, S., François, T., & Desmet, P. (2019). Discussing with a computer to practice a foreign language: Research synthesis and conceptual framework of dialogue-based CALL. *Computer Assisted Language Learning*, *32*(8), 827–877. doi:10.1080/09588221.2018.1535508

Bibauw, S., Van den Noortgate, W., François, T., & Desmet, P. (2022). Dialogue Systems for Language Learning: A MetaAnalysis. *Language Learning & Technology*, *26*(1), 1–24. https://hdl.handle.net/10125/73488

Bilquise, G., Ibrahim, S., & Shaalan, K. (2022). Emotionally Intelligent Chatbots: A Systematic Literature Review. [Reference Link]. *Human Behavior and Emerging Technologies*, *2022*, 2022. doi:10.1155/2022/9601630

Bird, S., Klein, E., & Loper, E. (2009). *Natural language processing with Python: analyzing text with the natural language toolkit*. O'Reilly Media, Inc. [Reference Link]

Biswas, S. S. (2023). Potential Use of Chat GPT in Global Warming. *Annals of Biomedical Engineering*, *51*(6), 1126–1127. doi:10.1007/s10439-023-03171-8 PMID:36856927

Brandtzaeg, P. B., & Følstad, A. (2017). Why people use chatbots. In I. Kompatsiaris (Ed.), Lecture Notes in Computer Science: Vol. 10673. *Internet Science. INSCI 2017*. Springer. doi:10.1007/978-3-319-70284-1_30

Brandtzaeg, P. B., & Følstad, A. (2018). Chatbots: User Changing Needs and Motivations. *Interactions (New York, N.Y.)*, *25*(5), 38–43. Advance online publication. doi:10.1145/3236669

Brin, D., Sorin, V., Vaid, A., Soroush, A., Glicksberg, B. S., Charney, A. W., Nadkarni, G., & Klang, E. (2023). Comparing ChatGPT and GPT-4 performance in USMLE soft skill assessments. *Scientific Reports*, *13*(1), 16492. doi:10.1038/s41598-023-43436-9 PMID:37779171

Brown, T. B., Mann, B., Ryder, N., Subbiah, M., Kaplan, J., Dhariwal, P., & Amodei, D. (2020). *Language Models are Few-Shot Learners.* arXiv preprint arXiv:2005.14165.

Brown, P. F., Pietra, V. J. D., Pietra, S. A. D., & Mercer, R. L. (1993). The mathematics of statistical machine translation: Parameter estimation. *Computational Linguistics*, *19*(2), 263–311.

Buchanan, B. G. (2005). A (Very) Brief History of Artificial Intelligence. *AI Magazine*, *26*(4), 4. doi:10.1609/aimag.v26i4.1848

Caldarini, G., Jaf, S., & McGarry, K. (2022). A literature survey of recent advances in chatbots. *Information (Basel)*, *13*(1), 41. doi:10.3390/info13010041

Calvaresi, D., Ibrahim, A., Calbimonte, J.-P., Schegg, R., Fragniere, E., & Schumacher, M. 2021. The Evolution of Chatbots in Tourism: A Systematic Literature Review. In Information and Communication Technologies in Tourism 2021. Springer. doi:10.1007/978-3-030-65785-7_1

Calvaresi, D., Ibrahim, A., Calbimonte, J. P., Fragniere, E., Schegg, R., & Schumacher, M. I. (2023). Leveraging Inter-Tourists Interactions via Chatbots to Bridge Academia, Tourism Industries and Future Societies. *Journal of Tourism Futures*, *9*(3), 311–337. doi:10.1108/JTF-01-2021-0009

Can, I., Gelmez-Burakgazi, S., & Celik, I. (2019). An investigation of uses and gratifications for using web 2.0 technologies in teaching and learning processes. [IOJET]. *International Online Journal of Education & Teaching*, *6*(1), 88–102. https://www.iojet.org/index.php/IOJET/article/view/504

Canöz, K., İrez, B., & Kaya, K. K. (2023). Halkla İlişkiler, Yapay Zekâ ve Hegemonya: Eleştirel Bir Değerlendirme. *Karatay Sosyal Araştırmalar Dergisi*, *11*(11), 335–352. doi:10.54557/karataysad.1312694

Capacity, T. (2023). *ECommerce Chatbots: The Complete Guide.* Capacity. https://capacity.com/learn/ai-chatbots/ecommerce-chatbot/

Casilli, A. A. (2019). *En attendant les robots. Enquête sur le travail du clic.* Editions Seuil.

Castillo, D., Canhoto, A. I., & Said, E. (2021). The dark side of AI-powered service interactions: Exploring the process of co-destruction from the customer perspective. *Service Industries Journal*, *41*(13–14), 900–925. doi:10.1080/02642069.2020.1787993

Castle-Green, T., Reeves, S., Fischer, J. E., & Koleva, B. (2020, July). Decision trees as sociotechnical objects in chatbot design. In *Proceedings of the 2nd Conference on Conversational User Interfaces* (pp. 1-3). ACM. 10.1145/3405755.3406133

Celesti, A., Fazio, M., Giacobbe, M., Puliafito, A., & Villari, M. (2016). Characterizing Cloud Federation in IoT. *30th International Conference on Advanced*. IEEE.

Celesti, A., Fazio, M., Giacobbe, M., Puliafito, A., & Villari, M. (2016). Characterizing Cloud Federation in IoT. In *2016 30th International Conference on Advanced Information Networking and Applications Workshops (WAINA)*, (pp. 93-98). IEEE. 10.1109/WAINA.2016.152

Ceylan, N. B. (Director). (2023, September 29). *Kuru Otlar Üstüne* [Drama]. NBC Film, Memento Films Production, Komplizen Film.

Chamberlain, W. (1984). *The policeman's beard is half constructed*. Warner Books.

Chang, J.-W., Yen, N., & Hung, J. C. (2022). Design of a NLP-empowered finance fraud awareness model: The anti-fraud chatbot for fraud detection and fraud classification as an instance. *Journal of Ambient Intelligence and Humanized Computing*, *13*(10), 4663–4679. doi:10.1007/s12652-021-03512-2

Chang, K.-W., Prabhakaran, V., & Ordonez, V. (2019). Bias and fairness in natural language processing. *Proceedings of the 2019 Conference on Empirical Methods in Natural Language Processing and the 9th International Joint Conference on Natural Language Processing (EMNLP-IJCNLP): Tutorial Abstracts*. IEEE.

Chat OpenAI. (2023). Chat OpenAI. https://chat.openai.com/auth/login

Chatbots. (2023). *Parry*. Chatbots. https://www.chatbots.org/chatbot/parry/

Chen, J. S., Le, T. T. Y., & Florence, D. (2021). Usability and responsiveness of artificial intelligence chatbot on online customer experience in e-retailing. *International Journal of Retail & Distribution Management*, *49*(11), 1512–1531. doi:10.1108/IJRDM-08-2020-0312

Chien, Y. C., Wu, T. T., Lai, C. H., & Huang, Y. M. (2022). Investigation of the influence of artificial intelligence markup language-based LINE ChatBot in contextual English learning. *Frontiers in Psychology*, *13*, 13. doi:10.3389/fpsyg.2022.785752 PMID:35465562

Chong, T., Yu, T., Keeling, D. I., & de Ruyter, K. (2021). AI-chatbots on the services frontline addressing the challenges and opportunities of agency. *Journal of Retailing and Consumer Services*, *63*, 102735. doi:10.1016/j.jretconser.2021.102735

Chung, M., Ko, E., Joung, H., & Kim, S. J. (2020). Chatbot e-service and customer satisfaction regarding luxury brands. *Journal of Business Research*, *117*, 587–595. doi:10.1016/j.jbusres.2018.10.004

Ciechanowski, L., Przegalinska, A., Magnuski, M., & Gloor, P. (2019). In the shades of the uncanny valley: An experimental study of human–chatbot interaction. [Reference Link]. *Future Generation Computer Systems*, *92*, 539–548. doi:10.1016/j.future.2018.01.055

Čižmešija, A., Horvat, A., & Vukovac, D. P. (2021). Improving student engagement and course completion using Chatbot application. In *INTED2021 Proceedings* (pp. 8346-8354). IATED. 10.21125/inted.2021.1697

Clark, S. (2023, September 1). *The evolution of AI chatbots: Past, present, and future*. CMSWire. https://www.cmswire.com/digital-experience/the-evolution-of-ai-chatbots-past-present-and-future/

Clark, L., Pantidi, N., Cooney, O., Doyle, P., Garaialde, D., Edwards, J., Spillane, B., Gilmartin, E., Murad, C., Munteanu, C., Wade, V., & Cowan, B. R. (2019). What makes a good conversation?: Challenges in designing truly conversational agents. *Proceedings of the 2019 CHI Conference on Human Factors in Computing Systems*, (pp. 1–12). ACM. 10.1145/3290605.3300705

Clark, P. (2019). *Chatbot marketing: The ultimate guide*. Springer.

Cnet, (2023). *You can now try Google's bard charbot*. Cnet. https://www.cnet.com/tech/computing/you-can-now-try-googles-bard-chatbot-an-alternative-to-chatgpt/

Colby, K. M., Hilf, F. D., Weber, S., & Kraemer, H. C. (1972). Turing-like indistinguishability tests for the validation of a computer simulation of paranoid processes. *Artificial Intelligence*, *3*, 199–221. doi:10.1016/0004-3702(72)90049-5

Coniam, D. (2014). The linguistic accuracy of chatbots: Usability from an ESL perspective. *Text & Talk*, *34*(5), 545–567. doi:10.1515/text-2014-0018

Cooper, G. (2023). Examining Science Education in ChatGPT: An Exploratory Study of Generative Artificial Intelligence. *Journal of Science Education and Technology*, *32*(3), 444–452. doi:10.1007/s10956-023-10039-y

Courey, A. (2020). *The Future Of Customer Service: Artificial Intelligence*. Data Driven Investor.

Cox, S. R., Lee, Y., & Ooi, W. (2023). Comparing How a Chatbot References User Utterances from Previous Chatting Sessions: An Investigation of Users' Privacy Concerns and Perceptions. *Proceedings of the 11th International Conference on Human-Agent Interaction*. ACM. 10.1145/3623809.3623875

Cui, W., Xiao, Y., Wang, H., Song, Y., Hwang, S. W., & Wang, W. (2019). KBQA: learning question answering over QA corpora and knowledge bases. *arXiv prepri*.

Customer Satisfaction template. (n.d.). ChatBot. https://www.chatbot.com/chatbot-templates/customer-satisfaction-template/

Dai, Z., Yang, Z., Yang, Y., Carbonell, J., Le, Q. V., & Salakhutdinov, R. (2019). Transformer-XL: Attentive Language Models Beyond a Fixed-Length Context. In *Proceedings of the 57th Annual Meeting of the Association for Computational Linguistics* (pp. 2978-2988). ACL. 10.18653/v1/P19-1285

Dale, R. (2016). The return of the chatbots. *Natural Language Engineering*, *22*(5), 811–817. doi:10.1017/S1351324916000243

Daniel, G., Cabot, J., Deruelle, L., & Derras, M. (2020). Xatkit: A Multimodal Low-Code Chatbot Development Framework. *IEEE Access : Practical Innovations, Open Solutions*, *8*, 15332–15346. doi:10.1109/ACCESS.2020.2966919

Dash, M., & Bakshi, S. (2019). An exploratory study of customer perceptions of usage of chatbots in the hospitality industry. *International Journal on Customer Relations*, *7*(2), 27–33.

Davis, F. D. (1985). *A technology acceptance model for empirically testing new end-user information systems: Theory and results* [Doctoral dissertation, Massachusetts Institute of Technology].

Davis, M., McInnes, B., & Ahmed, I. (2022). Forensic Investigation of Instant Messaging Services on Linux OS: Discord and Slack as Case Studies. *Forensic Science International Digital Investigation*, *42*, 301401. doi:10.1016/j.fsidi.2022.301401

De Sanctis, M., Bucchiarone, A., & Marconi, A. (2020). Dynamic adaptation of service-based applications: A design for adaptation approach. *Journal of Internet Services and Applications*, *11*(1), 1–29. doi:10.1186/s13174-020-00123-6

Delipetrev, B., Tsinaraki, C., & Kostić, U. (2020). *AI Watch, historical evolution of artificial intelligence: Analysis of the three main paradigm shifts in AI*. Publications Office. https://data.europa.eu/doi/10.2760/801580

Deng, J., Sun, H., Zhang, Z., Cheng, J., & Huang, M. (2023). Recent advances towards safe, responsible, and moral dialogue systems: A survey. *ArXiv Preprint ArXiv:2302.09270*.

Deng, J., & Lin, Y. (2023). The Benefits and Challenges of ChatGPT: An Overview. *Frontiers in Computing and Intelligent Systems*, *2*(2), 81–83. doi:10.54097/fcis.v2i2.4465

Deng, L., & Liu, Y. (2018). *Deep learning in natural language processing*. Springer. doi:10.1007/978-981-10-5209-5

Devlin, J. (2018). *BERT: Pre-training of deep bidirectional transformers for language understanding*. arXiv preprint arXiv:1810.04805.

Devlin, J., Chang, M. W., Lee, K., & Toutanova, K. (2018). *BERT: Pre-training of Deep Bidirectional Transformers for Language Understanding.* arXiv preprint arXiv:1810.04805.

Dignum, V., & Dignum, F. (2018). *Responsible artificial intelligence: How to develop and use AI in a responsible way.* Springer.

Dinh, H., & Tran, T. K. (2023). EduChat: An AI-based chatbot for university-related information using a hybrid approach. *Applied Sciences (Basel, Switzerland), 13*(22), 12446. doi:10.3390/app132212446

Divya, S., Indumathi, V., Ishwarya, S., Priyasankari, M., & Devi, S. K. (2018). A self-diagnosis medical chatbot using artificial intelligence. *Journal of Web Development and Web Designing, 3*(1), 1–7.

Domingos, P. (2015). *The master algorithm: How the quest for the ultimate learning machine will remake our world.* Basic Books.

Duque, J. (2021). *Mastering Conversational AI with IBM Watson: Design and Develop Conversational Solutions with IBM Watson Assistant.* Packt Publishing.

Dwivedi, Y. K., Kshetri, N., Hughes, L., Slade, E. L., Jeyaraj, A., Kar, A. K., Baabdullah, A. M., Koohang, A., Raghavan, V., Ahuja, M., Albanna, H., Albashrawi, M. A., Al-Busaidi, A. S., Balakrishnan, J., Barlette, Y., Basu, S., Bose, I., Brooks, L., Buhalis, D, & Wright, R. (2023). Opinion Paper: "So what if ChatGPT wrote it?" Multidisciplinary perspectives on opportunities, challenges and implications of generative conversational AI for research, practice and policy. *International Journal of Information Management, 71*, 102642. doi:10.1016/j.ijinfomgt.2023.102642

Dwivedi, Y. K., & Wang, Y. (2022). Guest editorial: Artificial intelligence for B2B marketing: Challenges and opportunities. *Industrial Marketing Management, 105*, 109–113. doi:10.1016/j.indmarman.2022.06.001

Ebadi, S., & Amini, A. (2022). Examining the roles of social presence and humanlikeness on Iranian EFL learners' motivation using artificial intelligence technology: A case of CSIEC chatbot. *Interactive Learning Environments*, 1–19. doi:10.1080/10494820.2022.2096638

Ebel, P., Söllner, M., Leimeister, J. M., Crowston, K., & De Vreede, G.-J. (2021). Hybrid intelligence in business networks. *Electronic Markets, 31*(2), 313–318. doi:10.1007/s12525-021-00481-4

Engati. (2023). *Wechat Bot.* Engati. https://www.engati.com/glossary/wechat-bot

Epstein, R., Roberts, G., & Beber, G. (2007). *Parsing the Turing Test: Philosophical and Methodological Issues in the Quest for the Thinking Computer.* Springer Science & Business Media.

Evans data. (2016). *Evans Data Corporation |Internet of Things – Vertical Research Service.* Evans. http://www.evansdata.com/reports/viewRelease.php?reportID=38

Evans, D. (2012). *The Internet of Things How the Next Evolution of the Internet is Changing Everything (April 2011).* IEEE.

Facebook. (2020). *WhatsApp Business API.* Developers.Facebook.Com.

Fan, X., Chao, D., Zhang, Z., Wang, D., Li, X., & Tian, F. (2021). Utilization of self-diagnosis health chatbots in real-world settings: Case study. *Journal of Medical Internet Research, 23*(1), e19928. doi:10.2196/19928 PMID:33404508

Fapal, A., Kanade, T., Janrao, B., Kamble, M., & Raule, M. (2021). Personal Virtual Assistant for Windows Using Python. *International Research Journal of Modernization in Engineering.*

Ferri, C., Hernández-Orallo, J., & Modroiu, R. (2009). An experimental comparison of performance measures for classification. *Pattern Recognition Letters, 30*(1), 27–38. doi:10.1016/j.patrec.2008.08.010

Fitria, T. N. (2023). Artificial intelligence (AI) technology in OpenAI ChatGPT application: A review of ChatGPT in writing English essay. *ELT Forum: Journal of English Language Teaching, 12*(1), 44–58. 10.15294/elt.v12i1.64069

Floridi, L., & Chiriatti, M. (2020). GPT-3: Its nature, scope, limits, and consequences. *Minds and Machines, 30*(4), 681–694. doi:10.1007/s11023-020-09548-1

Fogg, B. J., & Tseng, H. (1999, May). The elements of computer credibility. In *Proceedings of the SIGCHI conference on Human Factors in Computing Systems* (pp. 80-87). ACM. 10.1145/302979.303001

Forman, G., & Scholz, M. (2010). Apples-to-apples in cross-validation studies: Pitfalls in classifier performance measurement. *SIGKDD Explorations, 12*(1), 49–57. doi:10.1145/1882471.1882479

Fortune. (2019). Apple, Google, and Amazon May Have Violated Your Privacy by Reviewing Digital Assistant Commands. *Fortune.*

Foster, M. E. (2019). Natural language generation for social robotics: opportunities and challenges. *Philosophical Transactions of the Royal Society B, 374*(1771), 20180027.

Frangoudes, F., Hadjiaros, M., Schiza, E. C., Matsangidou, M., Tsivitanidou, O., & Neokleous, K. (2021, July). An overview of the use of chatbots in medical and healthcare education. In *International Conference on Human-Computer Interaction* (pp. 170-184). Cham: Springer International Publishing. 10.1007/978-3-030-77943-6_11

Frieder, S., Pinchetti, L., Chevalier, A., Griffiths, R.-R., Salvatori, T., Lukasiewicz, T., Petersen, P. C., & Berner, J. (2023). *Mathematical Capabilities of ChatGPT* (arXiv:2301.13867). arXiv. https://doi.org//arXiv.2301.13867 doi:10.48550

Fryer, L., & Nakao, K. (2009). Assessing chatbots for EFL learner use. In A. Stoke (Ed.), *Proceedings from JALT2008 Conference.* Tokyo: JALT.

Galitsky, B., & Goldberg, S. (2019). Explainable Machine Learning for Chatbots. In B. Galitsky (Ed.), *Developing Enterprise Chatbots: Learning Linguistic Structures* (pp. 53–83). Springer International Publishing. doi:10.1007/978-3-030-04299-8_3

García-Méndez, S., De Arriba-Pérez, F., González-Castaño, F. J., Regueiro-Janeiro, J. A., & Gil-Castiñeira, F. (2021). Entertainment chatbot for the digital inclusion of elderly people without abstraction capabilities. *IEEE Access : Practical Innovations, Open Solutions, 9*, 75878–75891. doi:10.1109/ACCESS.2021.3080837

Garcia, N., Otani, M., Chu, C., & Nakashima, Y. (2020). KnowIT VQA: Answering knowledge-based questions about videos. In *Proceedings of the AAAI Conference on Artificial Intelligence*, New York, NY, USA, Volume 34, pp. 10826–10834. 10.1609/aaai.v34i07.6713

GENÇ, N. (2023). Artificial Intelligence in Physical Education and Sports: New Horizons with ChatGPT. *Akdeniz Spor Bilimleri Dergisi, 6*(1-Cumhuriyet'in 100. Yılı Özel Sayısı), 17–32. doi:10.38021/asbid.1291604

Gibbs, S. (2017). Amazon's Alexa escapes the Echo and gets into cars. *The Guardian.*

Gilardi, F., Alizadeh, M., & Kubli, M. (2023). ChatGPT outperforms crowd workers for text-annotation tasks. *Proceedings of the National Academy of Sciences of the United States of America, 120*(30), e2305016120. doi:10.1073/pnas.2305016120 PMID:37463210

Go, E., & Sundar, S. S. (2019). Humanizing chatbots: The effects of visual, identity and conversational cues on humanness perceptions. *Computers in Human Behavior, 97*, 304–316. doi:10.1016/j.chb.2019.01.020

Göktaş, L. S. (2023). The role of ChatGPT in vegetarian menus. *Tourism and Recreation, 5*(2), 79–86. doi:10.53601/tourismandrecreation.1343598

Goldberg, L. R. (2019). *The Book of Why: The New Science of Cause and Effect: by Judea Pearl and Dana Mackenzie, Basic Books (2018)*. Taylor & Francis.

Goleman, D. (1995). Emotional intelligence, imagination, cognition and personality. *Personality and Individual Differences, 9*, 185–211.

Gondwe, G. (2023). CHATGPT and the Global South: How are journalists in sub-Saharan Africa engaging with generative AI? *Online Media and Global Communication, 2*(2), 228–249. doi:10.1515/omgc-2023-0023

Google assistant, (2023). Google. https://assistant.google.com/

Google. (2016). *Overview of Internet of things.* Google Developers. https://cloud.google.com/solutions/iot-overview

Graves, A., Mohamed, A. R., & Hinton, G. (2013). Speech recognition with deep recurrent neural networks. In Acoustics, speech and signal processing (ICASSP), 2013 IEEE international conference (pp. 6645-6649). IEEE. doi:10.1109/ICASSP.2013.6638947

Guida, S. (2021). Privacy policies between perception and learning through legal design: ideas for an educational chatbot combining rights' awareness, optimized user experience and training efficacy. *Symposium on Psychology-Based Technologies.*

Güzeldere, G, & Franchi, S. (1995). Dialogues with Colorful 'Personalities' of Early AI. *Stanford Humanities Review, 4*(2).

Hand, D. J., Christen, P., & Kirielle, N. (2021). F*: An interpretable transformation of the F-measure. *Machine Learning, 110*(3), 451–456. doi:10.1007/s10994-021-05964-1 PMID:33746357

Hao, A. W., Paul, J., Trott, S., Guo, C., & Wu, H.-H. (2019). Two decades of research on nation branding: A review and future research agenda. *International Marketing Review, 38*(1), 46–69. doi:10.1108/IMR-01-2019-0028

Harilal, N., Shah, R., Sharma, S., & Bhutani, V. (2020). CARO: an empathetic health conversational chatbot for people with major depression. In *Proceedings of the 7th ACM IKDD CoDS and 25th COMAD* (pp. 349-350). ACM. 10.1145/3371158.3371220

Haristiani, N., & Danuwijaya, A. A. (2019). Gengobot: A chatbot-based grammar application on mobile instant messaging as language learning medium. *Journal of Engineering Science and Technology, 14*(6), 3158–3173.

Haristiani, N., & Rifa'i, M. M. (2020). Combining Chatbot and Social Media: Enhancing Personal Learning Environment (PLE) in Language Learning. *Indonesian Journal of Science and Technology, 5*(3), 487–506. doi:10.17509/ijost.v5i3.28687

Harrison, D. E., Ajjan, H., Hair, J. F., Ryan, S., Myers, C., Drewes, P., & Disch, W. (2022). The Essentials of Marketing Analytics: Teaching, Research and Practice—An Abstract. In F. Pantoja & S. Wu (Eds.), *From Micro to Macro: Dealing with Uncertainties in the Global Marketplace* (pp. 1–2). Springer International Publishing. doi:10.1007/978-3-030-89883-0_1

Hasal, M., Nowaková, J., Ahmed Saghair, K., Abdulla, H., Snášel, V., & Ogiela, L. (2021). Chatbots: Security, privacy, data protection, and social aspects. *Concurrency and Computation, 33*(19), e6426. doi:10.1002/cpe.6426

He, X., Shen, X., Chen, Z., Backes, M., & Zhang, Y. (2024). *MGTBench: Benchmarking Machine-Generated Text Detection* (arXiv:2303.14822). arXiv. http://arxiv.org/abs/2303.14822

Heo, M., & Lee, K. J. (2018). Chatbot as a new business communication tool: The case of naver talktalk. *Business Communication Research and Practice, 1*(1), 41–45. doi:10.22682/bcrp.2018.1.1.41

Hirschberg, J., & Manning, C. D. (2015). Advances in natural language processing. *Science, 349*(6245), 261–266. doi:10.1126/science.aaa8685 PMID:26185244

Ho, A., Hancock, J., & Miner, A. S. (2018). Psychological, relational, and emotional effects of self-disclosure after conversations with a chatbot. *Journal of Communication*, *68*(4), 712–733. doi:10.1093/joc/jqy026 PMID:30100620

Holopainen, J., & Räisänen, T. (2019). Designing Chatbots for Better User Experience. In *International Conference on Human-Computer Interaction* (pp. 155-174). Springer.

Hong, W. C. H. (2023). The impact of ChatGPT on foreign language teaching and learning: Opportunities in education and research. *Journal of Educational Technology and Innovation*, *5*(1), 1. https://jeti.thewsu.org/index.php/cieti/article/view/103

Ho, R. C. (2021). Chatbot for online customer service: customer engagement in the era of artificial intelligence. In *Impact of globalization and advanced technologies on online business models* (pp. 16–31). IGI Global. doi:10.4018/978-1-7998-7603-8.ch002

Horton, J. J., & Chilton, L. B. (2010). The labor economics of paid crowdsourcing. *Proceedings of the 11th ACM conference on Electronic commerce. EC '10*. New York, New York, USA: ACM Press. 10.1145/1807342.1807376

How to make a chatbot ? (2022b, March 11). AppMaster - Ultimate All-in No-code Platform. https://appmaster.io/blog/how-make-chatbot

Hoy, M. B. (2018). Alexa, Siri, Cortana, and More: An Introduction to Voice Assistants. *Medical Reference Services Quarterly*, *37*(1), 81–88. doi:10.1080/02763869.2018.1404391 PMID:29327988

Hsieh, P. J., & Lai, H. M. (2020). Exploring peoples intentions to use the health passbook in self-management: An extension of the technology acceptance and health behavior theoretical perspectives in health literacy. *Technological Forecasting and Social Change*, *161*, 120328. doi:10.1016/j.techfore.2020.120328

HsuI.LiaoA. (2022). Sentiment-based chatbot using machine learning for recommendation system. doi:10.21203/rs.3.rs-1468604/v1

Hsu, M. H., Chen, P. S., & Yu, C. S. (2023). Proposing a task-oriented chatbot system for EFL learners speaking practice. *Interactive Learning Environments*, *31*(7), 4297–4308. doi:10.1080/10494820.2021.1960864

Huang, T., Smith, C., McGuire, B., & Yang, G. (2006). *The History of Artificial Intelligence*. Semantic Scholar. https://www.semanticscholar.org/paper/The-History-of-Artificial-Intelligence-Huang-Smith/085599650ebfcfba0dcb-434bc50b7c7c54fdbf05

Huang, D., Markovitch, D. G., & Stough, R. A. (2024). Can chatbot customer service match human service agents on customer satisfaction? An investigation in the role of trust. *Journal of Retailing and Consumer Services*, *76*, 103600. doi:10.1016/j.jretconser.2023.103600

Huh, J., Nelson, M. R., & Russell, C. A. (2023). ChatGPT, AI Advertising, and Advertising Research and Education. *Journal of Advertising*, *52*(4), 477–482. doi:10.1080/00913367.2023.2227013

Hu, M., & Liu, B. (2004). Mining and summarizing customer reviews. *Proceedings of the Tenth ACM SIGKDD International Conference on Knowledge Discovery and Data Mining*, (pp. 168–177). IEEE. 10.1145/1014052.1014073

Hussain, S., Ameri Sianaki, O., & Ababneh, N. (2019). A survey on conversational agents/chatbots classification and design techniques. In *Web, Artificial Intelligence and Network Applications: Proceedings of the Workshops of the 33rd International Conference on Advanced Information Networking and Applications (WAINA-2019) 33* (pp. 946-956). Springer International Publishing.

Hussain, K., Khan, M. L., & Malik, A. (2024). Exploring audience engagement with ChatGPT-related content on YouTube: Implications for content creators and AI tool developers. *Digital Business*, *4*(1), 100071. doi:10.1016/j.digbus.2023.100071

Hutto, C., & Gilbert, E. (2014). *Vader: A parsimonious rule-based model for sentiment analysis of social media text.* 8(1).

Hwang, W. Y., Guo, B. C., Hoang, A., Chang, C. C., & Wu, N. T. (2022). Facilitating authentic contextual EFL speaking and conversation with smart mechanisms and investigating its influence on learning achievements. *Computer Assisted Language Learning*, 1–27. doi:10.1080/09588221.2022.2095406

Ikemoto, Y., Asawavetvutt, V., Kuwabara, K., & Huang, H. H. (2019). Tuning a Conversation Strategy for Interactive Recommendations in a Chatbot Setting. *Journal of Information and Telecommunication*, 3(2), 180–195. doi:10.1080/24751839.2018.1544818

Illescas-Manzano, M. D., López, N. V., González, N. A., & Rodríguez, C. C. (2021). Implementation of Chatbot in Online Commerce, and Open Innovation. *Journal of Open Innovation*, 7(2), 125. doi:10.3390/joitmc7020125

Ischen, C., Araujo, T., Voorveld, H., van Noort, G., & Smit, E. (2020). Privacy Concerns in Chatbot Interactions. In A. Følstad, T. Araujo, S. Papadopoulos, E. L.-C. Law, O.-C. Granmo, E. Luger, & P. B. Brandtzaeg (Eds.), *Chatbot Research and Design* (pp. 34–48). Springer International Publishing. doi:10.1007/978-3-030-39540-7_3

Ivanov, S. (2019). Ultimate Transformation: How Will Automation Technologies Disrupt the Travel, Tourism and Hospitality Industries? *Zeitschrift für Tourismuswissenschaft*, 11(1), 25–43. doi:10.1515/tw-2019-0003

Jaf, S., & Caldarini, G. (2023). Recent advances in chatbot algorithms, techniques, and technologies: Designing chatbots. In Trends, Applications, and Challenges of Chatbot Technology (pp. 245-273). IGI Global. doi:10.4018/978-1-6684-6234-8.ch011

Jain, A., & Srivastava, S. (2020). *Building Enterprise Chatbots: A Step by Step Approach*. Apress.

Jeong, S. S., & Seo, Y. S. (2019). Improving Response Capability of Chatbot Using Twitter. *Journal of Ambient Intelligence and Humanized Computing*. Advance online publication. doi:10.1007/s12652-019-01347-6

Jeon, J. (2022). Exploring a self-directed interactive app for informal EFL learning: A self-determination theory perspective. *Education and Information Technologies*, 27(4), 5767–5787. doi:10.1007/s10639-021-10839-y

Jeon, J. (2023). Chatbot-assisted dynamic assessment (CA-DA) for L2 vocabulary learning and diagnosis. *Computer Assisted Language Learning*, 36(7), 1338–1364. doi:10.1080/09588221.2021.1987272

Jeon, J., Lee, S., & Choe, H. (2023). Beyond ChatGPT: A conceptual framework and systematic review of speech-recognition chatbots for language learning. *Computers & Education*, 206, 104898. doi:10.1016/j.compedu.2023.104898

Jia, J., & Ruan, M. (2008). Use chatbot CSIEC to facilitate the individual learning in English instruction: A case study. In *International Conference on Intelligent Tutoring Systems* (706–708). Springer. Berlin, Heidelberg. 10.1007/978-3-540-69132-7_84

Jin, J., Walker, J., & Reczek, R. W. (n.d.). Avoiding embarrassment online: Response to and inferences about chatbots when purchases activate self-presentation concerns. *Journal of Consumer Psychology*. doi:10.1002/jcpy.1414

Jordan, M. I., & Mitchell, T. M. (2015). Machine learning: Trends, perspectives, and prospects. *Science*, 349(6245), 255–260. doi:10.1126/science.aaa8415 PMID:26185243

Jurafsky, D., & Martin, J. H. (2018). *Speech and Language Processing: An Introduction to Natural Language Processing*. Computational Linguistics, and Speech Recognition.

Jurafsky, D., & Martin, J. H. (2019). *Speech and language processing* (3rd ed.). Prentice Hall.

K., G. P., Ranjan, S., Ankit, T., & Kumar, V. (2019). A personalized medical assistant chatbot: Medibot. *Int. J. Sci. Technol. Eng*, 5(7).

Kadu, O., Sihasane, S., Naik, S., Katariya, V., & Gutte, V. S. (2019). Intelligent healthbot for transforming healthcare. [IJTSRD]. *Int. J. Trend Sci. Res. Dev.*, *3*(3), 1576–1579.

Kalantari, M., & Rauschnabel, P. (2018). Exploring the early adopters of augmented reality smart glasses: The case of Microsoft HoloLens. In *Augmented reality and virtual reality* (pp. 229–245). Springer. doi:10.1007/978-3-319-64027-3_16

Kalla, D., & Samiuddin, V. (2020). Chatbot for medical treatment using NLTK Lib. *IOSR Journal of Computer Engineering*, 22.

Kaplan, A. M., & Haenlein, M. (2010). Users of the world, unite! The challenges and opportunities of Social Media. *Business Horizons*, *53*(1), 59–68. doi:10.1016/j.bushor.2009.09.003

Kaplan, A., & Haenlein, M. (2019). Siri, Siri, in my hand: Who's the fairest in the land? On the interpretations, illustrations, and implications of artificial intelligence. *Business Horizons*, *62*(1), 15–25. doi:10.1016/j.bushor.2018.08.004

Karimov, Z., Allahverdiyev, I., Agayarov, O. Y., Demir, D., & Almuradova, E. (2024). ChatGPT vs UpToDate: Comparative study of usefulness and reliability of Chatbot in common clinical presentations of otorhinolaryngology–head and neck surgery. *European Archives of Oto-Rhino-Laryngology*, *281*(4), 2145–2151. doi:10.1007/s00405-023-08423-w PMID:38217726

Karl, R. (2016). *Applying Chatbots to the Internet of Things: Opportunities and Architectural Elements*. Research Gate.

Kecht, C., Egger, A., Kratsch, W., & Röglinger, M. (2023). Quantifying chatbots' ability to learn business processes. [Reference Link]. *Information Systems*, *113*, 102176. doi:10.1016/j.is.2023.102176

Kela, P. (2024, March 21). *What is CRM Integration? Everything you need to know*. SoftwareSuggest Blog. https://www.softwaresuggest.com/blog/crm-integration/

Khan, A. (2019). NEEV : An Education Informational Chatbot. [IRJET]. *International Research Journal of Engineering and Technology*, *6*(4), 492–495.

Khan, R., & Das, A. (2018). Introduction to chatbots. In *Build better chatbots*. Apress., doi:10.1007/978-1-4842-3111-1_1

Kim, H. S., Cha, Y., & Kim, N. Y. (2020). Impact of mobile interactions with AI on writing performance. *Modern English Education*, *21*(2), 1–13. doi:10.18095/meeso.2020.21.2.1

Kim, N. (2017). Effects of different types of chatbots on EFL learners' speaking competence and learner perception. *Cross Cultural Studies*, *48*, 223–252. doi:10.21049/ccs.2017.48..223

Kim, N. Y. (2019). A Study on the use of Artificial Intelligence Chatbots for Improving English Grammar Skills. *Journal of Digital Convergence*, *17*(8), 37–46. doi:10.14400/JDC.2019.17.8.037

Kim, N.-Y., Cha, Y., & Kim, H.-S. (2019). Future English learning: Chatbots and artificial intelligence. *Multimedia Assisted Language Learning*, *22*(3), 32–53.

Kim, T. W., Jiang, L., Duhachek, A., Lee, H., & Garvey, A. (2022). Do You Mind if I Ask You a Personal Question? How AI Service Agents Alter Consumer Self-Disclosure. *Journal of Service Research*, *25*(4), 649–666. doi:10.1177/10946705221120232

King, M. R. (2023). The future of AI in medicine: A perspective from a Chatbot. *Annals of Biomedical Engineering*, *51*(2), 291–295. doi:10.1007/s10439-022-03121-w PMID:36572824

Kizilgeçi, T. (2023). Yapay Zekâ Sohbet Robotu Chatgpt İle İnanç- İnançsızlık, Doğal Afet Ve Ölüm Konuları Üzerine Nitel Bir Araştırma: Din Ve Maneviyatın Psikolojik Sağlığa Etkileri. *Ağrı İbrahim Çeçen Üniversitesi Sosyal Bilimler Enstitüsü Dergisi*, *9*(1), 137–172. doi:10.31463/aicusbed.1275061

Klyshbekova, M. (2023). ChatGPT and Language Learning. SSRN *Electronic Journal*. doi:10.2139/ssrn.4488587

Kohnke, L. (2023). L2 learners' perceptions of a chatbot as a potential independent language learning tool. *International Journal of Mobile Learning and Organisation*, *17*(1-2), 214–226. doi:10.1504/IJMLO.2023.128339

Kohnke, L., Moorhouse, B. L., & Zou, D. (2023). ChatGPT for language teaching and learning. *RELC Journal*, 00336882231162868.

Kohnke, L., Moorhouse, B. L., & Zou, D. (2023). ChatGPT for Language Teaching and Learning. *RELC Journal*, *54*(2), 537–550. doi:10.1177/00336882231162868

Kong, X., Liu, S., & Zhu, L. (2024). Toward Human-centered XAI in Practice: A survey. *Machine Intelligence Research*, (pp. 1–31). IEEE.

Kou, G., Yang, P., Peng, Y., Xiao, F., Chen, Y., & Alsaadi, F. E. (2020). Evaluation of feature selection methods for text classification with small datasets using multiple criteria decision-making methods. *Applied Soft Computing*, *86*, 105836. doi:10.1016/j.asoc.2019.105836

Kounev, S., Lange, K.-D., & Von Kistowski, J. (2020). *Systems Benchmarking*. Springer. doi:10.1007/978-3-030-41705-5

Krippendorff, K. (2019). *Content Analysis: An Introduction to Its Methodology*. SAGE Publications, Inc., doi:10.4135/9781071878781

Krishna, A., Herd, K. B., & Aydınoğlu, N. Z. (2019). A Review of Consumer Embarrassment as a Public and Private Emotion. *Journal of Consumer Psychology*, *29*(3), 492–516. doi:10.1002/jcpy.1086

Kristensen-McLachlan, R. D., Canavan, M., Kardos, M., Jacobsen, M., & Aarøe, L. (2023). *Chatbots Are Not Reliable Text Annotators* (arXiv:2311.05769). arXiv. http://arxiv.org/abs/2311.05769

Kröger, J. L., Lutz, O. H.-M., & Raschke, P. (2020). "Privacy Implications of Voice and Speech Analysis – Information Disclosure by Inference". Privacy and Identity Management. Data for Better Living: AI and Privacy. *IFIP Advances in Information and Communication Technology*, *576*, 242–258. doi:10.1007/978-3-030-42504-3_16

Kuhail, M. A., Alturki, N., Alramlawi, S., & Alhejori, K. (2023). Interacting with educational chatbots: A systematic review. *Education and Information Technologies*, *28*(1), 973–1018. doi:10.1007/s10639-022-11177-3

Kumar, V., Rajan, B., Venkatesan, R., & Lecinski, J. (2019). Understanding the role of artificial intelligence in personalized engagement marketing. *California Management Review*, *2019*(61), 135–155. doi:10.1177/0008125619859317

Kushwaha, A. K., Kumar, P., & Kar, A. K. (2021). What impacts customer experience for B2B enterprises on using AI-enabled chatbots? Insights from Big data analytics. [Reference Link]. *Industrial Marketing Management*, *98*, 207–221. doi:10.1016/j.indmarman.2021.08.011

Kvale, K., Freddi, E., Hodnebrog, S., Sell, O. A., & Følstad, A. (2020). Understanding the user experience of customer service chatbots: what can we learn from customer satisfaction surveys? In *International Workshop on Chatbot Research and Design* (pp. 205-218). Cham: Springer International Publishing.

LaCroix, T., & Bengio, Y. (2019). Learning from learning machines: optimisation, rules, and social norms. *ArXiv Preprint ArXiv:2001.00006*.

Lai, S.-T., Leu, F.-Y., & Lin, J.-W. (2019). A Banking Chatbot Security Control Procedure for Protecting User Data Security and Privacy. In L. Barolli, F.-Y. Leu, T. Enokido, & H.-C. Chen (Eds.), *Advances on Broadband and Wireless Computing, Communication and Applications* (pp. 561–571). Springer International Publishing. doi:10.1007/978-3-030-02613-4_50

La, L. (2017). *Everything Google Assistant can do on the Pixel"*. CNET.

Lasek, M., & Jessa, S. (2013). CHATBOTS FOR CUSTOMER SERVICE ON HOTELS' WEBSITES. *Information Systems Management, 2*.

Laurillard, D. (2013). *Teaching as a design science: Building pedagogical patterns for learning and technology.* Routledge. doi:10.4324/9780203125083

Leavy, S. (2018). Gender bias in artificial intelligence: The need for diversity and gender theory in machine learning. *Proceedings of the 1st International Workshop on Gender Equality in Software Engineering*, (pp. 14–16). ACM. 10.1145/3195570.3195580

Li, B., Jiang, N., Sham, J., Shi, H., & Fazal, H. (2019). Real-World Conversational AI for Hotel Bookings. In *Proceedings - 2019 2nd International Conference on Artificial Intelligence for Industries, AI4I 2019.* ACM. 10.1109/AI4I46381.2019.00022

Li, Y., Ott, M., Du, J., Goyal, N., Joshi, M., Chen, D., & Stoyanov, V. (2020). *Scaling Up Natural Language Understanding with Large LLMs.* arXiv preprint arXiv:2005.14165.

Liao, L., Yang, G. H., & Shah, C. (2023). Proactive conversational agents in the post-ChatGPT world. In *Proceedings of the 46th International ACM SIGIR Conference on Research and Development in Information Retrieval (SIGIR'23)*, (pp. 1-4). ACM, New York, NY, USA. 10.1145/3539618.3594250

Lin, C. J., & Mubarok, H. (2021). Learning analytics for investigating the mind map-guided AI chatbot approach in an EFL flipped speaking classroom. *Journal of Educational Technology & Society, 24*(4), 16–35.

Li, S., Kao, C. Y., & Wang, Q. (2017). Building a Chatbot with Serverless Computing and Machine Learning. In *2017 IEEE International Conference on Web Services (ICWS)* (pp. 758-761). IEEE.

Liu, Y., Ott, M., Goyal, N., Du, J., Joshi, M., Chen, D., & Zettlemoyer, L. (2019). *RoBERTa: A Robustly Optimized BERT Pretraining Approach.* arXiv preprint arXiv:1907.11692.

Liu, B., Ding, M., Shaham, S., Rahayu, W., Farokhi, F., & Lin, Z. (2021). When machine learning meets privacy: A survey and outlook. *ACM Computing Surveys, 54*(2), 1–36. doi:10.1145/3436755

Liu, B., & Sundar, S. S. (2018). Should machines express sympathy and empathy? Experiments with a health advice chatbot. *Cyberpsychology, Behavior, and Social Networking, 21*(10), 625–636. doi:10.1089/cyber.2018.0110 PMID:30334655

Liu, G., & Ma, C. (2023). Measuring EFL learners' use of ChatGPT in informal digital learning of English based on the technology acceptance model. *Innovation in Language Learning and Teaching*, 1–14.

Liu, H., Wang, Y., Fan, W., Liu, X., Li, Y., Jain, S., Liu, Y., Jain, A., & Tang, J. (2022). Trustworthy ai: A computational perspective. *ACM Transactions on Intelligent Systems and Technology, 14*(1), 1–59. doi:10.1145/3546872

Li, Y., Li, Y., Chen, Q., & Chang, Y. (2024). Humans as teammates: The signal of human–AI teaming enhances consumer acceptance of chatbots. *International Journal of Information Management, 76*, 102771. doi:10.1016/j.ijinfomgt.2024.102771

Lucas, G. M., Rizzo, A., Gratch, J., Scherer, S., Stratou, G., Boberg, J., & Morency, L.-P. (2017). Reporting Mental Health Symptoms: Breaking Down Barriers to Care with Virtual Human Interviewers. *Frontiers in Robotics and AI, 4*, 51. doi:10.3389/frobt.2017.00051

Machiraju, S., & Modi, R. (2018). *Developing Bots with Microsoft Bots Framework.* Developing Bots with Microsoft Bots Framework. doi:10.1007/978-1-4842-3312-2

Macinka, M., & Maly, F. (2019). Comparison of the Development of Native Mobile Applications and Applications on Facebook Platform. In. Lecture Notes in Computer Science: Vol. 11673. *Including Subseries Lecture Notes in Artificial Intelligence and Lecture Notes in Bioinformatics)*. LNCS. doi:10.1007/978-3-030-27192-3_7

Maddala, C. (2023, September 6). *What is PEFT (Parameter Efficient Fine Tuning)?* iGebra.ai. https://genai.igebra.ai/concepts/what-is-peft-parameter-efficient-fine-tuning/#:~:text=September%206%2C%202023,subset%20of%20the%20model%E2%80%99s

Magistretti, S., Dell'Era, C., & Petruzzelli, A. M. (2019). How Intelligent Is Watson? Enabling Digital Transformation through Artificial Intelligence. *Business Horizons*, *62*(6), 819–829. doi:10.1016/j.bushor.2019.08.004

Magni, D., Del Gaudio, G., Papa, A., & Della Corte, V. (2023). Digital humanism and artificial intelligence: The role of emotions beyond the human–machine interaction in Society 5.0. *Journal of Management History*. doi:10.1108/JMH-12-2022-0084

Magni, D., Palladino, R., Papa, A., & Cailleba, P. (2022). Exploring the journey of Responsible Business Model Innovation in Asian companies: A review and future research agenda. *Asia Pacific Journal of Management*, 1–30. doi:10.1007/s10490-022-09813-0

Magni, D., Scuotto, V., Pezzi, A., & Del Giudice, M. (2021). Employees' acceptance of wearable devices: Towards a predictive model. *Technological Forecasting and Social Change*, *172*, 121022. doi:10.1016/j.techfore.2021.121022

Mahajanetal, S. (2018). Design and implementation of IoT enabled personal air quality assistant on instant messenger. In: *Proceedings of the 10th International Conference on Management of Digital EcoSystems*, (pp. 165–170). ACM. 10.1145/3281375.3281398

Mahmud, T. R., & Porntrakoon, P. (2023, August). The Use of AI Chatbots in Mental Healthcare for University Students in Thailand: A Case Study. In *2023 7th International Conference on Business and Information Management (ICBIM)* (pp. 48-53). IEEE. 10.1109/ICBIM59872.2023.10303025

Malhotra, T. (2023, September 27). *Researchers from MIT and CUHK propose LongLoRA (Long Low-Rank Adaptation), An efficient fine-tuning AI approach for long context Large Language Models (LLMs)*. Reddit. https://www.reddit.com/r/hash

Malik, S. I., Ashfque, M. W., Tawafak, R. M., Al-Farsi, G., Usmani, N. A., & Khudayer, B. H. (2022). A Chatbot to Facilitate Student Learning in a Programming 1 Course: A Gendered Analysis. [IJVPLE]. *International Journal of Virtual and Personal Learning Environments*, *12*(1), 1–20. doi:10.4018/IJVPLE.310007

Manning, C. D., Raghavan, P., & Schütze, H. (2009). *Introduction to Information Retrieval* (1st ed.). Cambridge University Press., doi:10.1017/CBO9780511809071

Manning, C., & Schutze, H. (1999). *Foundations of statistical natural language processing*. MIT press.

Mariani, M. M., Hashemi, N., & Wirtz, J. (2023). Artificial intelligence empowered conversational agents: A systematic literature review and research agenda. *Journal of Business Research*, *161*, 161. doi:10.1016/j.jbusres.2023.113838

Markoff, J., & Mozour, P. (2015). For Sympathetic Ear, More Chinese Turn to Smartphone Program. *The New York Times*.

Marsden, T., Gormley, G., Hyken, S., Munch-Andersen, S., Yang, J., Gelhaar, L., Miron, U., & Condell, M. (2022). *Customer service trends 2022: The pivot to personalization*. Ultimate.ai. https://www.ultimate.ai/guides/customer-service-trends-2022

Marsico, M. D., & Budiu, R. (2018). *Chatbots: what they are and how to build one (with examples)*. Nielsen Norman Group.

McGee, R. W. (2023). Gender Discrimination Arguments and Non Sequiturs: A Chatgpt Essay. SSRN *Electronic Journal*. doi:10.2139/ssrn.4413432

McHugh, M. L. (2012). Interrater reliability: The kappa statistic. *Biochemia Medica*, *22*(3), 276–282. doi:10.11613/BM.2012.031 PMID:23092060

Mckitterick, W. (2015). *The Messaging App Report: How instant Messaging can be monetized*. Business Insider.

McTear, M. (2022). *Conversational ai: Dialogue systems, conversational agents, and chatbots*. Springer Nature.

McTear, M., Callejas, Z., & Griol, D. (2016). Conversational interfaces: Past and present. In *The conversational interface*. Springer. doi:10.1007/978-3-319-32967-3_4

Melián-González, S., Gutiérrez-Taño, D., & Bulchand-Gidumal, J. (2021). Predicting the intentions to use chatbots for travel and tourism. *Current Issues in Tourism*, *24*(2), 192–210. doi:10.1080/13683500.2019.1706457

Mende, M., Scott, M. L., van Doorn, J., Grewal, D., & Shanks, I. (2019). Service Robots Rising: How Humanoid Robots Influence Service Experiences and Elicit Compensatory Consumer Responses. *JMR, Journal of Marketing Research*, *56*(4), 535–556. doi:10.1177/0022243718822827

Michalski, R. S., Carbonell, J. G., & Mitchell, T. M. (2013). *Machine Learning: An Artificial Intelligence Approach*. Springer Science & Business Media.

Michaud, L. N. (2018). Observations of a New Chatbot: Drawing Conclusions from Early Interactions with Users. *IT Professional*, *20*(5), 40–47. doi:10.1109/MITP.2018.053891336

Miner, A., Chow, A., Adler, S., Zaitsev, I., Tero, P., Darcy, A., & Paepcke, A. (2016). Conversational agents and mental health: Theory-informed assessment of language and affect. *Proceedings of the Fourth International Conference on Human Agent Interaction*, (pp. 123–130). ACM. 10.1145/2974804.2974820

Misischia, C. V., Poecze, F., & Strauss, C. (2022). Chatbots in customer service: Their relevance and impact on service quality. [Reference Link]. *Procedia Computer Science*, *201*, 421–428. doi:10.1016/j.procs.2022.03.055

Mogaji, E., Balakrishnan, J., Nwoba, A. C., & Nguyen, N. P. (2021). Emerging-market consumers' interactions with banking chatbots. *Telematics and Informatics*, *65*, 101711. doi:10.1016/j.tele.2021.101711

Mohammad, S. M. (2020). Artificial Intelligence in Information Technology. SSRN *Electronic Journal*. doi:10.2139/ssrn.3625444

Mohammad, S., & Turney, P. (2013). Crowdsourcing a Word-Emotion Association Lexicon. *Computational Intelligence*, *29*(3), 436–465. doi:10.1111/j.1467-8640.2012.00460.x

Muller, M., Chilton, L. B., Kantosalo, A., Martin, C. P., & Walsh, G. (2022). GenAICHI: Generative AI and HCI. *CHI Conference on Human Factors in Computing Systems Extended Abstracts*, 1–7. 10.1145/3491101.3503719

Murphy, K. P. (2012). *Machine learning: a probabilistic perspective*. MIT press.

Murtarelli, G., Gregory, A., & Romenti, S. (2021). A Conversation-Based Perspective for Shaping Ethical Human–Machine Interactions: The Particular Challenge of Chatbots. *Journal of Business Research*, *129*, 927–935. doi:10.1016/j.jbusres.2020.09.018

Nadarzynski, T., Miles, O., Cowie, A., & Ridge, D. (2019). Acceptability of artificial intelligence (AI)-led chatbot services in healthcare: A mixed-methods study. *Digital Health*, *5*, 2055207619871808. doi:10.1177/2055207619871808 PMID:31467682

Naqvi, M. H. A., Hongyu, Z., Naqvi, M. H., & Kun, L. (2023). Impact of service agents on customer satisfaction and loyalty: Mediating role of Chatbots. [Reference Link]. *Journal of Modelling in Management*.

Nasir, S., & Yurder, Y. (2015). Consumers' and physicians' perceptions about high tech wearable health products. *Procedia: Social and Behavioral Sciences*, *195*, 1261–1267. doi:10.1016/j.sbspro.2015.06.279

Nath, M. P., & Sagnika, S. (2020). Capabilities of Chatbots and Its Performance Enhancements in Machine Learning. In D. Swain, P. K. Pattnaik, & P. K. Gupta (Eds.), *Machine Learning and Information Processing* (pp. 183–192). Springer. doi:10.1007/978-981-15-1884-3_17

Nguyen-Mau, T., Le, A.-C., Pham, D.-H., & Huynh, V.-N. (2024). An information fusion based approach to context-based fine-tuning of GPT models. *Information Fusion*, *104*, 102202. doi:10.1016/j.inffus.2023.102202

Nigam, B., Mehra, N., & Niranjanamurthy, M. (2022). Self-Diagnosis in Healthcare Systems Using AI Chatbots. *IoT and AI Technologies for Sustainable Living: A Practical Handbook*, 79. Research Gate.

Ni, J., Young, T., Pandelea, V., Xue, F., & Cambria, E. (2023). Recent advances in deep learning based dialogue systems: A systematic survey. *Artificial Intelligence Review*, *56*(4), 3055–3155. doi:10.1007/s10462-022-10248-8

Nimavat, K., & Champaneria, T. (2017). Chatbots: An Overview Types, Architecture, Tools and Future Possibilities. *International Journal of Scientific Research and Development*, *5*(7), 1019–1026.

Nithyanandam, S. D., Kasinathan, S., Radhakrishnan, D., & Jebapandian, J. (2021). NLP for Chatbot Application: Tools and Techniques Used for Chatbot Application, NLP Techniques for Chatbot, Implementation. In Deep Natural Language Processing and AI Applications for Industry 5.0 (pp. 142-168). IGI Global.

Nithyanandam, S. D., Kasinathan, S., Radhakrishnan, D., & Jebapandian, J. (2021). NLP for chatbot application. *Advances in Computational Intelligence and Robotics*, 142–168. doi:10.4018/978-1-7998-7728-8.ch008

Nivethan, S. (2020). Sentiment Analysis and Deep Learning Based Chatbot for User Feedback. In *Lecture Notes on Data Engineering and Communications Technologies, 33*. . doi:10.1007/978-3-030-28364-3_22

Norelus, E. (2022, January 27). Designing a chatbot with IBM Watson Assistant. *Medium*. https://ernesenorelus.medium.com/designing-a-chatbot-with-ibm-watson-assistant-7e11b94c2b3d

Novelli, C., Taddeo, M., & Floridi, L. (2023). Accountability in artificial intelligence: What it is and how it works. *AI & Society*, 1–12. doi:10.1007/s00146-023-01635-y

Noy, S., & Zhang, W. (2023). Experimental Evidence on the Productivity Effects of Generative Artificial Intelligence. SSRN *Electronic Journal*. doi:10.2139/ssrn.4375283

Nunuk Wahyuningtyas, & Koentjoro. (2020). Android-based educational learning game for children based on Android. *JOINCS (Journal of Informatics, Network, and Computer Science)*, *3*(2), 38-43. https://doi.org/ doi:10.21070/joincs.v4i0.724

Oguntosin, V., & Olomo, A. (2021). Development of an e-commerce chatbot for a university shopping mall. *Applied Computational Intelligence and Soft Computing*, *2021*, 1–14. doi:10.1155/2021/6630326

Okonkwo, C. W., & Ade-Ibijola, A. (2021). Chatbots applications in education: A systematic review. *Computers and Education: Artificial Intelligence*, *2*, 100033. doi:10.1016/j.caeai.2021.100033

Ooi, K.-B., Tan, G. W.-H., Al-Emran, M., Al-Sharafi, M. A., Capatina, A., Chakraborty, A., Dwivedi, Y. K., Huang, T.-L., Kar, A. K., Lee, V.-H., Loh, X.-M., Micu, A., Mikalef, P., Mogaji, E., Pandey, N., Raman, R., Rana, N. P., Sarker, P., Sharma, A., & Wong, L.-W. (2023). The Potential of Generative Artificial Intelligence Across Disciplines: Perspectives and Future Directions. *Journal of Computer Information Systems*, 1–32. doi:10.1080/08874417.2023.2261010

Ovuakporaye, K. (2022). The Impact, Comparison and Usefulness of Digital Marketing Communications Tools on Organizational Profit Maximization Using Facebook. *Asian Journal of Research in Computer Science*. . doi:10.9734/ajrcos/2022/v13i430321

Özpolat, Z., Yildirim, Ö., & Karabatak, M. (2023). Artificial Intelligence-Based Tools in Software Development Processes: Application of ChatGPT. *European Journal of Technic*. doi:10.36222/ejt.1330631

Padghan, V. (2021, December 6). How to develop a chat bot using Amazon Lex? *Medium*. https://medium.com/edureka/how-to-develop-a-chat-bot-using-amazon-lex-a570beac969e

Palomino, N., & Arbaiza, F. (2023). The Role of a Chatbot Personality in the Attitude of Consumers Towards a Banking Brand. In Á. Rocha, C. H. Fajardo-Toro, & J. M. Riola (Eds.), *Developments and Advances in Defense and Security* (pp. 205–215). Springer Nature. doi:10.1007/978-981-19-7689-6_18

Panchal, V., & Kurup, L. (2023). Educational chatbot on data structures and algorithms for the visually impaired. 2023 5th Biennial International Conference on Nascent Technologies in Engineering (ICNTE). IEEE. 10.1109/ICNTE56631.2023.10146702

Pantano, E., & Pizzi, G. (2020). Forecasting Artificial Intelligence on Online Customer Assistance: Evidence from Chatbot Patents Analysis. *Journal of Retailing and Consumer Services*, *55*, 102096. doi:10.1016/j.jretconser.2020.102096

Park, H., Kim, H., & Kim, P. (2020). Development of electronic library chatbot system using SNS-based mobile chatbot service*. *The 9th International Conference on Smart Media and Applications*. ACM. 10.1145/3426020.3426134

Park, D. M., Jeong, S. S., & Seo, Y. S. (2022). Systematic Review on Chatbot Techniques and Applications. *Journal of Information Processing Systems*, *18*(1), 26–47.

Paul, S. C., Bartmann, N., & Clark, J. L. (2021). Customizability in conversational agents and their impact on health engagement. *Human Behavior and Emerging Technologies*, *3*(5), 1141–1152. doi:10.1002/hbe2.320

Pereira, J., & Nogueira, A. (2018). Chatbots in educational environments: A systematic review. *Computers & Education*, *124*, 74–89.

Pérez, J. Q., Daradoumis, T., & Puig, J. M. (2020). Rediscovering the use of chatbots in education: A systematic literature review. *Computer Applications in Engineering Education*, *28*(6), 1549–1565. doi:10.1002/cae.22326

Perez-Soler, S., Juarez-Puerta, S., Guerra, E., & De Lara, J. (2021). Choosing a Chatbot Development Tool. *IEEE Software*, *38*(4), 94–103. Advance online publication. doi:10.1109/MS.2020.3030198

Pimmer, C., Abiodun, R., Daniels, F., & Chipps, J. (2019). "I felt a sense of belonging somewhere". Supporting graduates' job transitions with WhatsApp groups. *Nurse Education Today*, *81*, 57–63. doi:10.1016/j.nedt.2019.06.010 PMID:31330403

Pizzi, G., Scarpi, D., & Pantano, E. (2021). Artificial intelligence and the new forms of interaction: Who has the control when interacting with a chatbot? *Journal of Business Research*, *129*, 878–890. doi:10.1016/j.jbusres.2020.11.006

Plocher, T., Rau, P. L. P., Choong, Y. Y., & Guo, Z. (2021). Cross-Cultural Design. Handbook of human factors and ergonomics, 252-279. Wiley.

Przegalinska, A., Ciechanowski, L., Stroz, A., Gloor, P., & Mazurek, G. (2019). In Bot We Trust: A New Methodology of Chatbot Performance Measures. *Business Horizons*, *62*(6), 785–797. doi:10.1016/j.bushor.2019.08.005

Punjabi, S., Sethuram, V., & Ramachandran, V., boddu, R., & Ravi, S. (2019). Chat bot Using API: Human To Machine Conversation. *2019 Global Conference for Advancement in Technology (GCAT)*, (pp. 1–5). IEEE. 10.1109/GCAT47503.2019.8978336

Qaffas, A. A. (2019). Improvement of Chatbots Semantics Using Wit.ai and Word Sequence Kernel: Education Chatbot as a Case Study. International Journal of Modern Education and Computer Science (IJMECS). MECS.

Radford, A., Wu, J., Child, R., Luan, D., Amodei, D., & Sutskever, I. (2019). Language Models are Unsupervised Multitask Learners. *OpenAI Blog, 1*(8).

Radford, A., Wu, J., Child, R., Luan, D., Amodei, D., & Sutskever, I. (2019). Language models are unsupervised multitask learners. *OpenAI Blog*, *1*(8), 1–24.

Raffel, C., Shazeer, N., Roberts, A., Lee, K., Narang, S., Matena, M., & Liu, P. J. (2020). Exploring the Limits of Transfer Learning with a Unified Text-to-Text Transformer.

Rafiq, F., Dogra, N., Adil, M., & Wu, J. Z. (2022). Examining Consumer's Intention to Adopt AI-Chatbots in Tourism Using Partial Least Squares Structural Equation Modeling Method. *Mathematics*, *10*(13), 2190. doi:10.3390/math10132190

Rajendran, V., & Prasanna, S. R. M. (2018). Intelligent Chatbot for Enabling e-Governance: A Case Study. In *2018 IEEE Calcutta Conference (CALCON)* (pp. 174-177). IEEE.

Rani, S., Bhambri, P., & Kataria, A. (2023b). Integration of IoT, Big Data, and Cloud Computing Technologies. *Big Data, Cloud Computing and IoT: Tools and Applications*.

Rani, S., Bhambri, P., Kataria, A., & Khang, A. (2023a). Smart City Ecosystem: Concept, Sustainability, Design Principles, and Technologies. In AI-Centric Smart City Ecosystems (pp. 1-20). CRC Press.

Rani, S., Pareek, P. K., Kaur, J., Chauhan, M., & Bhambri, P. (2023c). Quantum Machine Learning in Healthcare: Developments and Challenges. *Paper presented at the International Conference on Integrated Circuits and Communication Systems,* (pp. 1-7). IEEE. 10.1109/ICICACS57338.2023.10100075

Ranoliya, B. R., Raghuwanshi, N., & Singh, S. (2017). Chatbot for university related FAQs. *2017 International Conference on Advances in Computing, Communications and Informatics (ICACCI)*. IEEE. 10.1109/ICACCI.2017.8126057

Rapp, A., Curti, L., & Boldi, A. (2021). The human side of human-chatbot interaction: A systematic literature review of ten years of research on text-based chatbots. [Reference Link]. *International Journal of Human-Computer Studies*, *151*, 102630. doi:10.1016/j.ijhcs.2021.102630

RathjeS.MireaD.-M.SucholutskyI.MarjiehR.RobertsonC.Van BavelJ. J. (2023). *GPT is an effective tool for multilingual psychological text analysis*. PsyArXiv. doi:10.31234/osf.io/sekf5

Redesign UI. (n.d.). UpLabs. https://www.uplabs.com/posts/chat-gpt-redesign-ui

Rese, A., & Tränkner, P. (2024). Perceived conversational ability of task-based chatbots – Which conversational elements influence the success of text-based dialogues? *International Journal of Information Management*, *74*, 102699. doi:10.1016/j.ijinfomgt.2023.102699

Reshmi, S. (2016). Implementation of an Inquisitive Chatbot for Database Supported Knowledge Bases. *Sadhana - Academy Proceedings in Engineering Sciences, 41*(10). . doi:10.1007/s12046-016-0544-1

Retail chatbots use cases for improving your sales. (n.d.). ChatBot Blog. https://www.chatbot.com/blog/retail-chatbots

Review: Ready for Robots?: How to Think About the Future of AI on JSTOR. (n.d.). jStor. https://www.jstor.org/stable/26798238

Ribino, P. (2023). The role of politeness in human–machine interactions: A systematic literature review and future perspectives. *Artificial Intelligence Review*, 56(S1, Suppl 1), 445–482. doi:10.1007/s10462-023-10540-1

Rinker, T. (2018). *Sentimentr* (2.6.1) [R]. https://github.com/trinker/sentimentr

Roppelt, J. S., Kanbach, D. K., & Kraus, S. (2023). Artificial intelligence in healthcare institutions: A systematic literature review on influencing factors. *Technology in Society*, 102443.

Rozado, D. (2023). The political biases of chatgpt. *Social Sciences (Basel, Switzerland)*, 12(3), 148. doi:10.3390/socsci12030148

Rukavina, A. (2024, March 15). *From hype to hero: How chatbots can revolutionize your bank's customer experience.* Infobip. https://www.infobip.com/blog/revolutionize-your-banks-customer-experience-with-chatbots

Russell, S. J., & Norvig, P. (2010). *Artificial intelligence a modern approach.*

Russell, S. J., Norvig, P., Canny, J. F., Malik, J. M., & Edwards, D. D. (2003). *Artificial intelligence: a modern approach* (Vol. 2). Prentice hall.

Sadasivan, C., Cruz, C., Dolgoy, N., Hyde, A., Campbell, S., McNeely, M., Stroulia, E., & Tandon, P. (2023). Examining Patient Engagement in Chatbot Development Approaches for Healthy Lifestyle and Mental Wellness Interventions: Scoping Review. *Journal of Participatory Medicine*, 15, e45772. doi:10.2196/45772 PMID:37213199

Saini, P., Tajammul, M., & School of Computer Science and IT, Jain University, Jayanagar, Bangalore, Karnataka, India. (2022). Conversational AI powered chatbot using LEX and AWS. In *International Journal of Trend in Scientific Research and Development, 6*(3), 1622–1627). https://www.ijtsrd.com/papers/ijtsrd49722.pdf

Sanh, V., Debut, L., Chaumond, J., & Wolf, T. (2020). *DistilBERT, a distilled version of BERT: smaller, faster, cheaper and lighter.*

Sapna, R. C., M. (2019). Recommendence and Fashionsence Online Fashion Advisor for Offline Experience. In *ACM International Conference Proceeding Series*. ACM. 10.1145/3297001.3297035

Schario, M. E., Bahner, C. A., Widenhofer, T. V., Rajaballey, J. I., & Thatcher, E. J. (2022). Chatbot-assisted care management. *Professional Case Management*, 27(1), 19–25. doi:10.1097/NCM.0000000000000504 PMID:34846321

Schermer, B. W. (2007). *Software agents, surveillance, and the right to privacy: a legislative framework for agent-enabled surveillance.* Leiden University Press. doi:10.5117/9789087280215

Schmidthuber, L., Maresch, D., & Ginner, M. (2020). Disruptive technologies and abundance in the service sector-toward a refined technology acceptance model. *Technological Forecasting and Social Change*, 155, 119328. doi:10.1016/j.techfore.2018.06.017

Schneider, P., Klettner, M., Jokinen, K., Simperl, E., & Matthes, F. (2024). Evaluating large language models in semantic parsing for conversational question answering over knowledge graphs. *Proceedings of the 16th International Conference on Agents and Artificial Intelligence*. ACM. 10.5220/0012394300003636

Schuetzler, R. M., Grimes, G. M., & Scott Giboney, J. (2020). The impact of chatbot conversational skill on engagement and perceived humanness. *Journal of Management Information Systems*, 37(3), 875–900. doi:10.1080/07421222.2020.1790204

Seitz, L., Bekmeier-Feuerhahn, S., & Gohil, K. (2022). Can we trust a chatbot like a physician? A qualitative study on understanding the emergence of trust toward diagnostic chatbots. *International Journal of Human-Computer Studies*, *165*, 102848. doi:10.1016/j.ijhcs.2022.102848

Selamat, M. A., & Windasari, N. A. (2021). Chatbot for SMEs: Integrating customer and business owner perspectives. [Reference Link]. *Technology in Society*, *66*, 101685. doi:10.1016/j.techsoc.2021.101685

Selman, R. L. (2003). *Promotion of Social Awareness: Powerful Lessons for the Partnership of Developmental Theory and*. Russell Sage Foundation.

Sen BhattacharyaB. (2023). Assistive chatbots for healthcare: A succinct review. https://doi.org/ doi:10.36227/techrx-iv.23741469.v1

Sepahpour, T. (2020). *Ethical considerations of chatbot use for mental health support* [Doctoral dissertation, Johns Hopkins University].

Serban, I. V. (2017). A deep reinforcement learning chatbot. arXiv preprint arXiv:1709.02349.

Sestino, A., & D'Angelo, A. (2023). My doctor is an avatar! The effect of anthropomorphism and emotional receptivity on individuals' intention to use digital-based healthcare services. *Technological Forecasting and Social Change*, *191*, 122505. doi:10.1016/j.techfore.2023.122505

Shadiev, R., & Liu, J. (2023). Review of research on applications of speech recognition technology to assist language learning. *ReCALL*, *35*(1), 74–88. doi:10.1017/S095834402200012X

Shaikh, S., Yayilgan, S. Y., Klimova, B., & Pikhart, M. (2023). Assessing the usability of ChatGPT for formal english language learning. *European Journal of Investigation in Health, Psychology and Education*, *13*(9), 1937–1960. doi:10.3390/ejihpe13090140 PMID:37754479

Shawar, B. A., & Atwell, E. (2015). ALICE Chatbot: Trials and Outputs. *Computación y Sistemas*, *19*(4). doi:10.13053/cys-19-4-2326

Shawar, B. A., & Atwell, E. S. (2005). Using Corpora in Machine-Learning Chatbot Systems. *International Journal of Corpus Linguistics*, *10*(4), 489–516. Advance online publication. doi:10.1075/ijcl.10.4.06sha

Shereen, A. (2022, November 21). *What is a Key Differentiator of Conversational AI? - Freshchat Blog*. Freshchat Blog. https://www.freshworks.com/live-chat-software/chatbots/key-differentiator-of-conversational-ai-blog/

Sheth, J. (2020). Impact of Covid-19 on consumer behavior: Will the old habits return or die? *Journal of Business Research*, *117*, 280–283. doi:10.1016/j.jbusres.2020.05.059 PMID:32536735

Shevchuk, R., & Pastukh, Y. (2019). Improve the Security of Social Media Accounts. *2019 9th International Conference on Advanced Computer Information Technologies (ACIT)*. IEEE. 10.1109/ACITT.2019.8779963

Shumanov, M., & Johnson, L. (2021). Making conversations with chatbots more personalized. *Computers in Human Behavior*, *117*, 106627. doi:10.1016/j.chb.2020.106627

Singh, G., Singh, M., & Bhambri, P. (2020). Artificial Intelligence based Flying Car. In *Proceedings of the International Congress on Sustainable Development through Engineering Innovations* (pp. 216-227). Springer.

Singh, G., Singh, M., & Bhambri, P. (2020). Artificial Intelligence based Flying Car. In *Proceedings of the International Congress on Sustainable Development through Engineering Innovations* (pp. 216-227). IEEE.

Singh, H., Bhangare, A., Singh, R., Zope, S., & Saindane, P. (2023). Chatbots: A Survey of the Technology. In J. Hemanth, D. Pelusi, & J. I.-Z. Chen (Eds.), *Intelligent Cyber Physical Systems and Internet of Things* (pp. 671–691). Springer International Publishing. doi:10.1007/978-3-031-18497-0_49

Singh, M., Bhambri, P., Dhanoa, I. S., Jain, A., & Kaur, K. (2021). Data Mining Model for Predicting Diabetes. *Annals of the Romanian Society for Cell Biology*, *25*(4), 6702–6712.

Singh, R., Paste, M., Shinde, N., Patel, H., & Mishra, N. (2018). Chatbot Using TensorFlow for Small Businesses. In *Proceedings of the International Conference on Inventive Communication and Computational Technologies, ICICCT 2018*. IEEE. 10.1109/ICICCT.2018.8472998

Skrebeca, J., Kalniete, P., Goldbergs, J., Pitkevica, L., Tihomirova, D., & Romanovs, A. (2021, October). Modern development trends of chatbots using artificial intelligence (ai). In *2021 62nd International Scientific Conference on Information Technology and Management Science of Riga Technical University (ITMS)* (pp. 1-6). IEEE.

Smith, J. (2023). Enhancing Chatbot Interactions through Natural Language Processing (NLP). *Journal of AI Applications*, *10*(3), 45–58.

SnatchBot. (n.d.). *Education — Enhancing the Classroom with Chatbots*. SnatchBot. https://snatchbot.me/education

Sokolova, M., & Lapalme, G. (2009). A systematic analysis of performance measures for classification tasks. *Information Processing & Management*, *45*(4), 427–437. doi:10.1016/j.ipm.2009.03.002

Solanki, N., Singh, N., & Garg, D. (2023). Human mental experience through chatbots. *Edge-AI in Healthcare*, 143-158. doi:10.1201/9781003244592-11

Solanki, R. K., Rajawat, A. S., Gadekar, A. R., & Patil, M. E. (2023). Building a Conversational Chatbot Using Machine Learning: Towards a More Intelligent Healthcare Application. In *Handbook of Research on Instructional Technologies in Health Education and Allied Disciplines* (pp. 285–309). IGI Global. doi:10.4018/978-1-6684-7164-7.ch013

Song, M., Du, J., Xing, X., & Mou, J. (2022). Should the chatbot "save itself" or "be helped by others"? The influence of service recovery types on consumer perceptions of recovery satisfaction. *Electronic Commerce Research and Applications*, *55*, 101199. doi:10.1016/j.elerap.2022.101199

Song, M., Zhang, H., Xing, X., & Duan, Y. (2023). Appreciation vs. apology: Research on the influence mechanism of chatbot service recovery based on politeness theory. *Journal of Retailing and Consumer Services*, *73*, 103323. doi:10.1016/j.jretconser.2023.103323

Sophia, J. J., & Jacob, T. P. (2021). EDUBOT-A Chatbot for education in Covid-19 pandemic and VQAbot comparison. In *Proceedings of the Second International Conference on Electronics and Sustainable Communication Systems (IC-ESC-2021)* (pp. 1707-1714). IEEE. https://doi.org/xx.xxx/ICESC.2021.CFP21V66-ART

Stefanowicz, B. (2024, March 7). *5 Best Shopping Bots [Examples and How to Use Them]*. Tidio. https://www.tidio.com/blog/shopping-bot/

Stefanowicz, B. (2024, March 7). *NLP Chatbot: Complete Guide & How to Build Your Own*. Tidio. https://www.tidio.com/blog/nlp-chatbots/

Step 3: Build and test the bot . (n.d.) Amazon.. https://docs.aws.amazon.com/lex/latest/dg/gs2-build-and-test.html

Suhel, S. F., Shukla, V. K., Vyas, S., & Mishra, V. P. (2020). Conversation to Automation in Banking Through Chatbot Using Artificial Machine Intelligence Language. *2020 8th International Conference on Reliability, Infocom Technologies and Optimization (Trends and Future Directions) (ICRITO)*, (pp. 611–618). IEEE. 10.1109/ICRITO48877.2020.9197825

Sun, Y., Chen, J., & Sundar, S. S. (2024). Chatbot ads with a human touch: A test of anthropomorphism, interactivity, and narrativity. *Journal of Business Research*, *172*, 114403. doi:10.1016/j.jbusres.2023.114403

Sutskever, I., Vinyals, O., & Le, Q. V. (2014). Sequence to sequence learning with neural networks. In Advances in neural information processing systems (pp. 3104-3112). Research Gate.

Taecharungroj, V. (2023). "What Can ChatGPT Do?" Analyzing Early Reactions to the Innovative AI Chatbot on Twitter. *Big Data and Cognitive Computing*, *7*(1), 1. doi:10.3390/bdcc7010035

Tai, T. Y., & Chen, H. H. J. (2020). The impact of Google Assistant on adolescent EFL learners' willingness to communicate. *Interactive Learning Environments*. doi:10.1080/10494820.2020.1841801

Tallyn, E., Fried, H., Gianni, R., Isard, A., & Speed, C. (2018). The ethnobot: Gathering ethnographies in the age of IoT. In *Proceedings of the 2018 CHI conference on human factors in computing systems* (pp. 1-13). IEEE. 10.1145/3173574.3174178

Tan, J., Westermann, H., & Benyekhlef, K. (2023). *ChatGPT as an Artificial Lawyer?* AI4AJ@ICAIL. https://www.semanticscholar.org/paper/ChatGPT-as-an-Artificial-Lawyer-Tan-Westermann/11a55f5fac2f9078281fd24756bca2dff59bb374

Tang, I., Zhang, E., & Gu, R. (2023). *Point-PEFT: Parameter-efficient fine-tuning for 3D pre-trained models*. ArXiv, abs/2310.03059.

Tan, K. L., Lee, C. P., & Lim, K. M. (2023). A survey of sentiment analysis: Approaches, datasets, and future research. *Applied Sciences (Basel, Switzerland)*, *13*(7), 4550. doi:10.3390/app13074550

Tan, P. K., & Lim, C. M. (2023). Factors That Affect User Satisfaction of Using E-Commerce Chatbot: A Study on Generation Z. *International Journal of Business and Technology Management*, *5*(1), 292–303.

Tazl, O. A., & Wotawa, F. (2019). Using Model-Based Reasoning for Enhanced Chatbot Communication. In. Lecture Notes in Computer Science: Vol. 11606. *Including Subseries Lecture Notes in Artificial Intelligence and Lecture Notes in Bioinformatics*). LNAI. doi:10.1007/978-3-030-22999-3_67

Team, L. (2024, March 22). *The best conversational AI platform for business*. LivePerson. https://www.liveperson.com/

Telner, J. (2021). Chatbot User Experience: Speed and Content Are King. In T. Z. Ahram, W. Karwowski, & J. Kalra (Eds.), Advances in Artificial Intelligence, Software and Systems Engineering (pp. 47–54). Springer International Publishing. doi:10.1007/978-3-030-80624-8_6

Thorat, S. A., & Jadhav, V. (2020, April). A review on implementation issues of rule-based chatbot systems. In *Proceedings of the international conference on innovative computing & communications (ICICC)*. IEEE.

Thorne, S. L., & Black, R. W. (2007). Language and literacy development in computer-mediated contexts and communities. *Annual Review of Applied Linguistics*, *27*, 133–160. doi:10.1017/S0267190508070074

Thosani, P. (2020). A Self Learning Chat-Bot from User Interactions and Preferences. *2020 4th International Conference on Intelligent Computing and Control Systems (ICICCS)*. IEEE. 10.1109/ICICCS48265.2020.9120912

Toosi, A., Bottino, A. G., Saboury, B., Siegel, E., & Rahmim, A. (2021). A Brief History of AI: How to Prevent Another Winter (A Critical Review). *PET Clinics*, *16*(4), 449–469. doi:10.1016/j.cpet.2021.07.001 PMID:34537126

Tranfield, D., Denyer, D., & Smart, P. (2003). Towards a methodology for developing evidence-informed management knowledge by means of systematic review. *British Journal of Management*, *14*(3), 207–222. doi:10.1111/1467-8551.00375

Tudor Car, L., Dhinagaran, D. A., Kyaw, B. M., Kowatsch, T., Joty, S., Theng, Y. L., & Atun, R. (2020). Conversational agents in health care: Scoping review and conceptual analysis. *Journal of Medical Internet Research*, *22*(8), e17158. doi:10.2196/17158 PMID:32763886

Turgut, E. (2024). Genel Veri Koruma İlkelerinin Yapay Zekâ Karşısında Uygulanabilirliği Sorunu. *Türkiye Adalet Akademisi Dergisi, YOK*(57), 247–282. https://doi.org/ doi:10.54049/taad.1418236

Turing, A. M. (1950). Computing machinery and intelligence. *Mind, LIX*(236), 433–460. doi:10.1093/mind/LIX.236.433

VaddadiS.AsriS.GhemiY.AythaR. (2020). Developing chatbot wrapper for online shopping: A case study of using generic mobile messaging system. https://doi.org/ doi:10.36227/techrxiv.12061602

van Velsen, L., van der Geest, T., & Klaassen, R. (2017). From usability to user experience: A systematic framework for chatbot design. *Proceedings of the 21st International Academic Mindtrek Conference*, (pp. 126-133). Research Gate.

van Velsen, L., van der Geest, T., & Klaassen, R. (2017). From usability to user experience: A systematic framework for chatbot design. *Proceedings of the 21st International Academic Mindtrek Conference*, (pp. 126-133). IEEE.

Vander Meulen, R. (2015). Gartner Says 6.4 Billion Connected 'Things' Will Be in Use in 2016, Up 30 Percent From 2015. Stamford.

Vankadara, S. (2022, March 30). Build Chatbot using Amazon Lex.. *Medium*. https://medium.datadriveninvestor.com/build-chatbot-using-amazon-lex-ed3db80b27d0

Vaswani, A., Bengio, S., Brevdo, E., Chollet, F., Chintala, S., Cisse, M., & De Sa, C. (2018). *Tensor2tensor for neural machine translation*. arXiv preprint arXiv:1803.07416.

Vaswani, A., Shazeer, N., Parmar, N., Uszkoreit, J., Jones, L., Gomez, A. N., & Polosukhin, I. (2017). Attention is all you need. *Advances in Neural Information Processing Systems*, *30*, 5998–6008.

Vaziri, M., Mandel, L., Shinnar, A., Siméon, J., & Hirzel, M. (2017). Generating chat bots from web API specifications. *Proceedings of the 2017 ACM SIGPLAN International Symposium on New Ideas, New Paradigms, and Reflections on Programming and Software*, (pp. 44–57). ACM. 10.1145/3133850.3133864

Venkatesh, V., & Zhang, X. (2010). Unified theory of acceptance and use of technology: US vs. China. *Journal of Global Information Technology Management*, *13*(1), 5–27. doi:10.1080/1097198X.2010.10856507

Viera, A. J., & Garrett, J. M. (2005). Understanding interobserver agreement: The kappa statistic. *Family Medicine*, *37*(5), 360–363. PMID:15883903

Vyawahare, S., & Chakradeo, K. (2020). Chatbot Assistant for English as a Second Language Learners. In *2020 International Conference on Convergence to Digital World - Quo Vadis, ICCDW 2020*. IEEE. 10.1109/ICCDW45521.2020.9318672

Wallace, M. (2016). *Fragmentation is the enemy of the Internet of Things | Qualcomm*. Qualcomm.

Wallace, R. S. (2009). *The anatomy of ALICE*. Springer Netherlands. doi:10.1007/978-1-4020-6710-5_13

Wang, E. L., Matsumura, L. C., Correnti, R., Litman, D., Zhang, H., Howe, E., Magooda, A., & Quintana, R. (2020). Students' revision of text evidence use in an automated writing evaluation system. *Assessing Writing*, *44*, 100449. doi:10.1016/j.asw.2020.100449

Wang, X., Lin, X., & Shao, B. (2022). How does artificial intelligence create business agility? Evidence from chatbots. *International Journal of Information Management*, *66*, 102535. doi:10.1016/j.ijinfomgt.2022.102535

Weizenbaum, J. (1966). ELIZA—A computer program for the study of natural language communication between man and machine. *Communications of the ACM, 9*(1), 36–45. doi:10.1145/365153.365168

Wiangsamut, S., Chomphuwiset, P., & Khummanee, S. (2019). Chatting with Plants (Orchids) in Automated Smart Farming using IoT, Fuzzy Logic and Chatbot. Advances in Science, Technology and Engineering Systems Journal. doi:10.25046/aj040522

Widianingtyas, N., Mukti, T. W. P., & Silalahi, R. M. P. (2023). ChatGPT in Language Education: Perceptions of Teachers - A Beneficial Tool or Potential Threat? [Voices of English Language Education Society]. *VELES, 7*(2), 279–290. doi:10.29408/veles.v7i2.20326

Wirtz, J., Patterson, P. G., Kunz, W. H., Gruber, T., Lu, V. N., Paluch, S., & Martins, A. (2018). Brave new world: Service robots in the frontline. *Journal of Service Management, 29*(5), 907–931. doi:10.1108/JOSM-04-2018-0119

Wirtz, J., & Zeithaml, V. (2018). Cost-effective service excellence. *Journal of the Academy of Marketing Science, 46*(1), 59–80. doi:10.1007/s11747-017-0560-7

Wolf, T.. (2019). *HuggingFace's transformers: State-of-the-art Natural Language Processing.* arXiv preprint arXiv:1910.03771.

Wolf, T., Sanh, V., Chaumond, J., & Delangue, C. (2020). Transformers: State-of-the-Art Natural Language Processing. In *Proceedings of the 2020 Conference on Empirical Methods in Natural Language Processing: System Demonstrations* (pp. 38-45). IEEE.

Wollny, S., Schneider, J., Di Mitri, D., Weidlich, J., Rittberger, M., & Drachsler, H. (2021). Are we there yet?-a systematic literature review on chatbots in education. *Frontiers in Artificial Intelligence, 4*, 654924. doi:10.3389/frai.2021.654924 PMID:34337392

Wu, T., He, S., Liu, J., Sun, S., Liu, K., Han, Q. L., & Tang, Y. (2023). A brief overview of ChatGPT: The history, status quo and potential future development. *IEEE/CAA Journal of Automatica Sinica, 10*(5), 1122-1136.

Wu, W., Guo, Z., Zhou, X., Wu, H., Zhang, X., Lian, R., & Wang, H. (2019). Proactive Human-Machine Conversation with Explicit Conversation Goal. *Proceedings of the 57th Annual Meeting of the Association for Computational Linguistics*, (pp. 3794–3804). ACL. 10.18653/v1/P19-1369

Xiao, Y., & Zhi, Y. (2023). An Exploratory Study of EFL Learners' Use of ChatGPT for Language Learning Tasks: Experience and Perceptions. *Languages (Basel, Switzerland), 8*(3), 212. doi:10.3390/languages8030212

Xing, X., Song, M., Duan, Y., & Mou, J. (2022). Effects of different service failure types and recovery strategies on the consumer response mechanism of chatbots. *Technology in Society, 70*, 102049. doi:10.1016/j.techsoc.2022.102049

Xu, A., Liu, Z., Guo, Y., Sinha, V., & Akkiraju, R. (2017). A New Chatbot for Customer Service on Social Media. *Proceedings of the 2017 CHI Conference on Human Factors in Computing Systems*, (pp. 3506–3510). ACM. 10.1145/3025453.3025496

Xue, J., Wang, Y.-C., Wei, C., Liu, X., Woo, J., & Kuo, C.-C. J. (2023). Bias and fairness in chatbots: An overview. *ArXiv Preprint ArXiv:2309.08836.*

Xu, L., Hristidis, V., & Le, N. X. T. (2019). Clustering-based summarization of transactional chatbot logs. In *2019 IEEE International Conference on Humanized Computing and Communication (HCC)* (pp. 60-67). IEEE. 10.1109/HCC46620.2019.00017

Yang, Y., & Liu, X. (1999). A re-examination of text categorization methods. *Proceedings of the 22nd Annual International ACM SIGIR Conference on Research and Development in Information Retrieval*, (pp. 42–49). IEEE. 10.1145/312624.312647

Ye, B. J., Kim, J. Y., Suh, C., Choi, S. P., Choi, M., Kim, D. H., & Son, B. C. (2021). Development of a chatbot program for follow-up management of workers' general health examinations in korea: A pilot study. *International Journal of Environmental Research and Public Health, 18*(4), 2170. doi:10.3390/ijerph18042170 PMID:33672158

Yin, Q., & Satar, M. (2020). English as a Foreign Language Learner Interactions with Chatbots: Negotiation for Meaning. *International Online Journal of Education & Teaching, 7*(2), 390–410.

Young, S., Gašić, M., Thomson, B., & Williams, J. D. (2013). Pomdp-based statistical spoken dialog systems: A review. [Reference Link]. *Proceedings of the IEEE, 101*(5), 1160–1179. doi:10.1109/JPROC.2012.2225812

Zahour, O. (2020). Towards a chatbot for educational and vocational guidance in Morocco: Chatbot E-orientation. *International Journal of Advanced Trends in Computer Science and Engineering, 9*(2), 2479–2487. doi:10.30534/ijatcse/2020/237922020

Zaib, M., Zhang, W. E., Sheng, Q. Z., Mahmood, A., & Zhang, Y. (2022). Conversational question answering: A survey. *Knowledge and Information Systems, 64*(12), 3151–3195. doi:10.1007/s10115-022-01744-y

Zaremba, A., & Demir, E. (2023). ChatGPT: Unlocking the future of NLP in finance. *Modern Finance, 1*(1), 93–98. doi:10.61351/mf.v1i1.43

Zhang, B., Zhu, J., & Su, H. (2023). Toward the third generation artificial intelligence. *Science China. Information Sciences, 66*(2), 121101. doi:10.1007/s11432-021-3449-x

Zhang, S., Shan, C., Lee, J. S. Y., Che, S., & Kim, J. H. (2023). Effect of chatbot-assisted language learning: A meta-analysis. *Education and Information Technologies, 28*(11), 1–21. doi:10.1007/s10639-023-11805-6

Zhu, X., Li, R. Y. M., Crabbe, M. J. C., & Sukpascharoen, K. (2022). Can a chatbot enhance hazard awareness in the construction industry? *Frontiers in Public Health, 10*, 993700. doi:10.3389/fpubh.2022.993700 PMID:36530655

About the Contributors

Munir Ahmad, Ph.D. in Computer Science, brings over 24 years of invaluable expertise in the realm of spatial data development, management, processing, visualization, and quality assurance. His unwavering commitment to open data, big data, crowdsourced data, volunteered geographic information, and spatial data infrastructure has solidified him as a seasoned professional and a trusted trainer in cutting-edge spatial technologies. With a profound passion for research, Munir has authored more than 30 publications in his field, culminating in the award of his Ph.D. in Computer Science from Preston University Pakistan in 2022. His dedication to propelling the industry forward and sharing his extensive knowledge defines his mission.

Muhammad Akram is a PhD scholar passionate about safeguarding privacy and enabling accurate location services in mobile networks. Their research delves into the intricate dance between user privacy and the power of location data. During their BS (Hons) and MS studies, Muhammad Akram explored innovative techniques for location estimation, laying the groundwork for their current doctoral research, which focuses on Location Privacy in Social Networks.

Pankaj Bhambri is affiliated with the Department of Information Technology at Guru Nanak Dev Engineering College in Ludhiana. Additionally, he fulfills the role of the Convener for his Departmental Board of Studies. He possesses nearly two decades of teaching experience. He is an active member of IE India, ISTE New Delhi, IIIE Navi Mumbai, IETE New Delhi and CSI Mumbai. He has contributed to the various research activities while publishing articles in the renowned SCIE and Scopus journals and conference proceedings. He has also published several international patents. Dr. Bhambri has garnered extensive experience in the realm of academic publishing, having served as an editor/author for a multitude of books in collaboration with esteemed publishing houses such as CRC Press, Elsevier, Scrivener, and Bentham Science. Dr. Bhambri has been honored with several prestigious accolades, including the ISTE Best Teacher Award in 2023 and 2022, the I2OR National Award in 2020, the Green ThinkerZ Top 100 International Distinguished Educators award in 2020, the I2OR Outstanding Educator Award in 2019, the SAA Distinguished Alumni Award in 2012, the CIPS Rashtriya Rattan Award in 2008, the LCHC Best Teacher Award in 2007, and numerous other commendations from various government and non-profit organizations. He has provided guidance and oversight for numerous research projects and dissertations at the postgraduate and Ph.D. levels. He successfully organized a diverse range of educational programmes, securing financial backing from esteemed institutions such as the AICTE, the TEQIP, among others. Dr. Bhambri's areas of interest encompass machine learning, bioinformatics, wireless sensor networks, and network security.

Neepa Biswas has done her B.Tech in Information Technology from WBUT, M.E. in Information Technology from IIEST Shibpur, She has completed PhD from Jadavpur University. Her research Interest Data Warehousing, Data mining, Ad-hoc Network, Machine Learning etc. Currently she is working as Assistant Professor in Narula Institute of Technology, in West Bengal, Kolkata, India.

Sudarsan Biswas has completed his Bachelor of Engineering (IT) from Bengal Engineering and Science University, Shibpur in 2006 and his Master of Engineering (IT) from Bengal Engineering and Science University, Shibpur in 2010. Currently he is serving as an Assistant Professor Department of IT, RCC Institute of Information Technology, Kolkata, West Bengal, India. His research domain is Data mining, Data warehousing and Cryptography.

Neslihan Bulur graduated from Anadolu University, Faculty of Communication Sciences, Department of Communication Design and Management in 2017. She graduated from the Sociology Department, which is a double major program at Anadolu University, and the International Relations undergraduate program at Anadolu University, which she studied as a second university, in 2018. In 2020, she graduated from Galatasaray University Strategic Communication Management master's program. She is currently doing her PhD at Marmara University Communication Sciences program.

Zindan Çakıcı graduated as the valedictorian from the Department of Public Relations and Publicity at Kadir Has University Faculty of Communication in 2018. He completed his master's degree in 2020 within the discipline of Strategic Communication Management at Galatasaray University Institute of Social Sciences. In 2024, Dr. Çakıcı attained the doctoral title by presenting a thesis entitled "Visual Representation of Irregular Migration in the Turkish Press: Afghan Migration After the Taliban Administration" at the Galatasaray University Institute of Social Sciences, Department of Media and Communication Studies. Throughout the course of his academic trajectory, Dr. Çakıcı garnered a total of 9 accolades from esteemed institutions such as KalDer, Tühid, TRT, and KKB, acknowledging his contributions to projects in the realms of communication and social responsibility. His areas of scholarly pursuit and investigation encompass studies on migration and emerging media

Sadettin Demirel completed his undergraduate education in the Public Relations at Kadir Has University in 2016. He obtained his first master's degree in the New Media at Kadir Has University in 2018. In 2019, as a recipient of a scholarship from the Swedish Institute, he completed his second master's degree in Investigative Journalism at the University of Gothenburg, Sweden. In 2023, he received the title of PhD in the field of Journalism at Istanbul University, with his dissertation titled "Unraveling the Relationship between Sentiments and User Engagements in Twitter News: A Multimethod Study." Dr. Demirel's academic interests encompass various areas, including new media, text mining, computational social sciences, sentiment analysis, social networks, and data journalism. Actively engaged in civil society activities, he is the founder and a board member of the Data Literacy Association (VOYD), based in Istanbul. This organization is established with the mission of promoting data literacy in Turkey and supporting data journalism and open data initiatives.

Gulnara Z. Karimova created a few theories in the field, such as an innovative framework for AI-based product promotion and design. Having a Ph.D. in Communications and an impressive roster of publications, her credentials are further enriched by certifications for such tech companies as IBM. Beyond offering consultancy to diverse corporations, she shares her wealth of knowledge with eager learners.

Yevgeniya Kim is a Senior Lecturer at KIMEP University, Kazakhstan. She teaches undergraduate and graduate courses in operations management, logistics, and information systems. Her interests lie in e-commerce and logistics. She was a fellow at Chonbuk National University (South Korea) and Eindhoven Technical University (The Netherland).

Domitilla Magni Ph.D., is Associate Professor in Management and Marketing at eCampus University. She obtained her Ph.D. in "Management, Banking and Commodity Sciences" at Sapienza, University of Rome. With a distinguished academic background, she has served as a Visiting Professor at renowned institutions worldwide, including New York University, Montpellier Business School, South-Western University of Finance and Economics, and La Salle University. Her research focuses on Innovation and Technology Management, Sustainability, and Knowledge Management. She has authored numerous books, book chapters, and articles published in international journals, covering a range of topics in management, innovation, and energy research. She actively participates in the peer-review procedures of numerous esteemed international journals, contributing her expertise to evaluate and enhance the quality of scholarly submissions.

Froilan Mobo is a Doctor of Public Administration graduate from the Urdaneta City University Class of 2016 and a graduate of the 2nd Doctorate Degree (Ph.D.) in Development Education program at the Central Luzon State University, Nueva Ecija, Philippines, Class of 2022. After obtaining his Doctorate Degree, he was promoted to the position of Associate Professor V in the Philippine Merchant Marine Academy (PMMA), and this allowed him to work with different international research institutions, such as the Director / Research Consultant of the IKSAD Research Institute, Turkey; At present, he is in the process of finishing his 3rd Masters's degree leading to Social Studies Education at Bicol University.

Muhammad Khizar Hayat Naeem is a distinguished Ph.D. candidate affiliated with the School of Management at Harbin Institute of Technology in Harbin, China. His notable contributions to the academic realm are underscored by a prolific publication record in both national and international journals, reflecting his dedication to advancing knowledge in his field. In addition to his scholarly achievements, Mr. Naeem has established himself as a respected figure in the research community. He actively engages with esteemed journals and publishing houses, such as Sage Publications, IGI Global and Frontiers Inn, where he serves as a conscientious reviewer. This role underscores his commitment to maintaining the highest standards of academic rigor and contributing to the peer-review process. Mr. Naeem's research pursuits center around the intricate domains of consumer behavior, travel, and tourism. His expertise extends to the proficient use of analytical tools, including SPSS, AMOS, and Smart-PLS, showcasing his adeptness in employing advanced methodologies. Mr. Muhammad Khizar Hayat Naeem continues to make substantial strides in academia, leaving an indelible mark on the field of management science.

Kaushikkumar Patel is a distinguished leader known for his exceptional contributions at the intersection of finance and technology. As a key figure at TransUnion, he leverages Big Data to transform decision-making processes and financial strategies, with expertise spanning Data Analytics, FinTech, and Digital Transformation. Based in the United States, Mr. Patel is renowned for his strategic insights in addressing complex challenges like data privacy and risk assessment, ensuring compliance in dynamic financial landscapes. An influential thought leader, Mr. Patel's work has been internationally recognized, earning him the prestigious ET Leadership Excellence Award for his groundbreaking achievements in Data-Driven Financial Strategies. His unique blend of technical prowess and strategic acumen establishes him as a visionary in his field, continually pushing the boundaries of what's possible in finance and technology.

Rajesh Kanna R is an Assistant Professor in the Department of Computer Science at CHRIST (Deemed to be University) since 2022. He possesses 16 years of teaching experience, specializing in Artificial Intelligence and Machine Learning. Dr. Rajesh has authored 32 articles in various Scopus/WoS indexed peer-reviewed journals. Dr. Rajesh has secured Grant-in-Aid from esteemed funding agencies such as DST-SERB, ICSSR, IKST-Indo Korea, and FSL India, totalling worth 2.5 million. Additionally, he has submitted funding proposals amounting to Rs. 3.5 billion. He holds memberships in the IEEE,ACM and other Information technology related forums across the world. He has authored 8 books and 6 book chapters.

Sita Rani works in the Department of Computer Science and Engineering at Guru Nanak Dev Engineering College, Ludhiana. She earned her Ph.D. in Computer Science and Engineering from I.K. Gujral Punjab Technical University, Kapurthala, Punjab in 2018. She has also completed Post Graduate Certificate Program in Data Science and Machine Learning from Indian Institute of Technology, Roorkee in 2023. She has completed her Postdoc from Big Data Mining and Machine Learning Lab, South Ural State University, Russia in August, 2023. She has more than 20 years of teaching experience. She is an active member of ISTE, IEEE and IAEngg. She is the receiver of ISTE Section Best Teacher Award- 2020, and International Young Scientist Award-2021. She has contributed to the various research activities while publishing articles in the renowned SCI and Scopus journals and conference proceedings. She has published several international patents and authored/edited/coedited 8 books. Dr. Rani has delivered many expert talks in A.I.C.T.E. sponsored Faculty Development Programs and key note talks in many National and International Conferences. She has also organized many International Conferences during her 20 years of teaching experience. She is the member of Editorial Board and reviewer of many international journals of repute. She is also the vice-president of SME and MSME (UT Council), Women Indian Chamber of Commerce and Industry (WICCI) from last 3 years. Her research interest includes Parallel and Distributed Computing, Data Science, Machine Learning, Internet of Things (IoT), and Smart Healthcare.

Mohana Priya T, currently an Assistant Professor in the Department of Computer Science at CHRIST (Deemed to be University) in Bangalore, boasts over 14 years and 11 months of extensive experience in academia. Holding a Ph.D. from Bharathiar University and an M.Phil. from Vinayaka Missions University, she has demonstrated a steadfast commitment to advancing knowledge and educational excellence. Dr. Mohana Priya has made significant contributions to research, particularly in Artificial Intelligence, Machine Learning and Data Mining, evident through her numerous publications in reputable journals and innovative patents in healthcare and industrial IoT. Additionally, she has successfully secured research funds totaling 1.5 million from various agencies.

Gülin Zeybek is a doctor in ELT and is currently working in School of Foreign Languages at Isparta University of Applied Sciences. She earned her BA degree in English Language Teaching at Boğaziçi University and holds two MA degrees in both areas of Foreign Language Education and Educational Technologies. Her research interests center on pre-service teacher education, Multimodal Mobile Assisted Language Learning, and various technology integrations such as Augmented Reality and Artificial Intelligence into foreign language teaching. She has worked as a foreign language teacher trainer for over 10 years. She has published various research papers nationally and internationally.

Index

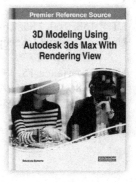

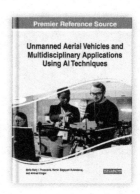

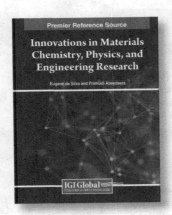

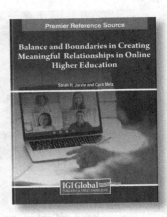

Submit an Open Access Book Proposal

Have Your Work Fully & Freely Available Worldwide After Publication

Seeking the Following Book Classification Types:

Authored & Edited Monographs • Casebooks • Encyclopedias • Handbooks of Research

Gold, Platinum, & Retrospective OA Opportunities to Choose From

Easily Track Your Work in Our Advanced Manuscript Submission System With **Rapid Turnaround Times**

Double-Blind Peer Review by Notable Editorial Boards (*Committee on Publication Ethics* (COPE) Certified

Publications Adhere to All **Current OA Mandates & Compliances**

Affordable APCs *(Often 50% Lower Than the Industry Average)* Including Robust Editorial Service Provisions

Direct Connections with **Prominent Research Funders** & OA Regulatory Groups

Institution Level OA Agreements Available (Recommend or Contact Your Librarian for Details)

Join a **Diverse Community of 150,000+ Researchers Worldwide** Publishing With IGI Global

Content Spread Widely to Leading Repositories (AGOSR, ResearchGate, CORE, & More)

 Retrospective Open Access Publishing

You Can Unlock Your Recently Published Work, Including Full Book & Individual Chapter Content to Enjoy All the Benefits of Open Access Publishing

Learn More

Printed in the United States
by Baker & Taylor Publisher Services